CONSTRUCTION ACCOUNTING AND FINANCIAL MANAGEMENT

Steven J. Peterson, MBA, PE
Weber State University

PEARSON

Prentice
Hall

Upper Saddle River, New Jersey
Columbus, Ohio

Library of Congress Cataloging-in-Publication Data

Peterson, Steven J.
  Construction accounting and financial management / Steven J. Peterson.
       p. cm.
  Includes bibliographical references and index.
  ISBN 0-13-110939-1
  1. Construction industry—Accounting. 2. Construction
industry—Finance. 3. Managerial accounting. I. Title.

  HF5686.B7P48 2005
  624'.068'1—dc22

                                                          2004003199

Editor in Chief: Stephen Helba
Executive Editor: Ed Francis
Editorial Assistant: Jennifer Day
Production Editor: Holly Shufeldt
Project Coordination: *The GTS Companies*/York, PA Campus
Design Coordinator: Diane Ernsberger
Cover Designer: Linda Sorrells-Smith
Cover art: Index Stock
Production Manager: Matt Ottenweller
Marketing Manager: Mark Marsden

This book was set in ITC Mendoza Roman by *The GTS Companies*/York, PA Campus. It was
printed and bound by R.R. Donnelley & Sons Company. The cover was printed by The Lehigh Press, Inc.

Pearson Prentice Hall™ is a trademark of Pearson Education, Inc.
Pearson® is a registered trademark of Pearson plc
Prentice Hall® is a registered trademark of Pearson Education, Inc.

Pearson Education Ltd.   Pearson Education Australia Pty. Limited
Pearson Education Singapore Pte. Ltd.   Pearson Education North Asia Ltd.
Pearson Education Canada, Ltd.   Pearson Educación de Mexico, S. A. de C.V.
Pearson Education—Japan   Pearson Education Malaysia Pte. Ltd.

10 9 8 7 6
0-13-110939-1

To my wife, Corrine, for her help and patience while writing this book.

PREFACE

A few years ago I was asked to teach a course on construction accounting and finance. The course was to cover the fundamental principles needed by construction managers to successfully manage the finances of construction companies. In preparing to teach this course I found that these principles were scattered among many disciplines, including business management, engineering economics, accounting, estimating, project management, and scheduling. After I reviewed the available textbooks, two things were apparent. First, the material was often presented in a generic fashion and failed to address how the principles applied to the construction industry. For example, in most accounting textbooks only a few pages were devoted to the accounting procedures for long-term contracts, which comprise a bulk of the projects for general construction companies. Second, with the topics scattered among many disciplines and textbooks, the topic of how the different components of construction financial management were interrelated and interacted was being ignored.

Financial management may be defined as the use of a company's financial resources and encompasses all decisions that affect a company's financial health. Many everyday decisions affect a company's financial health. The difference between a marginally profitable and a very profitable company is good financial management. Business schools teach the fundamental principles of financial management; however, because of the many unique characteristics of the construction industry, the usefulness of these financial principles as taught by business schools is limited. To be useful, these principles must be adapted specifically to the construction industry. For example, in the construction industry equipment is mobile and may be needed for multiple jobs during a single month. Traditional accounting methods and financial statements do not allow a company to properly manage and account for its equipment.

This book was written to help construction professionals—both those who are working in the construction industry and those seeking a degree in construction management—learn how the principles of financial management can be adapted to and used in the management of construction companies. This book will be most useful for general managers and owners of companies who are responsible for managing the finances of the entire company; however, many of these principles are useful to project managers and superintendents. For the project manager or superintendent who desires to stand out in a company, there is no better way than to improve the profitability of their project through the principles of sound financial management. The book also discusses how owners and general managers can manage construction projects by sound management of their project managers, superintendents, and crew foreperson.

This book explains common financial principles, demonstrating how these principles may be applied to a construction situation and how these principles affect the financial performance of a company. Many of the examples included in this book are based on actual situations encountered by the author.

This book is organized in five parts: introduction to construction financial management, accounting for financial resources, managing costs and profits, managing cash flows, and making financial decisions.

> *The first part*—comprising Chapter 1—introduces the reader to construction financial management, explains why construction financial management is different than financial management in other industries, and defines the role of a construction financial manager.
>
> *The second part*—comprising Chapters 2 through 6—describes how to account for a company's financial resources. Accounting for these resources is built around a company's accounting system.
>
> *The third part*—comprising Chapters 7 through 11—examines how to manage the costs and profits of a construction company. This must be done at the project level as well as at the company level.
>
> *The fourth part*—comprising Chapters 12 through 16—looks at how to manage a company's cash flows and how to evaluate different sources of funding cash needs.
>
> *The fifth part*—comprising Chapters 17 and 18—explores ways to quantitatively analyze financial decisions.

After reading this book, you should have a better understanding of the following:

- ❑ The basic financial principles that are widely used in the business world and how to modify them so that they work for the construction industry. Application of these principles will help you better manage your business.
- ❑ Construction accounting systems, which will help you manage the accounting systems and use accounting information to manage a company.
- ❑ Financial and accounting principles, so that you may interact with accountants and bankers at a professional level.

This textbook brings all of the key financial management principles needed by construction managers under one cover, addressing how they are applied in the construction industry and how they interact. Many of the examples in this book are based on my fourteen years of experience in construction financial management. Join me on a journey of discovery as we discuss the fundamental principles of financial management that are needed to make a construction company a financial success.

Particular thanks are due to Laura Lucas (Indiana University–Purdue University, Indianapolis), Jonathan Shi (Illinois Institute of Technology), and Brent H. Weidman (Brigham Young University) for their assistance with the text review.

Best Wishes,

Steven J. Peterson, MBA, PE

CONTENTS

PART II ACCOUNTING FOR FINANCIAL RESOURCES 15

CHAPTER 2

CONSTRUCTION ACCOUNTING SYSTEMS 17

CHAPTER 3

ACCOUNTING TRANSACTIONS 45

CHAPTER 4

MORE CONSTRUCTION ACCOUNTING   77

CHAPTER

DEPRECIATION   91

CHAPTER 6

ANALYSIS OF FINANCIAL STATEMENTS   117

PART III MANAGING COSTS AND PROFITS   145

CHAPTER 7

CHAPTER 8

CHAPTER

MANAGING GENERAL OVERHEAD COSTS   183

CHAPTER

SETTING PROFIT MARGINS FOR BIDDING   209

CHAPTER 11

PROFIT CENTER ANALYSIS   223

PART IV MANAGING CASH FLOWS   243

CHAPTER 12

CASH FLOWS FOR CONSTRUCTION PROJECTS   245

CHAPTER 13

PROJECTING INCOME TAXES   279

CHAPTER 14

CASH FLOWS FOR CONSTRUCTION COMPANIES   297

CHAPTER 15

TIME VALUE OF MONEY   325

CHAPTER 16

PART V MAKING FINANCIAL DECISIONS   407

CHAPTER 17

CHAPTER 18

INCOME TAXES AND FINANCIAL DECISIONS   457

APPENDIX A   COMPUTERIZED ACCOUNTING SYSTEMS   479

APPENDIX B   TREND ANALYSIS   485

INTRODUCTION TO CONSTRUCTION FINANCIAL MANAGEMENT

In this section we introduce you to construction financial management, how it is different from financial management in other industries, and why construction companies need to use good financial management. This section includes:

❏ Chapter 1: Construction Financial Management

CONSTRUCTION FINANCIAL MANAGEMENT

In this chapter you will learn what financial management is and why the financial management of construction companies is different from financial management of most other companies.

In 1997, 10,867[1] construction companies in the United States failed, bringing the total for the eight-year period beginning in 1990 to more than 80,000[2] construction companies. These failures include only those business failures that resulted in a loss to their creditors and do not include contractors who closed their doors without leaving their creditors with a loss. The 1997 failure rate translates to 118 failures per 10,000[3] construction companies or 1.18% of the construction companies. These failures are divided among companies of all ages. Figure 1-1 shows the breakdown of these failures by age of the business. During 1997 the greatest number of business failures was for construction companies that had been operating for longer than 10 years.[4]

---

[1]Dun & Bradstreet, *Business Failure Record*, 1986–97, annually as quoted by The Center to Protect Worker's Rights, *The Construction Chart Book*, 3rd Edition, September 2002. Note: Dun & Bradstreet stopped publishing business failure data after 1997.

[2]Dun & Bradstreet, *Business Failure Record*, 1986–97, annually as quoted by Surety Information Office, *Why Do Contractors Fail?*, downloaded from http://www.sio.org/html/whyfail.html downloaded on April 3, 2003.

[3]Dun & Bradstreet, *Business Failure Record*, 1986–97, annually as quoted by The Center to Protect Worker's Rights, *The Construction Chart Book*, 3rd Edition, September 2002.

[4]Dun & Bradstreet, *Business Failure Record*, 1986–97, annually as quoted by The Center to Protect Worker's Rights, *The Construction Chart Book*, 3rd Edition, September 2002.

Figure 1-1 Business Failure by Age[5]

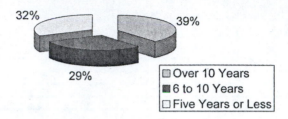

32%

39%

29%

☐ Over 10 Years
■ 6 to 10 Years
☐ Five Years or Less

Since 1988 the construction industry has experienced a higher-than-average business failure rate when compared to the failure rate of all businesses.[6]

The number of construction companies doing business in the United States declined from 709,590 in 2000 to 698,898 in 2001,[7] resulting in a net decline of 10,692 companies or 1.5% for the year. This statistic does not represent the true number of companies that went out of business during the year because the actual number of construction companies that went out of business is offset by the number of new construction companies that were started during the year.

In 2002, two of Japan's largest construction companies—Sato Kogy Company and Nissan Construction—filed for bankruptcy in the same month.[8] Also in the same month, Germany's second-largest construction company, Philipp Holzmann AG, which had been in business for longer than 150 years, filed for bankruptcy.[9]

Large and small, old and new, domestic and foreign construction companies are among the statistics of failed construction companies. What are the sources of failure for construction companies? The Surety Information Office—an office that collects data on surety bonds—has identified six broad warning signs that a construction company is in trouble. They are "ineffective financial management systems . . . bank lines of credit constantly borrowed to the limits . . . poor estimating and/or job cost reporting . . . poor project management . . . no comprehensive business plan . . . [and] communication problems."[10] Four of these six

---

[5]Dun & Bradstreet, *Business Failure Record, 1986–97*, annually as quoted by The Center to Protect Worker's Rights, *The Construction Chart Book*, 3rd Edition, September 2002.

[6]Dun & Bradstreet, *Business Failure Record, 1986–97*, annually as quoted by The Center to Protect Worker's Rights, *The Construction Chart Book*, 3rd Edition, September 2002.

[7]U.S. Census Bureau, *CBP United States Economic Profiles*, 2000 and 2001 downloaded from http://www.census.gov/epcd/cbp/view/cbpus.html.

[8]The Associated Press, *Nissan Construction to File for Bankruptcy*, The New York Times on the Web, April 1, 2002, and Ken Belson, *Contractor in Japan Is Seeking Bankruptcy*, The New York Times on the Web, March 5, 2002.

[9]Edmund L. Andrews, *Kirch in Danger of Bankruptcy After Rescue Talks Break Down*, The New York Times on the Web, April 3, 2002, and Skyscrapers.com.

[10]Surety Information Office, *Why Do Contractors Fail?*, downloaded from http://www.sio.org/html/whyfail.html downloaded on April 3, 2003.

sources of failure are directly related to the financial management of the company. Without sound financial management, construction companies are setting themselves up for failure.

WHAT IS FINANCIAL MANAGEMENT?

Financial management is the use of a company's financial resources. This includes the use of cash and other assets—such as equipment. Many everyday decisions affect a company's financial future. For example, the decision to bid on a large project can have great impact on the finances of a company. When deciding whether to bid on a project, a manager may need to address the following questions: Does the company have enough cash resources to perform this work or will the company need outside financing? Can the company get bonded for this work? If not, what changes need to be made in the company's financial structure so the company can get a bond for the project? Should the company hire employees to perform the work or should the company subcontract out this labor? Should the company lease or purchase the additional equipment needed for this project? If the company purchases the equipment, how should it be financed? Will this project require the company to increase its main office overhead? And, finally, what profit and overhead markup should be added to the bid? The answers to all of these questions will affect the company's finances. The answer to one of the questions may change the available options to other questions. For example, if the manager decides to hire employees to perform the work on the project, the project will require more financial resources than if the company had hired subcontractors to perform the labor and may leave the company with insufficient resources to purchase the additional equipment, leaving leasing the equipment as the only option.

WHY IS CONSTRUCTION FINANCIAL MANAGEMENT DIFFERENT?

Construction companies are different from most other companies and are faced with many unique challenges and problems not faced by other companies in other industries. Although the construction industry is producing a product—as do manufacturing plants—the construction of buildings, roads, and other structures is different from manufacturing of most other products. Because of these unique characteristics the financial management principles applied to other product-producing industries often need to be modified before they are applied to the construction industry, otherwise they are useless.

To understand the unique characteristics and challenges faced by the managers of construction industries, let's compare the management of a construction company to the management of a manufacturing plant. For this example we look at the manufacturing of fiberglass insulation. The manufacturing of fiberglass batt insulation can be summarized in the following steps:

1. Sand and other ingredients necessary to make glass are delivered to the plant and stored in silos.
2. The glass-making ingredients, delivered to the mixing bin by conveyor belts or other means, are mixed in the specified proportions.
3. After mixing, the ingredients are fed into a furnace, where they are heated to make molten glass.
4. The molten glass is passed through a machine that spins the glass into fibers, cools the fibers, and adds liquid binders which causes the glass fibers to stick together.
5. The spun glass is placed on a conveyor belt, where the speed of the conveyor belt controls the thickness of the insulation.
6. As the insulation proceeds along the conveyor belt, it is cut to width, and paper backing is added if required.
7. Finally, the insulation is cut to length, packaged, and stored for shipment.

Now that you have a basic understanding of the process used to manufacture fiberglass insulation, let's compare the management of this process to the management of a construction company.

Project Oriented

The insulation manufacturer is process oriented, whereas the construction company is project oriented. Although the insulation manufacturer produces different types of insulation, the range of products that they produce is limited. In the above example the insulation produced may be of different thickness or R values, different widths, and with or without paper backing and packaged in rolls or bundles of 8-foot batts. All of these products are similar with slight variations. For many construction companies, each product is unique but often the products are very different. It is not uncommon for a construction company to be working on a tenant finish in a high-rise tower, a fire station, and an apartment complex at the same time. Even when a construction company is working on similar products—such as a homebuilder or a company building a number of convenience stores—the projects are often different due to site conditions and locations, which affects the availability of labor and materials.

Because insulation manufacturers have a limited number of products they produce repeatedly, it is easier for them to determine their production costs. When a manager has produced a million square feet of R-11 insulation with paper backing packaged in a 15-inch-wide by 40-foot-long roll it is easier to project the cost to produce the next 10,000 square feet than it is if the product has never been produced before. Construction companies often give clients fixed prices for a product that the company has never built or for a product that the company has never built using the local group of suppliers and subcontractors available at the project location.

The insulation manufacturer sells the same product to a wide variety of buyers at locations other than the place the insulation is manufactured. In the construction industry, projects are often custom built for a specific owner on a specific location. The insulation manufacturer can deal with fluctuation in demand by producing and storing extra products when demand is slower for use when the demand is higher. It is relatively easy to store 5,000 square feet of insulation for immediate shipment to meet some future demand. With most of a construction company's work occurring at the individual project's location, the construction company cannot store unused production during slow times for use on future projects. How can you store 500 cubic yards of excavation for immediate use on some future project? To deal with this, the construction company must constantly bid new work to keep the company's employees workforce fully utilized or build speculative projects—projects without owners or buyers. Speculative building is a risky venture for the company because the product cannot be moved and often must be modified before it can be sold to another buyer.

No other industry is as project based as is the construction industry. Almost everything a construction company does is a project. Because of this, a construction company must keep accurate construction costs for each and every project that it constructs. Not only must the cost be kept for each project, but also the cost must be kept for each group of components on a project. This data is necessary to control the costs of the current project and also so the cost of the components may be used in the bidding of future projects. With each project requiring a different mix of labor, materials, and equipment, knowing the cost of the components of a project is necessary to bid future projects.

Decentralized versus Centralized Projection

The insulation manufacturers perform all of their work at a centralized location, whereas the construction company performs its work at a number of decentralized locations. Insulation manufacturing plants are set up at a fixed location with the equipment being dedicated to a specific manufacturing process for years. Employees come to the same plant year after year. In the construction industry the equipment and employees are seldom dedicated to a single project year after year. Equipment and employees may move from job to job on a regular basis. As a result, the location of each employee and piece of equipment must be tracked to ensure that their costs are charged to the correct job. Additionally, each crew and piece of equipment must be managed as a project center.

Payment Terms

The insulation manufacturer bills the buyer at the time the insulation is shipped or when it is ordered with the expectation that the buyer will pay the full bill within a specified number of days. For many construction companies, their work consists of long-term contracts for individual projects with monthly progress payments being made by the owner as the project is being built. Additionally, the owners often withhold retention—funds used to ensure the contractor completes the construction project—thus deferring payment of a portion of the progress payment. As a result, construction companies have unusual cash flows and require modification to accounting and other financial procedures to handle retention.

Heavy Use of Subcontractors

The insulation manufacturer would never subcontract out a step in its manufacturing process, yet many construction companies rely heavily on subcontractors' work. The use of subcontractors allows a construction company to tap into a subcontractor's financial assets during the construction process. The use of subcontractors has a great impact on the finances of a construction company.

Because of these unique characteristics it is important for the manager of a construction company to have a sound understanding not only of financial management but also of how financial management principles are applied to the construction industry. The tools that financial managers are taught in business schools must be modified to take into account the unique characteristics of the construction industry if they are to be useful to construction managers.

WHO IS RESPONSIBLE FOR CONSTRUCTION MANAGEMENT?

The person ultimately responsible for the financial management of a construction company is often the owner or general manager. Often (especially in smaller companies) many of these tasks are delegated to estimators, superintendents, or project managers—particularly those tasks that are project specific. For this reason, and because many project managers, superintendents, and estimators aspire to move up within the company or start their own construction business, it is important for all construction management students to understand the principles of financial success for a construction company. Nothing will put an employee on the fast track to success within a company faster than increasing the company's profitability through sound construction financial management. In this book the term *financial manager* is used to designate superintendents, project managers, estimators, general managers, or owners who are responsible for all or part of the financial management of a construction company.

WHAT DOES A FINANCIAL MANAGER DO?

The financial manager is responsible for seeing that the company uses its financial resources wisely. A financial manager's responsibilities may be broken down into four broad areas that include accounting for financial resources, managing costs and profits, managing cash flows, and making financial decisions.

Accounting for Financial Resources

Financial managers are responsible for accounting or tracking how the company's financial resources are used, including the following:

❏ Making sure that project and general overhead costs are accurately tracked through the accounting system.

❏ Ensuring that a proper construction accounting system has been set up and is functioning properly.

❏ Projecting the costs at completion for the individual projects and ensuring that unbilled committed costs—costs that the company has committed to pay but have not received a bill for—are included in these projections.

❏ Determining whether the individual projects are over- or underbilled.

❏ Making sure that the needed financial statements have been prepared.

❏ Reviewing the financial statements to ensure that the company's financial structure is in line with the rest of the industry and trying to identify potential financial problems before they become a crisis.

Chapters 2 through 6 will help prepare you to fulfill these functions.

In chapter 2 you will be introduced to the structure of construction financial statements, including the different ledgers used by construction accounting systems. You will also learn the difference between accounting systems that are used for cost reporting and systems that are used for controlling costs, as well as the different accounting methods available to construction companies. Because of the unique characteristics of construction companies, there are some key differences between accounting systems and financial statements for the construction industry and other industries. Before you can understand how to read construction company financial statements or understand how construction costs are tracked and managed, you must understand how construction accounting systems operate.

In chapter 3 you will gain a better understanding how different accounting transactions are processed in the accounting system. There are a number of unique transactions that take place in construction accounting that do not occur in other industries. Most of these transactions are a result of the construction industry's focus on job costing, equipment tracking, and accounting for long-term contracts. Understanding these transactions is important for three reasons: First, some project costs—such as labor burden and equipment costs—are often generated by the accounting system rather than an invoice or time card. Understanding how these costs are obtained will help you gain a better understanding how to estimate these costs and incorporate them in the financial analysis of the project. Second, financial managers must review the accounting reports for errors—improperly billed costs and omitted costs—and ensure that the necessary corrections are made. Understanding how the costs are generated will help you better understand how to interpret the accounting reports. Finally, for the general manager and owner, understanding construction accounting is necessary to ensure that the accounting system is set up to meet the needs of the company. Many construction companies are using substandard accounting systems because the management does not understand how accounting systems should be structured to meet the needs of the construction industry.

In chapter 4 you will increase your understanding of construction accounting systems. You will learn to track committed costs outside the accounting system if your company's accounting system does not track committed costs, which will also help you understand how accounting systems track committed costs. You will learn to use committed costs to project the estimated cost and profit at completion for projects. You will also learn to calculate over- and underbillings. Finally, you will learn about the internal controls needed to protect your financial resources and what to look for in computerized construction accounting systems.

In chapter 5 you will learn the differences among the methods available for depreciating construction assets, including the methods used for tax purposes. Understanding the difference in depreciation methods is necessary for a manager to interpret the financial statement and financial ratios, which is covered in the next chapter. Simply put, changing the method of depreciation can have significant impact on the company's financial statements. It is also necessary when preparing income tax projections, which is discussed in chapter 13.

In chapter 6 you will learn to use financial ratios to analyze the company's financial statements, including comparing the company's ratios to industrial averages. This will include adapting commonly used ratios to the unique characteristics of the construction industry. Analysis of the financial statements will help the financial manager identify problems before they become a crisis. These problems may be life threatening to the company (such as realizing that the company will not be able to pay its bills in the upcoming months) or simple planning issues (such as identifying that the company's equipment is aging and that funds need to be set aside to replace this equipment in the next few years).

Managing Costs and Profits

Financial managers are responsible for managing the company's costs and earning a profit for the company's owners. Financial managers rely heavily on the reports from the accounting system in their management of costs. Managing the company's costs and profits includes the following duties:

❑ Controlling project costs.
❑ Monitoring project and company profitability.
❑ Setting labor burden markups.
❑ Developing and tracking general overhead budgets.
❑ Setting the minimum profit margin for use in bidding.

❑ Analyzing the profitability of different parts of the company and making the necessary changes to improve profitability.

❑ Monitoring the profitability of different customers and making the necessary marketing changes to improve profitability.

Chapters 7 through 11 will help to prepare you to fulfill these functions.

In chapter 7 you will learn to monitor and control construction costs for materials, labor, subcontractors, equipment, other costs, and general overhead. You will also learn to measure the success of the project by monitoring profitability, using the schedule performance index, the cost performance index, and project close-outs. These skills help financial managers determine the success of projects and identify problem areas on projects, regardless of whether you are a project manager or superintendent who wants to know how your project is doing or a general manager or owner who wants to know how well your project managers and superintendents are running their projects.

In chapter 8 you will learn to determine the labor burden markup. This helps you better understand how to project these costs, whether they are to be used to bid a new job, price a change order, or project the cost to complete the project. This helps the general manager and owner determine the labor costs needed to prepare a general overhead budget.

In chapter 9 you will learn how to prepare a general overhead budget that may be used to track overhead costs. It is easy for a company to squander its profits by failing to control general overhead costs. Construction managers often spend enormous amounts of time and effort budgeting, tracking, and controlling construction costs while ignoring general overhead costs. Just as a project manager or superintendent tracks and manages construction costs on a project, the general manager or owner needs to track and manage the general overhead costs. The key to doing this is to set and follow a general overhead budget. A general overhead budget is also needed to prepare the company's annual cash flow projection, which is discussed in chapter 14.

In chapter 10 you will learn to set profit margins for use in bidding and how the profit changes as the volume of work changes. You will also learn to determine the volume of construction work and profit and overhead markup necessary to cover the costs associated with the general overhead. Profits are used to pay for general overhead costs and provide the owners with a profit. If the profits are insufficient to cover the general overhead costs the company will consume its available cash and fail. If the profits fail to provide the owner with a reasonable profit, the owner may decide there are better places to invest his or her money and the company will lose financing.

In chapter 11 you will learn to analyze the profitability of different parts of the company and identify where the company needs to make changes to improve profitability. You will learn to choose between hiring a subcontractor and self-performing work. You will also learn to monitor the profitability of different customers and identify which customers should be developed and which customers your company would be better off without.

Managing Cash Flows

Financial managers are responsible for managing the cash flows for the company. Many profitable companies fail because they simply run out of cash and are unable to pay their bills. The duties of a financial manager include the following:

- ❑ Matching the use of in-house labor and subcontractors to the cash available for use on a project.
- ❑ Ensuring that the company has sufficient cash to take on an additional project.
- ❑ Preparing an income tax projection for the company.
- ❑ Preparing and updating annual cash flow projections for the company.
- ❑ Arranging for financing to cover the needs of the construction company.

Chapters 12 through 16 will help prepare you to perform these functions.

In chapter 12 you will learn to develop a cash-flow projection for a construction project from both the perspective of a construction company that is receiving progress payments or draws from the project's owner and from the perspective of a construction company that receives a single payment when the project is sold—such as is the case with many homebuilders. For companies in either of these situations, the company must pay for some or all of the construction costs—especially labor—from the company's funds before being reimbursed for these costs. To cover these costs the company needs cash. Because inadequate funding of the construction company can spell doom to a construction project as well as to all of the companies involved, it is important that managers accurately project both the amount and timing of the cash required by a construction project. Understanding the cash flow for a construction project is a prerequisite to preparing a cash flow for an entire construction company, which is discussed in chapter 14.

In chapter 13 you will learn the fundamentals of income taxes and how to prepare an income tax projection. Income taxes are a significant expense to the company and need to be included in the company's annual cash flow projection. Having an unexpected income tax bill can reduce the funds available for use on construction projects to a dangerously low level.

In chapter 14 you will learn how to prepare an annual cash flow projection for a construction company. This is necessary to ensure that the company has sufficient cash for the upcoming year. Should a financial manager find that there are insufficient funds, he or she will have time to arrange for the necessary financing to provide the necessary funds. Annual cash flow projections for a company are prepared by projecting the annual revenues and construction costs for the construction company by combining the cash flows from the individual jobs or are based on historical data. The financial manager must then combine the projected revenues, construction costs, the general overhead budget, and the projected income taxes with the company's available cash to determine the cash needs of the company.

In chapter 15 you will learn to convert cash flows occurring in one time period to an equivalent cash flow occurring at another time period or into a uniform series of cash flows occurring over successive periods. Understanding the time value of money is a prerequisite to understanding debt financing and how to compare two or more financial options, which are the topics of chapters 16, 17, and 18. Additionally, you will learn how to adjust interest rates for inflation.

In chapter 16 you will learn about financial instruments that can be used to provide the necessary cash for a construction company's operation. You will also learn to compare debt instruments with different conditions and learn how loan provisions and closing costs can increase the effective interest rate on a loan or line of credit. An understanding of these principles helps you reduce borrowing costs and determine the best way to provide the cash needed to operate a construction company. Success in obtaining financing for a company can allow the company to take on additional projects, whereas failure to obtain financing can spell the doom of a company.

Choosing among Financial Alternatives

Financial managers are responsible for selecting among financial alternatives. These decisions include the following:

- ❑ Selecting which equipment to purchase.
- ❑ Deciding to invest the company's limited resources in which area of the business.

There are many financial tools that are available to quantitatively analyze the alternatives. In chapters 17 and 18 you will learn to use these tools.

In chapter 17 you will learn ten quantitative methods that may be used to analyze financial alternatives and choose the alternative that is best for the company. Without some quantitative method it is hard for managers to determine which option is best. Understanding these skills is necessary for any manager who must decide where to invest limited capital.

In chapter 18 you will learn how income taxes can influence the choice of financial decisions and how to incorporate income taxes into the decision-making tools from chapter 17. If income taxes affected all alternatives in the same way, income taxes would not be an issue; however, income taxes can make some financial alternatives preferable. With income tax rates of up to 38.6% financial managers must take income taxes into account by weighing financial alternatives.

ACCOUNTING FOR
FINANCIAL RESOURCES

In this section we look at how to account for the company's financial resources. Accounting for these resources is built around a company's accounting system. This section includes the following chapters:

CONSTRUCTION
ACCOUNTING SYSTEMS

In this chapter you will be introduced to the structure of construction financial statements, including the different ledgers used by construction accounting systems. You will also learn the difference between accounting systems that are used for cost reporting and systems that are used for controlling costs, as well as the different accounting methods available to construction companies. Because of the unique characteristics of construction companies, there are some key differences between accounting systems and financial statements for the construction industry and other industries. Before you can understand how to read construction company financial statements or understand how construction costs are tracked and managed, you must understand how construction accounting systems operate.

Construction accounting systems include the software, hardware, and personnel necessary to operate a construction accounting system. Construction accounting systems serve four purposes.

First, the accounting system processes the cash receipts (collecting payments) and disbursements (paying bills) for the company. The accounting system should ensure that revenues are billed and collected in a timely fashion and that timely payments are made only for bona fide expenses incurred by the company. Failure to collect revenues or careless payment of bills can quickly deplete the cash reserves of a company and, if left unchecked, can bankrupt a company.

Second, the accounting system collects and reports the data needed to prepare company financial statements that are used to report the financial status of the company to shareholders and lending institutions. These reports are

17

needed to assure shareholders and lending institutions that the company is solvent and is managing its financial assets in a wise manner.

Third, the accounting system collects and reports the data needed to prepare income taxes, employment taxes, and other documents required by the government. Failure to pay taxes and file other required documents—such as W-2s and 1099s—on time results in the assessment of penalties.

And, finally, the accounting system collects and provides the data needed to manage the finances of the company, including data for the company as a whole, each project, and each piece of heavy equipment. To successfully manage the company's financial resources, the accounting system must provide this data quickly enough for management to analyze the data and make corrections in a timely manner. Accounting systems that fail to do this are simply reporting costs.

COST REPORTING VERSUS COST CONTROL

Cost reporting is where the accounting system provides management with the accounting data after the opportunity has passed for management to respond to and correct the problems indicated by the data. When companies wait to enter the cost of their purchases until the bills are received, management does not know if they are under or over budget until the bills are entered, at which time the materials purchased have been delivered to the project and may have been consumed. The extreme case of cost reporting is where companies only look at the costs and profit for each project after the project is finished. Cost reporting is typified by the accounting reports showing where a company has been financially without giving management an opportunity to proactively respond to the data.

Cost control is where the accounting system provides management with the accounting data in time for management to analyze the data and make corrections in a timely manner. Companies that enter material purchase orders and subcontracts, along with their associated costs, into their accounting system as committed costs before issuing the purchase order or subcontract allow management time to address cost overruns before ordering the materials or work. Committed costs are those costs that the company has committed to pay and can be identified before a bill is received for the costs. For example, when a contractor signs a fixed-price subcontract he or she has committed to pay the subcontractor a fixed price once the work has been completed and, short of any change orders, knows what the work is going to cost. Accounting systems that track committed costs give management time to identify the cause of the overrun early on, identify possible solutions, and take corrective action. Cost control is typified by identifying problems early and giving management a chance to proactively address the problem. A lot of money can be saved by addressing pervasive problems—such as excessive waste—early in the project.

If a company's accounting system is going to allow management to control costs rather than just report costs, the accounting system must have the following key components:

First, the accounting system must have a strong job cost and equipment tracking system. The accounting system should update and report costs, including committed costs and estimated cost at completion on a weekly basis. Having timely, up-to-date costs for the project and the equipment is a must if management is going to manage costs and identify problems early.

Second, the accounting system must utilize the principle of management by exception. It can be easy for managers to get lost in the volumes of data generated by the accounting system. The accounting system should provide reports that allow management to quickly identify problem areas and address the problems. For example, as soon as bills are entered into the accounting system, management should get a report detailing all bills that exceed the amount of their purchase order or subcontract. Problems that are buried in volumes of accounting data are often never addressed because management seldom has time to pour through all of the data to find the problems or if they are found they are often found too late for management to address the problem. Providing reports that flag transactions that fall outside the acceptable limits is a necessity if management is going to control costs. By having reports that flag items that fall outside acceptable limits, management can make addressing these items a priority.

Third, accounting procedures need to be established to ensure that things do not fall through the cracks. These procedures should include things such as who can issue purchase orders and what to do when a bill is received for a purchase order that has not been issued. The procedures should also identify the acceptable limits for different types of transactions. Procedures ensure that the accounting is handled in a consistent manner and give management confidence in the data that it is using to manage the company.

Finally, the data must be easily and quickly available to management and other employees who are directly responsible for controlling costs. It does little good to collect cost data for use in controlling costs if the data cannot be accessed. Where possible the reports should be automatically prepared by the accounting software. This eliminates the time and effort needed to prepare the reports manually. Additionally, frontline supervisors who are responsible for control costs should readily have access to their costs. Holding supervisors responsible for costs at the end of a job while not giving them access to their costs throughout the project denies them the opportunity to proactively control costs.

The accounting system for many construction companies consists of three different ledgers: the general ledger, the job cost ledger, and the equipment ledger. The general ledger tracks financial data for the entire company and is used to prepare the company's financial statements and income taxes. The job cost ledger is used to track the financial data for each of the construction projects. The equipment ledger is used to track financial data for heavy equipment and vehicles. All construction companies should have a general ledger and a job cost ledger. Companies with lots of heavy equipment or vehicles should have an equipment ledger.

THE GENERAL LEDGER

Like all other companies, construction company accounting systems have a general ledger. The general ledger consists of all of the accounts necessary to track the financial data needed to prepare the balance sheet, income statement, and income taxes. A chart of accounts lists all of the accounts in the general ledger. A sample chart of accounts is shown in Figure 2-1. In the chart of accounts, the accounts for the balance sheet are listed before the accounts for the income statement. In Figure 2-1, accounts 110 through 430 are used for the balance sheet and accounts 500 through 950 are used for the income statement. The accounts on the chart of accounts appear in the order they appear in on the balance sheet and income statement; however, not all accounts from the chart of accounts appear on the balance sheet or income statement because successive accounts may be rolled up into a summary account that appears on the balance sheet or income statement. Other items—such as profit—appear on the balance sheet and income statement that are not included in the chart of accounts because they are calculated from accounts on the chart of accounts. The way transactions are handled in the general ledger is based on the accounting method used by the construction company.

METHOD OF ACCOUNTING

There are four methods of accounting available to construction companies. They are: cash, accrual, percentage of completion, and completed contract. The cash and accrual methods are two widely used accounting methods and are used in many industries. The percentage-of-completion and completed contract methods are used when companies enter long-term contracts, which are defined by the Internal Revenue Code as "any contract for the manufacture, building, installation, or construction of property if such contract is not completed within the taxable year in which such contract is entered into."[11] The key difference between these methods is how and when they recognize income, expenses, and profits. A construction company may use a different method of accounting when preparing its financial statements than it does when it is preparing its income taxes. Let's look at these accounting methods.

Cash

Cash is the easiest of the accounting methods to use. Revenue is recognized when the payment from the owner is received and expenses are recognized when bills are paid. Profit at any point equals the cash receipts less the cash disbursements. Because of the easiness of its use, it is often a favorite of small construction

---

[11]Title 26, Subtitle A, Chapter 1, Subchapter E, Part II, Subpart B, Section 460.

CHART OF ACCOUNTS

110	Cash		730	Repairs and Maintenance
120	Accounts Receivable-Trade		740	Fuel and Lubrication
121	Accounts Receivable-Retention		750	Taxes, Licenses, and Insurance
130	Inventory		798	Equipment Costs Charged to Employees
140	Costs and Profits in Excess of Billings		799	Equipment Costs Charged to Jobs
150	Notes Receivable			
160	Prepaid Expenses		805	Advertising
199	Other Current Assets		806	Promotion
			810	Car and Truck Expenses
210	Building and Land		811	Computer and Office Furniture
220	Construction Equipment		812	Repairs and Maintenance
230	Trucks and Autos		819	Depreciation
240	Office Equipment		820	Employee Wages and Salaries
250	Less Acc. Depreciation		821	Employee Benefits
260	Capital Leases		822	Employee Retirement
299	Other Assets		823	Employee Recruiting
			824	Employee Training
310	Accounts Payable-Trade		825	Employee Taxes
311	Accounts Payable-Retention		830	Insurance
320	Billings in Excess of Costs and Profits		835	Taxes and Licenses
330	Notes Payable		840	Office Supplies
340	Accrued Payroll		841	Office Purchase
341	Accrued Payables		842	Office Rent
342	Accrued Taxes		843	Office Utilities
343	Accrued Insurance		844	Postage and Delivery
344	Accrued Vacation		845	Janitorial and Cleaning
350	Capital Leases Payable		846	Telephone
360	Warranty Reserves		850	Charitable Contributions
379	Other Current Liabilities		855	Dues and Memberships
380	Long-Term Liabilities		860	Publications and Subscriptions
			865	Legal and Professional Services
410	Capital Stock		870	Meals and Entertainment
420	Retained Earnings		875	Travel
430	Current Period Net Income		880	Bank Fees
			881	Interest Expense
500	Revenue		885	Bad Debts
			891	Unallocated Labor
610	Materials		892	Unallocated Materials
620	Labor		893	Warranty Expense
630	Subcontract		898	Miscellaneous
640	Equipment		899	Overhead Charged to Jobs
650	Other			
			910	Other Income
710	Rent and Lease Payments		920	Other Expense
720	Depreciation		950	Income Tax

FIGURE 2-1   Chart of Accounts

companies. Another advantage of the cash method of accounting is that it can easily be used to defer income tax. For example, to decrease the company's tax liability for the year all the company has to do is to have any of the project's owners who are going to make payments during the last few weeks of the company's fiscal year hold the checks until the beginning of the next fiscal year. This moves the revenues from the current year into the next year, reduces the profit for the year, and thereby reduces the income tax liability for the year. The company can further reduce the profit by paying any bills that are due during the first few weeks of the next year on the last day of the current year. Regular "C" corporations whose average annual receipts for the last three taxable years are more than $5,000,000 may not use the cash method of accounting for income tax purposes.

The big disadvantage of the cash method is that financial statements based on the cash method are of little use for financial management because of the delay in recognizing revenue and expenses. Because of this, many financial institutions will not accept financial statements based on the cash accounting method. Construction companies that use the cash method of accounting for income tax purposes often use another accounting method for preparing financial statements for use in financial management.

Accrual

The accrual method tries to provide a more accurate financial picture by recognizing revenues when the company has the right to receive the revenues and by recognizing the expenses when the company is obligated to pay for the expenses, rather than when its cash flows occur. Revenues are usually recognized when the company bills the project's owners. Because the company does not have the right to receive the retention until the project is complete, the revenue associated with the retention is usually not recognized until the project is complete and the company has the right to receive the retention. Expenses are often recognized when the company receives a bill from the supplier or subcontractors. Because the accrual accounting method recognizes revenues and expenses before the revenues are received and the bills have been paid, financial statements prepared using the accrual method are more useful for financial management. Use of the accrual accounting method may also result in the payment of income taxes on revenues not received. Furthermore, companies that front-end load their contracts—put most or all of the profit at the beginning of the contract—may be paying income taxes on imaginary or unearned profits.

Percentage of Completion

The percentage-of-completion method requires construction companies to recognize revenues, expenses, and estimated profits on a construction project through the course of the project. Revenues are recognized when the company bills the project's owners. The revenue associated with the retention is recognized, along with the revenues from the bill, unlike with the accrual accounting method, which allows the company to defer recognizing retention as revenue until it has the right to receive the retention. Expenses are recognized when the company receives a bill from the supplier or subcontractors. Under the percentage-of-completion method the estimated profits must be equally distributed over the entire project based on the expected cost of the project. Revenues, expenses, and the estimated profits are calculated based on the percentage of the project that is complete. For example, if the project were 40% complete a company would recognize 40% of the expected revenue, 40% of the expected costs, and 40% of the expected profit. At the completion of the project the construction company must look back over the life of the project and determine if income taxes were overpaid or underpaid for each tax year. For underpayments of income taxes the construction company must pay interest to the Internal Revenue Service on the amount underpaid in addition to paying the underpaid taxes. For overpayment the Internal Revenue Service must pay interest to the construction company on the overpayment in addition to refunding the overpaid taxes. Larger construction companies are required to allocate general overhead to the individual projects when using the percentage-of-completion method. The percentage-of-completion method provides the best picture of the company's financial situation.

Completed Contract

The completed contract method recognizes revenues and expenses at the completion of the project. The benefit of recognizing revenues and expenses at the completion of the project is that the revenues and expenses are known. Historically, speculative builders used the completed contract method because the contract amount was not known until the project was sold. The disadvantage of the completed contract method is that it creates large swings in income.

To get the best picture of a company's financial health, a construction company should use the method that best matches its costs to its revenues and profits. For most general contractors this is the percentage-of-completion method. For smaller companies the added cost and complexity of using the percentage-of-completion method may not be warranted and the company may use the cash method.

For tax purposes construction companies must use the percentage-of-completion accounting method for long-term contracts except for (1) contracts entered into by a construction company whose average annual receipts for the last three taxable years is less than $10,000,000 and who estimates that the contract can be completed within a two-year period beginning at the contract commencement date or (2) home construction contracts, including improvements to dwelling units and the construction of new dwelling units in buildings containing no more than four dwelling units. Because the income tax regulations are very complex and ever changing, it is a good idea for construction companies to employ the services of a certified public accountant when determining what method of accounting to use for financial and tax purposes.

THE BALANCE SHEET

The balance sheet is a snapshot of a company's financial assets, liabilities, and the value of the company to its owner—often referred to as net worth or equity—at a specific point in time. Balance sheets are commonly prepared at the end of each month and at the end of the fiscal year. A typical balance sheet for a construction company using the percentage-of-completion accounting method is shown in Figure 2-2.

The balance sheet is divided into three sections: assets, liabilities, and owner's equity. The balance sheet reports the values of each of the accounts in the balance sheet portion of the chart of accounts at the time the balance sheet is printed. For example, the amount reported as cash on the balance sheet in Figure 2-2 comes from account number 110 from the chart of accounts shown in Figure 2-1. To prevent the balance sheet from becoming too complicated multiple accounts may be summarized by combining two or more consecutive accounts into a single line on the balance sheet. Other items on the balance sheet may be calculated from other lines on the balance sheet. For example, the Total Current Assets is the sum of the Cash, Accounts Receivable-Trade, Accounts Receivable-Retention, Costs and Profits in Excess of Billings, Notes Receivable, Prepaid Expenses, and Other Current Assets or accounts 110 through 199 on the chart of accounts in Figure 2-1. Not all companies will use all the accounts shown in Figure 2-1. For example, the construction company in Figure 2-2 does not use the inventory account.

On the balance sheet the relationship between assets, liabilities, and equity is as follows:

$$\text{Assets} = \text{Liabilities} + \text{Equity} \hspace{3cm} (2\text{-}1)$$

Assets

Assets are those resources held by the company that will probably lead to some future cash inflows. For example, a piece of property is an asset because it could be sold to produce a cash inflow. A pallet of custom framing brackets left over from a job would not be considered an asset unless there was a reasonable chance that the brackets could be used on a future job for which the company would be paid to build. Assets are divided into three broad categories: current assets, long-term assets, and other assets.

Current assets are the most liquid assets. Current assets are those assets that are expected to be converted to cash, exchanged, or consumed within one year. Common current assets include cash, accounts receivable, inventory, cost and profit in excess of billings, notes receivable, prepaid expenses, and other assets. Let's look at what would be included in each of these categories.

CASH: Cash includes demand deposits (such as savings and checking accounts), time deposits (such as certificates of deposits) with a maturity of one year or less, and petty cash.

BIG W CONSTRUCTION
BALANCE SHEET

	Current Year	Last Year
ASSETS		
CURRENT ASSETS		
Cash	200,492	144,254
Accounts Receivable-Trade	402,854	308,253
Accounts Receivable-Retention	25,365	21,885
Costs and Profits in Excess of Billings	32,586	15,234
Notes Receivable	12,548	0
Prepaid Expenses	5,621	4,825
Other Current Assets	11,254	7,225
Total Current Assets	690,720	501,676
FIXED AND OTHER ASSETS		
Building and Land	175,862	175,862
Construction Equipment	95,284	95,284
Trucks and Autos	51,245	31,556
Office Equipment	56,896	42,546
Total Fixed Assets	379,287	345,248
Less Acc. Depreciation	224,512	182,990
Net Fixed Assets	154,775	162,258
Other Assets	178,544	171,256
Total Assets	1,024,039	835,190
LIABILITIES		
Current Liabilities		
Accounts Payable-Trade	325,458	228,585
Accounts Payable-Retention	22,546	18,254
Billings in Excess of Costs and Profits	5,218	11,562
Notes Payable	15,514	45,250
Accrued Payables	15,648	16,658
Accrued Taxes	10,521	8,254
Accrued Vacation	3,564	3,002
Other Current Liabilities	25,438	35,648
Total Current Liabilities	423,907	367,213
Long-Term Liabilities	153,215	99,073
Total Liabilities	577,122	466,286
OWNER'S EQUITY		
Capital Stock	10,000	10,000
Retained Earnings	436,917	358,904
Current Period Net Income	0	0
Total Equity	446,917	368,904
Total Liabilities and Equity	1,024,039	835,190

FIGURE 2-2   Balance Sheet for Big W Construction

ACCOUNTS RECEIVABLE: Accounts receivable are invoices owed to the company that will likely be paid within one year and have not been formalized by a written promise to pay, such as a note receivable. For construction companies the monthly bills or draws to the owners of the construction projects constitute an account receivable until the bill is paid. When retention is held, it is common practice to divide the accounts receivable into two categories: accounts receivable-trade and accounts receivable-retention. The retention that is being held by the project's owner for which the company has not met the requirements for its release is recorded in the accounts receivable-retention category. The monthly bills—less retention—and retention for which the company has met the requirements for its release are recorded in the accounts receivable-trade category. This separation lets management quickly see which of the receivables are tied up in the form of retention, whose release is contingent on the completion of construction projects.

INVENTORY: Inventory includes materials that are available for sale or are available and expected to be incorporated into a construction project within the next year. Many construction companies have little or no inventory. Subcontractors are the most likely group of contractors to carry inventory.

COSTS AND PROFITS IN EXCESS OF BILLINGS: Costs and profits in excess of billings may also be referred to as costs and estimated earnings in excess of billings or underbillings. Construction companies using the percentage-of-completion accounting method are required to recognize the estimated profits on a construction project as the project is being completed rather than at the completion of the project. In these situations, the estimated profits must be equally distributed over the entire project based on the expected cost of the project. Costs and profits in excess of billings occur when the company bills less than the costs incurred plus the estimated profits or earnings associated with the completed work. If the billings are in excess of the costs and estimated profits, the difference is recorded as a liability under the billings in excess of costs and profits category. Costs and profits in excess of billings can be the result of cost overruns on the completed work or as a result of the profit not being equally spread over the items listed on the schedule of values. For companies using the completed contract accounting method, this category is replaced with a category entitled cost in excess of billings. For companies using the cash or accrual accounting method this category is not included on the financial statements.

NOTES RECEIVABLE: Notes receivable includes all invoices due to the company that will likely be paid within one year and have been formalized by a written promise to pay. Invoices, short-term loans, or advances to employees that have been formalized by a written promise to pay and are likely to be paid within a year are considered notes receivable.

PREPAID EXPENSES: Prepaid expenses are payments that have been made for future supplies and services. Examples of prepaid expenses include prepaid taxes, insurance premiums, rent, and deposits.

OTHER CURRENT ASSETS: Other current assets are all current assets not recorded elsewhere.

TOTAL CURRENT ASSETS: Total current assets represent the total value of the current assets.

Fixed and other assets include assets with an expected useful life of more than one year at the time of their purchase. Fixed assets are recorded on the balance sheet at their purchase price and with the exception of land are depreciated for financial purposes. Fixed and other assets include fixed assets, accumulated depreciation, net fixed assets, and other assets. Let's look at what would be included in each of these categories.

FIXED ASSETS: On the balance sheet shown in Figure 2-2 the fixed assets have been broken down into the following categories: building and land, construction equipment, trucks and autos, and office equipment. Building and land include all real property (real estate) owned by the company. Construction equipment includes heavy construction equipment, such as excavators and dump trucks, and other depreciable construction tools, such as compressors. Trucks and autos include pickup trucks and automobiles used by office and field personnel. Office equipment includes all depreciable office equipment and furnishings such as desks and computers. These subcategories are then summed up to get the total fixed assets.

ACCUMULATED DEPRECIATION: The losses in value to date of the fixed assets are recorded as accumulated depreciation. The depreciation method used in financial statements may be different from the depreciation method used for tax purposes. The depreciation taken for a fixed asset may never exceed the purchase price of the asset. The accumulated depreciation account is a contra account because it is subtracted from another account.

NET FIXED ASSETS: The net fixed assets equals the total fixed assets less the accumulated depreciation. The net fixed assets is also known as the book values for all of the fixed assets or the value of the fixed assets on the accounting books.

OTHER ASSETS: Other assets include assets not elsewhere classified. Common other assets include inventory that will not be sold within a year, investment in other companies, and the cash value of life insurance policies.

TOTAL ASSETS: Total assets represent the total value of the current, fixed, and other assets.

Liabilities

Liabilities are obligations for a company to transfer assets or render services at some future time for which the company is already committed to. Loans and warranty reserves are common liabilities. Liabilities are divided into two broad categories: current liabilities and long-term liabilities.

Current liabilities are those liabilities that are expected to be paid within one year. Current assets are usually used to pay current liabilities. Current liabilities include accounts payable, billings in excess of costs and estimated earnings, notes payable, accrued payables, capital lease payments, warranty reserves, and other current liabilities.

ACCOUNTS PAYABLE: Accounts payables are debts that the company owes and expects to pay within one year that are not evidenced by a written promise to pay. For construction companies the monthly bills that they receive from their suppliers and subcontractors constitute accounts payable until the bill has been paid. When retention is withheld from the subcontractor payments, it is common practice to divide accounts payable into two categories: accounts payable-trade and accounts payable-retention. The retention that is being withheld from the supplier or subcontractor's payments on projects that the requirements for release of the retention have not been met is recorded in the accounts payable-retention category. The monthly bills from the suppliers and subcontractors, less retention, and retention on projects where the requirements for release of the retention have been met are recorded in the accounts payable-trade category. The separation of these two categories allows management to see quickly how much of its accounts payable are being held until the requirements for the release of retention have been met.

BILLINGS IN EXCESS OF COSTS AND PROFITS: Billings in excess of costs and profits may also be referred to as billings in excess of costs and estimated earnings or over-billings. Billings in excess of costs and estimated profits is the opposite of costs and profits in excess of billings. Construction companies using the percentage-of-completion accounting method are required to recognize the estimated profits on a construction project as the project is being completed rather than at the completion of the project. In these situations, the estimated profits must be equally distributed over the entire project based on the expected cost of the project. Billings in excess of costs and estimated profits occur when the company bills more than the costs incurred plus the estimated profits or earnings associated with the completed work. If the costs and estimated profits are greater than the billings, the difference is recorded as an asset under the costs and profits in excess of billings category. Billings in excess of costs and profits can be the result of cost savings on the completed work or as a result of the profit not being equally spread over the items listed on the schedule of values. For companies using the completed contract accounting method, this category is replaced with a category entitled billings in excess of costs. For companies using the cash or accrual accounting method this category is not included on the financial statements.

NOTES PAYABLE: Notes payable includes all debts that will likely be paid within one year and have been formalized by a written promise to pay.

ACCRUED PAYABLES: Accrued payables are monies owed for supplies and services that have not been billed. They include accrued taxes, rents, wages, and employee vacation time that have not been paid. For example, from the time an employee's hours are entered into the accounting system until the payroll check is prepared, the wages due to the employee are recorded as an accrued payable. On the balance sheet in Figure 2-2 the accrued payables have been broken down into accrued payables, accrued taxes, and accrued vacation.

CAPITAL LEASE PAYMENTS: Capital leases must be recorded as a liability. Capital leases include all leases that are noncancelable and meet at least one of the following conditions: (1) the lease extends for 75% or more of the equipment or property's useful life, (2) ownership transfers at the end of the lease, (3) ownership is likely to transfer at the end of the lease through a purchase option with a heavily discounted price, or (4) the present value of the lease payments at market interest rates exceeds 90% of the fair market value of the equipment or property.

WARRANTY RESERVES: Warranty reserves are funds set aside to cover the foreseeable cost of warranty work. When a company has a foreseeable expense associated with providing warranty work on a completed construction project, the foreseeable expenses should be included as a liability on the balance sheet. Many homebuilders should be able to forecast their expected warranty costs based on past warranty experience.

OTHER CURRENT LIABILITIES: Other current liabilities include all other current liabilities that are not recorded elsewhere.

TOTAL CURRENT LIABILITIES: Total current liabilities represent the sum of all the current liabilities.

LONG-TERM LIABILITIES: Long-term liabilities include all debts that are not expected to be paid within one year. Common long-term liabilities include loans.

TOTAL LIABILITIES: Total liabilities represent the total of both current and long-term liabilities.

Owner's Equity

Owner's equity is the claim of the company's owner or shareholders on the assets that remain after the liabilities are paid. Owner's equity may also be referred to as net worth. Owner's equity is recorded differently on the balance sheet for corporations, sole proprietors, and partnerships.

For corporations the owner's equity is commonly broken down into three categories: capital stock, retained earnings, and current period net income. The capital stock represents the initial investment in the company by the shareholders. The retained earnings represent prior accounting period's profits or earnings retained by the corporation to invest in company operations rather than be distributed to the shareholders. The current period net income represents the profits or losses incurred during the current accounting period.

For sole proprietors the owner's equity is listed as a single sum and is known as the owner's capital. For partnerships, the owner's equity is listed for each partner separately and is known as owner's capital.

THE INCOME STATEMENT

The income statement shows a company's revenues, expenses, and the resulting profit generated over a period of time. Income statements span a period of time between two balance sheets and record all transactions that occur during the period. Income statements are commonly prepared for each month and the fiscal year. A typical income statement for a construction company using the percentage-of-completion accounting method is shown in Figure 2-3.

The income statement includes the following items: revenue, cost of construction, equipment costs, overhead, other income and expense, and income tax.

FIGURE 2-3   Income Statement for Big W Construction

BIG W CONSTRUCTION INCOME STATEMENT		
REVENUE	3,698,945	100.0%
CONSTRUCTION COSTS		
Materials	712,564	19.3%
Labor	896,514	24.2%
Subcontract	1,452,352	39.3%
Equipment	119,575	3.2%
Other	5,452	0.1%
Total Construction Costs	3,186,457	86.1%
EQUIPMENT COSTS		
Rent and Lease Payments	35,425	1.0%
Depreciation	32,397	0.9%
Repairs and Maintenance	21,254	0.6%
Fuel and Lubrication	29,245	0.8%
Taxes, Licenses, and Insurance	1,254	0.0%
Equipment Costs Charged to Jobs	119,575	3.2%
Total Equipment Costs	0	0.0%
GROSS PROFIT	512,488	13.9%
OVERHEAD	422,562	11.4%
NET PROFIT FROM OPERATIONS	89,926	2.4%
OTHER INCOME AND EXPENSE	21,521	0.6%
PROFIT BEFORE TAX	111,447	3.0%
INCOME TAX	33,434	0.9%
PROFIT AFTER TAX	78,013	2.1%

The income statement reports the value of each of the accounts in the income state-ment portion of the chart of accounts. Like the balance sheet, multiple accounts on the income statement may be combined and unneeded accounts left out.

Revenue

Revenue is the income recognized from the completion of part or all of a con-struction project. For a company using the percentage-of-completion or accrual accounting methods, revenue is recognized at the time the project's owner is billed for the work. For a company using the completed contract method, revenue is rec-ognized at the completion of the project. For a company using the cash method, revenue is recognized when the company is paid for the work by the project's owner. Revenue may also be referred to as contract revenue on a construction com-pany's income statement and is equivalent to net sales used by other industries. Income from nonconstruction operations is usually classified as other income.

Construction Costs

Construction costs include both direct costs and indirect costs. Construction costs are the same as cost of sales in other industries.

Direct costs are the cost of materials, labor, and equipment that are incorpo-rated into the construction of a project. Direct costs can be specifically identified to the completion of a specific construction component of a specific construction project, such as a wall, a road, a tree, and so forth. Direct costs include the cost of all materials incorporated into the completed construction project and the cost of the labor and equipment to install them. For example, for the task of installing a door the direct costs would include the material cost for the door—including sales tax and delivery costs—and the labor cost with burden to install the door. Most work in Divisions 2 through 16 of the MasterFormat[12] is specified as direct costs. The key is that direct costs can be billed to a specific component of a specific project.

Indirect costs consist of those costs that can be specifically identified to the completion of a specific construction project but cannot be identified with the completion of a specific construction component on that project. Indirect costs may also be referred to as indirect project costs, project overhead, or direct over-head costs. For example, job supervision and the jobsite trailer are indirect costs. Although these costs are required to complete the construction project, they are not directly incorporated into the construction project. Most work in Division 1 of the MasterFormat is specified as indirect costs. The key is that indirect costs can be billed to a specific project but cannot be billed to a specific component on the project.

All construction costs should be charged to a specific construction project. Construction costs are commonly broken down into five types or groups that

---

[12]MasterFormat is a registered trademark of Construction Specification Institute (CSI).

include materials, labor, subcontract, equipment, and other costs. Some companies break labor down into labor and labor burden and equipment down into equipment rental and equipment owned. One reason for this breakdown is that a company often pays a different liability insurance rate on each of these types of costs.

MATERIALS: The materials cost type includes supplies or material that are purchased by the company and incorporated into the finished project, such as lumber, windows, and concrete. The transportation and storage of the materials should be included in the cost of the materials as well as any sales tax on the purchase. The materials cost type does not include any labor for the installation of the material. Purchases that include labor would be considered a subcontract cost type.

LABOR: The labor cost type includes only the labor that is processed through the construction company's payroll system and is charged to a construction project. Labor includes all labor burden costs, including social security, Medicare, Federal Unemployment Tax (FUTA), State Unemployment Tax (SUTA), vacation allowance, company-paid health insurance, company-paid union fees, and other company-paid benefits. Labor that does not pass through the company's payroll system, including temporary labor services, would be considered a subcontract cost type. When the labor cost type is separated into labor and labor burden, the employee's wages would be considered a labor cost type, whereas all burden costs would be considered a labor burden cost type.

SUBCONTRACT: The subcontract cost type includes work that is performed by subcontractors for a construction project. Subcontracts must always include labor being performed by the subcontractor and may include the supplying of materials, equipment, and other items. Subcontract does not include labor that is processed through the contractor's payroll system.

EQUIPMENT: The equipment cost type includes equipment costs that have been charged to a construction project. These charges come from the equipment cost section of the income statement. When equipment is charged directly to the construction costs section of the income statement it should be categorized as an other cost type or the company should break the equipment cost type into equipment rented and equipment owned. When this is done, the equipment that is charged directly to the construction costs section of the income statement is categorized as an equipment rented cost type, whereas charges coming from the equipment cost section of the income statement are categorized as an equipment owned cost type. When a company does not use the equipment portion of the income statement, all equipment costs are charged directly to the jobs as an equipment cost type and there is no need to break down the equipment category. This separation is necessary to maintain checks and balances within the accounting system.

OTHER: The other cost type includes all costs that are not classified as labor, materials, equipment, or subcontract cost types and are performed on a construction project. Other costs include services (such as surveying, temporary toilets, and utilities) and materials that are not incorporated into the construction project (such as materials used on temporary office facilities).

Equipment Costs

When equipment is used on multiple construction projects the allocation of equipment costs to construction jobs is much more complicated than the billing of materials, labor, and subcontractor's services. When equipment is used on a single construction project, all costs go to the project. When a construction company spends $5,000 on tires for a front-end loader that is used on dozens or maybe hundreds of jobs during the life of the tires, it becomes unclear which construction project should be charged for the costs of the tires. Suppose the front-end loader was used on a construction project for two days. After the first day the company's maintenance personnel came to the project and changed the tires on the front-end loader. Even though the costs associated with the new tires occurred while the front-end loader was on the project, it would be unfair to charge the entire cost of the tires to the project. To do so would unfairly skew the costs of the project and render the data obtained from the accounting systems less meaningful. To fairly handle construction equipment costs, the costs must be allocated. The equipment costs portion of the income statement is where these costs are held until they can be allocated to specific projects. In the case of the front-end loader, the cost of the tires would be recorded under equipment costs and then would be allocated to the individual jobs based on the project's usage of the equipment.

The equipment cost portion of the income statement is a unique feature of income statements for construction companies that own their own equipment. Equipment costs are considered construction costs that have yet to be allocated or charged to specific projects and should not be confused with company overhead costs. Some companies and accountants require that all of the equipment costs be allocated by the end of the company's fiscal year.

Let's look at how the equipment section of the income statement works. Suppose that your company had a front-end loader whose costs for depreciation, taxes, licenses, and insurance were $3,200 per month and whose preventative maintenance, fuel, and lubrication were $35 per billable hour. During the month of April the tires were replaced on the loader at a cost of $6,000. No other costs were incurred during the year. The loader was only used during the months of April through October. The monthly costs and billable hours by job are shown in Table 2-1.

If a company were to bill the monthly costs to the jobs the loader worked on during the month, for the months of January, February, March, November, and December the monthly costs would go unbilled. During the remaining months the average hourly cost ranged from $52.78 to $150.00 per hour. To more evenly distribute the costs and to ensure all costs incurred during the year are billed to jobs,

TABLE 2-1   Loader Costs

Month	Monthly Costs ($)	Hourly Costs ($)	Tires ($)	Billable Hours by Job	Average Hourly Cost ($)
January	3,200	0	0	0	?
February	3,200	0	0	0	?
March	3,200	0	0	0	?
April	3,200	2,800	6,000	80 hr on Job 101	150.00
May	3,200	6,300	0	80 hr on Job 101	52.78
				100 hr on Job 102	
June	3,200	6,300	0	180 hr on Job 102	52.78
July	3,200	6,300	0	180 hr on Job 102	52.78
August	3,200	6,300	0	180 hr on Job 102	52.78
September	3,200	6,300	0	180 hr on Job 102	52.78
October	3,200	1,400	0	40 hr on Job 102	115.00
November	3,200	0	0	0	?
December	3,200	0	0	0	?

the monthly costs are charged to the equipment cost portion of the income statement in the month they are incurred and then the costs are allocated based on a projected hourly cost of the equipment and the billable hours to each project. Suppose the company in the above example were to project that the hourly cost of the loader was $80 per hour. During January, February, and March the monthly costs would be recorded to the equipment cost portion of the income statement, whereas no costs would be allocated to the jobs. At the end of March, the equipment cost portion of the income statement would have a balance of $9,600 in unallocated costs. During April $12,000 would be billed to the equipment cost portion of the income statement and $6,400 of these costs would be allocated to Job 101. This would continue through October, when at the end of the month the equipment cost portion of the income statement would be overallocated by $7,900. November and December's costs would reduce this overallocation to $1,500. This remaining overallocation at the end of December is due to the fact that the actual hourly cost was $78.53 per hour rather than the project cost of $80.00 per hour.

Equipment costs are often broken down into the following categories: rent and lease payments; depreciation; repairs and maintenance; fuel and lubrication; taxes, licenses, and insurance; and equipment costs charged to jobs. They may also be broken down in other ways.

RENT AND LEASE PAYMENTS: Rent and lease payments include the rental fees and lease payments for the use of equipment not owned by the construction company. Equipment that is rented or leased for a specific job may be billed directly to the job as an equipment rented cost type rather than being processed through the equipment cost portion of the income statement and subsequently allocated.

DEPRECIATION: Depreciation includes the loss in value of company-owned equipment over its useful life. The depreciation method used for allocating construction costs may be different from the depreciation method used for income tax purposes. Amortization of capital leases is included with depreciation costs. Depreciation methods are discussed in detail in chapter 5.

REPAIRS AND MAINTENANCE: Repairs and maintenance include repairs, routine maintenances, and the replacement of tires and other wear items. Repairs include repairs because of damage and abuse and other major repairs such as overhauls to extend the life of the equipment. Routine maintenance includes all regularly scheduled or preventative maintenance and includes oil and filter changes. Tires and other wear items include the replacement of tires, cutting edges, bucket teeth, and other items that frequently wear out. Repair and maintenance costs should include the materials, supplies, and labor involved in the repairs and maintenance.

FUEL AND LUBRICATION: Fuel and lubrication includes the fuel used to operate the equipment and lubricants consumed on the job, such as grease for the grease fittings. Lubricants added by the operator at the beginning of each shift are included in fuel and lubrication.

TAXES, LICENSES, AND INSURANCE: Taxes include all taxes and licensing fees assessed by government agencies. This includes property taxes on the equipment and licensing fees for vehicles that travel over public roads. Insurance includes insurance to protect against loss or damage to the equipment as well as insurance to cover the damage caused by the use of the equipment.

EQUIPMENT COSTS CHARGED TO JOBS: The equipment costs charged to jobs category is a contra account used to record the equipment costs that have been allocated or charged to the construction costs for a specific construction project. Equipment costs charged to jobs offset the cost categories in the equipment cost section of the income statement in the same way depreciation offsets the fixed assets on the balance sheet.

EQUIPMENT COSTS CHARGED TO EMPLOYEES: The equipment costs charged to employees includes all costs reimbursements from employees for the personal use of company vehicles. Employees must be charged for personal use of company vehicles--including travel to and from work—or the company must include the value of the employees' use of company vehicles as a taxable benefit in the employees' benefit package. Like equipment costs charged to jobs, equipment costs charged to employees is a contra account used to offset the cost categories in the equipment cost section of the income statement.

GROSS PROFIT: Gross profit equals the revenues less the construction costs and equipment costs.

Overhead

Overhead are those costs that cannot be charged to a specific construction project or be included in the equipment costs section of the income statement. Overhead is often referred to as general overhead, general and administrative expense, or indirect overhead. Because the term *project overhead* is often use to describe indirect costs, this book often uses the term *general overhead* in the place of *overhead* to avoid confusion. In other businesses general overhead is often referred to as *operating expenses*. General overhead includes all main office and supervisory costs that cannot be billed to a specific construction project. General overhead is discussed in detail in chapter 9. Some large companies may be required to allocate general overhead to the individual construction projects.

NET PROFIT FROM OPERATIONS: Net profit from operations equals the gross profit less the overhead and also equals the revenues less the construction costs, equipment costs, and overhead.

Other Income and Expenses

Other income and expenses is a catchall category that includes all income and expenses not associated with construction operations. A common source of other income and expenses is interest and the operation of a rental property.

PROFIT BEFORE TAX: Profit before tax or before-tax profit equals the net profit from operations less other income and expenses.

Income Tax

Income tax consists of income tax liabilities as well as deferred income taxes. Income tax consists of income taxes levied by the federal, state, and local governments. Some companies pay income taxes at the corporate level, whereas other companies pass their tax liability on to their shareholders. Deferred income tax occurs when a construction company uses a different accounting method for income tax purposes than they do for financial purposes. For example, a company may use the cash accounting method for income tax purposes because it allows the company to defer income tax, but uses the percentage-of-completion method for preparation of financial statements because it provides the most accurate financial picture of the company. In this case, the difference in the income tax calculated using the cash method and the percentage-of-completion method would be reported on the financial statement as deferred income tax. Income taxes are discussed in chapter 13.

There are three key relationships that must be maintained in the general ledger. First, the sum of the asset accounts on the balance sheet must equal the sum of the liability and the equity accounts on the balance sheet. For a company using the chart of accounts in Figure 2-1, the sum of accounts 110 through 299 must equal the sum of accounts 310 to 430. Second, the profit for the period reported on the income statement must equal the total revenue for the period—including other income—less the sum of the expenses, including all construction costs, equipment costs, overhead costs, other expenses, and income tax. For the company using the chart of accounts in Figure 2-1, the profit would be equal to the sum of accounts 500 and 910 less the sum of accounts 610 through 899, 920, and 950. Third, the profit for any period must equal the change in equity for that same period. For a company using the chart of accounts in Figure 2-1, the change in equity would occur in accounts 410 through 430. Changes in the equity that occur throughout a period are usually recorded in the current period net income category and are then transferred to another equity category at the end of the period.

PROFIT AFTER TAX: Profit after tax equals the profit before tax less income tax.

THE JOB COST LEDGER

For management to monitor and control the cost of construction projects, the costs for each project must be tracked against a budget. Additionally, management needs detailed cost information to prepare bids for future projects. Although construction costs are recoded in the general ledger, the general ledger lacks the necessary details to meet these two needs. These needs are met through the job cost ledger. The job cost ledger tracks the costs for each project as well as individual components within each of the projects. The job cost ledger tracks costs using a cost coding system based on a company's work breakdown structure. Most accounting systems allow for four levels of tracking: project, phase or area, cost code, and cost type. A graphical representation of the breakdown of the job cost ledger is shown in Figure 2-4.

FIGURE 2-4 Breakdown of Job Cost Ledger

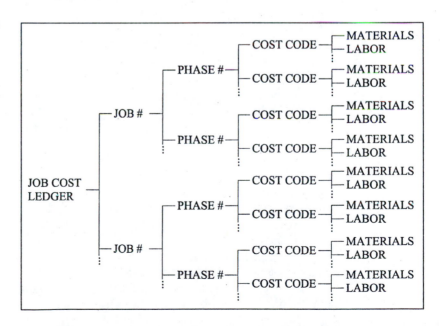

The first level of breakdown is by project. Each construction project is assigned a project code and is tracked separately. An easy way to set up project codes is to use the first one or two digits of the project code to represent the year that the project was started. The remaining digits are assigned sequentially starting with 1 for the first project of the year, 2 for the second project of the year, and so forth.

Each project may then be broken down into phases, which are assigned a number. The phases may be used to separate different structures within a project—such as different apartment buildings within an apartment complex—or may be used to separate the costs into groups—such as site costs versus building costs. Some companies may not separate the projects into phases.

The phases—if phases are not used, the projects—are then broken down into cost codes. Sample cost codes are found in Figure 2-5. A cost code often consists of two parts, with the first two digits representing a group of codes and the remaining digits representing a cost category within that group. The jobs cost codes are often based on the MasterFormat or the Uniformat. The first two digits of the cost codes in Figure 2-5 correspond with the divisions of the MasterFormat. The last three digits of the cost code loosely follow the MasterFormat. Modifications were made to the MasterFormat numbers to prevent the cost codes from bunching up and to meet the individual needs of the company. Not all of these cost codes are used for every job—only those codes for which costs have been budgeted.

The cost codes are then broken down into a cost type. Typically the cost types should match the types used on the income statement. In the case of the income statement in Figure 2-3 the cost types would be materials, labor, subcontracts, equipment, and other.

A complete cost code—consisting of the job number, phase code, cost code, and cost type—is used to describe each account on the job cost ledger. The job cost code may be written as follows:

###.##.#####A

where the three numbers to the left of the first decimal point represent the job number, the two numbers between the decimal points represent the phase code, the five numbers to the right of the second decimal point represent the cost code, and the last alphanumeric character represents the cost type. For the company using the income statement in Figure 2-3 the cost types would be M, L, S, E, and O, representing materials, labor, subcontracts, equipment, and other. The job cost code of 102.01.07200L for a company using the cost codes in Figure 2-5 would represent the labor component for the insulation work on Phase 1 of Project 102. Delimiters other than dots, such as dashes, may be used in the job cost code. For example, the previous code could be written 102-01-07200L.

For the job cost coding system to work, the system must be standardized, follow a common-sense format, match the way the company does business, and allow for expansion. It is also important that all parties who use the system—estimators, field employees, the accounting department, and management—must be using the same coding and must be consistent in how items are coded. If field employees code

COST CODES

Code	Description	Code	Description
01000	GENERAL CONDITIONS	07000	THERMAL & MOIST. PROT.
01100	Supervision	07100	Waterproofing
01400	General Labor	07200	Insulation
01600	Temporary Facilities	07210	Foundation Insulation
01700	Temporary Utilities	07250	Fireproofing
01800	Temporary Phone	07300	Stucco
01900	Clean-Up	07400	Siding
		07450	Rain Gutters
02000	SITE WORK	07500	Roofing
02050	Demolition & Grubbing	07600	Flashings-Sheet Metal
02100	Grading & Excavation	07700	Roof Specialties
02400	Sanitary Sewer	07900	Caulking & Sealants
02450	Water Line		
02500	Storm Drain	08000	DOORS & WINDOWS
02550	Gas Lines	08110	Metal Doors & Frames
02560	Power Lines	08200	Wood Doors
02570	Telephone Lines	08300	Overhead Doors
02600	Asphalt	08400	Store Fronts
02610	Site Conc.-Labor	08700	Hardware
02620	Site Conc.-Concrete	08800	Glass & Glazing
02630	Retaining Walls		
02640	Rebar	09000	FINISHES
02670	Signage	09050	Metal Studs
02700	Landscaping	09100	Drywall
02800	Fencing	09200	Ceramic Tile
02810	Dumpster Enclosures	09300	Acoustical Treatment
02900	Outside Lighting	09400	Carpet & Vinyl
		09800	Paint
03000	CONCRETE	09850	Wall Coverings
03200	Under-slab Gravel		
03300	Footing & Found.-Labor	10000	SPECIALTIES
03400	Footing & Found.-Conc.	10400	Signage
03450	Concrete Pump	10700	Toilet Partitions
03500	Slab/Floor-Labor	10800	Toilet & Bath Accessories
03600	Slab/Floor-Concrete		
03650	Light-Weight Concrete	11000	EQUIPMENT
03700	Pre-cast Concrete	11100	Appliances
03900	Rebar		
		12000	FURNISHINGS
04000	MASONRY	12300	Cabinetry & Counter Tops
04100	Masonry	12350	Counter Tops
		12500	Window Treatments
05000	METALS		
05100	Structural Steel	14000	CONVEYING SYSTEMS
05300	Joist & Deck	14100	Elevators
05400	Misc. Steel		
05900	Erection	15000	MECHANICAL
		15100	Plumbing
06000	WOOD & PLASTICS	15300	HVAC
06110	Rough Carpentry	15500	Fire Sprinklers
06120	Lumber		
06150	Trusses	16000	ELECTRICAL
06210	Finish Carpentry	16100	Electrical

FIGURE 2-5   Sample Cost Codes

framing hardware to a different code than the estimators, tracking the projects costs against the estimator's budget will be of little use when trying to manage costs and cost data from past projects will be of little use to the estimating department when bidding future projects. For this consistency to occur there must be a written, companywide standard that explains the coding system and how items are to be coded. This document should include a list of the cost codes with a description of what is to be included in each cost code.

Developing a job cost coding system that follows an easy, common-sense format makes it easier to ensure that items are coded correctly. A hard-to-follow format will create confusion and increase the number of coding errors.

The job cost coding system must match the way the company buys out a construction project and tracks the costs on the project. Looking at the cost codes in Figure 2-5, we see that 02610 Site Conc.-Labor and 02620 Site Conc.-Concrete have been included under 02000 Site Work. The contractor set this up this way so that building costs could be easily separated from the site costs. In this case the building costs are 3000 Concrete through 16000 Electrical. Additionally, the contractor uses both subcontractors and in-house crews to form and pour the site concrete, but the contractor always provides the concrete. By separating the forming and pouring costs from the concrete costs the contractor can easily compare the cost of using a subcontractor to the cost of using in-house crews by charging all costs usually paid by the subcontractor to the labor cost code when the company's work crews pour the concrete. For example, if the concrete subcontractor typically includes the cost of forms and tie wire in its bids, when the company uses in-house crews to pour the concrete, the cost of forms and tie wire is billed to the 02610 Site Conc.-Labor. This makes it possible for management to directly compare the cost of performing the work in-house versus subcontracting out the work. If the form and tie wire costs were included in 02620 Site Conc.-Concrete when in-house crews poured the concrete it would be difficult to compare cost of the in-house crew to the cost of subcontracting out the work.

Finally, the system must allow for expansion. Companies often set up a coding system to fit their current business operations. Later they find that their business has expanded, requiring additional codes that cannot be supported by their current coding system. The company then must change its coding system, which leads to confusion and coding problems. Common mistakes in this area are not leaving enough space between cost codes to allow for the addition of cost codes between two codes and not setting up the project and phase codes with enough places to allow for the increase in the number of projects or phases.

For the job cost ledger to be of use, budget must be recorded for each cost code. These budgets come from the cost estimate for the project that was generated when the project was bid and must be updated when changes occur. Whenever a cost is recorded to the general ledger as a construction cost it should also be recorded to the job cost ledger. Many job cost ledgers also allow revenues to be credited to individual jobs. Many job cost ledgers allow the company to track committed costs. Committed costs should be tracked to get a more accurate picture of the project's financial status. If the job cost ledger does not allow for the tracking of committed costs, the project's management should perform these calculations on a regular basis. Committed costs are discussed in detail in chapter 4.

Two key relationships must be maintained between the general ledger and the job cost ledger. First, the total of the revenue on the job cost ledger must equal the revenue from the core business—exclusive of interest received and other income—on the income statement for a specific period of time. For the company using the chart of accounts in Figure 2-1, the amount in account 500 Revenue must be equal to the total revenue recorded on the job cost ledger for the period. Second, the total of the costs—exclusive of committed costs that have not been recognized as an expense—on the job cost ledger must equal the construction costs on the income statements for a specific period of time.

The total in each of the five subcategories—labor, material, equipment, subcontract, and other—on the job cost ledger must equal the construction costs on the general ledger in the associated account for any given period. For the company using the chart of accounts in Figure 2-1, the amount in accounts 610 Materials, 620 Labor, 630 Subcontract, 640 Equipment, and 650 Other must equal the costs recorded in the job cost ledger for the period. Additionally, 610 Materials must equal the total of all costs on the job cost ledger with a material cost type, 620 Labor must equal the total of all costs on the job cost ledger with a labor cost type, 630 Subcontract must equal the total of all costs on the job cost ledger with a subcontract cost type, 640 Equipment must equal the total of all costs on the job cost ledger with an equipment cost type, and 650 Other must equal the total of all costs on the job cost ledger with an other cost type for a specific period. Again, committed costs that have not been recognized as expenses are not included in these calculations. At the end of each month, the company's accountant should verify that these relationships are being adhered to and make the necessary corrections. It is important to note that the costs on the job cost ledger span multiple months or years; therefore, the cost comparison between the job cost ledger and the general ledger must only include the costs recorded during a specific month, quarter, or year.

THE EQUIPMENT LEDGER

Many construction companies have major investments in equipment that is moved from job to job. Some equipment, such as a dump truck, may be on multiple jobs during one day. For a construction company to effectively manage equipment and to ensure that the equipment costs are being billed to projects and that they are making enough money on each piece of equipment to warrant the investment in the equipment, the costs and billings for each piece of equipment must be tracked. This tracking is accomplished through the equipment ledger.

The equipment ledger is broken down into two and sometimes three levels. A graphical representation of this breakdown in shown in Figure 2-6. The first

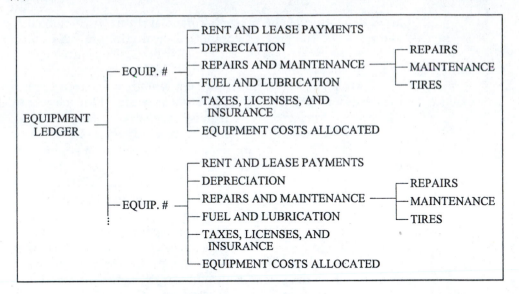

FIGURE 2-6   Breakdown of Equipment Ledger

level of breakdown is by piece of equipment. Each piece of construction equipment is assigned a code and is tracked separately. The equipment costs and equipment costs charged to jobs for each piece of equipment are tracked in the equipment ledger. The second level of breakdown is by the accounts found in the equipment section of the income statement. For the company using the chart of accounts in Figure 2-1 these accounts include 710 Rent and Lease Payments; 720 Depreciation; 730 Repairs and Maintenance; 740 Fuel and Lubrication; and 750 Taxes, Licenses, and Insurance. Also at this level the equipment costs charged to the job are tracked. For the company using the chart of accounts in Figure 2-1 the costs charged to jobs and employees is recorded in accounts 798 and 799, respectively. The third level of breakdown is where an account from the income statement is broken down into smaller accounts. For example, in Figure 2-6, Repairs and Maintenance is broken down into repairs, maintenance, and tires. This allows for more detailed tracking.

Two key relationships must be maintained between the general ledger and the equipment ledger. First, the total of the costs allocated to jobs on the equipment ledger must be equal to the equipment contra accounts on the income statement for a specific period. For the company using the chart of accounts in Figure 2-1, the total of the costs allocated to jobs and employees on the equipment ledger must equal the amount in accounts 798 Equipment Costs Charged to Employees and 799 Equipment Costs Charged to Jobs for the year. Second, the costs on the equipment ledger must equal the total of the equipment cost on the income statement—exclusive of the contra accounts—for a specific period. For the company using the chart of accounts in Figure 2-1, the costs recorded in the equipment ledger must be equal to the costs in accounts 710 Rent and Lease Payments; 720 Depreciation; 730 Repairs and Maintenance; 740 Fuel and Lubrication; and 750 Taxes, Licenses, and Insurance for the period. Additionally, 710 Rent and Lease Payments from the income statement must equal the total of all of the cost in the rent and lease payment category for all of the equipment in the equipment ledger for a specific period. The same is true for the 720 Depreciation; 730 Repairs and Maintenance; 740 Fuel and Lubrication; 750 Taxes, Licenses, and Insurance; 798 Equipment Costs Charged to Employees; and 799 Equipment Costs Charged to Jobs. Like the job cost ledger, the general ledger spans multiple months or years; therefore, the cost comparison between the equipment ledger and the general ledger must include only the costs recorded during a specific month or year.

CONCLUSION

For management to manage costs, the company's accounting system must provide cost data in time for management to proactively respond to the data. For this to occur, the accounting system must have a strong job costing and equipment tracking system, the data must allow management to manage by exception, and the accounting data must be readily available to all employees who are responsible for controlling costs.

Construction accounting systems consist of a general ledger and a job cost ledger. They also consist of an equipment ledger when a company has heavy equipment or lots of vehicles. The general ledger is divided into two sections, the balance sheet and the income statement, and is used to prepare the balance sheet and income statement for the company. The job cost ledger provides a detailed breakdown of the construction costs recorded on the income statement. On the job cost ledger, costs are broken down by project, phase (if desired), cost code, and cost type. The job cost ledger is used by construction managers to manage the costs of the individual projects. The equipment ledger provides a detailed breakdown of equipment costs on the general ledger, is broken down by individual pieces of equipment, and is used to manage heavy equipment and vehicles.

There are four methods of accounting available to construction companies: cash, accrual, percentage of completion, and completed contract. Because long-term contracts—contracts that span more than one fiscal year—are very common in the construction industry, many construction companies are required to use the percentage-of-completion method. When using the percentage-of-completion method, companies are required to report their costs and profits in excess of billing (underbillings) and billings in excess of costs and profits (overbillings) on their financial statements. Additionally, these companies are required to recognize their estimated profits as they are earned even if they have not yet received these profits.

PROBLEMS

1. Describe the purposes of the accounting system.
2. Describe the difference between cost reporting and cost control.
3. What are the key components of an accounting system that facilitates cost control?
4. Describe the different accounting ledgers used by construction companies and explain their purpose.
5. Describe the relationship among the chart of accounts, the balance sheet, and the income statement.
6. Compare and contrast the different accounting methods that are available to construction companies.
7. Describe the key relationships that must be maintained within the general ledger.
8. Describe the key relationships that must be maintained between the general ledger and the job cost ledger.
9. Describe the key relationships that must be maintained between the general ledger and the equipment ledger.

ACCOUNTING TRANSACTIONS

In this chapter you will gain a better understanding how different accounting transactions are processed in the accounting system. There are a number of unique transactions that take place in construction accounting that do not occur in other industries. Most of these transactions are a result of the construction industry's focus on job costing, equipment tracking, and accounting for long-term contracts. Understanding these transactions is important for three reasons: First, some project costs—such as labor burden and equipment costs—are often generated by the accounting system rather than an invoice or time card. Understanding how these costs are obtained will help you gain a better understanding of how to estimate these costs and incorporate them in the financial analysis of the project. Second, financial managers must review the accounting reports for errors—improperly billed costs and omitted costs—and ensure that the necessary corrections are made. Understanding how the costs are generated will help you better understand how to interpret the accounting reports. Finally, for the general manager and owner, understanding construction accounting is necessary to ensure that the accounting system is set up to meet the needs of the company. Many construction companies are using substandard accounting systems because management does not understand how accounting systems should be structured to meet the needs of the construction industry.

Now that we have looked at the different ledgers used in a construction accounting system, it is important to understand how common construction transactions affect the different ledgers and how the ledgers are interrelated. These transactions may be referred to as journal entries. Transactions or journal entries that occur on the balance sheet portion of the general ledger consist of both debits and credits, with the total of the debits equaling the total of the credits. Debits increase the balance of asset accounts and decrease the balance of liability and owners' equity accounts, whereas credits decrease the balance of asset accounts and increase the balance of liability and owners' equity accounts. To make it easier to understand how a transaction affects the different accounts, this book indicates simply whether the transaction increases or decreases the balance of the account.

As we look at these transactions, we need to keep in mind the key relationships discussed in the previous chapter. Let's look at some common transactions that occur in construction companies. For these transactions we use the chart of accounts in Figure 2-1 and the cost codes in Figure 2-5. The chart of accounts will also be broken into its two separate components: the balance sheet and the income statement.

INVOICE CHARGED TO A JOB WITHOUT RETENTION

When a material, subcontract, or other cost type invoice that is billable to a construction project—on which the contractor will not hold retention from the payment—is received and entered into the accounting system it affects the income statement, balance sheet, and job cost ledger. Most commonly this type of invoice is an invoice for materials. For discussion purposes we look at how a material invoice is handled. On the income statement the material invoice is recorded as a cost in the material section of the construction costs. The increase in the construction costs decreases the profit on the income statement by the amount of the invoice. This decrease in profit is not offset until revenues are recorded. On the balance sheet the materials invoice is recorded as an accounts payable-trade in the liability section. This increase in liability results in a reduction in the current period net income equal to the amount of the invoice. As per the relationships previously discussed, the reduction in profit on the income statement is equal to the reduction in the current period net income on the balance sheet. On the job cost ledger the materials invoice is recorded as a cost with a material cost type against the job, phase, and cost code for which the materials were purchased. Subcontract and other types of invoices are handled the same way, except subcontract invoices are recorded as a subcontract cost type and other invoices are recorded as an other cost type.

> **Example 3-1:** Determine the change to the balance sheet, income statement, and job cost ledger of a $10,000 material invoice for 7/16 OBS charged to cost code 06120 Lumber on Phase 1 of Job Number 110. The company uses the chart of accounts in Figure 2-1.
>
> **Solution:** The changes are shown in Table 3-1.

INVOICE CHARGED TO A JOB WITH RETENTION

When a material, subcontract, or other cost type invoice that is billable to a construction project—on which the contractor will hold retention from the payment—is received and entered into the accounting system it affects the

TABLE 3-1   Invoice Charged to a Job without Retention

ACCOUNT	CHANGE IN AMOUNT ($)	
Balance Sheet		
310 Accounts Payable-Trade	10,000.00	Increase
430 Current Period Net Income	10,000.00	Decrease
Income Statement		
610 Materials	10,000.00	Increase
Profit	10,000.00	Decrease
Job Cost Ledger		
110.01.06120M	10,000.00	Increase

income statement, balance sheet, and job cost ledger much the same way as an invoice on which the contractor does not hold retention. The key difference is that the retention that will be withheld must be recorded in the accounts payable-retention account. Typically these invoices are from subcontractors; however, they may also be material or other type invoices. For discussion purposes, we look at how a subcontractor's invoice is handled. On the income statement the subcontractor's invoice is recorded as a cost in the subcontract section of the construction costs. The increase in the construction costs decreases the profit on the income statement by the amount of the invoice. On the balance sheet the retained portion of the subcontractor's invoice is recorded in the accounts payable-retention account and the remaining portion of the invoice is recorded in the accounts payable-trade account in the liability section of the balance sheet. These increases in liability result in a reduction in the current period net income equal to the amount of the invoice. As per the relationships previously discussed, the reduction in profit on the income statement is equal to the reduction in the current period net income on the balance sheet. On the job cost ledger the subcontractor's invoice is recorded as a cost with a subcontract cost type against the job, phase, and cost code for which the subcontractor performed the work. If the invoice covers multiple cost codes, the invoice is divided among the appropriate cost codes. Material and other types of invoices are handled the same way, except material invoices are recorded as a material cost type and other invoices are recorded as an other cost type.

Example 3-2:   Determine the change to the balance sheet, income statement, and job cost ledger of a $10,000 subcontractor's invoices for plumbing work charged to cost code 15100 Plumbing on Phase 1 of Job Number 110. When paying the bill the contractor will withhold 10% retention. The company uses the chart of accounts in Figure 2-1.

Solution: The contractor will withhold $1,000 ($10,000 × 0.10) as retention until the project is complete. The changes are shown in Table 3-2.

TABLE 3-2   Invoice Charged to a Job with Retention

ACCOUNT	CHANGE IN AMOUNT ($)	
Balance Sheet		
310 Accounts Payable-Trade	9,000.00	Increase
311 Accounts Payable-Retention	1,000.00	Increase
430 Current Period Net Income	10,000.00	Decrease
Income Statement		
630 Subcontract	10,000.00	Increase
Profit	10,000.00	Decrease
Job Cost Ledger		
110.01.15100S	10,000.00	Increase

PAYING INVOICES

So far invoices have been entered into the accounting system, but they have not been paid. When invoices are paid cash (an asset) is used to pay the accounts payable (a liability). Payment of an invoice affects the balance sheet by reducing the accounts payable-trade (a liability account) and at the same time reducing the cash account (an asset account). By reducing both an asset account and a liability account by the same amount the relationship between assets and liabilities on the balance sheet is maintained. Because the invoices have already been recorded as costs on the income statement and the job cost ledger, no changes occur on the income statement or job cost ledger.

Example 3-3:   Determine the changes to the balance sheet that occur when the invoices in Examples 3-1 and 3-2 are paid. The retention will not be released at this time. The company uses the chart of accounts in Figure 2-1.

Solution: The contractor will use a check drawn against the cash account to pay $10,000 from Example 3-1 and $9,000 from Example 3-2, for a total of $19,000. The changes are shown in Table 3-3.

TABLE 3-3   Paying Invoices

ACCOUNT	CHANGE IN AMOUNT ($)	
Balance Sheet		
110 Cash	19,000.00	Decrease
310 Accounts Payable-Trade	19,000.00	Decrease

LABOR CHARGED TO A JOB

When an employee's time—whose costs are to be charged to a project—is entered into the accounting system it affects the income statement, balance sheet, and job cost ledger. On the income statement the employee costs—including labor burden—are recorded as a cost in the labor section of the construction costs. The increase in the construction costs decreases the profit on the income statement by the total cost of the employee. On the balance sheet the employee costs will become accrued liabilities. For a company using the chart of accounts in Figure 2-1 the accrued liabilities have been broken down into five accounts: 340 Accrued Payroll, 341 Accrued Payables, 342 Accrued Taxes, 343 Accrued Insurance, and 344 Accrued Vacation. The amount due to the employee—after withholdings and deductions—is recorded in the 340 Accrued Payroll account. Social security taxes, Medicare taxes, FUTA, and SUTA paid by the employer; social security taxes and Medicare taxes paid by the employee; and state and federal withholding taxes withheld from the employee's paycheck are recorded in the 342 Accrued Taxes account. Workers' compensation insurance, liability insurance, and health insurance costs are recorded in the 343 Accrued Insurance account. Because it is unfair to charge an employee's vacation time to the job he or she is working on when the employee takes vacation, funds to pay for the employee's vacation must be accrued throughout the year. These funds are recorded in the 344 Accrued Vacation account. All other benefits would be recorded in the 341 Accrued Payables account. This increase in liability on the balance sheet results in a reduction in the current period net income equal to the total cost of the employee. As per the relationships previously discussed, the reduction in profit on the income statement is equal to the reduction in the current period net income on the balance sheet. On the job cost ledger the labor cost, including burden, is recorded as a cost with a labor cost type against the job, phase, and cost code for which labor was performed. If the employee performed work on multiple cost codes, the labor is divided among the appropriate cost codes.

Example 3-4: Determine the change to the balance sheet, income statement, and job cost ledger of a finish carpenter when his or her time is entered into the accounting system. The finish carpenter is to be paid $895.90 for a week's work. The employer has the following burden costs: $55.55 for social security tax, $12.99 for Medicare, $26.88 for SUTA, $7.17 for FUTA, $8.96 for liability insurance, $71.67 for workers' compensation, $24.00 for the health insurance premium, and $38.00 is set aside for vacation. The employee has the following withheld from his or her check: $55.55 for social security tax, $12.99 for Medicare, $75.25 as federal withholding, $33.86 for state withholding, and $76.08 for the employee's part of the health insurance premium. The labor is charged to cost code 06210 Finish

Carpentry on Phase 1 of Job Number 112. The company uses the chart of accounts in Figure 2-1.

Solution: The amount payable to the employee is recorded in the 340 Accrued Payroll account on the balance sheet. The amount payable to the employee equals wages less deduction and withholdings taken from wages and is calculated as follows:

$$\text{Payable} = \text{Wages} - \text{Social Security Tax} - \text{Medicare Tax}$$
$$- \text{Federal Withholding} - \text{State Withholding}$$
$$- \text{Health Insurance}$$

$$\text{Payable} = \$895.90 - \$55.55 - \$12.99 - \$75.25$$
$$- \$33.86 - \$76.08$$

$$\text{Payable} = \$642.17$$

Both the state and federal government taxes are recorded in the 342 Accrued Taxes account on the balance sheet. This includes both taxes paid by the employer and taxes withheld from the employee's check. Find the amount payable to the state government:

$$\text{Payable} = \text{SUTA} + \text{State Withholding} = \$26.88 + \$33.86 = \$60.74$$

Find the amount payable to the federal government:

$$\text{Payable} = \text{Social Security Tax}_{\text{Employer}} + \text{Medicare Tax}_{\text{Employer}}$$
$$+ \text{FUTA} + \text{Social Security Tax}_{\text{Employee}}$$
$$+ \text{Medicare Tax}_{\text{Employee}} + \text{Federal Withholding}$$

$$\text{Payable} = \$55.55 + \$12.99 + \$7.17 + \$55.55$$
$$+ \$12.99 + \$75.25$$

$$\text{Payable} = \$219.50$$

The total amount of taxes is \$280.24 (\$60.74 + \$219.50).

The liability insurance, workers' compensation insurance, and health insurance costs are recorded in the 343 Accrued Insurance account on the balance sheet. Find the amount payable to the health insurance carrier:

$$\text{Payable} = \text{Health Insurance}_{\text{Employer}} + \text{Health Insurance}_{\text{Employee}}$$

$$\text{Payable} = \$24.00 + \$76.08 = \$100.08$$

Find the total recorded to the 343 Accrued Insurance account:

$$\text{Total} = \text{Liability Insurance} + \text{Workers' Comp.} + \text{Health Insurance}$$

$$\text{Total} = \$8.96 + \$71.67 + \$100.08 = \$180.71$$

The money set aside for vacation pay is recorded in the 342 Accrued Vacation account on the balance sheet. The changes are shown in Table 3-4.

TABLE 3-4   Labor Charged to a Job

ACCOUNT	CHANGE IN AMOUNT ($)	
Balance Sheet		
340 Accrued Payroll	642.17	Increase
342 Accrued Taxes	280.24	Increase
343 Accrued Insurance	180.71	Increase
344 Accrued Vacation	38.00	Increase
430 Current Period Net Income	1,141.12	Decrease
Income Statement		
620 Labor	1,141.12	Increase
Profit	1,141.12	Decrease
Job Cost Ledger		
112.01.06210L	1,141.12	Increase

LABOR CHARGED TO GENERAL OVERHEAD

When an employee's—whose costs are to be charged to general overhead—time is entered into the accounting system, it affects the income statement and balance sheet. Because the employee's time is not charged to a job it does not affect the job cost ledger. On the income statement the employee costs, including labor burden, are recorded as a cost in the general overhead section of the income statement. For a company using the chart of accounts in Figure 2-1 the employees' labor costs are broken down into the following accounts: 820 Employee Wages and Salaries, 821 Employee Benefits, 822 Employee Retirement, 825 Employee Taxes, and 830 Insurance. The total wages—before withholdings and deductions are taken from the employee's check—are recorded in the 820 Employee Wages and Salaries account. The health insurance costs, vacation, and other benefits paid by the employer are recorded in the 821 Employee Benefits account. Retirement paid by the employer is recorded in the 822 Employee Retirement account. Social security taxes, Medicare taxes, FUTA, and SUTA paid by the employer are recorded in the 825 Employee Taxes account. Workers' compensation insurance and liability insurance are recorded in the 830 Insurance account. Health insurance premiums paid by the employee, social security and Medicare taxes paid by the employee, and state and federal withholding taxes withheld from the employee's paycheck are not recorded because they are costs to the employee and are taken out of the employee's wages. The increase in the overhead costs decreases the profit on the income statement by the cost of the employee, including burden. On the balance sheet the employee costs becomes an accrued liability and is handled the same way the costs for an employee whose costs are charged to a project were handled (see Labor Charged to a Job).

Example 3-5: Determine the change to the balance sheet, income statement, and job cost ledger of an estimator's time when that time is entered into the accounting system. The estimator is paid $895.90 each week. The employer has the following burden costs: $55.55 for social security tax, $12.99 for Medicare, $26.88 for SUTA, $7.17 for FUTA, $8.96 for liability insurance, $71.67 for workers' compensation, $24.00 for the health insurance premium, and $38.00 is set aside for vacation. The employee has the following amounts withheld from his or her check: $55.55 for social security tax, $12.99 for Medicare, $75.25 as federal withholding, $33.86 for state withholding, and $76.08 for the employee's part of the health insurance premium.

Solution: Because this example has the same wages and costs as Example 3-4, the changes to the balance sheet are the same for this example as they are for Example 3-4. The amount recorded in the 820 Employee Wages and Salaries account equals the employee's wages, which is $895.90.

The amount recorded in the 821 Employee Benefits account equals the employer's portion of the health insurance premium plus the funds set aside for vacation. These costs are calculated as follows:

$$\text{Benefits Cost} = \text{Health Insurance Premium} + \text{Vacation}$$
$$\text{Benefits Cost} = \$24.00 + \$38.00 = \$62.00$$

The state and federal taxes paid by the employer are recorded in the 825 Employee Taxes account. Find the amount of taxes paid by the employer.

$$\text{Taxes} = \text{Social Security Tax} + \text{Medicare Tax} + \text{FUTA} + \text{SUTA}$$
$$\text{Taxes} = \$55.55 + \$12.99 + \$7.17 + \$26.88 = \$102.59$$

The liability and workers' compensation insurance paid by the employer are recorded in the 830 Insurance account. Find the amount liability and workers' compensation insurance paid by the employer.

$$\text{Insurance} = \text{Liability Insurance} + \text{Workers' Comp.}$$
$$\text{Insurance} = \$8.96 + \$71.67 = \$80.63$$

The changes are shown in Table 3-5.

TABLE 3-5   Labor Charged to General Overhead

ACCOUNT	CHANGE IN AMOUNT ($)	
Balance Sheet		
340 Accrued Payroll	642.17	Increase
342 Accrued Taxes	280.24	Increase
343 Accrued Insurance	180.71	Increase
344 Accrued Vacation	38.00	Increase
430 Current Period Net Income	1,141.12	Decrease
Income Statement		
820 Employee Wages and Salaries	895.90	Increase
821 Employee Benefits	62.00	Increase
825 Employee Taxes	102.59	Increase
830 Insurance	80.63	Increase
Profit	1,141.12	Decrease

TABLE 3-6   Paying an Employee's Wages

Account	Change in Amount ($)	
Balance Sheet		
110 Cash	642.17	Decrease
340 Accrued Payroll	642.17	Decrease

PAYING AN EMPLOYEE'S WAGES

So far we have entered the employee's time into the accounting system, but the employee has yet to be paid. When an employee is paid for the work he or she has performed it affects the balance sheet. When an employee is paid a company uses cash—an asset—to pay an accrued liability. In the case of a company using the chart of accounts in Figure 2-1 the accrued liability is accrued payroll recorded in the 340 Accrued Payroll account. By reducing both asset accounts and liability accounts by the same amount the relationship between assets and liabilities on the balance sheet is maintained. No changes occur on the income statement or job cost ledger because the employee's costs have already been charged to the income statement and job cost ledger.

Example 3-6: Determine the changes to the balance sheet that occur when the employee in Example 3-4 is paid.

Solution: From Example 3-4, the employee is owed $642.17. The contractor will use a check drawn against the cash account to pay the employee $642.17. The changes are shown in Table 3-6.

PAYING PAYROLL TAXES

When the employee's costs were entered into the accounting system, a variety of state and federal taxes were set aside that have not yet been paid. When the state and federal taxes are paid, it affects the balance sheet. When taxes are paid, a company uses cash—an asset—to pay an accrued liability. In the case of a company using the chart of accounts in Figure 2-1 the accrued liability is accrued taxes recorded in the 342 Accrued Taxes account. By reducing both an asset account and a liability account by the same amount, the relationship between assets and liabilities on the balance sheet is maintained. No changes occur on the income statement or job cost ledger because the employee's costs have already been charged to the income statement and job cost ledger.

Example 3-7: Determine the changes to the balance sheet that occur when the federal taxes in Example 3-4 are paid.

TABLE 3-7   Paying Payroll Taxes

ACCOUNT	CHANGE IN AMOUNT ($)	
Balance Sheet		
110 Cash	219.50	Decrease
342 Accrued Taxes	219.50	Decrease

Solution: From Example 3-4, the company owes $219.50 in federal taxes on the employee's wages. This includes funds withheld from the employee's paycheck. The contractor uses a check drawn against the cash account to pay the federal government for the federal tax liability of all employees. Included in this amount is $219.50 for the weekly wages for the employee in Example 3-4. The changes resulting from the single week of wages for the employee in Example 3-4 are shown in Table 3-7.

PAYING FOR BENEFITS

When the employee's time was entered into the accounting system, funds were set aside to pay the health insurance premium for the employee but the premium has yet to be paid. When a company pays for a benefit, such as health insurance, it affects the balance sheet. When paying for benefits a company uses cash—an asset—to pay an accrued liability. In the case of a company using the chart of accounts in Figure 2-1 the accrued liability is accrued insurance recorded in the 343 Accrued Insurance account. By reducing both an asset account and a liability account by the same amount, the relationship between assets and liabilities on the balance sheet is maintained. No changes occur on the income statement or job cost ledger because these costs have already been charged to the income statement and job cost ledger.

Example 3-8: Determine the changes to the balance sheet that occur when the monthly health insurance premium for the employee in Example 3-4 is paid. The insurance is paid every month (4.3333 weeks).

Solution: From Example 3-4, the company owes $100.08 per week. The monthly premium is $433.68 ($100.08 per week × 4.3333 weeks per month). Each month the contractor will use a check drawn against the cash account to pay the health insurance premium. The health insurance premium includes the health insurance premiums for all employees. Included in this amount is $433.68 for the employee in Example 3-4. The changes resulting from paying the health insurance premium for the employee in Example 3-4 are shown in Table 3-8.

TABLE 3-8   Paying for Benefits

ACCOUNT	CHANGE IN AMOUNT ($)	
Balance Sheet		
110 Cash	433.68	Decrease
343 Accrued Insurance	433.68	Decrease

VACATION TIME FOR JOBSITE EMPLOYEES

In Example 3-4, when the employee's time was entered into the accounting system, funds were set aside to pay for the employee's vacation time. This was done because it would be unfair to charge all of an employee's vacation to the job he or she was working on when his or her vacation was taken. For example, if an employee worked on a job for one day then took a week's vacation and returned to the job for one day, it would distort the project costs to charge the job for seven days of work when only two days of work had been performed.

When a jobsite employee takes vacation, the employer pays him or her for not working. The cost of this time is paid from funds set aside and charged to the jobs the employee worked on throughout the year. When an employee is paid for vacation time it affects the balance sheet. No costs are incurred because the company has been accruing these costs throughout the year. As a result, no changes occur on the income statement or job cost ledger. On the balance sheet the employee costs become an accrued liability, the same as they did when we looked at Labor Charged to a Job. This increase in liability on the balance sheet is offset by an equivalent reduction in accrued liability in the form of accrued vacation. For a company using the chart of accounts in Figure 2-1, the company would have an increase in liability recorded in the 340 Accrued Payroll, 342 Accrued Taxes, and 343 Accrued Insurance accounts, which would be offset by a reduction in liability in the 344 Accrued Vacation account. By increasing some liability accounts while decreasing another liability account by the same amount the relationship between assets and liabilities on the balance sheet is maintained.

Example 3-9:   Determine the change to the balance sheet when the employee in Example 3-4 is paid for one week's vacation time.

Solution: The change to the 340 Accrued Payroll, 342 Accrued Taxes, and 343 Accrued Insurance accounts are the same as they were in Example 3-4. Money to cover these changes would be paid out of the 344 Accrued Vacation account. Any money set aside from this week's wages for accruing vacation would come from the 344 Accrued Vacation account and would be recorded in the same account that was covering its costs, effectively washing itself out. In this example, there would be an increase

TABLE 3-9   Vacation Time for Jobsite Employees

ACCOUNT	CHANGE IN AMOUNT ($)	
Balance Sheet		
340 Accrued Payroll	642.17	Increase
342 Accrued Taxes	280.24	Increase
343 Accrued Insurance	180.71	Increase
344 Accrued Vacation	1,103.12	Decrease

in the 344 Accrued Vacation account of $38.00 to cover the vacation accrued during the week and a decrease from the same account of $1,141.12 to cover the employee's costs for the week. This creates a net decrease in the 344 Accrued Vacation account of $1,103.12 ($1,141.12 − $38.00). The changes are shown in Table 3-9.

RECORDING OFFICE RENT

When a construction company rents office space for the general office—space that cannot be charged to a job—it is handled differently than it would be if it purchased the office. When a bill for office rent is entered into the accounting system it affects the income statement and the balance sheet. On the income statement the rent is recorded as a general overhead expense. In the case of a company that uses the chart of accounts in Figure 2-1, the invoice would be recorded to the 842 Office Rent account. This increase in general overhead cost decreases the profit on the income statement by the amount of the invoice. On the balance sheet the invoice is recorded as an account payable-trade in the liability section. This increase in liability results in a reduction in the current period net income equal to the amount of the general overhead invoice. As in the relationships previously discussed, the reduction in profit on the income statement is equal to the reduction in the current period net income on the balance sheet. Because the cost is part of the general overhead and is not charged to a job, the invoice does not affect the job cost ledger.

Example 3-10:   Determine the change to the balance sheet and income statement of a $2,000 invoice for office rent.

Solution: The changes are shown in Table 3-10.

Should the invoice cover more than one month's rent, the invoice may need to be treated as a prepaid expense. See an accountant for help in determining how to handle this transaction. When the rent invoice is paid, it will have the same effect on the balance sheet as paying any other invoice; namely, reducing both accounts payable-trade while reducing cash.

TABLE 3-10   Recording Office Rent

ACCOUNT	CHANGE IN AMOUNT ($)	
Balance Sheet		
310 Accounts Payable-Trade	2,000.00	Increase
430 Current Period Net Income	2,000.00	Decrease
Income Statement		
842 Office Rent	2,000.00	Increase
Profit	2,000.00	Decrease

RECORDING OFFICE DEPRECIATION

When the company owns the general office and cannot bill the cost of the office to the job, the company needs to record the loss in value or depreciation each month. When the loss in value is recorded, it affects the income statement and the balance sheet. On the income statement the depreciation is recorded as a general overhead expense. In the case of a company that uses the chart of accounts in Figure 2-1 the depreciation would be recorded to the 819 Depreciation account. This increase in general overhead cost decreases the profit on the income statement by the amount of the depreciation. On the balance sheet the depreciation is recorded in the less accumulated depreciation contra account in the asset section, which is used to offset the value of the fixed assets. This decrease in assets results in a reduction in the current period net income equal to the amount of the depreciation. As per the relationships previously discussed, the reduction in profit on the income statement is equal to the reduction in the current period net income on the balance sheet. Because the depreciation is part of the general overhead and is not charged to a job, the depreciation does not affect the job cost ledger.

Example 3-11:   Determine the change to the balance sheet and income statement of $2,000 of office depreciation.

Solution: The changes are shown in Table 3-11.

TABLE 3-11   Recording Office Depreciation

ACCOUNT	CHANGE IN AMOUNT ($)	
Balance Sheet		
250 Less Acc. Depreciation	2,000.00	Increase
430 Current Period Net Income	2,000.00	Decrease
Income Statement		
819 Depreciation	2,000.00	Increase
Profit	2,000.00	Decrease

TABLE 3-12 Paying General Overhead Invoices

ACCOUNT	CHANGE IN AMOUNT ($)	
Balance Sheet		
310 Accounts Payable-Trade	500.00	Increase
430 Current Period Net Income	500.00	Decrease
Income Statement		
846 Telephone	500.00	Increase
Profit	500.00	Decrease

RECORDING GENERAL OVERHEAD INVOICES

Recording general overhead invoices has the same effect on the income statement and balance sheet as recording office rent, except that they are recorded to the appropriate general overhead category.

Example 3-12: Determine the change of a $500 telephone bill to the balance sheet and income statement.

Solution: The telephone bill is charged to the 846 Telephone account in the general overhead section of the income statement. The changes are shown in Table 3-12.

When a general overhead invoice is paid it has the same affect on the balance sheet as paying any other invoice; namely, reducing both accounts payable-trade while reducing cash.

BILLING A CLIENT

In previous examples we have looked at how invoices and labor affected the accounting system. Now it is time to bill the client for these costs. When a company bills a client for work performed it affects the income statement, balance sheet, and the job cost ledger. On the income statement the bill to the client is recorded as revenue. In the case of a company using the chart of accounts in Figure 2-1 the bill is recorded in the 500 Revenue account. The increase in revenue increases the profit on the income statement by the amount of the invoice. The portion of the bill withheld by the client in the form of retention is recorded as an accounts receivable-retention and the remaining portion of the bill is recorded as an account receivable-trade in the asset portion of the balance sheet. This increase in accounts receivable results in an increase in the current period net income equal to the amount of the invoice. As in the relationships previously discussed, the increase in profit on the income statement is equal to the increase in the current period net income on the balance sheet. On the job cost ledger the

TABLE 3-13   Billing a Client

ACCOUNT	CHANGE IN AMOUNT ($)	
Balance Sheet		
120 Accounts Receivable-Trade	90,000.00	Increase
121 Accounts Receivable-Retention	10,000.00	Increase
430 Current Period Net Income	100,000.00	Increase
Income Statement		
500 Revenue	100,000.00	Increase
Profit	100,000.00	Increase
Job Cost Ledger		
120 Revenue	100,000.00	Increase

bill is credited to the job or jobs for which the bill represented. Not all companies track their revenues on the job cost ledger. In such a case, nothing is recorded to the job cost ledger.

Example 3-13:   Determine the change to the balance sheet, income statement, and job cost ledger of a $100,000 bill to a client for Job 120. The client holds 10% retention.

Solution: The client holds $10,000 ($100,000 × 0.10) as retention until the project is complete. The changes are shown in Table 3-13.

BILLING FOR RETENTION

In the previous example, retention was withheld by the client. When the company has met the requirement for the release of the retention it will need to recognize this in the accounting system. The company does this by sending a bill for the retention to the client. Billing for retention affects the balance sheet by moving the retention from the accounts receivable-retention account to the accounts receivable-trade account. Once the retention has been moved to the accounts receivable-trade account the company may begin tracking and treating it as a collectable invoice. Because the retention has already been recorded as income on the income statement and the job cost ledger, no change is made to either of these ledgers.

Example 3-14:   A contractor has completed a construction project on which the client is holding $10,000 in retention. Determine the changes to the balance sheet when the contractor bills the client for the outstanding retention.

Solution: The changes are shown in Table 3-14.

TABLE 3-14   Billing for Retention

ACCOUNT	CHANGE IN AMOUNT ($)	
Balance Sheet		
120 Accounts Receivable-Trade	10,000.00	Increase
121 Accounts Receivable-Retention	10,000.00	Decrease

TABLE 3-15   Receiving Payment from a Client

ACCOUNT	CHANGE IN AMOUNT ($)	
Balance Sheet		
110 Cash	90,000.00	Increase
120 Accounts Receivable-Trade	90,000.00	Decrease

RECEIVING PAYMENT FROM A CLIENT

Now that the contractor has billed the client, the next step is to see how receiving payment from the client affects the accounting system. When payment is received from the client it affects the balance sheet by changing an account receivable-trade into cash. Because the payment is already recorded as income on the income statement and the job cost ledger when the bill was prepared, no changes are made to either of these ledgers.

Example 3-15:   Determine the changes that occur on the balance sheet when the contractor receives payment for the $90,000.00 bill that was submitted in Example 3-13.

Solution: The changes are shown in Table 3-15.

PURCHASE OF EQUIPMENT WITH A LOAN

When a contractor purchases a piece of equipment or other asset with a loan, the company obtains a new asset with a new liability; therefore, the purchase of the asset affects only the balance sheet. On the balance sheet the cash account is decreased by any down payment the contractor makes. The asset purchased is recorded as a long-term asset in the asset section of the balance sheet. The loan used to purchase the asset is recorded as a long-term liability. If prepaid interest is included in the loan down payment, the prepaid interest may have to be amortized over the life of the loan. The net increase in the assets is offset by an equally large increase in the net liabilities.

Example 3-16:   Determine the changes that occur on the balance sheet when the contractor purchases a $120,000 hydraulic excavator with a $110,000 loan and a $10,000 cash down payment.

TABLE 3-16 Purchase of Equipment with a Loan

ACCOUNT	CHANGE IN AMOUNT ($)	
Balance Sheet		
110 Cash	10,000.00	Decrease
220 Construction Equipment	120,000.00	Increase
380 Long-Term Liabilities	110,000.00	Increase

Solution: The changes are shown in Table 3-16.

LOAN PAYMENT

When payments on a loan are made, the payments affect the income statement and the balance sheet. On the income statement the interest paid on the loan is recorded as interest expense in the general overhead portion of the income statement. In the case of a company using the chart of accounts in Figure 2-1 it would be recorded in the 881 Interest Expense account. Some companies may charge interest expense to other expenses rather than a general overhead account. The increase in the interest expense decreases the profit on the income statement by the amount of the interest. On the balance sheet the loan payment reduces the cash account by the amount of the payment. The portion of the payment that is used to reduce the principal decreases the long-term liability account. Here the company is using cash—an asset—to reduce the loan principal—a long-term liability. Because of this, the portion of the loan payment used to reduce the principal does not affect the income statement. The portion of the payment that is used to pay the interest on the loan reduces the current period net income on the balance sheet. As per the relationships previously discussed, the reduction in profit on the income statement is equal to the reduction in the current period net income on the balance sheet.

> **Example 3-17:** Determine the changes that occur on the balance sheet and income statement when the contractor makes the first payment on the excavator in Example 3-16. The amount of the payment is $2,230.40, which includes $1,497.10 in principal and $733.33 in interest.

Solution: The changes are shown in Table 3-17.

EQUIPMENT DEPRECIATION

As owned equipment is used, the company needs to record the loss in value or depreciation each month. When the loss in value is recorded it affects the income statement, the balance sheet, and the equipment ledger. On the income statement the depreciation is recorded as an equipment depreciation cost. In the case of a company that uses the chart of accounts in Figure 2-1 the depreciation is recorded

TABLE 3-17   Loan Payment

ACCOUNT	CHANGE IN AMOUNT ($)	
Balance Sheet		
110 Cash	2,230.40	Decrease
380 Long-Term Liabilities	1,497.07	Decrease
430 Current Period Net Income	733.33	Decrease
Income Statement		
881 Interest Expense	733.33	Increase
Profit	733.33	Decrease

in the 720 Depreciation account. This increase in equipment cost decreases the profit on the income statement by the amount of the depreciation. On the balance sheet the depreciation is recorded in the less accumulated depreciation contra account in the asset section, which is used to offset the value of the fixed asset. This decrease in assets results in a reduction in the current period net income equal to the amount of the depreciation. As in the relationships previously discussed, the reduction in profit on the income statement is equal to the reduction in the current period net income on the balance sheet. Because the equipment has not been charged to a job, the depreciation does not affect the job cost ledger. The depreciation is recorded as a cost to the equipment ledger. This maintains the relationship between the equipment portion of the income statement and the equipment ledger.

Example 3-18:   Determine the change to the balance sheet, income statement, and equipment ledger for one month's depreciation for the excavator in Example 3-16. The monthly depreciation is $2,000.

Solution: The changes are shown in Table 3-18.

TABLE 3-18   Equipment Depreciation

ACCOUNT	CHANGE IN AMOUNT ($)	
Balance Sheet		
250 Less Acc. Depreciation	2,000.00	Increase
430 Current Period Net Income	2,000.00	Decrease
Income Statement		
720 Depreciation	2,000.00	Increase
Profit	2,000.00	Decrease
Equipment Ledger		
Excavator 1-Depreciation	2,000.00	Increase

TABLE 3-19   Leased Equipment with an Operating Lease

ACCOUNT	CHANGE IN AMOUNT ($)	
Balance Sheet		
310 Accounts Payable-Trade	2,500.00	Increase
430 Current Period Net Income	2,500.00	Decrease
Income Statement		
710 Rent and Lease Payments	2,500.00	Increase
Profit	2,500.00	Decrease
Equipment Ledger		
Excavator 2-Rent and Lease Payments	2,500.00	Increase

LEASED EQUIPMENT WITH AN OPERATING LEASE

When equipment is leased on a month-to-month basis or with an operating lease and the equipment is charged to multiple jobs, the equipment should be charged to the equipment portion of the income statement and then charged out to the jobs that use the equipment. Leasing equipment with an operating lease affects the income statement, balance sheet, and equipment ledger. On the income statement the monthly lease payment is recorded to the equipment portion of the income statement. In the case of a company using the chart of accounts in Figure 2-1, the lease payment would be recorded in the 710 Rent and Lease Payments account. This increase in equipment cost decreases the profit on the income statement by the amount of the lease. On the balance sheet the lease payment is recorded as an account payable-trade. This increase in liability results in a reduction in the current period net income equal to the amount of the lease payment. As per the relationships previously discussed, the reduction in profit on the income statement is equal to the reduction in the current period net income on the balance sheet. Because the equipment has not been charged to a job, the lease payment does not affect the job cost ledger. The lease payment is recorded as a cost to the equipment ledger. When equipment is rented for a single job it could be treated as an invoice for that job.

Example 3-19:   Determine the change to the balance sheet, income statement, and equipment ledger for one month's rent of an excavator. The excavator rents for $2,500 per month and is used on multiple jobs.

Solution: The changes are shown in Table 3-19.

LEASED EQUIPMENT WITH A CAPITAL LEASE

Capital leases are noncancelable leases that meet at least one of the following conditions: (1) The lease extends for 75 percent or more of the equipment's useful life, (2) ownership transfers at the end of the lease, (3) ownership is likely

TABLE 3-20   Leased Equipment with a Capital Lease

ACCOUNT	CHANGE IN AMOUNT ($)	
Balance Sheet		
260 Capital Leases	120,000.00	Increase
350 Capital Lease Payable	120,000.00	Increase

to transfer at the end of the lease through a purchase option with a heavily discounted price, or (4) the present value of the lease payment at market interest rate exceeds 90% of the fair market value of the equipment. Capital leases look and act much like a loan and are treated similarly to a loan. When a company takes on a new capital lease it not only obtains an asset that it can use for the life of the lease but also takes on the liability to pay for the leased equipment for the life of the lease. As such when a new capital lease is obtained it is recorded as both an asset and liability on the balance sheet. The amount recorded equals the present value of the capital lease. The calculation of present value is covered in chapter 15. In the case of a company that uses the chart of accounts in Figure 2-1, the present value of the lease would be recorded in the 260 Capital Leases account on the asset portion of the balance sheet and in the 350 Capital Lease Payable account on the liability portion of the balance sheet. The increase in the assets is offset by the increase in liabilities.

Example 3-20:   Determine the changes that occur on the balance sheet when the contractor leases a front-end loader. The lease is considered a capital lease with a present value of $120,000.00.

Solution: The changes are shown in Table 3-20.

LEASE PAYMENTS ON A CAPITAL LEASE

As lease payments are made on a capital lease the payment must be split into two components: interest on the liability and reduction of the liability. The lease payment affects the income statement and the balance sheet. On the income statement the interest component of the lease must be recorded as an interest expense in the general overhead portion of the income statement. In the case of a company using the chart of accounts in Figure 2-1 it would be recorded in the 881 Interest Expense account. Some companies may charge interest expense to other expenses rather than a general overhead account. The increase in the interest expense decreases the profit on the income statement by the amount of the interest. On the balance sheet the lease payment reduces the cash account by the amount of the payment. The portion of the payment that is used to reduce the liability decreases the capital lease payable account. In the case of a company using the chart of accounts in Figure 2-1 it would be recorded in the 350 Capital Lease Payable account. Here the company is using cash—an asset—

TABLE 3-21 Lease Payments on a Capital Lease

ACCOUNT	CHANGE IN AMOUNT ($)	
Balance Sheet		
110 Cash	2,433.17	Decrease
350 Capital Lease Payable	1,633.17	Decrease
430 Current Period Net Income	800.00	Decrease
Income Statement		
881 Interest Expense	800.00	Increase
Profit	800.00	Decrease

to reduce the capital lease payable—a long-term liability. Because of this, the portion of the lease payment used to reduce the capital lease payable does not affect the income statement. The portion of the payment that is used to pay the interest on the liability reduces the current period net income on the balance sheet. As in the relationships previously discussed, the reduction in profit on the income statement is equal to the reduction in the current period net income on the balance sheet.

Example 3-21: Determine the changes that occur on the balance sheet and income statement when the contractor makes the first lease payment on the loader in Example 3-20. The amount of the payment is $2,433.17, of which $1,633.17 is used to reduce the capital lease payable and $800.00 is the interest on the liability.

Solution: The changes are shown in Table 3-21.

AMORTIZATION OF A CAPITAL LEASE

Over time the asset value of a capital lease decreases. As a result, the asset value of the capital lease must be amortized. The amortization of a capital lease behaves much the same as depreciation of an asset. When the amortization of a capital lease is recorded it affects the income statement, the balance sheet, and the equipment ledger. On the income statement the amortization is recorded as equipment lease costs. In the case of a company that uses the chart of accounts in Figure 2-1 the amortization would be recorded in the 710 Rent and Lease Payment account. This increase in equipment cost decreases the profit on the income statement by the amount of the amortization. The amortization reduces the capital lease asset on the balance sheet. Some companies may set up a contra account for capital leases. In the case of a company that uses the chart of accounts in Figure 2-1 the amortization would be recorded against the 260 Capital Lease account. This decrease in assets results in a reduction in the current period net income equal to the amount of the amortization. As in the

TABLE 3-22   Amortization of a Capital Lease

ACCOUNT	CHANGE IN AMOUNT ($)	
Balance Sheet		
260 Capital Leases	2,000.00	Decrease
430 Current Period Net Income	2,000.00	Decrease
Income Statement		
710 Rent and Lease Payment	2,000.00	Increase
Profit	2,000.00	Decrease
Equipment Ledger		
Loader 1-Rent and Lease Payments	2,000.00	Increase

relationships previously discussed, the reduction in profit on the income statement is equal to the reduction in the current period net income on the balance
sheet. Because the equipment has not been charged to a job, the amortization
does not affect the job cost ledger. The amortization is recorded as a cost to the
equipment ledger, thus maintaining the relationship between the income statement and the equipment ledger.

Example 3-22:   Determine the change to the balance sheet, income statement, and equipment ledger for one month's amortization for the loader in
Example 3-20. The monthly amortization is $2,000.

Solution: The changes are shown in Table 3-22.

INVOICE FOR EQUIPMENT REPAIRS

When an invoice for equipment repairs is received and entered into the accounting system it affects the income statement, balance sheet, and equipment ledger.
On the income statement the invoices are recorded as an equipment cost in the
equipment portion of the income statement. In the case of a company that uses
the chart of accounts in Figure 2-1 the invoice is recorded to the 730 Repairs and
Maintenance account. The increase in the equipment costs decreases the profit on
the income statement by the amount of the invoice. On the balance sheet the invoice is recorded as an accounts payable-trade in the liability section. This increase
in liability results in a reduction in the current period net income equal to the
amount of the invoice. As in the relationships previously discussed the reduction
in profit on the income statement is equal to the reduction in the current period
net income on the balance sheet. Because the equipment has not been charged to
a job, the invoice does not affect the job cost ledger. The invoice is recorded as a
cost to the equipment ledger against the piece of equipment that was repaired.
Large repairs—such as engine overhauls—may need to be recorded as an asset and
depreciated. A company's accountant can help to determine if a repair must be
depreciated. Maintenance, fuel, and other equipment invoices are handled in the

TABLE 3-23   Invoice for Equipment Repairs

ACCOUNT	CHANGE IN AMOUNT ($)	
Balance Sheet		
310 Accounts Payable-Trade	500.00	Increase
430 Current Period Net Income	500.00	Decrease
Income Statement		
730 Repairs	500.00	Increase
Profit	500.00	Decrease
Equipment Ledger		
Loader 1-Repairs and Maintenance	500.00	Increase

same manner; however, they may be recorded in a different equipment account on the income statement.

Example 3-23:   Determine the change to the balance sheet, income statement, and equipment ledger of a $500 invoice for repairs to the loader in Example 3-20.

Solution: The changes are shown in Table 3-23.

EQUIPMENT CHARGED TO A JOB

So far costs have been recorded to the equipment section of the income statement, but these costs have not been charged to a job. The goal at the end of the fiscal year is for all equipment costs to be charged to the individual jobs or employees. Equipment charges may be made to jobs based on the number of hours a piece of equipment was operated on a job or based on the number of days a piece of equipment was on a job, whether or not it was operating. Often a time card is kept for each piece of equipment, just as a company would keep a time card for its employees. When equipment is charged to a job it affects the income statement, the job cost ledger, and the equipment ledger. On the income statement the equipment charge is recorded as an equipment cost in the construction cost portion of the income statement. In the case of a company that uses the chart of accounts in Figure 2-1 the charge would be recorded to the 640 Equipment account. The charge is also recorded to the equipment costs charged to a job contra account in the equipment portion of the income statement, which offsets the equipment costs in the same way the depreciation account offsets the fixed assets. In the case of a company that uses the chart of accounts in Figure 2-1 the charge would be recorded to the 799 Equipment Costs Charged to Job account. On the job cost ledger the equipment charge is recorded as a cost with an equipment cost type against the job, phase, and cost code on which the equipment was used. On the equipment ledger the charge is recorded as a cost

TABLE 3-24   Equipment Charged to a Job

ACCOUNT	CHANGE IN AMOUNT ($)	
Income Statement		
640 Equipment	5,000.00	Increase
799 Equipment Costs Charged to Jobs	5,000.00	Increase
Job Cost Ledger		
105.01.02100E	5,000.00	Increase
Equipment Ledger		
Excavator 2-Equipment Costs Allocated	5,000.00	Increase

allocation for the piece of equipment. Because this is just an allocation of a previously recorded cost no changes are required on the balance sheet.

Example 3-24:   Determine the change to the income statement, the job cost ledger, and the equipment ledger of a $5,000 equipment charge to Job 105, Phase 1, cost code 02100 Grading and Excavation.

Solution: The changes are shown in Table 3-24.

EQUIPMENT CHARGED TO AN EMPLOYEE

The IRS requires that employers report an employee's personal use of company vehicles as compensation to the employee. The personal use of a company vehicle includes using the vehicle to commute to and from work. To do this many employers deduct a flat monthly rate for use of the vehicle from the employee's paycheck. Employers who do not want to charge the employee for use of the vehicle often add the monthly rate to the employee's base wages—so that the use of the vehicle is recorded as wages—and then deduct the same monthly rate from the employee's check. The deduction is made after taxes are deducted from the employee's paycheck. By doing this, the monthly charge for the vehicle is recorded as wages and the employee pays taxes on the use of the vehicle.

When equipment is charged to an employee it affects the balance sheet, income statement, and equipment ledger. On the balance sheet the wages due to the employee—which are recorded as an accrued payroll—are decreased by the amount of the deduction. In the case of a company that uses the chart of accounts in Figure 2-1 the charge would reduce the 340 Accrued Payroll account. The reduction in the accrued payroll increases the current period net income by the amount of the deduction. On the income statement the deduction is recorded to the equipment costs charged to the employee's contra account in the equipment portion of the income statement, which account offsets the equipment costs. In the case of a company that uses the chart of accounts in Figure 2-1 the charge would be recorded to

TABLE 3-25 Equipment Charged to an Employee

ACCOUNT	CHANGE IN AMOUNT ($)	
Balance Sheet		
340 Accrued Payroll	50.00	Decrease
430 Current Period Income	50.00	Increase
Income Statement		
798 Equipment Costs Charged to Employees	50.00	Increase
Profit	50.00	Increase
Equipment Ledger		
Truck 5-Equipment Costs Allocated	50.00	Increase

the 798 Equipment Costs Charged to Employees account. This charge increases the profit by the amount of the deduction. As per the relationships previously discussed the increase in profit on the income statement is equal to the increase in the current period net income on the balance sheet. On the equipment ledger the charge is recorded as a cost allocation for the piece of equipment.

Example 3-25: Determine the change to the balance sheet, income statement, and the equipment ledger of a $50 deduction from an employee's wages for personal use of a company vehicle.

Solution: The changes are shown in Table 3-25.

SALE OF EQUIPMENT

The last equipment transaction we look at is what happens when a piece of equipment is sold. When the sale of a piece of equipment occurs, an asset—recorded in the fixed asset and less accumulated depreciation accounts—is exchanged for cash. If the asset is sold for more or less than its book value, the gain or loss on the asset must be reported as an income or loss. The sale of equipment affects the balance sheet and if a gain or loss on the asset occurs, it also affects the income statement. On the balance sheet, when an asset is sold, the asset is removed from the fixed asset account and its depreciation is removed from the less accumulated depreciation account. This results in a change in the net fixed asset account equal to the book value of the asset. The sale of the asset increases the cash, note receivable, or other asset account depending on the terms of the sale. If the asset is financed, the sale decreases the note payable or long-term liability associated with paying off the asset's financing. If the asset is sold for a price different from the book value, the gain or loss on the sale will result in an increase or decrease in the current period net income equal to the gain or loss. On the income statement the gain or loss will be recorded as other income or other expense. Gains increase the profit on the income statement by the amount of the gain. Losses

TABLE 3-26   Sale of Equipment

ACCOUNT	CHANGE IN AMOUNT ($)	
Balance Sheet		
110 Cash	60,000.00	Increase
220 Construction Equipment	120,000.00	Decrease
250 Less Acc. Depreciation	62,400.00	Decrease
430 Current Period Net Income	2,400.00	Increase
Income Statement		
910 Other Income	2,400.00	Increase
Profit	2,400.00	Decrease

decrease the profit on the income statement by the amount of the loss. As per the relationships previously discussed, the reduction or increase in profit on the income statement is equal to the reduction or increase in the current period net income on the balance sheet.

Example 3-26: Determine the change to the balance sheet and income statement of the sale of a crane. The crane was sold for $60,000 in cash. The crane was purchased for $120,000 and $62,400 of depreciation has been taken.

Solution: The book value on the crane is $57,600 ($120,000 − $62,400). The gain on the sale is $2,400 ($60,000 − $57,600). The changes are shown in Table 3-26.

PURCHASE OF INVENTORY

When a company purchases materials and places them in inventory until they are ready to use them, the company is exchanging a liability (accounts payable) or an asset (cash) for an asset (inventory). When the materials are received they are recorded as an asset in the inventory category. In the case of a company that uses the chart of accounts in Figure 2-1 the cost of the materials would be recorded to the 130 Inventory account. If the materials were purchased on credit, the accounts payable-trade will increase by the amount of the purchase. If the materials were purchased with cash, the cash account would be reduced by the amount of the purchase. No changes are made to the income statement or job cost ledger until the materials are charged to a job.

Example 3-27: Determine the change to the balance sheet from the purchase of $5,000 of copper wiring on credit for use on future projects. The wiring will be held in inventory until it is needed on a job.

Solution: The changes are shown in Table 3-27.

TABLE 3-27   Purchase of Inventory

ACCOUNT	CHANGE IN AMOUNT ($)	
Balance Sheet		
130 Inventory	5,000.00	Increase
310 Accounts Payable-Trade	5,000.00	Increase

CHARGING INVENTORY TO A JOB

When inventoried materials are used on a job and subsequently charged to that job, it affects the balance sheet, income statement, and job cost ledger. On the balance sheet, the inventory is reduced by the amount of the purchase price of the materials. Because the same kind of materials may have been purchased at different times and different prices it can be difficult to determine the purchase price of the materials used on the project. Often the price is an assigned price rather than the actual price of the material. Two common methods of assigning prices are the first-in/first-out (FIFO) and last-in/first-out (LIFO) methods. Using the FIFO method, it is assumed that the materials are used in the order that they were purchased, regardless of the actual order of use. Using the LIFO method it is assumed that the most recently purchased materials are used first, again, regardless of the actual order of use. A contractor should consult with a certified public accountant when setting up an inventory system to ensure that he or she complies with all the tax rules covering inventory. The reduction in inventory is accompanied by a reduction in the current period net income. On the income statement and the job cost ledger the material purchased is recorded as if the material had been purchased directly from a supplier (see Invoice Charged to a Job without Retention).

Example 3-28:   Determine the change to the balance sheet, income statement, and job cost ledger when $2,000 of copper wire is billed from inventory to Job Number 172 for use in Phase 2. The wire is cost coded to 16100.

Solution: The changes are shown in Table 3-28.

TABLE 3-28   Charging Inventory to a Job

ACCOUNT	CHANGE IN AMOUNT ($)	
Balance Sheet		
130 Inventory	2,000.00	Decrease
430 Current Period Net Income	2,000.00	Decrease
Income Statement		
610 Materials	2,000.00	Increase
Profit	2,000.00	Decrease
Job Cost Ledger		
172.01.16100M	2,000.00	Increase

TABLE 3-29   Recording Changes in Cost and Profits in Excess of Billings

ACCOUNT	CHANGE IN AMOUNT ($)	
Balance Sheet		
140 Costs and Profits in Excess of Billings	5,000.00	Increase
430 Current Period Net Income	5,000.00	Increase
Income Statement		
500 Revenue	5,000.00	Increase
Profit	5,000.00	Increase

RECORDING CHANGES IN COSTS AND PROFITS IN EXCESS OF BILLINGS

When a company using the percentage-of-completion accounting method has costs and profits in excess of billing it has underbilled the revenue on its construction projects. Because it must recognize the revenues, costs, and profits throughout the project, it needs to recognize the underbilled revenues as revenues although it has not billed the client for them. This increase in revenues increases the company's profits. The underbilled revenues create an asset that is recorded in the current asset portion of the balance sheet, which in turn increases the current period net income. In the case of the company using the chart of accounts in Figure 2-1, the revenues would be recorded to the 500 Revenues account and the asset would be recorded to the 140 Costs and Profits in Excess of Billings account. The amount recorded each month is the difference between last month's underbillings and this month's underbillings. As in the relationships previously discussed, the reduction or increase in profit on the income statement is equal to the reduction or increase in the current period net income on the balance sheet. The calculation of the underbillings or costs and profits in excess of billings is covered in chapter 4.

Example 3-29:   At the end of last month the company's costs and profits in excess of billings was $10,000. At the end of this month it was $15,000. Determine the change to the balance sheet and income statement when this change is recorded.

Solution: The change in the cost and profit in excess of billings is an increase of $5,000 ($15,000 − $10,000). The changes are shown in Table 3-29.

RECORDING CHANGES IN BILLINGS IN EXCESS OF COSTS AND PROFITS

When a company using the percentage-of-completion accounting method has billings in excess of costs and profits it has overbilled the revenue on its construction projects. The overbilling should not be recognized as profits, yet the

TABLE 3-30   Recording Changes in Billings in Excess of Cost and Profits

ACCOUNT	CHANGE IN AMOUNT ($)	
Balance Sheet		
140 Costs and Profits in Excess of Billings	1,500.00	Increase
430 Current Period Net Income	1,500.00	Decrease
Income Statement		
500 Revenue	1,500.00	Decrease
Profit	1,500.00	Decrease

company has done so when it billed its projects. To correct this situation, the company must reduce its revenues by the overbilled amount. This decrease in revenues decreases the company's profits. The company also owes its clients for the work it has billed for but has yet to perform, which creates a liability recorded in the current liability portion of the balance sheet. The increase in the liability that results when an overbilling occurs reduces the current period net income. In the case of the company using the chart of accounts in Figure 2-1, the revenues would be recorded to the 500 Revenues account and the liability would be recorded to the 320 Billings in Excess of Costs and Profits account. The amount recorded each month is the difference between last month's overbillings and this month's overbillings. As in the relationships previously discussed, the reduction or increase in profit on the income statement is equal to the reduction or increase in the current period net income on the balance sheet. The calculation of the overbillings or billings in excess of costs and profits is covered in chapter 4.

Example 3-30:   At the end of last month the company's billings in excess of costs and profits was $10,000. At the end of this month it is $11,500. Determine the change to the balance sheet and income statement when this change is recorded.

Solution: The change in the billings in excess of costs and profits is an increase of $1,500 ($11,500 − $10,000). The changes are shown in Table 3-30.

CONCLUSION

There are a number of unique transactions that take place in construction accounting that do not occur in other industries. Most of these transactions are a result of the construction industry's focus on job costing, equipment tracking, and accounting for long-term contracts. In this chapter we looked at how accounting transactions affect the general ledger—balance sheet and income statement—as well as the job cost ledger and the equipment ledger, while maintaining the proper balance between these ledgers. Some of the unique transitions that we examined were accruing vacation time for field employees, recording and allocating equipment costs, recording costs and profits in excess of billings, and recording billings in excess of costs and profits.

PROBLEMS

1. The following invoices are being entered into the accounting system. Using the chart of accounts in Figure 2-1, determine the changes to the balance sheet, income statement, job cost ledger, and equipment ledger as the result of entering each of the following invoices:

   a. A $5,000 invoice for concrete charged to job cost code 302.01.02620M.

   b. A $12,350 invoice from a subcontractor for plumbing charged to job cost code 309.02.15100S. Ten percent retention is withheld from the invoice.

   c. A $255 phone bill charged to job cost code 315.01.01800O.

   d. A $1,352 bill for office rent.

   e. A $112 invoice for office supplies.

   f. A $375 invoice for repairs to Backhoe 2.

   g. A $563 invoice for nails. The nails will be placed in inventory until they are needed on the jobs, at which time they will be billed to the jobs.

   What are the changes to the balance sheet, income statement, job cost ledger, and equipment ledger as a result of all of these invoices?

2. Time cards are being entered into the accounting system for four employees. The costs for Employee 1 are to be billed to job cost code 302.01.01100L. Ten hours of Employee 2 time is to be billed to job cost code 302.01.06110L and the remaining 30 hours are to be billed to job cost code 302.01.06210L. Employee 3 took vacation this entire week and Employee 4 works in the main office. The employee costs and deductions withheld from the employee's check are shown below. Using the chart of accounts in Figure 2-1, determine the changes to the balance sheet, income statement, job cost ledger, and equipment ledger as the result of entering the employees' time into the accounting system:

	EMPLOYEE ($)				
	1	2	3	4	TOTAL
Employer's Costs					
Wages	600.00	400.00	350.00	500.00	1,850.00
Social Security	37.20	24.80	21.70	31.00	114.70
Medicare	8.70	5.80	5.08	7.25	26.83
SUTA	18.00	12.00	10.50	15.00	55.50
FUTA	4.80	3.20	2.80	4.00	14.80
Liability Insurance	12.00	8.00	7.00	10.00	37.00
Workers' Comp.	54.00	36.00	31.50	15.00	136.50
Health Insurance	40.00	40.00	40.00	40.00	160.00
Vacation	38.92	29.79	27.51	33.20	129.42
Total	813.62	559.59	496.09	655.45	2,524.75

(continued)

	Employee ($)				
	1	2	3	4	Total
Employee Deductions					
Social Security	37.20	24.80	21.70	31.00	114.70
Medicare	8.70	5.80	5.08	7.25	26.83
Federal Withholdings	59.85	29.85	22.35	44.85	156.90
State Withholdings	36.00	24.00	21.00	30.00	111.00
Health Insurance	60.00	60.00	60.00	60.00	240.00
Total	201.75	144.45	130.13	173.10	649.43

3. Using the chart of accounts in Figure 2-1, determine the changes to the balance sheet, income statement, job cost ledger, and equipment ledger as the result of paying the employees in Problem 2 for one week's work.

4. Using the chart of accounts in Figure 2-1, determine the changes to the balance sheet, income statement, job cost ledger, and equipment ledger as the result of paying a $5,000 invoice for concrete charged to job cost code 302.01.02620M, $2,273.80 for federal employment taxes, and $1,732 for health insurance. The invoices were previously entered into the accounting system.

5. Using the chart of accounts in Figure 2-1, determine the changes to the balance sheet, income statement, job cost ledger, and equipment ledger as the result of billing a client $368,264 for Job 313. The bill includes $249,996 for work performed during the last month and $118,268 for retention withheld from the previous month's payments. Retention will not be withheld on the $249,996.

6. Using the chart of accounts in Figure 2-1, determine the changes to the balance sheet, income statement, job cost ledger, and equipment ledger as the result of receiving payment from the owner for the bill in Problem 5.

7. Using the chart of accounts in Figure 2-1, determine the changes to the balance sheet, income statement, job cost ledger, and equipment ledger as the result of purchasing a new loader (Loader 3) to replace an existing loader (Loader 2). The new loader costs $115,200. The new loader will be paid for by trading in the existing loader for a credit of $15,200 and the remaining $100,000 will be financed through the dealership. The existing loader was purchased for $95,000 and $83,230 of depreciation had been taken.

8. Using the chart of accounts in Figure 2-1, determine the changes to the balance sheet, income statement, job cost ledger, and equipment ledger as the result of leasing a $32,000 backhoe (Backhoe 6). The backhoe may be returned to the lessor at any time without penalty. The lease payment is not paid at this time.

9. Using the chart of accounts in Figure 2-1, determine the changes to the balance sheet, income statement, job cost ledger, and equipment ledger as the result of leasing a $55,000 dump truck (Dump Truck 11). The lease

extends for five years at which time the dump truck may be purchased for $5,000. The present value of the lease is $55,000.

10. Using the chart of accounts in Figure 2-1, determine the changes to the balance sheet, income statement, job cost ledger, and equipment ledger as the result of paying a $1,312 loan payment and a $1,050 capital lease payment. For the loan, $270 of the payment is interest and for the capital lease $692 of the payment is used to reduce the capital lease payable.

11. Using the chart of accounts in Figure 2-1, determine the changes to the balance sheet, income statement, job cost ledger, and equipment ledger as the result of recording $2,500 in office depreciation, $1,920 in depreciation for Loader 3, and $917 in amortization on the capital lease for Dump Truck 11.

12. Using the chart of accounts in Figure 2-1, determine the changes to the balance sheet, income statement, job cost ledger, and equipment ledger as the result of billing $600 for Truck 22 to job cost code 302.01.01100L and $50 for personal use of Truck 22 to the superintendent of Job 302.

13. Using the chart of accounts in Figure 2-1, determine the changes to the balance sheet, income statement, job cost ledger, and equipment ledger as the result of billing $200 of nails to job cost code 302.01.06110M.

CHAPTER

4

MORE CONSTRUCTION ACCOUNTING

In this chapter you will increase your understanding of construction accounting systems. You will learn to track committed costs outside the accounting system in the event your company's accounting system does not track committed costs, which will also help you understand how accounting systems track committed costs. You will learn to use committed costs to project the estimated cost and profit at completion for projects. You will also learn to calculate over- and underbillings. Finally, you will learn about the internal controls that need to be set up to protect your financial resources and what to look for in computerized construction accounting systems.

What follows are a number of topics that will round out your understanding of construction accounting. Let's begin by looking at committed costs and estimated cost at completion.

COMMITTED COSTS AND ESTIMATED COST AT COMPLETION

To get a more accurate picture of a construction project's financial status, unbilled committed costs must be included with the invoiced costs in the job costs ledger and the estimated cost at completion needs to be projected.

Committed costs are those costs that the company has committed to pay. This occurs when the company issues a purchase order or signs a subcontract for a known amount. Often a company hires subcontractors for a major portion of a project. When the subcontractors are hired for a fixed price, the cost to complete the subcontracted work is known—barring any change orders—far in advance of the work being completed and the company receiving a bill for the work. Some accounting systems allow you to track committed costs in the job cost ledger, whereas others do not. Once a bill is received for a committed cost, it is included with the invoiced costs and tracked on the job cost ledger. If a company's accounting system does not track committed costs, unbilled committed costs must be manually combined with the job cost ledger to get an accurate picture of the project's financial status. In this section we look at how to use a spreadsheet to combine unbilled committed costs with the costs from the job cost ledger. This will help you understand how to include committed costs and how an accounting package handles committed costs, since they handle them in a similar manner.

We also look at projecting the estimated cost at completion. As a project is completed, estimated costs become actual costs. As cost over- and underruns occur on projects the estimated cost at completion, as well as the estimate profit, change for each of the projects. Additionally, as change orders occur they further change the estimated cost at completion and profit. It is important for management to track and manage the profitability of each project.

Including committed costs and estimating the cost at completion can be done with a simple spreadsheet similar to the one shown in Figure 4-1. Each project is done on a separate spreadsheet. Let's look at how to use this spreadsheet to include the committed costs and project the cost at completion for a project.

Each cost code is entered on a separate line. The cost codes may or may not be separated by cost type—labor, materials, equipment, subcontract, and other. The cost codes are entered in Column A with the associated description entered in Column B. The original estimated cost for each cost code is entered in Column C. Typically these are the costs used to generate the estimate. The changes that need to be made—positive or negative—to the original estimate as the result of change orders are entered in Column D. The change orders may be change orders submitted to the owner or internal change orders that are used to track changes to the original budget. The total estimated cost equals the original estimate plus the change orders; therefore, Column E equals Column C plus Column D. The committed costs for each cost code are entered in Column F. Committed costs commonly include subcontract amounts and purchase orders with known costs. The costs from the job cost ledger are then divided into two types: costs that are charged against committed costs and costs that are charged against noncommitted costs. The costs charged against committed costs are entered in Column G and costs charged against noncommitted costs are entered in Column H. When setting up

	A	B	C	D	E	F	G	H	I	J	K	L
1									Total		Total	
2									Committed		Estimated	
3								Non-	and Non-		Cost	Variance
4					Total		Committed	Committed	Committed	Cost	at	Over /
5			Original	Change	Estimate	Committed	Costs	Costs	Costs	to	Completion	(Under)
6	Code	Description	Estimate	Orders	(C + D)	Costs	Invoiced	Invoiced	(F + H)	Complete	(I + J)	(K - E)
7					-				-		-	-
8					-				-		-	-
9			-	-	-	-	-	-	-	-	-	

FIGURE 4-1　Committed Cost Worksheet

a company's cost codes, it is a good idea to set them up in such a manner that makes it easy to separate committed from noncommitted costs. The total committed and noncommitted costs are entered in Column I and are calculated by adding the committed costs in Column F to the noncommitted costs invoiced in Column H. These costs represent the total spent plus unbilled committed costs on the project thus far. The cost to complete the work covered by each cost code is entered in Column J. The cost to complete should include any costs the company anticipates spending between now and the completion of the project that the company has not already committed to. Committed costs should not be included because they have already been included in the worksheet. The total estimated cost at completion is entered in Column K and is calculated by adding the total committed and noncommitted costs in Column I to the cost to complete in Column J. Finally the variance is entered in Column L and is calculated by subtracting the total estimate in Column E from the total estimated cost at completion in Column K. Cost overruns are represented by a positive number and cost underruns are represented by a negative number. Once all of the values for each of the cost codes have been calculated, the project totals may be calculated by totaling each of the columns. Let's see how this works.

Example 4-1: A contractor has signed a contract to pour the footing, foundation, and slab floor for a building. The contractor uses the cost codes in Figure 2-5. The original estimate for the labor to complete the footing and foundation was $8,400 and the contractor has subcontracted this work out for $8,560. The subcontractor has billed the contractor for $2,700 for this work. No additional cost commitments are expected to be made for this line item. The original estimate for concrete to complete the footings and foundation is $9,270, no costs have been committed, and the contractor has received a bill for $3,960. The contractor estimates that it will cost an additional $5,310 to purchase the remaining concrete for the footings and foundations. The original estimate for the labor to complete the slab floor is $20,000 and a $100 change order has been approved for additional work. This work will by performed by in-house crews. The work has yet to be performed and the contractor estimates that the cost to complete the work is $20,100. The original estimate for the concrete to complete the slab floor is $23,456 and a $118 change order has been approved for additional work. The work has yet to be performed, but the contractor has been given a 1% price discount for the slab concrete from the supplier, which reduces the total estimated for this item by 1%. Determine the total estimated cost at completion for the project and the variance for each cost code.

Solution: The original estimate for the labor to complete the footings and foundation is $8,400. The total estimate (Column E) for the labor to complete the footings and foundation equals the original estimate (Column C) because no change orders have been issued. Because the contractor has hired a subcontractor for this work, the committed costs (Column F) are $8,560, of which $2,700 have been invoiced (Column G). The total committed and noncommitted costs (Column I) are calculated as follows:

Total Committed and Noncommitted Costs = $8,560 + $0 = $8,560

The total estimated cost at completion is equal to the total committed and noncommitted costs (Column I) because the estimated cost to complete (Column J) is zero. The variance (Column L) is equal to the total estimated cost at completion (Column K) less the total estimate (Column E) and is calculated as follows:

Variance = $8,560 − $8,400 = $160

This variance indicates that there is a cost overrun of $160 for this line item.

The original estimate for the concrete to complete the footings and foundation is $9,270. The total estimate (Column E) for the concrete to complete the footings and foundation equals the original estimate (Column C) because no change orders have been issued. Because no costs have been committed, the committed costs (Column F) are $0. The invoiced costs are noncommitted costs; therefore, the noncommitted costs invoiced (Column H) are $3,960. The total committed and noncommitted costs (Column I) are calculated as follows:

Total Committed and Noncommitted Costs = $0 + $3,960 = $3,960

The estimated cost to complete (Column J) is $5,310. The total estimated cost at completion (Column K) is equal to the total committed and noncommitted costs (Column I) plus the cost to complete (Column J) and is calculated as follows:

Total Estimated Cost at Completion = $3,960 + $5,310 = $9,270

Because the total estimated cost at completion is equal to the total estimate, the variance (Column L) is zero. This cost item is neither over nor under budget.

For the labor to complete the slab floor, the total estimate (Column E) equals the original estimate (Column C) plus the change orders (Column D) and is calculated as follows:

Total Estimate = $20,000 + $100 = $20,100

Because the work is being performed in-house, the costs are still unknown and are noncommitted costs. Because the costs have not occurred the noncommitted costs invoiced (Column H) is zero. The company estimates that the cost to complete (Column J) is $20,100.

The total estimated cost at completion (Column K) is equal to the total committed and noncommitted costs (Column I) plus the cost to complete (Column J) and is calculated as follows:

Total Estimated Cost at Completion = $0 + $20,100 = $20,100

Because the total estimated cost at completion is equal to the total estimate the variance is zero. This cost item is neither over nor under budget.

For the concrete to complete the slab floor, the total estimate (Column E) equals the original estimate (Column C) plus the change orders (Column D) and is calculated as follows:

$$\text{Total Estimate} = \$23,456 + \$118 = \$23,574$$

Because the work has yet to be performed and the actual quantity of concrete has not been determined, the costs are still unknown and are noncommitted costs. Because the costs have not occurred the noncommitted costs invoiced (Column H) are zero. The company has received a 1% discount from the supplier that is reflected in the estimated cost to complete and is calculated as follows:

$$\text{Estimated Cost to Complete} = \$23,574(1 - 1/100) = \$23,338$$

The total estimated cost at completion (Column K) is equal to the total committed and noncommitted costs (Column I) plus the cost to complete (Column J) and is calculated as follows:

$$\text{Total Estimated Cost at Completion} = \$0 + \$23,338 = \$23,338$$

The variance (Column L) is equal to the total estimated cost at completion (Column K) less the total estimate (Column E) and is calculated as follows:

$$\text{Variance} = \$23,574 - \$23,338 = -\$236$$

This variance indicates that there is a cost under run of $236 for this line item.

The total of each of the columns may then be summed for a project total. For the project the variance is calculated as follows:

$$\text{Variance} = \$160 + \$0 + \$0 + (-\$236) = -\$76$$

We see that the project has a projected cost savings of $76. The solution using a spreadsheet is found in Figure 4-2.

	A	B	C	D	E	F	G	H	I	J	K	L
1									Total		Total	
2									Committed		Estimated	
3							Non-		and Non-		Cost	Variance
4					Total		Committed	Committed	Committed	Cost	at	Over /
5			Original	Change	Estimate	Committed	Costs	Costs	Costs	to	Completion	(Under)
6	Code	Description	Estimate	Orders	(C + D)	Costs	Invoiced	Invoiced	(F + H)	Complete	(I + J)	(K - E)
7	3300	Footing & Found.-Labor	8,400	—	8,400	8,560	2,700	—	8,560	—	8,560	160
8	3400	Footing & Found.-Conc.	9,270	—	9,270	—	—	3,960	3,960	5,310	9,270	—
9	3500	Slab/Floor-Labor	20,000	100	20,100	—	—	—	—	20,100	20,100	—
10	3600	Slab/Floor-Conc.	23,456	118	23,574	—	—	—	—	23,338	23,338	(236)
11			61,126	218	61,344	8,560	2,700	3,960	12,520	48,748	61,268	(76)

FIGURE 4-2   Solution to Example 4-1

OVERBILLINGS AND UNDERBILLINGS

To prepare the monthly and annual balance sheets the overbillings and under-billings must be calculated for each project. In this section we look at how to calculate the under- and overbillings for a company using the percentage-of-completion method. For a company using the percentage-of-completion method the overbillings are recorded on the balance sheet as costs and profits in excess of billings and the underbillings are recorded as billings in excess of costs and profit. A simple spreadsheet used to calculate the over- and underbillings for a company using the percentage-of-completion method are shown in Figure 4-3. A single worksheet is used to calculate the over- and underbillings for the entire company. Let's look at how to use this worksheet to calculate the over- and underbillings.

Each project or job is entered on a separate line of the form and then the costs and profits in excess of billings and the billings in excess of costs and profit are totaled for the entire company. The job number for a project is entered in Column A. This should be the same number used in the job cost ledger. The job or project name is entered into Column B. The current contract amount is entered into Column C. This amount should include all approved change orders. The current total estimated cost at completion for the project is entered in Column D. The current total estimated cost at completion comes from the committed cost worksheet shown in Figure 4-1. The estimated profit on the project equals the current contract amount less the total estimated cost at completion; therefore, Column E equals Column C less Column D.

The actual costs to date for the project are entered in Column F. The actual costs should include all construction costs that are included in the income statement for the project. Unbilled committed costs should not be included in these costs. The earned profit equals the percentage complete times the estimated profit. Most often the percentage complete is calculated by dividing the actual costs to date by the estimated costs at completion for the project; therefore, Column G—earned profit—is calculated by multiplying Column E by Column F and dividing the resultant by Column D. Column H, cost and earned profit equals actual costs to date in Column F plus earned profit in Column G. The total billed to the client on the job is entered in Column I.

If costs and earned profits are greater than the total billed, the project has been underbilled and the costs and profits in excess of billings are entered in Column J,

	A	B	C	D	E	F	G	H	I	J	K	L
1										Costs &	Billings in	
2				Total		Actual		Costs &		Profits in	Excess of	
3			Current	Estimated	Estimated	Costs	Earned	Earned		Excess of	Costs &	Percentage
4	Job		Contract	Cost at	Profit	to	Profit	Profit	Total	Billings	Profits	Complete
5	#	Job Name	Amount	Completion	(C - D)	Date	(E x F / D)	(F + G)	Billed	(H - I)	(I - H)	(F x 100 / D)
6					—			—		—	—	—
7					—			—		—	—	—
8										—	—	

FIGURE 4-3   Overbillings and Underbillings Worksheet

where Column J equals costs and earned profit recorded in Column H less total billed recorded in Column I. A zero is entered into Column J if costs and earned profits are less than or equal to the total billed. The total costs in excess of billings for the company is found by summing Column J for all of the company's projects.

If costs and earned profits are less than the total billed, the project has been overbilled and the billings in excess of costs and profits are entered in Column K, where Column K equals total billed in Column I less costs and earned profit in Column H. A zero is entered into Column K if costs and earned profits are greater than or equal to the total billed. The billings in excess of costs and profits for the company are found by summing Column K for all of the company's projects.

Finally, the percentage complete is entered in Column L, which is calculated by multiplying actual costs to date in Column F by 100 and dividing the resultant by the total estimated cost at completion in Column D.

Example 4-2: Determine over- and underbillings for a company with the following information:

Job Number: 301
Job Name: Henderson Remodel
Current Contract Amount: $122,500
Total Estimate Cost at Completion: $101,256
Actual Costs to Date: $95,265
Total Billed: $110,687

Job Number: 302
Job Name: Weston Offices
Current Contract Amount: $25,265
Total Estimate Cost at Completion: $18,000
Actual Costs to Date: $11,542
Total Billed: $17,253

Job Number: 303
Job Name: Johnson Warehouse
Current Contract Amount: $255,202
Total Estimate Cost at Completion: $229,564
Actual Costs to Date: $35,264
Total Billed: $41,200

Solution: First let's look at the Henderson remodel. The contract amount is $122,500 and is entered in Column A. The total estimated cost at completion is $101,256 and is entered in Column B. The estimated profit is calculated by subtracting the current contract amount from the total estimated cost at completion as follows:

Estimated Profit = $122,500 − $101,256 = $21,244

The estimated profit is recorded in Column C. The actual costs to date are $95,265 and are entered in Column D. Earned profit is calculated as follows:

$$\text{Earned Profit} = \text{Estimated Profit}(\text{Actual Costs to Date})/$$
$$\text{Total Estimated Costs at Completion}$$
$$\text{Earned Profit} = \$21,244(\$95,265)/\$101,256 = \$19,987$$

The earned profit is recorded in Column G. Costs and earned profit are calculated as follows:

$$\text{Costs and Earned Profit} = \$95,265 + \$19,987 = \$115,252$$

The costs and earned profit are recorded in Column H. The total billed for the job is $110,687 and is entered in Column I. Because the job has been billed less than the costs and earned profit the job is underbilled or has costs and profits in excess of billings. The underbillings are calculated by subtracting the total billed from the costs and earned profits as follows:

$$\text{Underbillings} = \$115,252 - \$110,687 = \$4,565$$

The underbillings are recorded in Column J. Billings in excess of costs and profits—Column K—are zero, because the job is underbilled. The percentage complete is calculated as follows:

$$\text{Percentage Complete} = \text{Actual Costs to Date}(100)/$$
$$\text{Total Estimated Costs at Completion}$$
$$\text{Percentage Complete} = \$95,265(100)/\$101,256 = 94\%$$

The percentage complete is recorded in Column L. The Weston Offices and Johnson Warehouse are calculated in the same manner except both projects are overbilled. As a result, both the project's costs and profits in excess of billings are zero. The billings in excess of costs and profit for the Weston Offices are $1,053 and for the Johnson Warehouse are $1,998. For the entire company, the total costs and profits in excess of billings are $4,565 ($4,564 + $0 + $0) and the total billings in excess of costs and profits are $3,051 ($1,053 + $1,998). The spreadsheet solution is shown in Figure 4-4.

	A	B	C	D	E	F	G	H	I	J	K	L
1										Costs &	Billings in	
2				Total		Actual		Costs &		Profits in	Excess of	
3			Current	Estimated	Estimated	Costs	Earned	Earned		Excess of	Costs &	Percentage
4	Job		Contract	Cost at	Profit	to	Profit	Profit	Total	Billings	Profits	Complete
5	#	Job Name	Amount	Completion	(C - D)	Date	(E x F / D)	(F + G)	Billed	(H - I)	(I - H)	(F x 100 / D)
6	301	Henderson Remodel	122,500	101,256	21,244	95,265	19,987	115,252	110,687	4,565	—	94
	302	Weston Offices	25,265	18,000	7,265	11,542	4,658	16,200	17,253	—	1,053	64
7	303	Johnson Warehouse	255,202	229,564	25,638	35,264	3,938	39,202	41,200	—	1,998	15
8										4,565	3,050	

FIGURE 4-4   Solution to Example 4-2

INTERNAL CONTROLS

When setting up an accounting system it is important to set up internal controls to protect the company against internal theft and misappropriation of financial resources. Each year many companies run into financial difficulties—some even ending up in bankruptcy—because a trusted employee is stealing from the company or misappropriating financial resources. The internal controls vary with the size of the company. A small company with two office employees will need different internal controls than a large company. The following are some key principles to keep in mind when setting up internal controls.

The first key principle is separation of duties. The duties should be separated such that any significant theft—say over $100—requires the collaboration of two or more of the company's employees. Activities such as purchase approval, receiving, check preparation, and check signing should be done by separate persons. By separating these activities, it prevents someone—such as a superintendent—from issuing a purchase order for a fictitious purchase to a friend, signing off on the receipt of the purchase even though nothing was purchased, and sharing the money with the friend when the company pays the bill. Now it is unrealistic for the superintendent to seek approval for every small item purchased, so it is common to allow the superintendent to approve purchase orders to some limit—say $100—thus limiting the potential theft from inadequate separation of duties to small amounts. Procedures should be established to identify each employee's duties and what authority he or she has to approve purchases, disbursements, and other critical transactions.

The second key principle is maintaining a proper paper trail so that it is difficult to hide a theft by not documenting transactions or by destroying the paper trail. For this reason, purchase orders and checks should be prenumbered. Additionally, all checks issued by the company should be backed up by the proper documentation—such as a signed time card or invoice—and the documentation should be canceled by the person signing the check to prevent the duplicate payment of an invoice. Standard document processing procedures should be developed and followed for things such as receiving payments and issuing credits. This should not be delegated to out-of-house accounting firms because they usually are not familiar enough with the day-to-day operations of the company to adequately perform this audit, although they can help an owner or manager through the process.

The third key principle is that the owner, manager, or other appropriate person should review the transactions and reconciliations performed by the accounting staff as well as other cash receipts and disbursement procedures. As a part of this review process the owner, manager, or other appropriate person should hand deliver payroll checks to all employees at least annually to verify that the employees exist.

The fourth key is that all assets should be tracked and accounted for. This includes marking the physical assets with identification tags and periodically identifying the location of the company's assets.

When setting up internal controls the company should seek the help of a certified public accountant. There are internal control questionnaires prepared for the construction industry to help the accountant and contractor develop proper internal controls.

COMPUTERIZED ACCOUNTING SYSTEMS

There are many accounting systems that have been specifically developed for the construction industry. These systems are often sold in modules or pieces. Commonly these modules include a general ledger, accounts receivable, accounts payable, payroll, job cost, equipment, inventory, and purchase orders. The systems are sold in modules because not all contractors will need all of the modules. For example, a contractor that leases its employees will not need the payroll module. Similarly, a contractor that has limited amounts of equipment will not need the equipment module.

Before selecting a software package you need to decide what features your company needs in the accounting package and what features it can do without. Companies with limited inventories may find that it takes more time to implement and maintain an inventory module than it would take to track the inventory manually outside the accounting system. If you don't have a clear picture of what you want in an accounting system you risk being sold a lot of extra features that your company doesn't need and will not use. Appendix A contains a list of some of the features that are available in accounting modules, which may be used when determining what features your accounting system needs.

When looking at an accounting system one should take the following into account:

Reliability: A company should look for an accounting package with a performance history without a lot of problems and that is virtually bug free. You don't want your company to be the first to try a system, only to spend hours working with the software vendor to solve software problems.

Cost: The cost of the software should take into account the purchase price of the software, the cost of training and support, the cost of software upgrades, and setup costs. Most accounting packages require training and support during the software implementation. Often the cost of this training and support is in addition to the cost of the software modules. Additionally, your company will need to periodically purchase upgrades to the software to fix problems and limitations with the software and maintain compatibility with computer operating systems. The cost of upgrades may be a fixed rate per year or so much every time an upgrade comes out. Different software packages often require a different amount of effort and time commitment from your company's employees during the implementation of the system. They may also require your company to purchase new computer hardware to run the software. All of these costs need to be included in the cost of the accounting system.

Training and Technical Support: Good training and support make implementation and operation of the accounting system easier, whereas poor training and support may result in a company abandoning a software package because it cannot get it to operate correctly. Good training and technical support come at a price and it is not a good idea to cut corners in these areas.

Ease of Use: The easier and more natural an accounting package is to use the easier it will be to implement. The system should be easy enough that management personnel can access the system and generate its own reports. Easy-to-use accounting packages require less training and technical support than do complex, difficult-to-use packages.

System Protection: The system should have multiple levels of password protection. Management personnel should be able to access the system and generate reports for their projects, without being able to access other projects or make changes in the accounting system. Data-entry personnel should be able to enter data into the system without accessing other areas. Good accounting systems allow users to see only those commands and projects that they have been granted access to.

Integration of Modules: The modules should be integrated in such a way that they do not require items to be entered separately in different modules. An example of good integration is an accounting system that allows you to bill an employee's truck to the jobs it worked on at the same time you bill the employee's hours to the jobs, thus reducing the need to take a separate step allocating the truck's time to the jobs.

Backup and Recovery Procedures: The systems should allow for easy backup and recovery in the event of a loss of data due to virus, hardware failure, or another unexpected event. The data in the accounting system is valuable to a construction company and duplicate copies need to be maintained and stored in a safe, off-site location. Backups should be done on a daily and weekly basis.

Customization: The software should allow the user to create custom reports without having the software vendor modify the program. Many packages come with a report writer—which allows the user to create custom reports—and a means of exporting data into spreadsheets and word processors.

CONCLUSION

To get an accurate picture of the financial status of a project, unbilled committed costs must be included with the costs to date. This may be done by the accounting package or may be done in a separate spreadsheet. Additionally, committed costs should be used to estimate the cost and profit at completion for each project. To prepare the monthly and annual balance sheet, the overbillings or under-billings must be calculated for each project, which may be done in a simple spread-sheet. To protect the company's financial assets, internal controls for the company must be implemented to prevent theft and misuse of the assets. Finally, there are many accounting systems designed just for contractors. Construction companies should carefully choose the package that best fits the company's needs.

PROBLEMS

1. A contractor has a contract to construct the sanitary sewer, water line, storm drain, and street lighting for a new subdivision. The contractor uses the cost codes in Figure 2-5. The original estimate for the sewer was $25,000 and a $3,200 change order has been approved to add a manhole. The sewer work has been completed at a cost of $27,365. The original estimate for the water line was $31,000 and no changes have been made to the budget. The costs to date for the water line are $31,300 and it is estimated that it will take another $450 to complete the water line. The original estimate for the storm drain was $17,000 and no changes have been made to the budget. The contractor has paid $7,236 for materials and estimates that it will cost $9,764 to install the storm drain. The original estimate for the outside lighting was $23,600 and no changes have been made to the budget. The contractor has subcontracted the outside lighting for $23,600. The subcontractor has billed $11,230 for materials. Determine the total estimated cost at completion for the project and the variance for each cost code.

2. A contractor has a contract to remove and replace the existing landscape and sidewalks around an office building. The work includes demolition of the existing landscaping and sidewalks, importing fill and grading around the office building, constructing new concrete sidewalks, and new landscaping. The contractor uses the cost codes in Figure 2-5. The original estimate for the demolition was $30,000 and a $5,000 change order has been approved to remove some unexpected debris found during the demolition. The demolition work has been completed at a cost of $33,562. The original estimate for the fill and grading was $17,500 and a $2,000 change order for importing additional fill to replace the debris has been approved. The fill and grading costs to date are $17,264 and the cost to complete has been estimated at $2,236. The original budget for the labor to pour the concrete was $19,200 and no changes have been made. The concrete labor has been subcontracted out for $19,200, for which the contractor has received a bill for $15,200. The original budget for the concrete for the sidewalks was $9,900 and no changes have been made. The contractor has spent $7,425 for concrete and estimates that $1,950

of concrete will be needed to complete the project. The original estimate for the landscaping was $37,500 and no changes have been made. The landscape work has been subcontracted out for $37,500. The landscaping work has yet to start and no bills have been received. Determine the total estimated cost at completion for the project and the variance for each cost code.

3. Determine over- and underbillings for a company with the following information:

> Job Number: 318
> Job Name: Mountain Peak Office Remodel
> Current Contract Amount: $256,852
> Total Estimated Cost at Completion: $225,236
> Actual Costs to Date: $202,138
> Total Billed: $252,253

> Job Number: 319
> Job Name: East Street Restaurant
> Current Contract Amount: $350,199
> Total Estimated Cost at Completion: $310,564
> Actual Costs to Date: $152,364
> Total Billed: $178,256

> Job Number: 320
> Job Name: Market Street Warehouse
> Current Contract Amount: $55,123
> Total Estimated Cost at Completion: $45,224
> Actual Costs to Date: $5,211
> Total Billed: $5,500

4. Determine over- and underbillings for a company with the following information:

> Job Number: 311
> Job Name: Smith Remodel
> Current Contract Amount: $22,530
> Total Estimated Cost at Completion: $17,264
> Actual Costs to Date: $16,538
> Total Billed: $21,000

> Job Number: 316
> Job Name: Redd Remodel
> Current Contract Amount: $35,624

Total Estimated Cost at Completion: $28,221
Actual Costs to Date: $22,345
Total Billed: $28,500

Job Number: 318
Job Name: Winter Remodel
Current Contract Amount: $17,954
Total Estimated Cost at Completion: $14,567
Actual Costs to Date: $4,562
Total Billed: $6,000

Job Number: 322
Job Name: Richardson Remodel
Current Contract Amount: $5,213
Total Estimated Cost at Completion: $3,721
Actual Costs to Date: $1,956
Total Billed: $0

5. Create a spreadsheet to solve Problem 1.
6. Create a spreadsheet to solve Problem 2.
7. Create a spreadsheet to solve Problem 3.
8. Create a spreadsheet to solve Problem 4.

DEPRECIATION

In this chapter you will learn the differences among the methods available for depreciating construction assets, including the methods used for tax purposes. Understanding the difference in depreciation methods is necessary for a manager to interpret the financial statement and financial ratios, which is covered in the next chapter. Simply put, changing the method of depreciation can have significant impact on the company's financial statements. Understanding depreciation is also necessary when preparing income tax projections, which is discussed in chapter 13.

Suppose a year ago your business purchased a new $30,000 truck to haul materials to various construction sites. If your company were to sell that truck today, could the company sell it for $30,000? The answer is no. The truck is worth less today than it was a year ago due to wear and tear, the age of the equipment, and obsolescence. This loss in equipment value over time is known as depreciation.

For the owners of depreciable assets, such as equipment and buildings, it is important to estimate the depreciation of the assets for three reasons:

1. For a company to prepare its financial statements the company managers must accurately determine the value of the company's assets. The value of the company's depreciable assets equals the price paid for the assets less the depreciation of the assets. In the case of the truck, when it was purchased it would have been listed as an asset with a value of $30,000 on the company's balance sheet. As the truck gets older, the value of the asset is offset by its depreciation.

2. For a company to allocate the cost of owning the assets used to complete construction projects and support company operations, the annual cost of owning these assets must be determined. The asset's depreciation is a significant cost of owning an asset.

3. In most cases the Internal Revenue Service (IRS) requires that cost of a depreciable asset be spread over the useful life of the asset. Depreciation for tax purposes must follow the rules set forth in the Internal Revenue Code. Many of these rules can be found in *Instructions for Form 4562*, published by the IRS. Because of the complexity of the tax code, it is recommended that the service of a Certified Public Accountant (CPA) be employed in the calculation of depreciation for tax purposes.

Because the depreciation method required by the Internal Revenue Code may not accurately reflect the actual depreciation of an asset, a different method of depreciation or a different useful life may be used to determine the value of the asset for financial statements or cost allocations than was used for tax purposes.

The useful life of an asset is the number of years it is useful to a company and is most often a function of economics rather than the number of years an asset can be used. Although an asset may continue to function, it may no longer be economical to use the asset and the asset may be replaced by a more economical asset. In this case, economics govern the useful life of the asset rather than whether the asset continues to function.

The three commonly used methods to calculate depreciation are the straight-line method, the sum-of-the-years method, and the declining-balance method. Each of these depreciation methods uses the following variables:

P = the purchase price of the asset.

F = the salvage value of the asset which is the estimated resale value of the asset at some time in the future when it is sold. For tax purposes, the salvage value is assumed to be zero.

N = the recovery period which is the number of years over which the asset is to be depreciated. For tax purposes, the Internal Revenue Code identifies the recovery period for different classes of assets. For other purposes, the recovery period is often equal to the useful life of the asset.

R_m = the depreciation rate or percentage of depreciation taken in year m.

D_m = the depreciation for year m.

BV_m = the book value or the value of the asset as it is listed on the accounting books at the end of year m. The book value equals the purchase price less the depreciation recorded to date.

The book value and depreciation may be calculated for each year of an asset's useful life. A tabular listing of the annual book value and annual depreciation is known as the depreciation schedule.

STRAIGHT-LINE METHOD

The straight-line method of depreciation assumes that an asset loses value at a constant rate. The annual depreciation rate is calculated by dividing 1 by the recovery period as follows:

$$R_m = 1/N \qquad\qquad (5\text{-}1)$$

The annual depreciation rate for the straight-line method is constant for all years of the recovery period. The annual depreciation is calculated by taking the purchase price less the salvage value of the equipment and multiplying the result by the annual depreciation rate as follows:

$$D_m = (P - F)R_m \qquad\qquad (5\text{-}2)$$

By substituting Eq. (5-1) into Eq. (5-2) the annual depreciation is calculated as follows:

$$D_m = (P - F)/N \qquad\qquad (5\text{-}3)$$

The book value of the asset decreases at a uniform rate each year and is calculated for the end of year m as follows:

$$BV_m = P - m(D_m) \qquad\qquad (5\text{-}4)$$

The book value for an asset at the end of year m is calculated from the previous year's book value, as follows:

$$BV_m = BV_{m-1} - D_m \qquad\qquad (5\text{-}5)$$

If we were to plot the book values for an asset these values would fall on a straight line; hence, the name of the method.

Example 5-1: A dump truck is purchased for $110,000 and has an estimated salvage value of $10,000 at the end of the recovery period. Prepare a depreciation schedule for the dump truck using the straight-line method with a recovery period of five years.

Solution: Using Eq. (5-1), the annual depreciation rate is calculated as follows:

$$R_m = 1/5$$

Using Eq. (5-3), the annual depreciation is calculated as follows:

$$D_m = (\$110{,}000 - \$10{,}000)/5 = \$20{,}000$$

Using Eq. (5-4), the book values at the end of years 1 through 5 is calculated as follows:

$$BV_1 = \$110{,}000 - 1(\$20{,}000) = \$90{,}000$$
$$BV_2 = \$110{,}000 - 2(\$20{,}000) = \$70{,}000$$
$$BV_3 = \$110{,}000 - 3(\$20{,}000) = \$50{,}000$$
$$BV_4 = \$110{,}000 - 4(\$20{,}000) = \$30{,}000$$
$$BV_5 = \$110{,}000 - 5(\$20{,}000) = \$10{,}000$$

TABLE 5-1   Depreciation Schedule for Example 5-1

m	R_m	D_m ($)	BV_m ($)
0			110,000
1	1/5	20,000	90,000
2	1/5	20,000	70,000
3	1/5	20,000	50,000
4	1/5	20,000	30,000
5	1/5	20,000	10,000

Alternately, they may be calculated from the previous year book value using Eq. (5-5) as follows:

$$BV_1 = \$110{,}000 - \$20{,}000 = \$90{,}000$$
$$BV_2 = \$90{,}000 - \$20{,}000 = \$70{,}000$$
$$BV_3 = \$70{,}000 - 20{,}000 = \$50{,}000$$
$$BV_4 = \$50{,}000 - 20{,}000 = \$30{,}000$$
$$BV_5 = \$30{,}000 - 20{,}000 = \$10{,}000$$

Organizing the annual depreciation rates, annual depreciation, and annual book values in table form is known as the depreciation schedule. The depreciation schedule for Example 5-1 is shown in Table 5-1.

SUM-OF-THE-YEARS METHOD

The sum-of-the-years (SOY) method is used to accelerate the depreciation of an asset. The annual depreciation rate is calculated by dividing the number of years left in the recovery period by the sum of the years in the recovery period as follows:

$$R_m = (N - m + 1)/SOY \tag{5-6}$$

where

$$SOY = N(N + 1)/2 \tag{5-7}$$

With the sum-of-the-years method the annual depreciation is calculated by taking the purchase price less the salvage value of the equipment and multiplying the resultant by the annual depreciation rate as follows:

$$D_m = (P - F)R_m \tag{5-8}$$

By substituting Eq. (5-6) into Eq. (5-8) we get the following:

$$D_m = (P - F)(N - m + 1)/SOY \tag{5-9}$$

SIDEBAR 5-1

CALCULATING STRAIGHT-LINE DEPRECIATION USING A TI BA II PLUS CALCULATOR

The yearly depreciation and book values for straight-line depreciation is calculated as shown below. For this sidebar we use Example 5-1.

TASK	KEYSTROKES	DISPLAY	
1. Set Variables to Defaults	[2nd] [RESET] [ENTER]	RST	0.00
2. Select Depreciation Worksheet	[2nd] [DEPR]	SL	
3. Enter Life (years)	[↓] 5 [ENTER]	LIF =	5.00
4. Enter Starting Month	[↓] 1 [ENTER]	MO1 =	1.00
5. Enter Cost	[↓] 110000 [ENTER]	CST =	110,000.00 0
6. Enter Salvage Value	[↓] 10000 [ENTER]	SAL =	10,000.00
7. Select Year's Values to Calculate	[↓] 1 [ENTER]	YR =	1.00
8. View Depreciation	[↓]	DEP =	20,000.00
9. View (Remaining) Book Value	[↓]	RBV =	90,000.00
10. View Remaining Depreciable Value	[↓]	RDV =	80,000.00
11. Return to Select Year's Values to Calculate	[↓]	YR =	1.00
12. Repeat Steps 7-11 for Each of the Remaining Years			

In this example the keystrokes for entering all variables are shown to provide a generic example that can be used for any problem by changing the numbers entered into the calculator. If the display is already shown as indicated you may type [↓] to continue to the next step.

The book value for the end of year m is calculated as follows:

$$BV_m = P - (P - F)[m(N - m/2 + 0.5)/SOY] \tag{5-10}$$

When preparing a depreciation table it is often easier to subtract the annual depreciation from the previous year's book value using the following equation:

$$BV_m = BV_{m-1} - D_m \tag{5-11}$$

Example 5-2: A dump truck is purchased for $110,000 and has an estimated salvage value of $10,000 at the end of the recovery period. Prepare a depreciation schedule for the dump truck using the sum-of-the-years method with a recovery period of five years.

Solution: The sum of the years is calculated using Eq. (5-7) as follows:

$$SOY = 5(5 + 1)/2 = 15$$

The annual depreciation rate for the first year is calculated using Eq. (5-6) as follows:

$$R_1 = (5 - 1 + 1)/15 = 5/15$$

The annual depreciation for the first year is calculated using Eq. (5-8) as follows:

$$D_1 = (\$110,000 - \$10,000)5/15 = \$33,333$$

The book value at the end of the first year is calculated using Eq. (5-11) as follows:

$$BV_1 = \$110,000 - \$33,333 = \$76,667$$

The annual depreciation rate for the second year is calculated using Eq. (5-6) as follows:

$$R_2 = (5 - 2 + 1)/15 = 4/15$$

The annual depreciation for the second year is calculated using Eq. (5-8) as follows:

$$D_2 = (\$110,000 - \$10,000)4/15 = \$26,667$$

The book value at the end of the second year is calculated using Eq. (5-11) as follows:

$$BV_2 = \$76,667 - \$26,667 = \$50,000$$

The remaining years are calculated in a similar manner. The annual depreciation rates, annual depreciation, and annual book values for Example 5-2 are shown in Table 5-2.

TABLE 5-2   Depreciation Schedule for Example 5-2

m	R_m	D_m (\$)	BV_m (\$)
0		0	110,000
1	5/15	33,333	76,667
2	4/15	26,667	50,000
3	3/15	20,000	30,000
4	2/15	13,333	16,667
5	1/15	6,667	10,000

SIDEBAR 5-2

CALCULATING SUM-OF-THE-YEARS DEPRECIATION USING A TI BA II PLUS CALCULATOR

The yearly depreciation and book values for sum-of-the-years depreciation is calculated as shown below. The same steps are used to solve this problem as were used in Sidebar 5-1 except after selecting the depreciation worksheet you must select the sum-of-the-years depreciation method. For this sidebar we use Example 5-2.

TASK	KEYSTROKES	DISPLAY	
1. Set Variables to Defaults	[2nd] [RESET] [ENTER]	RST	0.00
2. Select Depreciation Worksheet	[2nd] [DEPR]	SL	
3. Select Depreciation Method	[2nd] [SET]	SYD	
4. Enter Life (years)	[↓] 5 [ENTER]	LIF =	5.00
5. Enter Starting Month	[↓] 1 [ENTER]	MO1 =	1.00
6. Enter Cost	[↓] 110000 [ENTER]	CST =	110,000.00
7. Enter Salvage Value	[↓] 10000 [ENTER]	SAL =	10,000.00
8. Select Year's Values to Calculate	[↓] 1 [ENTER]	YR =	1.00
9. View Depreciation	[↓]	DEP =	33,333.33
10. View (Remaining) Book Value	[↓]	RBV =	76,666.67
11. View Remaining Depreciable Value	[↓]	RDV =	66,666.67
12. Return to Select Year's Values to Calculate	[↓]	YR =	1.00
13. Repeat Steps 8-12 for Each of the Remaining Years			

In this example the keystrokes for entering all variables are shown to provide a generic example that can be used for any problem by changing the numbers entered into the calculator. If the display is already shown as indicated you may type [↓] to continue to the next step.

DECLINING-BALANCE METHOD

The declining-balance method is used to accelerate the depreciation of an asset. The annual depreciation is calculated from the previous year's book value. The annual depreciation rate is based on a declining-balance factor between 1.25 and

2.00, which is divided by the recovery period. The most common annual depreciation rates for the declining-balance method are calculated as follows:

$$R_m = 2.00/N \quad \text{for 200\% declining-balance or}$$
$$\text{double-declining-balance} \quad (5\text{-}12)$$
$$R_m = 1.50/N \quad \text{for 150\% declining-balance} \quad (5\text{-}13)$$

The annual depreciation equals last year's book value multiplied by the annual depreciation rate and can be calculated as follows:

$$D_m = (BV_{m-1})R_m \quad (5\text{-}14)$$

The book value at the end of year m is calculated using one of the following formulas:

$$BV_m = P(1 - R_m)^m \quad \text{provided that } BV_m \geq F \text{ and } m \text{ is a whole number}$$
$$(5\text{-}15)$$
$$BV_m = BV_{m-1} - D_m \quad \text{provided that } BV_m \geq F \quad (5\text{-}16)$$

Because this depreciation method does not automatically produce a book value equal to the salvage value at the end of the recovery period, the book value must be forced to intersect the salvage value. This is done by switching to the straight-line method and depreciating the current book value over the years remaining in the recovery period. The switch to straight-line depreciation occurs when the annual depreciation calculated by the straight-line method exceeds the depreciation calculated by the declining-balance method or when the depreciation calculated by the declining-balance method would produce a book value less than the salvage value. Switching to the straight-line method ensures that the depreciation is equal to the book value at the end of the recovery period and that the book value does not fall below the salvage value.

Example 5-3: A dump truck is purchased for $110,000 and has an estimated salvage value of $10,000 at the end of the recovery period. Prepare a depreciation schedule for the dump truck using the 200% declining-balance method with a recovery period of five years.

Solution: Using Eq. (5-12), the annual depreciation rate for each year under the 200% declining-balance method is as follows:

$$R_m = 2.00/5 = 0.40$$

Using Eq. (5-14) and the 200% declining-balance method, the annual depreciation for the first year is as follows:

$$D_1 = (\$110,000)0.40 = \$44,000$$

Using Eq. (5-3), the annual depreciation for the first year using the straight-line method is as follows:

$$D_1 = (\$110,000 - \$10,000)/5 = \$20,000$$

Using Eq. (5-16) and the larger of the two depreciations, the book value at the end of the first year is as follows:

$$BV_1 = \$110,000 - \$44,000 = \$66,000$$

The depreciation using the 200% declining-balance method, the depreciation using the straight-line method, and the book value for years 2 through 4 are calculated in the same manner as follows:

$$D_2 = (\$66,000)0.40 = \$26,400$$
$$D_2 = (\$66,000 - \$10,000)/4 = \$14,000$$
$$BV_2 = \$66,000 - \$26,400 = \$39,600$$
$$D_3 = (\$39,600)0.40 = \$15,840$$
$$D_3 = (\$39,600 - \$10,000)/3 = \$9,867$$
$$BV_3 = \$39,600 - \$15,840 = \$23,760$$
$$D_4 = (\$23,760)0.40 = \$9,504$$
$$D_4 = (\$23,760 - \$10,000)/2 = \$6,880$$
$$BV_4 = \$23,760 - \$9,504 = \$14,256$$

Using Eq. (5-14) and the 200% declining-balance method, the annual depreciation for the fifth year is as follows:

$$D_5 = (\$14,256)0.40 = \$5,702$$

Because the dump truck has been in service for four years, there in one year left in its recovery period. Using Eq. (5-3), the annual depreciation for the fifth year using the straight-line method is as follows:

$$D_m = (\$14,256 - \$10,000)/1 = \$4,256$$

Using Eq. (5-16) and the larger of the two depreciation amounts, the book value at the end of the fifth year is as follows:

$$BV_5 = \$14,256 - \$5,702 = \$8,554$$

Because the 200% declining-balance method produces a book value less than the salvage value, we must switch to the straight-line method. Using Eq. (5-5) and the depreciation calculated by the straight-line method, the book value for the fifth year is as follows:

$$BV_5 = \$14,256 - \$4,256 = \$10,000$$

Switching to the straight-line depreciation method in the fifth year allows the book value to be equal to the salvage value at the end of the fifth year, which is the end of the recovery period.

The annual depreciation rates, annual depreciation, and annual book values for Example 5-3 are shown in Table 5-3.

TABLE 5-3   Depreciation Schedule for Example 5-3

m	R_m	D_m ($)	BV_m ($)
0		0	110,000
1	0.40	44,000	66,000
2	0.40	26,400	39,600
3	0.40	15,840	23,760
4	0.40	9,504	14,256
5	0.40	4,256	10,000

SIDEBAR 5-3

CALCULATING DECLINING-BALANCE CHANGING TO STRAIGHT-LINE DEPRECIATION USING A TI BA II PLUS CALCULATOR

The yearly depreciation and book values for declining-balance changing to straight-line depreciation may be calculated as shown below. The same steps are used to solve this problem as were used in Sidebar 5-1 except after selecting the depreciation worksheet you must select the declining-balance changing to straight-line depreciation method and set the declining-balance factor. For this sidebar we use Example 5-3.

Task	Keystrokes	Display	
1. Set Variables to Defaults	[2nd] [RESET] [ENTER]	RST	0.00
2. Select Depreciation Worksheet	[2nd] [DEPR]	SL	
3. Select Depreciation Method	[2nd] [SET] [2nd] [SET] [2nd] [SET]	DBX =	200.00
4. Set Declining-Balance Factor	200 [ENTER]	DBX =	200.00
5. Enter Life (years)	[↓] 5 [ENTER]	LIF =	5.00
6. Enter Starting Month	[↓] 1 [ENTER]	MO1 =	1.00
7. Enter Cost	[↓] 110000 [ENTER]	CST =	110,000.00
8. Enter Salvage Value	[↓] 10000 [ENTER]	SAL =	10,000.00
9. Select Year's Values to Calculate	[↓] 1 [ENTER]	YR =	1.00
10. View Depreciation	[↓]	DEP =	44,000.00
11. View (Remaining) Book Value	[↓]	RBV =	66,000.00
12. View Remaining Depreciable Value	[↓]	RDV =	56,000.00
13. Return to Select Year's Values to Calculate	[↓]	YR =	1.00
14. Repeat Steps 9-13 for Each of the Remaining Years			

In this example the keystrokes for entering all variables are shown to provide a generic example that can be used for any problem by changing the numbers entered into the calculator. If the display is already shown as indicated you may type [↓] to continue to the next step.

FIGURE 5-1 Comparison of Depreciation Methods

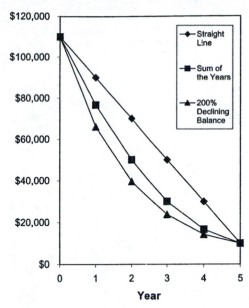

Figure 5-1 shows the depreciation of an $110,000 dump truck with a salvage value of $10,000 and a recovery period of five years using the straight-line, sum-of-the-years, and 200% declining-balance methods.

PLACING IN SERVICE AND DISPOSING OF AN ASSET

For tax purposes, a full year's depreciation is not allowed by the IRS during the tax year the asset is placed in service or disposed of. In most cases, the IRS assumes that the asset was placed in service or disposed of in the middle of the year and allows taxpayers to take 50% of the annual depreciation for the first and last years of service. This is known as the half-year convention. The half-year convention does not apply to real property.

Should the taxpayer place more than 40% of the year's depreciable assets—excluding real property—in service during the last quarter, the IRS assumes that the individual assets were placed in service or disposed of in the middle of the quarter that the asset was placed in service or disposed of. For equipment placed in service during the year, the taxpayer is allowed to take one-eighth of the annual depreciation in the quarter the asset was placed in service and one-fourth of the annual depreciation during the remaining quarters of their tax year. For disposal of the equipment, the taxpayer is allowed to take one-eighth of the annual depreciation in the quarter the asset was disposed of and one-fourth of the annual depreciation during the proceeding quarters of the tax year. This is known as the midquarter convention. Under the midquarter convention, the percentages of

TABLE 5-4[13]   Depreciation Percentages for the Midquarter Convention

QUARTER	PLACED IN SERVICE	DISPOSED OF
1st	0.875	0.125
2nd	0.625	0.375
3rd	0.375	0.625
4th	0.125	0.875

depreciation allowed are shown in Table 5-4. The midquarter convention does not apply to real property (real estate).

For real estate, the IRS assumes that the real estate was placed in service or disposed of in the middle of the month it was placed in service or disposed of. For real estate placed in service during the year, the taxpayer is allowed to take one-twenty-fourth of the annual depreciation in the month the real estate was placed in service and one-twelfth of the annual depreciation during the following months of the tax year. For the disposal of real estate, the taxpayer is allowed to take one-twenty-fourth of the annual depreciation in the month the real estate was disposed of and one-twelfth of the annual depreciation during the proceeding months of the tax year. This is known as the midmonth convention. The percentages of depreciation allowed under the midmonth convention are shown in Table 5-5.

TABLE 5-5[14]   Depreciation Percentages for the Midmonth Convention

MONTH	PLACED IN SERVICE	DISPOSED OF
1st	0.9583	0.0417
2nd	0.8750	0.1250
3rd	0.7917	0.2083
4th	0.7083	0.2917
5th	0.6250	0.3750
6th	0.5417	0.4583
7th	0.4583	0.5417
8th	0.3750	0.6250
9th	0.2917	0.7083
10th	0.2083	0.7917
11th	0.1250	0.8750
12th	0.0417	0.9583

[13]IRS, *Instructions for Form 4562*, 2002, p. 6.
[14]IRS, *Instructions for Form 4562*, 2002, p. 6.

IRS Standard Recovery Periods and Depreciation Methods

For tax purposes, the IRS has set up standard recovery periods. The IRS recognizes the following standard recovery periods or classes of property:

Three-year: Rent-to-own property.

Five-year: Automobiles, light general propose trucks, calculators, copiers, and computer equipment.

Seven-year: Office furniture, office equipment, and railroad tracks.

Ten-year: Vessels, barges, tugs, and other water transportation equipment.

Fifteen-year: Retail motor fuel outlets.

Twenty-year: Farm buildings.

Twenty-five-year: Municipal sewers, water treatment plants, and water distribution lines.

Twenty-seven-and-a-half-year: Residential real estate where more than 80% of the rent is derived from the dwelling units.

Thirty-nine-year: Nonresidential real estate.

Fifty-year: Railroad roadbeds, right-of-ways, and tunnels.

For tax purposes, 200% declining-balance depreciation switching to straight-line depreciation when the annual straight-line depreciation rate exceeds the depreciation from the 200% declining-balance method is used for properties with a standard recovery period of 3, 5, 7, or 10 years. Table 5-6 shows the annual

TABLE 5-6[15]   Depreciation Rates for 200% Declining Balance Using the Half-Year Convention

YEAR	3 YEARS (%)	5 YEARS (%)	7 YEARS (%)	10 YEARS (%)
1	33.33	20.00	14.29	10.00
2	44.45	32.00	24.49	18.00
3	14.81	19.20	17.49	14.40
4	7.41	11.52	12.49	11.52
5	NA	11.52	8.93	9.22
6	NA	5.76	8.92	7.37
7	NA	NA	8.93	6.55
8	NA	NA	4.46	6.55
9	NA	NA	NA	6.56
10	NA	NA	NA	6.55
11	NA	NA	NA	3.28

[15]IRS, *Instructions for Form 4562*, 2001, p. 10.

TABLE 5-7   Depreciation Rates for 200% Declining Balance Using the Midquarter Convention; the Asset Is Placed in Service during the First Quarter

YEAR	3 YEARS (%)	5 YEARS (%)	7 YEARS (%)	10 YEARS (%)
1	58.33	35.00	25.00	17.50
2	27.78	26.00	21.43	16.50
3	12.35	15.60	15.31	13.20
4	1.54	11.01	10.93	10.56
5	NA	11.01	8.75	8.45
6	NA	1.38	8.74	6.76
7	NA	NA	8.75	6.55
8	NA	NA	1.09	6.55
9	NA	NA	NA	6.56
10	NA	NA	NA	6.55
11	NA	NA	NA	0.82

depreciation rates for 3-, 5-, 7-, and 10-year property using the half-year convention and the 200% declining-balance method. The depreciation rates in Table 5-6 are expressed as a percentage of the purchase price rather than the previous year's book value.

Tables 5-7 through 5-10 show the annual depreciation rates for 3-, 5-, 7-, and 10-year property using the midquarter convention and the 200% declining-balance method. Table 5-7 shows assets placed in service during the first quarter, Table 5-8 shows assets placed in service during the second quarter, Table 5-9 shows assets placed in service during the third quarter, and Table 5-10 shows assets placed in service during the fourth quarter. The depreciation rates in

TABLE 5-8   Depreciation Rates for 200% Declining Balance Using the Midquarter Convention; the Asset Is Placed in Service during the Second Quarter

YEAR	3 YEARS (%)	5 YEARS (%)	7 YEARS (%)	10 YEARS (%)
1	41.67	25.00	17.86	12.50
2	38.89	30.00	23.47	17.50
3	14.14	18.00	16.76	14.00
4	5.30	11.37	11.97	11.20
5	NA	11.37	8.87	8.96
6	NA	4.26	8.87	7.17
7	NA	NA	8.87	6.55
8	NA	NA	3.33	6.56
9	NA	NA	NA	6.55
10	NA	NA	NA	6.55
11	NA	NA	NA	2.46

TABLE 5-9   Depreciation Rates for 200% Declining Balance Using the Midquarter Convention; the Asset Is Placed in Service during the Third Quarter

YEAR	3 YEARS (%)	5 YEARS (%)	7 YEARS (%)	10 YEARS (%)
1	25.00	15.00	10.71	7.50
2	50.00	34.00	25.51	18.50
3	16.67	20.40	18.22	14.80
4	8.33	12.24	13.02	11.84
5	NA	11.30	9.30	9.47
6	NA	7.06	8.85	7.58
7	NA	NA	8.86	6.55
8	NA	NA	5.53	6.56
9	NA	NA	NA	6.55
10	NA	NA	NA	6.55
11	NA	NA	NA	4.10

Tables 5-7 through 5-10 are expressed as a percentage of the purchase price rather than the previous year's book value.

For property with a standard recovery period of 3, 5, 7, or 10 years, the property owner may make an irrevocable election to use 150% declining-balance depreciation switching to straight-line depreciation when the annual straight-line depreciation rate exceeds the depreciation calculated by the 150% declining-balance method. This election must apply to all property within its class that is placed in service during the year.

For property with a 15-year or 20-year recovery period, 150% declining-balance depreciation switching to straight-line depreciation when the annual straight-line depreciation rate exceeds the 150% declining-balance depreciation

TABLE 5-10   Depreciation Rates for 200% Declining Balance Using the Midquarter Convention; the Asset Is Placed in Service during the Fourth Quarter

YEAR	3 YEARS (%)	5 YEARS (%)	7 YEARS (%)	10 YEARS (%)
1	8.33	5.00	3.57	2.50
2	61.11	38.00	27.55	19.50
3	20.37	22.80	19.68	15.60
4	10.19	13.68	14.06	12.48
5	NA	10.94	10.04	9.98
6	NA	9.58	8.73	7.99
7	NA	NA	8.73	6.55
8	NA	NA	7.64	6.56
9	NA	NA	NA	6.55
10	NA	NA	NA	6.56
11	NA	NA	NA	5.73

TABLE 5-11[16]   Depreciation Rates for 150% Declining Balance Using the Half-Year Convention

YEAR	5 YEARS (%)	7 YEARS (%)	10 YEARS (%)	15 YEARS (%)
1	15.00	10.71	7.50	5.00
2	25.50	19.13	13.88	9.50
3	17.85	15.03	11.79	8.55
4	16.66	12.25	10.02	7.70
5	16.66	12.25	8.74	6.93
6	8.33	12.25	8.74	6.23
7	NA	12.25	8.74	5.90
8	NA	6.13	8.74	5.90
9	NA	NA	8.74	5.91
10	NA	NA	8.74	5.90
11	NA	NA	4.37	5.91
12	NA	NA	NA	5.90
13	NA	NA	NA	5.91
14	NA	NA	NA	5.90
15	NA	NA	NA	5.91
16	NA	NA	NA	2.95

rate is used as the depreciation method. Table 5-11 shows the annual depreciation rates for 5-, 7-, 10-, 15-, and 20-year property using the half-year convention and 150% declining-balance method. The depreciation rates are expressed as a percentage of the purchase price rather than the previous year's book value.

Straight-line depreciation must be used for property with a recovery period of 25 years or more and for all real estate. It is important to note that when depreciating real estate, only the building and improvements may be depreciated. The cost of the land is not depreciated.

Example 5-4:   Prepare a depreciation schedule to be used for tax purposes for a $30,000 truck using the 200% declining-balance method and the half-year convention.

Solution: For tax purposes, the recovery period for the truck is five years and the salvage value is zero. From Table 5-6 the depreciation rate for the first year is 20%. The first year's depreciation is calculated as follows:

$$D_1 = (\$30,000)0.2000 = \$6,000$$

Using Eq. (5-16), the book value at the end of the first year is as follows:

$$BV_1 = \$30,000 - \$6,000 = \$24,000$$

---

[16]IRS, *Instructions for Form 4562*, 2001, p. 10.

TABLE 5-12 Depreciation Schedule for Example 5-4

m	D_m ($)	BV_m ($)
0	0	30,000
1	6,000	24,000
2	9,600	14,400
3	5,760	8,640
4	3,456	5,184
5	3,456	1,728
6	1,728	0

The depreciation rate and book value for the second through the sixth years are calculated in the same manner and are as follows:

$$D_2 = (\$30,000)0.3200 = \$9,600$$
$$BV_2 = \$24,000 - \$9,600 = \$14,400$$
$$D_3 = (\$30,000)0.1920 = \$5,760$$
$$BV_3 = \$14,400 - \$5,760 = \$8,640$$
$$D_4 = (\$30,000)0.1152 = \$3,456$$
$$BV_4 = \$8,640 - \$3,456 = \$5,184$$
$$D_5 = (\$30,000)0.1152 = \$3,456$$
$$BV_5 = \$5,184 - \$3,456 = \$1,728$$
$$D_6 = (\$30,000)0.0576 = \$1,728$$
$$BV_6 = \$1,728 - \$1,728 = \$0$$

The annual depreciation and annual book values are shown in Table 5-12.

Example 5-5: Prepare a depreciation schedule to be used for tax purposes for a $30,000 truck using the 200% declining-balance method and the midquarter convention. The truck is placed in service during the fourth quarter of the company's tax year.

Solution: For tax purposes, the recovery period for the truck is five years and the salvage value is zero. From Table 5-4 we see that we can only take 0.125 (12.5%) of the depreciation in the first year because we are using the midquarter convention. From Table 5-10, the depreciation rate for the first year is 5%. The first year's depreciation may be calculated as follows:

$$D_1 = (\$30,000)0.0500 = \$1,500$$

Using Eq. (5-16), the book value at the end of the first year is as follows:

$$BV_1 = \$30,000 - \$1,500 = \$28,500$$

SIDEBAR 5-4

CALCULATING DECLINING BALANCE CHANGING TO STRAIGHT-LINE DEPRECIATION FOR TAXES USING A TI BA II PLUS CALCULATOR

The procedures in Sidebar 5-3 may be used to calculate the yearly depreciation and book values for declining balance changing to straight-line depreciation for tax purposes. For the half-year convention the starting month is the seventh month. For the midquarter convention and assets placed in service during the first quarter the starting month is the 2.5 month. For assets placed in service during the second, third, and fourth quarter the starting months are 5.5, 8.5, and 11.5, respectively. For depreciation using the midmonth convention add 0.5 to the month to get the starting month. For example, the starting month for the first month is 1.5 and the starting month for the last month of the year is 12.5. For this sidebar we use Example 5-4.

TASK	KEYSTROKES	DISPLAY	
1. Set Variables to Defaults	[2nd] [RESET] [ENTER]	RST	0.00
2. Select Depreciation Worksheet	[2nd] [DEPR]	SL	
3. Select Depreciation Method	[2nd] [SET] [2nd] [SET] [2nd] [SET]	DBX =	200.00
4. Set Declining-Balance Factor	200 [ENTER]	DBX =	200.00
5. Enter Life (years)	[↓] 5 [ENTER]	LIF =	5.00
6. Enter Starting Month	[↓] 7 [ENTER]	MO1 =	7.00
7. Enter Cost	[↓] 30000 [ENTER]	CST =	30,000.00
8. Enter Salvage Value	[↓] 0 [ENTER]	SAL =	0.00
9. Select Year's Values to Calculate	[↓] 1 [ENTER]	YR =	1.00
10. View Depreciation	[↓]	DEP =	6,000.00
11. View (Remaining) Book Value	[↓]	RBV =	24,000.00
12. View Remaining Depreciable Value	[↓]	RDV =	24,000.00
13. Return to Select Year's Values to Calculate	[↓]	YR =	1.00
14. Repeat Steps 9-13 for Each of the Remaining Years			

In this example the keystrokes for entering all variables are shown to provide a generic example that can be used for any problem by changing the numbers entered into the calculator. If the display is already shown as indicated you may type [↓] to continue to the next step.

TABLE 5-13 Depreciation Schedule for Example 5-5

m	D_m ($)	BV_m ($)
0	0	30,000
1	1,500	28,500
2	11,400	17,100
3	6,840	10,260
4	4,104	6,156
5	3,282	2,874
6	2,874	0

The depreciation rate and book value for the second through the sixth years are calculated in the same manner and are as follows:

$$D_2 = (\$30,000)0.3800 = \$11,400$$
$$BV_2 = \$28,500 - \$11,400 = \$17,100$$
$$D_3 = (\$30,000)0.2280 = \$6,840$$
$$BV_3 = \$17,100 - \$6,840 = \$10,260$$
$$D_4 = (\$30,000)0.1368 = \$4,104$$
$$BV_4 = \$10,260 - \$4,104 = \$6,156$$
$$D_5 = (\$30,000)0.1094 = \$3,282$$
$$BV_5 = \$6,156 - \$3,282 = \$2,874$$
$$D_6 = (\$30,000)0.0958 = \$2,874$$
$$BV_6 = \$2,874 - \$2,874 = \$0$$

The annual depreciation and annual book values are shown in Table 5-13.

Example 5-6:   Prepare a depreciation schedule to be used for tax purposes for a $1,170,000 office building, excluding the cost of the land. The office building is placed in service during the third month of the company's tax year.

Solution: For tax purposes, the recovery period for the office building is 39 years with a salvage value of zero at the end of the 39 years. By tax code, straight-line depreciation must be used. Using Eq. (5-3), the annual depreciation using the straight-line method is as follows:

$$D_m = (\$1,170,000 - \$0)/39 = \$30,000$$

From Table 5-5 we see that only 0.7917 (79.17%) of the annual depreciation may be taken the first year because we are required to use the midmonth convention; therefore, the depreciation is as follows:

$$D_1 = \$30,000(0.7917) = \$23,751$$

Using Eq. (5-5), the book value at the end of the first year is as follows:

$$BV_1 = \$1,170,000 - \$23,751 = \$1,146,249$$

Using Eq. (5-5), the book value at the end of the second year is as follows:

$$BV_2 = \$1,146,249 - \$30,000 = \$1,116,249$$

The book values at the end of the third through thirty-ninth years are calculated in a similar manner. At the end of the thirty-ninth year the book value is $6,249 and the asset has been depreciated for 38.7917 years, leaving 0.2083 years in its useful life. The depreciation for the fortieth year is calculated as follows:

$$D_{40} = \$30,000(0.2083) = \$6,249$$

Using Eq. (5-5), the book value at the end of the fortieth year is as follows:

$$BV_{40} = \$6,249 - 6,249 = \$0$$

The annual depreciation and annual book values are shown in Table 5-14.

TABLE 5-14   Depreciation Schedule for Example 5-6

m	D_m ($)	BV_m ($)	m	D_m ($)	BV_m ($)
0	0	1,170,000	21	30,000	546,249
1	23,751	1,146,249	22	30,000	516,249
2	30,000	1,116,249	23	30,000	486,249
3	30,000	1,086,249	24	30,000	456,249
4	30,000	1,056,249	25	30,000	426,249
5	30,000	1,026,249	26	30,000	396,249
6	30,000	996,249	27	30,000	366,249
7	30,000	966,249	28	30,000	336,249
8	30,000	936,249	29	30,000	306,249
9	30,000	906,249	30	30,000	276,249
10	30,000	876,249	31	30,000	246,249
11	30,000	846,249	32	30,000	216,249
12	30,000	816,249	33	30,000	186,249
13	30,000	786,249	34	30,000	156,249
14	30,000	756,249	35	30,000	126,249
15	30,000	726,249	36	30,000	96,249
16	30,000	696,249	37	30,000	66,249
17	30,000	666,249	38	30,000	36,249
18	30,000	636,249	39	30,000	6,249
19	30,000	606,249	40	6,249	0
20	30,000	576,249			

When an asset is sold for more or less than its book value that was used for tax purposes, an adjustment must be made during the tax year the asset is disposed of. If the asset is sold for more than its book value, the difference between the sales price and the book value is recorded as a capital gain on the sale of an asset. If an asset is sold for less than its book value, the difference between the sales price and the book value is recorded as a capital loss on the sale of an asset.

Example 5-7:   The truck in Example 5-4 was sold for $8,000 at the end of the fourth year. What is the gain or loss on the sale of this truck?

Solution: From Example 5-4, the book value at the end of year four was $5,184. Because the asset was sold for more than the book value there is a capital gain on the sale of the asset. The gain on the sale of the truck is $2,816 ($8,000 − $5,184).

SECTION 179 EXCEPTION

Under Section 179 of the Internal Revenue Code some taxpayers may expense up to $24,000 of equipment without having to depreciate the equipment for the 2002 tax year. This is scheduled to be increased to $25,000 in 2003.[17] This is a good example of a time when a business owner would want to use a different depreciation schedule for financial purposes than was used for tax purposes.

DEPRECIATION FOR NONTAX PURPOSES

As indicated earlier in the chapter, depreciation is calculated differently for financial statements and for use in the billing of equipment than the depreciation calculated for tax purposes. The calculations may differ for any of the following reasons:

1. A different depreciation method is being used.
2. A different recovery period is being used.
3. The salvage value has been included in the calculations.
4. The asset is exempt from depreciation under Section 179 but is depreciated for other purposes.
5. Special depreciation allowances are available for tax purposes, which allow even faster depreciation of an asset than is used for financial purposes. For example, for qualified property purchased between September 11, 2001, and September 11, 2004, which is placed in service before January 1, 2005, a special depreciation allowance of 30% is available.[18] This special allowance

---

[17]IRS, *Highlights of 2001 Tax Changes*, Publication 553, 2002, p. 12.

[18]http://www.irs.gov/formspubs/page/0,,id%3D83709,00.html

must be taken after any Section 179 exceptions have been taken. When taking the special depreciation allowance, an additional depreciation allowance of 30% is taken during the first year and the remaining 70% of the asset's value is depreciated using the depreciation rules and rates previously discussed. This type of provision is often used to stimulate the national economy. This special depreciation allowance will be ignored in the examples and problems at the end of the chapter.

Because of these differences, the depreciation schedule for an asset may be very different for each of these purposes.

Example 5-8: Prepare a depreciation schedule to be used for the financial statements for the truck in Example 5-4 using the 200% declining-balance method. The truck was placed in service during the first month of the company's tax year and a full year's depreciation may be taken during the first year. The company estimates that the truck's useful life is six years. At the end of six years the estimated salvage value of the truck is $5,000. Compare the depreciation calculated for the financial statements to the depreciation calculated for tax purposes in Example 5-4.

Solution: Using Eq. (5-12), the annual depreciation rate for each year under the 200% declining-balance method is as follows:

$$R_m = 2.00/6 = 0.33333$$

Using Eq. (5-14) and the 200% declining-balance method, the annual depreciation for the first year is as follows:

$$D_1 = (\$30,000)0.33333 = \$10,000$$

Using Eq. (5-3), the annual depreciation for the first year using the straight-line method is as follows:

$$D_1 = (\$30,000 - \$0)/6 = \$5,000$$

Using Eq. (5-16) and the larger of the two depreciation amounts, the book value at the end of the first year is as follows:

$$BV_1 = \$30,000 - \$10,000 = \$20,000$$

The depreciation using the 200% declining-balance method, the depreciation using the straight-line method, and the book value for years 2 through 4 are calculated in the same manner as follows:

$$D_2 = (\$20,000)0.33333 = \$6,667$$
$$D_2 = (\$20,000 - \$5,000)/5 = \$3,000$$
$$BV_2 = \$20,000 - \$6,667 = \$13,333$$
$$D_3 = (\$13,333)0.33333 = \$4,444$$
$$D_3 = (\$13,333 - \$5,000)/4 = \$2,083$$
$$BV_3 = \$13,333 - \$4,444 = \$8,889$$

$$D_4 = (\$8,889)0.33333 = \$2,963$$
$$D_4 = (\$8,889 - \$5,000)/3 = \$1,296$$
$$BV_4 = \$8,889 - \$2,963 = \$5,926$$

Using Eq. (5-14) and the 200% declining-balance method, the annual depreciation for the fifth year is as follows:

$$D_5 = (\$5,926)0.33333 = \$1,975$$

Because the truck has been in service for four years, there are two years left in its recovery period. Using Eq. (5-3), the annual depreciation for the fifth year using the straight-line method is as follows:

$$D_5 = (\$5,926 - \$5,000)/2 = \$463$$

Using Eq. (5-16) and the larger of the two depreciation amounts, the book value at the end of the fifth year is as follows:

$$BV_5 = \$5,926 - \$1,975 = \$3,951$$

Because the 200% declining-balance depreciation method produces a book value less than the salvage value, we must switch to the straight-line depreciation method. Using Eq. (5-5) and the depreciation calculated by the straight-line method, the book value at the end of the fifth year is as follows:

$$BV_5 = \$5,926 - \$463 = \$5,463$$

Because we switched to straight-line depreciation in the fifth year, the straight-line depreciation for the sixth year is the same as that for the fifth year, which was $463. Using Eq. (5-5) and the depreciation calculated by the straight-line method, the book value at the end of the fifth year is as follows:

$$BV_6 = \$5,463 - \$463 = \$5,000$$

Switching to the straight-line depreciation method in the fifth year allows the book value to be equal to the salvage value at the end of the sixth year, which is the end of the recovery period. The annual depreciation and annual book values are shown in Table 5-15.

TABLE 5-15   Depreciation Schedule for Example 5-8

m	D_m ($)	BV_m ($)
0	0	30,000
1	10,000	20,000
2	6,667	13,333
3	4,444	8,889
4	2,963	5,926
5	463	5,463
6	464	5,000

FIGURE 5-2   Book Values Comparison for Example 5-8

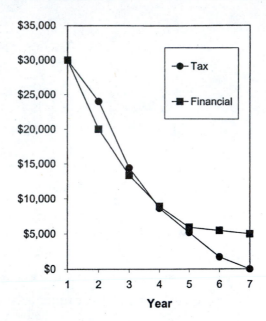

The greatest difference occurs in the sixth and seventh years because the depreciation for financial purposes includes a salvage value, whereas the depreciation for tax purposes ignores the salvage value. A comparison of the two depreciation schedules is shown in Figure 5-2.

CONCLUSION

Depreciation is the loss in value of a piece of equipment or real property. Different depreciation schedules may be used for the preparation of financial statements, the billing of equipment, and the preparation of income taxes, which may result in very different depreciation rates. For the preparation of financial statements and the billing of equipment there are three commonly used methods. They are the straight-line method, the sum-of-the-years method, and the declining-balance method. For tax purposes the IRS has set up standard recovery periods for assets and has identified the depreciation methods that may be used for each of the recovery periods. The depreciation methods allowed by the IRS include the straight-line, 200% declining-balance, and 150% declining-balance methods. The IRS has also established three standard conventions that are used to determine the percentage of the annual depreciation allowed when equipment or property is placed in service or disposed of. They are the half-year convention, the midquarter convention, and the midmonth convention. A business owner may expense some equipment under Section 179 of the Internal Revenue Code without having to depreciate the equipment.

PROBLEMS

1. A piece of equipment is purchased for $110,000 and has an estimated salvage value of $10,000 at the end of the recovery period. Prepare a depreciation schedule for the piece of equipment using the straight-line method with a recovery period of seven years.

2. A piece of equipment is purchased for $40,000 and has an estimated salvage value of $1,000 at the end of the recovery period. Prepare a depreciation schedule for the piece of equipment using the straight-line method with a recovery period of five years.

3. A piece of equipment is purchased for $110,000 and has an estimated salvage value of $10,000 at the end of the recovery period. Prepare a depreciation schedule for the piece of equipment using the sum-of-the-years method with a recovery period of seven years.

4. A piece of equipment is purchased for $40,000 and has an estimated salvage value of $1,000 at the end of the recovery period. Prepare a depreciation schedule for the piece of equipment using the sum-of-the-years method with a recovery period of five years.

5. A piece of equipment is purchased for $110,000 and has an estimated salvage value of $10,000 at the end of the recovery period. Prepare a depreciation schedule for the piece of equipment using the 200% declining-balance method with a recovery period of seven years.

6. A piece of equipment is purchased for $40,000 and has an estimated salvage value of $1,000 at the end of the recovery period. Prepare a depreciation schedule for the piece of equipment using the 200% declining-balance method with a recovery period of five years.

7. A piece of equipment is purchased for $110,000 and has an estimated salvage value of $10,000 at the end of the recovery period. Prepare a depreciation schedule for the piece of equipment using the 150% declining-balance method with a recovery period of seven years.

8. A piece of equipment is purchased for $40,000 and has an estimated salvage value of $1,000 at the end of the recovery period. Prepare a depreciation schedule for the piece of equipment using the 150% declining-balance method with a recovery period of five years.

9. Prepare a depreciation schedule to be used for tax purposes for a $110,000 railroad spur (track) using the 200% declining-balance method and a half-year convention. Ignore any special depreciation allowances.

10. Prepare a depreciation schedule to be used for tax purposes for $40,000 of computer equipment using the 150% declining-balance method and a half-year convention. Ignore any special depreciation allowances.

11. Prepare a depreciation schedule to be used for tax purposes for a $110,000 railroad spur (track) using the 200% declining-balance method and the

midquarter convention. The equipment was placed in service during the second quarter of the company's tax year. Ignore any special depreciation allowances.

12. Prepare a depreciation schedule to be used for tax purposes for $40,000 of computer equipment using the 200% declining-balance method and a midquarter convention. The equipment was placed in service during the third quarter of the company's tax year. Ignore any special depreciation allowances.

13. Prepare a depreciation schedule to be used for tax purposes for a $1,170,000 office building. The office building is placed in service in the fifth month of the company's tax year. The cost of the land is not included in the $1,170,000. Ignore any special depreciation allowances.

14. Prepare a depreciation schedule to be used for tax purposes for a $495,000 apartment building. The apartment building is placed in service in the ninth month of the company's tax year. The cost of the land is not included in the $495,000. Ignore any special depreciation allowances.

15. The truck in Example 5-4 was sold for $4,000 at the end of the fifth year. What is the capital gain or loss on the sale of the truck?

16. The truck in Example 5-4 was sold for $12,000 at the end of the second year. What is the capital gain or loss on the sale of the truck?

17. Create a computer spreadsheet to calculate the depreciation schedule for Problem 9. The spreadsheet should allow you to change the purchase price by changing a single cell.

18. Create a computer spreadsheet to calculate the depreciation schedule for Problem 13. The spreadsheet should allow you to change the purchase price by changing a single cell. Additionally, you should be able to change the month placed in service by changing a single cell.

19. Create a computer spreadsheet to calculate the depreciation schedule for Problem 14. The spreadsheet should allow you to change the purchase price by changing a single cell. Additionally, you should be able to change the month placed in service by changing a single cell.

REFERENCE

IRS, *Instructions for Form 4562*, 2001.

ANALYSIS OF FINANCIAL STATEMENTS

In this chapter you will learn to use financial ratios to analyze a company's financial statements, including comparing the company's ratios to industrial averages. This includes adapting commonly used ratios to the unique characteristics of the construction industry. Analysis of the financial statements helps the financial manager identify problems before they become a crisis. These problems may be life threatening to the company (such as realizing that the company will not be able to pay its bills in the upcoming months) or simple planning issues (such as identifying that the company's equipment is aging and that funds need to be set aside to replace this equipment in the next few years).

The most common tools used to track and measure a company's financial health are the company's balance sheet and the income statement. The financial health of a company is determined by not only the values shown on the financial statements but also the relationships among these values. These relationships are known as financial ratios. Good construction financial management includes monitoring the critical financial ratios and comparing them to other companies in the industry. In this chapter we look at ratios that are commonly used to measure the performance of a company, regardless of its industrial segment. Where necessary, these ratios are adapted to the unique characteristics found in the construction industry. We also look at recommended target ratios for the construction industry.

Analysis of financial statements is done by dividing one category or group of categories on the company's financial statement by another category or group of categories on the company's financial statement. By making this calculation we create a ratio that can be compared to other companies within the industry. These ratios represent the relationship between the two categories or among groups of categories and are often expressed as the ratio to 1, as in 2.00 to 1. At other times

117

the ratios are expressed as a percentage or may represent the number of times an event occurs during a period, such as the number of times a company turns over working capital during the year. These ratios can provide insights into a company's ability to pay bills, how efficiently it uses its financial resources, profitability, and the capital structure of the company.

When calculating ratios that include categories on the income statement and categories on the balance sheet, one must use the average balance for the categories from the balance sheet rather than the ending balance. This is necessary because the income statement represents all transactions between two points in time, whereas the balance sheet represents the separate points in time. The most common method of obtaining the average balance for a category on the balance sheet is to take the average of the balance of the category at the beginning of the period represented by the income statement and the balance of the category at the end of the period represented by the income statement.

Sometimes the amounts reported on the balance sheet at the beginning and ending of the year are not representative of the average balance for the year. This is the case for excavation companies whose fiscal year is the same as the calendar year and who shutdown for the winter months because of poor working conditions. While the company is shut down, its accounts receivable and accounts payable are significantly lower than they were during the construction season, as are many other accounts on the balance sheet. To get a more accurate picture of the company's financial health, one should use the average monthly balance for the accounts. The monthly average balance is calculated as follows:

$$\text{Average} = A_1/24 + A_2/12 + \cdots + A_{12}/12 + A_{13}/24 \tag{6-1}$$

where

A_1 through A_{12} = Amounts at the beginning of the 12 months during the year

A_{13} = Amount at the beginning of the next year or end of this year

As ratios are discussed, when data are available, typical ratios for construction companies in the single-family residence, commercial, heavy and highway, and specialty trades sectors are given. These data are based on the data from financial statements for over 62,000 companies for the years 1996 through 2000 as reported by Dun & Bradstreet, Inc.[19] Data are also published by the Risk Management Association, Standard and Poor's, Robert Morris Associates, and others. When comparing ratios to industrial averages, companies should obtain current data for their sector of the construction industry.

The data reported include a typical median and a typical range for the years studied. The median is the point where half of the companies are above the

[19]Dun & Bradstreet, Inc., *Industrial Norms and Key Business Ratios One Year—Desk Top Edition SIC #0100-8999*, years 1997 through 2001.

median and half are below the median, which should not be confused with the average or mean. The typical range is based on the upper and lower quartiles and represents the range of values for which half of the construction company falls within, with 25% of the companies performing better than the range and 25% of the companies performing below the range.

Single-family residential includes construction of new single-family homes and remodels, repairs, and additions to single-family homes performed by construction companies. Single-family residential excludes the construction of single-family homes built by speculative builders and developers.[20]

Commercial[21] construction includes the construction of multifamily housing, hotels, industrial buildings, warehouses, and other commercial construction by construction companies. Commercial construction excludes construction projects built by developers. Data on more specific classes of commercial construction are available from Dun & Bradstreet, Inc., as well as other sources.

Heavy and highway construction[22] includes the construction of streets, highways, elevated highways, bridges, tunnels, water lines, sewers, pipelines, communications, and power lines. Data on specific classes of heavy and highway construction are available from Dun & Bradstreet, Inc., as well as other sources.

Specialty trades[23] includes most subcontractor work and includes the following specific classes of specialty trades: plumbing, heating, and air-conditioning; paint and paper hanging; electrical work; masonry, stone setting, and other stone work; plastering, drywall, acoustical, and insulation work; terrazzo, tile, marble, and mosaic work; carpentry work; floor laying and other floor work not elsewhere classified; roofing, siding, and sheet metal work; concrete work; water well drilling; structural steel erection; glass and glazing work; excavation work; wrecking and demolition work; installing or erecting building equipment not elsewhere classified; and specialty trade not elsewhere classified. Data on specific classes of specialty trades are available from Dun & Bradstreet, Inc., as well as other sources.

DEPRECIATION AND FINANCIAL ANALYSIS

In Chapter 5 we saw that there were a variety of ways a company may depreciate a piece of equipment. When preparing financial statements the depreciation method used should be the method that best matches the equipment's actual loss in value. When the depreciation method used differs greatly from the actual loss in value, the depreciation of the fixed assets is overstated in the financial statements. When the depreciation is overstated or understated, the net fixed assets are understated or overstated as well as the total assets and owners' equity. For example, let's look at a small

---

[20]Includes all of U.S. Standard Industrial Classification (SIC) 1521.

[21]Weighted average for SIC 1522, 1541, and 1542.

[22]Includes all of SIC 16.

[23]Includes all of SIC 17.

company that purchases only one piece of depreciable equipment during the year for $100,000. The purchase takes place in the eighth month of its tax year. By using special depreciation allowances for equipment purchased between September 11, 2001, and September 11, 2004, the company could depreciate for tax purposes 44% of the asset's value during the remaining four months of the tax year. In reality the actual depreciation is closer to 10% for this four-month period. If the company were to use the depreciation calculated for tax purposes the depreciation on the income statement would be overstated by about $34,000, whereas the net fixed assets, total assets, and owner's equity would be understated by about $34,000. For a small company this would be a significant change in its financial statements.

Because the depreciation method can have a great impact on the financial statements, it is important to know which depreciation method is being used. When looking at financial ratios any ratio that includes depreciation, net fixed assets, total assets, or owners' equity is affected by the depreciation method used when preparing the financial statements. In this chapter, eight of the financial ratios include depreciation, net fixed assets, total assets, or owners' equity in the calculations. They are current liabilities to net worth ratio, debt to equity ratio, fixed assets to net worth ratio, current assets to total assets ratio, assets to revenues ratio, return on assets, return on equity, and the degree of fixed asset newness.

QUICK RATIO

The quick ratio is a measurement of a company's ability to pay current (short-term) liabilities with cash or other near cash assets—assets that can quickly be turned into cash. The quick ratio may also be referred to as the acid test ratio. The quick ratio is calculated as follows:

$$\text{Quick Ratio} = (\text{Cash} + \text{Accounts Receivable})/\text{Current Liabilities} \qquad (6\text{-}2)$$

When calculating the quick ratio a company should not include accounts receivable in the form of retention because often retention cannot be converted to cash quickly. Similarly, accounts receivable that are unlikely to be collected—often recorded as an allowance for bad debt—should not be included in the accounts receivable.

A company with a quick ratio of 1.00 to 1 or greater is considered liquid. A company with a ratio below 1.00 to 1 will need to convert inventory, notes receivable, other current or long-term assets to cash or raise cash through debt or equity financing to pay its current liabilities. A ratio greater than 1.50 to 1 may be an indication that the company has too much cash and should be investing its capital elsewhere or should be disbursing it to its shareholders. A quick ratio greater than 1.00 to 1 does not guarantee that a company can pay its current liabilities on time because its current liabilities may be due before its accounts receivable are received. Typical quick ratios for construction companies are found in Table 6-1.

Example 6-1: Determine the quick ratio for the commercial construction company in Figures 2-2 and 2-3. What insight does this give you into the company's financial operations?

TABLE 6-1 Typical Quick Ratios

INDUSTRY SECTOR	MEDIAN	RANGE
Single-Family Residential	0.9	2.1–0.3
Commercial	1.2	2.1–0.6
Heavy and Highway	1.2	2.1–0.8
Specialty Trades	1.4	2.5–0.9

Solution: The accounts receivable-retention should not be used in the calculation of the quick ratio because they may not be converted to cash quickly. The quick ratio is calculated using Eq. (6-2) as follows:

$$\text{Quick Ratio} = (\$200,492 + \$402,854)/\$423,907 = 1.42$$

The quick ratio is slightly higher than the median for a commercial construction company but well within the typical range. Because the quick ratio is less than 1.50 to 1 it does not appear that the company has too much cash or near cash assets.

CURRENT RATIO

The current ratio is a measurement of a company's ability to use current assets to pay for current liabilities. The current ratio is calculated as follows:

$$\text{Current Ratio} = \text{Current Assets}/\text{Current Liabilities} \qquad (6\text{-}3)$$

A current ratio of 2.00 to 1 is considered a strong indication that a company is able to pay current liabilities. If a company's current ratio is below 1.00 to 1 it is an indication that the company does not expect to receive enough revenue over the next year to pay its current liabilities. To pay these liabilities the company needs to sell long-term assets or raise cash through debt or equity financing. If a company's current ratio is below 1.50 to 1 the company is undercapitalized and may run into financial problems during the next year. If a company's current ratio is over 2.50 to 1, the company may have too much of its assets tied up in current assets and should possibly be investing its assets in other long-term ventures or distributing them to its shareholders. Typical current ratios for construction companies are found in Table 6-2.

TABLE 6-2 Typical Current Ratios

INDUSTRY SECTOR	MEDIAN	RANGE
Single-Family Residential	1.6	3.2–1.1
Commercial	1.5	3.1–1.2
Heavy and Highway	1.7	2.8–1.2
Specialty Trades	1.8	3.3–1.3

Example 6-2: Determine the current ratio for the commercial construction company in Figures 2-2 and 2-3. What insight does this give you into the company's financial operations?

Solution: The current ratio is calculated using Eq. (6-3) as follows:

Current Ratio = $690,720/$423,907 = 1.63

The current ratio is slightly higher than the median for a commercial construction company but well within the typical range. Because the current ratio is greater than 1.00 to 1 it appears that the company will meet its short-term cash needs and because the current ratio is less than 2.50 to 1 it does not appear that the company has too much of its assets tied up in current assets.

CURRENT LIABILITIES TO NET WORTH RATIO

The current liabilities to net worth ratio is a measurement of the risk that short-term creditors are taking by extending credit to the company compared to the risk the company's owners are taking in the company. For example, in the case of a construction company with current liabilities greater than the company's net worth or equity, the short-term creditors would have more capital at risk than the owners. Short-term creditors include suppliers and subcontractors who provide materials, labor, and equipment on credit. The current liabilities to net worth ratio is often expressed as a percentage of net worth and is calculated as follows:

Current Liabilities to Net Worth = Current Liabilities/Net Worth   (6-4)

For most industries it is recommended that care be taken when short-term credit is extended to companies with a current liabilities to net worth ratio of 67%. The construction industry consistently exceeds this recommended level because of the construction industry's heavy reliance on trade financing from suppliers and subcontractors. Typical current liabilities to net worth ratios for construction companies are found in Table 6-3.

Commercial construction companies have a higher current liabilities to net worth ratio because of their extensive use of suppliers and subcontractors to perform their work.

TABLE 6-3   Typical Current Liabilities to Net Worth Ratios (percentages)

INDUSTRY SECTOR	MEDIAN	RANGE
Single-Family Residential	88	29–241
Commercial	112	32–240
Heavy and Highway	65	29–132
Specialty Trades	71	29–153

Example 6-3: Determine the current liabilities to net worth ratio for the commercial construction company in Figures 2-2 and 2-3. What insight does this give you into the company's financial operations?

Solution: The current liabilities to net worth ratio is calculated using Eq. (6-4) as follows:

Current Liabilities to Net Worth = $423,907/$446,917 = 0.95
Current Liabilities to Net Worth = 95%

The current liabilities to net worth ratio is slightly worse than the median for a commercial construction company but well within the typical range. Because the ratio is less than 100% the short-term creditors do not have more capital at risk than the owners of the construction company, which is a good position to be in.

Debt to Equity Ratio

The debt to equity ratio is a measurement of the risk in the company all creditors are taking compared to the risk the company's owners are taking. It is also known as the debt to worth ratio or the total liabilities to net worth ratio. The debt to equity ratio is calculated as follows:

$$\text{Debt to Equity} = \text{Total Liabilities/Net Worth} \qquad (6\text{-}5)$$

The desired range for the debt to equity ratio is less than 2.00 to 1. If the debt to equity ratio exceeds 2.00 to 1, one begins to question whether the company can service its debt, particularity during a downturn in the industry. A debt to equity ratio that is less than 1.00 to 1 may indicate that the company is averse to debt financing and is not using debt to expand the company's business. Typical debt to equity ratios for construction companies are found in Table 6-4.

Example 6-4: Determine the debt to equity ratio for the commercial construction company in Figures 2-2 and 2-3. What insight does this give you into the company's financial operations?

TABLE 6-4   Typical Total Liabilities to Net Worth Ratios

INDUSTRY SECTOR	MEDIAN	RANGE
Single-Family Residential	1.2	0.4–3.0
Commercial	1.3	0.5–2.7
Heavy and Highway	1.0	0.4–1.9
Specialty Trades	0.9	0.4–1.9

Solution: The debt to equity ratio is calculated using Eq. (6-5) as follows:

Debt to Equity = $577,122/$446,917 = 1.30

The debt to equity ratio is at the median for a commercial construction company. Because the ratio is less than 2.00 to 1 it appears that the company will be able to service their debt.

FIXED ASSETS TO NET WORTH RATIO

The fixed assets to net worth ratio is a measurement of the amount of the owner's equity that is tied up in fixed assets, such as construction equipment, building, and vehicles. The fixed assets to net worth ratio is often expressed as a percentage and is calculated as follows:

Fixed Assets to Net Worth = Net Fixed Assets/Net Worth   (6-6)

A high number indicates a company has a heavy investment in fixed assets. Fixed assets require a constant stream of income to offset their loss in value. Construction companies—especially those in the heavy and highway sectors—that have significant investment in construction equipment are more dependent on maintaining a constant flow of work than those companies that have little invested in construction equipment. During a downturn in the industry, companies with a large investment in construction equipment usually suffer the most. Typical fixed assets to net worth ratios for construction companies are found in Table 6-5.

As expected, the heavy and highway sector, which uses a lot of expensive excavating equipment, has the highest fixed assets to net worth ratios—nearly double the next closest sector.

Example 6-5:   Determine the fixed assets to net worth ratio for the commercial construction company in Figures 2-2 and 2-3. What insight does this give you into the company's financial operations?

Solution: The fixed assets to net worth ratio is calculated using Eq. (6-6) as follows:

Fixed Assets to Net Worth = $154,775/$446,917 = 0.35 or 35%

TABLE 6-5   Typical Fixed Assets to Net Worth Ratios (percentages)

INDUSTRY SECTOR	MEDIAN	RANGE
Single-Family Residential	38	14–90
Commercial	24	8–64
Heavy and Highway	68	36–117
Specialty Trades	36	17–75

The fixed assets to net worth ratio is higher than the median for a commercial construction company but well within the typical range. Because the ratio is greater than the median the company has more fixed assets than the average company and therefore is more dependent on maintaining a steady stream of work to pay for these fixed assets.

CURRENT ASSETS TO TOTAL ASSETS RATIO

The current assets to total assets ratio is a measurement of how liquid a construction company's assets are. The current assets to total assets ratio is calculated as follows:

$$\text{Current Assets to Total Assets} = \text{Current Assets/Total Assets} \qquad (6\text{-}7)$$

A company with a high ratio would have most of its assets in the form of current assets and would be very liquid. A company with a low ratio would have most of its assets tied up in long-term assets, such as fixed and other assets. The ratio varies by sector. For single-family residential, commercial, and most specialty trades the average current assets to total asset ratio runs between 0.70 and 0.80. For heavy and highway the average runs between 0.55 and 0.65 because of their large investment in excavation equipment. Notable exceptions from the specialties trades are concrete work with an average of 61, wrecking and demolition with an average of 55, and excavation with an average of 46.

Remembering that fixed assets require a constant stream of income to offset their loss in value, construction companies that have significant investments in construction equipment are more dependent on maintaining a constant flow of work than those companies that have little invested in construction equipment. During a downturn in the industry, companies with a large investment in construction equipment usually suffer the most.

Example 6-6: Determine the current assets to total assets ratio for the commercial construction company in Figures 2-2 and 2-3. What insight does this give you into the company's financial operations?

Solution: The current assets to total assets ratio is calculated using Eq. (6-7) as follows:

$$\text{Current Assets to Total Assets} = \$690,720/\$1,024,039 = 0.67$$

The current assets to total assets ratio is slightly outside and below the range for a commercial construction company. This indicates that the company has a heavier investment in fixed assets than most commercial construction companies.

COLLECTION PERIOD

The collection period is a measurement of the average time it takes a company to collect its accounts receivable or the average number of days that capital is tied up in accounts receivable. The collection period is also a measure of how long the company's capital is being used to finance client's construction projects. It may also be referred to as the average age of accounts receivable. The collection period is calculated as follows:

$$\text{Collection Period} = \text{Accounts Receivable} (365)/\text{Revenues} \qquad (6\text{-}8)$$

For the construction industry the collection period is affected by retention. Retention held is recorded as an accounts receivable when the work is completed but will not be available for release until the project is completed. This has the effect of lengthening the collection period. The greater the percentage of retention being held and the longer the project the greater this effect is. For an accurate measure of how long capital is being used to finance client's construction projects it is necessary to include the accounts receivable that are in the form of retention because retention is a source of capital to the project's owner. However, including the accounts receivable that are in the form of retention in the calculation of the collection period distorts the collection period as a measure of how well a company is collecting the accounts receivable that are due to it. This is because no matter how aggressive a company collects its accounts receivable it cannot collect the retention until the project is complete. A better measure of how well a company is collecting its accounts receivable is to exclude the accounts receivable that are in the form of retention from the calculations. When a company has met the requirement for receipt of the retention, the retention should be moved to the accounts receivable trade account, thus reflecting that the retention is now collectable.

A company's collection period should be less than 45 days. A collection period of more than 45 days indicates that the company has poor collection policies or has extended generous payment terms to its clients. For a company whose clients do not hold retention, this time should be reduced to 30 days. Reducing the collection period reduces a company's need for cash and may reduce the company's need for debt and the interest charges that accompany debt. Generous payment terms and slow collections often increase a company's reliance on debt, which increases its interest expenses and thereby reduces its profitability. Typical collection periods for construction companies are shown in Table 6-6 and include accounts receivable in the form of retention.

A closely related ratio is the receivable turns. The receivable turns represent the number of times the receivables are turned over during a year and is calculated as follows:

$$\text{Receivable Turns} = 365/\text{Collection Period} \qquad (6\text{-}9)$$

Because of the mathematical relationship between the collection period and the receivable turns it is unnecessary to measure both ratios.

TABLE 6-6   Typical Collection Period (days)

INDUSTRY SECTOR	MEDIAN	RANGE
Single-Family Residential	23	8–45
Commercial	48	22–75
Heavy and Highway	51	31–73
Specialty Trades	50	31–72

Example 6-7: Determine the collection period—with and without retention—and receivable turns for the commercial construction company in Figures 2-2 and 2-3. What insight does this give you into the company's financial operations?

Solution: Because we are comparing the value of an account on the balance sheet to an account on the income statement, we need to use the average of the beginning and ending balance for the accounts on the balance sheet. Including retention, the average for the accounts receivable is calculated as follows:

Accounts Receivable
$$= [(\$402,854 + \$25,365) + (\$308,253 + \$21,885)]/2$$
Accounts Receivable $= \$379,178$

The collection period is calculated using Eq. (6-8) as follows:

Collection Period $= \$379,178(365)/\$3,698,945 = 37.4$ days

The receivable turns is calculated using Eq. (6-9) as follows:

Receivable Turns $= 365/37.4 = 9.8$

Excluding retention, the average for the accounts receivable is calculated as follows:

Accounts Receivable $= (\$402,854 + \$308,253)/2 = \$355,554$

The collection period is calculated using Eq. (6-8) as follows:

Collection Period $= \$355,554(365)/\$3,698,945 = 35.1$ days

The receivables turn is calculated using Eq. (6-9) as follows:

Receivable Turns $= 365/35.1 = 10.4$

The collection period is better than the median for a commercial construction company and is within the typical range. It is also below the recommended 45 days. On average, the company is funding the construction costs to the client for 37.4 days. On average, it takes the company 35 days to collect the payment on a bill sent to a client.

AVERAGE AGE OF ACCOUNTS PAYABLE

The average age of accounts payable represents the average time it takes a company to pay its bills and is a measure of how extensively a company is using trade financing. The average accounts age of accounts payable is the average amount of accounts payable divided by the total of the invoices that pass through the accounts payable for the period. The average age of accounts payable is often calculated as follows:

Average Age of Accounts Payable

$$= \text{Accounts Payable} (365)/(\text{Materials} + \text{Subcontract}) \quad (6\text{-}10)$$

The underlying assumption is that the bulk of the invoices that pass through the accounts payable for the period are material and subcontract construction costs. When a significant amount of invoices for equipment, other construction costs, or general overhead pass through the accounts payable, they will lengthen out the average age of accounts payable because they will increase the numerator in Eq. (6-10) without changing the denominator. To get a realistic measure of the average age of accounts payable a company may need to increase the materials and subcontract amount by the estimated amount of invoices from equipment, other construction costs, and general overhead that pass through the accounts payable account.

When the average age of accounts payable is greater than 45 days this is an indication that the construction company is slow to pay its bills and may receive less favorable credit terms and pricing from its suppliers and subcontractors. When the average age of accounts payable is shorter than 20 days—unless a construction company is taking advantage of trade discounts—it may be an indication that a company is underutilizing trade financing. If the average age of accounts payable is equal to or slightly greater than the collection period—calculated with retention—it is an indication that the construction company is using its suppliers and subcontractors to fund the construction work. If the average age of accounts payable is much greater than the collection period it may be an indication that the construction company is withholding payments from its suppliers and subcontractors even after it has received payment for the work. If the average age of accounts payable is less than the collection period, the construction company is in the habit of using its working capital to pay bills before it has received payment from the owner. It is desirable for the average age of accounts payable to be equal to or slightly greater than the collection period.

A closely related ratio is the payable turns. The payable turns represent the number of times the payables are turned over during a year and is calculated as follows:

$$\text{Payable Turns} = 365/\text{Average Age of Accounts Payable} \quad (6\text{-}11)$$

Because of the mathematical relationship between the payable turns and average age of accounts payable it is unnecessary to measure both ratios.

Example 6-8:   Determine the average age of accounts payable and payable turns for the commercial construction company in Figures 2-2 and 2-3. Use only the material and subcontract construction costs to calculate the average of accounts payable. What insight does this give you into the company's financial operations?

Solution: Because we are comparing the value of an account on the balance sheet to an account on the income statement, we need to use the average of the beginning and ending balance for the account on the balance sheet. The average for the accounts payable is calculated as follows:

Accounts Payable
$$= [(\$325,458 + \$22,546) + (\$228,585 + \$18,254)]/2$$
Accounts Payable = $297,422

The average age of accounts payable is calculated using Eq. (6-10) as follows:

Average Age of Accounts Payable
$$= \$297,422(365)/(\$712,564 + \$1,452,352)$$
Average Age of Accounts Payable = 50.1

The payable turns are calculated using Eq. (6-11) as follows:

Payable Turns = 365/50.1 = 7.3

The average age of accounts payable is greater than 45 days, indicating that the company is slow to pay its bills. The average age of accounts payable is 15 days greater than its collection period—with retention included—which is an indication that the construction company is withholding payments from its suppliers and subcontractors even after the project's owner has paid them for the work. It is likely that the average age of accounts payable is overstated because the accounts receivable includes bills other than material and subcontractor construction costs. From Figure 2-3 we see that there were $21,254 in equipment repairs and maintenance costs and $29,245 in fuel and lubrication equipment costs. If we include these costs in our calculations, the average age of accounts payable drops to 49.0. Other costs that pass through the accounts payable account may be hidden in the general overhead and other areas of the income statement. The company needs to work on paying suppliers and subcontractors in a more timely fashion.

ASSETS TO REVENUES RATIO

Assets to revenues ratio is a measurement of how efficiently the company is using its assets. It is also known as the assets to sales ratio. The assets to revenues ratio is often expressed as a percentage and is calculated as follows:

Assets to Revenues = Total Assets/Revenues   (6-12)

TABLE 6-7   Typical Assets to Revenues Ratios (percentages)

INDUSTRY SECTOR	MEDIAN	RANGE
Single-Family Residential	29	17–49
Commercial	29	19–55
Heavy and Highway	46	34–62
Specialty Trades	32	24–44

The recommended range for the ratio varies from industry to industry. Typical assets to revenues ratios for construction companies are shown in Table 6-7.

Companies with assets to revenues ratios above the upper end of the typical range may be performing too much work for their assets, which may be a sign of pending financial difficulties if left uncorrected. Companies with assets to revenues ratios below the lower end of the range are underutilizing their assets and should consider taking on more work. Heavy and Highway have a higher median assets to revenues ratio because of its extensive investment in construction equipment.

Example 6-9:   Determine the assets to revenues ratio for the commercial construction company in Figures 2-2 and 2-3. What insight does this give you into the company's financial operations?

Solution: Because we are comparing the value of an account on the balance sheet to an account on the income statement, we need to use the average of the beginning and ending balance for the account on the balance sheet. The average for the total assets is calculated as follows:

Total Assets = ($1,024,039 + $835,190)/2 = $929,614

The assets to revenues ratio is calculated using Eq. (6-12) as follows:

Assets to Revenues = $929,614/$3,698,945 = 0.25 or 25%

The assets to revenues ratio is almost midway between the median and upper limit of the range for a commercial construction company. It does not appear that the company is performing too much work with its assets.

WORKING CAPITAL TURNS

Working capital turns is a measurement of how efficiently a company is using its working capital. Working capital is defined as current assets less current liabilities and may be calculated as follows:

Working Capital = Current Assets − Current Liabilities   (6-13)

TABLE 6-8   Typical Working Capital Turns

INDUSTRY SECTOR	MEDIAN	RANGE
Single-Family Residential	11.7	26–5.8
Commercial	12.1	23–6.1
Heavy and Highway	8.8	17–4.9
Specialty Trades	8.8	16–5.3

The working capital represents those funds available for future operations or for the reduction of long-term liabilities. The working capital turns is also known as the revenues to net working capital ratio or sales to net working capital ratio. The working capital turns is calculated as follows:

$$\text{Working Capital Turns} = \text{Revenues/Working Capital} \qquad (6\text{-}14)$$

When a company passes payments on from the owners to subcontractors, a better measurement of working capital turns is obtained by subtracting the subcontractor payments from the revenues as follows:

$$\text{Working Capital Turns}$$
$$= (\text{Revenues} - \text{Subcontractor})/\text{Working Capital} \qquad (6\text{-}15)$$

A firm with a high number of turns is undercapitalized and needs to reduce its level of sales or increase the availability of current assets. Typical working capital turns for construction companies are shown in Table 6-8.

Example 6-10:   Determine the working capital turns for the commercial construction company in Figures 2-2 and 2-3. What insight does this give you into the company's financial operations?

Solution: Because we are comparing the value of an account on the balance sheet to an account on the income statement, we need to use the average of the beginning and ending balance for the account on the balance sheet. The average of the company's working capital is calculated using Eq. (6-13) as follows:

$$\text{Working Capital}$$
$$= (\$690,720 + \$501,676)/2 - (\$423,907 + \$367,213)/2$$
$$\text{Working Capital} = \$200,638$$

The working capital turn is calculated using Eq. (6-15) as follows:

$$\text{Working Capital Turns} = (\$3,698,945 - \$1,452,352)/\$200,638$$
$$= 11.2$$

The working capital turns is slightly less than the average but well within the typical range. The company appears to be properly capitalized.

ACCOUNTS PAYABLE TO REVENUE RATIO

The accounts payable to revenue ratio is a measurement of how much a company is using its suppliers and subcontractors as a source of funds. It is also known as accounts payable to sales. The accounts payable to revenue ratio is calculated as follows:

$$\text{Accounts Payable to Revenue} = \text{Accounts Payable/Revenue} \qquad (6\text{-}16)$$

When calculating the accounts payable to revenue ratio, the accounts payable in the form of retention should be included because retention held from a supplier or subcontractor is a form of funding to the contractor.

The higher the percentage the greater the funding the company is receiving from its suppliers and subcontractors. Typical accounts payable to revenue ratios for construction companies are shown in Table 6-9.

Example 6-11: Determine the accounts payable to revenue ratio for the commercial construction company in Figures 2-2 and 2-3. What insight does this give you into the company's financial operations?

Solution: Because we are comparing the value of an account on the balance sheet to an account on the income statement, we need to use the average of the beginning and ending balances for the account on the balance sheet. We include both accounts payable trade and accounts payable retention. The average for the accounts payable is calculated as follows:

Accounts Payable
$$= [(\$325,458 + \$22,546) + (\$228,585 + \$18,254)]/2$$
Accounts Payable = \$297,422

The accounts payable to revenue ratio is calculated using Eq. (6-16) as follows:

Accounts Payable to Revenue = \$297,422/\$3,698,945 = 0.080
Accounts Payable to Revenue = 8.0%

The accounts payable to revenue ratio is approximately equal to the median for a commercial construction company. The company is properly using its suppliers and subcontractors as a source of funding.

TABLE 6-9 Typical Accounts Payable to Revenue Ratios (percentages)

INDUSTRY SECTOR	MEDIAN	RANGE
Single-Family Residential	4.1	1.9–7.4
Commercial	7.9	2.9–13.0
Heavy and Highway	5.6	2.8–9.6
Specialty Trades	4.8	2.6–8.1

TABLE 6-10   Typical Gross Profit Margins (percentages)

INDUSTRY SECTOR	MEDIAN
Single-Family Residential	24
Commercial	17
Heavy and Highway	25
Specialty Trades	32

GROSS PROFIT MARGIN

The gross profit margin is the percentage of the revenues left after paying construction costs and equipment costs and is a measure of what percentage of each dollar of revenue is available to cover general overhead expenses and provide the company with a profit. It is also known as the gross profit ratio. The gross profit margin is calculated as follows:

$$\text{Gross Profit Margin} = \text{Gross Profit/Revenue} \qquad (6\text{-}17)$$

Typical gross profit margins for construction companies are shown in Table 6-10.

Example 6-12:   Determine the gross profit margin for the commercial construction company in Figures 2-2 and 2-3. What insight does this give you into the company's financial operations?

Solution: The gross profit margin is calculated using Eq. (6-17) as follows:

$$\text{Gross Profit Margin} = \text{Gross Profit/Revenue}$$
$$\text{Gross Profit Margin} = \$512,488/\$3,698,945 = 0.139 \text{ or } 13.9\%$$

In this case, the gross profit margin may be read directly off of the income statement in Figure 2-3.

The company spent 86.1% of its revenue on construction costs and retained 13.9% of its revenue to cover overhead expenses and provide a profit for the company's shareholders. The company's gross profit margin is less than the median for commercial construction companies. The company needs to increase its profit and overhead markup or exercise better control over its construction costs.

GENERAL OVERHEAD RATIO

General overhead ratio is the percentage of the revenues used to pay the general overhead expense. It is also known as the general and administrative cost ratio. The general overhead ratio is calculated as follows:

$$\text{General Overhead} = \text{General Overhead/Revenue} \qquad (6\text{-}18)$$

As a rule of thumb, the general overhead ratio for commercial construction companies should be less than 10%. Single-family residential construction companies' ratios would be higher when sales commissions are included in the general overhead.

Example 6-13: Determine the general overhead ratio for the commercial construction company in Figures 2-2 and 2-3. What insight does this give you into the company's financial operations?

Solution: The general overhead ratio is calculated using Eq. (6-18) as follows:

General Overhead Ratio = $422,562/$3,698,945 = 0.114 or 11.4%

In this case, the general overhead ratio may be read directly from the income statement in Figure 2-3.

The company spent 11.4% of its revenue on general overhead. Because the general overhead percentage is over 10% the company needs to decrease its general overhead expenses or increase its revenues without increasing the general overhead.

PROFIT MARGIN

The profit margin is the percentage of the revenues that becomes profit and may be measured before or after income taxes. It is also known as the return on revenues or return on sales. The profit margin is a measurement of how well a construction company can withstand changes in the construction market, such as reduced prices, higher costs, and less demand. The pretax profit margin is calculated as follows:

Pretax Profit Margin = Net Profit Before Taxes/Revenues   (6-19)

A good target for a pretax profit margin is 5%. The pretax profit margin is discussed further in Chapter 10.

The after-tax profit margin is calculated as follows:

After-Tax Profit Margin = Net Profit After Taxes/Revenues   (6-20)

Typical after-Tax profit margins for construction companies are shown in Table 6-11.

Example 6-14: Determine the pretax and after-tax profit margins for the commercial construction company in Figures 2-2 and 2-3. What insight does this give you into the company's financial operations?

TABLE 6-11 Typical After-Tax Profit Margins (percentages)

INDUSTRY SECTOR	MEDIAN	RANGE
Single-Family Residential	3.3	8.1–0.9
Commercial	2.2	8.7–0.6
Heavy and Highway	3.2	7.3–1.0
Specialty Trades	2.8	6.7–0.8

Solution: The pretax profit margin is calculated using Eq. (6-19) as follows:

Pretax Profit Margin = $111,447/$3,698,945 = 0.030 or 3.0%

The after-tax profit margin is calculated using Eq. (6-20) as follows:

After-Tax Profit Margin = $78,013/$3,698,945 = 0.021 or 2.1%

In this case, the pretax profit margin and after-tax profit margin may be read directly off of the income statement in Figure 2-3.

The pretax profit margin for the company is less than the recommended 5%. The after-tax profit margin is slightly less than the median for a commercial construction company but well within the range. The company needs to work on its profitability. This may be done by cutting costs or increasing the profit and overhead markup.

RETURN ON ASSETS

The return on assets is a measurement of how efficiently a construction company is using its assets and is often expressed as a percentage. The return on assets is calculated as follows:

Return on Assets = Net Profit After Taxes/Total Assets   (6-21)

Efficiently run companies will have a high return on assets, whereas companies that are poorly run will have a low return on assets. Typical returns on assets ratios for construction companies are shown in Table 6-12.

Example 6-15: Determine the return on assets for the commercial construction company in Figures 2-2 and 2-3. What insight does this give you into the company's financial operations?

Solution: Because we are comparing the value of an account on the balance sheet to an account on the income statement, we need to use the average of the beginning and ending balances for the account on the balance sheet. The average for the total assets is calculated as follows:

Total Assets = ($1,024,039 + $835,190)/2 = $929,614

TABLE 6-12 Typical Return on Assets Ratios (percentages)

INDUSTRY SECTOR	MEDIAN	RANGE
Single-Family Residential	8.7	24.1–2.3
Commercial	6.5	21.7–2.0
Heavy and Highway	6.5	14.7–2.0
Specialty Trades	7.9	19.0–2.4

The return on assets ratio is calculated using Eq. (6-21) as follows:

$$\text{Return on Assets} = \$78,013/\$929,614 = 0.084 \text{ or } 8.4\%$$

The return on assets for the company is better than the median for a commercial construction company but well below the upper end of the range. Improvement in the after-tax profit margin will help increase this percentage.

RETURN ON EQUITY

Return on equity is the return the company's shareholders received on their invested capital. It is also known as return on investment. The return on equity may be measured before or after income tax. The pretax return on equity is calculated as follows:

$$\text{Pretax Return on Equity} = \text{Net Profit Before Taxes/Equity} \qquad (6\text{-}22)$$

A good target for the pretax return on equity is 15%. The after-tax return on equity is calculated as follows:

$$\text{After-Tax Return on Equity} = \text{Net Profit After Taxes/Equity} \qquad (6\text{-}23)$$

Typical after-tax returns on equity ratios for construction companies are shown in Table 6-13.

Pretax and after-tax returns for a construction company should be greater than the pretax or after-tax returns of investing the capital in the stock market or other saving instruments.

TABLE 6-13 Typical Return on Equity (percentages)

INDUSTRY SECTOR	MEDIAN	RANGE
Single-Family Residential	25.9	62–8.1
Commercial	16.7	53–5.4
Heavy and Highway	14.6	31–4.7
Specialty Trades	17.4	42–5.6

Example 6-16: Determine the pretax return on equity and after-tax return on equity for the commercial construction company in Figures 2-2 and 2-3. What insight does this give you into the company's financial operations?

Solution: Because we are comparing the value of an account on the balance sheet to an account on the income statement, we need to use the average of the beginning and ending balances for the account on the balance sheet. The average for the equity is calculated as follows:

$$Equity = (\$446,917 + \$368,904)/2 = \$407,910$$

The pretax return on equity is calculated using Eq. (6-22) as follows:

$$Pretax\ Return\ on\ Equity = \$111,447/\$407,910 = 0.273\ or\ 27.3\%$$

The after-tax return on equity is calculated using Eq. (6-23) as follows:

$$After\text{-}Tax\ Return\ on\ Equity = \$78,013/\$407,910 = 0.191\ or\ 19.1\%$$

The after-tax return on equity for the company is better than the median for a commercial construction company but well below the upper end of the range. Improvement in the after-tax profit margin will help increase this percentage.

DEGREE OF FIXED ASSET NEWNESS

The degree of fixed asset newness is a measurement of how new a company's assets are. The degree of fixed asset newness is calculated as follows:

$$Degree\ of\ Fixed\ Asset\ Newness = Net\ Fixed\ Assets/Total\ Fixed\ Assets\ \ (6\text{-}24)$$

Remembering that the net fixed assets equals the total assets at their purchase price less the depreciation taken, the degree of fixed asset newness represents the percentage of the asset's original value that has not depreciated. The depreciation method used for the financial statement will have a great effect on this ratio, the faster the depreciation the lower the ratio. For a company with a single fixed asset, when the asset is first purchased the company's degree of fixed asset newness would be 100%. When the asset has been completely depreciated, the company's degree of asset newness would be 0%. A good target range for a construction company is between 60% and 40% or near the middle. A company with a degree of fixed asset newness ratio greater than 60% would have a lot of new, shiny equipment, which is often accompanied by large loan payments and represents a large investment of capital in equipment. A company with a degree of fixed asset newness ratio less than 40% would have a lot of older equipment, often indicating that the company will need to invest heavily in fixed assets to maintain its operations. As a reminder, the depreciation method used when preparing the financial statements should be matched to the actual depreciation of the equipment. It is possible to replace all of a company's equipment in the eighth month of its tax year, use the special depreciation allowances, and end the year with a degree of fixed asset newness ratio of 56—even though its equipment is only four months old—by using its tax depreciation when preparing the financial statements.

Example 6-17:   Determine the degree of fixed asset newness for the commercial construction company in Figures 2-2 and 2-3. What insight does this give you into the company's financial operations?

Solution: The degree of fixed asset newness is calculated using Eq. (6-24) as follows:

Degree of Fixed Asset Newness = \$154,775/\$379,287 = 0.408
Degree of Fixed Asset Newness = 40.8%

The degree of fixed asset newness lies between 40% and 60%. The company's equipment is neither too new nor too old.

CONCLUSION

The withholding of retention is common in the construction industry. When retention is withheld, the accounts receivable is separated into two categories, one for retention and for the rest of the accounts receivable. Accounts payable are similarly split into two accounts. The standard financial ratios must be modified to take retention into account. The retention portion of the accounts receivable is ignored when calculating the quick ratio and the collection period used measuring the effectiveness of the company's collection efforts.

Subcontractors are used as a source of capital for construction companies. As a result, when calculating the working capital turns, the revenues are reduced by the amount of money that is paid to the subcontractor when the contractor gets paid by the owner.

PROBLEMS

1. Determine the quick ratio for the construction company in Figures 6-1 and 6-2. What insight does this give you into the company's financial operations?
2. Determine the current ratio for the construction company in Figures 6-1 and 6-2. What insight does this give you into the company's financial operations?
3. Determine the current liabilities to net worth ratio for the construction company in Figures 6-1 and 6-2. What insight does this give you into the company's financial operations?

WEST MOUNTAIN CONSTRUCTION
BALANCE SHEET

	Current Year	Last Year
ASSETS		
CURRENT ASSETS		
Cash	32,387	34,826
Accounts Receivable-Trade	74,526	38,212
Accounts Receivable-Retention	6,888	4,235
Inventory	0	0
Costs and Profits in Excess of Billings	9,177	4,549
Notes Receivable	3,139	0
Prepaid Expenses	735	1,061
Other Current Assets	3,114	1,119
Total Current Assets	129,966	84,002
FIXED AND OTHER ASSETS		
Construction Equipment	39,229	39,229
Trucks and Autos	8,981	8,981
Office Equipment	8,057	8,057
Total Fixed Assets	56,267	56,267
Less Acc. Depreciation	46,562	39,889
Net Fixed Assets	9,705	16,378
Other Assets	45,996	50,462
Total Assets	185,667	150,842
LIABILITIES		
Current Liabilities		
Accounts Payable-Trade	38,682	35,772
Accounts Payable-Retention	3,768	3,536
Billings in Excess of Costs and Profits	1,424	2,022
Notes Payable	4,022	5,791
Accrued Payables	4,574	2,254
Accrued Taxes	2,718	2,405
Accrued Vacation	606	308
Other Current Liabilities	6,605	5,330
Total Current Liabilities	62,399	57,418
Long-Term Liabilities	61,544	48,916
Total Liabilities	123,943	106,334
OWNER'S EQUITY		
Capital Stock	10,000	10,000
Retained Earnings	51,724	34,508
Current Period Net Income	0	0
Total Equity	61,724	44,508
Total Liabilities and Equity	185,667	150,842

FIGURE 6-1   Balance Sheet for West Mountain Construction

FIGURE 6-2   Income
Statement for West
Mountain Construction

WEST MOUNTAIN CONSTRUCTION INCOME STATEMENT	
REVENUE	789,839
CONSTRUCTION COSTS	
Materials	92,214
Labor	199,690
Subcontract	401,948
Equipment	20,833
Other	1,352
Total Construction Costs	716,037
EQUIPMENT COSTS	
Rent and Lease Payments	3,773
Depreciation	6,673
Repairs and Maintenance	2,734
Fuel and Lubrication	7,289
Taxes, Licenses, and Insurance	364
Equipment Costs Charged to Jobs	20,833
Total Equipment Costs	0
GROSS PROFIT	73,802
OVERHEAD	53,827
NET PROFIT FROM OPERATIONS	19,975
OTHER INCOME AND EXPENSE	1,162
PROFIT BEFORE TAX	21,137
INCOME TAX	3,921
PROFIT AFTER TAX	17,216

4. Determine the debt to equity ratio for the construction company in Figures 6-1 and 6-2. What insight does this give you into the company's financial operations?

5. Determine the fixed assets to net worth ratio for the construction company in Figures 6-1 and 6-2. What insight does this give you into the company's financial operations?

6. Determine the current assets to total assets ratio for the construction company in Figures 6-1 and 6-2. What insight does this give you into the company's financial operations?

7. Determine the collection period—with and without retention—and receivable turns for the construction company in Figures 6-1 and 6-2. What insight does this give you into the company's financial operations?

8. Determine the average age of accounts payable and payable turns for the construction company in Figures 6-1 and 6-2. Use only the material and subcontract construction costs to calculate the average of accounts payable. What insight does this give you into the company's financial operations?

9. Determine the assets to revenues ratio for the construction company in Figures 6-1 and 6-2. What insight does this give you into the company's financial operations?

10. Determine the working capital turns for the construction company in Figures 6-1 and 6-2. What insight does this give you into the company's financial operations?

11. Determine the accounts payable to revenue ratio for the construction company in Figures 6-1 and 6-2. What insight does this give you into the company's financial operations?

12. Determine the gross profit margin for the construction company in Figures 6-1 and 6-2. What insight does this give you into the company's financial operations?

13. Determine the general overhead ratio for the construction company in Figures 6-1 and 6-2. What insight does this give you into the company's financial operations?

14. Determine the pretax and after-tax profit margins for the construction company in Figures 6-1 and 6-2. What insight does this give you into the company's financial operations?

15. Determine the return on assets for the construction company in Figures 6-1 and 6-2. What insight does this give you into the company's financial operations?

16. Determine the pretax return on equity and after-tax return on equity for the construction company in Figures 6-1 and 6-2. What insight does this give you into the company's financial operations?

17. Determine the degree of fixed asset newness for the commercial company in Figures 6-1 and 6-2. What insight does this give you into the company's financial operations?

18. Determine the quick ratio for the construction company in Figures 6-3 and 6-4. What insight does this give you into the company's financial operations?

19. Determine the current ratio for the construction company in Figures 6-3 and 6-4. What insight does this give you into the company's financial operations?

20. Determine the current liabilities to net worth ratio for the construction company in Figures 6-3 and 6-4. What insight does this give you into the company's financial operations?

21. Determine the debt to equity ratio for the construction company in Figures 6-3 and 6-4. What insight does this give you into the company's financial operations?

```
                    EASTSIDE CONTRACTORS
                       BALANCE SHEET

                                        Current      Last
                                         Year        Year
ASSETS
 CURRENT ASSETS
  Cash                                   118,626     78,470
  Accounts Receivable-Trade             243,300    171,734
  Accounts Receivable-Retention          12,905     12,929
  Inventory                                   0          0
  Costs and Profits in Excess of Billings 17,507    10,562
  Notes Receivable                         6,441          0
  Prepaid Expenses                         3,398      2,463
  Other Current Assets                     6,228      3,792
    Total Current Assets                 408,405    279,950

 FIXED AND OTHER ASSETS
  Building and Land                      106,006    106,006
  Construction Equipment                  56,727     56,727
  Trucks and Autos                        31,159     31,159
  Office Equipment                        35,193     35,193
    Total Fixed Assets                   229,085    229,085
    Less Acc. Depreciation               133,314    112,393
  Net Fixed Assets                        95,771    116,692
  Other Assets                           110,345    115,952
    Total Assets                         614,521    512,594

LIABILITIES
 Current Liabilities
  Accounts Payable-Trade                 191,046    142,789
  Accounts Payable-Retention              14,945     10,159
  Billings in Excess of Costs and Profits  2,961      7,935
  Notes Payable                            8,330     13,293
  Accrued Payables                         9,278     11,394
  Accrued Taxes                            6,294      4,985
  Accrued Vacation                         1,960      1,802
  Other Current Liabilities               16,973     23,863
    Total Current Liabilities            251,787    216,220
 Long-Term Liabilities                    81,668     49,781
    Total Liabilities                    333,455    266,001

OWNER'S EQUITY
 Capital Stock                            10,000     10,000
 Retained Earnings                       271,066    236,593
 Current Period Net Income                     0          0
    Total Equity                         281,066    246,593
 Total Liabilities and Equity            614,521    512,594
```

FIGURE 6-3   Balance Sheet for Eastside Contractors

FIGURE 6-4   Income
Statement for Eastside
Contractors

EASTSIDE CONTRACTORS
INCOME STATEMENT

REVENUE	2,225,379
CONSTRUCTION COSTS	
Materials	414,840
Labor	564,783
Subcontract	932,250
Equipment	68,506
Other	2,761
Total Construction Costs	1,983,140
EQUIPMENT COSTS	
Rent and Lease Payments	21,654
Depreciation	18,203
Repairs and Maintenance	10,805
Fuel and Lubrication	16,982
Taxes, Licenses, and Insurance	862
Equipment Costs Charged to Jobs	68,506
Total Equipment Costs	0
GROSS PROFIT	242,239
OVERHEAD	207,805
NET PROFIT FROM OPERATIONS	34,434
OTHER INCOME AND EXPENSE	7,813
PROFIT BEFORE TAX	42,247
INCOME TAX	7,774
PROFIT AFTER TAX	34,473

22. Determine the fixed assets to net worth ratio for the construction company in Figures 6-3 and 6-4. What insight does this give you into the company's financial operations?

23. Determine the current assets to total assets ratio for the construction company in Figures 6-3 and 6-4. What insight does this give you into the company's financial operations?

24. Determine the collection period—with and without retention—and receivable turns for the construction company in Figures 6-3 and 6-4. What insight does this give you into the company's financial operations?

25. Determine the average age of accounts payable and payable turns for the construction company in Figures 6-3 and 6-4. Use only the material and subcontract construction costs to calculate the average of accounts payable. What insight does this give you into the company's financial operations?

26. Determine the assets to revenues ratio for the construction company in Figures 6-3 and 6-4. What insight does this give you into the company's financial operations?

27. Determine the working capital turns for the construction company in Figures 6-3 and 6-4. What insight does this give you into the company's financial operations?

28. Determine the accounts payable to revenue ratio for the construction company in Figures 6-3 and 6-4. What insight does this give you into the company's financial operations?

29. Determine the gross profit margin for the construction company in Figures 6-3 and 6-4. What insight does this give you into the company's financial operations?

30. Determine the general overhead ratio for the construction company in Figures 6-3 and 6-4. What insight does this give you into the company's financial operations?

31. Determine the pretax and after-tax profit margins for the construction company in Figures 6-3 and 6-4. What insight does this give you into the company's financial operations?

32. Determine the return on assets for the construction company in Figures 6-3 and 6-4. What insight does this give you into the company's financial operations?

33. Determine the pretax return on equity and after-tax return on equity for the construction company in Figures 6-3 and 6-4. What insight does this give you into the company's financial operations?

34. Determine the degree of fixed asset newness for the construction company in Figures 6-3 and 6-4. What insight does this give you into the company's financial operations?

35. Setup a spreadsheet to calculate the financial ratios for Examples 6-1 to 6-17 for the company in Figures 2-2 and 2-3.

PART

III

MANAGING COSTS AND PROFITS

In this section we look at how to manage the costs and profits of a construction company. This must be done at the project level as well as at the company level. This section includes the following chapters:

MANAGING COSTS

In this chapter you will learn to monitor and control construction costs for materials, labor, subcontractors, equipment, other costs, and general overhead. You will also learn to measure the success of the project by monitoring profitability using the schedule performance index, the cost performance index, and project closeouts. These skills help financial managers determine the success of projects and identify problem areas on projects, regardless of whether you are a project manager or superintendent who wants to know how your project is doing or a general manager or owner who wants to know how well your project managers and superintendents are running their projects.

> In this chapter we look at monitoring and controlling the individual costs as well as monitoring the costs of the individual project.

MONITORING AND CONTROLLING CONSTRUCTION COSTS

For management to control costs, it must actively monitor costs, looking for potential problems and proactively address the problems. In this section we look at the five different types of costs—materials, labor, subcontracts, equipment, and other—as well as general overhead to see how management can monitor and control costs.

Material Purchases

Prior to making any material purchases, employees should obtain a purchase order for the purchase. The purchase order should include the quantity of materials ordered and the cost of the materials. Purchase orders should be approved by the project manager. The superintendent should be allowed to approve small purchases up to a specified limit—say $100 or $200—without approval of the project manager.

The approval of the purchase order gives management a chance to check and see if the material costs are in line with the budget and to ensure that only needed materials are ordered for the job. Small purchase orders for stopgap materials may be processed without costs but should include the quantity of the items needed. This is often necessary to keep the job moving. On every job some stopgap purchase orders are needed; however, a persistent pattern of stopgap purchase orders is a sign of inadequate planning, which is a major enemy to good cost controls. Material purchases may be handled as shown in Figure 7-1.

FIGURE 7-1   Material Purchases

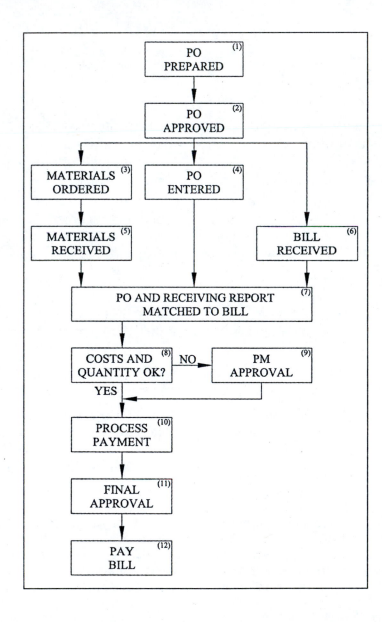

A purchase order is prepared (step 1) for the materials needed and should include the quantity of materials, type of materials, the material costs, and the date the materials are needed. This may be done by field personnel, the estimator at the time of buyout, or the project manager.

The purchase order is checked against the budget and approved or denied by the project manager or, if allowed, by the superintendent (step 2). This gives the project manager and the superintendent the opportunity to seek other sources for the materials if the purchase order exceeds the budget amount before the materials have been ordered. For the project manager to check the purchase order against the budget, the total committed and noncommitted costs to date must be available. At the time the purchase order is approved the materials are coded to a job cost code. After the purchase order has been approved the materials may be ordered (step 3) by the party requesting the purchase and the purchase order is entered into the accounting system as a committed cost (step 4) by the accounting department.

When the materials are received, the site personnel should notify the accounting department that the materials have been received (step 5). This notice of receipt should include listing any missing or damaged materials. This notice is often done by sending a copy of the shipping invoice to the accounting department.

After the bill is received (step 6) it is entered into the accounting system and matched to the notice of receipt and the purchase order (step 7) by the accounting department. The quantities and prices on the bill are compared to the notice of receipt and the purchase order (step 8). If the material quantities or costs on the bill exceed the amounts on the purchase order or notice of receipt, or if the purchase order lacks costs, a copy of the bill, the notice of receipt, and the purchase order are sent to the project manager for reconciliation and approval (step 9). If the material quantities on the bill are less than the amounts on the purchase order and there are additional deliveries expected, the quantities received are noted on the purchase order so that they may be added to future deliveries. This is a common occurrence when ordering large quantities of material that cannot be delivered in a single shipment. The accounting system should allow for receipt and payment of partial shipments. If the material quantities on the bill are less than the amounts on the purchase order and no additional deliveries are expected, the purchase order is closed so that additional purchases cannot be credited against the purchase order. All bills that do not exceed the quantities or costs on the purchase order or notice of receipt do not need approval of the project manager (step 9) and are processed for payment (step 10). It is redundant to have the project manager approve all bills that do not exceed the quantities or costs approved by the project manager on the purchase order because the project manager has already approved these quantities and costs.

Prior to payment of the bill, the accounting department should send a list of suppliers to be paid to the project manager for final approval (step 11). This gives the project manager one last chance to withhold payment in the event there were problems with the materials supplied. Once final approval is received the accounting department may pay the bill (step 12).

Labor

Labor is much more difficult to control than materials. With materials, the project manager has the opportunity to approve a purchase along with costs before the materials are purchased. With labor, the costs are not available to the project manager until the work has been performed and the employees' time has been entered into the accounting system, which may occur a week or more after the work has been performed.

A key to controlling labor cost is for the project manager to hold the superintendent and crew forepersons responsible for the productivity and costs of their crew. Labor may be handled as shown in Figure 7-2.

The employees keep track of their time on a time card (step 1). The time should be separated by the type of work being performed and should be consistent with the company's cost coding system and the budget for the project. The foreperson and superintendent check and approve the time card (step 2). The superintendent should make sure that the work has been coded to the correct job cost code. The superintendent will have better control of the labor costs if he or she reviews the labor hours daily. Once the time cards have been approved, the superintendent sends the time cards to the accounting department, where the time is into the accounting system (step 3). The number of hours worked, along with the costs, are then sent to the project manager for approval (step 4) and payroll checks are processed (step 5). With the new costs entered into the accounting system, the project manager may

FIGURE 7-2   Labor

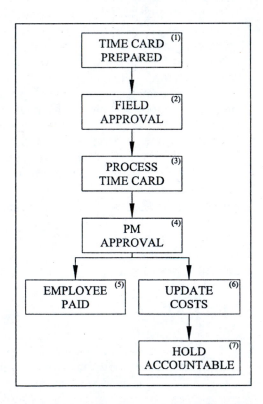

update the cost to complete and the total estimated cost at completion (step 6). Finally, the project manager should review the costs with the superintendent and the crew foreperson and hold them accountable for the weekly labor costs (step 7). If the project manager does not hold field personnel responsible for their costs, the company is simply reporting costs rather than controlling costs.

Subcontracts

Unlike purchase orders, all bills from subcontractors must be reviewed by the project manager prior to processing the payment. This is because most subcontracts require progress payments, which are based on the amount of work that is complete. Determining the amount of work completed is more difficult than determining the amount of materials that have been delivered to the project. For this reason the project manager must make the final decision as to whether the bill from the subcontractor is fair. Subcontracts may be processed as shown in Figure 7-3.

FIGURE 7-3   Subcontracts

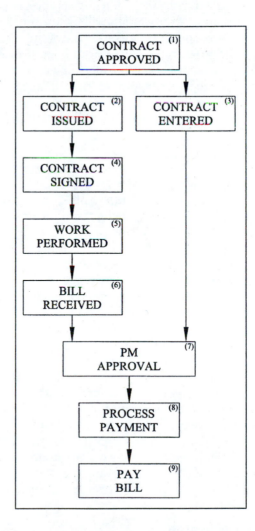

The subcontractors' bids or proposals are checked against the scope of work and the budget. After selecting the best bid or proposal, a subcontract is prepared and approved by the project manager (step 1). This gives the project manager the opportunity to check the cost of the work against the budget, to seek other bids, make corrections to the scope of work, and negotiate the finer point of the contract before issuing the subcontract. Once this is completed, the contract is issued to the subcontractor (step 2) and is entered into the accounting system as a committed cost (step 3) by the accounting department. On receipt of a signed contract from the subcontractor (step 4) the project manager notifies the superintendent that the subcontractor can work on the project (step 5). The project manager should send the superintendent a copy of the contract so that the superintendent is aware of the contractor and subcontractor's responsibilities under the contract.

At the end of a billing period, the subcontractor submits a progress bill to the contractor (step 6). The project manager, often in consultation with the superintendent, reviews the bill and approves it for payment, resolving any differences in the amount of the work the subcontractor has billed for and the amount of the work performed on the job. The review of the bill may include a trip to the jobsite to inspect the progress or may rely on progress reports from the jobsite. When reviewing the bill, the project manager should check the bill against the contract amount. At the time the bill is approved, the bill is coded to a job cost code. After approval the payment is processed (step 8) and paid (step 9) by the accounting department. Change orders to the contract are handled in the same manner as was the original contract.

Equipment

Equipment, like labor, is a difficult cost to control. A time card should be prepared for each piece of equipment. If an employee is always using a piece of equipment—such as a superintendent and his or her truck—the employee's time card may be used in lieu of a time card for the piece of equipment. The equipment time cards are processed in the same manner as the labor time cards.

Equipment may be billed to a job based on the number of hours spent working on the job or the number of days that the equipment is present at the job. When being charged for equipment based on the equipment being at the project, the project manager should make sure that unneeded equipment is returned promptly to reduce equipment costs.

When equipment is charged to a project, the expected cost of the piece of equipment is allocated to the project. It is important to note that the costs being billed to the projects are not the actual costs but the expected or projected average hourly or daily costs for the year. There is a great deal of uncertainty in the expected costs because of the uncertainty in the number of billable hours or days that will occur during the year and the uncertainty in some of the costs. The ownership costs—rent and lease payments, depreciation, taxes, licenses, and insurance—are easily projected; however, the hourly or daily ownership costs are quite uncertain because of the uncertainty in the number of billable hours or days over which these costs will be recovered. The operation costs—repairs, maintenance, fuel, and lubrication—vary with equipment use and are much more difficult to quantify because they are a function of the conditions under which the equipment is working and may vary from operator to operator. Because of the uncertainty of the expected costs, the cost allocation and projected number of billable hours or days for the year must be reviewed monthly to determine the appropriateness of the expected costs. At the end of the year the allocation of equipment costs should equal the actual costs. If management overallocates costs—the expected costs are too high—this will increase the project costs and may show that a budget item is over budget when all that is happening is the equipment costs have been overallocated. If management underallocates costs—the expected costs are too low—this will decrease the project costs and may show that a budget item is on or under budget when in reality the item is over budget, yet management does not know it because the equipment costs have been underallocated.

Other

Where possible, the other cost type items should have purchase orders and be handled in the same manner as material purchases. However, there are many items—such as utility bills—that cannot be handled in this manner. Bills such as these should be sent to the project manager for approval and cost coding before processing and paying the bill.

Monitoring and Controlling General Overhead Costs

General overhead costs should be handled in the same manner as project costs with the general manager approving the purchase orders and contracts. Like monitoring project costs the general overhead costs should be compared to a budget on a weekly or monthly basis. The procedures for preparing a general overhead budget are discussed in chapter 9. Costs that are not actively monitored and controlled will quickly become out of control.

MONITORING JOB PROFITABILITY

The costs for each job should be monitored at least weekly. During the buyout process—the process of hiring subcontractors and procuring materials—costs are often monitored on a more frequent basis. The monitoring should include monitoring the job costs against a budget as well as updating the cost to complete and the estimated cost at completion for each budget item. All costs should include committed costs. A sample job cost report is shown in Figure 7-4. If the accounting system does not provide a report with committed costs and the estimated cost at completion—as is the case in the job cost report shown in Figure 7-4—these costs should be entered into a spreadsheet similar to the one shown in Figure 4-1.

When the estimated cost at completion exceeds the budget for a line item, the project manager should investigate the source of the overrun. Common problem

Job: 317 Weston Apartments							July 16, 2004	
	Contract	Billed	----------------Costs----------------			--------------Hours-----------		
Code	Description	Amount	to Date	Actual	Budget	Overrun	Actual	Budget	Overrun
	Phase 1: Bldg 1								
06110	Rough Carpentry	35,000.00	25,000.00	29,375.21	29,200.00	175.21	1,295	1,300	-5
06120	Lumber	42,000.00	39,000.00	36,579.32	37,000.00	-420.68	0	0	0
06150	Trusses	15,000.00	0.00	13,560.00	13,560.00	0.00	0	0	0
	Phase Total	92,000.00	64,000.00	79,514.53	79,760.00	-245.47	1,295	1,300	-5
	Phase 2: Bldg 2								
06110	Rough Carpentry	35,000.00	0.00	11,526.33	29,200.00	-17,673.67	526	1,300	-774
06120	Lumber	42,000.00	0.00	18,265.35	37,000.00	0.00	0	0	0
06150	Trusses	15,000.00	0.00	0.00	13,560.00	-13,560.00	0	0	0
	Phase Total	92,000.00	0.00	29,791.68	79,760.00	-31,233.67	526	1,300	-774
	Job Total	184,000.00	64,000.00	109,306.21	159,520.00	-31,479.14	1,821	2,600	-779

FIGURE 7-4   Sample Job Cost Report

types to look for include clerical errors (such as bills that have been miscoded or incorrectly entered into the accounting system), budgeting and estimating errors, unexpected conditions (such as an unexpectedly cold winter), and poor execution of the work (such as bad planning or poor productivity).

When clerical errors are found they should be sent to the accounting department for correction. After the corrections have been made the cost should be updated to make sure that the correction did not result in any other categories exceeding their budgeted amounts.

When budgeting and estimating errors are found, an internal change order should be issued to move money from the contingency to the category in which the error occurred to maintain a realistic budget for the project. An internal change order is a change order that is not approved by the project's owner because it changes neither the scope nor the cost of the project. Similarly, when a budget category is found to have excess funds during the buyout process, an internal change order should be generated to move the excess funds for the budget line item into the contingency. It is important to have a realistic budget to monitor the progress against. Budgets that have plenty of waste built into them do not require the company to exercise good cost controls. Budgets that have insufficient funds hold employees responsible for meeting costs that they cannot possibly achieve, which often results in the employees becoming demoralized. The budgets should be set at a point where the costs are achievable when good cost control principles are used.

Unexpected conditions do arise, but with careful review of the bid documents and careful planning their impact can be minimized. Many unexpected conditions—such as unexpected ground condition—are billable as a change order to the project's owners. Unexpected conditions should not include winter snow in an area that is prone to snow during the winter but should be reserved for only those conditions for which there was no way that the conditions could have been foreseen. For example, the snowiest year on record would be an unexpected condition, whereas a winter with an above-average snowfall would not. When truly unexpected conditions occur, the cost of the unexpected conditions should be covered by the contingency or an internal change order should be issued to move money from the contingency to the category that is affected by the unexpected condition to cover the cost of the unexpected condition. Once again it is necessary to maintain a realistic budget for the project. Care must be taken when dealing with unexpected conditions to protect against workers charging all overruns to the unexpected condition regardless of the cause of the overrun.

The final category for cost overruns is poor execution. The execution of the project is wholly within control of the project's management. When a realistic budget has been set for a project, then the cost overruns are due to poor execution and cost underruns are due to good execution on the part of the project's management. The project's management, including the project manager, should be held accountable on a weekly basis for the financial success of the project as well its progress. Not only should they be held accountable for the costs, but also the labor hours, the productivity of the employees, and the schedule for the project. Labor hours should be tracked and recorded in the accounting reports. Good scheduling is a part of controlling costs because schedule overruns increase project costs by increasing project overhead costs, whereas beating the schedule reduces project costs by reducing project overhead costs. A common way of measuring the schedule and the cost efficiency of a project is through the use of earned value. Earned value uses two indexes to measure the performance of a project: the schedule performance index and the cost performance index. Three values are needed to calculate the schedule performance index and the cost performance index. They are the actual cost of the work performed, the budgeted cost of the work scheduled, and the budgeted cost of the work performed.

The actual cost of the work performed comes from the accounting system and represents the actual costs spent on the construction work to a specific date. The actual costs of the work performed should be measured at the same date as the budgeted cost of the work performed and the budgeted cost of the work scheduled. When determining the actual cost of the work performed, cost for work that has not been performed—such as materials whose costs are included in the accounting reports that have not been incorporated into the construction project—should not be included in the costs. Additionally, care must be taken to ensure that costs for all of the completed work are included in the actual costs. Often subcontractors may bill only once a month. If the actual costs are measured between subcontractor's bills, work has been completed by the subcontractor for which the company does not have costs. It is important that the costs are up-to-date for the management to accurately determine the cost performance index.

The budgeted cost of the work scheduled comes from the cost-loaded schedule and is the budgeted or estimated cost for each of the tasks in the schedule that should have been completed or partially completed as of the date selected. For partially completed tasks the budgeted cost is determined by multiplying the budgeted cost for the task by the task's scheduled percentage of completion. For example, if the task of installing doors has a budget of $5,000 and is scheduled to be 20% complete, then the budgeted cost of the work scheduled for the task is $1,000 ($5,000 × 0.20). It is important to note that the costs used here are budgeted costs, not actual costs.

The budgeted cost of the work performed is determined by taking the budget cost from the cost-loaded schedule for each of the activities on the schedule and multiplying them by their percentage of completion as of the date selected. Again, it is important to note that the costs used here are budgeted costs, not actual costs.

Before we can calculate the schedule performance index and cost performance index we must know how to prepare a cost-loaded schedule.

Cost-Loaded Schedule

A cost-loaded schedule is a schedule that shows not only the time frame when a task is to be completed but also the cost of the work so that the cost of the work completed each week or month can be estimated. A cost-loaded schedule is prepared by first preparing a schedule for the project and then assigning dollar estimates to each of the tasks. The costs for each task are spread out over the duration of the task, resulting in a weekly or monthly cost for each of the tasks. The total cost of the work performed for each week or month may be obtained by adding up the weekly or monthly costs for each of the individual tasks.

> **Example 7-1:**   Determine the estimated cost of the work performed each week given the tasks—with their associated costs and schedules—shown in Table 7-1. When a task spans more than one week the costs should be divided equally among the weeks.

TABLE 7-1   Schedule and Costs for Example 7-1

		WEEK	
TASK	COST ($)	START	FINISH
Mobilization	2,000	1	1
Grubbing	5,000	1	1
Bridge Excavation	2,000	2	2
Install Prefabricated Bridge	47,000	2	2
Back Fill Bridge	2,000	2	2
Install Culverts	10,000	3	3
Rough Excavate Roadway	112,000	3	6
Install Sanitary Sewer	57,000	6	7
Install Water Lines	69,000	7	8
Install Storm Drains	15,000	8	8
Grade and Roll Sub Grade	12,000	8	9
Place and Compact Road Base	42,000	9	9
Place and Compact Asphalt	48,000	9	9
Grade Shoulders	3,000	10	10
Clean Up	1,000	10	10
Demobilize	2,000	10	10

TABLE 7-2   Cost-Loaded Schedule for Example 7-1

WEEK	COST ($)	WEEK	COST ($)
1	7,000	6	56,500
2	51,000	7	63,000
3	38,000	8	55,500
4	28,000	9	96,000
5	28,000	10	6,000

Solution: During Week 1, mobilization and grubbing will be completed at a cost of $7,000 ($2,000 + $5,000). During Week 2, bridge excavation, installation of the prefabricated bridge, and back filling the bridge will be completed at a cost of $51,000 ($2,000 + $47,000 + $2,000). The costs to rough excavate the roadway must be equally spread out over Weeks 3 through 6 for a cost of $28,000 ($112,000/4) per week. During Week 3 the installation of the culvers will occur and the rough excavation of the roadway will begin at a cost of $38,000 ($10,000 + $28,000). The remaining weeks are calculated in a similar manner and are shown in Table 7-2.

A cost-loaded schedule may be developed in a scheduling software package such as Microsoft Project or SureTrak. A cost-loaded schedule may also be developed in Microsoft Excel as shown in Figure 7-5.

Schedule Performance Index

The schedule performance index (*SPI*) measures the success of a project's management to complete the work on time. The schedule performance index is based on the relationship between the budgeted cost of the work performed (*BCWP*) and the budgeted cost of the work scheduled (*BCWS*) using the following formula:

$$SPI = BCWP/BCWS \qquad (7\text{-}1)$$

If the budgeted cost of the work performed is greater than the budgeted cost of the work scheduled, more work—as measured by budgeted costs—has been performed than was scheduled and the corresponding schedule performance index is greater than one, indicating that the project is ahead of schedule. A schedule performance index of one indicates that the project is on schedule and a schedule performance index of less than one indicates that the project is behind schedule. The strength of the schedule performance index is that it takes all tasks with costs into account when determining if the project is on schedule, not just those tasks on the critical path. When measuring a project's progress using the critical path, it is possible to be on schedule with the tasks on the critical path while ignoring all tasks that are not on the critical path until they become critical. Using the schedule performance index does not allow noncritical tasks to be ignored. The weakness of the schedule performance index is that it does not take into account if the project's critical path is on schedule. It is possible to have a schedule performance

Task	Cost	Start	Finish	Week 1	Week 2	Week 3	Week 4	Week 5	Week 6	Week 7	Week 8	Week 9	Week 10
Mobilization	2,000	Week 1	Week 1	2,000									
Grubbing	5,000	Week 1	Week 1	5,000									
Bridge Excavation	2,000	Week 2	Week 2		2,000								
Install Prefabricated Bridge	47,000	Week 2	Week 2		47,000								
Back Fill Bridge	2,000	Week 2	Week 2		2,000								
Install Culverts	10,000	Week 3	Week 3			10,000							
Rough Excavate Roadway	112,000	Week 3	Week 6			28,000	28,000	28,000	28,000				
Install Sanitary Sewer	57,000	Week 6	Week 7						28,500	28,500			
Install Water Lines	69,000	Week 7	Week 8							34,500	34,500		
Install Storm Drains	15,000	Week 8	Week 8								15,000		
Grade and Roll Sub Grade	12,000	Week 8	Week 9								6,000	6,000	
Place and Compact Road Base	42,000	Week 9	Week 9									42,000	
Place and Compact Asphalt	48,000	Week 9	Week 9									48,000	
Grade Shoulders	3,000	Week 10	Week 10										3,000
Clean Up	1,000	Week 10	Week 10										1,000
Demobilize	2,000	Week 10	Week 10										2,000
	429,000			7,000	51,000	38,000	28,000	28,000	56,500	63,000	55,500	96,000	6,000

FIGURE 7-5   Cost-Loaded for Example 7-1

index greater than one while being behind on the critical path. Another weakness of the schedule performance index is that it ignores tasks that have a budgeted cost of zero, such as tasks dealing with submittals and the ordering of materials. Because of these reasons the schedule performance index should be used in conjunction with the critical path to determine the success of a project's management to complete the work on time.

> **Example 7-2:**   A project consists of three tasks. Task A is scheduled to begin at the start of Week 1 and finish at the end of Week 2. Task B is scheduled to begin at the start of Week 1 and finish at the end of Week 1. Task C is scheduled to begin at the start of Week 2 and end at the end of Week 2. The budgeted cost for Task A is $3,000, for Task B is $1,000, and for Task C is $500. At the end of the first week Task A is 45% complete, Task B is 100% complete, and Task C is 10% complete. What is the schedule performance index for the project at the end of the first week?

> **Solution:**   For tasks that are scheduled to be in progress, the budgeted cost of the work scheduled must be prorated. Task A should be 50% complete at the end of the first week; therefore, its budgeted cost of the work scheduled is $1,500 ($3,000 × 0.50). The budgeted cost of the work scheduled for Task B is 100% of its costs because it was to be completed by the end of the first week. The budgeted cost of the work scheduled for Task C is zero because it was not scheduled to be started by the end of the first week. The budgeted cost of the work scheduled for the project is as follows:

> BCWS = $1,500 + $1,000 + $0 = $2,500

The budgeted cost of the work performed is calculated by taking the budgeted cost of the work for each task and multiplying it by the percentage of completion for the task as follows:

> BCWP = $3,000(0.45) + $1,000(1.00) + $500(0.10) = $2,400

The schedule performance index is calculated using Eq. (7-1) as follows:

> SPI = $2,400/$2,500 = 0.96

The project is behind schedule.

Cost Performance Index

The cost performance index (*CPI*) measures the success of the project's management to complete the work under budget. The cost performance index is based on the relationship between the budgeted cost of the work performed (*BCWP*) and the actual cost of the work performed (*ACWP*) using the following formula:

CPI = BCWP/ACWP   (7-2)

If the budgeted cost of the work performed is greater than the actual cost of the work performed, the anticipated cost of the work performed is greater than the actual cost of the work and the corresponding cost performance index is greater than one, indicating that the project is under budget. A cost performance index of one indicates that the project is on budget, and a cost performance index of less than one indicates that the project is over budget.

Example 7-3: The actual cost of the work performed at the end of the first week for the project in Example 7-2 is $2,350. Determine the cost performance index for the project.

Solution: The cost performance index is calculated using Eq. (7-2) as follows:

CPI = $2,400/$2,350 = 1.02

The project is under budget.

The cost performance index may be used to determine the estimated cost at completion for a project or task that is in progress using the following formula:

Total Estimated Cost at Completion = Total Estimate/CPI   (7-3)

The underlying assumption is that the cost performance index will remain the same throughout the remainder of the project or task. This may or may not be true. If the cost performance index is below one, management should take corrective action and improve the cost performance index. The total estimated cost at completion may then be used to determine the cost to complete by subtracting the actual costs to date from the total estimated cost at completion.

Example 7-4: Determine the total estimated cost at completion and estimated cost to complete for the project in Example 7-3, assuming the cost performance index remains the same through the remainder of the job.

Solution: The total estimated cost is $4,500 ($3,000 + $1,000 + $500). The total estimated cost at completion is calculated using Eq. (7-3) as follows:

Total Estimated Cost at Completion = $4,500/1.02 = $4,412

The cost to complete is $2,012 ($4,412 – $2,400).

TARGET LEVELS FOR CPI AND SPI

What are the best target levels for the cost performance index and the schedule performance index? One would think that the higher the number for these indices the better; however, a high number for either of these indices probably indicates that either the schedule or the budget was unrealistic. For example, a cost performance index of two would indicate that the actual cost of the work performed was half of the budgeted cost of the work performed. It is unlikely that the cost savings of 50% was solely a result of good cost management on the project but instead was a result of an unrealistically high budget. When analyzing the cost performance index and the schedule performance index, management should look at two things: the value of the indices and the trend in these values.

On a project, the costs may be deterministic or probabilistic. The deterministic costs are those costs that management can determine before they occur. Fixed prices from subcontractors, where there is little chance that the cost will change, are considered deterministic costs. Deterministic costs include all committed costs. Probabilistic costs are those costs that management cannot determine before they occur, such as is the case with in-house labor. Probabilistic costs may be represented by a statistical curve such as the normal or bell curve. Although these costs are unknown through analysis of historical data, an expected value and a standard deviation may be determined for each of the costs, provided there is sufficient information. The expected value is the most likely value—in the case of the normal distribution is equal to the mean or average with it being equally likely that the actual cost will exceed the expected value as it is that the actual costs will be less than the expected value. Although the costs are not known they are expected to fall within the distribution curve. The standard deviation represents how much the actual costs could vary from the expected costs. By nature all durations on the schedule are probabilistic.

The ideal target range for the cost performance index and the schedule performance index is within one standard deviation of the expected values. Projects that are between one and two standard deviations from the expected values should be a cause for concern and projects that are more than two standard deviations from the expected values need immediate attention from management. One would expect that a project that consists of mostly deterministic costs would stay closer to the expected values than would a project consisting of mostly probabilistic costs. Because of this it is impossible to set a single target range for all projects.

If the budget and schedule used for the cost performance index and the schedule performance index are based on the expected values then the cost performance index and schedule performance index should be within one standard deviation for both indices. If the indices are based on another value—for example, the costs may be set at a level where the probability of exceeding the costs is 25%—the indices should be within one standard deviation of the index values that represent the expected values. For example, if the costs were set at the level where the probability of exceeding the costs is 25%, both indices should be centered around a cost performance index and a schedule performance index greater than one. Determining the standard deviation for the cost performance index and the schedule performance index is beyond the scope of this book.

The second measure that management should look at when using the cost performance and schedule performance indexes is the trend of these indices over time. To do this, the indices may be graphed with the *x* axis representing the schedule performance index and the *y* axis representing the cost performance index as shown

Figure 7-6 Graphing the CPI and SPI

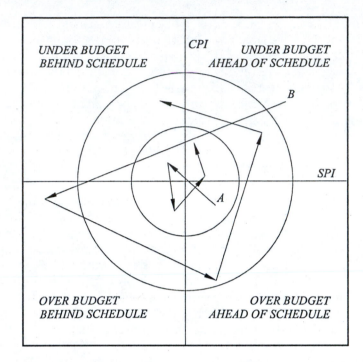

in Figure 7-6.[24] In Figure 7-6 the inner circle represents one standard deviation from the expected values of one for both the cost performance index and schedule performance index. The outer circle represents two standard deviations. A project that has a high degree of consistency in its schedule performance and cost performance indices is being managed in a more consistent manner and is more likely to stay in control than a project whose indices vary widely from period to period. In Figure 7-6 Project A is in better control and more likely to stay within the inner circle than Project B, which is all over the place—sometimes ahead of schedule and other times behind schedule—sometimes under budget and other times over budget.

Project Closeout Audit

At the completion of every project—after all the costs and revenues have been recorded—it is important to perform a project closeout audit. The purpose of the project closeout audit is to identify those things that helped to control costs so that they may be repeated on other projects and to identify problems that were encountered so that management can find ways to avoid these problems in the future. It is important that the project closeout audit focuses on finding and fixing problems rather than blaming people. If the project closeout audit becomes

[24]See Hemsath, James R., PE and Ra, Dr. Jang W., *Multiple Project Performance with Graphical Performance Indicators*, 46th Annual Meeting of AACE International, June 2002.

a blame-placing game, personnel will hide the problems rather than identify the problems and find ways to avoid them in the future. Project teams need to learn from their mistakes and learn what works well so that it can be repeated.

The project closeout audit consists of three steps. First, the project costing data must be validated. This validation includes looking at the cost data in detail and verifying that the costs were charged to the appropriate project and category and that all costs are included. If the project manager has been approving the costs throughout the project, there should be very few problems with inaccurate data. Inaccurate data may cause problems to go unidentified and then lead to erroneous results. Second, management must look at those areas of the project where they performed better than expected—the areas where they really shone—and determine what factors led to their success. Once they have identified these factors they should look at ways to incorporate these factors in all of their projects. For example, if they found that holding weekly subcontractor meetings on the job reduced the conflicts on the job and helped coordinate the schedule, they should look at holding weekly subcontractor meetings on all of their projects. Third, management must look at those areas of the project where they encountered problems. When identifying the problems, management should identify the source of the problem. Was the problem a result of problems with the estimate or buyout? Was it the result of a management decision? Was it due to poor project management? Poor production? Excessive waste? Once it has identified the problems it can explore ways to avoid these problems in the future. For example, if management found that doors were not ordered on time—causing construction delays and cost overruns—it could make sure that ordering doors is included as a task on the schedule for future projects. Project teams who do not review and learn from their past projects are condemned to repeat their mistakes.

CONCLUSION

To manage construction costs appropriate cost control procedures need to be implemented. When controlling costs, the earlier in the process the costs can be checked and approved against a budget the easier it is to control costs. For most material purchases, the purchase should be approved by a purchase order before the materials are ordered. Costs should be entered into the accounting system as soon as possible after the costs are known. For subcontracts and most material purchases the costs should be entered as committed costs shortly after the contract or purchase order is issued. By doing so accurate, up-to-date cost information is maintained in the accounting system. At a minimum, the cost reports from the accounting system should be reviewed on a weekly basis for all projects and for the general overhead. In addition to using accounting reports, earned value may be used to measure the scheduling and cost efficiency of a project. The schedule performance index is used to measure the scheduling efficiency and the cost performance index is used to measure the cost efficiency of the project. At the completion of each project, management should perform a project closeout audit, during which time it learns from what was done right and from its mistakes.

PROBLEMS

1. Determine the estimated cost of the work performed each week given the tasks—with their associated costs and schedules—shown in the following table. When a task spans more than one week, the costs should be divided equally among the weeks.

		WEEK	
TASK	COST ($)	START	FINISH
Mobilization	1,000	1	1
Grubbing	4,000	1	1
Rough Excavate Roadway	24,000	2	4
Grade and Roll Sub Grade	1,000	4	4
Place and Compact Road Base	8,000	5	5
Place and Compact Asphalt	12,000	5	5
Grade Shoulders	1,000	6	6
Clean Up	1,000	6	6
Demobilize	1,000	6	6

2. Determine the estimated cost of the work performed each week given the tasks—with their associated costs and schedules—shown in the following table. When a task spans more than one week, the costs should be divided equally among the weeks.

		WEEK	
TASK	COST ($)	START	FINISH
Excavation	2,200	1	1
Footings and Foundation	19,600	2	3
Waterproofing	900	3	3
Backfill and Under Slab Gravel	2,000	4	4
Slab on Grade	22,300	4	4
Masonry	54,000	5	7
Structural Steel	2,400	8	8
Joist and Deck	11,900	8	8
Hollow Metal Doors and Hardware	2,100	9	9
Overhead Doors	10,100	9	9
Skylights	5,800	9	9
Roof Insulation	5,600	10	10
Membrane Roofing	13,000	10	10
Heating	15,600	11	11
Electrical	29,800	11	12
Cleanup	1,000	12	12

3. A project consists of three tasks. Task A is scheduled to begin at the start of Week 1 and finish at the end of Week 3. Task B is scheduled to begin at the start of Week 1 and finish at the end of Week 2. Task C is scheduled to begin at the start of Week 2 and end at the end of Week 3. The budgeted cost for Task A is $22,000, for Task B is $17,000, and for Task C is $15,000. At the end of the second week Task A is 65% complete, Task B is 95% complete, and Task C is 60% complete. What is the schedule performance index for the project at the end of the second week?

4. A project consists of six tasks. Task A is scheduled to begin at the start of Week 1 and finish at the end of Week 4. Task B is scheduled to begin at the start of Week 1 and finish at the end of Week 2. Task C is scheduled to begin at the start of Week 3 and end at the end of Week 4. Task D is scheduled to begin at the start of Week 1 and end at the end of Week 1. Task E is scheduled to begin at the start of Week 2 and end at the end of Week 4. Task F is scheduled to begin at the start of Week 4 and end at the end of Week 4. The budgeted cost for Task A is $10,000, for Task B is $2,000, for Task C is $3,000, for Task D is $1,000, for Task E is $6,000, and for Task F is $4,000. At the end of the third week Task A is 80% complete, Task B is 100% complete, Task C is 40% complete, Task D is 100% complete, Task E is 55% complete, and Task F has not started. What is the schedule performance index for the project at the end of the third week?

5. The actual cost of the work performed at the end of the second week for the project in Problem 3 is $37,900. Determine the cost performance index for the project.

6. The actual cost of the work performed at the end of the third week for the project in Problem 4 is $16,500. Determine the cost performance index for the project.

7. Determine the total estimated cost at completion and estimated cost to complete for the project in Problem 5, assuming the cost performance index remains the same through the remainder of the job.

8. Determine the total estimated cost at completion and estimated cost to complete for the project in Problem 6, assuming the cost performance index remains the same through the remainder of the job.

9. Set up a spreadsheet to solve Problem 1.

10. Set up a spreadsheet to solve Problem 2.

DETERMINING LABOR BURDEN

In this chapter you will learn to determine the labor burden markup. This helps you better understand how to project these costs, whether they are to be used to bid a new job, price a change order, or project the cost to complete the project. This helps the general manager and owner determine the labor costs needed to prepare a general overhead budget.

To project costs or prepare a general overhead budget we must estimate the labor wages and burden for the employees. The estimated labor wages should include the wages paid to the employees, including all bonuses, and should include any anticipated raises that may occur during the budgetary period. Employees may be separated into two groups based on how their wages are calculated. The first group includes all employees who are paid an hourly wage based on the number of hours they work during the pay period. These employees are often referred to as hourly employees. To estimate the wages for hourly employees one must first estimate the number of hours each employee will work during an average pay period. Remember that pay rates for hourly employees may be different for overtime, holidays, and weekends. The wage rates for hourly employees and the rules governing overtime may be set forth by union contracts or government regulatory agencies. Federal Davis–Bacon wages—wage rates that must be used on contracts with federal funding—vary by state, county, and type of work being performed (for example, road work will have different wages than residential construction). These rates are published as General Decision by the U.S. Department of Labor. A sample General Decision is found in Figure 8-1. To ensure that you are using the correct General Decision for a specific project you should obtain the decisions from the contracting officer for the project. The total wages for an employee or group of employees is calculated by multiplying the number of hours by the wage rate for these hours and adding any anticipated bonuses.

FIGURE 8-1 General
Decision

GENERAL DECISION **UT020008** 05/17/2002 UT8

Date: May 17, 2002
General Decision Number **UT020008**

Superseded General Decision No. UT010008

State: Utah

Construction Type:
HEAVY

County(ies):
SALT LAKE

HEAVY CONSTRUCTION PROJECTS (including Water & Sewer Line
Construction Projects and Wastewater Treatment Plants).

Modification Number	Publication Date
0	03/01/2002
1	05/17/2002

COUNTY(ies):
SALT LAKE

ELEC0354A 06/01/2001

	Rates	Fringes
ELECTRICIANS	23.43	6.32+4.2%

----

* IRON0027C 01/01/2002

	Rates	Fringes
IRONWORKERS:		
Ornamental, Structural,		
and Reinforcing	20.27	8.36

PLUM0019G 08/01/2001

	Rates	Fringes
PIPEFITTERS	24.25	6.36

SUUT2001A 10/07/1991

	Rates	Fringes
CARPENTERS	14.15	2.43
CEMENT MASONS	14.40	2.41
LABORERS:		
General laborer	10.41	2.64
Asphalt raker	12.40	2.81
Pipelayer	10.41	2.64
Flagger	7.05	1.60

FIGURE 8-1   continued

	Rates	Fringes
PLUMBERS	15.07	2.49
POWER EQUIPMENT OPERATORS:		
Asphalt screed	16.29	7.08
Backhoe	13.73	5.33
Bulldozer, all sizes	10.28	5.20
Cranes, all sizes	20.40	7.08
Loader, all sizes	15.03	7.08
Roller	15.99	7.08
Scraper	12.82	4.92
TRUCK DRIVERS:		
Dump Trucks—Water Level Capacity (Bottom, End, and Side), Including Dumpster Truck, Turnawagons, Turnarockers and Dumpcrete:		
8 cu. yds. and less than 14 cu. yds.	15.99	5.72
Water truck, single axle	15.99	5.72

TEAM0222A 07/01/1990

	Rates	Fringes
TRUCK DRIVERS:		
Dump Trucks—Water Level Capacity (Bottom, End, and Side), Including Dumpster Truck, Turnawagons, Turnarockers and Dumpcrete:		
14 cu yds. and less than 35 cu. yds.	16.69	6.52

WELDERS - Receive rate prescribed for craft performing operation to which welding is incidental.

==

Unlisted classifications needed for work not included within the scope of the classifications listed may be added after award only as provided in the labor standards contract clauses [(29 CFR 5.5(a)(1)(v))].

In the listing above, the "SU" designation means that rates listed under that identifier do not reflect collectively bargained wage and fringe benefit rates. Other designations indicate unions whose rates have been determined to be prevailing.

   WAGE DETERMINATION APPEALS PROCESS

1.) Has there been an initial decision in the matter? This can be:

(*continued*)

FIGURE 8-1   continued

* an existing published wage determination
* a survey underlying a wage determination
* a Wage and Hour Division letter setting forth a
  position on a wage determination matter
* a conformance (additional classification and rate)
  ruling

On survey related matters, initial contact, including requests
for summaries of surveys, should be with the Wage and Hour
Regional Office for the area in which the survey was conducted
because those Regional Offices have responsibility for the
Davis–Bacon survey program. If the response from this initial
contact is not satisfactory, then the process described in 2.)
and 3.) should be followed.

With regard to any other matter not yet ripe for the formal
process described here, initial contact should be with the Branch
of Construction Wage Determinations. Write to:

> Branch of Construction Wage Determinations
> Wage and Hour Division
> U.S. Department of Labor
> 200 Constitution Avenue, N.W.
> Washington, D.C. 20210

2.) If the answer to the question in 1.) is yes, then an
interested party (those affected by the action) can request
review and reconsideration from the Wage and Hour Administrator
(see 29 CFR Part 1.8 and 29 CFR Part 7). Write to:

> Wage and Hour Administrator
> U.S. Department of Labor
> 200 Constitution Avenue, N.W.
> Washington, D.C. 20210

The request should be accompanied by a full statement of the
interested party's position and by any information (wage payment
data, project description, area practice material, etc.) that the
requestor considers relevant to the issue.

3.) If the decision of the Administrator is not favorable, an
interested party may appeal directly to the Administrative Review
Board (formerly the Wage Appeals Board). Write to:

> Administrative Review Board
> U.S. Department of Labor
> 200 Constitution Avenue, N.W.
> Washington, D.C. 20210

4.) All decisions by the Administrative Review Board are final.
                END OF GENERAL DECISION

Example 8-1: The secretary for your company makes $8.50 per hour and last year was paid for an average of 45 hours per week. The secretary is expected to work the same number of hours this year. Time-and-a-half is paid on any work over 40 hours per week. In the past the secretary has received a $200 Christmas bonus. Determine the average wages paid to the secretary during a one-year period.

Solution: The secretary will be paid $8.50 per hour for the first 40 hours each week and $12.75 ($8.50 × 1.5) per hour for the remaining 5 hours (45 − 40) for 52 weeks. The wages are calculated as follows:

$$\text{Wages} = 52 \text{ weeks/year}[\$8.50/\text{hr} (40 \text{ hr/week})$$
$$+ \$12.75/\text{hr} (5 \text{ hr/week})] + \$200/\text{year}$$
$$\text{Wages} = \$21{,}195/\text{year}$$

The second group includes all employees who are paid a flat rate per pay period and are known as salaried employees. To estimate the wages for salaried employees you need not know how many hours each employee works. The total wages for an employee or group of employees is calculated by summing the salaries of the employees and adding any anticipated bonuses.

Burden includes all payroll taxes, unemployment insurance, workers' compensation insurance, general liability insurance, and fringe benefits or their cash equivalent paid for by the employer. Let's look at how labor burden is calculated.

Cash Equivalents and Allowances

Cash equivalents and allowances include cash paid in lieu of providing fringe benefits or cash paid as an allowance. In some cases where a company is required to provide fringe benefits, it may be allowed to pay the cash equivalent of those benefits. Allowances are used to help the employee cover out-of-pocket associated job expenses. For example, a company located in an out-of-the-way place or a company that requires its employees to use their personal vehicles during work hours may pay the employees a vehicle allowance. An allowance differs from reimbursing the employees for expenses or mileage because it is not based on the actual cost or mileage. Reimbursements are not considered part of the labor wages and burden but are costs that can be billed to the appropriate general overhead budget category. For example, mileage reimbursement is part of the Car and Truck Expense line item.

Cash equivalents and allowances are treated as regular wages for the purpose of payroll taxes, unemployment insurance, workers' compensation insurance, and general liability insurance.

Example 8-2: The secretary in Example 8-1 is paid a $100 per month vehicle allowance to cover use of a personal vehicle for company business. Determine the annual wages, including allowances paid to the secretary, during a one-year period.

Solution: From Example 8-1, the secretary is paid $20,995 plus allowances. The wages with allowances are calculated as follows:

$$\text{Allowances} = \$100/\text{month}(12\,\text{month/year}) = \$1{,}200/\text{year}$$
$$\text{Wages and Allowances} = \$21{,}195/\text{year} + \$1{,}200/\text{year}$$
$$\text{Wages and Allowances} = \$22{,}395/\text{year}$$

PAYROLL TAXES

The Federal Insurance Contributions Act (FICA) requires employers to pay social security and Medicare taxes for each employee. For the year 2002, the employer pays a social security tax of 6.2% of each employee's first $84,900 in wages.[25] Although the tax rate has not changed for many years, the amount of wages on which social security is paid increases yearly. Be sure to check with your tax advisor or the Internal Revenue Service for the current rates. For the year 2002, the employer pays a Medicare tax of 1.45% of the employee's entire wages.[26] The employee is required to match these payments. The social security and Medicare taxes paid by the employee are deducted from his or her wages and are not a cost to the employer. Cash equivalents and allowances must be included when calculating these taxes; however, in some cases the amount the employee pays for benefits may be excluded.

Example 8-3: Determine the social security and Medicare taxes paid by the employer during the 2002 year for the secretary in Example 8-2. The secretary pays $150 per month for health insurance, which is not subject to social security and Medicare taxes.

Solution: The wages used in calculating the social security and Medicare tax must include the allowances paid to the secretary. From Example 8-2 the annual wages, including allowances, for the secretary are $22,395. This may be reduced by the $1,800 ($150/month $\times$ 12 months) per year the secretary pays for health insurance. The secretary's wages that are subject to social security and Medicare taxes are $20,595 ($22,395 − $1,800). Because the secretary's wages are less than $84,900, the employer must pay 6.2% for social security tax on the secretary's entire wages. The social security taxes are calculated as follows:

$$\text{Social Security Tax} = 0.062(\$20{,}595/\text{year}) = \$1{,}276.89/\text{year}$$

The Medicare tax is 1.45% of the secretary's wages and is calculated as follows:

$$\text{Medicare Tax} = 0.0145(\$20{,}595/\text{year}) = \$298.62/\text{year}$$

---

[25]See IRS, *Circular E, Employer's Tax Guide,* Publication 15, p. 1.

[26]See IRS, *Circular E, Employer's Tax Guide,* Publication 15, p. 1.

The secretary will have these same amounts deducted from his or her paycheck. The government will receive $2,553.78 ($1,276.89 × 2) per year in social security taxes and $597.24 ($298.62 × 2) per year in Medicare taxes because of the secretary's employment.

Example 8-4: Determine the social security and Medicare taxes paid during the year 2002 on a general manager whose annual wages are $125,000.

Solution: Because the general manager's wages are more than $84,900, the employer must pay 6.2% on $84,900 for social security tax. The social security taxes are calculated as follows:

$$\text{Social Security Tax} = 0.062(\$84,900/\text{year}) = \$5,263.80/\text{year}$$

The Medicare tax is 1.45% of the general manager's wages and is calculated as follows:

$$\text{Medicare Tax} = 0.0145(\$125,000/\text{year}) = \$1,812.50/\text{year}$$

The general manager will have these same amounts deducted from his or her paycheck.

UNEMPLOYMENT INSURANCE

By law, employers are required to pay federal unemployment tax (FUTA) and state unemployment tax (SUTA) if a state program exists.

For the year 2002 the federal unemployment tax rate was 6.2% on the first $7,000 of each employee's wages paid during the year.[27] When a company pays into a state unemployment program, a company may be eligible for a credit of up to 5.4%. To receive the entire 5.4% a company must pay its state unemployment tax on time and the maximum state rate to any company must be at least 5.4%.[28] When eligible for the full credit, the federal unemployment tax rate for a company is reduced to 0.8% of the first $7,000 of each employee's wages paid during the year.

A company's state unemployment tax rate is based in part on its claims history and must be obtained from the state agency that administers the state unemployment tax. The maximum rate a state charges and the amount of the employees' wages that are subject to tax vary from state to state. For example, for the year 2002, Texas' minimum rate was 0.30% and the maximum rate was 6.54%, and companies paid these rates on the first $9,000 of each employee's wages paid during the year. Arizona's minimum rate was 0.05% and the maximum rate was 5.40%, and companies paid these rates on the first $7,000 of each employee's

---

[27]See IRS, *Circular E, Employer's Tax Guide*, Publication 15, p. 27.

[28]See *Federal Unemployment Tax Act*, Title 26, Chapter 23, Section 3302.

wages paid during the year. Utah's minimum rate was 0.10% and the maximum rate was 8.1%, and companies paid these rates on the first $22,000 of each employee's wages paid during the year.

Example 8-5: Determine the state unemployment and federal unemployment taxes paid by the employer during the 2002 year for the secretary in Example 8-2. The company's state unemployment rate is 2.0% on the first $9,000 and the state's maximum rate exceeds 5.40%. All state unemployment taxes were paid on time.

Solution: The wages used in calculating the unemployment taxes must include the allowances paid to the secretary. From Example 8-2 the annual wages, including allowances, for the secretary are $22,395. Because the secretary's wages are more than $9,000, the employer must pay 2.0% on $9,000 for state unemployment tax. The state unemployment tax is calculated as follows:

$$SUTA = 0.02(\$9,000/year) = \$180.00/year$$

Because the company paid its state unemployment on time and the state rate exceeds 5.4% the company may take the entire 5.4% credit, thus reducing the federal unemployment rate to 0.8% on the first $7,000. The federal unemployment tax is calculated as follows:

$$FUTA = 0.008(\$7,000/year) = \$56.00/year$$

The total unemployment tax paid is $236.00 ($180.00 + $56.00). The underlying assumption in these calculations is that the same person fills the secretary position for the entire year.

Example 8-6: The secretary in Example 8-5 was replaced during the year. The first secretary was paid $18,095 and the replacement secretary was paid $4,100. Determine the state unemployment and federal unemployment taxes paid by the employer during the 2002 year for the secretary position. The company's state unemployment rate is 2.0% on the first $9,000 and the state's maximum rate exceeds 5.40%. All state unemployment taxes were paid on time.

Solution: Because the first secretary's wages are more than $9,000, the employer must pay 2.0% on $9,000 for state unemployment tax. The state unemployment tax for the first secretary is calculated as follows:

$$SUTA_1 = 0.02(\$9,000/year) = \$180.00/year$$

Because the replacement secretary's wages are less than $9,000, the employer must pay 2.0% on the wages paid ($4,100) to the replacement secretary for state unemployment tax. The state unemployment tax for the replacement secretary is calculated as follows:

$$SUTA_R = 0.02(\$4,100/year) = \$82.00/year$$

The total state unemployment tax paid for the secretarial position is $262.00 ($180.00 + $82.00) per year.

Because the company paid its state unemployment on time and the state rate exceeds 5.4% the company may take the entire 5.4% credit, thus reducing the federal unemployment rate to 0.8% on the first $7,000 for each employee. The federal unemployment tax for the first secretary is calculated as follows:

$$FUTA_1 = 0.008(\$7,000/year) = \$56.00/year$$

The federal unemployment tax for the replacement secretary is calculated as follows:

$$FUTA_R = 0.008(\$4,100/year) = \$32.80/year$$

The total federal unemployment tax paid for the secretarial position is $88.80 ($56.00 + $32.80) per year.

The total unemployment tax paid for the secretary's position is $350.80 ($262.00 + $88.80) per year. The increase of $114.80 ($350.80 − $236.00) is due to turnover in the secretarial position.

WORKERS' COMPENSATION INSURANCE

By law all employers are required to provide their employees with workers' compensation insurance. Workers' compensation insurance is governed by the individual states and requirements may vary from state to state.

Workers' compensation insurance covers reasonable medical costs as well as some of the lost wages for employees who are injured on the job or who contract an occupational illness. For employees who are killed on the job, workers' compensation insurance may pay part of the burial expense and may provide surviving family members a weekly or monthly benefit.

The cost of the insurance is to be paid entirely by the employer. The premium is based on the gross payroll, the type of work performed by the employees, the company's accident history, and other factors. Employees are grouped into a standard set of classifications set by the National Council on Compensation Insurance (NCCI) based on the type of work they do. The NCCI sets a standard Lost Cost Factor for each job classification, which is modified by the individual states to take into account local variances in losses and regulations. The premium rate is based on the lost cost factor and is expressed in dollars per $100 of payroll.

The premium rate may be modified by an experience modifier, which is done by multiplying the premium rate by the experience modifier. Experience modifiers are calculated by NCCI and reflect the relationship between the company's actual losses and the expected losses for similar companies. An experience modifier greater than one indicates that a company had higher than expected losses, whereas an experience modifier of less than one indicates that a company had lower than expected losses. The experience modifiers are based on the past three years' losses not including the most recent policy year. For example, the experience modifier for the year 2005 would be based on the years 2001, 2002, and 2003. For companies to receive an experience modification they must meet a minimum level of premiums, thus companies with small payrolls are often not given experience modifiers. Experience modifiers may be as low as 0.6 and as high as 2.0.

The workers' compensation insurance premiums may also be adjusted based on the safety practices of the company. Other discounts may be offered for such items as policy size.

Throughout the year, companies pay workers' compensation insurance premiums based on the estimated payroll. At the end of the year or more frequently, the insurance carrier will audit the payroll of the company and make adjustments in the premiums to reflect the actual payroll. It is important to note that this is an adjustment in the total premium, not the premium rate.

Example 8-7:   Determine the cost of workers' compensation insurance for the secretary in Example 8-2. The company's workers' compensation insurance rate for office personnel is $1.24 per $100.00 in wages.

Solution: The wages used in calculating the workers' compensation insurance must include the allowances paid the secretary. From Example 8-2 the annual wages, including allowances, for the secretary are $22,395. The workers' compensation insurance cost is calculated as follows:

$$\text{Workers' Compensation} = (\$1.24/\$100)(\$22,395/\text{year})$$
$$\text{Workers' Compensation} = \$277.70/\text{year}$$

GENERAL LIABILITY INSURANCE

General liability insurance protects the company against claims due to negligent business activities and failure to use reasonable care. The types of claims include bodily injury, property damage or loss, and other personal injury such as slander or damage to reputation. Like workers' compensation insurance, the cost of the insurance is based on gross revenues by workers' class.

Throughout the year, companies pay general liability insurance premiums based on the estimated payroll. At the end of the year or more frequently, the insurance carrier will audit the payroll of the company and make adjustments in the premiums to reflect the actual payroll.

Example 8-8:   Determine the cost of general liability insurance for the secretary in Example 8-2. The company's general liability insurance rate for office personnel is 0.51% of wages.

Solution: The wages used in calculating the general liability insurance must include the allowances paid to the secretary. From Example 8-2 the annual wages, including allowances, for the secretary are $22,395. The general liability insurance cost is calculated as follows:

$$\text{Liability Insurance} = 0.0051(\$22,395/\text{year}) = \$114.21/\text{year}$$

INSURANCE BENEFITS

As part of the employee benefit package, the employer may provide health, dental, life, and disability insurance for which employees and their families are beneficiaries. The employer may pay the entire cost of the benefits, split the cost with employees, or require employees to pay the entire amount. The amount the employees pay is deducted from their wages and does not represent a cost to the employer. The part of the costs that is paid by the employer is a real cost to the employer and needs to be included in the cost of the benefits.

Example 8-9: Determine the cost of health insurance for the secretary in Example 8-2. The company pays $100 per month toward health insurance for its employees. An additional $250 is deducted from the employee's paycheck.

Solution: The cost of the health insurance only includes those costs paid by the employer and is calculated as follows:

$$\text{Health Insurance} = \$100/\text{month}(12\,\text{month/year}) = \$1,200.00/\text{year}$$

RETIREMENT

As part of the employee benefit package, the employer may provide a traditional pension plan, pay funds to a union to provide pension benefits, or participate in a profit-sharing plan such as a 401(k). Like insurance benefits, the employer may pay all, part, or none of the cost of the retirement. The amount the employees pay are deducted from their wages and do not represent a cost to the employer. The part of the cost that is paid by the employer is a real cost to the employer and needs to be included in the cost of the benefits.

Example 8-10: Determine the cost of retirement for the secretary in Example 8-2. For retirement the company has provided the employee with access to a 401(k) plan and matches the employee's contributions to the plan at a rate of $0.50 per $1.00 contributed by the employee on the first 6% of the employee's wages—including allowances—for a maximum matching contribution of 3% of the employee's wages. The secretary is expected to make a wage contribution of at least 6% to the 401(k) plan.

Solution: From Example 8-2 the annual wages, including allowances, for the secretary are $22,395. The cost of retirement is calculated as follows:

$$\text{Retirement} = (\$0.50/\$1.00)0.06(\$22,395/\text{year}) = \$671.85/\text{year}$$

UNION PAYMENTS

Employee unions often require the employer to make payments directly to the union which are used to provide benefits and training for union employees. Payments to unions are governed by the contract between the company and the union. Union costs paid by the employer should be included in the cost of the benefits. Unions may also require the employer to deduct union dues from the employees' paycheck. The amounts the employees pay do not represent a cost to the employer and should not be included in the cost of the benefits.

OTHER BENEFITS

The employer may provide other benefits not covered in one of the categories mentioned earlier. Where possible the costs of these benefits should be included.

The total cost of the employee's burden may be determined by summing the individual burden items. The total cost may then be divided by the wages paid to the employee to get the burden markup. For an hourly employee, the average hourly cost may be determined by dividing the total cost of the employee during the period by the number of hours worked during the period.

Example 8-11: Determine annual cost, average hourly cost, and the burden markup for the secretary in Example 8-1 using Examples 8-2, 8-3, 8-5, 8-7, 8-8, 8-9, and 8-10. Assume the same person fills the secretary position during the entire year. The secretary is given 15 days off in the form of vacation, sick leave, and holidays.

Solution: From Examples 8-1, 8-2, 8-3, 8-5, 8-7, 8-8, 8-9, and 8-10 we calculated the following costs:

Wages = $21,195/year
Allowances = $1,200/year
Social Security Tax = $1,277/year
Medicare Tax = $299/year
SUTA = $180/year
FUTA = $56/year
Workers' Compensation = $278/year
Liability Insurance = $114/year

Health Insurance = $1,200/year

Retirement = $672/year

The total cost of burden is $5,276 (1,200 + $1,277 + $299 + $180 + $56 + $278 + $114 + $1,200 + $672) per year. The annual cost of the secretary is $26,471 ($21,195 + $5,276) per year.

Next we must find the number of hours the secretary works during the year, taking into account the time the secretary is given off for vacation, sick leave, and holidays. The secretary will be paid for eight hours per day when using vacation, holiday, and sick leave. The number of hours worked is calculated as follows:

$$\text{Hours Worked} = 45 \text{ hour/week}(52 \text{ weeks/year})$$
$$- 15 \text{ days}(8 \text{ hours/day})$$
$$\text{Hours Worked} = 2,220 \text{ hours}$$

The hourly cost is calculated as follows:

$$\text{Hourly Costs} = \text{Total Cost/Hours Worked}$$
$$\text{Hourly Costs} = (\$26,471/\text{year})/2,220 \text{ hours} = \$11.92$$

The burden markup is calculated by taking the total cost of the employee and dividing it by the wages paid for work performed and subtracting 1. The work performed equals the wages paid to the employee less the wages paid for time off. This allows us to include the cost of vacation, holidays, and sick leave in the markup. The wages in Example 8-1 must be reduced by $1,020 (15 days $\times$ 8 hours/day $\times$ $8.50/hour) for time off. The burden markup is calculated as follows:

$$\text{Burden Markup} = \text{Total Cost}/(\text{Wages}_{\text{Total}} - \text{Wages}_{\text{Time Off}}) - 1$$
$$\text{Burden Markup} = (\$26,471/\text{year})/(\$21,195/\text{year}$$
$$- \$1,020/\text{year}) - 1$$
$$\text{Burden Markup} = 0.312 \text{ or } 31.2\%$$

It is important to note that we cannot take the base hourly rate of $8.50 and add the burden markup to get the hourly cost because for five hours a week the secretary is earning 1.5 times the base rate. The overtime rate is not included in the burden markup.

CONCLUSION

When projecting costs that include labor it is important to include all of the costs associated with employees. The cost of employees includes their wages and the associated labor burden. Employees' wages may be determined by market rates, union contracts, or Federal Davis–Bacon wages decisions. Labor burden includes cash equivalents and allowances paid to the employees, payroll taxes, unemployment insurance, workers' compensation insurance, general liability insurance, insurance benefits, retirement, union payments, and other benefits.

PROBLEMS

1. Determine the annual cost, average hourly cost, and burden markup of an hourly employee given the following information. Assume the employee takes full advantage of the 401(k) benefit. The employee gets 10 days off per year in the form of vacation, sick leave, and holidays. The employee's health insurance is paid for entirely by the employer.

ITEM	COST
Wages	$12/hr for 42 hrs/week
Bonus	$500
Allowances	None
Social Security	6.2% of wages to $84,900
Medicare	1.45% of wages
FUTA	0.8% of wages to $7,000
SUTA	2.0% of wages to $20,000
Workers' Comp.	$0.85 per $100 of wages
General Liability	0.65% of wages
401(k)	50% match up to 6% of wages
Health Insurance	$200/month

2. Determine the annual cost, monthly cost, and burden markup for a salaried employee given the following information. Assume the employee takes full advantage of the 401(k) benefit.

ITEM	COST
Wages	$80,000
Bonus	$10,000
Allowances	$500 per month for vehicle
Social Security	6.2% of wages to $84,900
Medicare	1.45% of wages
FUTA	0.8% of wages to $7,000
SUTA	3.0% of wages to $7,000
Workers' Comp.	$4.25 per $100 of wages
General Liability	1.02% of wages
401(k)	100% match up to 6% of wages
Health Insurance	$175/month

3. Set up a worksheet to calculate the annual cost, average hourly cost, and the burden markup of an hourly employee. The spreadsheet should allow you to enter the hourly wages, the average number of hours paid for each week, number of days off per year, annual bonus ($/year), monthly allowances ($/month), the amount of employee expenses that are not subject to social security and Medicare taxes, social security percentage rate and limit, Medicare percentage rate, FUTA percentage rate and limit, SUTA percentage rate and limit, workers' compensation insurance rate ($/$100), general liability percentage rate, 401(k) matching rate and limit, monthly health insurance payment, monthly union payments, and other monthly benefits. Assume the employee takes full advantage of the 401(k) benefit. Check your answer against Example 8-11.

4. Set up a worksheet to calculate the annual cost, the monthly cost, and the burden markup of a salaried employee. The spreadsheet should allow you to enter the annual salary, annual bonus ($/year), monthly allowances ($/month), the amount of employee expenses that are not subject to social security and Medicare taxes, social security percentage rate and limit, Medicare percentage rate, FUTA percentage rate and limit, SUTA percentage rate and limit, workers' compensation insurance rate ($/$100), general liability percentage rate, 401(k) matching rate and limit, monthly health insurance payment, monthly union payments, and other monthly benefits. Assume the employee takes full advantage of the 401(k) benefit. Check your answer against Problem 2.

MANAGING GENERAL OVERHEAD COSTS

In this chapter you will learn how to prepare a general overhead budget that is used to track overhead costs. It is easy for a company to squander its profits by failing to control general overhead costs. Construction managers often spend enormous amounts of time and effort budgeting, tracking, and controlling construction costs while ignoring general overhead costs. Just as a project manager or superintendent tracks and manages construction costs on a project, the general manager or owner needs to track and manage the general overhead costs. The key to doing this is to set and follow a general overhead budget. A general overhead budget is also needed to prepare the company's annual cash flow projection, which is discussed in chapter 14.

It is not uncommon for a construction company to spend 10 to 25% of its revenues on general overhead while retaining less than 5% of its revenues as profit. In chapter 6 we saw that the average commercial construction company spent 83% of its revenues on direct and indirect construction costs, leaving 17% to cover overhead, pay taxes, and provide a profit for the owners. With the average commercial construction company earning less than 5% profit before taxes, the difference of 12% is consumed as general overhead; in other words, over two-thirds of the gross profit from the jobs is used to pay for the general overhead. Because general overhead costs are a major expense to a construction company, construction managers should manage the general overhead costs just as they would direct and indirect construction costs.

WHAT IS GENERAL OVERHEAD?

General overhead consists of those costs that cannot be specifically identified to the completion of a construction project. General overhead may also be referred to as indirect costs. General overhead includes all main office and supervisory costs that cannot be billed to a specific construction project. General overhead costs are controlled on a companywide basis. The responsibility for controlling these costs falls on the owner of the construction company or the company's general manager.

When preparing bids for construction projects all direct costs and project overhead should be included as line item costs in the bid or project's budget. The budget for these costs can then be monitored and tracked during the course of the project. With computerized accounting systems it is easy to bill materials, equipment, and labor—including burden—costs to specific construction projects. Each bid should include a markup for profit and overhead. This markup is used to cover the general overhead for the construction company and provide the company with a profit. The profit and overhead markup should not be used to cover project overhead costs. The profit and overhead markup is discussed in chapter 10.

The difference between a project overhead and general overhead may vary from project to project based on what is billable to the project's owner under the construction contract with the owner. For example, one contract may specifically allow the construction company to bill the cost of the project manager to the project, whereas another may specifically prohibit it and require that the project manager be paid out of the profit and overhead markup. This is very important to the construction company that is engaged in a cost-plus contract. If the project manager is included as part of the project overhead, the construction company can be reimbursed for the costs of the project manager by billing the cost of the project manager to the project. Whereas if the project manager is considered part of the general overhead, the construction company must pay the cost of the project manager out of the profit and overhead markup for the project. The profit and overhead markup is the source of the gross profit discussed in earlier chapters.

THE GENERAL OVERHEAD BUDGET

Because both profit and general overhead come out of the gross profit, the smaller the overhead costs, the greater the profit. To control these costs, a budget should be prepared for the general overhead and the general overhead costs should be tracked, just as one prepares budgets for and tracks direct and indirect construction costs for each project. The general overhead budget is a plan of all expenditures for the company that cannot be billed to a construction project. The general overhead budget should be used when making day-to-day decisions that involve the expenditure of company funds. The preparation and use of a general overhead budget helps to control general overhead costs and thereby increase profits.

Experience has shown that companies that use sound budgeting principles to manage their general overhead are more profitable than companies that do not. Use of a general overhead budget requires daily vigilance, vigilance that many construction companies fail to exercise.

General overhead budgets may be prepared for two specific reasons: projection of cash needs and projection of profits. The difference in these two general overhead budgets is in how we handle capital costs and loans.

When preparing a general overhead budget for projection of the company's cash needs, we want to include the actual cash flows for all capital assets and loans. For example, if a company purchased a $25,000 truck for use by the general manager and paid cash for the truck, the company would see a cash expenditure of $25,000 during the budgetary period and the company would have to have sufficient cash to cover this expenditure. If the company were to purchase this same truck with a five-year loan, the expenditure for the truck would be spread out over five years and the required cash would be divided into sixty monthly payments instead of occurring in a single budgetary period. In this case, the goal is to project the actual cash flows so that management can make sure that the company has adequate cash to fund its overhead.

When preparing a general overhead budget for use in projecting a company's profit, a company needs to recognize that capital assets have a value that often extends beyond the period in which the cash flows associated with its purchase occur. For capital assets, the cost of producing the revenues that result in profits is not the cash flow associated with the capital asset but the loss in value of the asset. This loss in value is known as depreciation. Rather than including the cash flow associated with the capital asset in the budget, the budget must include the depreciation of the asset. In the case of the aforementioned truck, the truck will be consumed or depreciated at the same rate regardless of whether it was purchased outright or purchased through a loan. Additionally, the only portion of a loan payment that would be included in the budget is the portion that goes toward paying the interest. The payment of the principal is just using an asset (cash) to reduce a liability (loan balance). In chapter 10 we use this type of general overhead budget to analyze the relationship among the volume of work, the profit margin, and the general overhead.

ITEMS TO INCLUDE IN THE GENERAL OVERHEAD BUDGET

Like a project budget, the general overhead budget should be broken down into a number of categories. There are three things to keep in mind when deciding what details to include in the general overhead budget. First, the budget should have enough detail to allow management to track and manage costs. If the general overhead budget lacks sufficient details it is difficult to know where the money is being spent and to identify what expenses management needs to watch more carefully to better control costs. Second, the budget should not have so much detail that management spends a lot of extra time and effort tracking costs or gives up trying to track costs because it is too difficult. Often it is not worth the effort to bill out office employees to different budget line items according to the task they are doing at the moment. Office labor costs are often combined into a single budgetary category. For example, if management is going to budget $500 of office labor to prepare a direct mail advertisement, management needs to be able to track these costs and bill them against the budget for advertising. If management is not going to track and bill these costs to the advertising budget then these costs should be lumped together with other office employees' expenses. Third, the budget needs to provide the information necessary to prepare financial statements and income tax returns. For income tax purposes, meals and entertainment are treated differently from other general overhead expenses and as a result should be tracked separately so that the information is readily available. It is a good idea to include a company's tax advisor in the selection of general overhead categories.

The categories included in a general overhead budget will vary from company to company. Small companies often have much simpler general overhead budgets than larger companies. The following is a list of items that could be included in a general overhead budget:

Advertising: Advertising includes all costs to market the construction company through printed materials, such as trade journals and newspapers, and direct mail. These costs should include the design and preparation of advertising materials, printing, postage, and the cost of ad space. It may also include signage for trucks and projects. When project signage is specific to a single project, it should be billed to the project rather than to the general overhead. Advertising for employees should be included in the Employee Recruiting line item.

Bad Debts: Bad debts include the writing off of bad debts. For companies that do a lot of one-time work for many different owners—such as an HVAC construction company that does residential system replacements and services—the budget cost for this category could be a significant amount. The cost of lawyers and collection agencies used in the collection process is included in the Legal and Professional Services line item.

Bank Fees: Bank fees include all fees charged by the bank to provide banking services and include returned check fees.

Car and Truck Expenses: Car and truck expenses should include all vehicle costs associated with office and general management personnel. The car and truck expenses associated with employees working on the construction projects should not be included in the general overhead budget but should be billed to the construction projects. Car and truck expenses include taxes, insurance, parking, tires, fuel, maintenance, and repairs for the vehicles. When preparing a budget for use in projection of a company's cash requirements, car and truck expenses should include all lease payments, loan payments, and the purchase price of any vehicle that is purchased outright. When preparing a budget for the purpose of projecting profit, the lease payments, loan payments, and the purchase price are included in the Depreciation and the Interest Expense line items rather than in Car and Truck Expenses.

Charitable Contributions: Charitable contributions are any donations that are donated to a qualified organization. Qualified organizations include churches, nonprofit schools and hospitals, public parks and recreation facilities, and other nonprofit charitable organizations.[29] Charitable donations may be in the form of cash or property. For a construction company, the cost of labor and material donated to qualified charitable organizations to renovate office space may be deductible. Charitable contributions must be tracked separately because there may be limits to their tax deductibility.

Computer and Office Furniture: When preparing a budget for use in projection of a company's cash requirements, computer and office furniture should include all costs associated with the purchase or lease of personal property used in the main office. Computer and office furniture used at jobsites should be billed to the construction projects. When preparing a budget for the purpose of projecting profit, these costs are included in the Depreciation line item.

Depreciation: When preparing a budget for the purpose of projecting profit, depreciation includes the depreciation of vehicles, computer and office furniture, and the office building. When preparing a budget for use in projection of a company's cash requirements, depreciation is replaced with the actual cash flow resulting from the purchase of capital assets. The cash flows are placed on the appropriate budget line item and the depreciation line is zero.

Dues and Memberships: Dues and memberships include the fees paid to professional organizations, such as the Associated General Contractors and Associated Builders and Contractors.

Employee Wages and Salaries: Employee wages and salaries should include all wages and salaries paid to office and general management personnel. For hourly personnel, this should include any overtime at time-and-a-half or other required rate. Performance, Christmas, and other bonuses should be included in this item. Pay for sick leave and vacation may be included in employee wages and salaries or may be included as an employee benefit. For tax purposes, employee benefits and retirement should be budgeted and tracked separately. The wages for employees who work on construction projects should be billed to the project.

Employee Benefits: Employee benefits should include all "bona fide" fringe benefits paid to office and general management personnel except pension and profit-sharing plans. Benefits include life insurance, health

---

[29]See IRS, *Charitable Contributions,* Publication 526.

insurance, vacation, holidays, sick leave, and dependent care assistance programs. The cost of sick leave and vacation may be included in employee wages and salaries rather than employee benefits. Matching costs paid by the employee should not be included in this line item because they are deducted from the employees' wages, which are included in the Employee Wage and Salaries line item. The costs of employee pensions and profit-sharing programs should be budgeted and tracked separately for tax purposes. The benefits for employees who work on construction projects should be billed to the project, which can be easily accomplished with many construction accounting systems.

Employee Retirement: Employee retirement should include all costs associated with providing pensions and profit-sharing plans—401(k) plans—to office and general management personnel. This should not include any funds paid by the employees into retirement accounts because they are deducted from the employees' wages. Pension and profit-sharing plans for employees who work on construction projects should be billed to the project, which can be easily accomplished with many construction accounting systems.

Employee Recruiting: Typical employee recruiting costs include the cost of newspaper and other advertising to find employees and hiring personnel agencies and other costs incurred during the hiring process. Meals and travel associated with the hiring process should be budgeted under the Meals and Entertainment and the Travel line items, respectively.

Employee Training: Employee training should include the cost of seminars and classes used to improve the employees' skills. Meals and travel associated with the training should be budgeted under the Meals and Entertainment line item and Travel line item, respectively.

Employee Taxes: Employee taxes should include all taxes paid by the employer for office and general management personnel. The taxes include social security, Medicare, state unemployment tax (SUTA), and federal unemployment tax (FUTA). This should not include social security, Medicare, federal withholding, and state withholding taxes paid by employees because they are deducted from the employee's wages. Employee taxes for employees who work on construction projects should be billed to the project, which can be easily accomplished with many construction accounting systems.

Insurance: Insurance includes general liability insurance, key man life insurance policies (life insurance on key employees where the company is the beneficiary), workers' compensation insurance, and other insurance not covered elsewhere. Vehicle insurance should be included in the Car and Truck Expense line item and insurance provided as an employee benefit should be included in Employee Benefits line item.

Interest Expense: When preparing a budget for the purpose of projecting profit, interest expense includes the interest on loans. When preparing a budget for use in projection of a company's cash requirements, interest expense is replaced with the actual cash flow resulting from the purchase of capital assets. The cash flows are placed on the appropriate budget line item and the interest expense line is zero.

Janitorial and Cleaning: Janitorial and cleaning include the cost of regular cleaning services. It also includes the occasional cleaning of the carpets and other infrequent cleaning costs.

Legal and Professional Services: Legal and professional services include the cost of legal services used in the set up of the company, collection of bills, review of contracts, dealing with lien rights, and other legal matters. It also includes professional accounting services used in the preparations of financial statements, preparations of taxes, set up and review of accounting systems, and bookkeeping services. It also can include fees paid to professional engineers and architects that cannot be billed to a construction project.

Meals and Entertainment: Meals and entertainment must be tracked separately because it is only partially deductible for tax purposes. If your company pays for meals and entertainment that is not deductible for tax purposes, you may want to divide this line item into two groups, one for partially deductible meals and entertainment and one for nondeductible meals and entertainment. Meals that are partially deductible may include meals that are associated with business and are consumed in the presence of a company employee.[30]

Office Supplies: Office supplies include consumable supplies used by office and general management personnel, such as paper, printer cartridges, pens, and so forth. Office supplies used by employees working on construction projects should not be included in the general overhead budget but should be billed to the construction projects.

Office Purchases: When preparing a budget for use in projection of a company's cash requirements, office purchases should include all loan payments and the purchase price of any office space that is purchased outright. When preparing a budget for the purpose of projecting profit, these costs are included in the Depreciation and Interest Expense line items. Real-property office space—for example, a nearby office building or home—that is obtained, used, and disposed of for a single construction project should be billed to the construction project. Personal property office space—for example, a trailer—used on construction projects should be billed to the construction project in the same way that equipment is billed to the project.

Office Rent: Office rent should include the cost of all rented office space, except office space that is obtained for a single construction project, which should be billed to the construction projects.

---

[30]See IRS, *1040 Instructions for Schedule C—Profit or Loss From Business,* 2001, p. C-5.

Office Utilities: Office utilities include water, sewer, natural gas, electricity, garbage collection, and other utility costs associated with the main office or that cannot be billed to a construction project. The cost of telephone services is included in the Telephone line item.

Postage and Delivery: Postage and delivery include the cost of postage, overnight mail, and other delivery services that are not billed to a construction project. Where appropriate these costs should be billed to a construction project.

Promotion: Promotion includes items given away to promote the company, such as hats, shirts, and cups printed with the company's name and logo.

Publications and Subscriptions: Publications and subscriptions include the cost of trade magazines and newspapers used to keep the company's staff up-to-date with respect to potential projects and with other changes in the industry. This also includes newspapers and publications used in the waiting area.

Repairs and Maintenance: Repairs and maintenance include the cost of maintaining office facilities and the associated capital equipment—computers and furnishings—covered under the general overhead budget. The cost of vehicle maintenance is included in the Car and Truck Expense line item.

Taxes and Licenses: Taxes and licenses include property taxes, business licenses, and other government-mandated permits required to operate a business.

Telephone: Telephone includes the cost of telephone services, long-distance services, mobile phones, and radios that are not billed to a construction project.

Travel: Travel includes the cost of lodging and transportation for office and general management personnel while they are away from the office. It includes the costs associated with rental cars and mileage reimbursement but does not include the costs associated with company-owned vehicles inasmuch as their costs are included in the Car and Truck Expense line item.

Unallocated Labor: Unallocated labor includes the costs of employees who normally work on a construction project but are not billable to a construction project.

Unallocated Materials: Unallocated materials include the costs of materials that are purchased for construction projects but are not billable to a construction project. This includes inventory shrinkage.

Miscellaneous: Miscellaneous includes all costs not included elsewhere. This line item should be used for infrequent or unusual costs; otherwise, a new cost category should be set up for the costs.

After preparing a budget, a list of what is included in each budget line item should be prepared to help make sure that the costs are billed to the appropriate budget line item. Failure to be consistent during the budget and billing processes quickly renders the budget useless as a management tool.

ESTIMATING GENERAL OVERHEAD

Estimating general overhead requires management to project today what expenses are going to occur in the future. The best sources of data for future costs are historical costs; however, these costs must be adjusted to take into account the uniqueness of each year's financial objectives. For example, if the company is going to expand its business next year, the general overhead budget needs to be adjusted to take into account the expansion of the business. The general overhead budget should be compatible with the company's goals or it is useless. The projected costs should also be adjusted for inflation and changes in the market. For example, if the trend in the market is to provide employees with health insurance—which a company has not provided in the past—it may need to add the cost of health insurance into its budget to remain competitive with the market and retain its employees. Alternately, if the company has paid for its employees' health insurance it would need to increase the budget line item for health insurance to reflect the increasing cost of health insurance. Historical costs are easily obtained from past accounting reports.

> **Example 9-1:** Determine the annual budget for office utilities using the data from the past twelve months shown in Figure 9-1. Utility costs are expected to increase by 5% per year due to inflation. None of the company's goals are expected to affect the utility costs.

> **Solution:** The total cost of utilities for the past twelve months was $1,745.59. Increasing this by 5% we get $1,833. For budgetary purposes we round this to $1,850.

To accurately project and control costs, the general overhead budget must be estimated line by line. By doing this managers are forced to look at each line item and estimate how their goals, the market conditions, and inflation affect each line item. This results in a more accurate budget, which makes tracking the budget more meaningful. Additionally, this process forces the manager to look at how each of the company's goals affect the day-to-day operations of the company and helps the manager clarify what is required to achieve each of the goals. For example, if the company is going to expand its business, will this require the company to increase its office support staff and as a result increase its office space requirements? This also allows the manager to identify the costs associated with each goal and allows the manager to determine if the goal is worth the cost. For example, if the company needs to move its office to a new building to accommodate the increase in office staff that is necessary to support the goal of expansion, when preparing the general overhead budget the manager has the

```
12/14/04                                                              Page 1


                               EXPENSE REPORT


  From 12/1/03 to 11/30/04


    Ck Num        Date        Payee             Account           Amount
     5068       01/14/04    Gas Company       Office Utilities     137.18
     5069       01/14/04    Power Company     Office Utilities      66.44
     5079       02/13/04    Gas Company       Office Utilities     190.35
     5080       02/13/04    Power Company     Office Utilities      66.05
     5088       03/12/04    Gas Company       Office Utilities     162.82
     5089       03/12/04    Power Company     Office Utilities      66.47
     5099       04/09/04    Gas Company       Office Utilities     128.17
     5101       04/09/04    Power Company     Office Utilities      53.18
     5113       05/15/04    Power Company     Office Utilities      56.50
     5115       05/15/04    Gas Company       Office Utilities      96.71
     5123       06/09/04    Power Company     Office Utilities      48.54
     5124       06/09/04    Gas Company       Office Utilities      55.40
     5137       07/14/04    Power Company     Office Utilities      62.66
     5138       07/14/04    Gas Company       Office Utilities      46.44
     5147       08/06/04    Gas Company       Office Utilities      28.35
     5148       08/06/04    Power Company     Office Utilities      69.02
     5162       09/09/04    Power Company     Office Utilities      64.42
     5163       09/09/04    Gas Company       Office Utilities      31.24
     5179       10/16/04    Gas Company       Office Utilities      33.46
     5182       10/16/04    Power Company     Office Utilities      57.39
     5234       11/05/04    Gas Company       Office Utilities      39.48
     5235       11/05/04    Power Company     Office Utilities      51.02
     5244       12/10/04    Gas Company       Office Utilities      65.84
     5248       12/10/04    Power Company     Office Utilities      68.46
                                                                _____
                                                 Total            1,745.59
```

FIGURE 9-1   Past 12 Months' Costs

opportunity to determine if expansion of the business is worth the cost of relocating the business.

Many companies will benefit by breaking down the annual general overhead budget into monthly overhead budgets. This provides monthly milestones that the manager can measure performance against, rather than waiting until the end of the year. When preparing a monthly budget one cannot simply allocate the annual budget equally over twelve months because many of the costs occur quarterly or annually. For example, association dues are often only paid annually. If we allocated the annual budget for the dues paid to an association equally over twelve months, during the months prior to the payment of the dues there would be an excess of funds in the budget. However, starting with the month that the dues are paid the line item would be over budget for the remainder of the year.

TYPES OF COSTS

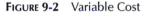

Overhead costs may be divided into three types of costs: variable costs, fixed costs, and mixed costs. Variable costs are those costs that tend to vary with the volume of work, which is most commonly expressed as a percentage of the revenues from construction projects. For example, for a residential remodeling construction company that pays its sales force a commission in the form of a percentage of sales, the commission paid to the sales force would be a variable cost. The relationship between cost and revenues for variable costs is shown in Figure 9-2.

Fixed costs are those costs that tend to be fixed over a specific range of revenues. For example, if a company currently has two salaried employees working as estimators, the cost of these employees is fixed over the volume of work that can be won by these employees. Another example of this is if a company currently has two office employees and rents office space that can accommodate three employees. The cost of office rent is fixed unless the volume of work increases such that the company needs to hire two more office employees. Here the office rent is fixed over the range of revenues that may be supported by three or less office employees. If the company rented an adjacent office to increase its office space to handle six employees because of an increase in the volume of work, the new cost of office rent would be fixed over the range of revenues that may be supported by

FIGURE 9-2   Variable Cost

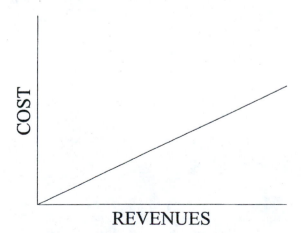

COST

REVENUES

FIGURE 9-3   Fixed Cost

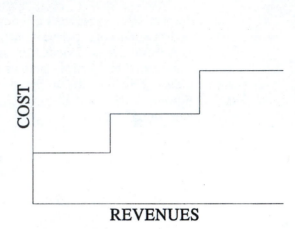

four to six employees. Hence, fixed costs increase in steps with each step representing the fixed cost for a range of revenues. The relationship between cost and
revenues for fixed costs is shown in Figure 9-3.

Mixed costs are costs that contain both a variable cost component and a
fixed cost component. For example, if a company paid its estimators a base salary
plus a bonus based on the volume of work won, the cost of the estimators is a
mixed cost. The salary is a fixed cost, whereas the bonus is a variable cost. The relationship between cost and revenues for mixed costs is shown in Figure 9-4.

Because variable and mixed costs vary with the volume of work and the fixed
costs are for a specific range of work volume, the general overhead budget must
be prepared for a specified volume of work. When the volume of work changes,
the general budget must be adjusted accordingly.

When multiple years of data are available trend analysis may be used to project future costs. Trend analysis involves determining the annual inflation rate (f)
and an initial cost that represents the growth of costs over the years represented
by the data using regression, with exponential regression being the most common.

FIGURE 9-4   Mixed Cost

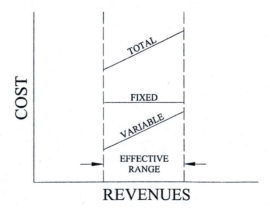

Exponential regression is used to determine the exponential curve that best fits the actual data. Appendix B discusses the procedures for performing trend analysis using exponential regression. Because the exponential curve does not necessarily pass through each point, the initial cost calculated by regression is often different than the initial cost from the actual data. Future costs may then be projected by using the following equation:

$$Cost_n = Cost_0(1 + f)^n \qquad\qquad (9\text{-}1)$$
$$Cost_0 = \text{Initial Cost}$$
$$f = \text{Annual Inflation Rate}$$

Example 9-2: Determine the projected costs for utilities in year 10. The inflation rate has been determined to be 0.193 (19.3%) and the initial cost is $1.013.

Solution: The expected cost in year 10 is calculated using Eq. (9-1) as follows:

$$Cost_n = \$1.013(1 + 0.193)^{10} = \$5.916$$

SAMPLE OF A GENERAL OVERHEAD BUDGET

Now we are ready to prepare a complete general overhead budget.

Example 9-3: Prepare a general overhead budget for a company given the following. The company's revenues are shown below.

MONTH	REVENUES ($)	MONTH	REVENUES ($)
Jan.	768,000	July	500,000
Feb.	712,000	Aug.	391,000
March	785,000	Sept.	342,000
April	769,000	Oct.	460,000
May	560,000	Nov.	492,000
June	545,000	Dec.	516,000

The advertising budget is to be 1% of revenues. The budget for promotions is to include $8,000 in July for a company picnic, $5,000 in December for Christmas cards and gifts, and $10,000 in December for a company Christmas party. The company leases two vehicles for $350 per month per vehicle. The monthly fuel and maintenance cost for these vehicles is estimated to be $200 per month per vehicle. In July, the company plans on purchasing a new computer system for $18,000.

The company employs five workers: the owner, a project manager/estimator, a secretary/receptionist, a bookkeeper, and an accounting clerk.

The owner is paid $8,000 per month. The project manager/estimator is paid $5,000 per month. The secretary/receptionist is paid $12.00 per hour and works an average of 42 hours per week. The bookkeeper is paid $18.00 per hour and works an average of 45 hours per week. The accounting clerk is paid $9.00 per hour and works an average of 42 hours per week. All of the hourly employees are paid for 52 weeks per year. Time-and-a-half must be paid to hourly employees for work over 40 hours per week. The company contributes $150 per month per employee—including the owner—for health insurance. It also deposits 50 cents into an employee's 401(k) account for every dollar the employee deposits. The maximum the company would deposit is 3% of an employee's wages. This match includes the company's owner. Historically, the employees have taken full advantage of this benefit. The current social security rate is 6.2% to $84,900 of wages per employee. The current Medicare rate is 1.45%. The company's FUTA rate is 0.8% on the first $7,000 of wages per employee and the SUTA rate is 2% on the first $22,000 of wages per employee.

The company is charged 0.5% of revenues, 1% of wages for hourly employees, and 3% of wages for salaried employees for general liability insurance. In January the company pays $100 for a business license. It is anticipated that office supplies will cost $500 per month. Rent for the office space is $500 per month. Office utilities are expected to run $50 per month for water and sewer; $250 per month for power in June, July, and August and $150 per month during the remaining months of the year; and $150 per month for natural gas during November, December, January, and February and $50 per month during the remaining months of the year. It is anticipated that the company will spend $100 per month for postage and $100 per week for janitorial services. The estimated telephone costs are $200 per month for telephone and long-distance service and $240 per month to provide mobile phone service for the salaried employees. In December the company plans on making a $3,000 charitable contribution to a local food bank. In April the company must pay $1,500 for its annual plan-room membership. The company plans on spending $1,000 at the first of each quarter for accounting services to close the previous quarter's books and an additional $2,000 in April for tax services. The estimated cost of meals and entertainment is $200 per week. Bank fees are $50 per month. Allow $100 per month for miscellaneous expenses. Assume that all of the months are the same length—four and one-third weeks.

Solution: The budget is grouped by the categories found earlier in this chapter.

The monthly budget for advertising is 1% of revenues. January's budget for advertising is calculated as follows:

$$\text{Advertising}_{\text{Jan}} = \$768,000(0.01) = \$7,680$$

The advertising budget for the remaining months of the year is calculated in a similar manner. The monthly budgets are shown in Table 9-1.

TABLE 9-1 Advertising Budget

MONTH	BUDGET ($)	MONTH	BUDGET ($)
Jan.	7,680	July	5,000
Feb.	7,120	Aug.	3,910
March	7,850	Sept.	3,420
April	7,690	Oct.	4,600
May	5,600	Nov.	4,920
June	5,450	Dec.	5,160
		Total	68,400

The promotional budget for July is $8,000 and for December is $15,000 ($5,000 + $10,000). The promotional budget for the remaining months of the year is zero. The annual promotional budget is $23,000.

The monthly budget for car and truck expenses includes the lease payment and the fuel and maintenance costs. The monthly budget for car and truck is $1,100 ($350 + $350 + $200 + $200). The annual budget for car and truck expenses is $13,200.

July's budget for computer and office furniture is the cost of the computer system or $18,000. The budget for the remaining months is zero.

The monthly budget for employee wages and salaries are the same for each month because of the assumption that all months are equal. For hourly employees time-and-a-half is paid for work over 40 hours per week. The monthly wages for the secretary/receptionist are as follows:

$$\text{Wages}_{\text{Jan-Dec}} = \$12/\text{hour}(40\text{ hours/week})(52\text{ weeks/12 month})$$
$$+ \$12/\text{hour}(1.5)(2\text{ hours/week})(52\text{ weeks/12 month})$$
$$\text{Wages}_{\text{Jan-Dec}} = \$2,236$$

The monthly wages for the bookkeeper are as follows:

$$\text{Wages}_{\text{Jan-Dec}} = \$18/\text{hour}(40\text{ hours/week})(52\text{ weeks/12 month})$$
$$+ \$18/\text{hour}(1.5)(5\text{ hours/week})(52\text{ weeks/12 month})$$
$$\text{Wages}_{\text{Jan-Dec}} = \$3,705$$

The monthly wages for the accounting clerk are as follows:

$$\text{Wages}_{\text{Jan-Dec}} = \$9/\text{hour}(40\text{ hours/week})(52\text{ weeks/12 month})$$
$$+ \$9/\text{hour}(1.5)(2\text{ hours/week})(52\text{ weeks/12 month})$$
$$\text{Wages}_{\text{Jan-Dec}} = \$1,677$$

The monthly budget for employee wages and salaries is as follows:

$$\text{Wages}_{\text{Jan-Dec}} = \$8,000 + \$5,000 + \$2,236 + \$3,705 + \$1,677$$
$$= \$20,618$$

The annual budget for employee wages and salaries is $247,416.

The only employee benefit is the company's contribution to health insurance at $150 per month per employee—including the owner. The monthly budget for employee benefits is $750, and the annual budget is $9,000.

The maximum monthly payment for employee retirement is 3% of wages or $619 ($20,618 × 0.03) per month. Because the employees have historically taken full advantage of this benefit, the monthly budget should be equal to the maximum monthly payment. The annual budget for employee retirement is $7,428.

The budget for employee taxes includes social security, Medicare, FUTA, and SUTA. The company pays 6.2% on the first $84,900 of each employee's wages. The employees making $7,075 ($84,900/12) per month or less do not reach the social security limit and the amount of social security is the same for all of the months. Only the owner makes more than $7,075 per month. During the eleventh month—November—the owner's wages exceed the social security limit. The social security paid by the company on the owner's wages is calculated as follows:

$$\text{Social Security}_{\text{Jan-Oct}} = \$8,000(0.062) = \$496$$
$$\text{Social Security}_{\text{Nov}} = [\$84,900 - \$8,000(10)]0.062 = \$304$$
$$\text{Social Security}_{\text{Dec}} = \$0$$

The social security tax is calculated in the same manner for the remaining employees. The social security taxes for the year are shown in Table 9-2.

The company pays 1.45% on all wages for Medicare. The Medicare taxes paid by the company are calculated as follows:

$$\text{Medicare}_{\text{Jan-Dec}} = \$20,618(0.0145) = \$299$$

The company pays 0.8% on the first $7,000 of each employee's wages for federal unemployment tax (FUTA). The employees making $583.33 ($7,000/12)

TABLE 9-2 Social Security Taxes

MONTH	OWNER ($)	ESTIMATOR ($)	SECRETARY ($)	BOOK. ($)	CLERK ($)	TOTAL ($)
Jan.	496	310	139	230	104	1,279
Feb.	496	310	139	230	104	1,279
March	496	310	139	230	104	1,279
April	496	310	139	230	104	1,279
May	496	310	139	230	104	1,279
June	496	310	139	230	104	1,279
July	496	310	139	230	104	1,279
Aug.	496	310	139	230	104	1,279
Sept.	496	310	139	230	104	1,279
Oct.	496	310	139	230	104	1,279
Nov.	304	310	139	230	104	1,087
Dec.	0	310	139	230	104	783

per month or less do not reach the FUTA limit and the amount of FUTA is the same for all of the months. All employees make more than $583.33. During the first month—January—the owner's wages exceed the FUTA limit. The FUTA paid by the company on the owner's wages is calculated as follows:

$$FUTA_{Jan} = \$7,000(0.008) = \$56$$
$$FUTA_{Feb-Dec} = \$0$$

The FUTA tax is calculated in the same manner for the remaining employees. The FUTA taxes for the year are shown in Table 9-3.

The company pays 2% on the first $22,000 of each employee's wages for state unemployment taxes (SUTA). The employees making $1,833.33 ($22,000/12) per month or less do not reach the SUTA limit and the amount of SUTA is the same for all of the months. Only the accounting clerk makes $1,833.33 or less. During the third month—March—the owner's wages exceed the SUTA limit. The SUTA paid by the company on the owner's wages is calculated as follows:

$$SUTA_{Jan-Feb} = \$8,000(0.02) = \$160$$
$$SUTA_{March} = [\$22,000 - \$8,000(2)]0.02 = \$120$$
$$SUTA_{April-Dec} = \$0$$

The SUTA tax is calculated in the same manner for the remaining employees. The SUTA taxes for the year are shown in Table 9-4.

The total budget for employee taxes will be the sum of the payments for social security, Medicare, FUTA, and SUTA. January is calculated as follows:

$$Employee\ Taxes_{Jan} = \$1,279 + \$299 + \$157 + \$413 = \$2,148$$

TABLE 9-3   FUTA Taxes

MONTH	OWNER ($)	ESTIMATOR ($)	SECRETARY ($)	BOOK. ($)	CLERK ($)	TOTAL ($)
Jan.	56	40	18	30	13	157
Feb.	0	16	18	26	13	73
March	0	0	18	0	13	31
April	0	0	2	0	13	15
May	0	0	0	0	2	2
June	0	0	0	0	0	0
July	0	0	0	0	0	0
Aug.	0	0	0	0	0	0
Sept.	0	0	0	0	0	0
Oct.	0	0	0	0	0	0
Nov.	0	0	0	0	0	0
Dec.	0	0	0	0	0	0

TABLE 9-4   SUTA Taxes

MONTH	OWNER ($)	ESTIMATOR ($)	SECRETARY ($)	BOOK. ($)	CLERK ($)	TOTAL ($)
Jan.	160	100	45	74	34	413
Feb.	160	100	45	74	34	413
March	120	100	45	74	34	373
April	0	100	45	74	34	253
May	0	40	45	74	34	193
June	0	0	45	70	34	149
July	0	0	45	0	34	79
Aug.	0	0	45	0	34	79
Sept.	0	0	45	0	34	79
Oct.	0	0	38	0	34	72
Nov.	0	0	0	0	34	34
Dec.	0	0	0	0	34	34

The budgets for employee taxes for the remaining months of the year are calculated in a similar manner. The monthly budgets for employee taxes for the year are shown in Table 9-5.

The monthly budget for insurance is a result of the liability insurance. The company is charged 0.5% of revenues, 1% of wages for hourly employees, and 3% of wages for salaried employees for general liability insurance. The wages for hourly employees is estimated to be $7,618 ($2,236 + $3,705 + $1,677) per month and the wages for salaried employees is $13,000 ($8,000 + $5,000) per month. January's budget for insurance is calculated as follows:

$$\text{Insurance}_{Jan} = \$768,000(0.005) + \$7,618(0.01) + \$13,000(0.03)$$
$$\text{Insurance}_{Jan} = \$4,306$$

The insurance budgets for the remaining months of the year are calculated in a similar manner. The monthly budgets for insurance for the year are shown in Table 9-6.

TABLE 9-5   Employee Taxes Budget

MONTH	BUDGET ($)	MONTH	BUDGET ($)
Jan.	2,148	July	1,657
Feb.	2,064	Aug.	1,657
March	1,982	Sept.	1,657
April	1,846	Oct.	1,650
May	1,773	Nov.	1,420
June	1,727	Dec.	1,116
		Total	20,697

TABLE 9-6 Insurance Budget

MONTH	BUDGET ($)	MONTH	BUDGET ($)
Jan.	4,306	July	2,966
Feb.	4,026	Aug.	2,421
March	4,391	Sept.	2,176
April	4,311	Oct.	2,766
May	3,266	Nov.	2,926
June	3,191	Dec.	3,046
		Total	39,792

The budget for taxes and licenses for January is the cost of the business licenses or $100. The budget for taxes and licenses for the remaining months of the year is zero.

The monthly budget for office supplies is $500 and the annual budget is $6,000.

The monthly budget for office rent is $500 and the annual budget is $6,000.

The monthly budget for office utilities includes sewer and water, power, and natural gas. The monthly budgets are calculated as follows:

$$\text{Office Utilities}_{\text{Jan-Feb}} = \$50 + \$150 + \$150 = \$350$$
$$\text{Office Utilities}_{\text{March-May}} = \$50 + \$150 + \$50 = \$250$$
$$\text{Office Utilities}_{\text{June-Aug}} = \$50 + \$250 + \$50 = \$350$$
$$\text{Office Utilities}_{\text{Sept-Oct}} = \$50 + \$150 + \$50 = \$250$$
$$\text{Office Utilities}_{\text{Nov-Dec}} = \$50 + \$150 + \$150 = \$350$$

The annual budget for office utilities is $3,700.

The monthly budget for postage and delivery is $100 and the annual budget is $1,200.

The monthly budget for janitorial and cleaning is $433 ($100 × 52/12) and the annual budget is $5,196.

The telephone budget includes the telephone bill, long distance, and mobile phones for the office personnel. The monthly budget for telephone is $440 and the annual budget is $5,280.

The budget for charitable contributions consists of one contribution to a local food bank in December in the amount $3,000. The budget for the remaining months is zero.

The annual budget for dues and memberships consists of their annual plan-room fee of $1,500, which is paid in April. The budget for the remaining months is zero.

The monthly budget for legal and professional services include services provided by the company's accounting firm. The monthly budget for January, July, and October is $1,000 each month. The monthly budget for April is $3,000 for a total annual budget of $6,000.

TABLE 9-7 Monthly General Overhead Budget

MONTH	BUDGET ($)	MONTH	BUDGET ($)
Jan.	41,661	July	63,050
Feb.	39,637	Aug.	34,415
March	40,550	Sept.	33,580
April	44,674	Oct.	36,343
May	36,966	Nov.	35,693
June	36,795	Dec.	53,749
		Total	497,113

Social Security Rate:	6.20%
Social Security Limit:	84,900
Medicare Rate:	1.45%
FUTA Rate:	0.80%
FUTA Limit:	7,000
SUTA Rate:	2.00%
SUTA Limit:	22,000

Item	Jan.	Feb.	March	April	May	June	July	Aug.	Sept.	Oct.	Nov.	Dec.	Total
Owner													
Wages	8,000	8,000	8,000	8,000	8,000	8,000	8,000	8,000	8,000	8,000	8,000	8,000	96,000
Social Security	496	496	496	496	496	496	496	496	496	496	304	—	5,264
Medicare	116	116	116	116	116	116	116	116	116	116	116	116	1,392
FUTA	56	—	—	—	—	—	—	—	—	—	—	—	56
SUTA	160	160	120	—	—	—	—	—	—	—	—	—	440
Project Manager/Estimator													
Wages	5,000	5,000	5,000	5,000	5,000	5,000	5,000	5,000	5,000	5,000	5,000	5,000	60,000
Social Security	310	310	310	310	310	310	310	310	310	310	310	310	3,720
Medicare	73	73	73	73	73	73	73	73	73	73	73	73	870
FUTA	40	16	—	—	—	—	—	—	—	—	—	—	56
SUTA	100	100	100	100	40	—	—	—	—	—	—	—	440
Office Salaries	13,000	13,000	13,000	13,000	13,000	13,000	13,000	13,000	13,000	13,000	13,000	13,000	156,000
Secretary/Receptionist													
Hours Per Week	42	42	42	42	42	42	42	42	42	42	42		
Wage Rate	12	12	12	12	12	12	12	12	12	12	12		
Wages	2,236	2,236	2,236	2,236	2,236	2,236	2,236	2,236	2,236	2,236	2,236	2,236	26,832
Social Security	139	139	139	139	139	139	139	139	139	139	139	139	1,664
Medicare	32	32	32	32	32	32	32	32	32	32	32	32	389
FUTA	18	18	18	2	—	—	—	—	—	—	—	—	56
SUTA	45	45	45	45	45	45	45	45	45	38	—	—	440
Bookkeeper													
Hours Per Week	45	45	45	45	45	45	45	45	45	45	45	45	
Wage Rate	18	18	18	18	18	18	18	18	18	18	18	18	
Wages	3,705	3,705	3,705	3,705	3,705	3,705	3,705	3,705	3,705	3,705	3,705	3,705	44,460
Social Security	230	230	230	230	230	230	230	230	230	230	230	230	2,757
Medicare	54	54	54	54	54	54	54	54	54	54	54	54	645
FUTA	30	26	—	—	—	—	—	—	—	—	—	—	56
SUTA	74	74	74	74	74	69	—	—	—	—	—	—	440
Accounting Clerk													
Hours Per Week	42	42	42	42	42	42	42	42	42	42	42	42	
Wage Rate	9	9	9	9	9	9	9	9	9	9	9	9	
Wages	1,677	1,677	1,677	1,677	1,677	1,677	1,677	1,677	1,677	1,677	1,677	1,677	20,124
Social Security	104	104	104	104	104	104	104	104	104	104	104	104	1,248
Medicare	24	24	24	24	24	24	24	24	24	24	24	24	292
FUTA	13	13	13	13	2	—	—	—	—	—	—	—	56
SUTA	34	34	34	34	34	34	34	34	34	34	34	34	402
Hourly Wages	7,618	7,618	7,618	7,618	7,618	7,618	7,618	7,618	7,618	7,618	7,618	7,618	91,416
Total Wages	20,618	20,618	20,618	20,618	20,618	20,618	20,618	20,618	20,618	20,618	20,618	20,618	247,416
Taxes													
Social Security	1,278	1,278	1,278	1,278	1,278	1,278	1,278	1,278	1,278	1,278	1,086	782	14,652
Medicare	299	299	299	299	299	299	299	299	299	299	299	299	3,588
FUTA	157	74	31	16	2	—	—	—	—	—	—	—	280
SUTA	412	412	372	252	192	148	78	78	78	71	34	34	2,162
TOTAL	2,147	2,063	1,981	1,845	1,772	1,725	1,656	1,656	1,656	1,648	1,419	1,115	20,682

FIGURE 9-5 Employee Costs

Item	Jan.	Feb.	March	April	May	June	July	Aug.	Sept.	Oct.	Nov.	Dec.	Total
							General Overhead						
Advertising	7,680	7,120	7,850	7,690	5,600	5,450	5,000	3,910	3,420	4,600	4,920	5,160	68,400
Promotion	—	—	—	—	—	—	8,000	—	—	—	—	15,000	23,000
Car and Truck Expenses	1,100	1,100	1,100	1,100	1,100	1,100	1,100	1,100	1,100	1,100	1,100	1,100	13,200
Computer and Office Furniture	—	—	—	—	—	—	18,000	—	—	—	—	—	18,000
Employee Wages and Salaries	20,618	20,618	20,618	20,618	20,618	20,618	20,618	20,618	20,618	20,618	20,618	20,618	247,416
Employee Benefits	750	750	750	750	750	750	750	750	750	750	750	750	9,000
Employee Retirement	619	619	619	619	619	619	619	619	619	619	619	619	7,422
Employee Taxes	2,147	2,063	1,981	1,845	1,772	1,725	1,656	1,656	1,656	1,648	1,419	1,115	20,682
Insurance	4,306	4,026	4,391	4,311	3,266	3,191	2,966	2,421	2,176	2,766	2,926	3,046	39,794
Taxes & Licenses	100												100
Office Supplies	500	500	500	500	500	500	500	500	500	500	500	500	6,000
Office Rent	500	500	500	500	500	500	500	500	500	500	500	500	6,000
Office Utilities	350	350	250	250	250	350	350	350	250	250	350	350	3,700
Postage and Delivery	100	100	100	100	100	100	100	100	100	100	100	100	1,200
Janitorial and Cleaning	433	433	433	433	433	433	433	433	433	433	433	433	5,200
Telephone	440	440	440	440	440	440	440	440	440	440	440	440	5,280
Charitable Contributions	—	—	—	—	—	—	—	—	—	—	—	3,000	3,000
Dues and Memberships	—	—	—	1,500	—	—	—	—	—	—	—	—	1,500
Legal and Professional Services	1,000	—	—	3,000	—	—	1,000	—	—	1,000	—	—	6,000
Meals and Entertainment	867	867	867	867	867	867	867	867	867	867	867	867	10,400
Bank Fees	50	50	50	50	50	50	50	50	50	50	50	50	600
Miscellaneous	100	100	100	100	100	100	100	100	100	100	100	100	1,200
Total Overhead	41,659	39,636	40,549	44,673	36,965	36,793	63,048	34,413	33,578	36,341	35,691	53,748	497,094

FIGURE 9-6 General Overhead Budget

The monthly budget for meals and entertainment is $867 ($200 × 52/12) and the annual budget is $10,404.

The monthly budget for bank fees is $50 and the annual budget is $600.

The monthly budget for miscellaneous is $100 and the annual budget is $1,200.

The total monthly budgets for general overhead are shown in Table 9-7.

The employee costs and general overhead budget may also be calculated in spreadsheet format as shown in Figures 9-5 and 9-6. There are small differences between the numbers shown in Figures 9-5 and 9-6 and the calculations in Example 9-3, which are due to rounding in the example.

CONCLUSION

General overhead costs include those costs that cannot be tied to a specific construction project. A company should prepare a general overhead budget and track general overhead costs just as it tracks project costs. The general overhead budget is a valuable tool in controlling the costs of overhead. Historical data are the best for use in preparing a general overhead budget. When preparing the budget, managers must take into account changes in their business and inflation. When the volume of business changes, the general overhead costs may remain fixed over the change in volume, vary with the change in volume, or both. When a cost does not change with a change in volume it is considered a fixed cost. When a cost changes with the volume of work it is considered a variable cost. A cost that contains both fixed and variable cost components is known as a mixed cost. When projecting costs, exponential or linear regression may be used to project inflation into future costs when multiple periods of historical data are available.

PROBLEMS

1. Determine the annual budget for office utilities using the data from the past 12 months shown in Figure 9-7. Utility costs are expected to increase by 8% per year due to inflation. None of the company's goals are expected to affect the utility costs.

2. Determine the annual budget for office utilities using the data from the past 12 months shown in Figure 9-7. Utility costs are expected to increase by 7% per year due to inflation. The company is planning on doubling its office space in July by expanding into some unoccupied space adjacent to its existing office space.

3. Determine the projected costs for utilities in year 5. The inflation rate has been determined to be 0.222 and the initial cost is $57.39.

```
12/14/04                                                        Page 1

                         EXPENSE REPORT

From 12/1/03 to 11/30/04


    Ck Num      Date      Payee           Account          Amount
     4990     01/07/04   Gas Company     Office Utilities   231.13
     5004     01/21/04   Power Company   Office Utilities   100.35
     5029     02/06/04   Gas Company     Office Utilities   291.01
     5035     02/20/04   Power Company   Office Utilities    99.56
     5036     03/05/04   Gas Company     Office Utilities   273.12
     5047     03/19/04   Power Company   Office Utilities   105.22
     5073     04/02/04   Gas Company     Office Utilities   206.65
     5103     04/16/04   Power Company   Office Utilities    80.47
     5133     05/08/04   Power Company   Office Utilities    86.42
     5159     05/22/04   Gas Company     Office Utilities   159.23
     5181     06/02/04   Power Company   Office Utilities    80.21
     5182     06/16/04   Gas Company     Office Utilities    89.91
     5204     07/07/04   Power Company   Office Utilities   106.06
     5229     07/21/04   Gas Company     Office Utilities    71.51
     5233     07/30/04   Gas Company     Office Utilities    44.73
     5262     08/13/04   Power Company   Office Utilities   113.69
     5272     09/02/04   Power Company   Office Utilities    98.81
     5287     09/16/04   Gas Company     Office Utilities    48.72
     5295     10/09/04   Gas Company     Office Utilities    54.52
     5315     10/23/04   Power Company   Office Utilities    95.44
     5323     10/29/04   Gas Company     Office Utilities    62.94
     5344     11/12/04   Power Company   Office Utilities    77.10
     5366     12/07/04   Gas Company     Office Utilities   109.23
     5375     12/11/04   Power Company   Office Utilities   111.51

                                         Total            2,797.54
```

FIGURE 9-7   Utility Costs

4. Determine the projected costs for utilities in year 10. The inflation rate has been determined to be 0.076 and the initial cost is $56.27.
5. You have been running a construction company out of your home with your spouse helping you keep the books. The company has grown and has begun to take up too much of your and your spouse's time. The decision has been made to hire a part-time estimator to help you with the bidding and a full-time

office manager. The office manager's duties will include accounting, receptionist, and secretarial duties. By hiring the new personnel you will need to move the company's operations out of your home and into an office. Use the following cost information to prepare a cash flow budget for one year:

Item	Cost
Estimator's Wages	$15/hr for 20 hrs/week
Office Manager's Wages	$12/hr for 40 hrs/week
Social Security	6.2% of wages to $84,900
Medicare	1.45% of wages
FUTA	0.8% to $7,000 of wages per employee
SUTA	2.0% to $12,000 of wages per employee
Workers' Comp.	$1.25 per $100 of wages
General Liability	0.67% of wages
401(k)	50% match up to 6% of wages
Health Insurance	$150/month per employee
Vacation/Sick/Holidays	10 days per year
Rent	$12 per square foot per year
Utilities	$0.25 per square foot per month

The employees pay $200 per month toward their insurance, which is not subject to social security and Medicare taxes. The budget should include the following budget categories:

Advertising
Bad Debts
Bank Fees
Car and Truck Expenses
Charitable Contributions
Computer and Office Furniture
Depreciation
Dues and Memberships
Employee Wages and Salaries
Employee Benefits
Employee Retirement
Employee Recruiting
Employee Training
Employee Taxes
Insurance
Interest Expense
Janitorial and Cleaning

Legal and Professional Services
Meals and Entertainment
Office Supplies
Office Purchases
Office Rent
Office Utilities
Postage & Delivery
Promotion
Publications and Subscriptions
Repairs and Maintenance
Taxes and Licenses
Telephone
Travel
Unallocated Labor
Unallocated Materials
Miscellaneous

A budget of "0" for a category is acceptable. Present your budget in the following format:

CATEGORY	AMOUNT $/YEAR	JUSTIFICATION
Advertising		
. . .		

SETTING PROFIT MARGINS FOR BIDDING

In this chapter you will learn to set profit margins for use in bidding and how the profit changes as the volume of work changes. You will also learn to determine the volume of construction work and profit and overhead markup necessary to cover the costs associated with the general overhead. Profits are used to pay for general overhead costs and provide the owners with a profit. If the profits are insufficient to cover the general overhead costs the company will consume its available cash and fail. If the profits fail to provide the owners with a reasonable profit, the owners may decide there are better places for them to invest their money and the company will lose financing.

A key goal for any construction company is to make money or profit. The investors in a construction company expect that the money they have invested in the company will be used to supply the cash needed to operate the construction company and that the company will generate a profit, thus increasing the value of their investment. To successfully operate a construction company, the company's managers must understand how a construction company generates profit. We limit our discussion of profit to a company's core business of building construction projects; in other words, the profit from construction operations. For the company's income statement shown in Figure 2-3, this profit is recorded as net profit from operations. As such, we ignore other incomes and expenses and income taxes. Additionally, we will assume that all of the equipment costs will be allocated to the construction costs during the course of the year; therefore, the company equipment costs will be zero.

THE PROFIT EQUATION

For a construction company the revenues are in the form of payments from the project owners or from the sale of projects. These revenues are then used for three key items: to pay the construction costs, to pay the general overhead costs, and to provide the profit for the investors in the construction company. The use of the revenues is shown in Figure 10-1.

The construction costs include both the direct and indirect (project overhead) costs from all of the construction projects when all equipment costs have been allocated to the construction costs. The general overhead costs include those costs discussed in chapter 9 and are costs that are not attributable to any specific construction project. The general overhead budget used to calculate the profit from operations should be the budget prepared for estimating profit rather than the general overhead budget prepared for cash flow projections. From Figure 10-1 we see that:

$$\text{Revenues} = \text{Construction Costs} + \text{Overhead} + \text{Profit} \qquad (10\text{-}1)$$

The profit is calculated by solving Eq. (10-1) for the profit as follows:

$$\text{Profit} = \text{Revenues} - \text{Construction Costs} - \text{Overhead} \qquad (10\text{-}2)$$

This is known as the profit equation.

> **Example 10-1:**   For the company's income statement shown in Figure 2-3, determine the company's profit from operations for the year and the percentage of the construction revenues that became profits.

FIGURE 10-1   Use of Revenues

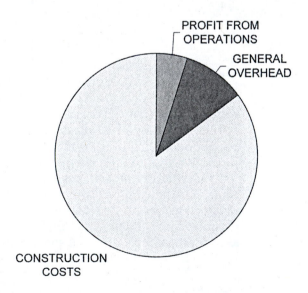

PROFIT FROM OPERATIONS

GENERAL OVERHEAD

CONSTRUCTION COSTS

Solution: From Figure 2-3 the company's revenues are $3,698,945, the construction costs are $3,186,457, and overhead costs are $422,562. Substituting these values into Eq. (10-2) to find the profits for the year we get the following:

$$\text{Profit} = \$3,698,945 - \$3,186,457 - \$422,562 = \$89,926$$

The percentage of the construction revenues that became profits is calculated by dividing the profits by the revenues and expressing the answer in percentage form, as follows:

$$\text{Profit \%} = \$89,926/\$3,698,945 = 0.024 \text{ or } 2.4\%$$

In this case, both of these values may be read directly from the income statement in Figure 2-3.

CONTRIBUTION MARGIN

Remembering that general overhead costs may be broken down into its variable and fixed components as follows:

$$\text{Overhead} = \text{Variable Overhead} + \text{Fixed Overhead} \qquad (10\text{-}3)$$

we can express Eq. (10-2) as follows:

$$\text{Profit} = \text{Revenues} - \text{Construction Costs} - \text{Variable Overhead} \\ - \text{Fixed Overhead} \qquad (10\text{-}4)$$

The contribution margin is the amount of money that a project or projects contributes to the company to be used to pay for the fixed overhead and provide a profit for the stakeholders. The contribution margin is what is left over from the revenues after paying the construction costs—which are considered a variable cost—and the variable portion of the overhead. The equation for the contribution margin may be written as follows:

$$\text{Contribution Margin} = \text{Revenues} - \text{Construction Costs} \\ - \text{Variable Overhead} \qquad (10\text{-}5)$$

Dividing the contribution margin by revenues we get the contribution margin ratio. The equation for the contribution margin ratio may be written as follows:

$$\text{CM Ratio} = \text{Contribution Margin}/\text{Revenues} \qquad (10\text{-}6)$$

Substituting Eq. (10-5) into Eq. (10-6) we get the following:

$$\text{CM Ratio} = \text{Revenues}/\text{Revenues} - \text{Construction Costs}/\text{Revenues} \\ - \text{Variable Overhead}/\text{Revenues} \\ \text{CM Ratio} = 1 - \text{Construction Costs}/\text{Revenues} \\ - \text{Variable Overhead}/\text{Revenues} \qquad (10\text{-}7)$$

Because all of the variable costs in Eq. (10-5) are considered to vary directly with revenues, the contribution margin varies directly with revenues and the contribution margin ratio may be considered to be a fixed percentage of the revenues. Alternately, Eq. (10-6) may be written as follows:

$$\text{Contribution Margin} = \text{CM Ratio}(\text{Revenues}) \qquad (10\text{-}8)$$

Substituting Eqs. (10-5) and (10-8) into Eq. (10-4) we get the following:

$$\text{Profit} = \text{Contribution Margin} - \text{Fixed Overhead}$$
$$\text{Profit} = \text{CM Ratio}(\text{Revenues}) - \text{Fixed Overhead} \qquad (10\text{-}9)$$

Example 10-2: What are the contribution margin and the contribution margin ratio for the company's income statement shown in Figure 2-3 if $45,000 of the overhead is considered variable overhead?

Solution: Using Eq. (10-5) to get the contribution margin we get the following:

$$\text{Contribution Margin} = \$3,698,945 - \$3,186,457 - \$45,000$$
$$\text{Contribution Margin} = \$467,488$$

The contribution margin ratio may be calculated by using Eq. (10-6) as follows:

$$\text{CM Ratio} = \$467,488/\$3,698,945 = 0.126 \text{ or } 12.6\%$$

The contribution margin ratio is used to calculate the break-even volume of work or the volume of work may be used to calculate the break-even contribution margin ratio.

PROJECTING BREAK-EVEN VOLUME OF WORK

Once a company has established a general overhead budget for a year, it can use the historical contribution margin ratio to determine the break-even volume of work that it needs to produce during the year to cover overhead costs and provide a specified profit. The historical contribution margin ratio may be calculated from the company income statement for the previous year as it was done in Example 10-2. The historical contribution margin ratio may need to be adjusted to take into account changing market conditions. For example, during an economic downturn contribution margin ratios often shrink, whereas during a rapidly growing economy, when construction work is plentiful, contribution margin ratios often increase.

By setting profit in Eq. (10-9) equal to zero we can determine the break-even volume of work for a specific contribution margin and fixed overhead. The break-even volume of work is expressed in dollars of revenue.

Example 10-3: Determine the break-even volume of work for a company with a fixed overhead of $350,000 and a contribution margin ratio of 9.5%.

Solution: Using Eq. (10-9) and setting the profit equal to zero we get the following:

$$\$0 = 0.095(\text{Revenues}) - \$350,000$$

Solving for revenues we get the following:

$$0.095(\text{Revenues}) = \$350,000$$
$$\text{Revenues} = \$350,000/0.095 = \$3,684,211$$

The company in Example 10-3 will need to generate $3,684,211 in revenues to cover its fixed overhead. If it generates less than $3,684,211 the company will not cover the fixed overhead and will lose money on construction operations. For the revenues in excess of $3,684,211, the entire contribution margin will be profit from operations.

Alternately, a company may have a required level of profit. By setting profit in Eq. (10-9) equal to the required level of profit we can determine the break-even volume of work for a specific contribution margin and fixed overhead. The break-even volume of work is expressed in dollars of revenue.

Example 10-4:   Determine the break-even volume of work for a company with a fixed overhead of $350,000, a contribution margin ratio of 9.5%, and a required level of profit of $190,000.

Solution: Using Eq. (10-9) and setting the profit equal to $190,000 we get the following:

$$\$190,000 = 0.095(\text{Revenues}) - \$350,000$$

Solving for revenues we get the following:

$$0.095(\text{Revenues}) = \$540,000$$
$$\text{Revenues} = \$540,000/0.095 = \$5,684,211$$

The company in Example 10-4 will need to generate $5,684,211 in revenues to cover its fixed overhead and make $190,000 in profit. If it generates less than $5,684,211 it will not meet its profit requirements. If the company generates more than $5,684,211 it will exceed its profit requirements.

Projecting Break-Even Contribution Margin Ratio

Once a company has established a general overhead budget for a year, it can use the anticipated volume of work to project the required contribution margin ratio. The volume of work may be estimated by looking at historical levels of work and making adjustments to reflect the economic conditions. Alternately, the volume of work may be projected based on the work the company thinks it can get during the upcoming year.

By setting profit in Eq. (10-9) equal to zero we can determine the break-even contribution margin ratio for a specific level of revenues and fixed overhead.

Example 10-5: Determine the break-even contribution margin ratio for a company with a fixed overhead of $350,000 and revenues of $3,250,000.

Solution: Using Eq. (10-9) and setting the profit equal to zero we get the following:

$0 = CM Ratio($3,250,000) − $350,000

Solving for contribution margin ratio we get the following:

CM Ratio($3,250,000) = $350,000
CM Ratio = $350,000/$3,250,000 = 0.1077 or 10.77%

The company in Example 10-5 will need to maintain a contribution margin ratio of 10.77% to cover its fixed overhead. If its contribution margin ratio is less than 10.77% the company will not cover its fixed overhead costs and will lose money on construction operations. If the contribution margin ratio is greater than 10.77%, the difference between the actual contribution margin ratio and 10.77% will be profit. For example, if the contribution margin ratio were 15%, 4.23% (15.00 − 10.77) of the company's revenues would be profit from construction operations.

Alternately, a company may have a required level of profit. By setting profit in Eq. (10-9) equal to the required level of profit we can determine the break-even contribution margin ratio for a specific level of revenues and fixed overhead.

Example 10-6: Determine the break-even contribution margin ratio for a company with a fixed overhead of $350,000, revenues of $3,250,000, and a required level of profit of $190,000.

Solution: Using Eq. (10-9) and setting the profit equal to $190,000 we get the following:

$190,000 = CM Ratio($3,250,000) − $350,000

Solving for contribution margin ratio we get the following:

CM Ratio($3,250,000) = $540,000
CM Ratio = $540,000/$3,250,000 = 0.1662 or 16.62%

The company in Example 10-6 will need to maintain a contribution margin ratio of 16.62% in order to meet profit requirements. If the contribution margin ratio is less than 16.62% the company will not meet its profit requirement. If the contribution margin ratio is greater than 16.62% the company will exceed its profit requirement.

When a company has multiple divisions or profit centers, the break-even volume of work or break-even contribution margin may be established for each division or profit center by allocating the general overhead to the divisions or profit centers and solving for the break-even volume of work or break-even contribution margin for each division or profit center. Different profit and overhead markups may be established for materials, labor, subcontractors, equipment, and other cost types in the same manner. Allocation of general overhead is discussed in chapter 11.

Adjusting the Financial Mix

If the calculated break-even volume of work exceeds the volume of work that the company thinks it can perform, the contribution margin ratio needs to be increased. This may be done by raising prices; however, this often results in a reduced volume of work. If the company's clients are not price sensitive, raising prices may solve the problem. If the company's clients are price sensitive—as is the case when clients solicit multiple bids for their work—raising prices may further reduce the volume of work and may only aggravate the problem. When raising prices is not an option, the company must reduce the fixed overhead costs or increase the contribution margin ratio by reducing construction costs or variable overhead costs.

When the break-even contribution margin ratio exceeds the historical contribution margin ratio, prices need to be raised or construction costs need to be reduced to achieve the contribution margin. After raising prices and reducing construction costs, if the break-even contribution margin ratio exceeds the contribution margin ratio that the company thinks it can obtain from its customers, the contribution margin needs to be decreased. This may be done by increasing the volume of work, thereby spreading the overhead and required profit over a higher volume of work. Alternately, the contribution margin may be decreased by decreasing overhead costs or profit expectations.

Remembering that a key goal of any construction company should be to make a profit, the object of looking at the profit equation and performing a break-even volume of work or break-even contribution margin ratio analysis is to clarify how the company is going to make a profit. The outcome of this analysis is for the company's management to set target levels for the company's revenues, gross profit margin, general overhead costs, and profit from operations, along with a realistic plan outlining how it is going to achieve these target levels. This plan—along with the target levels—should guide the company's marketing strategy. If the plan is inconsistent with the company's current marketing strategy, the company needs to revise the plan or be committed to change its marketing strategy. When making a change in a company's marketing strategy it is often better to phase in the new strategy over time rather than make an abrupt change.

Too often a company is focused on increasing the volume of its work rather than on its profitability. When a company focuses on volume of work without taking into account profit, it often settles for smaller profit margins or takes unprofitable work in order to increase its volume of work. These increases in the volume of work are often accompanied by the need to increase its main office support, thus increasing general overhead. It is not uncommon for companies that pursue this strategy to find that significant increases in the size of the company and the volume of work that it performs have been seen, yet its profits have improved little or actually declined.

Many companies have found that profits could increase by being more selective as to the type of project that is bid on, in essence specializing in certain areas of the construction market. This specialization allows the company to learn the ins and outs of a few specific segments of the market. As similar work is performed over and over the company and its employees move down the learning curve, learning where the common pitfalls occur and how to successfully avoid them. By reducing the number of construction problems that occur, the company can reduce the time it takes to construct the project and reduce the project overhead. Additionally, it learns to avoid costly construction mistakes.

To demonstrate this, let's compare two companies both performing a small office remodel in a high-rise building. The first company has performed many projects in high-rise buildings and has learned by experience that doorframes for double-hung doors often must be ordered in pieces (so that they can be transported up the elevator) and fabricated on site. The first company orders materials and schedules the work with this in mind. The second company, with little experience working in high-rise buildings, orders the doorframes for the double-hung doors fully fabricated, not taking into account the size limitations of the elevators. The doorframes arrive on the day they are to be installed. When trying to get the doorframes to their final location the second company realizes that the doorframes will not fit in the elevator. As a result construction has to be delayed while someone is found to cut the frames and then weld them back together once they arrive at their final destination or new doorframes have to be ordered; meanwhile progress on the project grinds to a halt.

In addition to learning to avoid the common pitfalls, specialization allows companies to learn better ways of performing the work. This includes time-saving shortcuts as well as changes that can be made in the design that will achieve the same structural and aesthetic quality, while cutting costs and construction time. Companies also learn more efficient ways to schedule the work as well as the optimum crew size or mix.

Specialization also allows companies the opportunity to develop relationships with suppliers and subcontractors who share the same area of specialization. These relationships can result in better pricing from subcontractors and suppliers, which in turn may be used as a competitive edge when bidding or used to increase a company's profit.

There are two common pitfalls when trying to focus on profits rather than the volume of work. First, because of the highly competitive nature of the construction industry most owners of construction companies are highly competitive. Many owners have a hard time losing a bid, even if there is little or no profit in the job. Owners need to change the way they measure their success from winning every bid to the profitability of their company. Second, when most construction companies start up, owners need to take every job they can get just to survive. As a company grows, it continues to think that it needs to take every job and fails to specialize. Once a company has enough work to survive it needs to begin to focus on specializing and increasing its profitability. This may require passing on a long-time customer who has provided marginally profitable work to another contractor. In chapter 11 we look at customers as profit centers.

Once a company has set a target level for the gross profit margin it often requires that all projects meet a minimum gross profit margin, which is included in its bids in the form of a profit and overhead markup (P&O Markup).

PROFIT AND OVERHEAD MARKUP

The profit and overhead markup is not the same as the gross profit margin; however, they are mathematically related. If we were to look at a construction project with revenues of $1,000,000 and construction costs of $850,000, the gross profit equals the revenues less the construction costs or $150,000 ($1,000,000 − $850,000). The gross profit margin is calculated using Eq. (6-17) as follows:

Gross Profit Margin = $150,000/$1,000,000 = 0.150 or 15.0%

If we were to mark up the construction costs by 15% to get the bid price (revenue from the project) we would get the following:

Revenue = $850,000(1 + 0.15) = $977,500

which is $22,500 ($1,000,000 − $977,500) less than the actual revenues from the project. The gross profit margin and the profit and overhead markup are related by the following equation:

P&O Markup = Gross Profit Margin/(1 − Gross Profit Margin)   (10-10)

The profit and overhead markup that is equal to a 15% gross profit margin is calculated by using Eq. (10-10) as follows:

P&O Markup = Gross Profit Margin/(100 − Gross Profit Margin)
P&O Markup = 15/(100 − 15) = 17.65%

Applying a profit and overhead markup of 17.65 to the construction costs of $850,000 we get the following:

Revenue = $850,000(1 + 0.1765) = $1,000,025

with the difference being due to the rounding of the profit and overhead markup.

For the company that has determined its break-even contribution margin ratio, the gross profit margin is calculated from the contribution margin ratio as follows:

Gross Profit Margin = CM Ratio + Variable Overhead/Revenues   (10-11)

Example 10-7:   Determine the profit and overhead markup for a company that wants to maintain a 16% gross profit margin.

Solution: Using Eq. (10-10) to find the profit and overhead markup we get:

P&O Markup = 16/(100 − 16) = 0.1905 or 19.05%

When preparing a bid, the profit and overhead markup has the advantage of being easier to calculate than the gross profit margin because it is expressed as a percentage of construction costs rather than a percentage of the total bid.

Not all projects can or should be bid at the same profit and overhead markup. A company should set a minimum profit and overhead markup and then increase the markup when condition warrants. The hard part is to determine when the conditions warrant an increase in the profit and overhead markup. There are some common reasons for increasing the profit and overhead markup.

First, the company is submitting a bid as a courtesy to the customer but really doesn't want the project unless it is profitable. This may happen when a company is asked to bid on a project that is outside its geographical area or area of specialization.

Second, the project is a difficult project, has a high degree of risk, or the project owners are difficult to work with. The level of risk may be increased by poor document quality, short construction schedules, high liquid damages, and uncertainty that may lead to cost or schedule overruns. In this case the risk and headaches of the project are only acceptable to the construction company if there is a higher level of profit.

Third, the company is bidding on the project to check its prices but really doesn't want the project unless it is profitable. When starting to bid after not bidding for a few months or bidding in a new market, it is wise to bid on two or three projects to get a feel for the market and to get back into a bidding rhythm. This gives the company's management a chance to get a feel for the level of profit and overhead markup that it can add to its bids, as well as give estimators a chance to warm up. Should they win the job by accident, the project usually has a good profit margin.

Fourth, the other companies bidding on the project are expected to be charging a higher profit and overhead markup or have higher construction costs. When competition in the market is stiff, companies can seldom charge more than the minimum profit and overhead markup; however, when competition is meager companies can often increase profit and overhead markup. To assist in determining when to charge a higher profit and overhead markup, a company must track how a competitor's prices compared to its own. The easiest way to do this is to keep a record of all of the competitors who have bid against the company along with each of the bids and the profit and overhead markup that our company would have had to add to our construction costs for our bid to equal the competitor's bid. This may be done by using the following equation:

$$P\&O \text{ Markup} = \text{Bid}/\text{Construction Costs} - 1 \qquad (10\text{-}12)$$

Example 10-8: Your construction company recently bid against ABC Construction Company. Your construction costs were $157,260 and you added a 15% profit and overhead markup for a total bid of $180,849. ABC's bid was $179,249. What profit and overhead markup would you need to add to your construction costs to get ABC's bid?

Solution: The profit and overhead markup is determined as follows using Eq. (10-12).

$$P\&O \text{ Markup} = \$179,249/\$157,260 - 1 = 0.1398 \text{ or } 13.98\%$$

When tracking changes it is important to keep track of the name of the project and the date bid as well as the competitor's bid and your construction costs. Competitors may be tracked using the simple spreadsheet format shown in Figure 10-2.

When deciding whether to increase the profit and overhead markup you need to take into account the size of the project, type of project, and the bid date. It is important to take size into account because as the project's size increases the profit and overhead markup tends to decrease. It is important to take the type of project into account because some companies may bid different types of projects at different profit and overhead markups. Finally, it is important to take the bid date for the data into account because projects bid in the spring—when companies are looking for this year's work—are often bid at a lower rate than projects later in the year when contractors begin filling up.

	A	B	C	D	E
1	ABBCO				
2	Project	Date	Bid	Costs	P&O
3	West City Park	6/24/2002	$ 875,256	$ 798,952	9.55%
4	Platt Park Restrooms	8/14/2002	$ 52,326	$ 42,165	24.10%
5					
6					
7	ABC Construction				
8	Project	Date	Bid	Costs	P&O
9	South Street Improvements	3/15/2002	$ 179,249	$ 157,260	13.98%
10	West City Park	6/24/2002	$ 859,462	$ 798,952	7.57%
11	East Side Community Center	7/22/2002	$ 1,152,634	$ 1,092,215	5.53%

FIGURE 10-2 Spreadsheet for Tracking Competitors' Bids

Example 10-9: Your construction company is bidding against the two construction companies shown in Figure 10-2 on a municipal project with an engineer's estimate of $750,000 to $850,000. Your company's minimum profit and overhead markup is 8%. What are the chances of increasing your profit and overhead markup above the minimum 8%?

Solution: Your company bid against ABC Construction on the West City Park—a municipal project of similar size—where their bid was 7.57% above your costs. It is unlikely that you will be able to raise your profit and overhead markup and still be competitive with ABC Construction. You also bid against ABBCO on the same project, where their bid was 9.55% above your costs. If ABC Construction were not to bid, you might be able to raise your profit and overhead a little.

The construction bidding market is constantly changing. Contractors who are winning work and feeling less pressure to get work may raise their profit and overhead markups, while other contractors are completing projects and need more work and may lower their profit and overhead markups to get this work. Meanwhile contractors are adjusting the profit and overhead on courtesy bids or when they perceive that a project has a higher degree of risk. All of this makes it hard to predict where contractors are going to bid. By tracking your competitors you increase your odds of reading the market right.

CONCLUSION

Revenues from operations are used to pay construction costs, pay overhead costs, and provide a profit for the investors. By dividing overhead into a fixed and variable portion, the percentage of construction revenues available for paying the fixed overhead costs and to provide a profit to the investors may be determined. This percentage is known as the contribution margin ratio. The break-even volume of work may be calculated from the contribution margin ratio, the fixed overhead, and required profit. Alternately, the break-even contribution margin ratio may be calculated from the volume of work, the fixed overhead, and required profit. These break-even analyses may be used to help the managers of construction companies set target level for revenues, gross profit margin, general overhead costs, and profit from operations for the upcoming year.

The gross profit margin is incorporated into the construction project by adding a profit and overhead markup. The gross profit margin is not the same as the profit and overhead markup; however, they are mathematically related by Eq. (10-10). Companies should set a minimum profit and overhead markup, which may be raised when conditions warrant. Tracking a company's competitors helps a manager determine when to increase the profit and overhead markup.

PROBLEMS

1. A construction company has total revenues of $650,000, total construction costs of $509,000, and general overhead costs of $65,000 for the year. Determine the company's total profit for the year and the percentage of the construction revenues that became profits.

2. A construction company has total revenues of $1,150,000, total construction costs of $956,000, and general overhead costs of $159,000 for the year. Determine the company's total profit for the year and the percentage of the construction revenues that became profits.

3. What are the contribution margin and the contribution margin ratio for the company in Problem 1 if $15,000 of the overhead is considered variable overhead?

4. What are the contribution margin and the contribution margin ratio for the company in Problem 2 if $53,000 of the overhead is considered variable overhead?

5. Determine the break-even volume of work for a company with a fixed overhead of $250,000 and a contribution margin ratio of 11.3%.

6. Determine the break-even volume of work for a company with a fixed overhead of $72,000 and a contribution margin ratio of 14.0%.

7. Determine the break-even volume of work for a company with a fixed overhead of $138,000, a contribution margin ratio of 8.9%, and a required level of profit of $100,000.

8. Determine the break-even volume of work for a company with a fixed overhead of $63,000, a contribution margin ratio of 11.0%, and a required level of profit of $60,000.

9. A construction company has a fixed overhead of $100,000 and a variable overhead of 2% of revenue. Historically, construction costs have been 90% of revenue. What is the minimum amount of sales that are required to break even?

10. A construction company has a fixed overhead of $60,000 and a variable overhead of 2.5% of revenue. Historically, construction costs have been 88% of revenue. What is the minimum amount of sales that are required to break even?

11. Determine the break-even contribution margin ratio for a company with a fixed overhead of $115,000 and revenues of $1,500,000.

12. Determine the break-even contribution margin ratio for a company with a fixed overhead of $92,000 and revenues of $450,000.

13. Determine the break-even contribution margin ratio for a company with a fixed overhead of $115,000, revenues of $1,500,000, and a required level of profit of $85,000.

14. Determine the break-even contribution margin ratio for a company with a fixed overhead of $92,000, revenues of $450,000, and a required level of profit of $45,000.

15. Determine the profit and overhead markup for a company that wants to maintain an 8% gross profit margin.

16. Determine the profit and overhead markup for a company that wants to maintain a 12% gross profit margin.

17. Your construction company recently bid against ABC Construction Company. Your construction costs were $265,815 and you added an 11% profit and overhead markup for a total bid of $295,055. ABC's bid was $301,251. What profit and overhead markup would you need to add to your construction costs to get ABC's bid?

18. Your construction company recently bid against ABC Construction Company. Your construction costs were $1,125,572 and you added a 6% profit and overhead markup for a total bid of $1,193,106. ABC's bid was $1,179,999. What profit and overhead markup would you need to add to your construction costs to get ABC's bid?

PROFIT CENTER ANALYSIS

In this chapter you learn to analyze the profitability of different parts of the company and identify where the company needs to make changes to improve profitability. You will learn to select between hiring a subcontractor and self-performing work. You will also learn to monitor the profitability of different customers and identify which customers should be developed and which customers your company would be better off without.

It is important for financial managers to identify where the company's profit is generated. This would be easy if all activities produced the same gross profit margin. This, however, is not the case. Profit center analysis is where management looks at different activities of the company as profit centers that generate company's profits. Profit center analysis helps management determine if certain activities of the company are meeting its goals, identifies places for change, and provides a quantitative analysis that helps management make decisions, such as whether the company will self-perform work or subcontract the work out to other companies. Before profits can be allocated to different activities we must understand two things. First, we must understand the sources of profit on the company's core business: building construction projects. Second, we must understand how to allocate the general overhead costs to the different profit centers. Let's look at the sources of profit.

SOURCES OF PROFIT

There are up to four sources of profit on a construction project. They are as follows: minimum profit and overhead markup required by the company, profit from the bidding and buyout process, profit from individual crews, and profit from project management. For profit calculation to be accurate, the budget must be a realistic estimate of the cost to complete the project. Budgets that are fat, have large contingencies, are missing items, or have underestimated costs distort the profit analysis. It is important that budgets are carefully and accurately prepared.

The first source of profit is the minimum profit and overhead markup. Each company should establish a minimum profit and overhead markup that each project needs to meet to make it worthwhile for the company to construct the project. The profit and overhead markup, including marking up labor and equipment, may be different for different cost categories—materials, labor, subcontract, equipment, and other. This profit and overhead markup is used to cover the costs of the general overhead and provide a minimum profit for the company's shareholders. Chapter 10 discussed how to determine the minimum profit and overhead markup. The profit from the minimum profit and overhead markup is easily determined by multiplying the project budget by the minimum profit and overhead markup using the following equation:

$$\text{Profit}_{\text{Min}} = \text{Budget(Profit and Overhead Markup)} \qquad (11\text{-}1)$$

If the profit and overhead markup was different for each cost category, the profit for each cost category would be calculated and the profit from the categories would be added together.

Example 11-1: Your company bid a project for $1,000,000 that had a budget of $820,000. The company's minimum profit and overhead markup is 15% for all cost categories. What is the profit generated from the profit and overhead markup?

Solution: The profit is calculated using Eq. (11-1) as follows:

$$\text{Profit}_{\text{Min}} = \$820,000(0.15) = \$123,000$$

The second source of profit or loss is profit or loss generated during the bidding and buyout process by the estimator. The title of estimator is used to describe the person who prepares the estimate regardless of his or her job title. This is profit in addition to the minimum profit and overhead markup and is a result of skillful bidding, subcontracting, and purchasing by the estimator. One way to increase the markup is to identify those times when the market will allow contractors to charge higher than normal prices for their work. The tracking of competitors' bidding habits was discussed at the end of chapter 10 as a way to help the company determine when this opportunity exists. Another way is to reduce construction costs while maintaining prices to the project's owners. This may be done by getting price concessions from suppliers and subcontractors or finding cheaper sources for materials and subcontract work. The markup may also be increased by decreasing costs faster than prices are decreased.

The profit generated by the bidding and buyout process equals the price charged the owner—which is the bid accepted by the owner or the contract amount with the owner—less the budget for the project less the minimum profit and overhead markup. This profit is calculated by the following equation:

$$\text{Profit}_{\text{Est}} = \text{Price} - \text{Budget} - \text{Profit and Overhead Markup} \qquad (11\text{-}2)$$

Conversely, if the estimator does a poor job during the bidding and buyout process there could be a loss instead of a profit. A loss occurs any time that the bidding and buyout process fails to include enough profit to exceed the minimum profit and overhead markup. This may occur because of bidding the job too cheaply, poor estimation of costs, or error in the estimate.

Example 11-2: Determine the profit from the bidding and buyout process for Example 11-1.

Solution: The profit is calculated using Eq. (11-2) as follows:

$$\text{Profit}_{Est} = \$1,000,000 - \$820,000 - \$123,000 = \$57,000$$

The third source of profit is profit from the management of labor and equipment by the crew's foreperson. Equipment is included as part of the crews when the equipment is used and managed by the crews. The profit earned by the foreperson as part of management of the crews is the difference between the budget for the work performed by the crew and the cost to perform the work. This profit is calculated using the following equation:

$$\text{Profit}_{Crew} = \text{Budget} - \text{Cost} \tag{11-3}$$

The profit earned by the management of the crews is a function of two factors: the number of hours—labor and equipment—it takes to complete the task and the hourly rates for the labor and equipment. Profit occurs when the work is managed in such a way that the workers are productive and the proper class of employees is assigned to each task. Conversely, if the foreperson poorly manages the labor and equipment a loss can occur. This may be due to poor scheduling so that the task takes more hours to complete than it should or because the hourly costs were higher than were needed due to using the wrong class of workers to complete the work.

Example 11-3: Your company's excavation crew completed the excavation work on the project in Example 11-1 for $125,000. The budget for this item is $130,000. What is the profit that resulted because of good management on the part of the foreperson?

Solution: The profit is calculated using Eq. (11-3) as follows:

$$\text{Profit}_{Crew} = \text{Budget} - \text{Cost} = \$130,000 - \$125,000 = \$5,000$$

The fourth and final source of profit is profit from management of the project. Equipment is included as part of the management of the project when the equipment is used by the entire project and is managed by the project's management team. The profit earned by the project's management team is the difference between the budget and the cost for the entire project, except for the work performed by the crews, and is calculated using the following equation:

$$\text{Profit}_{Mgt} = \text{Budget} - \text{Cost} \tag{11-4}$$

Profit can be generated by good project management in the form of controlling material waste and reducing overhead costs. One way to reduce overhead costs is to reduce the duration of the project. On the other hand, poor management can reduce profit by poor scheduling and excessive material waste.

Example 11-4:   Your company completed the project in Example 11-1 for $812,000, of which $125,000 was performed by in-house crews. The budgeted cost for the in-house work was $130,000. What is the profit from the management of the project?

Solution: The budgeted cost for the work—excluding the work performed by in-house crews—is $690,000 ($820,000 − $130,000). The cost for the work—excluding the work performed by in-house crews—is $687,000 ($812,000 − $125,000). The profit from the project management is determined using Eq. (11-4) as follows:

$$\text{Profit}_{Mgt} = \text{Budget} - \text{Cost} = \$690,000 - \$687,000 = \$3,000$$

The total profit on the project in Examples 11-1 through 11-4 is $188,000 ($1,000,000 − $812,000). Of this, $123,000 is from the profit and overhead markup, $57,000 is from good estimating practices, $5,000 is from good management of the excavation crew, and $3,000 is from good project management. When properly calculated, the total of the profit and overhead markup required by the company, profit from the bidding and buyout process, profit from the individual crews, and profit from project management should equal the total profit on the project.

The project's management can affect the cost to perform in-house work by poor scheduling, among other things. In order for profit center analysis to work, the in-house crews must be treated and act as subcontractors to the project. When poor coordination on the part of the project's management increases the time needed to complete the task or their costs, the crew's management should be discussing these issues with the project's management. Just as subcontractors request a change order when the scope of work changes, the in-house crews should request change orders. If the project's management is not responsible for the costs of the in-house crews and the crews are not treated as subcontractors, the crew can become a source of funds that the project's management team can tap without being held accountable for the use of the funds.

Example 11-5:   Your company completed building a garage for the Winstons. The costs are shown in Figure 11-1. The work in the grading and excavation, landscaping, roofing, and overhead door cost categories was done by subcontractors. All concrete labor was performed by the company's concrete crew and the framing was done by the company's framing crew. The company's minimum profit and overhead markup is 20%. Determine the profit generated by the estimator, project management, the concrete crew, and the framing crew on this project.

```
┌─────────────────────────────────────────────────────────────────────────────┐
│ Job: 408  Winston Garage                                    August 21, 2004   │
│                                                                               │
│                              Contract   Billed   ----------Costs----------    │
│ Code   Description           Amount     to Date   Actual   Budget   Overrun   │
│ 1000   General Conditions                          3,275    3,400     -125    │
│ 2100   Grading and Excavation                      2,000    1,900      100    │
│ 2700   Landscape                                     152      200      -48    │
│ 3300   Footing and Found.-Labor                      462      450       12    │
│ 3400   Footing and Found.-Concrete                   475      550      -75    │
│ 3500   Slab/Floor-Labor                              395      400       -5    │
│ 3600   Slab/Floor-Concrete                         1,964    2,000      -36    │
│ 3900   Rebar                                         225      200       25    │
│ 6110   Rough Carpentry                             1,522    1,700     -178    │
│ 6120   Lumber                                      2,257    2,200       57    │
│ 7500   Roofing                                       850      850        0    │
│ 8110   Metal Doors and Frames                        243      250       -7    │
│ 8300   Overhead Door                                 392      400       -8    │
│ 9800   Paint                                         700      700        0    │
│               Job Total   20,000   20,000        14,912   15,200     -288    │
└─────────────────────────────────────────────────────────────────────────────┘
```

FIGURE 11-1   Costs for Winston Garage

Solution: The minimum profit and overhead for the project is calculated using Eq. (11-1) as follows:

$$\text{Profit}_{Min} = \$15{,}200(0.20) = \$3{,}040$$

The profit generated by the estimator is calculated using Eq. (11-2) as follows:

$$\text{Profit}_{Est} = \$20{,}000 - \$15{,}200 - \$3{,}040 = \$1{,}760$$

In Figure 11-1, the difference between the actual costs and the budget costs is recorded as a cost overrun, with positive numbers indicating a cost overrun or a loss and negative numbers indicating a cost savings. The profit earned by the concrete crew is the cost savings for the footings and foundation labor and the slab/floor labor or a loss of $7 (−5 + 12). The profit earned by the framing crew is the cost saving for the rough carpentry or a profit of $178. The profit earned by the project management is the cost savings on the remaining items or a profit of $117 ($288 − $178 + $7). The total profit on the project is $5,088 ($20,000 − $14,912). The sum of the profits is $5,088 [$3,040 + $1,760 + (−$7) + $178 + $117].

ALLOCATION OF GENERAL OVERHEAD

Often in a profit center analysis the general overhead needs to be allocated to the profit centers. Because we are dealing with profits, the overhead that should be allocated is the overhead budget or costs based on profits rather than cash flows (see chapter 9). There are a number of methods for allocating general overhead. When allocating the general overhead each account of the general overhead should be allocated separately using the method that is most appropriate for that account. Let's look at the different methods.

The first method is to allocate the general overhead based on the percentage of a company's revenue generated by the profit center. The underlying assumption is that there is a relationship between the amount of revenue generated by a profit center and the amount of general overhead resources that the profit center uses. This is not always the case. For example, profit centers that rely heavily on in-house labor often use more of the general overhead than profit centers that rely heavily on a few subcontractors.

The second method is to allocate the general overhead based on the labor costs or labor hours for each profit center. In the days before computerized accounting packages, the labor burden for project labor was not charged to the jobs but was included as a general overhead item and then allocated to the jobs based on the labor costs or labor hours of each job. This was done because the calculations needed to charge the costs to the jobs are complex and time consuming. With the advent and use of computerized construction accounting systems, the computer can effortlessly perform these calculations, allowing companies to track labor burden costs as construction costs rather than treating them as general overhead costs. Currently, all labor burden for labor performed on the projects should be charged to the projects. Where possible, general management labor costs should be charged to the project on which the crews they manage spend their time. For example, in the case where all of the in-house crews report to a company manager who spends all of his or her time managing the crews—assigning the crews to the various projects and seeing that they have the necessary materials and personnel—the manager should track the time he or she spends supporting each crew so his or her time can be billed as part of the crew costs. This is not always possible, but when possible it should be done because it gives a more accurate picture of the cost of performing the work in-house. When this is not possible, allocating the cost based on labor costs or labor hours is the next best method. Another place this method is commonly used is when allocating unallocated labor—labor for field employees that cannot be charged to a job. This occurs when employees are paid for traveling between projects.

The third method is to allocate the general overhead based on the material costs for each profit center. This method is used when there is a relationship between general overhead costs and the use of materials. This method is commonly used when allocating general overhead costs associated with maintaining an inventory and includes such items as unallocated materials, storage costs, delivery costs not charged to jobs, and the labor costs associated with maintaining an inventory.

The fourth method is to allocate the general overhead based on the estimated usage of the general overhead by the profit center. Here management makes a judgment call as to how much of the general overhead was used by each profit center.

The fifth method is to determine the incremental general overhead cost of each of the profit centers with remaining costs being assigned to the core profit center. Many construction companies consist of a core business—say, general contracting—and then have a number of small profit centers that have been created to support the core business—such as an excavation or framing crew. In this method the general overhead costs are allocated based on the increases in the general overhead costs that are associated with the existence of the individual profit center. This method is useful when determining if a profit center is to be eliminated. When determining the incremental general overhead that is associated with each profit center, the manager determines how much general overhead would be eliminated if the profit center were eliminated. In chapter 9, it was determined that general overhead costs might be fixed over a certain range. If the changes as a result of the profit center are not significant enough to move the company out of the range the fixed overhead costs remains the same. For example, a framing crew requires 10% of the payroll clerk's time. If by eliminating the framing crew the company is unable to reduce the number of hours the clerk works, the incremental cost of the clerk is zero. If by eliminating the framing crew the company could eliminate the two hours of overtime the clerk worked each week, the incremental cost of the clerk would be the cost of the two hours of overtime. All general overhead costs not allocated as incremental costs are allocated to the core business. This is because the core business is the primary reason the company exists, which if it were eliminated would likely be the end of the company.

The final method is an arbitrary assignment of general overhead costs to the profit centers. Here the costs are allocated using some method where there is not a relationship between the costs allocated to the profit centers and the profit centers use of the general overhead resources. For example, management might decide to allocate general overhead costs based on the profit centers ability to pay the costs, thus using the more profitable profit centers to subsidize the less profitable profit centers.

Example 11-6: A company has two divisions. The first division consists of project management and generated $4,523,367 of revenue during the year. The second division consists of three framing crews that generated $1,080,238 in revenues during the year. Management has decided to allocate the office overhead of $562,256 based on the percentage of the company's revenues generated by each of the profit centers, with one exception—$8,264 of unallocated labor that will be allocated entirely to the second division. Determine the overhead allocated to each of the divisions.

Solution: Of the overhead, $553,992 ($562,256 − $8,264) will be allocated based on percentage of revenues. The total revenues for the company are $5,603,605 ($4,523,367 + $1,080,238) for the year. The general overhead allocated to the first division is calculated as follows:

$$\text{Overhead} = \$553,992(\$4,523,367/\$5,603,605) = \$447,196$$

The general overhead allocated to the second division is calculated as follows:

$$\text{Overhead} = \$553,992(\$1,080,238/\$5,603,605) + \$8,264$$
$$\text{Overhead} = \$115,060$$

Profit Center Analysis

Previously, we saw that the profit from a project may be divided up into the profit from the minimum profit and overhead markup, profit from the bidding and buy-out process, profit from the management of crews, and profit from the management of the project. By doing this for all of the projects and totaling the profit, the profit from operations may be used to measure the successfulness of the estimator, each crew, and each project management team. There are two additional ways of dividing the profit from operations: by project type and by customer type. Additionally, management can look at the profitability of each piece of heavy equipment.

One of the important duties of management is to hold the managers or supervisors of the profit centers accountable for the profitability of their profit center. Before they can be held accountable for the profitability of their profit centers they need to be given the authority and resources necessary to succeed. Without the authority to make decisions or if their decisions are constantly being overturned by upper management, the managers of the profit center are simply carrying out orders from upper management and cannot be held accountable for the decisions made by upper management. For the profit center managers to be held accountable, they must have the authority to make decisions and fail—within reasonable limits—because success cannot exist unless there is the possibility of failure. Additionally, without the necessary resources—which include the proper training and support from the main office—managers cannot be held accountable for the operation of the profit center. This does not mean upper management does not set limits on the authority and resources available to the managers of the profit centers, but rather that when those reasonable limits have been established upper management allows the profit center managers to operate within those limits. Neither does it mean that once the limits have been set that upper management can ignore the profit center managers. Upper management must be available to help teach, train, and guide the managers to success without interfering with the managers' ability to operate their profit center.

When supervising the managers of the profit centers it is important to remember that what gets measured and rewarded is what gets done. If the profit center managers are only rewarded for meeting the schedule, they will have little incentive to meet profitability and quality objectives. When evaluating profit centers management should look at three areas: schedule, quality, and financial performance. Let's look at how management may evaluate different profit centers.

Crews as Profit Centers

Crews as profit centers may be evaluated against a company standard or against the cost of replacing the crew with a subcontractor.

When comparing crews to a company standard, the performance of a crew may be determined by comparing their performance to the performance of other crews. For example, it is very easy to compare one framing crew to the other framing crews, especially when they are framing similar types of buildings. Alternately, they may be compared to a minimum standard that applies to the whole company or to an individual goal for each crew. For example, one crew may have the goal to increase their profitability by 10%, whereas another crew may have the goal to operate at a profit rather than a loss. When measuring performance management must look at scheduling, quality, and financial performance.

Schedule performance may be measured by determining the success rate in meeting scheduled milestones. For crews that work on a single project for a long time, it is also useful to measure their schedule performance index (see chapter 7) at regular intervals (say, at the end of every week) and determine the average schedule performance index for a set period of time (say, the quarter) as a measure of the ability to stay on schedule between the milestones.

Quality performance may be measured by performing standardized quality inspections and by using the results of these inspections to determine how the crew did compared to a set standard. For example, a crew may be evaluated against a standard checklist, where the number of noncomplying items are measured. Care must be taken to ensure that there is consistence in how the noncomplying items are handled. For example, are multiple defects in the drywall throughout a room or building counted as an individual item or is each defect counted as an item? Additionally, the items may be weighted based on their importance. It is important that the quality standard is based on the expected quality of the customers. For example, there would be a higher quality standard for a high-end, custom home than there would be for entry-level housing.

Financial performance may be measured against the budget, which is used to determine the profit for the crew. Once these three performance measurements have been taken they may be compared to the performance measurement of other crews, to a set standard, or to a goal for the crew.

Crews should be compared to costs to subcontract the work out to determine if it is cost effective to continue using the crew or if the company would be better off subcontracting the work out. This decision should be reviewed periodically—quarterly or annually—for each crew.

Management must look at schedule, quality, and financial performance when comparing in-house crews to subcontracting the work out. It may be wise to pay more to perform the work in-house—thereby sacrificing financial performance—for improved schedule and quality performance. Improved schedule performance may reduce the duration of the project and the associated reduction in the project overhead may offset some or all of the extra cost of performing the work in-house. Improved schedule and quality performance may translate into higher customer satisfaction and may result in more work from the client. Additionally, management must determine if having the extra personnel on staff is worth the effort. Saving a few dollars a month for the same schedule and quality performance may not be worth the time it takes management to support the crews.

The schedule and quality performance is measured as discussed above. When comparing crews to subcontracting the work out, the profit on labor is the difference between the fair market value of the labor and the cost of performing the labor in-house rather than the difference between the budget and the costs. The fair market value of the labor is the cost at which the work could be subcontracted out and should include all costs that would be born by a subcontractor. For example, if a framing subcontractor typically provides the labor (including labor burden), nails and fasteners, hand tools, and the forklift to frame a building, all of these costs should be included in the cost of in-house framing crews. The reason that rough carpentry is separate from lumber in the cost codes shown in Figure 2-5 is so that all costs that would be born by a framing subcontract can be recorded to 06110 Rough Carpentry, including materials such as nails and fasteners, whereas all costs borne by the general contractor for materials can be recorded to 06120 Lumber. The same is true for 02610 Site Concrete Labor, 03300 Footings and Foundation Labor, and 03500 Slab/Floor Labor, which are used to record the costs of in-house crews. This makes it easy to make a comparison between the rates for in-house crews and the market for the work. When determining the fair market value, all change orders should be included.

Evaluating the crew is important not only so that management can hold the supervisor accountable or determine if the crew should continue to exist but also to know the strength and weakness of each crew so that the most appropriate crew can be assigned to the projects. For example, management would like the crews with the strongest scheduling performance to work on the most time-sensitive projects. In addition, when management knows the weaknesses of each of the crew it knows where more teaching and training would be most beneficial and where corrective action is needed.

Project Management as Profit Centers

Project management teams may be evaluated by comparing their performance to other project management teams, a minimum standard, or to an individual goal for the team. Evaluations must include scheduling, quality, and financial performance. The management team's scheduling, quality, and financial performance may be measured in the same way that the crews' performance was measured. This performance may be measured on a single job or a group of jobs occurring over a period of time. Additionally, its performance should include some measurement of the customers' satisfaction with the management team's performance in these three areas. The customers' satisfaction with the scheduling performance should include items such as how well the management team met turnover dates, how quickly the punch list was completed, and how well the team coordinated with the owners' representatives when dealing with change orders, owner submittals, owner-supplied equipment, and so forth. The customers' satisfaction with the quality performance should include whether the project's quality met the customers' expectations and how the management team handled quality problems. Finally, the customers' satisfaction with the financial performance of the team should include the following: Were change orders handled fairly? Was the billing fair and accurate? And for contracts without a fixed price, was the budget met? Like evaluating the crew, evaluating management teams is important so that management can get the most appropriate crew assigned to the projects, identify areas where more training is needed, and take corrective action.

Estimators as Profit Centers

Estimators are a source of profit or loss within a company. Estimators should be rewarded for the profit that they generate, with estimators who consistently generate above-average profits rewarded more than those who do not. However, if their performance is measured based only on profit, profit will come at the sacrifice of schedule and quality. The cheapest subcontractors and suppliers will be chosen without regard to their ability to meet the schedule and desired levels of quality. Remember, what gets measured and rewarded is what gets done. Estimators' performance should also be determined by their performance in finding subcontractors and suppliers who understand, are committed to, and are contractually tied to scheduling and quality standards required for the project. Evaluating estimators is important so that management can get the most appropriate estimator assigned to the projects, identify areas where more training is needed, and take corrective action.

Types of Jobs as Profit Centers

In chapter 10 we saw that one way to increase profitability is to specialize in certain areas of the construction market. To identify those areas of the market that are more profitable and to monitor the profitability of the company's different market segments, each area of specialization may be treated as a profit center. When treating types of jobs as profit centers, jobs that have a similar set of characteristics are grouped together and the profitability for the group of jobs is calculated. Jobs may be grouped by one or more of the following characteristics: similar customer base (such as residential customers), similar use (such as manufacturing), similar types of buildings (such as Type V wood framed buildings), similar location (such as a city or state), and so forth. When grouping the jobs into profit centers, management must make sure that the types are similar. For example, building apartments and building condominiums are very different types of jobs even though they may be built from virtually identical plans and in the same area of a city. This is because their customers and their uses are very different. With apartments there is a single customer—the owner of the apartments—who wants to rent the apartments for business income. Whereas with condominiums there are multiple owners, many of whom have been saving for years to fulfill the dream of home ownership. When grouping jobs by type, the groups often cross management team boundaries and include jobs from more than one team. The groups may not include all of the jobs performed by one team, unless separate divisions or teams have been established for each type of project.

Once the groups have been established the profitability may be calculated for each group and compared to other project groups, a minimum standard that applies to the whole company or to a target level for the individual group. This comparison may be based on one of the following methods:

> First, the comparison may be made based on the actual gross profit margin or the actual profit and overhead markup at the completion of the projects. Because the gross profit margin and the profit and overhead markup are mathematically related, either method may be used. The gross profit margin compares the gross profit to the revenue from the project (the cost of the project to the owner), whereas the profit and overhead markup compares the gross profit to the construction costs of the project. The comparison should be based on the revenue and gross profit for projects over a specified period of time. Completed projects and in-progress projects—where the revenues (or costs) and gross profit can accurately be estimated—should be included in this analysis. By using this comparison, management may find that it obtains a higher gross profit margin on one type of project and as a result it wants to place a greater focus on obtaining the type of project that has the higher gross margin.

Example 11-7: Your company worked on the projects shown in Table 11-1 during the last year.

The duration in Table 11-1 represents the number of months during the year that the project was under construction. Analyze the different profit centers based on their gross profit margins.

Solution: The gross profit and revenue for the apartment profit center is as follows:

$$\text{Gross Profit} = \$153{,}000 + \$110{,}000 + \$75{,}000 = \$338{,}000$$
$$\text{Revenue} = \$3{,}000{,}000 + \$2{,}017{,}000 + \$1{,}542{,}000$$
$$\text{Revenue} = \$6{,}559{,}000$$

The gross profit margin is calculated using Eq. (6-17) as follows:

$$\text{Gross Profit Margin} = \$338{,}000/\$6{,}559{,}000 = 0.0515 \text{ or } 5.15\%$$

TABLE 11-1 Work Performed During the Year

PROFIT CENTER	REVENUE ($)	GROSS PROFIT ($)	AVERAGE MONTHLY INVESTMENT ($)	DURATION MONTHS
Apartment	3,000,000	153,000	187,000	8
Apartment	2,017,000	110,000	183,000	11
Apartment	1,542,000	75,000	108,000	5
Condo	642,000	51,000	88,000	7
Condo	1,600,000	110,000	160,000	10

The gross profit margin for the condominium profit center is calculated in the same manner:

$$\text{Gross Profit} = \$51,000 + \$110,000 = \$161,000$$
$$\text{Revenue} = \$642,000 + \$1,600,000 = \$2,242,000$$
$$\text{Gross Profit Margin} = \$161,000/\$2,242,000 = 0.0718 \text{ or } 7.18\%$$

Based on the gross profit margin, the condominium projects are more profitable.

Second, the comparison may be made based on the return on the cash invested in the projects constructed by the profit centers. By using this comparison, management may find that certain types of projects have a lower return on investment even though they have a higher than average gross profit margin because the projects require more cash investment. This may be due to slow payments from the owners, owners who require a higher retention rate, or that the projects use fewer subcontractors. As a result, management may want to increase the profit and overhead markup for this group of projects. The return on investment for the profit center may be estimated by dividing the profit for a specified period of time—often a year—by the average investment in the jobs that make up that profit center for that same period of time.

Example 11-8: Analyze the different profit centers in Table 11-1 based on their return on cash invested in the projects.

Solution: From Example 11-7, the sum of the gross profit for the apartment profit center is $338,000. The average investment for the apartment profit center is the weighted average of the average monthly investments in each of the projects. For example, the average monthly investment for the first project is only invested eight months of the year during the time it was under construction. The average monthly investment for the apartment profit center is as follows:

$$\text{Investment} = \$187,000(8/12) + \$183,000(11/12)$$
$$+ \$108,000(5/12)$$
$$\text{Investment} = \$337,417$$

The return on cash investment in the apartment profit center projects is as follows:

$$\text{Return} = \$338,000/\$337,417 = 1.0017 \text{ or } 100.17\%$$

The average monthly investment and the return on cash investment in the condominium profit center projects are as follows:

$$\text{Investment} = \$88,000(7/12) + \$160,000(10/12) = \$184,667$$
$$\text{Return} = \$161,000/\$184,667 = 0.8718 \text{ or } 87.18\%$$

Based on the return on cash invested in the apartment projects, they are more profitable. It is important to note that this return ignores general overhead, which will greatly reduce the return for the company.

Finally, the comparison may be made based on the amount of management time the project consumes. Management's time is a limited resource that limits the number of jobs that a company can perform. If projects consume more of management's time than is available, then additional management must be hired, increasing the cost of general overhead. If additional management is not hired, the effectiveness of existing management is reduced, resulting in higher cost due to poor cost control. By looking at this comparison, management may determine if they could earn more profit by focusing on obtaining projects that do not consume a lot of management's time or if they should increase the profit and overhead markup on projects that require a lot of management's time. This calculation is done by determining the expected profit that a management team will achieve running at full capacity.

Example 11-9: Analyze the different profit centers in Table 11-1 based on their use of management's time. One project manager can oversee four apartment projects or two condominium projects.

Solution: The monthly profit generated by each apartment project is as follows:

$$\text{Profit}_1 = \$153,000/8 = \$19,125$$
$$\text{Profit}_2 = \$110,000/11 = \$10,000$$
$$\text{Profit}_3 = \$75,000/5 = \$15,000$$

The average monthly profit generated by an apartment project is as follows:

$$\text{Profit} = (\$19,125 + \$10,000 + \$15,000)/3 = \$14,708$$

On average an apartment project takes 25% of a project manager's time. Running at full capacity a project manager would generate the following profit per month:

$$\text{Profit} = \$14,708/0.25 = \$58,832$$

The monthly profit generated by each condominium project is as follows:

$$\text{Profit}_1 = \$51,000/7 = \$7,286$$
$$\text{Profit}_2 = \$110,000/10 = \$11,000$$

The average monthly profit generated by a condominium project is as follows:

$$\text{Profit} = (\$7,286 + \$11,000)/2 = \$9,143$$

On average a condominium project takes 50% of a project manager's time. Running at full capacity a project manager would generate the following profit per month:

$$\text{Profit} = \$9,143/0.50 = \$25,618$$

Based on the use of management's time the apartment projects are more profitable. Each project manager can generate more than twice as much profit when working on apartment projects versus condominiums.

From Examples 11-7 through 11-9 we can see that apartment projects generated more profits based on the limited resources of cash and management's time even though the condominium projects had a higher gross profit margin. In an environment where there is a surplus of projects to build and limited amount of management personnel, the company should focus on building apartments. The company may want to focus on getting additional apartment projects because of their profitability; however, focusing on apartments must be weighed against the risk associated with only operating in one area of the market. Alternately, the company may want to increase its gross profit margin on condominium projects.

Customers as Profit Centers

Each customer should be treated as a profit center. To do this management needs to determine the volume and profit attributed to each customer. Once the data have been collected, the customers are plotted on the matrix as shown in Figure 11-2.

Customers in Quadrant I are the company's best customers. They provide a high volume of work at a high profit margin. In short, they are the company's most profitable customers. Where possible, the company should try to expand the volume of work performed for their existing Quadrant I customers. The company should take precautions to ensure that these customers' needs are being met and that these customers have no reason to take their business elsewhere.

Customers in Quadrant II are customers who provide an occasional job at a high profit margin. Where possible, the company should try to increase the business of these customers. An occasional high-profit job can be a nice bonus. High-maintenance customers in this quadrant may require more of the company's general overhead than it generates in profit or they require so much of management's time

FIGURE 11-2 Customer Matrix

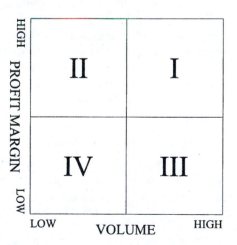

that they do not have time to service Quadrant I customers and develop other customers. When this happens, management must increase the profitability of the customers, convert them into low-maintenance customers, or get rid of the customers. When customers are so high maintenance that they prevent management from taking care of the Quadrant I customers, management must choose if they want to keep the high-maintenance customers and risk losing their Quadrant I customers or get rid of the high-maintenance customers and focus on their Quadrant I customers. The best way to get rid of customers is to pass them along to another contractor who may be in a position to meet their needs while making a profit.

Customers in Quadrant III are customers who provide a steady flow of work at a low gross profit margin. A lot of profit can be generated by customers in this quadrant provided the customers are low maintenance. Where possible, the company should try to increase the profit margin provided by customers in this quadrant. The risk that the company takes by increasing the profit margin is that these customers may take some or all of their business elsewhere, which must be weighed against the increased profit margin. The company may find that it is better off taking fewer selective jobs from customers at a higher gross profit margin than it is trying to do all of the customers' work. This is especially true when customers require many different types of work, some of which are outside the company's area of specialization. However, just like the Quadrant II customers, if customers in this quadrant distract the company's focus from serving the Quadrant I customers or if they are high-maintenance customers, the company should consider getting rid of them.

Customers in Quadrant IV should be moved into one of the other quadrants or dropped. It is not uncommon to buy a customer's business—bid the work at a low profit margin—when trying to establish a relationship with the customer. As soon as possible these customers should be moved to another quadrant; otherwise, they will distract management from taking care of the customers in the other quadrants. Some customers are habitual Quadrant IV customers, running from company to company based on who has the best prices. No company can survive on Quadrant IV customers.

Elimination of a few customers who are less profitable or too high maintenance may allow management the time and resources to develop one customer into a customer that produces more profit than the eliminated customers. It is better to be small and highly profitable than large and marginally profitable. It is not uncommon for a small company to double and triple in size while seeing its total profit stay the same or shrink because it is taking on less-profitable jobs while increasing general overhead costs.

Equipment as Profit Centers

Each piece of heavy equipment may be treated as a profit center. To do this management needs to know the revenues and the costs of each piece of equipment. These revenues and costs are tracked within the equipment ledger. There are a number of reasons for treating the equipment as profit centers.

First, management must decide if the company is using the equipment enough to justify owning the equipment or if the company would be better off renting the equipment on a monthly, weekly, or daily basis. It is important to note that if management is looking at hiring a subcontractor to provide the equipment, it is looking at replacing a crew because they would be replacing both equipment and labor. When making this decision, the cost of owning the equipment is compared to the fair market value of renting the equipment. The fair market value of the equipment is the cost to rent the equipment from the local equipment rental business. This decision is made for each piece of equipment and should be made periodically, for example, annually.

Second, management must decide if the company is spending so much on the repair of the old equipment that it would be better to replace the old equipment with new equipment. This decision is made by comparing the historical costs of the company's equipment to the projected costs of the new equipment. When comparing the different life expectancies of the new and old equipment, management must take into account the difference in their costs and the time value of money when making these decisions. Quantitative methods that may be used in making this decision are discussed in chapters 17 and 18.

Third, management must decide if the equipment is seeing a lot of unnecessary repairs due to abuse or poor maintenance practices. To address this issue, costs for unexpected repairs must be tracked separately from the cost of routine maintenance and expected repairs—such as engine overhauls that occur every 200,000 miles. In Figure 2-6, the repairs and maintenance category is subdivided into repairs, maintenance, and tires subcategories. The repairs subcategory would be used to track unexpected repairs. Routine maintenance and expected repairs would be tracked in the maintenance category.

And, finally, management must decide if the company is spending enough on tire repairs to see if it would be more economical to foam-fill the tires or replace the equipment with a tracked vehicle. To address this issue the money spent on tires must be tracked. In Figure 2-6, the tire cost would be tracked in the tires subcategory under repairs and maintenance.

CONCLUSION

It is important for management to know where the company is making its profit. This allows management to focus on those areas that are most profitable, identify those areas that need improvement, identify unprofitable work that may be eliminated or subcontracted out, and identify unprofitable customers. Profit may be increased above the company's minimum profit and overhead markup by skillful bidding and buying out of the project, good management of the crews, and by good project management. When analyzing the sources of profit, the company may be divided up in several ways. The profit may be divided among the minimum profit and overhead markup, the crews, the project teams, and the estimators, with the crews, project teams, and the estimators being the profit centers. Alternately, the profit may be divided among the different types of jobs, with each type of job being treated as a profit center. Finally, the profit may be divided up by customer, with each customer becoming a profit center. When analyzing profit, management often needs to allocate overhead. Overhead may be allocated based on the revenue generated, labor costs, material costs, usage of general office support, the incremental (change in overhead) associated with the profit center, or by some arbitrary assignment of the costs.

PROBLEMS

1. Your company completed the site work for the South Pointe office complex. The costs are shown in Figure 11-3. The site concrete labor and landscaping were done by subcontractors. The demolition and grubbing and the grading and excavation were done by the company's excavation crew. The company's minimum profit and overhead markup is 15%. Determine the profit generated by the estimator, project management, and the excavation crew on this project.

2. Your company completed the East Side subdivision. The costs are shown in Figure 11-4. The site concrete labor and outside lighting were done by subcontractors. The grading and excavation, sanitary sewer, water line, and storm drain were done by the company's excavation crew. The company's minimum profit and overhead markup is 15%. Determine the profit generated by the estimator, project management, and the excavation crew on this project.

Job: 411 South Pointe Site Work					May 15, 2004
		Contract	Billed	-------------Costs------------		
Code	Description	Amount	to Date	Actual	Budget	Overrun
2050	Demolition & Grubbing			33,562	35,000	−1,438
2100	Grading & Excavation			20,500	19,500	1,000
2610	Site Conc.-Labor			19,200	19,200	0
2620	Site Conc.-Concrete			9,375	9,900	−525
2700	Landscaping			37,500	37,500	0
	Job Total	138,000	128,000	120,137	121,100	−963

FIGURE 11-3 Costs for South Point Site Work

```
Job: 424  East Side Subdivision                                    Sept. 1, 2004

                         Contract    Billed   -------------------Costs--------------------
Code   Description        Amount    to Date    Actual    Budget    Overrun
2100   Grading & Excavation                    57,800    59,000    -1,200
2400   Sanitary Sewer                          27,365    28,200      -835
2450   Water Line                              31,750    31,000       750
2500   Storm Drain                             16,850    17,000      -150
2610   Site Conc.-Labor                        19,200    19,200         0
2620   Site Conc.-Concrete                     21,265    20,900       365
2900   Outside Lighting                        23,600    23,600         0
            Job Total    234,699   234,699    197,830   198,900    -1,070
```

FIGURE 11-4   Costs for South Pointe Site Work

profit Margin Analysis   16.52

3. Your company worked on the projects shown as follows during the last year. Analyze the different profit centers based on their gross profit margins, their return on cash invested in the projects, and their use of management's time. One project manager can oversee three office remodel projects or one new construction project.

PROFIT CENTER	REVENUE ($)	GROSS PROFIT ($)	AVERAGE MONTHLY INVESTMENT ($)	DURATION MONTHS
Office Remodel	150,000	22,272	37,500	4
Office Remodel	75,000	13,854	25,000	3
Office Remodel	55,000	10,120	27,500	2
New Construction	375,000	41,659	23,000	8
New Construction	325,000	35,555	20,000	8
New Construction	270,000	32,338	24,000	6

16.52 (Office Remodel), *11.29* (New Construction)

4. Your company worked on the projects shown as follows during the last year. Analyze the different profit centers based on their gross profit margins, their return on cash invested in the projects, and their use of management's time. One project manager can oversee four subdivisions or one road construction project.

PROFIT CENTER	REVENUE ($)	GROSS PROFIT ($)	AVERAGE MONTHLY INVESTMENT ($)	DURATION MONTHS
Subdivision	500,000	73,334	83,333	6
Subdivision	375,000	46,954	75,000	5
Subdivision	177,000	17,079	44,250	4
Road	1,123,000	137,968	140,375	8
Road	1,564,800	112,660	156,480	10

PART

IV

MANAGING CASH FLOWS

In this section we look at how to manage the company's cash flows and how to evaluate different sources of funding its cash needs. This section includes the following chapters:

CHAPTER 12

Cash Flows for Construction Projects

In this chapter you learn to develop a cash-flow projection for a construction project from both the perspective of a construction company that is receiving progress payments or draws from the project's owner and from the perspective of a construction company that receives a single payment when the project is sold—such as is the case with many homebuilders. For companies in either of these situations, the company must pay for some or all of the construction costs—especially labor—from the company's funds before being reimbursed for these costs. To cover these costs the company needs cash. Because inadequate funding on the part of the construction company can spell doom to a construction project as well as to all of the companies involved, it is important that managers accurately project both the amount and timing of the cash required by a construction project. An understanding of the cash flow for a construction project is a prerequisite to preparing a cash flow for an entire construction company, which is discussed in chapter 14.

There are two primary threats to a construction company's financial future. The first threat is a lack of profitability. The second threat is insufficient cash. Insufficient cash is where the company lacks sufficient funds to pay the bills that are due. A company may be profitable and still fail because it lacks sufficient cash. In this chapter we look at the cash needed to construct individual projects.

The cash generated by a project is equal to the cash receipts less the cash disbursements. If the cash disbursements are less than the cash receipts for a project, the project will be generating cash for use by the company on other projects, to cover general overhead, or provide a profit to the owners. When a project is generating cash the cash flow will be positive. If the cash disbursements exceed the cash receipts on a project, the company will need to supply cash to fund the project and the cash flow will be negative. Most construction projects require the investment of cash at the beginning of the project and, if they are profitable, generate cash near the end of the project.

With a large portion of a company's financial assets tied up in the form of cash used to fund construction projects, it is important that a construction manager understands how the decisions he or she makes regarding individual construction projects affect the project's need for cash and as a result the company's cash flow. The construction company's needs for cash stem from the company's need to pay bills before receiving payment from the owner for the work associated with these bills. A lack of sufficient cash hurts a construction company in many ways. First, when a company cannot pay its bills on time because of a lack of cash, the company may have to pay late charges, pay higher prices, or may have to pre-pay for materials and subcontractor services. When the company pays late charges and higher prices, this reduces a company's profits and reduces a company's ability to compete based on price. When a company has to prepay for materials and services due to lack of cash, this increases its need for cash and further aggravates the problem. Second, the amount of cash a construction company has greatly affects the amount of work the company can perform. This can be in the form of limits placed on a company from the bonding and insurance carriers or because the company cannot acquire the necessary materials and subcontractor services necessary to complete the project because it lacks the cash necessary to obtain credit. If the lack of cash is great enough, an otherwise profitable company may be forced into bankruptcy.

In this chapter we look at the project's cash flow and cash requirements from two perspectives whose cash requirements differ greatly. The first perspective is from the construction company that is receiving a monthly payment from the project's owner. The second perspective is from a construction company that receives a single payment when the project is sold. This perspective is applicable to homebuilders who get paid when the house is sold or construction companies that are developing a property. In both of these cases a company needs to fund the construction until the project is sold or permanent, long-term financing can be obtained for the project.

CASH FLOW FOR PROJECTS WITH PROGRESS PAYMENTS

For construction projects where a construction company receives monthly progress payments the cash flow from the project has three unique characteristics. First, the cash receipts for the project usually occur only once during each month. As a result, there is a single point in time during the month when the cash a construction company has invested in the project rapidly decreases, which coincides with the receipt of the payment from the owner. Second, a construction company can often defer paying some of the costs associated with the construction on these types of projects until it receives payment from the owner. As a result, much of the payment from the owner is immediately paid out to suppliers and subcontractors. In effect, some of the cash associated with these projects quickly passes from the project's owner through the construction company's banking accounts to the suppliers and sub-contractors. Third, the owner holds back part of the payments due to the construction company in the form of retention, which is held until the project is completed. At the completion of the project, the owner pays the construction company the retention. Retention on a project can often exceed the expected profits on a project. These three factors all affect a construction company's need for cash on a project with progress payments.

To determine the needed cash for a project we need to look at the timing of the cash flows for the project; specifically, the cash flows associated with the payments from the owner versus the payment of the construction bills.

One of the biggest factors in determining the cash needs for a project is the schedule of payments from the owner. A construction company will need more cash to complete a project when the owner pays the monthly bill 60 days after receipt of the bill than it would need if the owner paid the monthly bill 15 days after receipt. Often the final payment has a different payment schedule than the progress payments.

Another big factor in determining the cash needs for a construction project is retention. Retention is often held by the owner to ensure that a construction company completes a project. Most commonly, retention is expressed as a percentage of the cost of the work billed to the owner. Common retention rates include 5 and 10%. In some cases, the owner may hold retention only on the first half of the contract. For example, the owner may hold 10% retention until the contract is 50% complete, at which time no additional retention is withheld. In this example, at the completion of the project the owner would be holding retention equal to 5% of the contract amount. The retention is often paid to the construction company at the time of the final payment although it may be paid at a later date. When negotiating a construction contract, the contractor should negotiate the retention terms as well as the contract price.

One of the greatest needs for cash on a project comes from labor performed by the company on the project. Typically, labor for a project is paid weekly or every two weeks. Often, contracts—especially government contracts—require that employees are paid weekly. When paying weekly, the construction company pays for the labor performed for the previous week during the current week. For a construction company that bills the owner on a monthly basis this means that the company will pay up to four weeks of labor before it can bill the owner for the labor and then the construction company has to wait for the owner to pay the bill. If the owner pays one month after the bill is received, the construction company will need enough cash to cover two months of labor. If the payment schedule for the owner is increased to 45 days, the contractor will be funding two and a half months of payroll. Conversely, if the payment terms are reduced to 15 days the contractor will reduce funding needs to one and a half months of payroll. Because retention cannot be held from employees' wages, the construction company also must have sufficient cash to cover the retention held on wages. One way a construction company may reduce the cash required to cover labor costs is to subcontract the labor out, thereby utilizing the subcontractor's cash rather than its own.

Example 12-1: Payroll due to the employees on a project is $10,594 for the week of May 12 through 18. The employees will be paid on May 21. The construction company can bill the owner for this labor on May 31 and will be paid for the labor on June 25. How long must the construction company fund the labor?

Solution: The company must fund the $10,594 of labor from May 21 to June 25 or for 35 days.

Another need for cash comes from the use of materials on the project. The payment terms with material suppliers vary from company to company. Material suppliers often require that they be paid without taking into account whether the construction company has received payment from the owner. Commonly, suppliers require that they be paid 10, 15, or 30 days after issuing the bill. How often the supplier bills the construction company has a great effect on the cash needs of the construction company. For example, a project where the owner pays the monthly bills within 15 days of receipt and the suppliers bill monthly—just in time for the construction company to submit the monthly bill to the owner— and the suppliers allow the construction company 30 days to pay the bill, the construction company would not need cash to pay the supplier's bills. This is because the construction company receives payment from the owner before it has to pay the suppliers. Whereas if the supplier on the same project bills on a weekly basis, the construction company would need cash to cover the bills received during the first part of the monthly billing period. Bills received after the middle of the month will not require funding by the construction company. When dealing with large purchases or when the construction company is one of the supplier's largest customers, the construction company may be able to negotiate for the supplier to be paid when the owner pays the construction company. Like subcontracting, this allows the construction company to use the supplier's cash rather than its own. Most often material suppliers will not allow retention to be held from their payments, leaving the construction company to supply the cash needed to cover retention on the materials. Some suppliers offer discounts for early payment. Determining whether a company should take advantage of the discounts is discussed in chapter 16.

Example 12-2: A $5,000 material bill for lumber is received on May 7 and is due 30 days from its billing date of May 1. An $800 material bill for lumber is received on May 27 and is due 30 days from its billing date of May 23. The construction company can bill the owner for these material bills on May 31 and will be paid on June 15. How long must the construction company fund the costs of these material bills?

Solution: The $5,000 bill must be paid by May 31; therefore, the company must fund the bill from May 31 to June 15 or for 15 days. The $800 bill must be paid by June 22, after the construction company receives payment from the owner for this bill; therefore, it will not need to fund the payment of this bill.

Additional cash may be needed to pay for materials because the point in time when the materials become a billable item to the construction company may be different than the point in time when the materials become a billable item to the project's owner. Materials may become a billable item to the construction company when it orders the materials or when the materials are delivered to the project. The same materials may become a billable item to the project's owner when they are ordered, delivered, or incorporated into the construction project. For example, a supplier of custom-built materials may require that the construction company place a deposit on or prepayment for the materials before fabrication begins. However, the project's owner may require that the materials be incorporated into the project before the construction company can bill the owner for the materials. This would require the construction company to fund the cash paid to the supplier from the time the order was placed until after the materials were incorporated into the project. When dealing with expensive mechanical and electrical equipment, a large sum of cash could be tied up for many months. Similarly, when a project's owner does not pay for materials until they are incorporated into the construction, additional cash is required when materials are delivered to the site before the work crews are ready to incorporate them into the project. When calculating the needed cash for a project, the construction manager should understand when he or she is allowed to bill the project's owner for materials used in the construction project.

Additional cash is needed to cover the cost of the equipment used to construct the project. When equipment is rented on a short-term basis—daily or weekly—the equipment creates the same need for cash as does the materials. When the equipment is leased, the payment of the lease is required on a monthly basis. This requires the construction company to use its cash to cover the cost of the equipment until the owner pays for the work performed by the equipment. When owned equipment is purchased on a loan it behaves much as a lease because there are still monthly payments to make. When the equipment is owned outright the projects that use the equipment are expected to generate a cash flow to cover cash outlays used to purchase equipment; therefore, it behaves much as a lease or purchase with a loan. Many companies set up a separate leasing company for equipment and bill the projects as if the equipment was leased. When setting up a separate leasing company, companies should consult a tax professional to make sure that they understand the tax implications of setting up such a company are understood.

One of the advantages of using subcontractors is that subcontractors are often paid when the contractor gets paid. This allows the contractor to use the subcontractor's cash for the materials, labor, and equipment supplied by the subcontractor rather than using its own cash. The contractor often holds retention from the subcontractor, further reducing the contractor's need for cash.

FIGURE 12-1   Cost Curve

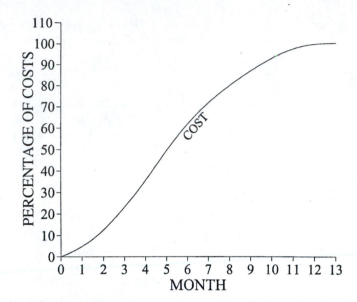

Other costs must be looked at on a case-by-case basis. For some items, the construction company may have to pay up front, such as for a building permit. Other items, such as mobilization, the contractor may have to pay for and recoup the cost as the equipment is used on the project.

There are four steps a construction manager must follow when developing a cash flow for a construction project.

In the first step, the manager must prepare a cost-loaded schedule for the project. The preparation of a cost-loaded schedule was covered in chapter 7. The rate of progress on a project usually starts out slowly, picks up speed through the middle of the project, and slows down as the project nears completion. Commonly, the rate of progress at the end of the project is slower than at the beginning of the project. A graph showing the cost-loaded schedule for a typical project is shown in Figure 12-1. The graph is based on the cost of the work performed. The months shown on the x axis of the graph represent the end of the months. This cost curve is often referred to as the S curve.

In the second step, the manager must determine when the construction company will pay for the items in the cost-loaded schedule. To do this, the costs on the cost-loaded schedule must be grouped based on their payment terms. For example, labor costs that will be paid during the week following the week the costs were incurred need to be separated from the costs that will be paid when payment is received from the project's owner. Additionally, costs that will be paid in full need to be separated from those costs that retention can be withheld from until the completion of the project, usually subcontractor costs. A graph showing the payment of costs for a project is shown in Figure 12-2. The graph is based on 25% of the costs being materials, 25% being labor, and 50% being subcontractors. The material bills are paid in full when payment is received from

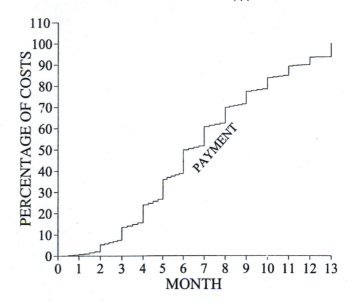

FIGURE 12-2 Payment Curve

the project's owner. The labor is paid weekly. The subcontractors are paid when payment is received, less 10% retention that is withheld until the retention is released by the owner.

In the third step, the manager must determine when payment will be received from the project's owner for the work in the cost-loaded schedule. This is done by determining when the costs in the cost-loaded schedule will be billed to the owner and then determining when payment will be received. The payments must be reduced by the retention withheld by the project's owner and the release of retention must be included in the cash flows at the end of the project. The costs and payments shown in Figures 12-1 and 12-2 include the only the construction costs, while excluding the profit and overhead markup. When billing the project's owner the profit and overhead markup is included in the progress payments. In addition to the cost of the work, Figure 12-3 shows the value of the work, which includes an 8% profit and overhead markup along with the cash receipts (payments) from the project's owner, both of which are expressed as a percentage of costs. The receipts are based on the owner being billed at the end of the month for the work being performed during the month and the project's owner paying the bills at the end of the following month, while withholding a 10% retention. In this example, the costs incurred during the first month are billed at the end of the first month and payment is received from the owner for these costs at the end of the second month. The retention is released at the end of the thirteenth month. If the project's owner paid the bills 15 days after receipt, the receipt curve would move one-half of a month to the left. If payments were received 45 days after receipt of the bill, the receipt curve would move one-half of a month to the right.

In the final step, the manager must determine the difference between the cash inflows to the project (receipts from the owner) and the cash outflows from

FIGURE 12-3   Receipt
Curve

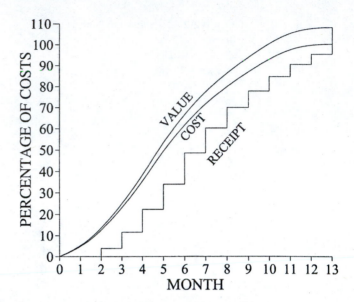

the project (payment to labor, suppliers, and subcontractors). The vertical distance between the payment and receipt lines represents the cash provided by the construction company and is shown as the shaded area in Figure 12-4. In this example, the project first experiences a cash surplus during the tenth month—which is eliminated by labor payments during the month—and by the twelfth month a constant cash surplus on the project occurs.

FIGURE 12-4   Cash
Provided by Construction
Company

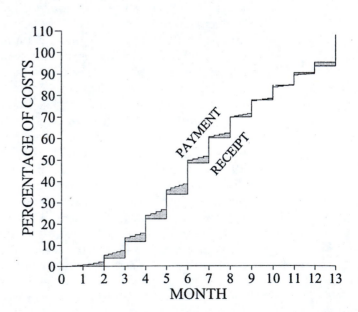

The cash is provided in the form of actual cash used to cover the costs of the work and the deferral of the profit and overhead markup on part of the construction company. The profit and overhead markup needs to be included as part of the cash provided for the project for three reasons. First, the profit and overhead markup is needed to cover the costs of the general overhead. If the profit and overhead markup were not paid until the end of the project, the construction company would still need to supply cash to cover the project's portion of the general overhead costs until the payment of the profit and overhead markup. Second, the profit and overhead markup provides the company with profit that is invested in other company operations or distributed to company's owners. When payment of the profit and overhead markup is deferred, the company is—by default—investing in the project while forgoing investing in other company operations or distributing the profit to the company's owners. Third, because many construction companies use the percentage-of-completion accounting method for tax purposes, the company is recording the profits and paying income taxes on those profits throughout the project, even when the profits have not been paid.

The cash provided consists of two components. First, it consists of costs that have been incurred and billed to the owner for which payment has not been received. For the construction company, this is their accounts receivable. Second, it consists of costs incurred during the current billing period that have not been billed to the owner.

The vertical distance between the value and the receipt lines represents the cash provided by the construction company, labor, the suppliers, and the subcontractors and is shown as the shaded area in Figure 12-5.

There are three conclusions that can be made about the amount of cash provided by the construction company. First, during each month the greatest need for cash occurs just prior to receipt of the payment from the owner. From Figure 12-4

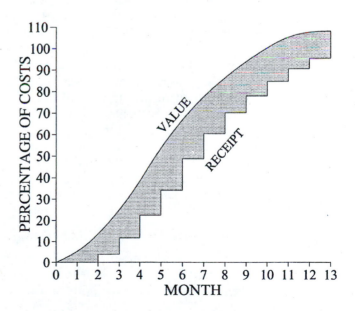

Figure 12-5 Cash Provided by Construction Company, Labor, Suppliers, and Subcontractors

we see that when payments are received there is a quick drop in the amount of cash needed. As a result, the cash needed at the end of the month is often less than the peak amount of cash needed during the month. Second, the amount of cash tied up in retention increases as the project is completed. In the above example the cash needed to fund the retention starts out at 0% of the total value of the project and increases to 10% of the total value of the project by the twelfth month. Third, the amount of cash needed—excluding retention—is greatest when the rate of progress is greatest. In other words, the faster the construction company completes the project the more cash it needs.

The monthly cash flow may be characterized by measuring the monthly cash flows to date at two points in time during the month. The first point in time is at the end of each month. This is referred to as the monthly cash flow. The second point in time is when the project requires the greatest investment of cash during the month, which usually occurs just before the payment is received from the project's owner. This is referred to as the peak cash flow and represents the most negative cash flow during the month. Cash flows measured at this point in time are designated by the prime mark, as in n'. These two monthly cash flows are used in chapter 14 to get a picture of the financial status of the construction company. If we were to look only at the cash flow or cash invested at the end of the month, we would greatly understate the cash needs for many projects.

The monthly cash flow for the project for a specific month equals the cash receipts less the cash disbursements for the month and is calculated as follows:

$$\text{Cash Flow}_n = \text{Cash Receipts}_n - \text{Cash Disbursements}_n \qquad (12\text{-}1)$$

The peak cash flow for a month—which usually occurs just prior to receipt of payment from the project's owner—is calculated by using Eq. (12-1), where only the cash disbursements included are those that occur prior to receipt of the payment from the owner. The cash receipts would be zero at this point in time.

The total cash generated by a project at a specified date may be measured at the end of each month and at the point in time when the monthly peak cash flow occurs. The total cash generated is calculated by summing all of the cash flows that have occurred prior to the specified date. A negative number represents an investment of cash in the project. The total cash generated as of the end of any month is calculated by summing the monthly cash flows through the end of the month. For example, if we were calculating the total cash generated as of the end of the month of June we would sum the monthly cash flows for all prior months and add the monthly cash flow for June to this sum. Alternately, we could calculate the total cash generated as of the end of the month of June by adding June's monthly cash flow to the total cash generated as of the end of the month of May—the previous month. The cash flow generated is calculated as follows:

$$\text{Cash}_n = \text{Cash}_{n-1} + \text{Cash Flow}_n \qquad (12\text{-}2)$$

The peak amount of cash required by projects often occurs just prior to receipt of payment from the project's owner. When calculating the total cash generated ($\text{Cash}_{n'}$) just prior to receipt of payment from the project's owner, we would add this month's cash flows (Cash Flow$_{n'}$) that occur before payment is received from the owner to the total cash generated as of the end of the previous month. The total cash generated just prior to receipt of payment from the project's owner is calculated as follows:

$$\text{Cash}_{n'} = \text{Cash}_{n-1} + \text{Cash Flow}_{n'} \tag{12-3}$$

Estimating the cash flows and cash generated is shown in the following example. In this example, the cash flows are prepared on a monthly basis. With a little more effort, the example could be solved by preparing the cash flows on a weekly basis.

Example 12-3: A construction company is negotiating on a construction project with a six-month duration. On the last day of each month the construction company may bill the owner for the work completed during the month. The owner pays the monthly bills one month after they are received. For example, the construction company receives payment for work completed during June on July 31. The owner also holds 10% retention. Final payment is expected one month after completion of the project and will include payment of the retention. The construction company pays material suppliers in full when it receives payment from the owner. The construction company pays subcontractors when it receives payment from the owner but withholds 10% from the subcontractor's payment. The construction company pays for labor weekly. The projected monthly material, labor, and subcontractor costs, as well as the amount the construction company will bill the project's owner each month, are shown in Table 12-1. Determine the monthly cash flows and the total cash generated by the project at the end of each month and just before each payment is received from the project's owner. What is the maximum amount of cash invested by the company during the completion of the project?

Solution: To analyze the cash needs of this project we begin at the beginning of the project and work our way to the end of the project, calculating the cash flow and total cash generated at the end of each month and just before each payment is received from the project's owner.

TABLE 12-1 Monthly Costs and Billings for Example 12-3

	COSTS			
MONTH	MATERIALS ($)	LABOR ($)	SUB. ($)	BILL TO OWNER ($)
1	30,400	34,900	54,700	129,600
2	57,300	48,900	123,800	248,400
3	80,500	73,100	136,400	313,200
4	29,200	34,000	106,800	183,600
5	27,800	26,200	66,000	129,600
6	15,400	11,300	43,300	75,600
Total	240,600	228,400	531,000	1,080,000

Because the first payment from the owner is not received until the second month, the first point in time where we calculate the total cash generated by the project is at the end of the first month. For the first month, the peak cash flow occurs at the end of the month. Because material suppliers and subcontractors are paid only when the construction company receives payment from the owner, no material or subcontractor payments are made during the first month. Payments are made to labor during the month. To simplify calculations we assume that all labor is paid during the month the work is performed although some of the costs may be paid during the first week of the following month. At the end of the first month the construction company has paid $34,900 to cover the cost of the labor. The cash flow for the first month is calculated using Eq. (12-1) as follows:

$$\text{Cash Flow}_n = \text{Cash Receipts}_n - \text{Cash Disbursements}_n$$
$$\text{Cash Flow}_n = \text{Cash Receipts}_n - (\text{Material Payments}_n$$
$$+ \text{ Labor Payments}_n + \text{ Subcontractor Payments}_n)$$
$$\text{Cash Flow}_1 = \$0 - (\$0 + \$34{,}900 + \$0) = -\$34{,}900$$

The total cash generated by the project by the end of the first month is calculated using Eq. (12-2) as follows:

$$\text{Cash}_1 = \text{Cash}_0 + \text{Cash Flow}_1$$
$$\text{Cash}_1 = \$0 + (-\$34{,}900) = -\$34{,}900$$

At the end of the first month the construction company will have $34,900 of cash invested in the project.

The next point in time where we need to calculate total cash generated by the project is just before receipt of the first payment from the owner, which occurs at the end of the second month. No additional payments have been made to suppliers and subcontractors during this part of the month. The construction company has paid out $48,900 to cover the cost of the labor performed during the second month. This cash flow is calculated using Eq. (12-1) as follows:

$$\text{Cash Flow}_{2'} = \$0 - (\$0 + \$48{,}900 + \$0) = -\$48{,}900$$

The total cash generated by the project just before the first payment is received from the project's owner is calculated using Eq. (12-3) as follows:

$$\text{Cash}_{2'} = \text{Cash}_1 + \text{Cash Flow}_{2'}$$
$$\text{Cash}_{2'} = -\$34{,}900 + (-\$48{,}900) = -\$83{,}800$$

Just before the construction company receives payment from the owner during the second month, the construction company will have $83,800 of cash invested in the project.

At the end of the second month the construction company will have received the first payment from the owner. The payment will be equal to the work billed at the end of the first month less the 10% retention. The payment received from the owner during the second month is calculated as follows:

$$\text{Cash Receipt}_n = \text{Bill}_{n-1}(1 - \text{Retention Rate})$$
$$\text{Cash Receipt}_2 = \$129,600(1 - 0.10) = \$116,640$$

During the month the construction company will have paid out $30,400 to material suppliers, $48,900 to cover the cost of the labor, and the first month's subcontractor costs—less the 10% retention. The subcontractor payments for the second month are as follows:

$$\text{Subcontractor Payments}_2 = \$54,700(0.90) = \$49,230$$

The cash flow for the second month is calculated using Eq. (12-1) as follows:

$$\text{Cash Flow}_2 = \$116,640 - (\$30,400 + \$48,900 + \$49,230)$$
$$\text{Cash Flow}_2 = -\$11,890$$

The total cash generated by the project by the end of the second month is calculated using Eq. (12-2) as follows:

$$\text{Cash}_2 = -\$34,900 + (-\$11,890) = -\$46,790$$

The maximum amount of cash needed during the second month is $37,010 ($83,800 − $46,790) more than the amount of cash needed at the end of the month.

The cash flows and the amount of cash needed for the third through the sixth month are calculated in a similar manner and are shown in Table 12-2.

The next point in time where we need to calculate total cash generated by the project is just before receipt of the last payment from the owner, which occurs at the end of the seventh month. By this time the construction company has not paid any additional costs; therefore, the total cash generated by the project equals the total cash generated by the project at the end of the previous month for a total of $11,430.

TABLE 12-2 Monthly Cash Flow and Cash Invested for Example 12-3

MONTH	MONTHLY CASH FLOW ($)		CASH GENERATED ($)	
	n'	n	n'	n
1	−34,900	−34,900	−34,900	−34,900
2	−48,900	−11,890	−83,800	−46,790
3	−73,100	−18,260	−119,890	−65,050
4	−34,000	44,620	−99,050	−20,430
5	−26,200	13,720	−46,630	−6,710
6	−11,300	18,140	−18,010	11,430
7	0	68,570	11,430	80,000

The payment received from the owner during the seventh month will include the full amount of the bill from the sixth month plus the retention withheld from the previous months. The retention held during the first six months is as follows:

$$\text{Retention} = \$0 + \$129,600(0.10) + \$248,400(0.10)$$
$$+ \$313,200(0.10) + \$183,600(0.10) + \$129,600(0.10)$$
$$\text{Retention} = \$100,440$$

The seventh month's payment from the owner is as follows:

$$\text{Cash Receipt}_7 = \$100,440 + \$75,600 = \$176,040$$

During the month the construction company will have paid out $15,400 to material suppliers and will have to pay for the sixth month's subcontractor costs plus all of the retention held during the first six months. The retention held from the subcontractor payments during the first six months is as follows:

$$\text{Retention} = \$0 + \$54,700(0.10) + \$123,800(0.10)$$
$$+ \$136,400(0.10) + \$106,800(0.10) + \$66,000(0.10)$$
$$\text{Retention} = \$48,770$$

The seventh month's payment to the subcontractors is as follows:

$$\text{Subcontractor Payments}_7 = \$48,770 + \$43,300 = \$92,070$$

The cash flow for the seventh month is calculated using Eq. (12-1) as follows:

$$\text{Cash Flow}_7 = \$176,040 - (\$15,400 + \$0 + \$92,070) = \$68,570$$

The total cash generated by the project at the end of the seventh month is calculated using Eq. (12-2) as follows:

$$\text{Cash}_7 = \$11,430 + \$68,570 = \$80,000$$

At this point the project is complete. At the completion of the project the cash generated by the project should equal the profit and overhead realized on the project, which equals the profit and overhead markup for this example. The monthly cash flow and the cash generated at the end of each month are shown in Table 12-2. The cash generated by the project just before payment from the owner and at the end of the month are shown in Figure 12-6.

The maximum amount of cash invested in the project by the construction company occurs in the third month and is $119,890, which is greater than the profit and overhead markup on the project. For the construction company to complete this project, it would need about $120,000 in cash.

Example 12-3 may be solved using a spreadsheet. The spreadsheet solution for Example 12-3 is found in Figure 12-7.

From the previous example we see that the cash requirements just before payment was received from the project's owner were consistently greater than the cash requirements at the end of the month. Had we projected the amount of cash

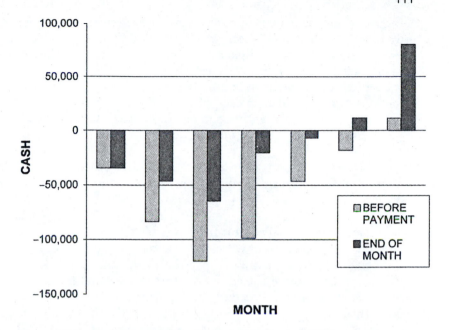

FIGURE 12-6 Cash Generated by the Project in Example 12-3

Retention Rate: 10%							
Month	1	2	3	4	5	6	7
Bill to Owner	129,600	248,400	313,200	183,600	129,600	75,600	—
Materials	30,400	57,300	80,500	29,200	27,800	15,400	—
Labor	34,900	48,900	73,100	34,000	26,200	11,300	—
Subcontractor	54,700	123,800	136,400	106,800	66,000	43,300	—
Total Costs	120,000	230,000	290,000	170,000	120,000	70,000	—
P&O	9,600	18,400	23,200	13,600	9,600	5,600	—
Receipts	—	116,640	223,560	281,880	165,240	116,640	176,040
Payments							
Materials	—	30,400	57,300	80,500	29,200	27,800	15,400
Labor	34,900	48,900	73,100	34,000	26,200	11,300	—
Subcontractor	—	49,230	111,420	122,760	96,120	59,400	92,070
Total Payments	34,900	128,530	241,820	237,260	151,520	98,500	107,470
Cash Flow Before Payment		(48,900)	(73,100)	(34,000)	(26,200)	(11,300)	—
Total Cash Before Payment		(83,800)	(119,890)	(99,050)	(46,630)	(18,010)	11,430
Cash Flow at Month's End	(34,900)	(11,890)	(18,260)	44,620	13,720	18,140	68,570
Total Cash at Month's End	(34,900)	(46,790)	(65,050)	(20,430)	(6,710)	11,430	80,000

FIGURE 12-7 Spreadsheet Solution for Example 12-3

needed to complete the project based on the cash needed at the end of the months we would have come up short by as much as $78,620.

In the previous example there were five things that affected the amount of cash needed to complete the project. They are material payments, labor payments, subcontractor payments, retention held by the owner, and the profit and overhead markup. Let's look at how each of these affects the project's cash requirements. Retention will be dealt with separately rather than lumped in with material payments, labor payments, and subcontractor payments so that we can see the effects of retention.

Material payments did not affect the project's cash requirements because the material bills were paid in full when the company received payment from the owner.

Labor payments had a great effect on the project's cash requirements. Just before receiving the payment from the owner, the construction company had paid out almost two months of wages. For the labor performed during the first month the construction company will pay the wages during the first month, bill the owner for the wages at the end of the first month, and receive payment from the owner at the end of the second month. During this time the owner will have to cover the costs of the wages for the second month. The maximum amount of cash needed to cover the costs of labor during the project occurs in the third month. At this time the construction company has to cover the second and third month's wages for a total of $122,000.

Subcontractor payments were paid when the company received payment from the owner; however, the payment was reduced by the 10% retention. As a result, the subcontractors became a source of cash that offsets the cash consumed by retention held by the owners. By the seventh month, the subcontractors had provided $48,770 of cash to the construction company, which is the amount of retention withheld from the subcontractors during the first six months.

Retention is an extensive use of cash. By the seventh month the owner had withheld $100,400 in retention from the contractor.

Profit and overhead markup was a source of cash. By the end of the project it provided the company with $80,000 in cash. However, this cash is needed to cover the costs of the general overhead, provide cash for investment, and provide a profit to the company's shareholders.

In the previous example there are three ways the construction company could reduce the project's cash requirements. First, the construction company could increase its use of subcontractors as a way to reduce the materials and labor that it provides. By using subcontractors in lieu of in-house labor, the construction company uses the subcontractor's cash to cover the cost of labor and increases its cash by withholding retention from the subcontractors on the labor supplied. By having the subcontractors provide materials, the construction company increases its cash by withholding retention from the subcontractors on the materials supplied. Second, the construction company could negotiate a more favorable retention rate. The greatest benefit of reducing the retention rate comes when the construction company is providing most of the labor and materials, while minimizing the use of subcontractors.

TABLE 12-3   Monthly Costs and Billings for Example 12-4

MONTH	COSTS			
	MATERIALS ($)	LABOR ($)	SUB. ($)	BILL TO OWNER ($)
1	17,700	19,000	83,300	129,600
2	31,600	26,300	172,100	248,400
3	47,700	40,100	202,200	313,200
4	15,500	17,800	136,700	183,600
5	14,200	14,600	91,200	129,600
6	8,300	6,300	55,400	75,600
Total	135,000	124,100	740,900	1,080,000

When subcontractors are supplying most of the labor and materials and the construction company is withholding retention on the subcontractors, there is little benefit gained by reducing the retention rate because the construction company passes the lower retention rate on to its subcontractors. The savings in cash due to the reduced retention rate is offset by a loss of cash being provided by the subcontractors in the form of retention. Third, the construction company could increase the profit and overhead markup.

Example 12-4:   How would the project's cash requirements change for the construction company in Example 12-3 if it increased the amount of work performed by subcontractors from 53.1 to 74.1% as shown in Table 12-3?

Solution: This example may be solved in the same manner that Example 12-3 was solved. The monthly cash flow and the cash generated at the end of each month for this example are shown in Table 12-4.

A comparison of the maximum cash invested in the project for each of the months for Examples 12-3 and 12-4 is shown in Figure 12-8. A comparison of the cash invested at the end of each of the months for Examples 12-3 and 12-4 is shown in Figure 12-9.

TABLE 12-4   Monthly Cash Flow and Cash Invested for Example 12-4

MONTH	MONTHLY CASH FLOW ($)		CASH GENERATED ($)	
	n'	n	n'	n
1	−19,000	−19,000	−19,000	−19,000
2	−26,300	−2,330	−45,300	−21,330
3	−40,100	−3,030	−61,430	−24,360
4	−17,800	34,400	−42,160	10,040
5	−14,600	12,110	−4,560	22,150
6	−6,300	14,060	15,850	36,210
7	0	43,790	36,210	80,000

FIGURE 12-8 Maximum Cash Invested for Examples 12-3 and 12-4

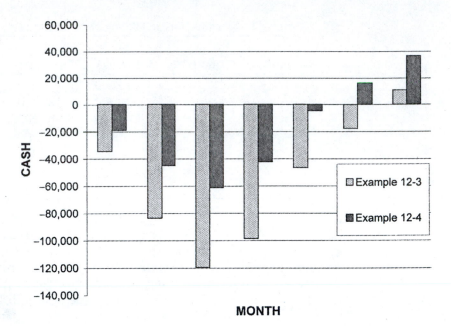

FIGURE 12-9 Cash Invested at the End of Each Month for Examples 12-3 and 12-4

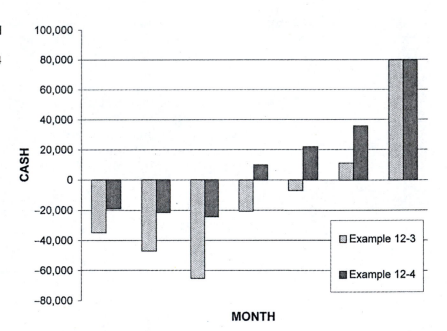

At the completion of the project the cash generated by both examples equals the profit and overhead markup. The peak amount of cash invested in the project by the construction company occurs in the third month and is $61,430 for Example 12-4 compared to the $119,890 that was required by Example 12-3. Example 12-4 required less cash investment and required this investment for a shorter period of time than did Example 12-3. This is because the construction company used the subcontractor's cash rather than its own to fund the project.

In Examples 12-3 and 12-4 we looked at the amount of cash a construction company needs to complete a project. In both of these examples the owner of the project received the benefit of using the construction company and its suppliers and subcontractor's cash rather than using his or her own cash. The benefit to the project's owner equals the amount of cash provided by the construction company, the labor, the suppliers, and the subcontractors, which equals the cost to the owner for the work performed (the value curve in Figure 12-5) less the payments received from the owner. The benefit for a specific month is calculated by taking the previous month's benefit and adding this month's costs less this month's receipts and may be written as follows:

$$\text{Cash}_n = \text{Cash}_{n-1} + \text{Bills}_n - \text{Receipt}_n \qquad (12\text{-}4)$$

Like the cash required by the construction company, the benefit to the owner may be measured just before the monthly payment to the construction company is made and at the end of the month. Now let's look at the benefit the owner receives from this.

Example 12-5: Determine the amount of cash that the construction company and its suppliers and subcontractors are providing to the project owner in Example 12-3.

Solution: We start at the beginning of the project and work our way to the end of the project, calculating the benefit to the owner at the end of each month and just before payment is made to the construction company.

Because the owner does not make a payment during the first month, the first point in time we calculate the benefit is at the end of the first month. From Example 12-3 the monthly bill to the owner is $129,600 and the monthly benefit is calculated using Eq. (12-4) as follows:

$$\text{Cash}_n = \text{Cash}_{n-1} + \text{Bills}_n - \text{Receipt}_n$$
$$\text{Cash}_1 = \$0 + \$129,600 - \$0 = \$129,600$$

At the end of the first month the construction company and its suppliers and subcontractors have provided the project's owner with $129,600 in funding for the project.

The next point in time we need to calculate the benefit to the owner is just before receipt of the first payment from the owner, which occurs at the end of the second month. The benefit just before the payment has been received is equal to the cash from the previous month plus the cost of the work completed between the end of the previous month and just before receipt of payment from the owner. The cost of the work completed between the end of the previous month and just before receipt of payment from the owner is approximately equal to the billing to the owner. The benefit is calculated using Eq. (12-4) as follows:

$$Cash_{1'} = \$129,600 + \$248,400 - 0 = \$378,000$$

The benefit for the end of the second month is calculated as follows:

$$Cash_2 = \$129,600 + \$248,400 - \$116,640 = \$261,360$$

The benefits for the third through seventh months are calculated as follows:

$$Cash_{3'} = \$261,360 + \$313,200 - \$0 = \$574,560$$
$$Cash_3 = \$261,360 + \$313,200 - \$223,560 = \$351,000$$
$$Cash_{4'} = \$351,000 + \$183,600 - \$0 = \$534,600$$
$$Cash_4 = \$351,000 + \$183,600 - \$281,880 = \$252,720$$
$$Cash_{5'} = \$252,720 + \$129,600 - \$0 = \$382,320$$
$$Cash_5 = \$252,720 + \$129,600 - \$165,240 = \$217,080$$
$$Cash_{6'} = \$217,080 + \$75,600 - \$0 = \$292,680$$
$$Cash_6 = \$217,080 + \$75,600 - \$116,640 = \$176,040$$
$$Cash_{7'} = \$176,040 + \$0 - \$0 = \$176,040$$
$$Cash_7 = \$176,040 + \$0 - \$176,040 = \$0$$

As expected, when the owner has paid for the project in full, the benefit provided by the construction company and its suppliers and subcontractors is zero. The maximum benefit provided by the construction company and its suppliers and subcontractors occurs during the third month and has a value in excess of half of the total cost of the project to the owner. In other words, during the third month the construction company and its suppliers and subcontractors are providing over half of the funds needed to construct the project.

Sometimes a project will receive progress payment from the project's owner at intervals other than monthly. For example, a project may receive progress payments at 25, 50, 75, and 100% complete. The procedures for calculating the project's cash needs are the same as for a project that receives monthly payments, with cash flows being calculated at the end of each month and just before each payment is received.

Let's look at a specialized cash flow that works for projects with multiple buildings of the same design. This type of cash flow often occurs when constructing office condominiums, warehouse complexes, residential condominiums, and residences where the construction contractor gets paid monthly, as is the case for many subcontractors. This type of cash flow is estimated by calculating a cash flow for each building type and then combining these cash flow projections with an estimated number of building starts for each month.

TABLE 12-5 Monthly Starts by Type

MONTH	TYPE 1	TYPE 2
June	1	2
July	2	1
Aug.	1	3
Sept.	3	1
Oct.	1	2
Nov.	2	2
Dec.	2	2

Example 12-6: A construction company is bidding on a contract to build homes for a developer. The project consists of two types of homes and is scheduled to begin in June. The first payment from the owner will occur in July. The expected monthly homes starts are shown in Table 12-5. The cash flow that occurs between the end of the previous month and receipt of payment from the owner along with the cash flow for the entire month is shown in Table 12-6. Determine the monthly cash flows and total cash generated by the project at the end of each month and just before each payment is received from the project's owner for the remaining months in the year. What is the maximum amount of cash invested by the company during the remaining months of the year?

Solution: As in the past problems, we begin our calculations in the first month—June—and work our way to the last month—December. Because the owner does not make a payment in June the first point in time we need to calculate the cash flow is at the end of June. The cash flow for June includes only the first month's cash flows for the June housing starts and is calculated as follows:

$$\text{Cash Flow}_{June} = \text{Type I Starts}_{June}(\text{Type I Cash Flow}_1)$$
$$+ \text{Type II Starts}_{June}(\text{Type II Cash Flow}_1)$$
$$\text{Cash Flow}_{June} = 1(-\$5,800) + 2(-\$6,700) = -\$19,200$$

TABLE 12-6 Cash Flow by Type

MONTH	BEFORE PAYMENT IS RECEIVED (n') ($)		END OF MONTH (n) ($)	
	TYPE 1	TYPE 2	TYPE 1	TYPE 2
1	−5,800	−6,700	−5,800	−6,700
2	−8,400	−9,500	−1,900	−2,500
3	−17,100	−20,200	7,500	9,700
4	−4,800	−4,800	2,300	3,000
5	−2,100	−1,900	3,100	3,600
6	0	0	10,500	12,800

The total cash invested at the end of the month of June is calculated using Eq. (12-2) as follows:

$$\text{Cash}_{\text{June}} = \$0 + (-\$19,200) = -\$19,200$$

The next point in time we calculate the cash flow is just before the payment is received in July. The cash flows for July includes the second month's cash flows (from the end of the previous month to the time the payment is received) for the June housing starts and the first month's cash flows (from the end of the previous month to the time the payment is received) for the July housing starts. This cash flow is calculated as follows:

$$\text{Cash Flow}_{\text{July}'} = \text{Type I Starts}_{\text{June}}(\text{Type I Cash Flow}_{2'})$$
$$+ \text{Type II Starts}_{\text{June}}(\text{Type II Cash Flow}_{2'})$$
$$+ \text{Type I Starts}_{\text{July}}(\text{Type I Cash Flow}_{1'})$$
$$+ \text{Type II Starts}_{\text{July}}(\text{Type II Cash Flow}_{1'})$$
$$\text{Cash Flow}_{\text{July}'} = 1(-\$8,400) + 2(-\$9,500) + 2(-\$5,800)$$
$$+ 1(-\$6,700)$$
$$\text{Cash Flow}_{\text{July}'} = -\$45,700$$

The total cash invested just prior to the July payment is calculated using Eq. (12-3) as follows:

$$\text{Cash}_{\text{July}'} = -\$19,200 + (-\$45,700) = -\$64,900$$

The next point in time we calculate the cash flow is at the end of July, which is calculated using the end of month cash flows as follows:

$$\text{Cash Flow}_{\text{July}} = \text{Type I Starts}_{\text{June}}(\text{Type I Cash Flow}_{2})$$
$$+ \text{Type II Starts}_{\text{June}}(\text{Type II Cash Flow}_{2})$$
$$+ \text{Type I Starts}_{\text{July}}(\text{Type I Cash Flow}_{1})$$
$$+ \text{Type II Starts}_{\text{July}}(\text{Type II Cash Flow}_{1})$$
$$\text{Cash Flow}_{\text{July}} = 1(-\$1,900) + 2(-\$2,500) + 2(-\$5,800)$$
$$+ 1(-\$6,700)$$
$$\text{Cash Flow}_{\text{July}} = -\$25,200$$

The total cash invested at the end of July is calculated using Eq. (12-2) as follows:

$$\text{Cash}_{\text{July}} = -\$19,200 + (-\$25,200) = -\$44,400$$

The monthly cash flows and the cash generated from the project are calculated in the same manner and are shown in Table 12-7.

The maximum amount of cash invested occurs in October with a value of $202,100. The cash generated by Example 12-6 is shown in Figure 12-10.

Example 12-6 could be solved using a spreadsheet by simply listing all of the houses to be started during the year in the rows and listing the month in the columns. For each of the housing starts the monthly cash flows are entered

TABLE 12-7   Monthly Cash Flow and Cash Invested for Example 12-6

MONTH	MONTHLY CASH FLOW ($)		CASH GENERATED ($)	
	n'	n	n'	n
June	−19,200	−19,200	−19,200	−19,200
July	−45,700	−25,200	−64,900	−44,400
Aug.	−109,700	−5,300	−154,100	−49,700
Sept.	−129,800	−500	−179,500	−50,200
Oct.	−151,900	27,100	−202,100	−23,100
Nov.	−149,200	57,500	−172,300	34,400
Dec.	−145,300	50,700	−110,900	85,100

under the month in which the cash flows occur. Finally, the monthly cash flows are added up and the total cash invested for each month is calculated. This is performed for both the end of the month and just before the payment is received. The spreadsheet solution for Example 12-6 is shown in Figure 12-11.

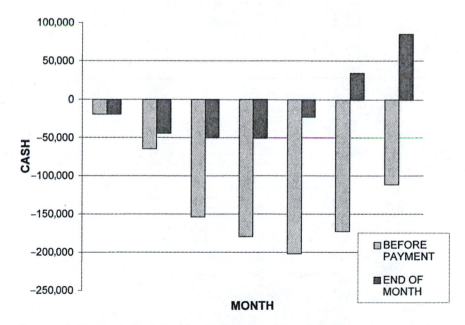

FIGURE 12-10   Cash Generated by the Project in Example 12-6

	A	B	C	D	E	F	G	H	I
1					Before Payment Is Received				
2		Starts	June	July	Aug.	Sept.	Oct.	Nov.	Dec.
3	June	Type 1	(5,800)	(8,400)	(17,100)	(4,800)	(2,100)	—	—
4		Type 2	(6,700)	(9,500)	(20,200)	(4,800)	(1,900)	—	—
5		Type 2	(6,700)	(9,500)	(20,200)	(4,800)	(1,900)	—	—
6	July	Type 1	—	(5,800)	(8,400)	(17,100)	(4,800)	(2,100)	—
7		Type 1	—	(5,800)	(8,400)	(17,100)	(4,800)	(2,100)	—
8		Type 2	—	(6,700)	(9,500)	(20,200)	(4,800)	(1,900)	—
9	Aug.	Type 1	—	—	(5,800)	(8,400)	(17,100)	(4,800)	(2,100)
10		Type 2	—	—	(6,700)	(9,500)	(20,200)	(4,800)	(1,900)
11		Type 2	—	—	(6,700)	(9,500)	(20,200)	(4,800)	(1,900)
12		Type 2	—	—	(6,700)	(9,500)	(20,200)	(4,800)	(1,900)
13	Sept.	Type 1	—	—	—	(5,800)	(8,400)	(17,100)	(4,800)
14		Type 1	—	—	—	(5,800)	(8,400)	(17,100)	(4,800)
15		Type 1	—	—	—	(5,800)	(8,400)	(17,100)	(4,800)
16		Type 2	—	—	—	(6,700)	(9,500)	(20,200)	(4,800)
17	Oct.	Type 1	—	—	—	—	(5,800)	(8,400)	(17,100)
18		Type 2	—	—	—	—	(6,700)	(9,500)	(20,200)
19		Type 2	—	—	—	—	(6,700)	(9,500)	(20,200)
20	Nov.	Type 1	—	—	—	—	—	(5,800)	(8,400)
21		Type 1	—	—	—	—	—	(5,800)	(8,400)
22		Type 2	—	—	—	—	—	(6,700)	(9,500)
23		Type 2	—	—	—	—	—	(6,700)	(9,500)
24	Dec.	Type 1	—	—	—	—	—	—	(5,800)
25		Type 1	—	—	—	—	—	—	(5,800)
26		Type 2	—	—	—	—	—	—	(6,700)
27		Type 2	—	—	—	—	—	—	(6,700)
28		Cash Flow	(19,200)	(45,700)	(109,700)	(129,800)	(151,900)	(149,200)	(145,300)
29		Cash	(19,200)	(64,900)	(154,100)	(179,500)	(202,100)	(172,300)	(110,900)
30									
31					End of Month				
32		Starts	June	July	Aug.	Sept.	Oct.	Nov.	Dec.
33	June	Type 1	(5,800)	(1,900)	7,500	2,300	3,100	10,500	—
34		Type 2	(6,700)	(2,500)	9,700	3,000	3,600	12,800	—
35		Type 2	(6,700)	(2,500)	9,700	3,000	3,600	12,800	—
36	July	Type 1	—	(5,800)	(1,900)	7,500	2,300	3,100	10,500
37		Type 1	—	(5,800)	(1,900)	7,500	2,300	3,100	10,500
38		Type 2	—	(6,700)	(2,500)	9,700	3,000	3,600	12,800
39	Aug.	Type 1	—	—	(5,800)	(1,900)	7,500	2,300	3,100
40		Type 2	—	—	(6,700)	(2,500)	9,700	3,000	3,600
41		Type 2	—	—	(6,700)	(2,500)	9,700	3,000	3,600
42		Type 2	—	—	(6,700)	(2,500)	9,700	3,000	3,600
43	Sept.	Type 1	—	—	—	(5,800)	(1,900)	7,500	2,300
44		Type 1	—	—	—	(5,800)	(1,900)	7,500	2,300
45		Type 1	—	—	—	(5,800)	(1,900)	7,500	2,300
46		Type 2	—	—	—	(6,700)	(2,500)	9,700	3,000
47	Oct.	Type 1	—	—	—	—	(5,800)	(1,900)	7,500
48		Type 2	—	—	—	—	(6,700)	(2,500)	9,700
49		Type 2	—	—	—	—	(6,700)	(2,500)	9,700
50	Nov.	Type 1	—	—	—	—	—	(5,800)	(1,900)
51		Type 1	—	—	—	—	—	(5,800)	(1,900)
52		Type 2	—	—	—	—	—	(6,700)	(2,500)
53		Type 2	—	—	—	—	—	(6,700)	(2,500)
54	Dec.	Type 1	—	—	—	—	—	—	(5,800)
55		Type 1	—	—	—	—	—	—	(5,800)
56		Type 2	—	—	—	—	—	—	(6,700)
57		Type 2	—	—	—	—	—	—	(6,700)
58		Cash Flow	(19,200)	(25,200)	(5,300)	(500)	27,100	57,500	50,700
59		Cash	(19,200)	(44,400)	(49,700)	(50,200)	(23,100)	34,400	85,100

FIGURE 12-11   Spreadsheet Solution to Example 12-6

CASH FLOW FOR PROJECTS WITH A SINGLE PAYMENT

Projects with a single payment differ in three ways from projects where the construction company receives progress payments from the project's owner. First, because there are no progress payments the peak amount of cash required is equal to the cash required at the end of the month for all but the last month when the payment is received. Second, retention is not held because there are no progress payments. Third, the construction company may also be paying some, if not all, of the soft costs. Soft costs include payments for the following: the purchase of the land; engineering and design fees; permitting and other fees charged by government entities; construction interest and loan fees; taxes and insurance; and other costs not typically included in the payments to the construction company.

Example 12-7: The construction company in Example 12-3 decides to act as the owner on the project. The construction company plans to sell the project for $1,350,600 at the end of the seventh month. In addition to the construction costs the construction company has the following soft costs: land purchase, $200,000; engineering and design fees, $30,000; building permits, $5,600; government fees, $20,000; and other miscellaneous costs, $15,000. The soft cost will be paid at the end of month zero. The construction company pays material suppliers in full on the last day of the month following the month the materials were supplied to the project. For example, materials supplied during the first month will be paid for at the end of the second month. The subcontractors will be paid on the same schedule as the suppliers; however, the construction company will withhold 10% retention from the subcontractors' payments, which will be paid to the subcontractors at the end of the seventh month. The construction company pays for labor weekly. Determine the monthly cash flows and total cash generated by the project at the end of each month and just before the payment is received. What is the maximum amount of cash invested by the company during the completion of the project?

Solution: As in the other examples we begin at the beginning of the project and work our way to the end of the project, calculating the cash flow and total cash generated as we go. Because only one payment is received for the project, which occurs during the seventh month, we need to calculate only the cash flow and total cash generated at the end of the month for the first six months. For the seventh month the cash flow and total cash generated will need to be calculated at the point in time just before the project is sold and after the project is sold.

Because the first costs occur during month zero we begin by calculating the cash flow for month zero. The total cash disbursements for the soft costs are as follows:

$$\text{Cash Disbursements}_0 = \$200{,}000 + \$30{,}000 + \$5{,}600$$
$$+ \$20{,}000 + \$15{,}000$$
$$\text{Cash Disbursements}_0 = \$270{,}600$$

The cash flow for month zero is calculated using Eq. (12-1) as follows:

$$\text{Cash Flow}_0 = \$0 - \$270{,}600 = -\$270{,}600$$

The total cash generated at the end of month zero is calculated using Eq. (12-2) as follows:

$$\text{Cash}_0 = \$0 + (-\$270{,}600) = -\$270{,}600$$

No payments to material suppliers or subcontractors will be made during the first month. During the first month the construction company will pay $34,900 for labor. The cash flow for the first month is calculated using Eq. (12-1) as follows:

$$\text{Cash Flow}_1 = \$0 - \$34{,}900 = -\$34{,}900$$

The total cash generated at the end of the first month is calculated using Eq. (12-2) as follows:

$$\text{Cash}_1 = -\$270{,}600 + (-\$34{,}900) = -\$305{,}500$$

At the end of the first month the construction company will need to have $305,500 of cash invested in the project.

During the second month the construction company will pay out $30,400 to material suppliers and $48,900 to cover the cost of the labor. The construction company will have to pay for the first month's subcontractor costs, less the 10% retention. The monthly subcontractor payments are as follows:

$$\text{Subcontractor Payments}_2 = \$54{,}700(0.90) = \$49{,}230$$

The cash flow for the second month is calculated using Eq. (12-1) as follows:

$$\text{Cash Flow}_2 = \$0 - (\$30{,}400 + \$48{,}900 + \$49{,}230) = -\$128{,}530$$

The total cash generated at the end of the second month is calculated using Eq. (12-2) as follows:

$$\text{Cash}_2 = -\$305{,}500 + (-\$128{,}530) = -\$434{,}030$$

The cash flow and cash generated for the third through the sixth months are calculated in a similar manner and are shown in Figure 12-9.

The next point in time when we need to perform our calculation is just before the payment is received for the project. By this time the construction company has paid no additional costs; therefore, the total cash generated is equal to the total cash generated at the end of the previous month, which is $1,163,130.

The payment of $1,350,600 for the project is received at the end of the seventh month. At the end of the seventh month the construction company will pay out $15,400 to material suppliers and will pay the subcontractors the retention held during the first six months plus the full amount of the work performed by the subcontractors during the sixth month. The retention held during the first six months is as follows:

$$\text{Retention} = \$0 + \$54,700(0.10) + \$123,800(0.10)$$
$$+ \$136,400(0.10) + \$106,800(0.10) + \$66,000(0.10)$$
$$\text{Retention} = \$48,770$$

The seventh month's payment to the subcontractors is as follows:

$$\text{Subcontractor Payments}_7 = \$48,770 + \$43,300 = \$92,070$$

The cash flow for the seventh month is calculated using Eq. (12-1) as follows:

$$\text{Cash Flow}_7 = \$1,350,600 - (\$15,400 + \$92,070) = \$1,243,130$$

The total cash generated at the end of the seventh month is calculated using Eq. (12-2) as follows:

$$\text{Cash}_7 = -\$1,163,130 + \$1,243,130 = \$80,000$$

At this point the project is complete. The monthly cash flow and the cash generated at the end of each month are shown in Table 12-8.

At the completion of the project the cash generated by the project should equal the profit and overhead realized on the project, which equals the profit and overhead markup for this example. The cash generated by the project is shown in Figure 12-12.

The maximum amount of cash needed by the construction company occurs just before the payment is received. For the construction company to complete this project, it would need at least $1,163,600 in cash.

TABLE 12-8 Monthly Cash Flow and Cash Invested for Example 12-7

MONTH	MONTHLY CASH FLOW ($)	CASH GENERATED ($)
0	−270,600	−270,600
1	−34,900	−305,500
2	−128,530	−434,030
3	−241,820	−675,850
4	−237,260	−913,110
5	−151,520	−1,064,630
6	−98,500	−1,163,130
7'	0	−1,163,130
7	1,243,130	80,000

Figure 12-12   Cash Generated by the Project in Example 12-7

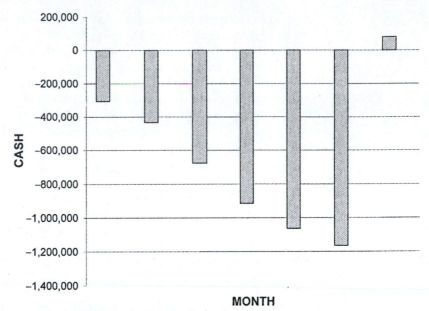

From this example we see that the construction company's needs for cash continue to increase throughout the life of the project with the maximum amount of cash required occurring just before the payment for the project is received, in this case when the project is sold.

Conclusion

A construction company needs cash to pay bills and labor costs while it waits to receive revenue from the construction project. A lack of cash is a major source of failure for construction companies.

For construction companies that receive progress payments, the greatest need for cash on an individual project occurs each month just before payment is received from the owner. Additionally, the amount of cash tied up in the form of retention increases as the work progresses. The cash needs—excluding cash tied up in the form of retention—is greatest when the rate of progress is greatest. A construction company can reduce its cash needs by increasing its use of subcontractors, thereby using the subcontractor's cash; reducing the retention rate; increasing its profit and overhead markup on the project; or decreasing the maximum rate of progress on the project. The latter may be accomplished by leveling the work so that it occurs at a more uniform rate or by performing the work over a greater period of time. Performing the work over a greater period of time causes other problems, such as increasing overhead costs.

For the construction company that receives a single payment at the completion of the project, the maximum cash requirement occurs just before the payment is received.

PROBLEMS

1. A construction company is negotiating on a construction project with a six-month duration. On the last day of each month the construction company may bill the owner for the work completed during the month. The owner pays the monthly bills one month after they are received. The owner also holds a 5% retention. Final payment is expected one month after completion of the project and includes payment of the retention. The construction company pays material suppliers in full when it receives payment from the owner. The construction company pays subcontractors when it receives payment from the owner but withholds 5% retention from the subcontractor's payment. The construction company pays for labor weekly. The projected monthly material, labor, and subcontractor costs as well as the amount the construction company will bill the project's owner each month are shown in the following table. Determine the monthly cash flows and the total cash generated by the project at the end of each month and just before each payment is received from the project's owner. What is the maximum amount of cash invested by the company during the completion of the project?

	COSTS			
MONTH	MATERIALS ($)	LABOR ($)	SUB. ($)	BILL TO OWNER ($)
1	8,800	8,100	13,100	33,000
2	14,200	11,900	31,400	63,200
3	21,000	19,800	31,700	79,800
4	6,800	7,600	28,100	46,800
5	5,100	7,000	17,900	33,000
6	4,100	4,100	9,300	19,200
Total	60,000	58,500	131,500	275,000

2. A construction company is negotiating on a construction project with a six-month duration. On the last day of each month the construction company may bill the owner for the work completed during the month. The owner pays the monthly bills 15 days after they are received. The owner also holds a 10% retention. Final payment is expected one month after completion of the project and includes payment of the retention. The construction company pays material suppliers in full when it receives payment from the owner. The construction company pays subcontractors when it receives payment from the owner but withholds 10% from the subcontractor's payment. The construction company pays for labor weekly. The projected monthly material, labor,

and subcontractor costs follow. Determine the monthly cash flows and the total cash generated by the project at the end of each month and just before each payment is received from the project's owner. What is the maximum amount of cash invested by the company during the completion of the project?

MONTH	COSTS			BILL TO OWNER ($)
	MATERIALS ($)	LABOR ($)	SUB. ($)	
1	33,700	25,300	35,600	101,200
2	54,100	42,400	125,200	237,200
3	69,600	77,900	93,600	258,000
4	17,200	17,900	105,700	150,700
5	14,700	21,900	60,400	103,800
6	11,600	12,700	35,600	64,100
Total	200,900	198,100	456,100	915,000

3. A construction company is bidding on a contract to build homes for a developer. The project consists of two types of homes and is scheduled to begin in September. The expected monthly housing starts, the cash flow that occurs between the end of the previous month and receipt of payment from the owner, and the cash flow for the entire month follow. Determine the monthly cash flows and total cash generated by the project at the end of each month and just before each payment is received from the project's owner for the remaining months in the year. What is the maximum amount of cash invested by the company during the remaining months of the year?

Monthly Starts by Type

MONTH	TYPE 1	TYPE 2
Sept.	2	4
Oct.	2	2
Nov.	3	3
Dec.	1	2

MONTH	BEFORE PAYMENT IS RECEIVED (n') ($)		END OF MONTH (n) ($)	
	TYPE 1	TYPE 2	TYPE 1	TYPE 2
1	−5,400	−6,500	−5,400	−6,500
2	−8,200	−8,700	−1,800	−2,400
3	−15,500	−19,800	7,300	9,300
4	−4,400	−4,400	2,200	2,800
5	−2,000	−1,700	3,000	3,400
6	0	0	9,500	11,900

4. The housing contract from Problem 3 continues on into the next year, with the last housing start occurring in April, as shown in the following table. Determine the monthly cash flows and total cash generated by the project at the end of each month and just before each payment is received from the project's owner for the remaining months in the year. What is the maximum amount of cash invested by the company during this year?

Monthly Starts by Type

MONTH	TYPE 1	TYPE 2
Jan.	4	2
Feb.	2	2
March	3	3
April	2	1

5. The construction company in Problem 1 decides to act as the owner on the project. The construction company will be paid $500,000 for the project at the end of the seventh month. In addition to the construction costs, the construction company has the following soft costs: land purchase, $150,000; engineering and design fees, $15,000; building permits, $3,000; government fees, $5,000; and other miscellaneous costs, $10,000. The soft costs will be paid at the end of month zero. The construction company pays material suppliers in full on the last day of the month following the month the materials were supplied to the project. The subcontractors will be paid on the same schedule as the suppliers; however, the construction company will withhold 5% retention from the subcontractors' payments, which will be paid to the subcontractors at the end of the seventh month. The construction company pays for labor weekly. Determine the monthly cash flows and total cash generated by the project at the end of each month and just before the payment is received. What is the maximum amount of cash invested by the company during the completion of the project?

6. The construction company in Problem 2 decides to act as the owner on the project. The construction company plans to sell the project for $1,250,000 at the end of the seventh month. In addition to the construction costs the construction company has the following soft costs: land purchase, $250,000; engineering and design fees, $30,000; building permits, $7,000; government fees, $15,000; and other miscellaneous costs, $10,000. The soft costs will be paid at the end of month zero. The construction company pays material suppliers in full on the fifteenth day of the month following the month the materials were supplied to the project. For example, materials supplied during the first month will be paid for on the fifteenth of the second month. The subcontractors will be paid on the same schedule as the suppliers; however, the construction company will withhold 10% retention from the subcontractors' payments, which will be paid to the subcontractors on the fifteenth day of the seventh month. The construction company pays

for labor weekly. Determine the monthly cash flows and total cash generated by the project at the end of each month and just before the payment is received. What is the maximum amount of cash invested by the company during the completion of the project?

7. Set up a spreadsheet to solve Problem 1.

8. Set up a spreadsheet to solve Problem 2.

9. Set up a spreadsheet similar to Figure 12-11 to solve Problem 3.

10. Set up a spreadsheet similar to Figure 12-11 to solve Problem 4.

11. Set up a spreadsheet to solve Problem 5.

12. Set up a spreadsheet to solve Problem 6.

13. Determine the monthly cash flows and total cash generated at the end of each month and just before the payment is received for the construction of a house with the following budget and schedule. On the last day of each month the construction company may bill the owner for the work completed during the month. The owner pays the monthly bills one month after they are received. The owner also holds a 10% retention. Final payment is expected one month after completion of the project and includes the retention. The construction company pays material suppliers in full when it receives payment from the owner. The construction company pays subcontractors when it receives payment from the owner but withholds a 10% retention from the subcontractor's payment. The construction company pays weekly for labor. Often costs will be paid throughout the month that costs are incurred. The projected monthly material, labor, subcontractor, and other costs follow. The construction company will add a 10% profit and overhead markup to these costs when billing the owner. Solve this problem using a spreadsheet.

ITEM	MAT. ($)	LABOR ($)	SUB. ($)	OTHER ($)	START	FINISH
Sanitary Sewer	0	0	1,500	0	4-Jun	4-Jun
Water Line	0	0	1,500	0	6-Jun	7-Jun
Excavation	0	0	2,500	0	8-Jun	11-Jun
Footing and Foundation	3,490	3,750	0	0	12-Jun	20-Jun
Sub-rough Plumbing	0	0	2,000	0	21-Jun	22-Jun
Slab/Floor	1,150	600	0	0	25-Jun	26-Jun
Rough Carpentary	18,560	12,340	0	0	27-Jun	31-Jul
Ext. Doors and Windows	4,800	1,000	0	0	1-Aug	3-Aug
Rough Plumbing	0	0	4,000	0	6-Aug	8-Aug
Rough HVAC	0	0	3,750	0	9-Aug	10-Aug
Rough Electrical	0	0	3,000	0	13-Aug	14-Aug
Insulation	0	0	1,650	0	17-Aug	17-Aug
Drywall	0	0	4,000	0	22-Aug	29-Aug

(continued)

ITEM	MAT. ($)	LABOR ($)	SUB. ($)	OTHER ($)	START	FINISH
Doors and Trim	6,250	1,000	0	0	30-Aug	4-Sep
Paint	0	0	2,500	0	5-Sep	12-Sep
Cabinetry	0	0	6,800	0	13-Sep	17-Sep
Overhead Door	0	0	600	0	13-Sep	13-Sep
Shower Surround	0	0	1,350	0	18-Sep	19-Sep
Hardware and Bath Access.	900	300	0	0	20-Sep	21-Sep
Ceramic Tile	0	0	2,500	0	24-Sep	27-Sep
Floor Coverings	0	0	5,000	0	28-Sep	2-Oct
Finish Plumbing	0	0	2,000	0	3-Oct	5-Oct
Finish Mechanical	0	0	1,250	0	8-Oct	8-Out
Finish Electrical	0	0	3,000	0	9-Oct	10-Oct
Appliances	2,300	200	0	0	11-Oct	11-Oct
Blinds	1,000	0	0	0	12-Oct	12-Oct
Roofing	0	0	2,070	0	17-Aug	21-Aug
Masonry	0	0	2,650	0	22-Aug	28-Aug
Siding	0	0	3,870	0	29-Aug	4-Sep
Rain Gutters	0	0	500	0	5-Sep	5-Sep
Site Concrete	1,365	1,220	0	0	6-Sep	12-Sep
Fencing	0	0	4,500	0	13-Sep	19-Sep
Landscaping	0	0	5,000	0	20-Sep	26-Sep
Supervision	0	2,000	0	0	1-Jun	18-Oct
Temporary Utilities	0	0	0	2,100	1-Jun	18-Oct
Trash Disposal	0	0	0	1,500	1-Jun	18-Oct
Building Permit	0	0	0	1,000	1-Jun	1-Jun
Clean Up	0	750	0	0	17-Oct	18-Oct
Total	39,815	23,160	67,490	4,600		

PROJECTING INCOME TAXES

In this chapter you learn the fundamentals of income tax and how to prepare an income tax projection. Income taxes are a significant expense to the company and need to be included in the company's annual cash flow projection. Having an unexpected income tax bill can reduce the funds available for use on construction projects to a dangerously low level.

The text that follows covers the basic principles of corporate and personal income tax. The purpose of this chapter is to give the reader a basic understanding of principles of income tax, not turn the reader into a tax professional. Because income tax law is constantly changing, the general principles of income tax as they apply to construction companies are discussed. Also, there are many exceptions to these rules that are beyond the scope of this chapter. For these reasons, the reader is advised to consult with a tax professional for the current regulations when dealing with income taxes.

CORPORATE VERSUS PERSONAL INCOME TAX

Income taxes can be separated into two distant classes: corporate income tax and personal income tax. Each class has its own set of rules. Traditional corporations—also known as C corporations—and some partnerships pay income taxes at the corporate level. When these companies pay dividends or distribute funds to their shareholders, the shareholders pay personal income taxes on the dividends and distributed funds. In this chapter, the term *corporation* is used to refer to C corporations and partnerships that pay corporate income tax. Limited liability companies (LLCs), S corporations, most partnerships, and sole proprietorships pass their taxable income through to their shareholders, which in turn pay personal income taxes on this income. As well, the term *individual* is used to refer to the shareholders who pay personal income tax on gains for limited liability companies, S corporations, partnerships, and sole proprietorships that pass their income through to their shareholders. Because the type of the company's structure affects how taxable income is taxed, it is important to seek the advice of a tax professional when setting up a company to insure that the tax implication resulting from the company's structure are clearly understood and the most advantageous company structure is used.

TAXABLE INCOME

Income taxes let the government share in the gains and losses of business. In essence the federal, state, and local governments may be viewed as partners in a business. In general, when a company receives revenue, its income tax liability is increased, and it owes more income taxes. And when a company incurs costs, its income tax liability is decreased, and it owes less income tax. The amount of income tax a company owes is based in part on the company's taxable income. Taxable income is equal to the company's income minus tax deductions and is written as follows:

$$\text{Taxable Income} = \text{Income} - \text{Tax Deductions} \tag{13-1}$$

When a company's taxable income is positive, the company is said to have a net income for the year. When a company's taxable income is negative, the company is said to have a net loss for the year.

In general, it is financially advantageous to take tax deductions—thereby reducing taxable income and tax liability—as soon as possible and postpone the payment of taxes as long as possible. This is not always the case, particularly for companies or individuals who are subject to the alternate minimum tax or whose taxable income varies greatly from year to year.

A company with a net loss for the tax year must use the loss in another tax year. In general, both corporations and individuals are required to carry their losses back, and if the losses are not used they may then carry their losses forward. In general the losses may be carried back five years and then carried forward up to 20 years. Some losses may be carried back only three years and carried forward five years.[31] When carrying back net losses to previous years, the tax for those years is recalculated. The company can apply for a refund if the recalculated tax is less than the tax paid.

> **Example 13-1:** A construction company is set up as a C corporation. The net income/loss for the first five years of the company's existence—before carrying back or forward any losses—are as follows: year 1, −$10,000; year 2, −$25,000; year 3, $20,000; year 4, $30,000; and year 5, $35,000. What

---

[31]See IRS, *Net Operating Losses (NOLs) for Individuals, Estates, and Trusts,* Publication 536, 2002, p. 7 and IRS, *Corporations,* Publication 542, 2001, pp. 5 and 8.

is the taxable income for the corporation after carrying back or carrying forward any losses for the years?

Solution: Because the losses occur in the first two years of the company's existence, the losses cannot be carried back and must be carried forward until there is a net income to offset the losses. During the first two years of the company's existence the company's taxable income is zero as well as its tax liability. The $10,000 loss that occurs in the first year must be carried forward to the second year. Because a loss occurs in the second year, the losses from the first and second years must be carried forward to the third year. In the third year, the entire $10,000 loss from the first and $10,000 of the loss from the second year are used to offset the $20,000 net income from the third year, leaving a $15,000 ($25,000 − $10,000) of the loss from the second year to be carried forward into the fourth year. In the fourth year, the net income of $30,000 is reduced by the unused $15,000 loss from the second year, leaving a net income of $15,000 in the fourth year. There are no losses to carry forward from the fourth year so the net income in the fifth year is $35,000.

In the previous example we saw that the tax savings from the losses that occurred in the first and second years were not available until the third and fourth years. In general, it is financially advantageous to take advantage of the tax savings as soon as possible.

If the company in Example 13-1 were a limited liability corporation owned by an individual with a net income greater than $10,000 for the first year, the individual may be able to use the first year's loss to offset the net income and incur the tax savings in the same year that the loss occurs. In some cases, the tax law creates different classes of taxable cash flows and only allows the losses in one class to offset taxable income in the same class. One such class is passive income. Generally, passive activities include all business activities in which the taxpayer did not materially participate in during the tax year and most rental activities.[32] For corporations the passive activity rules only apply to personal service corporations and closely held C corporations.[33] Losses from a passive activity may be used only to offset net income from other passive activities. However, there is a special allowance that may allow a taxpayer to deduct passive losses in excess of passive income—in other words, offset nonpassive income—during the current year for losses from the rental of real estate where the taxpayer actively participated. Should the losses from passive activities exceed the net income from passive activities during the year, the unused losses may be carried forward to future tax years and may be used to offset future gains from passive activities.

---

[32]See IRS, *Instruction for Form 8582—Passive Activity Loss Limitations*, 2001, p. 1 and IRS, *Corporations,* Publication 542, 2001, p. 9.

[33]See IRS, *Corporations,* Publication 542, 2001, p. 9.

The IRS refers to these unused losses as unallowed losses. When a passive investment is sold to an unrelated party, the passive losses may be used to offset other types of income.[34]

PAYMENT OF INCOME TAXES

Corporations are required to make installment payments on their estimated tax liability if the tax liability is expected to be more than $500 for the year. The estimated payments are due the fifteenth day of the fourth, sixth, ninth, and twelfth months of the corporate tax year. In the case of a corporation with a tax year ending December 31, their estimated tax payments would be due April 15, June 15, September 15, and December 15.[35] In general, individuals who expect to owe more than $1,000 of income tax and who expect their withholdings and credits to be less than the smaller of 90% of this year's tax liability or 100% of last year's tax liability are required to make installment payments on their estimated tax liability. The estimated payments for individuals are due on the fifteenth day of the fourth, sixth, and ninth month of the current year and the first month of the following year. For most taxpayers the tax year ends on December 31; therefore, their tax due dates are April 15, June 15, September 15, and January 15 of the following year.[36]

INCOME TAX RATES

All income tax rates are stepped such that the tax rate changes based on the amount of taxable income. Each of these steps is referred to as a tax bracket. The federal income tax rates for corporations for the year 2002 are found in Table 13-1.

     The tax rates shown in Table 13-1 are the rates that are applied to the taxable income within each of the tax brackets. The effective tax rate is the average tax rate paid on the taxable income.

> **Example 13-2:** Using the tax rates for the year 2002, determine the amount of federal income tax that is due for a C corporation that has a taxable income of $115,000.
>
> **Solution:** The corporation pays 15% on the first $50,000 of taxable income, 25% on the next $25,000 ($75,000 − $50,000), 34% of the next $25,000

---

[34]See IRS, *Instruction for Form 8582—Passive Activity Loss Limitations*, 2001, pp. 1 and 7. Also see IRS, *Passive Activity and At-Risk Rules*, Publication 925, 2001.

[35]See IRS, *Corporations*, Publication 542, 2001, p. 4.

[36]See IRS, *Tax Withholding and Estimated Tax*, Publication 505, 2002, pp. 16 and 21.

Table 13-1 Corporate Federal Income Tax Rates for the Year 2002[37]

TAXABLE INCOME		TAX
OVER ($)	BUT NOT OVER ($)	RATE (%)
0	50,000	15
50,000	75,000	25
75,000	100,000	34
100,000	335,000	39
335,000	10,000,000	34
10,000,000	15,000,000	35
15,000,000	18,333,333	38
18,333,333		35

($100,000 − $75,000), and 39% on the remaining $15,000 ($115,000 − $100,000) of taxable income. The taxable income is calculated as follows:

$$Tax = \$50,000(0.15) + \$25,000(0.25) + \$25,000(0.34) + \$15,000(0.39)$$

$$Tax = \$28,100$$

The company's tax liability for $115,000 of taxable income would be $28,100, which equates to an effective tax rate of 24.43% ($28,100/$115,000).

The federal income tax rates for personal income tax for the year 2002 for single persons are found in Table 13-2 and the tax rates for married persons filing jointly are found in Table 13-3.

The 2001 Economic Growth and Tax Relief Reconciliation Act bring many changes to Tables 7-2 and 7-3. The personal income tax rates are to be reduced in

Table 13-2 Personal Income Tax Rates for a Single Person for the Year 2002[38]

TAXABLE INCOME		TAX
OVER ($)	BUT NOT OVER ($)	RATE (%)
0	6,000	10.0
6,000	27,950	15.0
27,950	67,750	27.0
67,750	141,250	30.0
141,250	307,050	35.0
307,050		38.6

[37]See IRS, *Corporations*, Publication 542, 2001, p. 10.

[38]See IRS, *1040 Instructions*, 2002, p. 75.

TABLE 13-3 Personal Income Tax Rates for
Married Persons Filing Jointly for the Year 2002[39]

| TAXABLE INCOME | | TAX |
OVER ($)	BUT NOT OVER ($)	RATE (%)
0	12,000	10.0
12,000	46,700	15.0
46,700	112,850	27.0
112,850	171,950	30.0
171,950	307,050	35.0
307,050		38.6

the year 2004 to 10, 15, 26, 29, 34, and 37.6% and again in the year 2006 to 10, 15, 25, 28, 33, and 35%. The 15% tax bracket for married persons filing jointly will be raised over a five-year period beginning in 2005 and ending in 2009.[40] Additionally, the tax brackets are adjusted for inflation annually. Be sure to consult a tax advisor or IRS publications for the most current tax rates.

In addition to the federal government levying income tax most states levy income taxes. The federal government allows state income tax to be deducted from the taxable income when calculating the federal tax liability. A few local governments levy income taxes. Consult a tax advisor or state tax department to find out the state tax rates and regulations.

The stepped tax rates may favor companies that have a more consistent taxable income rather than a highly volatile taxable income, which is subject to a higher tax rate in the years the company produces a higher taxable income and a lower tax rate in the years the company produces a lower taxable income.

Example 13-3: Compare the tax paid by two C corporations. The first corporation has a taxable income of $10,000, $100,000, and $10,000 for the next three years. The second corporation has a taxable income of $35,000, $40,000, and $45,000 for the next three years. Determine the difference in federal income tax for these two corporations using the corporate tax rates for the year 2002.

Solution: The annual income taxes for the first corporation are calculated as follows:

$$Tax_1 = \$10,000(0.15) = \$1,500$$
$$Tax_2 = \$50,000(0.15) + \$25,000(0.25) + \$25,000(0.34)$$
$$Tax_2 = \$22,250$$
$$Tax_3 = \$10,000(0.15) = \$1,500$$
$$Tax = \$1,500 + \$22,250 + \$1,500 = \$25,250$$

[39]See IRS, *1040 Instructions*, 2002, p. 75.

[40]See IRS, *Highlights of 2001 Tax Changes*, Publication 553, 2001, p. 2.

The annual income taxes for the second corporation are calculated as follows:

$$\text{Tax}_1 = \$35{,}000(0.15) = \$5{,}250$$
$$\text{Tax}_2 = \$40{,}000(0.15) = \$6{,}000$$
$$\text{Tax}_3 = \$40{,}000(0.15) = \$6{,}750$$
$$\text{Tax} = \$5{,}250 + \$6{,}000 + \$6{,}750 = \$18{,}000$$

Although the total taxable income for the three years is the same for both corporations, the difference in federal income tax liability is $7,250 ($25,250 − $18,000). The company with a more consistent taxable income pays less federal taxes.

MARGINAL OR INCREMENTAL TAX RATE

The marginal or incremental tax rate is the tax rate paid on the last dollar of taxable income. The marginal tax rate is used when comparing financial alternatives that change the company's taxable income. When using the marginal tax rate, one must be careful that the cash flows do not change the tax bracket. In Example 13-2 the company's marginal tax rate for federal income tax was 39% because they paid 39% of the last dollar earned. The marginal tax rate works well for companies and persons who are well within the top tax bracket or where there is little chance that the cash flows from the alternative will change the income tax bracket.

The effect of state income tax—including their deductibility for the purpose of federal income tax—may be incorporated in the marginal tax rate by the following equation:

$$\text{Marginal Tax Rate} = (\text{Marginal Federal Rate})(1 - \text{Marginal State Rate}) \\ + \text{Marginal State Rate} \qquad (13\text{-}2)$$

Example 13-4: Determine the marginal tax rate for a corporation whose federal tax rate is 35% and whose state tax rate is 8%.

Solution: Using Eq. (13-2) we get the following:

$$\text{Marginal Tax Rate} = (0.35)(1 - 0.08) + 0.08 = 0.402$$

The corporation's marginal tax rate is 40.2%.

CAPITAL GAINS AND LOSSES

Capital gains and losses are gains and losses on the sale or disposition of capital assets, depreciable property, and real property (real estate).[41] Capital gains and losses are divided into different classes. Short-term capital gains and losses are

---

[41]See IRS, *Sales and Other Dispositions of Assets*, Publication 544, 2002, pp. 18 and 19.

gains and losses on capital assets held for one year or less. Long-term capital gains and losses are gains and losses on capital assets held for more than one year. Long-term gains on capital assets held for more than five years might also be classified as a qualified five-year gain.[42]

The treatment of capital gains and losses has changed as the tax law has changed. Short-term capital gains are taxed as ordinary income or at the standard income tax rate. Long-term capital gains have been treated as follows: ordinary income and taxed at the standard income tax rate, taxed at a lower rate, or only part of the capital gain has been tax as ordinary income.

In 2002, for capital gains not treated as ordinary income, the maximum capital gain rate could be 8, 10, 20, 25, or 28%. Beginning in 2006, 18% will be added to this list of rates.[43]

Like passive income, capital losses may only be used to offset capital gains. For corporate income tax, unused or unallowed capital losses may be carried back three years or carried forward five years as short-term capital losses.[44] When carrying back capital losses to previous years, the tax for those years is recalculated. If the recalculated tax is less than the tax paid, the company can apply for a refund. For personal income tax purposes, up to $3,000 ($1,500 for married persons who file separate returns) in capital losses may be used to offset ordinary income. The remaining losses may be carried forward until they are completely used up.[45]

Because of the complexity of determining the tax consequences of capital gains and losses, one should seek the help of a tax professional when dealing with these issues.

TAX CONSEQUENCES OF DEPRECIATION

Most assets—with a life of one year or more—purchased for use in business must be depreciated. The most notable exception to this is assets that are deducted under the Section 179 exception (see chapter 5). Depreciation takes the cost of the asset and spreads the cost over the assumed life of the asset. The Internal Revenue Service specifies the assumed life of the asset, as well as the allowable depreciation methods. These costs are then used to offset income— reducing taxable income and thereby reducing income taxes—over the life of the asset rather than at the time of its purchase. By depreciating assets, the tax savings that accompany the purchase of the assets are moved from the time the asset is purchased to future years.

---

[42]See IRS, *1040 Instruction for Schedule D—Capital Gains and Losses,* 2002, pp. D-1 and D-8.

[43]See IRS, *Sales and Other Dispositions of Assets,* Publication 544, 2002, p. 34 and IRS, *Highlights of 2001 Tax Changes,* Publication 553, 2001, pp. 3 and 11.

[44]See IRS, *Corporations,* Publication 542, 2001, p. 5.

[45]See IRS, *Investment Income and Expenses (Including Capital Gains and Losses),* Publication 550, 2002, p. 62 and IRS, *Sales and Other Dispositions of Assets,* Publication 544, 2002, p. 33.

Example 13-5: Calculate the annual difference between the cash flow and the deductibility for tax purposes of the purchase of a $10,000 computer system. The computer system is depreciated using the half-year convention and the 200% declining-balance method. The computer system is purchased outright.

Solution: The standard recovery period mandated by the IRS for computer systems is five years (see chapter 5). Using the depreciation rates for a five-year recovery period and the 200% declining-balance depreciation method found in Table 5-6, the depreciation for the computer system is calculated as follows:

$$D_1 = (\$10,000)0.2000 = \$2,000$$
$$D_2 = (\$10,000)0.3200 = \$3,200$$
$$D_3 = (\$10,000)0.1920 = \$1,920$$
$$D_4 = (\$10,000)0.1152 = \$1,152$$
$$D_5 = (\$10,000)0.1152 = \$1,152$$
$$D_6 = (\$10,000)0.0576 = \$576$$

Because the depreciation may be taken during the year the asset was purchased, the $10,000 spent on the outright purchase of the computer system occurs during the same period the $2,000 depreciation is taken. The difference between the cash flow and its deductibility for tax purposes for the first year is $8,000 ($10,000 − $2,000). For the second year it is −$3,200. The remaining differences are shown in Figure 13-1. Because we are allowed to depreciate the entire cost of the asset, the sum of the differences is zero.

FIGURE 13-1 Difference between Cash Flow and Deductibility for Example 13-5

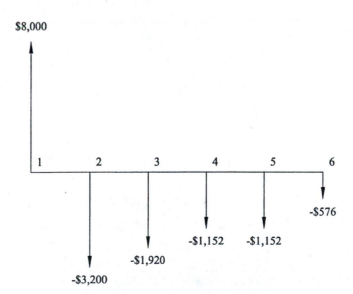

Depreciation does not reduce the amount we may deduct from the taxable income; it only defers the tax savings to future years.

Example 13-6: Using a marginal tax rate of 34%, calculate the annual difference in tax savings between deducting the entire $10,000 from Example 13-5 during the first year versus depreciating the computer system over six years. Assume that there is sufficient income that these deductions do not result in a loss that must be carried to prior years or carried forward.

Solution: If we were to deduct the entire $10,000 in the first year, the company would reduce their income tax by $3,400 ($10,000 × 0.34).

If we were to depreciate the $10,000, we would see the following tax savings over the next six years:

$$\text{Tax Savings}_1 = \$2,000(0.34) = \$680$$
$$\text{Tax Savings}_2 = \$3,200(0.34) = \$1,088$$
$$\text{Tax Savings}_3 = \$1,920(0.34) = \$653$$
$$\text{Tax Savings}_4 = \$1,152(0.34) = \$392$$
$$\text{Tax Savings}_5 = \$1,152(0.34) = \$392$$
$$\text{Tax Savings}_6 = \$576(0.34) = \$196$$

Note that other than rounding errors, the tax savings are equal in both cases. The difference is that we have to wait for six years to get the entire tax savings when depreciating the asset.

We see from Example 13-6 that companies that can avoid depreciating equipment can get the tax savings sooner than those who depreciate equipment.

Example 13-7: How would Example 13-6 change if we could use a three-year recovery period rather than a five-year?

Solution: From Table 5-6 the depreciation for the computer system is calculated as follows:

$$D_1 = (\$10,000)0.3333 = \$3,333$$
$$D_2 = (\$10,000)0.4445 = \$4,445$$
$$D_3 = (\$10,000)0.1481 = \$1,481$$
$$D_4 = (\$10,000)0.0741 = \$741$$

The tax savings over the four years are as follows:

$$\text{Tax Savings}_1 = \$3,333(0.34) = \$1,133$$
$$\text{Tax Savings}_2 = \$4,445(0.34) = \$1,511$$
$$\text{Tax Savings}_3 = \$1,481(0.34) = \$504$$
$$\text{Tax Savings}_4 = \$741(0.34) = \$252$$

Note that other than rounding errors, the tax savings are equal in both cases. In this example the difference is that we have to wait for four years rather than six years to get the tax savings.

We see from Examples 13-6 and 13-7 that companies that can depreciate equipment using a shorter recovery period gain the tax savings faster than companies that use longer recovery periods.

Example 13-8: How would Example 13-6 change if we were to use the 150% declining-balance depreciation method rather than the 200% declining-balance depreciation method?

Solution: From Table 5-11 the depreciation for the computer system is calculated as follows:

$$D_1 = (\$10,000)0.1500 = \$1,500$$
$$D_2 = (\$10,000)0.2550 = \$2,550$$
$$D_3 = (\$10,000)0.1785 = \$1,785$$
$$D_4 = (\$10,000)0.1666 = \$1,666$$
$$D_5 = (\$10,000)0.1666 = \$1,666$$
$$D_6 = (\$10,000)0.0833 = \$833$$

The tax savings over the six years are as follows:

$$\text{Tax Savings}_1 = \$1,500(0.34) = \$510$$
$$\text{Tax Savings}_2 = \$2,550(0.34) = \$867$$
$$\text{Tax Savings}_3 = \$1,785(0.34) = \$607$$
$$\text{Tax Savings}_4 = \$1,666(0.34) = \$566$$
$$\text{Tax Savings}_5 = \$1,666(0.34) = \$566$$
$$\text{Tax Savings}_6 = \$833(0.34) = \$283$$

Note that other than rounding errors the tax savings are equal in both cases. The difference is that using the 200% declining-balance depreciation method places larger tax savings in the earlier years.

From Figure 13-2 we can see that the 150% declining-balance depreciation method depreciates at a slower rate during the earlier years than the 200% declining-balance depreciation method and makes up for it in the later years. We see from Examples 13-6 and 13-8 that companies that can depreciate equipment using the 200% declining-balance method can get the tax savings from purchasing the equipment faster than companies that depreciate equipment using the 150% declining-balance method.

The rules that apply to depreciation are determined by the tax law in effect at the time of acquisition. It is also important to note that when personal or real property is leased, the lessee—the person using the property—cannot deduct the depreciation of the property but can deduct the lease payment as an expense,

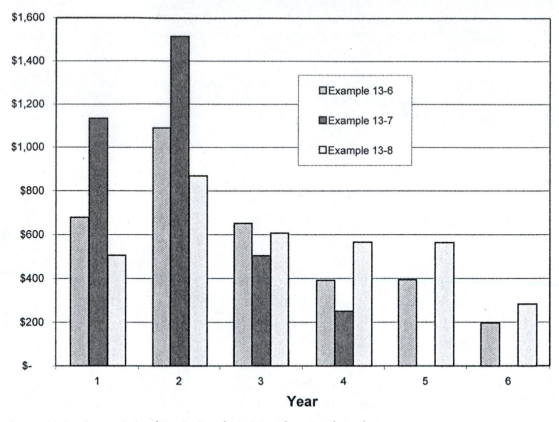

FIGURE 13-2   Comparison of Tax Savings from Examples 13-6 through 13-8

whereas the lessor—the person giving up use of the property in return for the lease payment—may claim the depreciation on the property.

NONDEDUCTIBLE EXPENSE/COSTS

Not all expenses are deductible when figuring the taxable income. For both corporations and individuals, generally only 50% of the cost of business-related meals and entertainment are deductible as an expense.[46] Meals and entertainment that are not business related may not be deducted.

> **Example 13-9:** Your company spent $2,500 last year on business-related meals and entertainment. Calculate the difference between the cash flow and the deductibility of these expenses for tax purposes.

[46]See IRS, *Instructions for Forms 1120 and 1120-A,* 2002, p. 12 and IRS, *1040 Instructions for Schedule C—Profit or Loss from Businesses,* 2002, p. C-5.

Solution: Only 50% of the costs of business-related meals and entertainment can be deducted from your taxable income. In this case it would be $1,250 ($2,500 × 0.50). The difference between the cash flow and the deductibility of these expenses for tax purposes is $1,250 ($2,500 − $1,250). This difference can never be recouped.

This rule must be taken into account when determining the taxable income while preparing an annual cash flow for the construction company.

For the purposes of corporate income tax, charitable contributions may be limited to 10% of the company's taxable income. Unused charitable contributions may be carried forward for up to five tax years.[47] This rule may come into play anytime a company disposes of an asset by giving it or selling it at a below market price to a charitable organization.[48] This rule can have a significant impact on the tax savings associated with disposition of an asset to a charitable organization by delaying the tax savings associated with the donation or by eliminating the deduction altogether if the deduction cannot be used within the allotted time.

TAX CREDITS

As an incentive to stimulate specific areas of the economy or to reward certain behaviors, the government gives tax credits for certain activities. Unlike deducting expenses that reduce a business's taxable income—which in turn reduces a business's tax liability—tax credits are used to directly reduce a business's tax liability.

In 2002 the following were some of the credits available to businesses that could be used to reduce its federal income tax liability: credit for federal tax on fuels used for certain nontaxable purposes, credit for prior year minimum tax, foreign tax credit, general business credit, nonconventional source fuel credit, and qualified electric vehicle credit. General business credits include work opportunity credit, welfare-to-work credit, credit for alcohol used as a fuel, credit for increasing research activities, low-income housing credit, enhanced oil recovery credit, disabled access credit, renewable electricity project credit, Indian employment credit, credit for employer social security and Medicare taxes paid on certain employee tips, orphan drug credit, new markets credit, credit for small employer pension plan startup costs, credit for employer-provided child care facilities and services, and credit for contributions to selected community development corporations.[49] Limits may be placed on how large a credit may be taken during any tax year. Unused tax credits may be carried back or forward. The rules differ for each of these credits. For specific information on each of these credits, see the rules governing each credit or talk to your tax advisor.

---

[47]See IRS, *Instructions for Forms 1120 and 1120-A*, 2002, p. 11.

[48]See IRS, *Sales and Other Dispositions of Assets*, Publication 544, 2002, pp. 3 and 4.

[49]See IRS, *Corporations*, Publication 542, 2001, p. 10 and IRS, *3800—General Business Credit*, 2002, pp. 1 and 3.

Example 13-10:   Your company paid employees eligible for work opportunity credit $10,000 last year. The credit is 40% of their wages. The company's wages expense must be reduced by the amount of the credit. If the company's marginal tax rate is 35%, how does this affect your company's taxes?

Solution: The tax credit is $4,000 ($10,000 × 0.40). The company must reduce its employee expenses by the $4,000 tax credit; therefore, it must pay income taxes on the tax credit. The taxes on the credit are $1,400 ($4,000 × 0.35). The net tax savings is $2,600 ($4,000 − $1,400).

ALTERNATE MINIMUM TAX

The tax laws discussed in this chapter can allow companies and individuals with large incomes to pay little or no taxes, especially when using tax credits. To ensure that companies and individuals pay a minimum amount of tax, the tax code includes provisions that require many companies and individuals to calculate their Alternate Minimum Tax liability and pay the higher of the Alternate Minimum Tax or their regular income tax. The effect of the Alternate Minimum Tax is that it can negate the tax savings gained by many of these tax provisions. Some small companies and many individuals do not need to calculate their Alternate Minimum Tax liability. Consult your tax advisor to see how the Alternate Minimum Tax provision affects you or your company.

PROJECTING TAXABLE INCOME

To prepare a cash flow projection for a company (chapter 14), the company's taxable income and income tax liability must be projected. Previously in this chapter we covered calculation of income tax liability from the taxable income. The taxable income may be projected from an income statement or from a company's cash flow projection.

When projecting the taxable income from an income statement the nontax deductible expenses must be adjusted out of the income statement. When calculating the before-tax profit the entire cost of meals and entertainment may be deducted for financial purposes; however, when calculating the before-tax profit only 50% of the costs of meals and entertainment may be deducted for tax purposes. The taxable income is calculated by taking the before-tax profits and adding back in any nondeductible expenses, such as the nondeductible portion of meals and entertainment. In addition, if the depreciation method or recovery periods are different for financial purposes than are allowed for tax purposes, further adjustments for these differences must be made.

Example 13-11:   A construction company has an estimated profit before taxes of $111,447 for the year. Included in the company's costs is $34,460 for meals and entertainment. Determine the taxable income for the company.

Solution: The profit before taxes included deducting $34,460 for meals and entertainment of which only $17,230 ($34,460 × 0.50) is deductible for tax purposes. To arrive at the taxable income we must add the nondeductible portion of the meals and entertainment back into the before-tax profit. The nondeductible portion of the meals and entertainment is $17,230 ($34,460 − $17,230). The taxable income for the company is $128,677 ($111,447 + $17,230).

When projecting the taxable income from a cash flow projection, the cash flow for depreciable assets—assets that must be depreciated for tax purposes—must be changed from a cash flow to the depreciation allowed for tax purposes in addition to adjusting for the nontax-deductible expenses. The adjustment for depreciable assets is done by replacing their cash flow with the allowed depreciation. This is done by adding the cash flow to the project cash flow for the company and subtracting the allowed depreciation along with any depreciation for depreciable assets purchased in prior periods. The adjustment for nondeductible expenses may be accomplished by adding back in any nondeductible expenses, as was done in the previous example. The calculation of the company's cash flow is covered in chapter 14.

Example 13-12: A construction company has a projected cash flow of $256,210 for the year. During the year it purchased $25,000 of assets that must be depreciated. The company may take $5,000 of depreciation for these assets and $17,500 for assets purchased during prior years. The company also spent $12,356 on meals and entertainment. Determine the taxable income for the company.

Solution: The cash flow projection included deducting the entire $25,000 used to purchase the depreciable assets. This must be added back into the cash flow. The cash flow may be reduced by the depreciation for the depreciable assets purchased this year as well as depreciation for depreciable assets purchased during prior years. Finally, the nondeductible portion of the meals and entertainment must be added to the cash flow. The nondeductible portion of the meals and entertainment is $6,178 ($12,356 − $12,356 × 0.5). The taxable income for the company is as follows:

$$\text{Taxable Income} = \$256,210 + \$25,000 - \$5,000 - \$17,000 + \$6,178$$
$$\text{Taxable Income} = \$264,888$$

CONCLUSION

The tax rules for income taxes are divided into two distinct classes, corporate and personal. C corporations and some partnerships pay corporate income tax. Limited liability companies, S corporations, most partnerships, and sole proprietorships pass income through to the shareholders, who in turn pay personal income tax.

Income tax is paid on a company's or individual's taxable income, which equals the income less allowable tax deductions. The cost of many assets may not be fully deducted during the year the assets are purchased but must be deducted over time by depreciating the asset.

When dealing with assets that must be depreciated, it is generally financially advantageous to depreciate the asset as fast as possible. Other items—such as meals and entertainment—may be partially or nondeductible for tax purposes. Any tax credits due to a company or individual are deducted from their tax liability rather than their taxable income. To ensure that they pay a minimum amount of tax, many corporations and individuals must calculate their Alternate Minimum Tax, which may render some tax savings unusable. Due to the complexity of the tax code, it is advisable for companies to seek the help of a tax accountant or other professional when dealing with income tax issues.

PROBLEMS

1. Using the tax rates for the year 2002, determine the amount of federal income tax that is due for a C corporation that has a taxable income of $356,000.

2. Using the tax rates for the year 2002, determine the amount of federal income tax that is due for an individual who is married filing jointly and has a taxable income of $356,000.

3. Determine the marginal tax rate for a corporation whose federal tax rate is 39% and whose state tax rate is 7.25%.

4. Determine the marginal tax rate for a corporation whose federal tax rate is 15% and whose state tax rate is 5%.

5. Calculate the annual difference between the cash flow and the deductibility for tax purposes of the purchase of a $20,000 truck. The truck is depreciated using the half-year convention and the 200% declining-balance method. The truck is purchased outright.

6. Calculate the annual difference between the cash flow and the deductibility for tax purposes of the purchase of $10,000 of office furniture. The furniture is depreciated using the half-year convention and the 200% declining-balance method. The furniture is purchased outright.

7. Your company spent $5,000 last year on business related meals and entertainment. Calculate the difference between the cash flow and the deductibility of these expenses for tax purposes.

8. Your company is planning on spending $15,000 on a company Christmas party. Calculate the difference between the cash flow and the deductibility of this party for tax purposes.

9. Your company paid employees who were eligible for work opportunity credit $25,000 last year. Of these wages, $21,000 is eligible for a tax credit of 40%

of the wages. The remaining wages are eligible for a tax credit of 25% of the wages. The company's wages expense must be reduced by the amount of the credit. If the company's marginal tax rate is 34%, how does this affect your company's taxes?

10. Your company spent $5,000 for building modifications to provide access required by the Americans with Disabilities Act. These expenditures are eligible for a tax credit of 50% of the cost of the modifications. How does this affect your company's taxes?

11. A construction company has an estimated profit, before taxes, of $256,452 for the year. Included in the company's costs is $25,622 for meals and entertainment. Determine the taxable income for the company.

12. A construction company has an estimated profit, before taxes, of $547,852 for the year. Included in the company's costs is $65,258 for meals and entertainment. Determine the taxable income for the company.

13. A construction company has a projected cash flow of $123,584 for the year. During the year it purchased $17,500 of assets that must be depreciated. The company may take $3,500 of depreciation for these assets and $7,500 for assets purchased during prior years. The company also spent $22,654 on meals and entertainment. Determine the taxable income for the company.

14. A construction company has a projected cash flow of $52,624 for the year. During the year it purchased $30,000 of assets that must be depreciated. The company may take $6,000 of depreciation for these assets and $22,546 for assets purchased during prior years. The company also spent $17,264 on meals and entertainment. Determine the taxable income for the company.

15. Create a computer spreadsheet to calculate the federal income tax liability from a company's taxable income using the tax rates in Table 13-1. The spreadsheet should allow you to change the taxable income by changing a single cell.

REFERENCES

IRS, *1040 Instruction*, 2002.

IRS, *1040 Instruction for Schedule C—Profit or Loss from Business*, 2002.

IRS, *1040 Instruction for Schedule D—Capital Gains and Losses*, 2002.

IRS, *1120 Schedule D—Capital Gains and Losses*, 2002.

IRS, *3800—General Business Credit*, 2002.

IRS, *5884 Work Opportunity Credit*, 2001.

IRS, *8826 Disabled Access Credit*, 2002.

IRS, *Charitable Contributions*, Publication 526, 2000.

IRS, *Corporations*, Publication 542, 2001.

IRS, *Highlights of 2001 Tax Change,* Publication 553, 2001.

IRS, *Instructions for Forms 1120 and 1220-A,* 2002.

IRS, *Instruction for Form 8810—Corporate Passive Activity Loss and Credit Limitations,* 2002.

IRS, *Instruction for Form 8582—Passive Activity Loss Limitations,* 2001.

IRS, *Investment Income and Expense (Including Capital Gains and Losses),* Publication 550, 2002.

IRS, *Net Operating Losses (NOLs) for Individuals, Estates, and Trusts,* Publication 536, 2002.

IRS, *Passive Activity and At-Risk Rules,* Publication 925, 2001.

IRS, *Sales and Other Dispositions of Assets,* Publication 544, 2002.

IRS, *Tax Withholding and Estimated Tax,* Publication 505, 2002.

IRS, *Travel, Entertainment, Gift, and Car Expense,* Publication 463, 2001.

CASH FLOWS FOR CONSTRUCTION COMPANIES

In this chapter you learn how to prepare an annual cash flow projection for a construction company. This is necessary to ensure that the company has sufficient cash for the upcoming year. Should a financial manager find that there are insufficient funds, he or she will have time to arrange for the necessary financing to provide the necessary funds. Annual cash flow projections for a company are prepared by projecting the annual revenues and construction costs for the construction company by combining the cash flows from the individual jobs or based on historical data. The financial manager must then combine the projected revenues, construction costs, the general overhead budget, and the projected income taxes with the company's available cash to determine the cash needs of the company.

Companies should not wait until the need for cash arises but should be actively looking into the future, trying to anticipate the need for cash well in advance of the arising need. Waiting for the need to arise is dangerous for two reasons. First, it takes time to arrange for the necessary funding. If one waits until the need arises the company must struggle financially while the financing is obtained. Second, financing is easier to get when a company does not need it. For companies with a surplus of cash, the preparation of a cash flow projection allows the company to wisely plan the investment of its surplus cash. After setting target levels for revenues, gross profit margin, general overhead costs, and profit from operations, management should prepare a cash flow projection to determine the amount of cash needed to meet these target levels and develop a plan of how it is going to obtain this cash. Sometimes management may find that the target levels need to be revised because it cannot obtain the required cash. In addition to preparing the annual cash flow projection, it is a good idea to update this projection a few months before the end of the year, thus allowing management time to implement year-end cash management and tax strategies. Careful planning helps a company's management more fully utilize the company's financial resources.

The process of developing an annual cash flow projection may be broken down into the following steps:

1. Project revenues, construction costs, cash receipts, and cash disbursements for the individual projects, as outlined in chapter 12. Combine the cash flow from the projects to get a cash flow for the company.
2. Determine the cash disbursement associated with the general overhead, as outlined in chapter 9. Combine this cash flow with the combined cash flow from the projects to get the cash flow from operations.
3. Incorporate other income and expenses—for example, interest—and income taxes, and determine the monthly cash flow (income tax was covered in chapter 13).
4. For companies that receive most of their revenue at the end of the month, check the minimum bank balance during the month.
5. Run what-if scenarios, sensitive analyses, and other simulations to determine how the company's needs change as the input parameters change.

Let's look at these steps.

INCORPORATING CONSTRUCTION OPERATIONS

Estimating the revenues, construction costs, cash receipts, and cash disbursements is the most difficult part of this process. The estimate should include not only current projects that will carry forward into the next year but also a realistic projection of new projects to be obtained during the year. For companies that rely heavily on open-market bidding, it is impossible to determine which projects they are going to win during the year. These companies must set target levels for each of these items as well as the amount of new work they will obtain during the year. The concepts discussed in chapter 10 may be used to set these target levels. For companies that work for a few select clients on a negotiated basis or rely heavily on design-build projects, it is easier to project what projects they will be constructing during the next year. This is because they are often involved in the project during the design phase, giving them a better picture of what is coming in the future. As you develop these projections it is important to remember that they are only projections and will need to be revised during the year because schedules change, projects are delayed or canceled, and new opportunities arise. Developing these projections in a computer spreadsheet makes it easier to make changes as circumstances change.

There are two things to keep in mind when developing the company cash flow projection from project cash flow projections. First, some of the projects will start before or finish after the period of time for which the company's cash flow is being projected. When this happens, only the revenues, construction costs, cash receipts, and cash disbursements that occur during the period of time for which the company's cash flow is being projected are included in the calculations. Care must be taken to ensure that unpaid revenues, unpaid retention, and unpaid bills are taken into account. For example, a project that is in progress before and finishes during the period of time for which the company's cash flow is being projected may have retention that was withheld prior to the period of time for which the company's cash flow is being projected. This retention will generate a cash flow that needs to be included in the company's cash flow projection. Second, the revenues, construction costs, cash receipts, and cash disbursements must be calculated for each individual project and then combined because the projects often have different payment schedules or retention rates.

Example 14-1: Determine the revenues, construction costs, cash receipts, and cash disbursements for a construction company that currently has three projects under contract for the next year and anticipates picking up a fourth project during the year.

For the first project, the project's owner is holding $50,000 in retention from this year's payments and will continue to hold 10% retention on all payments during the next year. The construction company is holding $26,000 retention on its subcontractors from the previous year's payments. The retention for this project is expected to be released in June. The estimated bill to the project's owner and construction costs for the first project are shown in Table 14-1.

For the second project, the project's owner is holding $150,000 in retention from this year's payments and will continue to hold 5% retention on all payments during the next year. The construction company is holding $82,000 retention on its subcontractors from the previous year's payments. The retention for this project is expected to be released the following year. The estimated bill to the project's owner and construction costs for the second project are shown in Table 14-2.

The third project is expected to start in February. The project's owner will hold a 10% retention on all payments during the year. The retention for this project is expected to be released in December. The construction company will withhold retention from the payments to its subcontractors. The estimated bill to the project's owner and construction costs for the third project are shown in Table 14-3.

TABLE 14-1   Bill to Owner and Construction Costs for the First Project

		COSTS			
MONTH	BILL TO OWNER ($)	MATERIAL ($)	LABOR ($)	SUB. ($)	OTHER ($)
Dec.	504,000	132,000	121,000	193,000	20,000
Jan.	448,000	98,000	109,000	192,000	15,000
Feb.	336,000	87,000	69,000	145,000	10,000
March	392,000	69,000	65,000	220,000	8,000
April	224,000	45,000	52,000	105,000	5,000
Total	1,904,000	431,000	416,000	855,000	58,000

TABLE 14-2　Bill to Owner and Construction Costs for the Second Project

Month	Bill to Owner ($)	Costs			
		Material ($)	Labor ($)	Sub. ($)	Other ($)
Dec.	160,000	54,000	55,000	18,000	15,000
Jan.	320,000	95,000	89,000	83,000	17,000
Feb.	256,000	85,000	85,000	38,000	20,000
March	288,000	85,000	81,000	69,000	21,000
April	320,000	82,000	76,000	104,000	22,000
May	320,000	75,000	81,000	107,000	21,000
June	320,000	65,000	69,000	127,000	23,000
July	320,000	62,000	59,000	139,000	24,000
Aug.	256,000	57,000	55,000	95,000	21,000
Sept.	192,000	45,000	49,000	58,000	18,000
Oct.	160,000	35,000	39,000	51,000	18,000
Nov.	192,000	30,000	33,000	92,000	15,000
Dec.	96,000	25,000	19,000	31,000	10,000
Total	3,200,000	795,000	790,000	1,012,000	245,000

The company anticipates picking up a fourth project from a current customer with a start date of October. The owner of this project will not hold retention. The estimated bill to the project's owner and construction costs for the fourth project are shown in Table 14-4.

The company's fiscal and tax year starts in January and December. The company uses the percentage-of-completion method of accounting. Cash receipts from the project's owner are received before the end of the month after the company bills its clients. Labor costs are paid weekly. Material bills are paid in full when the payment is received from the owner.

TABLE 14-3　Bill to Owner and Construction Costs for the Third Project

Month	Bill to Owner ($)	Costs			
		Material ($)	Labor ($)	Sub. ($)	Other ($)
Feb.	120,000	35,000	42,000	24,000	7,000
March	105,000	37,000	32,000	18,000	8,000
April	225,000	55,000	53,000	86,000	8,000
May	240,000	47,000	52,000	109,000	8,000
June	225,000	49,000	45,000	100,000	8,000
July	180,000	35,000	41,000	78,000	8,000
Aug.	135,000	39,000	36,000	39,000	8,000
Sept.	150,000	35,000	32,000	60,000	8,000
Oct.	120,000	22,000	29,000	50,000	7,000
Total	1,500,000	354,000	362,000	564,000	70,000

TABLE 14-4   Bill to Owner and Construction Costs for the Fourth Project

| MONTH | BILL TO OWNER ($) | COSTS | | | |
		MATERIAL ($)	LABOR ($)	SUB. ($)	OTHER ($)
Oct.	180,000	49,000	38,000	56,000	25,000
Nov.	300,000	75,000	67,000	111,000	27,000
Dec.	420,000	119,000	125,000	119,000	29,000
Total	900,000	243,000	230,000	286,000	81,000

Subcontractor bills are paid—less retention—when payment is received from the owner. The retention withheld from the subcontractor payments is based on the same retention rate that is held by the project's owner and will be paid to the subcontractor when the owner releases the retention. Other costs are paid at the end of the month the costs are incurred.

Solution: First, let's look at revenues. Because the company uses the percentage-of-completion method, the revenues are recognized when the company bills the owner; therefore, the monthly revenues equal the monthly billings to the project's owners. The revenues for January are calculated as follows:

$$\text{Revenues}_{\text{Jan}} = \$448,000 + \$320,000 + \$0 + \$0 = \$768,000$$

The revenues for the remaining months of the year are calculated in a similar manner. The revenues for next year are shown in Table 14-5.

Next, let's look at material costs. Because the company uses the percentage-of-completion method, the construction costs are recognized when the company receives the material bill; therefore, the material bills are received in the same month that the costs are recognized. This is true for labor, subcontractor, and other costs. We begin by calculating material costs in December of the current year, because these costs will be paid in January of next year and are needed to calculate January's cash flow. December's material costs are calculated as follows:

$$\text{Material}_{\text{Dec}} = \$132,000 + \$54,000 + \$0 + \$0 = \$186,000$$

TABLE 14-5   Revenues for Next Year

MONTH	REVENUES ($)	MONTH	REVENUES ($)
Jan.	768,000	July	500,000
Feb.	712,000	Aug.	391,000
March	785,000	Sept.	342,000
April	769,000	Oct.	460,000
May	560,000	Nov.	492,000
June	545,000	Dec.	516,000
		Total	6,840,000

TABLE 14-6   Material Costs for Next Year

MONTH	MATERIALS ($)	MONTH	MATERIALS ($)
Jan.	193,000	July	97,000
Feb.	207,000	Aug.	96,000
March	191,000	Sept.	80,000
April	182,000	Oct.	106,000
May	122,000	Nov.	105,000
June	114,000	Dec.	144,000
		Total	1,637,000

For this sample problem the material suppliers were paid when payment was received from the project's owner; therefore, they will be paid the month following receipt of their bill. When the payment terms for material suppliers are different from this, the cash flow should be adjusted to match the actual cash flow created by payment of their bills. The material costs for next year are calculated in a similar manner and are shown in Table 14-6.

Next, let's look at labor costs. To simplify calculations we assume all labor is recorded during the month that it was performed, although the labor costs for the last weeks of the month will be paid during the first week of the next month. If labor is paid every two weeks, a better assumption would be that half of this month's labor and half of last month's labor is paid during this month. The assumption should try to predict the actual cash flow without overcomplicating the calculations. We begin by calculating labor costs in January of next year because December's costs will be recorded and paid in December. The labor costs for January are calculated as follows:

$$\text{Labor Costs}_{Jan} = \$109,000 + \$89,000 + \$0 + \$0 = \$198,000$$

The labor costs for the remaining months of the year are calculated in a similar manner. The labor costs for next year are shown in Table 14-7.

Next, let's look at subcontractor costs. Because the company uses the percentage-of-completion method, the subcontractor costs are recognized when the company receives the subcontractor's bill. We begin by calculating

TABLE 14-7   Labor Costs for Next Year

MONTH	LABOR ($)	MONTH	LABOR ($)
Jan.	198,000	July	100,000
Feb.	196,000	Aug.	91,000
March	178,000	Sept.	81,000
April	181,000	Oct.	106,000
May	133,000	Nov.	100,000
June	114,000	Dec.	144,000
		Total	1,622,000

TABLE 14-8　Subcontractor Costs for Next Year

MONTH	SUB. ($)	MONTH	SUB. ($)
Jan.	275,000	July	217,000
Feb.	207,000	Aug.	134,000
March	307,000	Sept.	118,000
April	295,000	Oct.	157,000
May	216,000	Nov.	203,000
June	227,000	Dec.	150,000
		Total	2,506,000

subcontractor costs in December of the current year because these costs will be paid in January of next year and are needed to calculate January's cash flow. The subcontractor costs for December of the current year are calculated as follows:

$$\text{Sub. Costs}_{Dec} = \$193,000 + \$18,000 + \$0 + \$0 = \$211,000$$

The subcontractor costs for next year are calculated in a similar manner and are shown in Table 14-8.

Next, let's look at the other costs. Because the company uses the percentage-of-completion method, the construction costs are recognized when the company receives the bills. We begin by calculating the other costs in January of next year because December's costs will be recorded and paid in December. The other costs for January are calculated as follows:

$$\text{Other Costs}_{Jan} = \$15,000 + \$17,000 + \$0 + \$0 = \$32,000$$

The other costs for the remaining months of the year are calculated in a similar manner. The other costs for next year are shown in Table 14-9.

The total construction costs for each month of next year equal the sum of the material, labor, subcontract, and other costs for each month. The total construction costs for January are calculated as follows:

$$\text{Const. Costs}_{Jan} = \$193,000 + \$198,000 + \$275,000 - \$32,000$$
$$\text{Const. Costs}_{Jan} = \$698,000$$

TABLE 14-9　Other Costs for Next Year

MONTH	OTHER ($)	MONTH	OTHER ($)
Jan.	32,000	July	32,000
Feb.	37,000	Aug.	29,000
March	37,000	Sept.	26,000
April	35,000	Oct.	50,000
May	29,000	Nov.	42,000
June	31,000	Dec.	39,000
		Total	419,000

TABLE 14-10 Total Costs for Next Year

MONTH	TOTAL ($)	MONTH	TOTAL ($)
Jan.	698,000	July	446,000
Feb.	647,000	Aug.	350,000
March	713,000	Sept.	305,000
April	693,000	Oct.	419,000
May	500,000	Nov.	450,000
June	486,000	Dec.	477,000
		Total	6,184,000

The total costs for each month are calculated in a similar manner. The total costs for next year are shown in Table 14-10.

Next, let's look at cash receipts. The company expects that the cash receipts will occur in the month following the recognizing of the revenue and will be reduced by the retention held by the project's owner. The reason the cash receipt occurs in the following month is because revenue is recognized when the owner is billed rather than when the cash is received under the percentage-of-completion accounting method. An additional cash receipt will occur when the project's owner releases the retention. The cash receipts—except for the receipt when the project's owner releases retention—for each project are calculated as follows:

$$\text{Cash Receipt}_n = \text{Revenues}_{n-1}(1 - \text{Retention Rate})$$

When the project's owner releases retention, the cash receipt will equal the current month's payment plus all of the retention withheld by the project's owner.

For the first project, the owner holds a 10% retention; therefore, January's cash receipt from the project is as follows:

$$\text{Cash Receipt}_{\text{Jan}} = \$504,000(1 - 0.10) = \$453,600$$

The retention withheld from January's payments is calculated as follows:

$$\text{Retention}_n = \text{Revenues}_{n-1}(\text{Retention Rate})$$
$$\text{Retention}_{\text{Jan}} = \$504,000(0.10) = \$50,400$$

The cash receipts and retention held for February through May are calculated in a similar manner.

In June the retention will be released, which will include the $50,000 held during this year plus the retention held from next year's payments. The June cash receipt is calculated as follows:

$$\text{Cash Receipt}_{\text{June}} = \$50,000 + \$50,400 + \$44,800 + \$33,600$$
$$+ \ \$39,200 + \$22,400$$

$$\text{Cash Receipt}_{\text{June}} = \$240,400$$

The cash receipts and retention withheld for the first project are shown in Table 14-11.

TABLE 14-11 Cash Receipts and Retention for the First Project for Next Year

MONTH	CASH RECEIPT ($)	RETENTION ($)
Jan.	453,600	50,400
Feb.	403,200	44,800
March	302,400	33,600
April	352,800	39,200
May	201,600	22,400
June	240,400	0
Total	1,954,000	

For the second project, the owner holds a 5% retention; therefore, January's cash receipt is as follows:

$$\text{Cash Receipt}_{\text{Jan}} = \$160,000(1 - 0.05) = \$152,000$$

The retention withheld from January's payments is calculated as follows:

$$\text{Retention}_{\text{Jan}} = \$160,000(0.05) = \$8,000$$

The cash receipts and retention held for February through December are calculated in a similar manner. The cash receipts and retention withheld for the second project are shown in Table 14-12.

For the second project, retention will not be released during the year. At the end of the year the company would have been paid $2,948,800 on the project and there will be $155,200 withheld in retention.

TABLE 14-12 Cash Receipts and Retention for the Second Project for Next Year

MONTH	CASH RECEIPT ($)	RETENTION ($)
Jan.	152,000	8,000
Feb.	304,000	16,000
March	243,200	12,800
April	273,600	14,400
May	304,000	16,000
June	304,000	16,000
July	304,000	16,000
Aug.	304,000	16,000
Sept.	243,200	12,800
Oct.	182,400	9,600
Nov.	152,000	8,000
Dec.	182,400	9,600
Total	2,948,800	

TABLE 14-13   Cash Receipts and Retention for the Third Project for Next Year

MONTH	CASH RECEIPT ($)	RETENTION ($)
March	108,000	12,000
April	94,500	10,500
May	202,500	22,500
June	216,000	24,000
July	202,500	22,500
Aug.	162,000	18,000
Sept.	121,500	13,500
Oct.	135,000	15,000
Nov.	108,000	12,000
Dec.	150,000	0
Total	1,954,000	

For the third project, the first cash receipt will be received in March and the owners will hold a 10% retention. In December the retention withheld will be released. The cash receipts and retention withheld for the third project are calculated in the same way they were for the first project and are shown in Table 14-13.

For the fourth project, the first cash receipt will be received in November. The owner will not hold retention. The monthly cash receipts are as follows:

$$Cash\ Receipt_{Nov} = \$180,000$$
$$Cash\ Receipt_{Dec} = \$300,000$$

The total cash receipts for the fourth project for next year are $480,000.

The cash receipts for the company equal the sum of the cash receipts for the individual projects. The cash receipt for January is calculated as follows:

$$Cash\ Receipt_{Jan} = \$453,600 + \$152,000 + \$0 + \$0 = \$605,600$$

The cash receipts for the remaining month of the next year are calculated in a similar manner. The cash receipts for the next year are shown in Table 14-14.

Next, let's look at cash disbursements. Because the timing of the disbursements is different for materials, labor, subcontractors, and other costs, these costs need to be addressed separately. The cash disbursements for each project will be calculated separately because retention is withheld from the subcontractor's payments and the retention rates vary from project to project.

The cash disbursements for materials will occur in the month following the receipt of the bill for the materials. Because retention will not be withheld from the payments, the cash disbursement will equal the material

TABLE 14-14 Cash Receipts for Next Year

MONTH	CASH RECEIPTS ($)	MONTH	CASH RECEIPTS ($)
Jan.	605,600	July	506,500
Feb.	707,200	Aug.	466,000
March	653,600	Sept.	364,700
April	720,900	Oct.	317,400
May	708,100	Nov.	440,000
June	760,400	Dec.	632,400
		Total	6,882,800

costs from the previous month. January's cash disbursements for materials on the first project are $132,000.

The cash disbursements for labor will occur throughout the month the labor costs are incurred. To simplify calculation we assume all labor is recorded during the month that it was performed, although the labor costs for the last weeks of the month will be paid during the first week of the next month. January's cash disbursements for labor on the first project are $109,000.

The cash disbursements to subcontractors will occur in the month following the receipt of the bill from the subcontractors. For the first project a 10% retention is withheld from the subcontractor's payments; therefore, the cash disbursement for January is calculated as follows:

$$\text{Sub. Cash Disbursements}_n = \text{Sub.}_{n-1}(1 - \text{Retention Rate})$$
$$\text{Sub. Cash Disbursements}_{Jan} = \$193,000(1 - 0.10) = \$173,700$$

The retention withheld from January's payment to the subcontractors is calculated as follows:

$$\text{Retention}_n = \text{Revenues}_{n-1}(\text{Retention Rate})$$
$$\text{Retention}_{Jan} = \$193,000(0.10) = \$19,300$$

For other types of costs the cash disbursements will occur at the end of the month in which the other costs occur. January's cash disbursements for other costs on the first project are $15,000.

The total cash disbursements for the first project are the sum of the cash disbursements for materials, labor, subcontractors, and other costs. The cash disbursement for January is calculated as follows:

$$\text{Cash Disbursements}_{Jan} = \$132,000 + \$109,000 + \$173,00$$
$$+ \$15,000$$
$$\text{Cash Disbursements}_{Jan} = \$429,700$$

The cash disbursements for the remaining months are calculated in a similar manner, except for the cash disbursements to subcontractors for the month of June. In June the retention will be released to the subcontractors,

TABLE 14-15   Cash Disbursements for Projects

MONTH	FIRST ($)	SECOND ($)	THIRD ($)	FOURTH ($)
Jan.	429,700	177,100	0	0
Feb.	349,800	278,850	49,000	0
March	290,500	223,100	96,600	0
April	324,000	248,550	114,200	0
May	139,500	282,800	192,400	0
June	111,500	268,650	198,100	0
July	0	268,650	188,000	0
Aug.	0	270,050	149,200	0
Sept.	0	214,250	114,100	0
Oct.	0	157,100	125,000	63,000
Nov.	0	131,450	67,000	199,000
Dec.	0	146,400	56,400	340,000
Total	1,645,000	2,666,950	1,350,000	602,000

which will include the $26,000 held during the previous year and the retention held from this year's payments. June's cash disbursements to subcontractors are calculated as follows:

$$\text{Sub. Cash Disbursements}_{June} = \$26,000 + \$19,300 + \$19,200$$
$$+ \$14,500 + \$22,000 + \$10,500$$
$$\text{Sub. Cash Disbursements}_{June} = \$111,500$$

The cash disbursements for the remaining projects are calculated in the same manner. The cash disbursements for the projects are shown in Table 14-15.

The total cash disbursements for construction costs may be obtained by summing the cash disbursements for the individual projects. The monthly cash disbursements are shown in Table 14-16.

The revenues, construction costs, cash receipts, and cash disbursements may be calculated in spreadsheet format as shown in Figure 14-1.

TABLE 14-16   Total Cash Disbursements

MONTH	CASH DISBURSEMENTS ($)	MONTH	CASH DISBURSEMENTS ($)
Jan.	606,800	July	456,650
Feb.	677,650	Aug.	419,250
March	610,200	Sept.	328,350
April	686,750	Oct.	345,100
May	614,700	Nov.	397,450
June	578,250	Dec.	542,800
		Total	6,263,950

INCORPORATING GENERAL OVERHEAD

Once the cash receipts and disbursements have been calculated for each of the anticipated construction projects and have been combined for a company-wide total, we are ready to determine the cash disbursements associated with the general overhead. At this point we do not include other income and expenses that are not from construction operations—such as interest—and do not include income taxes. The preparation of a general overhead budget was covered in chapter 9. To prepare an annual cash flow, the general overhead budget must be prepared on a monthly basis and must be the general overhead budget prepared for cash flow purposes.

Example 14-2: Using the general overhead budget from Example 9-3, determine the cash disbursements associated with the general overhead budget for the company in Example 14-1. Assume that all overhead costs—except labor—are paid at the end of the month they occur. Labor will be paid weekly.

Solution: Because the costs are assumed to be paid in the month they occur, the general overhead budget is the same as the cash disbursement resulting from the general overhead budget. Using the general overhead budget from Example 9-3, we get the cash disbursements shown in Table 14-17 for the company in Example 14-1.

At this point we can determine the cash flow for the company from the construction operations and after accounting for the general overhead. This may be referred to as the cash flow from operations.

Example 14-3: Determine the monthly cash flow from operations for the company in Examples 14-1 and 14-2.

Solution: The cash flow equals the cash receipts less the cash disbursements resulting from construction costs less the cash disbursements from

TABLE 14-17   Monthly General Overhead Budget

MONTH	BUDGET ($)	MONTH	BUDGET ($)
Jan.	41,661	July	63,050
Feb.	39,637	Aug.	34,415
March	40,550	Sept.	33,580
April	44,674	Oct.	36,343
May	36,966	Nov.	35,693
June	36,795	Dec.	53,749
		Total	497,113

Project 1

Retention:	10%	
Previous Retention:	50,000	
Sub. Retention:	26,000	
Retention Paid in:	June	

Month	Dec.	Jan.	Feb.	March	April	May	June	July	Aug.	Sept.	Oct.	Nov.	Dec.	Total
Revenues	504,000	448,000	336,000	392,000	224,000									1,400,000
Construction Costs														
Materials	132,000	98,000	87,000	69,000	45,000									299,000
Labor	121,000	109,000	69,000	65,000	52,000									295,000
Subcontract	193,000	192,000	145,000	220,000	105,000									662,000
Other	20,000	15,000	10,000	8,000	5,000									38,000
Total	466,000	414,000	311,000	362,000	207,000									1,294,000
Cash Receipts		453,600	403,200	302,400	352,800	201,600	240,400							1,954,000
Cash Disbursements		429,700	349,800	290,500	324,000	139,500	111,500							1,645,000

Project 2

Retention:	5%	
Previous Retention:	150,000	
Sub. Retention:	82,000	
Retention Paid in:		

Month	Dec.	Jan.	Feb.	March	April	May	June	July	Aug.	Sept.	Oct.	Nov.	Dec.	Total
Revenues	160,000	320,000	256,000	288,000	320,000	320,000	320,000	320,000	256,000	192,000	160,000	192,000	96,000	3,040,000
Construction Costs														
Materials	54,000	95,000	85,000	85,000	82,000	75,000	65,000	62,000	57,000	45,000	35,000	30,000	25,000	741,000
Labor	55,000	89,000	85,000	81,000	76,000	81,000	69,000	59,000	55,000	49,000	39,000	33,000	19,000	735,000
Subcontract	18,000	83,000	38,000	69,000	104,000	107,000	127,000	139,000	95,000	58,000	51,000	92,000	31,000	994,000
Other	15,000	17,000	20,000	21,000	22,000	21,000	23,000	24,000	21,000	18,000	18,000	15,000	10,000	230,000
Total	142,000	284,000	228,000	256,000	284,000	284,000	284,000	284,000	228,000	170,000	143,000	170,000	85,000	2,700,000
Cash Receipts		152,000	304,000	243,200	273,600	304,000	304,000	304,000	304,000	243,200	182,400	152,000	182,400	2,948,800
Cash Disbursements		177,100	278,850	223,100	248,550	282,800	268,650	268,650	270,050	214,250	157,100	131,450	148,400	2,666,950

Project 3

Retention:	10%	
Sub. Retention:		
Previous Retention:		
Retention Paid in:	Dec.	

Month	Dec.	Jan.	Feb.	March	April	May	June	July	Aug.	Sept.	Oct.	Nov.	Dec.	Total
Revenues			120,000	105,000	225,000	240,000	225,000	180,000	135,000	150,000	120,000			1,500,000
Construction Costs														
Materials	—	—	35,000	37,000	55,000	47,000	49,000	35,000	39,000	35,000	22,000	—	—	354,000
Labor	—	—	42,000	32,000	53,000	52,000	45,000	41,000	36,000	32,000	29,000	—	—	362,000
Subcontract	—	—	24,000	18,000	86,000	109,000	100,000	78,000	39,000	60,000	50,000	—	—	564,000
Other	—	—	7,000	8,000	8,000	8,000	8,000	8,000	8,000	8,000	7,000	—	—	70,000
Total	—	—	108,000	95,000	202,000	216,000	202,000	162,000	122,000	135,000	108,000	—	—	1,350,000
Cash Receipts	—	—	—	108,000	94,500	202,500	216,000	202,500	162,000	121,500	135,000	108,000	150,000	1,500,000
Cash Disbursements	—	—	49,000	96,600	114,200	192,400	198,100	188,000	149,200	114,100	125,000	67,000	56,400	1,350,000

Project 4 Retention: 0%
Previous Retention:
Sub. Retention:
Retention Paid in:

Month	Dec.	Jan.	Feb.	March	April	May	June	July	Aug.	Sept.	Oct.	Nov.	Dec.	Total
Revenues	—	—	—	—	—	—	—	—	—	—	180,000	300,000	420,000	900,000
Construction Costs														
Materials	—	—	—	—	—	—	—	—	—	—	49,000	75,000	119,000	243,000
Labor	—	—	—	—	—	—	—	—	—	—	38,000	67,000	125,000	230,000
Subcontract	—	—	—	—	—	—	—	—	—	—	56,000	111,000	119,000	286,000
Other	—	—	—	—	—	—	—	—	—	—	25,000	27,000	29,000	81,000
Total	—	—	—	—	—	—	—	—	—	—	168,000	280,000	392,000	840,000
Cash Receipts	—	—	—	—	—	—	—	—	—	—	—	180,000	300,000	480,000
Cash Disbursements	—	—	—	—	—	—	—	—	—	—	63,000	199,000	340,000	602,000

TOTAL

Month	Dec.	Jan.	Feb.	March	April	May	June	July	Aug.	Sept.	Oct.	Nov.	Dec.	Total
Revenues	664,000	768,000	712,000	785,000	769,000	560,000	545,000	500,000	391,000	342,000	460,000	492,000	516,000	6,840,000
Materials	186,000	193,000	207,000	191,000	182,000	122,000	114,000	97,000	96,000	80,000	106,000	105,000	144,000	1,637,000
Labor	176,000	198,000	196,000	178,000	181,000	133,000	114,000	100,000	91,000	81,000	106,000	100,000	144,000	1,622,000
Subcontract	211,000	275,000	207,000	307,000	295,000	216,000	227,000	217,000	134,000	118,000	157,000	203,000	150,000	2,506,000
Other	35,000	32,000	37,000	37,000	35,000	29,000	31,000	32,000	29,000	26,000	50,000	42,000	39,000	419,000
Construction Costs	608,000	698,000	647,000	713,000	693,000	500,000	486,000	446,000	350,000	305,000	419,000	450,000	477,000	6,184,000
Cash Receipts	—	605,600	707,200	653,600	720,900	708,100	760,400	506,500	466,000	364,700	317,400	440,000	632,000	6,882,800
Cash Disbursements	606,800	606,800	677,650	610,200	686,750	614,700	578,250	456,650	419,250	328,350	345,100	397,450	542,800	6,263,950
Total Labor	176,000	198,000	196,000	178,000	181,000	133,000	114,000	100,000	91,000	81,000	106,000	100,000	144,000	1,622,000

Figure 14-1 Revenues, Construction Costs, Cash Receipts, and Cash Disbursements

TABLE 14-18   Monthly Cash Flow from Operations for Next Year

MONTH	BUDGET ($)	MONTH	BUDGET ($)
Jan.	−42,861	July	−13,200
Feb.	−10,087	Aug.	12,335
March	2,850	Sept.	2,770
April	−10,524	Oct.	−64,043
May	56,434	Nov.	6,857
June	145,355	Dec.	35,851
			121,737

the general overhead. January's cash flow from operations is calculated as follows:

$$\text{Cash Flow} = \text{Cash Receipts} - \text{Cash Disbursements} - \text{Overhead}$$
$$\text{Cash Flow}_{\text{Jan}} = \$605,600 - \$606,800 - \$41,661 = -\$42,861$$

The cash flows for February through December are calculated in a similar manner. The cash flows for each month of the year are shown in Table 14-18.

INCOME TAXES, INTEREST, LOAN PAYMENTS, AND CASH BALANCE

To get the monthly cash flow, the cash flow from operations needs to be reduced by the cash flows as a result of paying other expenses (such as loan payments) and income taxes and increased by the monthly cash flows resulting from other income (including interest).

The monthly cash flows will then affect the company's cash balance at the end of the month, which cash balance is stored in bank accounts. A negative cash flow for the month will reduce the company's cash balance, whereas a positive cash flow will increase the company's cash balance. Because the company's cash balance changes each month as a result of the monthly cash flows, which affects the amount of interest paid on the bank accounts, which in turn affects the next month's cash flow, incorporating interest is best done by starting at the first month and working through the year to the last month. When calculating the monthly interest we should use a cash balance that is representative of the average balance for the month. During the course of the month our beginning balance in the bank will be reduced by the bills paid during the month until the time the revenues are received. For many companies a representative balance may be calculated by averaging the beginning bank balance with the bank balance just before the revenues begin to occur. For the company in Examples 14-1 to 14-3, the balance just before the revenues occur may be approximated by reducing the beginning balance by the monthly labor costs, which are the only costs that are paid throughout the month. The balance may then be averaged with the beginning balance to get a representative average balance for the account.

If income taxes are paid during months other than the last month of the year, the payment of taxes will result in a cash flow that reduces the amount of cash in the bank, which reduces the amount of interest paid by the bank, which reduces the amount of taxes. This creates a loop or circular reference that can be solved only by iteration. This iteration is easily handled by spreadsheets; however, when preparing the calculations manually it is time consuming to use iteration to solve the problem.

Example 14-4: Determine the monthly cash flow and ending balance of the bank account for the company in Examples 14-1 to 14-3. The new computer system, included in the general overhead budget, will be subject to 200% declining-balance depreciation using the midyear convention and a five-year life. Depreciation from previous year's purchases of office equipment is $6,000 per year. The company has an outstanding loan with a payment of $1,626 per month. Of the entire year's loan payments, $10,900 will be in the form of interest and the remaining will reduce the outstanding loan balance. The surplus cash from each month will be placed in a bank account earning a monthly interest rate of 0.5%. Negative cash flows will be covered by funds in this bank account. At the beginning of the year the balance for the bank account will be $200,000. Inasmuch as the company is an S corporation, the estimated income taxes for the year will be distributed to the company's owners at the end of the year. The disbursement will be based on a marginal tax rate of 38.6%. Ignore underbillings and overbillings.

Solution: To get the cash flow for January we must add the interest from the bank account and subtract the loan payment. The interest on the loan is included in the loan payment and is included when we subtract the loan payment. To get the interest on the bank account we take the average of the beginning balance and the balance just before payment occurs, which will be approximated by reducing the beginning balance by the labor costs—the only costs that are paid throughout the month. The labor should include labor on the construction projects as well as general overhead labor. The average balance for January is calculated as follows:

$$\text{Average Balance} = [\text{Beginning Balance} + (\text{Beginning Balance} - \text{Labor})]/2$$
$$\text{Average Balance} = \text{Beginning Balance} - \text{Labor}/2$$
$$\text{Average Balance}_{Jan} = \$200,000 - (\$198,000 + \$20,618)/2$$
$$\text{Average Balance}_{Jan} = \$90,691$$

The interest on the bank account for January is calculated as follows:

$$\text{Interest} = \text{Average Balance}(\text{Interest Rate})$$
$$\text{Interest}_{Jan} = \$90,691(0.005) = \$453$$

The cash flow for January is calculated by adding the interest to the cash flow from operations and subtracting the monthly loan payment, as follows:

$$\text{Cash Flow}_{\text{Jan}} = -\$42{,}861 + \$453 - \$1{,}626 = -\$44{,}034$$

This cash will be withdrawn from the bank account leaving it with a balance of \$155,966 (\$200,000 − \$44,034). The average balance for February is calculated as follows:

$$\text{Average Balance}_{\text{Feb}} = \$155{,}966 - (\$196{,}000 + \$20{,}618)/2$$
$$\text{Average Balance}_{\text{Feb}} = \$47{,}657$$

The interest on the bank account for the month of February is calculated as follows:

$$\text{Interest}_{\text{Feb}} = \$47{,}657(0.005) = \$238$$

The cash flow for February is calculated as follows:

$$\text{Cash Flow}_{\text{Feb}} = -\$10{,}087 + \$238 - \$1{,}626 = -\$11{,}475$$

This cash will be withdrawn from the bank account, leaving it with a balance of \$144,491 (\$155,966 − \$11,475). The interest on the bank account, the monthly cash flow, and ending bank account balance for the months of March through November are calculated in a similar manner. At the end of November the balance in the bank account will be \$276,537.

The average balance for December is calculated as follows:

$$\text{Average Balance}_{\text{Dec}} = \$276{,}537 - (\$144{,}000 + \$20{,}618)/2$$
$$\text{Average Balance}_{\text{Dec}} = \$194{,}228$$

The interest on the bank account for the month of December is as follows:

$$\text{Interest}_{\text{Dec}} = \$194{,}228(0.005) = \$971$$

The total interest paid throughout the year is calculated as follows:

$$\text{Interest} = \$453 + \$238 + \$226 + \$226 + \$286 + \$609$$
$$+ \$1{,}366 + \$1{,}321 + \$1{,}406 + \$1{,}356 + \$1{,}050 + \$971$$
$$\text{Interest} = \$9{,}508$$

To get the cash flow for December we must include the cash distributed to the owners. This distribution is based on the estimated income taxes for the year, which equals the marginal tax rate times the taxable income. The estimated taxable income equals the revenues less construction costs less the portion of overhead that is tax deductible less other expenses (namely, interest paid) plus other income (namely, interest received). The easiest way to determine the portion of the overhead that is tax deductible is to begin with the cash flow from the overhead and make the necessary adjustments. The following adjustments must be made.

In the current overhead calculations 100% of meals and entertainment has been deducted, whereas only 50% of meals and entertainment is deductible.

This will decrease the tax-deductible overhead by 50% of the meals and entertainment cost or $5,202 ($10,404 × 0.50).

In the current overhead calculations the money spent on a new computer system has been deducted and depreciation has been ignored. The money spent on the computer system must be depreciated over five years using the 200% declining-balance method and the midyear convention. Because the company cannot deduct the cost of the computer system, these costs will decrease the company's tax-deductible overhead by $18,000. In lieu of writing off the costs the company may deduct 20% (see Table 5-6) of the purchase price during the first year as depreciation or $3,600 ($18,000 × 0.20). Additionally, the company has $6,000 in depreciation from previous year's purchases. Depreciation will increase the company's tax-deductible overhead by $9,600 ($3,600 + $6,000). The tax-deductible overhead is calculated as follows:

$$\text{Overhead} = \$497,113 - \$5,202 - \$18,000 + \$9,600 = \$483,511$$

The taxable income equals the revenues less construction costs less overhead less interest paid plus interest received and is calculated as follows:

$$\text{Taxable Income} = \$6,840,000 - \$6,184,000 - \$483,511$$
$$- \$10,900 + \$9,508$$

$$\text{Taxable Income} = \$171,097$$

The estimated taxes are 38.6% of the taxable income or $66,043 ($171,097 × 0.386). The taxable income and estimated taxes may be calculated in spreadsheet format as shown in Figure 14-2. There are small differences between the numbers shown in Figure 14-2 and the calculations in Example 14-4, which are due to rounding in the example.

FIGURE 14-2 Tax Calculations

Tax Rate	38.60%
Tax Calculations	
Revenues	6,840,000
Construction Costs	6,184,000
Gross Profit	656,000
Overhead—Cash Flow	497,094
Less 50% of Meals & Enter.	5,200
Less Office Equipment	18,000
Plus Past Depreciation	6,000
Plus New Depreciation	3,600
Total Deductible Overhead	483,494
Net Profit from Operations	172,506
Less Interest Paid	10,900
Plus Interest	9,509
Taxable Income	171,114
Estimated Taxes	66,050

TABLE 14-19　Monthly Balances, Interest, Income Tax, and Cash Flow

MONTH	BANK ACCOUNT			INCOME TAXES ($)	MONTHLY CASH FLOW ($)
	BEGINNING BALANCE ($)	INTEREST ($)	ENDING BALANCE ($)		
Jan.	200,000	453	155,966	0	−44,034
Feb.	155,966	238	144,491	0	−11,475
March	144,491	226	145,941	0	1,450
April	145,941	226	134,017	0	−11,924
May	134,017	286	189,111	0	55,094
June	189,111	609	333,449	0	144,338
July	333,449	1,366	319,989	0	−13,460
Aug.	319,989	1,321	332,019	0	12,030
Sept.	332,019	1,406	334,569	0	2,550
Oct.	334,569	1,356	270,256	0	−64,313
Nov.	270,256	1,050	276,537	0	6,281
Dec.	276,537	971	245,690	66,043	−30,847

In a spreadsheet the tax costs could be allocated to the months when tax payments are due; however, this will change the cash flow, which will change the monthly bank account balance, which will change the interest paid during the month, which will change the taxable income and income taxes due, which will change the tax payment. This circular loop can be solved using a spreadsheet. For manual calculations you would need to see if the changes caused by the circular loop were significant if you were going to spread out the tax payments throughout the year.

The cash flow for December is calculated as follows:

$$\text{Cash Flow}_{\text{Dec}} = \$35,851 + \$971 - \$1,626 - \$66,043$$
$$= -\$30,847$$

This cash will be withdrawn from the bank account, leaving it with a balance of $245,690 ($276,537 − $30,847). The beginning and ending bank account balances, monthly interest, income taxes, and monthly cash flows for the year are shown in Table 14-19.

From Example 14-4 we see that the smallest projected balance in the company's bank account at the end of each month during the year is $134,017, which occurs at the end of April.

DETERMINING THE MINIMUM MONTHLY BALANCE

For construction companies, the balances at the end of the month may or may not be representative of the company's needs for cash during the month. For construction companies whose cash receipts are distributed evenly throughout the month, the balances at the end of the month are often fairly representative of the entire month. For many medium- to large-volume homebuilders who have multiple sales spread throughout the month, this is the case. For many commercial construction companies, the bulk of their cash receipts occur during one week of the month, often near the end of the month. These companies have to fund cash disbursements that occur from the beginning of the month until the cash receipts begin. Because the company is using its cash to pay these bills, the available cash is reduced below the balances reported at the end of each month, often by a significant amount. Let's look at the company in Examples 14-1 through 14-4 that had a minimum balance in the bank account for the year of $134,017.

Example 14-5: Determine the minimum balance of the bank account for each month for the company in Examples 14-1 through 14-4. Does the company have sufficient funds for the next year?

Solution: Because all of our receivables occur at the end of the month, the bank account will be reduced during the courses of the month by the labor paid throughout the month. The minimum bank account balance during the month may be estimated by subtracting the monthly labor costs from the previous month's ending balance for the bank account, which is the same as this current month's beginning balance. The labor costs include the labor portion of the construction costs and the labor included in the general overhead. The minimum monthly balance for January is calculated as follows:

$$\text{Minimum Balance}_{Jan} = \$200,000 - \$198,000 - \$20,618$$
$$\text{Minimum Balance}_{Jan} = -\$18,618$$

The remaining months are calculated in a similar manner. The minimum monthly balances for the year are shown in Table 14-20.

The minimum balance for the bank account for the year occurs in February at $-\$60,652$. For the first five months of the year—January through May—the company has a negative balance in the bank just before it begins receiving payments from the owners. After May the bank account no longer has a negative balance each month because the retention is released from Project 1, which provides the company with an infusion of cash. To be on the safe side, the company should secure an additional $60,000 to $100,000 in cash for the upcoming year.

TABLE 14-20   Minimum Monthly Balances

MONTH	BUDGET ($)	MONTH	BUDGET ($)
Jan.	−18,618	July	212,831
Feb.	−60,652	Aug.	208,371
March	−54,127	Sept.	230,401
April	−55,677	Oct.	207,951
May	−19,601	Nov.	149,638
June	54,493	Dec.	111,919

							Annual Cash Flow from Operations						
Item	Jan.	Feb.	March	April	May	June	July	Aug.	Sept.	Oct.	Nov.	Dec.	Total
Cash Receipts	605,600	707,200	653,600	720,900	708,100	760,400	506,500	466,000	364,700	317,400	440,000	632,400	6,882,800
Cash Disbursements	606,800	677,650	610,200	686,750	614,700	578,250	456,650	419,250	328,350	345,100	397,450	542,800	6,263,950
Overhead:													
Advertising	7,680	7,120	7,850	7,690	5,600	5,450	5,000	3,910	3,420	4,600	4,920	5,160	68,400
Promotion	—	—	—	—	—	—	8,000	—	—	—	—	15,000	23,000
Car and Truck Expenses	1,100	1,100	1,100	1,100	1,100	1,100	1,100	1,100	1,100	1,100	1,100	1,100	13,200
Computer and Office Furniture	—	—	—	—	—	—	18,000	—	—	—	—	—	18,000
Employee Wages and Salaries	20,618	20,618	20,618	20,618	20,618	20,618	20,618	20,618	20,618	20,618	20,618	20,618	247,416
Employee Benefits	750	750	750	750	750	750	750	750	750	750	750	750	9,000
Employee Retirement	619	619	619	619	619	619	619	619	619	619	619	619	7,422
Employee Taxes	2,147	2,063	1,981	1,845	1,772	1,725	1,656	1,656	1,656	1,648	1,419	1,115	20,682
Insurance	4,306	4,026	4,391	4,311	3,266	3,191	2,966	2,421	2,176	2,766	2,926	3,046	39,794
Taxes & Licenses	100	—	—	—	—	—	—	—	—	—	—	—	100
Office Supplies	500	500	500	500	500	500	500	500	500	500	500	500	6,000
Office Rent	500	500	500	500	500	500	500	500	500	500	500	500	6,000
Office Utilities	350	350	250	250	250	350	350	350	250	250	350	350	3,700
Postage and Delivery	100	100	100	100	100	100	100	100	100	100	100	100	1,200
Janitorial and Cleaning	433	433	433	433	433	433	433	433	433	433	433	433	5,200
Telephone	440	440	440	440	440	440	440	440	440	440	440	440	5,280
Charitable Contributions	—	—	—	—	—	—	—	—	—	—	—	3,000	3,000
Dues and Memberships	—	—	—	1,500	—	—	—	—	—	—	—	—	1,500
Legal and Professional Services	1,000	—	—	3,000	—	—	1,000	—	—	1,000	—	—	6,000
Meals and Entertainment	867	867	867	867	867	867	867	867	867	867	867	867	10,400
Bank Fees	50	50	50	50	50	50	50	50	50	50	50	50	600
Miscellaneous	100	100	100	100	100	100	100	100	100	100	100	100	1,200
Total Overhead	41,659	39,636	40,549	44,673	36,965	36,793	63,048	34,413	33,578	36,341	35,691	53,748	497,094
Cash Flow from Operations	(42,859)	(10,086)	2,851	(10,523)	56,435	145,357	(13,198)	12,337	2,772	(64,041)	6,859	35,852	121,756
Interest Received	453	238	226	226	286	609	1,366	1,321	1,406	1,356	1,050	971	9,509
Loan Payments	1,626	1,626	1,626	1,626	1,626	1,626	1,626	1,626	1,626	1,626	1,626	1,626	19,512
Estimated Income Taxes												66,050	66,050
Cash Flow After Income Tax	(44,032)	(11,474)	1,451	(11,923)	55,095	144,340	(13,459)	12,032	2,552	(64,311)	6,282	(30,852)	45,702
Savings Account													
Beginning Balance	200,000	155,968	144,494	145,946	134,022	189,118	333,458	319,999	332,031	334,583	270,272	276,555	200,000
Deposit or (Withdrawal)	(44,032)	(11,474)	1,451	(11,923)	55,095	144,340	(13,459)	12,032	2,552	(64,311)	6,282	(30,852)	45,702
Ending Balance	155,968	144,494	145,946	134,022	189,118	333,458	319,999	332,031	334,583	270,272	276,555	245,702	
Monthly Labor Costs	218,618	216,618	198,618	201,618	153,618	134,618	120,618	111,618	101,618	126,618	120,618	164,618	
Minimum Monthly Bank Balance	(18,618)	(60,650)	(54,124)	(55,672)	(19,596)	54,500	212,840	208,381	230,413	207,965	149,654	111,937	

Figure 14-3 Spreadsheet for Examples 14–1 through 14–5

The revenues, construction costs, general overhead, interest, loan payments, income taxes, cash flow after income tax, savings account balances, and minimum monthly bank account balances may be calculated in spreadsheet format as shown in Figure 14-3. There are small differences between the numbers shown in Figure 14-3 and the calculations in Examples 14-1 through 14-5, which are due to rounding in the example. This spreadsheet can be combined with the spreadsheets in Figures 9-5, 14-1, and 14-2 to create a financial model that can be adjusted quickly to make changes in the assumption and input data.

From this example we see that the cash balance at the end of the month is not always representative of a company's cash balance during the month. In chapter 16 we discuss ways to supply the additional cash needs of a company.

FINE TUNING, WHAT IF, AND SENSITIVITY ANALYSIS

The calculations performed in Examples 14-1 through 14-5 are easily set up in a spreadsheet. Setting up a spreadsheet to perform the cash flow analysis for the company is less time consuming than performing the calculations manually. There are three additional reasons to set up the cash flow analysis in a spreadsheet.

First, it allows the user to easily change the input parameters and immediately see how the changes affect the cash flows. This is essential for fine-tuning a cash flow analysis. For example, after running the cash flow analysis, we decide that we need to reduce our overhead to ensure that we are profitable. This can be done quickly by changing the budgets for the individual overhead items until we meet our profitability goals.

Second, we can ask ourselves "What if . . ." and see what happens. For example, we may ask ourselves "What if the retention on Project 1 is released in July instead of June? How will that affect our need for cash during the next year?" By making the change we would see that although the cash flow for June and July changed, we still needed the same amount of cash for next year and it would not increase the number of months over which the additional cash was needed.

The third reason is so we can perform a sensitive analysis to determine which input variables the cash flow analysis is most sensitive to. By changing some variables by a large amount we may see little change in the cash flow analysis, whereas minor changes to other variables may make a major change in the cash flow analysis. For example, if we doubled bank fees from $50 to $100, little change would occur and we would say that the cash flow analysis is not very sensitive to the bank fees. However, if we reduce the amount of work subcontracted out on Project 1 during the month of February by 10% and perform that work with our labor, we increase the amount of additional cash we need from $60,652 to $75,150. Here we see that we are very sensitive to the amount of labor performed by our company during the month of February.

CONCLUSION

Companies should prepare an annual cash flow projection based on their target levels for revenues, gross profit margin, general overhead costs, and profit from operations to determine the amount of cash needed to meet these target levels and arrange for the necessary financing. Additionally, companies should prepare a cash flow projection for the remaining months in the year at the beginning of the last quarter of the year so that they have time to implement year-end cash flow and tax strategies.

It is best to prepare a company's cash flow projection in a computer spreadsheet so adjustments may be easily made to the spreadsheet, until the spreadsheet has been fine-tuned. Developing a cash flow projection may be broken down into the following steps:

1. Project revenues, construction costs, cash receipts, and cash disbursements for the individual projects, as outlined in chapter 12. Combine the cash flow from the projects to get a cash flow for the company.

2. Determine the cash disbursement associated with the general overhead, as outlined in chapter 9. Combine this cash flow with the combined cash flow from the projects to get the cash flow from operations.

3. Incorporate other income and expenses—for example, interest—and income taxes and determine the monthly cash flow.

4. For companies who receive most of their revenue at the end of the month, check the minimum bank balance during the month.

5. Run what-if scenarios, sensitive analyses, and other simulations to determine how the company's needs change as the input parameters change.

It is important to check the minimum cash balance during the month because for many construction companies, the balances at the end of the month are not representative of the company's need for cash during the month.

PROBLEMS

1. Set up Examples 14-1 to 14-5 in a spreadsheet.
2. How would the company's cash needs change for the company in Examples 14-1 to 14-5 if they subcontracted out $25,000 of labor per month for $26,000 per month on the first project for the months of January through April?

3. How would the company's cash needs change for the company in Examples 14-1 to 14-5 if the third project started in May instead of February and the retention was not released until the following year?

4. Other than borrowing more money—increasing the beginning balance of the bank account—what could the company in Examples 14-1 through 14-5 do to ensure that it had enough funds to prevent the bank account balance from going negative during the year?

5. Prepare a cash flow projection for a construction company that currently has two projects under contract for the next year and anticipates picking up a third and fourth project during the year.

For the first project, the project's owner is holding $24,200 in retention from this year's payments and will continue to hold a 10% retention on all payments during the next year. The construction company is holding $9,400 of retention on its subcontractors from this year's payments. The retention for this project is expected to be released in June. The estimated bill to the project's owner and construction costs for the first project are as follows:

| | | COSTS | | | |
MONTH	BILL TO OWNER ($)	MATERIAL ($)	LABOR ($)	SUB. ($)	OTHER ($)
Dec.	126,800	25,500	24,900	51,200	10,200
Jan.	52,900	9,900	10,100	22,400	4,100
Feb.	88,000	16,600	15,600	32,200	6,800
March	25,700	5,000	5,100	10,400	2,000
Total	293,400	57,000	55,700	116,200	23,100

The second project started last December and the owner has yet to make a payment. The project's owner will hold a 10% retention on this project and is expected to release the retention in August. The construction company will withhold retention from the payments to its subcontractors. The estimated bill to the project's owner and construction costs for the second project are as follows:

| | | COSTS | | | |
MONTH	BILL TO OWNER ($)	MATERIAL ($)	LABOR ($)	SUB. ($)	OTHER ($)
Dec.	11,900	3,400	3,700	1,400	1,300
Jan.	33,300	10,300	9,400	4,300	4,000
Feb.	42,200	11,100	10,700	4,900	4,400
March	44,600	14,700	14,500	6,300	5,400
April	70,000	21,500	19,100	9,500	7,600
May	32,200	8,900	8,800	3,600	3,100
June	45,300	12,800	12,800	5,400	5,000
July	15,200	4,600	4,100	1,900	1,700
Total	294,700	87,300	83,100	37,300	32,500

The third project is expected to start in April. The project's owner will hold a 5% retention on the project and the construction company will withhold retention from the payments to its subcontractors. The retention for this project is expected to be released in September. The estimated bill to the project's owner and construction costs for the third project are as follows:

| | | COSTS | | | |
MONTH	BILL TO OWNER ($)	MATERIAL ($)	LABOR ($)	SUB. ($)	OTHER ($)
April	36,300	6,400	9,400	6,300	4,000
May	50,800	9,400	12,400	7,600	5,500
June	61,800	10,800	15,100	10,300	6,500
July	36,100	7,400	8,600	6,000	3,900
Total	185,000	34,000	45,500	30,200	19,900

The fourth project is expected to start in August. The project's owner will hold a 10% retention on the project and the construction company will withhold retention from the payments to its subcontractors. The retention for this project will not be released this year. The estimated bill to the project's owner and construction costs for the fourth project are as follows:

| | | COSTS | | | |
MONTH	BILL TO OWNER ($)	MATERIAL ($)	LABOR ($)	SUB. ($)	OTHER ($)
Aug.	19,000	4,600	5,300	2,900	1,800
Sept.	53,200	16,500	16,200	8,700	5,000
Oct.	61,600	16,100	21,500	9,800	6,900
Nov.	73,700	19,900	21,300	11,800	7,600
Dec.	115,400	32,700	33,400	17,000	10,800
Total	322,900	89,800	97,700	50,200	32,100

The company's fiscal and tax years start in January and end in December. The company uses the percentage-of-completion method of accounting. Revenues are received before the end of the month after the month the company bills its clients. Labor costs are paid weekly. Material bills are paid in full when the payment is received from the owner. Subcontractor bills are paid—less retention—when payment is received from the owner. The retention withheld from the subcontractor payments is based on the same retention rate that is held by the project's owner and will be paid to the subcontractor when the owner releases the retention. Other costs are paid at the end of the month the costs are incurred.

Include in the general overhead budget the following. The budget for advertising is to be 0.5% of revenues. The budget for promotions is to include $1,000 in July for a company picnic, $200 in December for Christmas cards and gifts, and $1,300 in December for a company Christmas party. The monthly fuel and maintenance cost for the company vehicle driven by the owner is estimated to be $225 per month. In April, the company plans on purchasing a new copier for $2,000. The new copier will be subject to the 200% declining-balance depreciation method using the midyear convention and a five-year life.

The company employs three workers: the owner, an estimator, and a secretary/bookkeeper. The owner is paid $5,000 per month. The estimator is paid $15.00 per hour and works an average of twenty-five hours per week. The secretary/bookkeeper is paid $13.50 per hour and works an average of forty-five hours per week. All of the hourly employees are paid for fifty-two weeks of work per year. Time-and-a-half must be paid to hourly employees for work over 40 hours per week. The company contributes $175 per month per employee—including the owner—for health insurance. They also deposit $0.50 in an employee's 401(k) account for every dollar the employee deposits. The maximum the company would deposit is 3% of an employee's wages. The company's owner is included in this match. Historically, the employees have taken full advantage of this benefit. The current social security rate is 6.2% to $84,900 of wages per employee. The current Medicare rate is 1.45%. The company's FUTA rate is 0.8% on the first $7,000 of wages per employee and their SUTA rate is 2.5% on the first $9,000 of wages per employee.

The company is charged 0.45% of revenues, 0.65% of wages for hourly employees, and 1.5% of wages for salaried employees for general liability insurance. In January the company pays $25 for a business license. It is anticipated that office supplies will cost $150 per month. Rent for the office space is $425 per month and includes sewer and water. Office utilities are expected to run as follows: $150 per month for power in June, July, and August and $100 per month during the remaining months of the year; and $130 per month for natural gas during November, December, January, and February and $30 per month during the remaining months of the year. It is anticipated that the company will spend $50 per month for postage and $100 per month for janitorial services. The estimated telephone costs are $125 per month for telephone and long-distance service and $100 per month to provide mobile phone service for the owner. In December the company plans on making a $500 charitable contribution to a local university. In April the company must pay $500 for its annual plan room membership. The company plans on spending $250 at the first of each quarter for accounting services to close the previous quarter's books and an additional $500 in April for tax services. The estimated cost of meals and entertainments is $50 per week. Bank fees are $50 per month. Allow $75 per month for miscellaneous expenses.

Assume that all overhead costs—except labor—are paid at the end of the month they occur. Labor will be paid throughout the month that the costs occur. Also assume that all of the months are the same length—four and one-third weeks.

In addition to the above costs, the company depreciation from previous year's purchases of office equipment is $3,000 per year. The company has an outstanding loan with a payment of $575 per month. Of the monthly loan payments, $3,730 will be in the form of interest and the remaining will reduce the outstanding loan balance. The surplus cash from each month will be placed in a bank account earning a monthly interest rate of 0.45%. Negative cash flows will be covered by funds in this bank account. At the beginning of the year the balance for the bank account will be $55,000. Inasmuch as the company is an S corporation, the estimated income taxes for the year will be distributed to the company's owners at the end of the year. The disbursement will be based on a marginal tax rate of 27%. Ignore underbillings and overbillings.

Does the company have sufficient funds for the next year? If not, what changes can the company make to ensure that it has sufficient funds?

TIME VALUE OF MONEY

In this chapter you learn to convert cash flows occurring in one time period to an equivalent cash flow occurring at another time period or into a uniform series of cash flows occurring over successive periods. Understanding the time value of money is a prerequisite to understanding debt financing and how to compare two or more financial options, which are the topics of chapters 16, 17, and 18. Additionally, you learn how to adjust interest rates for inflation.

Suppose that I were to offer to give you $1,000 today or $1,000 a year from now. Which would you take? Most people would take the $1,000 today because a dollar today is worth more than a dollar tomorrow. Money's value is based not only on the amount of money received but also on when the money is received. In the case of the $1,000, the amount of money received is the same; however, the amounts are received at different points in time. Each of you could have taken the $1,000 today, invested it in the bank and at the end of the year had the original $1,000 plus the interest paid by the bank for the use of your money. If the bank were paying an interest rate of 5% compounded annually, the original $1,000 investment would have earned $50 ($1,000 × 0.05) interest for a total of $1,050 by the end of the first year. Therefore, $1,000 received today would be equivalent, although not equal in amount, to $1,050 received a year from now based on an interest rate of 5% compounded annually.

Now suppose that I were to offer to give you $1,000 today or $1,050 a year from now. Which would you take? First, we notice that the amounts of money received are different. The receipt a year from now is $50 greater. However, these receipts are equivalent when compared at an interest rate of 5% compounded annually because $1,000 invested today at an interest rate of 5% compounded annually would earn $50 interest and be worth $1,050 a year from now, which is the same as the payment a year from now.

EQUIVALENCE

Equivalent cash flows are cash flows that produce the same result over a specific period of time. In the example on the previous page you would have the same amount of cash at the end of the first year regardless of whether you chose to receive the $1,000 today and invest it at an interest rate of 5% compounded annually or you chose to receive the $1,050 a year from now. Equivalence is a function of the following:

1. The size of the cash flows,
2. The timing of the cash flows, and
3. The interest rate.

When analyzing cash flows it is important to take into account not only the amount or size of the cash flows but also the timing of the cash flows. To simplify the comparison of cash flows at different time periods, it is useful to convert the cash flows into their equivalent cash flows at a specific point in time based on a specified interest rate. The point in time may be now, at some time in the future, or a series of periodic cash flows over a specified period of time (for example, monthly or annual cash flows). By converting the cash flows to a specific point in time at a given interest rate, the timing of the cash flows and interest rate become fixed, leaving equivalence a function of the size of the cash flows. The cash flows then can be directly compared. For the purpose of determining equivalence, cash flows that occur in the same period of time may be added or subtracted.

A number of formulas have been developed to convert cash flows, which occur at different points in time, into their equivalent cash flows at some specific point or points in time. These formulas use the following variables:

P = the present value of a cash flow or the value of a cash flow at the present time. In the case of the $1,000, its present value is $1,000. When used in the equivalence formulas, the present value occurs at the beginning of the year, which is the same point in time as the end of the previous year. The present value may be used to refer to any point in time prior to a cash flow or series of cash flows for which we want to determine the equivalence of the cash flow or cash flows. This point may be now, in the past, or in the future.

F = the future value of a cash flow or the value of a cash flow at some specific point in the future. In the case of the $1,000, its future value in one year at an interest rate of 5% compounded annually is $1,050. The future value occurs at the end of the year. The future value may be used to refer to any point in time after a cash flow or series of cash flows for which we want to determine the equivalence of the cash flow or cash flows. The future value may also occur concurrently with the last cash flow in a uniform series of cash flows.

i = the periodic interest rate or interest rate for one period. The period may be any specified amount of time with years, quarters, and months being the most common. The period must be the same as the compounding period for the interest rate. In the case of the $1,000, the periodic interest rate was 5% and the period was one year. The compounding period was also one year.

n = the number of interest compounding periods of time. The length of the periods used to determine n must be the same as the length of the periods for the periodic interest rate. If the length of the compounding period is measured in months, then n equals the number of months. In the case of the $1,000, the number of periods was one and is measured in years.

A = the value of a single cash flow in a uniform series of cash flows that occurs at the end of each period and continues for n number of periods. These cash flows must be uniform or equal in amount (not equivalent), the cash flows must occur at the end of each and every period in the series, and the length of the periods must be the same length as the length of the periods for the periodic interest rate.

SINGLE-PAYMENT COMPOUND-AMOUNT FACTOR

Returning to the case of the $1,000, we saw that at the end of the first year the principal or original amount of money deposited in the bank had earned $50 ($1,000 × 0.05) interest for a total of $1,050. If this amount were to be left in the bank for an additional year it would have earned $52.50 ($1,050 × 0.05) interest during the second year for a total of $1,102.50 at the end of the second year. During the second year, interest was earned on the interest paid during the first year. This is known as compound interest. Compound interest is where interest is paid on the interest from the previous periods. With compound interest, interest is due at the end of each period. If the interest is not paid each period, then interest accrues on the unpaid interest. During the second year $2.50 ($50 × 0.05) of interest accrued on the unpaid interest from the first year. The future value at year n of a single cash flow is calculated by the following equation:

$$F = P(1 + i)^n \qquad (15\text{-}1)$$

This formula is known as the single-payment compound-amount factor. The derivation of Eq. (15-1) is found in Appendix C. The single-payment compound-amount factor converts a present value into a future value at a specified rate of interest and is shown in Figure 15-1.

Eq. (15-1) may also be written using shorthand notation as follows:

$$F = P(F/P, i, n) \qquad (15\text{-}2)$$

where

$$(F/P, i, n) = (1 + i)^n$$

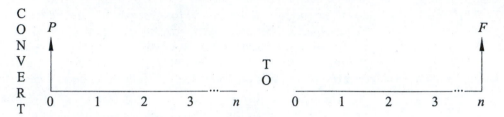

FIGURE 15-1   Single-Payment Compound-Amount Factor

The shorthand notation for the single-payment compound-amount factor and other cash-flow conversion formulas are written in the following standard format:

(Value Desired/Value to be Converted, Interest Rate, Number of Periods)

hence $(F/P,i,n)$ is used to get the future value from the present value using a periodic interest rate of i and n number of periods.

Values for $(F/P,i,n)$ for standard periodic interest rates and periods are found in Appendix D. To find a value one must first find the table in the appendix that corresponds to the interest rate. In the case of a 10% interest rate you would use Table D-16. The tables in Appendix D are read by finding the appropriate formula in the column headings and row that corresponds to the number of periods in the left column. Figure 15-2 shows the value for single-payment compound-amount factor $(F/P,i,n)$ for five periods at an interest rate of 10%, which is 1.6105.

The advantage of using the tables in Appendix D over Eq. (15-1) is that the math is less complex. The disadvantages are that the tables are quite limited in the number of interest rates and periods that are available and the tables may introduce rounding errors into the solutions.

Using Eq. (15-1) we find that by the end of ten years the $1,000 would have grown to $1,628.90. The calculation of this future value is as follows:

$$F_{10} = \$1,000(1 + 0.05)^{10} = \$1,628.89$$

Alternately, we may use Eq. (15-2) to solve for the future value at the end of the ten years as follows:

$$F_{10} = \$1,000(F/P,5,10) = \$1,000(1.6289) = \$1,628.90$$

The minor difference in the future value for year 10 is due to rounding that occurs in the tables located in Appendix D.

These equations are useful when we want to find the future value of a specific amount of money invested today, as in the case of the $1,000. It may also be used to find the future value of money invested at anytime.

Example 15-1:   What is the future value six years from now of a $1,000 cash flow that occurs one year from now using a periodic interest rate of 10% compounded annually?

Table D-16

Interest Factors for 10.00%

	Single Payment		Uniform Series			
	Compound-Amount Factor	Present-Worth Factor	Compound-Amount Factor	Sinking-Fund Factor	Present-Worth Factor	Capital-Recovery Factor
	Convert P to F	Convert F to P	Convert A to F	Convert F to A	Convert A to P	Convert P to A
n	(F/P,i,n)	(P/F,i,n)	(F/A,i,n)	(A/F,i,n)	(P/A,i,n)	(A/P,i,n)
1	1.1000	0.9091	1.0000	1.0000	0.9091	1.1000
2	1.2100	0.8264	2.1000	0.4762	1.7355	0.5762
3	1.3310	0.7513	3.3100	0.3021	2.4869	0.4021
4	1.4641	0.6830	4.6410	0.2155	3.1699	0.3155
5	1.6105	0.6209	6.1051	0.1638	3.7908	0.2638
6	1.7716	0.5645	7.7156	0.1296	4.3553	0.2296
7	1.9487	0.5132	9.4872	0.1054	4.8684	0.2054
8	2.1436	0.4665	11.4359	0.0874	5.3349	0.1874
9	2.3579	0.4241	13.5795	0.0736	5.7590	0.1736
10	2.5937	0.3855	15.9374	0.0627	6.1446	0.1627
11	2.8531	0.3505	18.5312	0.0540	6.4951	0.1540
12	3.1384	0.3186	21.3843	0.0468	6.8137	0.1468
13	3.4523	0.2897	24.5227	0.0408	7.1034	0.1408
14	3.7975	0.2633	27.9750	0.0357	7.3667	0.1357
15	4.1772	0.2394	31.7725	0.0315	7.6061	0.1315
16	4.5950	0.2176	35.9497	0.0278	7.8237	0.1278
17	5.0545	0.1978	40.5447	0.0247	8.0216	0.1247
18	5.5599	0.1799	45.5992	0.0219	8.2014	0.1219
19	6.1159	0.1635	51.1591	0.0195	8.3649	0.1195
20	6.7275	0.1486	57.2750	0.0175	8.5136	0.1175
21	7.4002	0.1351	64.0025	0.0156	8.6487	0.1156
22	8.1403	0.1228	71.4027	0.0140	8.7715	0.1140
23	8.9543	0.1117	79.5430	0.0126	8.8832	0.1126
24	9.8497	0.1015	88.4973	0.0113	8.9847	0.1113
25	10.8347	0.0923	98.3471	0.0102	9.0770	0.1102
26	11.9182	0.0839	109.1818	0.0092	9.1609	0.1092
27	13.1100	0.0763	121.0999	0.0083	9.2372	0.1083
28	14.4210	0.0693	134.2099	0.0075	9.3066	0.1075
29	15.8631	0.0630	148.6309	0.0067	9.3696	0.1067
30	17.4494	0.0573	164.4940	0.0061	9.4269	0.1061
35	28.1024	0.0356	271.0244	0.0037	9.6442	0.1037
40	45.2593	0.0221	442.5926	0.0023	9.7791	0.1023
45	72.8905	0.0137	718.9048	0.0014	9.8628	0.1014

FIGURE 15-2 Table D-16 from Appendix D

CONVERTING A PRESENT VALUE TO A FUTURE VALUE USING A TI BA II PLUS CALCULATOR

A present value is converted to a future value as shown below. Steps 4 through 6 may be entered in any order. For this sidebar we use Example 15-1.

TASK	KEYSTROKES	DISPLAY	
1. Set Variables to Defaults	[2nd] [RESET] [ENTER]	RST	0.00
2. Set Payment per Year to 1	[2nd] [P/Y] 1 [ENTER]	P/Y=	1.00
3. Return	[2nd] [QUIT]		0.00
4. Enter Number of Periods	5 [N]	N=	5.00
5. Enter Interest Rate	10 [I/Y]	I/Y=	10.00
6. Enter Present Value	1000 [PV]	PV=	1,000.00
7. Calculate Future Value	[CPT] [FV]	FV=	−1,610.51

The future value will always carry the opposite sign as the present value.

Solution: To solve this problem, a period with a length of one year is used because interest rate compounds annually. We would also use n equal to 5 periods because the $1,000 was invested for five years (6 years − 1 year). Substituting these values into Eq. (15-1) we get the following:

$$F = \$1,000(1 + 0.10)^5 = \$1,610.51$$

Alternately, Eq. (15-2) may be used to solve this problem as follows:

$$F = \$1,000(F/P,10,5) = \$1,000(1.6105) = \$1,610.50$$

Again, the difference in these two solutions is due to rounding that occurs in the tables of Appendix D.

The future value at the end of six years of the $1,000 invested a year from now is $1,610.51. Similarly, had we invested $1,000 one year from now in a bank account earning 10% compounded annually, by the end of the sixth year, the $1,000 would have been invested for five years and would have grown to $1,610.51, earning $610.51 ($1,610.51 − $1,000.00) of interest.

This equation may also be used when the compounding period is months. To do this the periodic interest rate must be compounded monthly and n would represent the number of months.

Example 15-2:   What is the future value a year from now of a $1,000 cash flow that occurs today using a periodic interest rate of 1% compounded monthly?

Solution: To solve this problem, a period with a length of one month is used because the interest rate compounds monthly. We would also use n equal to 12 periods, the number of months in a year. Substituting these values into Eq. (15-1) we get the following:

$$F = \$1,000(1 + 0.01)^{12} = \$1,126.83$$

Alternately, Eq. (15-2) may be used to solve this problem as follows:

$$F = \$1,000(F/P,1,12) = \$1,000(1.1268) = \$1,126.80$$

Again, the difference in these two solutions is due to rounding that occurs in the tables of Appendix D.

The future value of the $1,000 one year from now is $1,126.83. Similarly, $1,000 invested for one year, at an interest rate of 1% compounded monthly, would grow to $1,126.83 and would earn $126.83 ($1,126.83 − $1,000.00) of interest.

SINGLE-PAYMENT PRESENT-WORTH FACTOR

Conversely, we can find the present value of some future cash flow by solving Eq. (15-1) for P. Solving for P we get the following:

$$P = F/(1 + i)^n \qquad\qquad (15\text{-}3)$$

This equation is known as the single-payment present-worth factor. The single-payment present-worth factor converts a future value into a present value at a specified rate of interest and is shown in Figure 15-3.

Eq. (15-3) may also be written using shorthand notation as follows:

$$P = F(P/F,i,n) \qquad\qquad (15\text{-}4)$$

where

$$(P/F,i,n) = 1/(1 + i)^n$$

Values for $(P/F,i,n)$ for standard periodic interest rates and periods are found in Appendix D.

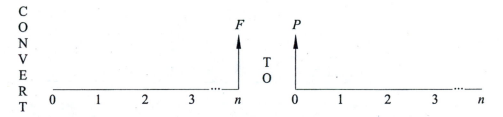

FIGURE 15-3   Single-Payment Present-Worth Factor

These equations are useful when we want to find out how much money needs to be set aside today in an interest-bearing account to make some payment in the future.

Example 15-3:   What is the present value of $1,000 received five years from now using a periodic interest rate of 10% compounded annually?

Solution: For this problem, the periodic interest rate is 10%, the period is one year, and the number of periods is 5. Substituting these values into Eq. (15-3) we get the following:

$$P = \$1,000/(1 + 0.10)^5 = \$620.92$$

Alternately, Eq. (15-4) may be used to solve this problem as follows:

$$P = \$1,000(P/F,10,5) = \$1,000(0.6209) = \$620.90$$

Again, the difference in these two solutions is due to rounding that occurs in the tables of Appendix D.

The present value of $1,000 received five years from now is $620.92. Similarly, had we set aside $620.92 today in a bank account earning an interest rate of 10% compounded annually, in five years it would have grown to $1,000 and earned $379.08 ($1,000 − $620.92) of interest.

Once a series of cash flows have been converted into their equivalent cash flows at a specific point in time, whether now or at some future time, they may be added to each other as shown in Example 15-4.

SIDEBAR 15-2

CONVERTING A FUTURE VALUE TO A PRESENT VALUE USING A TI BA II PLUS CALCULATOR

A future value is converted to a present value as shown below. Steps 4 through 6 may be entered in any order. For this sidebar we will use Example 15-3.

TASK	KEYSTROKES	DISPLAY	
1. Set Variables to Defaults	[2nd] [RESET] [ENTER]	RST	0.00
2. Set Payment per Year to 1	[2nd] [P/Y] 1 [ENTER]	P/Y=	1.00
3. Return	[2nd] [QUIT]		0.00
4. Enter Number of Periods	5 [N]	N=	5.00
5. Enter Interest Rate	10 [I/Y]	I/Y=	10.00
6. Enter Future Value	1000 [FV]	FV=	1,000.00
7. Calculate Present Value	[CPT] [PV]	PV=	−620.92

The future value will always carry the opposite sign as the present value.

Example 15-4: What is the present value of $1,000 cash flow one year from now and $1,000 cash flow two years from now using a 10% compounded annually interest rate?

Solution: To solve this example Eq. (15-3) will be used to convert both future cash flows into their present values. These values are as follows:

$$P_1 = \$1,000/(1 + 0.10)^1 = \$909.09$$
$$P_2 = \$1,000/(1 + 0.10)^2 = \$826.45$$

After finding the present values for these two future cash flows, they may be added together:

$$P = \$909.09 + \$826.45 = \$1,735.54$$

The present value of the two future cash flows is $1,735.54. Similarly, had we deposited $1,735.54 in a bank account earning 10% interest compounded annually, we could have withdrawn a $1,000 at the end of the first year and at the end of the second year there would have been $1,000 remaining in the bank account. During the first year the $1,735.54 in the bank account would have earned $173.55 ($1,735.54 × 0.10) in interest. After the interest is paid and the $1,000 is withdrawn, there would have remained $909.09 ($1,735.54 + $173.55 − $1,000.00) in the account. During the second year the $909.09 would have earned $90.91 ($909.09 × 0.10) in interest, leaving $1,000 ($909.09 + $90.91) in the account to be withdrawn at the end of the second year.

UNIFORM-SERIES COMPOUND-AMOUNT FACTOR

When faced with a long series of uniform cash flows, such as found in a thirty-year mortgage, it would be quite time consuming to calculate the present or future value for each individual cash flow and then add them together. To simplify these calculations, four formulas have been developed to deal with uniform cash flows. The first formula, the uniform-series compounding-amount factor, converts a series of uniform cash flows into a future value. For a series of cash flows to be uniform:

1. The cash flows must be uniform or equal in amount (not equivalent),
2. The cash flows must occur at the end of each and every period in the series,
3. The length of the periods in the series must be the same duration as the compounding period for the periodic interest rate, and
4. The length of the periods in the series must be the same length.

In a uniform series, the first cash flow occurs at the end of the first period, the second at the end of the second period, . . . , and the nth cash flow at the end of the nth period. The future value is calculated at the end of the nth period and

FIGURE 15-4   Uniform
Series of Cash Flows

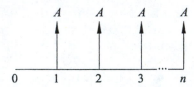

occurs at the same time as the last cash flow in the series. A uniform series of cash flows is shown in Figure 15-4.

Suppose we were to deposit $1,000 a year for the next three years in a bank account with an interest rate of 8% compounded annually. The deposits are to be made at the end of each year. How much money would be in the account at the end of the third year?

The first deposit will be made at the end of the first year and will accrue interest during the second and third years or for two periods. Using Eq. (15-1), the future value of the first cash flow is as follows:

$$F_1 = \$1,000(1 + 0.08)^2 = \$1,166.40$$

The second deposit will be made at the end of the second year and accrue interest during the third year or for one period. Using Eq. (15-1) the future value of the second cash flow is as follows:

$$F_2 = \$1,000(1 + 0.08)^1 = \$1,080.00$$

The third and final deposit will be made at the end of the third year, the same point in time for which we are calculating the future value; therefore, the third deposit will not earn any interest and its future value will be equivalent to the amount of the deposit. The future value for the third year is as follows:

$$F_3 = \$1,000(1 + 0.08)^0 = \$1,000.00$$

Summing the future values we get the following:

$$F = \$1,166.40 + \$1,080.00 + \$1,000.00 = \$3,246.40$$

Alternately, this future value may be calculated by the following equation:

$$F = A[(1 + i)^n - 1]/i \tag{15-5}$$

This equation is known as the uniform-series compound-amount factor. The derivation for Eq. (15-5) is found in Appendix C. The uniform-series compounding-amount factor converts a uniform series of cash flows into a future value at a specified rate of interest and is shown in Figure 15-5.

It is important to note that the future value is calculated at the same point in time as the final cash flow for the uniform series, period n.

Eq. (15-5) may also be written using shorthand notation as follows:

$$F = A(F/A,i,n) \tag{15-6}$$

where

$$(F/A,i,n) = [(1 + i)^n - 1]/i$$

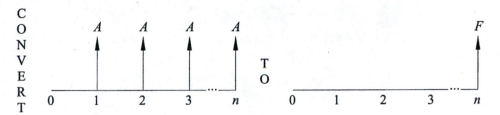

FIGURE 15-5   Uniform-Series Compound-Amount Factor

Values for $(F/P,i,n)$ for standard periodic interest rates and periods are found in Appendix D.

Using Eq. (15-5) to determine the future value of the three $1,000 payment cash flows, we get:

$$F = \$1,000[(1 + 0.08)^3 - 1]/0.08 = \$3,246.40$$

Eq. (15-5) produces the same result as solving for the future value for each of the cash flows and then adding them together; however, Eq. (15-5) is much quicker.

Example 15-5:   What is the future value ten years from now of ten $500 cash flows using a periodic interest rate of 9% compounded annually? The cash flows occur at the end of each year and begin a year from now.

Solution: For this problem, the annual cash flows equal $500, the periodic interest rate equals 9%, and the number of periods is 10. The future value is calculated as follows using Eq. (15-5):

$$F = \$500[(1 + 0.09)^{10} - 1]/0.09 = \$7,596.46$$

Alternately, Eq. (15-6) may be used to solve this problem as follows:

$$F = \$500(F/A,9,10) = \$500(15.1929) = \$7,596.45$$

Again, the difference in these two solutions is due to rounding that occurs in the tables of Appendix D.

The future value of this series of $500 cash flows is $7,596.46. Similarly, $500 invested at the end of the year for the next ten years in a bank account earning 9% compounded annually would have grown to $7,596.46 at the end of the tenth year, which is the time of the tenth deposit.

UNIFORM-SERIES SINKING-FUND FACTOR

Solving Eq. (15-5) for A we get the following:

$$A = Fi/[(1 + i)^n - 1] \tag{15-7}$$

This equation is known as the uniform-series sinking-fund factor. Equation (15-7) is based on the cash flows being uniform and occurring at the end of each

CONVERTING A UNIFORM SERIES TO A FUTURE VALUE USING A TI BA II PLUS CALCULATOR

A uniform series value is converted to a future value as shown below. Steps 4 through 6 may be entered in any order. For this sidebar we use Example 15-5.

TASK	KEYSTROKES	DISPLAY	
1. Set Variables to Defaults	[2nd] [RESET] [ENTER]	RST	0.00
2. Set Payment per Year to 1	[2nd] [P/Y] 1 [ENTER]	P/Y=	1.00
3. Return	[2nd] [QUIT]		0.00
4. Enter Number of Periods	10 [N]	N=	10.00
5. Enter Interest Rate	9 [I/Y]	I/Y=	9.00
6. Enter Uniform Series	500 [PMT]	PMT=	500.00
7. Calculate Future Value	[CPT] [FV]	FV=	−7,596.46

The future value will always carry the opposite sign as the uniform series.

period in the series. The uniform-series sinking-fund factor converts a future value to a series of annual values at a specified rate of interest and is shown in Figure 15-6.

It is important to note that the last cash flow for the uniform series occurs at the same point in time as the future value, period n.

Eq. (15-7) may also be written using shorthand notation as follows:

$$A = F(A/F,i,n) \tag{15-8}$$

where

$$(A/F,i,n) = i/[(1 + i)^n - 1]$$

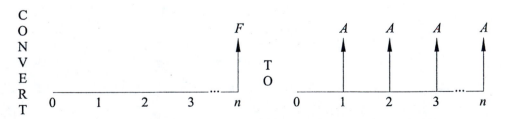

FIGURE 15-6   Uniform-Series Sinking-Fund Factor

Values for $(A/F,i,n)$ for standard periodic interest rates and periods are found in Appendix D.

Example 15-6: What uniform series of cash flows is equivalent to a $100,000 cash flow twenty years from now if the uniform cash flows occur at the end of the year for the next twenty years and the periodic interest rate is 10% compounded annually?

Solution: For this problem the number of periods is 20, the periodic interest rate is 10%, and the future value is $100,000. By substituting these amounts into Eq. (15-7) we get the following:

$$A = \$100,000(0.10)/[(1 + 0.10)^{20} - 1] = \$1,745.96$$

Alternately, Eq. (15-8) may be used to solve this problem as follows:

$$A = \$100,000(A/F,10,20) = \$100,000(0.0175) = \$1,750.00$$

Again, the difference in these two solutions is due to rounding that occurs in the tables of Appendix D.

A uniform series of $1,750 cash flows is equivalent to $100,000 twenty years from now at a 10% interest rate compounded annually. Similarly, had we invested $1,745.96 a year from now at a periodic interest rate of 10% compounded annually and an additional $1,745.96 were

---

S I D E B A R   1 5 - 4

CONVERTING A FUTURE VALUE TO A UNIFORM SERIES USING A TI BA II PLUS CALCULATOR

A future value is converted to a uniform series as shown below. Steps 4 through 6 may be entered in any order. For this sidebar we use Example 15-6.

TASK	KEYSTROKES	DISPLAY	
1. Set Variables to Defaults	[2nd] [RESET] [ENTER]	RST	0.00
2. Set Payment per Year to 1	[2nd] [P/Y] 1 [ENTER]	P/Y=	1.00
3. Return	[2nd] [QUIT]		0.00
4. Enter Number of Periods	20 [N]	N=	5.00
5. Enter Interest Rate	10 [I/Y]	I/Y=	10.00
6. Enter Future Value	100000 [FV]	FV=	100,000.00
7. Calculate Uniform Series	[CPT] [PMT]	PMT=	−1,745.96

The future value will always carry the opposite sign as the uniform series.

invested each year thereafter for a total of twenty years at the same interest rate, at the end of the twentieth year there would be $100,000 in the account. Of this, $34,919.20 ($1,745.96 × 20) would have been deposited over the years and $65,080.80 ($100,000.00 − $34,919.20) would have been earned as interest.

UNIFORM-SERIES PRESENT-WORTH FACTOR

To find the present value of a uniform series of annual cash flows we could use Eq. (15-5) to find the future value and then use Eq. (15-3) to convert the future value to a present value. By substituting Eq. (15-5) into Eq. (15-3) we get the following:

$$P = F/(1 + i)^n \quad \text{where } F = A[(1 + i)^n - 1]/i$$
$$P = A[(1 + i)^n - 1]/[i(1 + i)^n] \tag{15-9}$$

This equation is known as the uniform-series present-worth factor. The uniform-series present-worth factor converts a series of annual cash flows into a present value at a specified rate of interest and is shown in Figure 15-7.

It is important to note that the present value occurs one period prior to the first cash flow in the uniform series. Because the beginning of a period is the same point in time as the end of the previous period, the present value occurs at the beginning of the period containing the first cash flow in the uniform series.

Eq. (15-9) may also be written using shorthand notation as follows:

$$P = A(P/A,i,n) \tag{15-10}$$

where

$$(P/A,i,n) = [(1 + i)^n - 1]/[i(1 + i)^n]$$

Values for $(P/A,i,n)$ for standard periodic interest rates and periods are found in Appendix D.

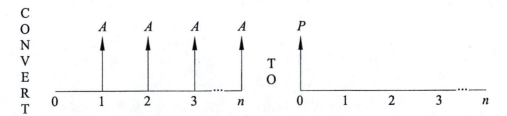

FIGURE 15-7   Uniform-Series Present-Worth Factor

SIDEBAR 15-5

CONVERTING A UNIFORM SERIES TO A PRESENT VALUE USING A TI BA II PLUS CALCULATOR

A uniform series is converted to a present value as shown below. Steps 4 through 6 may be entered in any order. For this sidebar we use Example 15-7.

TASK	KEYSTROKES	DISPLAY	
1. Set Variables to Defaults	[2nd] [RESET] [ENTER]	RST	0.00
2. Set Payment per Year to 1	[2nd] [P/Y] 1 [ENTER]	P/Y=	1.00
3. Return	[2nd] [QUIT]		0.00
4. Enter Number of Periods	5 [N]	N=	5.00
5. Enter Interest Rate	6 [I/Y]	I/Y=	6.00
6. Enter Uniform Series	500 [PMT]	PMT=	500.00
7. Calculate Present Value	[CPT] [PV]	PV=	−2,106.18

The present value will always carry the opposite sign as the uniform series.

Example 15-7: What is the present value of five $500 cash flows that occur at the end of each year for the next five years at a periodic interest rate of 6% compounded annually? The first cash flow occurs a year from now, the second cash flow occurs two years from now, ..., and the fifth cash flow occurs five years from now.

Solution: For this problem, the annual cash flow is $500, the number of periods is 5, and the periodic interest rate is 6%. Substituting these values into Eq. (15-9) we get the following:

$$P = \$500[(1 + 0.06)^5 - 1]/[0.06(1 + 0.06)^5] = \$2,106.18$$

Alternately, Eq. (15-10) may be used to solve this problem as follows:

$$P = \$500(P/A,6,5) = \$500(4.2124) = \$2,106.20$$

Again, the difference in these two solutions is due to rounding that occurs in the tables of Appendix D.

The present value of these cash flows is $2,106.20. Similarly, had we invested $2,106.20 in a bank account earning 6% interest compounded annually, we could have withdrawn $500 a year for the next five years with the withdrawals occurring at the end of the first, second, third, fourth, and fifth years. During the five-year existence of the bank account the original $2,106.18 would have earned $393.82 (5 × $500.00 − $2,106.18) of interest, allowing annual withdrawals of $500 each. The interest is earned on the money remaining in the account each year. The interest decreases each

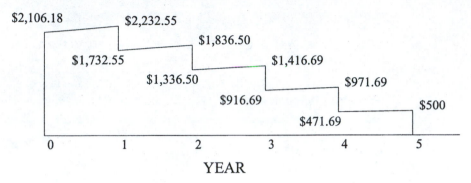

FIGURE 15-8   Value of Bank Account

year because the amount in the bank account decreases each year as withdrawals are made. The value of the bank account over time is shown in Figure 15-8.

UNIFORM-SERIES CAPITAL-RECOVERY FACTOR

Solving Eq. (15-9) for A we get the following:

$$A = P[i(1 + i)^n]/[(1 + i)^n - 1] \qquad (15-11)$$

This equation is known as the uniform-series capital-recovery factor. The uniform-series capital-recovery factor converts a present value into a uniform series of annual values at a specified rate of interest and is shown in Figure 15-9.

It is important to note that the first cash flow for the uniform series occurs one year after the present value.

Eq. (15-11) may also be written using shorthand notation as follows:

$$A = P(A/P,i,n) \qquad (15-12)$$

where

$$(A/P,i,n) = [i(1 + i)^n]/[(1 + i)^n - 1]$$

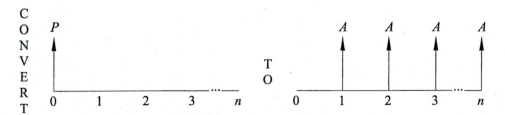

FIGURE 15-9   Uniform-Series Capital-Recovery Factor

Values for $(A/P,i,n)$ for standard periodic interest rates and periods are found in Appendix D.

> **Example 15-8:** What uniform series of cash flows is equivalent to a $10,000 cash flow occurring today if the uniform series of cash flows occur at the end of each month for the next five years and the periodic interest rate is 1% compounded monthly?
>
> **Solution:** For this problem, the present value is $10,000, the number of periods is sixty months, and the periodic interest rate is 1%. Substituting these values into Eq. (15-11) we get the following:
>
> $$A = \$10,000[0.01(1 + 0.01)^{60}]/[(1 + 0.01)^{60} - 1] = \$222.44$$
>
> Alternately, Eq. (15-12) may be used to solve this problem as follows:
>
> $$A = \$10,000(A/P,1,60) = \$10,000(0.0222) = \$222.00$$

Again, the difference in these two solutions is due to rounding that occurs in the tables of Appendix D.

The uniform series of cash flows is $222.00 per year. Similarly, had we borrowed $10,000 today at an interest rate of 1% compounded monthly and paid it off in sixty monthly cash flows occurring at the end of each month, we would have paid $13,320, of which $3,320 ($13,320 − $10,000) was interest.

SIDEBAR 15-6

CONVERTING A PRESENT VALUE TO A UNIFORM SERIES USING A TI BA II PLUS CALCULATOR

A present value is converted to a uniform series as shown below. Steps 4 through 6 may be entered in any order. For this sidebar we use Example 15-8.

TASK	KEYSTROKES	DISPLAY	
1. Set Variables to Defaults	[2nd] [RESET] [ENTER]	RST	0.00
2. Set Payment per Year to 1	[2nd] [P/Y] 1 [ENTER]	P/Y=	1.00
3. Return	[2nd] [QUIT]		0.00
4. Enter Number of Periods	60 [N]	N=	60.00
5. Enter Interest Rate	1 [I/Y]	I/Y=	1.00
6. Enter Present Value	10000 [PV]	PV=	10,000.00
7. Calculate Uniform Series	[CPT] [PMT]	PMT=	−222.44

The present value will always carry the opposite sign as the uniform series.

FIGURE 15-10 Cash Flow
Diagrams

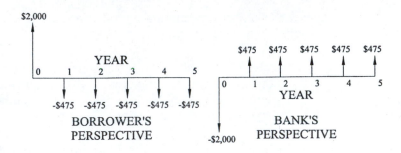

CASH FLOW DIAGRAMS

To visualize the cash flows it is often helpful to draw a cash flow diagram. In a cash flow diagram the periods are represented along the horizontal axis and the cash flows are drawn as vertical arrows next to the period in which they occur. Arrows drawn in the up direction represent cash receipts and arrows drawn in the down direction represent cash disbursements. Figure 15-10 shows the cash flow diagram for a $2,000 loan with an interest rate 6% compounded annually with the principal being paid back over five years, with a single payment at the end of each year. The cash flows are drawn from both the borrower's perspective and the bank's perspective.

These two cash flows are identical except for the direction that the cash is flowing. When the borrower borrows money from the bank, the borrower sees a receipt of cash, whereas the bank sees a disbursement of cash. When the borrower makes the annual payments, the bank sees a cash receipt and the borrower sees a cash disbursement. When reading a cash flow diagram it is important to know from which perspective the diagram is being drawn. Unless noted, all cash flow diagrams in this book are drawn from the construction company's perspective.

COMPLEX CASH FLOWS

Equivalent values for all cash flows can be calculated by using the equations in this chapter. Complex cash flows may require that multiple equations be used and their results added together.

Example 15-9: Determine the future value of a $2000 cash flow that occurs today and an additional $1,000 cash flow that occurs at the end of each of the next ten years using a periodic interest rate of 7% compounded annually.

Solution: The cash flow for this example is shown in Figure 15-11.

The future value of today's cash flow is calculated by using Eq. (15-1) as follows:

$$F_0 = \$2,000(1 + 0.07)^{10} = \$3,934.30$$

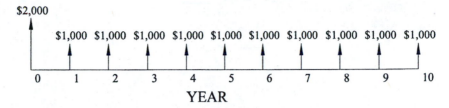

$2,000

$1,000 $1,000 $1,000 $1,000 $1,000 $1,000 $1,000 $1,000 $1,000 $1,000

0   1   2   3   4   5   6   7   8   9   10

YEAR

FIGURE 15-11   Cash Flow for Example 15-9

The future value of the cash flows for years 1 through 10 is calculated by using Eq. (15-5) as follows:

$$F_{1-10} = \$1,000[(1 + 0.07)^{10} - 1]/0.07 = \$13,816.45$$

Summing these two future values we get the following:

$$F = \$3,934.30 + \$13,816.45 = \$17,750.75$$

The future value is $17,750.75. Similarly, if we deposited the cash flows in Figure 15-11 in a bank account earning 7% interest compounded annually, at the end of the tenth year there would be $17,750.75 in the bank account, which includes the original $12,000.00 of principal plus $5,750.75 in interest.

Example 15-10:   Determine the future value at the end of August for the following cash flows using a periodic interest rate of 1.5% compounded monthly:

MONTH	CASH FLOW ($)
March	10,000
April	15,000
May	25,000
June	21,000
July	17,000

These cash flows occur at the end of the respective months.

Solution: The cash flows for Example 15-10 are shown in Figure 15-12.

FIGURE 15-12   Cash Flow for Example 15-10

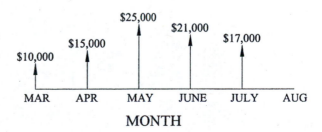

$25,000

$21,000

$15,000 $17,000

$10,000

MAR   APR   MAY   JUNE   JULY   AUG

MONTH

TABLE 15-1 Number of Compounding Periods

CASH FLOW	PERIODS
March	5
April	4
May	3
June	2
July	1

The number of compounding periods for each cash flow is shown in Table 15-1.

Using Eq. (15-1) we can calculate the future values of the money borrowed during each of the months. These calculations are as follows:

$$\text{March} = \$10,000(1 + 0.015)^5 = \$10,772.84$$
$$\text{April} = \$15,000(1 + 0.015)^4 = \$15,920.45$$
$$\text{May} = \$25,000(1 + 0.015)^3 = \$26,141.96$$
$$\text{June} = \$21,000(1 + 0.015)^2 = \$21,634.72$$
$$\text{July} = \$17,000(1 + 0.015)^1 = \$17,255.00$$

Adding the values together we get the following:

$$F = \$10,772.84 + \$15,920.45 + \$26,141.96 + \$21,634.72$$
$$+ \$17,255.00$$
$$F = \$91,724.97$$

The future value of the cash flows is $91,724.97. Similarly, if a contractor had borrowed these amounts at the end of the months indicated at a periodic interest rate of 1.5% compounded monthly, the contractor would have to pay back the $88,000 borrowed plus $3,724.97 interest for a total of $91,724.97.

Individual items in a cash flow may be treated as two separate cash flows to simplify the calculations. Figure 15-13 shows a nonuniform series of cash flows for which the present value needs to be calculated.

FIGURE 15-13 Cash Flow

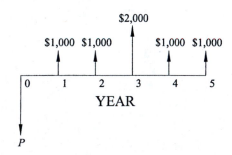

Figure 15-14 Equivalent
Cash Flow for Figure 15-13

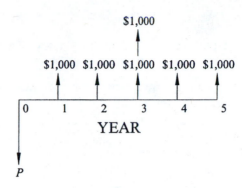

To simplify the calculations, the cash flow occurring in the third year may be treated as two $1,000 cash flows as shown in Figure 15-14.

The present value of the five $1,000 cash flows is determined by using Eq. (15-9) and the present value of the additional $1,000 cash flow that occurs in year 3 may be calculated by using Eq. (15-3). The present value of the entire cash flow is determined by adding these two present values together.

Example 15-11: Determine the present value of the cash flow shown in Figure 15-13 using a periodic interest rate of 12% compounded annually.

Solution: The present value of the five $1,000 cash flows is determined by using Eq. (15-9) as follows:

$$P_{1-5} = \$1,000[(1 + 0.12)^5 - 1]/[0.12(1 + 0.12)^5] = \$3,604.78$$

The present value for the additional $1,000 cash flow that occurs in year 3 is calculated by using Eq. (15-3) as follows:

$$P_3 = \$1,000/(1 + 0.12)^3 = \$711.78$$

The present value for the entire cash flow is determined by adding the two above present values together as follows:

$$P = \$3,604.78 + \$711.78 = \$4,316.56$$

The present value of the cash flow shown in Figure 15-13 at an interest rate of 12% compounded annually is $4,316.56.

The calculation of the present value, the future value, or the annual values for a complex cash flow is independent of the steps taken to calculate the equivalent cash flow. Figure 15-15 shows a cash flow for which the present value needs to be calculated.

At least two of the formulas in this chapter must be used to calculate the present value. The present value could be calculated by taking the present value of each of the individual cash flows using Eq. (15-3).

SIDEBAR 15-7

CONVERTING A NONUNIFORM SERIES TO A PRESENT VALUE USING A TI BA II PLUS CALCULATOR

A nonuniform series is converted to a present value as shown below. For this sidebar we use Example 15-11.

TASK	KEYSTROKES	DISPLAY	
1. Set Variables to Defaults	[2nd] [RESET] [ENTER]	RST	0.00
2. Select Cash Flow Worksheet	[CF]	CFo=	0.00
3. Enter First Two Cash Flows	[↓] 1000 [ENTER]	CF1=	1,000.00
	[↓] 2 [ENTER]	F01=	2.00
4. Enter Next Cash Flow	[↓] 2000 [ENTER]	CF2=	2,000.00
	[↓] 1 [ENTER]	F02=	1.00
5. Enter Last Two Cash Flows	[↓] 1000 [ENTER]	CF3=	1,000.00
	[↓] 2 [ENTER]	F03=	2.00
6. Enter Interest Rate	[NPV]	I=	0.00
	12 [ENTER]	I=	12.00
7. Calculate Present Value	[↓] [CPT]	NPV=	4,316.56

In this example the keystrokes for entering all variables are shown to provide a generic example that can be used for any problem by changing the numbers entered into the calculator. If the display is already shown as indicated you may type [↓] to continue to the next step.

Alternately, the cash flows could be treated as a uniform series for which the future value in year 5 could be calculated by using Eq. (15-5). This would create the equivalent cash flow shown in Figure 15-16.

The present value could then be calculated by taking the present value of the equivalent cash flow shown in Figure 15-16 using Eq. (15-3).

Alternately, the cash flows could be treated as a uniform series for which the present value in year 1 could be calculated by using Eq. (15-9). This would create the equivalent cash flow shown in Figure 15-17.

The present value could then be calculated by taking the present value of the equivalent cash flow shown in Figure 15-17 using Eq. (15-3).

FIGURE 15-15 Cash Flow

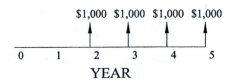

YEAR

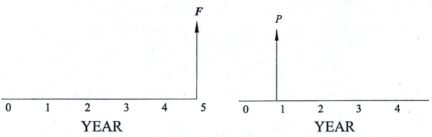

FIGURE 15-16 Equivalent Cash Flow for Figure 15-15

FIGURE 15-17 Equivalent Cash Flow for Figure 15-14

Example 15-12: Determine the present value of the cash flow shown in Figure 15-15 using an interest rate of 8% compounded annually.

Solution: The present value of each of the cash flows are calculated by using Eq. (15-3) as follows:

$$P_2 = \$1,000/(1 + 0.08)^2 = \$857.34$$
$$P_3 = \$1,000/(1 + 0.08)^3 = \$793.83$$
$$P_4 = \$1,000/(1 + 0.08)^4 = \$735.03$$
$$P_5 = \$1,000/(1 + 0.08)^5 = \$680.58$$

Summing these cash flows we get the following:

$$P = \$857.34 + \$793.83 + \$735.03 + \$680.58 = \$3,066.78$$

Alternately, the future value in year 5 of the four $1,000 cash flows may be determined by using Eq. (15-5), using four periods as follows:

$$F_5 = \$1,000[(1 + 0.08)^4 - 1]/0.08 = \$4,506.11$$

Next, the present value is calculated by taking the present value of the future value in year 5 using Eq. (15-3) as follows:

$$P = \$4,506.11/(1 + 0.08)^5 = \$3,066.78$$

Alternately, the value of the four $1,000 cash flows may be determined by using Eq. (15-9). Year 1 is regarded as the present time for the purposes of this calculation. The calculations are as follows:

$$P_1 = \$1,000[(1 + 0.08)^4 - 1]/[0.08(1 + 0.08)^4] = \$3,312.13$$

The value of the four $1,000 cash flows in year 1 is still one year into the future and is treated as a future value when converting the present value in year 1 to the present value in year 0. The present value is calculated by taking the present value in year 1 and substituting it into Eq. (15-3) as the future value as follows:

$$P = \$3,312.13/(1 + 0.08)^1 = \$3,066.79$$

We see that in all three cases the present value is the same, other than rounding errors. This is because when the calculations are completed we have performed the same mathematical calculations on the cash flows.

If we were to write a mathematical equation for converting the cash flow to a future value in year 5 and then convert it to its present value in year 0 for a generic annual value and periodic interest rate we would get the following:

$$P = F_5/(1 + i)^5 \quad \text{where } F_5 = A[(1 + i)^4 - 1]/i$$

Combining these two equations we get the following:

$$P = \{A[(1 + i)^4 - 1]/i\}/(1 + i)^5 = A[(1 + i)^4 - 1]/[i(1 + i)^5]$$

If we were to write a mathematical equation for converting the cash flow to a present value in year 1 and then convert it to its present value in year 0 for a generic annual value and periodic interest rate we would get the following:

$$P = P_1/(1 + i)^1 \quad \text{where } P_1 = A[(1 + i)^4 - 1]/[i(1 + i)^4]$$

Combining these two equations we get the following:

$$P = \{A[(1 + i)^4 - 1]/[i(1 + i)^4]\}/(1 + i)^1$$
$$P = A[(1 + i)^4 - 1]/[i(1 + i)^5]$$

We see that in both cases the resulting mathematical equation is the same.

FIND UNKNOWN PERIODIC INTEREST RATES

In some cases we may have cash receipts that are equivalent to cash disbursements at some unknown interest rate. The interest rate may be found by using Equations (15-1) through (15-12) to write an algebraic equation for the equivalence of the cash flows. The algebraic equation may then be solved for i. This is relatively simple when dealing with a single cash disbursement and single cash receipt.

Example 15-13:   At what periodic interest rate is a $1,000 cash disbursement occurring two years ago equivalent to cash receipt of $1,177.22 occurring today? The periodic interest rate is compounded annually.

Solution: The cash flow for this example is shown in Figure 15-18.

Because the interest compounds annually and the cash disbursement occurs two years before the cash receipt, the number of periods is two. For the purposes of this example, the time of the cash disbursement may be regarded as the present time and today may be regarded as the future time.

FIGURE 15-18   Cash Flow for Example 15-13

$1,177.22

-2   -1   0   1

YEAR

-$1,000.00

Substituting the cash disbursement as the present value and the cash receipt as the future value into Eq. (15-1) we get the following:

$$\$1,177.22 = \$1,000.00(1 + i)^2$$

Solving for i we get the following:

$$(1 + i)^2 = \$1,177.22/\$1,000.00$$
$$1 + i = (\$1,177.22/\$1,000.00)^{0.5}$$
$$i = (\$1,177.22/\$1,000.00)^{0.5} - 1 = 0.085$$

The periodic interest rate at which the cash receipts are equivalent to the cash disbursements is 8.5% compounded annually.

If the algebraic equation for the equivalence of the cash flows can be reduced to Eq. (15-6), Eq. (15-8), Eq. (15-10), or Eq. (15-12) the interest rate may

SIDEBAR 15-8

FINDING AN UNKNOWN INTEREST RATE FOR A PRESENT VALUE AND FUTURE VALUE USING A TI BA II PLUS CALCULATOR

An unknown interest rate for a present value and a future value is determined as shown below. The present value and the future value must have different signs (one positive and one negative). Steps 4 through 6 may be entered in any order. For this sidebar we use Example 15-13.

TASK	KEYSTROKES	DISPLAY	
1. Set Variables to Defaults	[2nd] [RESET] [ENTER]	RST	0.00
2. Set Payment per Year to 1	[2nd] [P/Y] 1 [ENTER]	P/Y=	1.00
3. Return	[2nd] [QUIT]		0.00
4. Enter Number of Periods	2 [N]	N=	5.00
5. Enter Present Value	1000 [+/−] [PV]	PV=	−1,000.00
6. Enter Future Value	1177.22 [FV]	FV=	1,177.22
7. Calculate Interest Rate	[CPT] [I/Y]	I/Y=	8.50

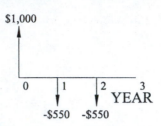

FIGURE 15-19   Cash Flow
for Example 15-14

be approximated by solving for $(F/A,i,n)$, $(A/F,i,n)$, $(P/A,i,n)$, or $(A/P,i,n)$ and estimating the value of i from the tables in Appendix D.

Example 15-14:   At what periodic interest rate is a $1,000 cash receipt occurring at the beginning of year 1 equivalent to two $550 cash disbursements, one occurring at the end of year 1 and the second occurring at the end of year 2? The periodic interest rate is compounded annually.

Solution: The cash flow for the problem is shown in Figure 15-19. Note that the beginning of year 1 is the same as the end of year 0.

This cash flow corresponds to Eq. (15-12) and is written as follows:

$$\$550.00 = \$1,000.00(A/P,i,2)$$

Solving for $(A/P,i,n)$ we get the following:

$$(A/P,i,2) = \$550.00/\$1,000.00$$
$$(A/P,i,2) = 0.5500$$

Using the tables located in Appendix D we see that the value 0.5500 falls between $(A/P,6,2)$, which has a value of 0.5454, and $(A/P,7,2)$, which is 0.5531. The interest rate may be approximated by linearly interoperating between these two values as follows:

$$i = (7 - 6)(0.5500 - 0.5454)/(0.5531 - 0.5454) + 6 = 6.597\%$$

The periodic interest rate at which the cash receipts are equivalent to the cash disbursements is 6.6% compounded annually.

Cash flows that cannot be solved algebraically must be solved by trial and error. To do this, an algebraic equation may be set up with a known value on the left side of the equation and the unknown interest rate on the right side of the equation. The interest rate is changed until the right side of the equation equals the known value on the left side of the equation.

Modern spreadsheet applications make solving trial-and-error problems easy. To use a spreadsheet to solve for the interest rate, the interest rate must be set up in one cell of the spreadsheet and the right side of the algebraic function—the side with the unknown interest rate—is set up in a second cell. The algebraic function, which is set up in the second cell, must reference the cell where the interest rate is located. The Goal Seek function in Microsoft Excel and the Solve For function in

FINDING AN UNKNOWN INTEREST RATE FOR A PRESENT VALUE AND UNIFORM SERIES USING A TI BA II PLUS CALCULATOR

An unknown interest rate for a present value and a uniform series is determined as shown below. The present value and uniform series must have different signs (one positive and one negative). Steps 4 through 6 may be entered in any order. For this sidebar we use Example 15-14.

TASK	KEYSTROKES	DISPLAY	
1. Set Variables to Defaults	[2nd] [RESET] [ENTER]	RST	0.00
2. Set Payment per Year to 1	[2nd] [P/Y] 1 [ENTER]	P/Y=	1.00
3. Return	[2nd] [QUIT]		0.00
4. Enter Number of Periods	2 [N]	N=	5.00
5. Enter Present Value	1000 [PV]	PV=	1,000.00
6. Enter Uniform Series	550.00 [+/−] [PMT]	PMT=	−550.00
7. Calculate Interest Rate	[CPT] [I/Y]	I/Y=	6.60

Corel Quattro Pro may be used to find the periodic interest rate that produces a result from the algebraic function which is equal to the left side of the equation.

Example 15-15: At what periodic interest rate is a $1,000 cash receipt occurring at the beginning of year 1 equivalent to a $500 cash disbursement occurring at the end of year 1 and a $600 cash disbursement occurring at the end of year 2? The periodic interest rate is compounded annually.

Solution: The cash flow for the problem is shown in Figure 15-20. Note that the beginning of year 1 is the same as the end of year 0.

Using Eq. (15-3) the present values for the two cash disbursements may be expressed algebraically as follows:

$$P_1 = \$500.00/(1 + i)^1$$
$$P_2 = \$600.00/(1 + i)^2$$

FIGURE 15-20   Cash Flow for Example 15-15

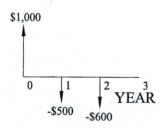

FIGURE 15-21 Spreadsheet
Set Up for Solving by Trial
and Error

	A	B
1	i	6.394%
2	P	$1,000:00

Summing these two present values we get the following:

$$\$1,000 = \$500.00/(1 + i)^1 + \$600.00/(1 + i)^2$$

To solve by trial and error, any value for *i* may be placed in cell B1 of the
spreadsheet. The right side of the previous equation is coded into cell B2 as
follows:

$$= 500/(1 + B1) + 600/(1 + B1)^\wedge 2$$

The Goal Seek function in Microsoft Excel and the Solve For function in
Corel Quattro Pro may be used to find the value of *i* by setting cell B2 to 1000
by changing cell B1. The result from setting up this spreadsheet is shown in
Figure 15-21. In cells A1 and A2 a title has been placed to indicate what the
accompanying cell represents.

The periodic interest rate at which the cash receipts are equivalent to
the cash disbursements is 6.394% compounded annually.

SIDEBAR 15-10

FINDING AN UNKNOWN INTEREST RATE FOR A PRESENT VALUE AND NONUNIFORM SERIES USING A TI BA II PLUS CALCULATOR

An unknown interest rate for a present value and a nonuniform series is determined
as shown below. The present value and the cash flows for the nonuniform series must
have different signs. Warning! Nonuniform cash flow with both positive and negative signs can create multiple solutions! For this sidebar we use Example 15-15.

TASK	KEYSTROKES	DISPLAY	
1. Set Variables to Defaults	[2nd] [RESET] [ENTER]	RST	0.00
2. Select Cash Flow Worksheet	[CF]	CFo=	0.00
3. Enter Initial Cash Flow	1000 [ENTER]	CFo=	1,000.00
4. Enter First Cash Flow	[↓] 500 [+/−] [ENTER]	CF1=	−500.00
	[↓] 1 [ENTER]	F01=	1.00
5. Enter Next Cash Flow	[↓] 600 [+/−] [ENTER]	CF2=	−600.00
	[↓] 1 [ENTER]	F02=	1.00
6. Calculate Interest Rate	[IRR] [CPT]	IRR=	6.39

In this example the keystrokes for entering all variables are shown to provide a
generic example that can be used for any problem by change in the numbers entered into the calculator. If the display is already shown as indicated you may
type [↓] to continue to the next step.

When the cash disbursements are equivalent to the cash receipts, they are equivalent regardless of the period of time chosen for the analysis. If receipts and disbursements are equivalent in the present time at a specified interest rate, they will also be equivalent at any point in the future or past at the same interest rate. Therefore, equivalence is independent of the time period chosen to evaluate equivalence. In Example 15-15 the $1,000 cash receipt was equivalent to the cash disbursements—the $500 cash disbursement at the end of year 1 and the $600 cash disbursement at the end of year 2—at an interest rate of 6.394% compounded annually. If we were to calculate the value of the cash receipts and the cash disbursements at the end of year 2 at an interest rate of 6.394% compounded annually the cash receipts should be equivalent to the cash disbursements.

Example 15-16: Compare the value of the cash receipts to the cash disbursement from Example 15-15 at the end of year 2 at a periodic interest rate of 6.394% compounded annually.

Solution: First, find the future value of the cash receipts at the end of year 2 using Eq. (15-1):

$$F = \$1,000.00(1 + 0.0639)^2 = \$1,131.97$$

Next, find the future value of the first cash disbursement at the end of year 2 using Eq. (15-1). The cash disbursement occurs one year before the end of year 2; therefore, the number of periods is one. The calculations are as follows:

$$F_1 = \$500.00(1 + 0.06394)^1 = \$531.97$$

The second cash disbursement occurs at the end of the second year, which is the same point in time for which we are calculating the future value; therefore, the number of periods is zero and its future value is $600.00. Summing these two future values we get the following:

$$F = \$531.97 + \$600.00 = \$1,131.97$$

At an interest rate of 6.394%, the cash receipts are equivalent to the cash disbursements.

INFLATION AND CONSTANT DOLLARS

While money is in the bank earning interest, inflation is eroding its purchasing power. During times of inflation, a dollar today will not purchase the same amount of goods that it would have purchased a year ago. If inflation were to be running 3% per year, it would take $1.03 today to purchase the same amount of goods that a $1.00 would have purchased a year ago. Money's value is also determined by what it can purchase. Using f to represent the inflation rate, we could write the following equation:

$$\text{Cost}_n = \text{Cost}_0(1 + f)^n \tag{15-13}$$

As inflation increases costs, purchasing power decreases. Because purchasing power is inversely related to costs we may write Eq. (15-13) as follows:

Future Purchasing Power $=$ Today's Purchasing Power$/(1 + f)^n$ (15-14)

Combining the effects of inflation with Eq. (15-1) we get the following:

$$F' = P(1 + i)^n/(1 + f)^n$$

where $(1 + i)^n$ is the increase in value due to interest, $(1 + f)^n$ is the decrease in purchasing power due to inflation, and F' is the future value in constant dollars. This formula not only produces equivalent cash flows at an interest rate of i but also cash flows in constant dollars or in dollars with the same purchasing power at an inflation rate of f.

To simplify the calculations, the periodic interest rate and inflation rate could be replaced with the constant dollar interest rate i', which incorporates both the periodic interest rate and the inflation rate as follows:

$$(1 + i') = (1 + i)/(1 + f)$$

Solving for i' we get the following:

$$i' = (1 + i)/(1 + f) - 1 \qquad\qquad (15-15)$$

The constant dollars interest rate (i') can be substituted for i into Eqs. (15-1) through (15-12) to get not only equivalent cash flows but also equivalent cash flows in constant dollars. The underlying assumption is that all cash flows are subject to the same inflation rate and the inflation rate is constant for all periods of time.

Example 15-17:   How much money needs to be set aside today to purchase a new piece of equipment in five years? The money is expected to earn 8% interest compounded annually and the price of the equipment is expected to increase by 3% per year. The present cost of the equipment is $10,000.

Solution: To solve this problem, we must first find the constant dollars interest rate for a periodic interest rate of 8% and an inflation rate of 3%. Substituting these values into Eq. (15-15) we get the following:

$$i' = (1 + 0.08)/(1 + 0.03) - 1 = 0.048544$$

Substituting i' into Eq. (15-3) and using five one-year periods we get the following:

$$P' = \$10,000/(1 + 0.048544)^5 = \$7,889.81$$

where P' is the present value in constant dollars.

In lieu of using the constant dollar inflation rate, we could have used Eq. (15-1) to find the future cost of the piece of equipment using the inflation rate in place of i as follows:

$$F' = \$10{,}000(1 + 0.03)^5 = \$11{,}592.74$$

We could then find the present value of the future cost of the piece of equipment by using Eq. (15-3):

$$P' = \$11{,}592.74/(1 + 0.08)^5 = \$7{,}889.82$$

During the five years that the $7,889.82 was invested, it would have earned $3,702.92 of interest, growing to $11,592.74. During this same time, the price of the piece of equipment would have increased by $1,592.74 to $11,592.74.

CONCLUSION

Money's value is based on the size of the cash flows, the timing of the cash flows, and the interest rate. Before cash flows can be added, subtracted, or compared the cash flows must be converted to an equivalent cash flow or series of uniform cash flows at a specific point or points in time. Equivalent cash flows are cash flows that produce the same results at the specified interest rate. There are six basic formulas that may be used to convert cash flows of different time periods. To simplify calculations a cash flow may be split into two or more cash flows. The point or points in time at which the cash flows are compared is unimportant because when the cash flows are equivalent at a specified interest rate and point in time, they are equivalent at all points in time at that interest rate. Inflation decreases the purchasing power of money. The constant dollar inflation rate adjusts the interest rate to take into account inflation and can be substituted into any of the six conversion equations.

PROBLEMS

1. What is the future value, ten years from now, of $1,000 invested today at a periodic interest rate of 12% compounded annually?
2. What is the future value, ten years from now, of $1,000 invested today at a periodic interest rate of 1% compounded monthly?
3. What is the present value of $1,000, received ten years from now, using a periodic interest rate of 12% compounded annually?
4. What is the present value of $1,000, received four years from now, using a periodic interest rate of 7.5% compounded annually?

5. What is the future value, ten years from now, of ten $1,000 cash flows using a periodic interest rate of 8% compounded annually? The cash flows are made at the end of each year.

6. What is the future value, five years from now, of sixty $100 cash flows using a periodic interest rate of 0.7% compounded monthly? The cash flows are made at the end of each month.

7. What uniform series of cash flows is equivalent to a $100,000 cash flow, ten years from now, if the uniform cash flows occur at the end of the year for the next ten years and the periodic interest rate is 11% compounded annually?

8. What uniform series of cash flows is equivalent to a $100,000 cash flow, fifteen years from now, if the uniform cash flows occur at the end of the year for the next fifteen years and the periodic interest rate is 8.5% compounded annually?

9. What is the present value of five $800 cash flows that occur at the end of each year for the next five years at a periodic interest rate of 8% compounded annually? The first cash flow occurs a year from now, the second cash flow occurs two years from now, . . . , and the fifth cash flow occurs five years from now.

10. What is the present value of twenty $500 cash flows that occur at the end of each year for the next twenty years at a periodic interest rate of 7.5% compounded annually? The first cash flow occurs a year from now, the second cash flow occurs two years from now, . . . , and the twentieth cash flow occurs twenty years from now.

11. What uniform series of cash flows is equivalent to a $15,000 cash flow occurring today if the uniform series of cash flows occur at the end of each year for the next five years and the periodic interest rate is 9% compounded annually?

12. What uniform series of cash flows is equivalent to a $150,000 cash flow occurring today if the uniform series of cash flows occur at the end of each month for the next fifteen years and the periodic interest rate is 0.62% compounded annually?

13. Draw a cash flow diagram for the following cash flow:

YEAR	0	1	2	3	4
Receipts ($)	0	1,000	2,000	2,000	1,000
Disbursements ($)	4,750	0	0	0	0

14. Draw a cash flow diagram for the following cash flow:

YEAR	0	1	2	3	4
Receipts ($)	0	5,000	0	5,000	5,000
Disbursements ($)	7,500	0	5,000	0	0

15. Determine the future value at the end of August for the following cash flows using a periodic interest rate of 1% compounded monthly:

MONTH	AMOUNT ($)
April	15,000
May	25,000
June	21,000
July	15,000

These cash flows occur at the end of the respective months.

16. Determine the future value at the end of June for the following cash flows using a periodic interest rate of 1% compounded monthly:

MONTH	AMOUNT ($)
Dec.	15,000
Jan.	22,000
Feb.	28,000
March	35,000
April	30,000
May	15,000

These cash flows occur at the end of the respective months.

17. Determine the present value in year 0 of the following cash flows using a periodic interest rate of 9% compounded annually:

YEAR	1	2	3	4	5
Receipts ($)	3,000	3,000	5,000	3,000	5,000

18. Determine the present value in year 0 of the following cash flows using a periodic interest rate of 11% compounded annually:

YEAR	1	2	3	4	5
Receipts ($)	5,000	5,000	0	5,000	5,000
Disbursements ($)	0	0	5,000	0	0

19. Determine the present value in year 0 of the following cash flows using a periodic interest rate of 5% compounded annually:

YEAR	5	6	7	8	9
Receipts ($)	6,000	6,000	6,000	6,000	6,000

20. Determine the present value in year 0 of the following cash flows using a periodic interest rate of 12% compounded annually:

YEAR	11	12	13	14	15
Receipts ($)	1,000	1,000	1,000	1,000	1,000

21. At what periodic interest rate is a $1,000 cash disbursement occurring four years ago equivalent to a cash receipt of $1,274.43 occurring today? The periodic interest rate is compounded annually.

22. At what periodic interest rate is a $5,000 cash disbursement occurring today equivalent to a cash receipt of $7,605.30 occurring five years from now? The periodic interest rate is compounded annually.

23. At what periodic interest rate is a $2,000 cash receipt occurring at the beginning of year 1 equivalent to four annual $600 cash disbursements? The first cash disbursement occurs at the end of year 1, the second occurs at the end of year 2, the third occurs at the end of year 3, and the fourth occurs at the end of year 4. The periodic interest rate is compounded annually.

24. At what periodic interest rate is a $4,000 cash receipt occurring at the beginning of year 1 equivalent to ten annual $750 cash disbursements? The first cash disbursement occurs at the end of year 1, the second occurs at the end of year 2, . . . , and the tenth occurs at the end of year 10.

25. What is the constant dollar interest rate for a periodic interest rate of 9% and an inflation rate of 4%?

26. What is the constant dollar interest rate for a periodic interest rate of 6% and an inflation rate of 3%?

27. How much money needs to be set aside today to purchase a new piece of equipment in five years? The money is expected to earn 5% interest compounded annually and the price of the equipment is expected to increase by 2% per year. The present cost of the equipment is $100,000.

28. How much money needs to be set aside today to purchase a new piece of equipment in three years? The money is expected to earn 9% interest compounded annually and the price of the equipment is expected to increase by 3% per year. The present cost of the equipment is $75,000.

29. Set up a computer spreadsheet to solve Problem 15. The spreadsheet should allow you to change the interest rate by changing a single cell. Set up your spreadsheet in the following format:

i	1%			
MONTH	APRIL	MAY	JUNE	JULY
Periods				
Amounts				
F				
			Total F	

30. Set up a computer spreadsheet to solve Problem 16. The spreadsheet should allow you to change the interest rate by changing a single cell. Set up your spreadsheet in a format similar to that in Problem 29.

31. At what periodic interest rate is a $2,000 cash receipt occurring at the beginning of year 1 equivalent to four cash disbursements: a $575 cash

disbursement occurring at the end of year 1, a $600 cash disbursement occurring at the end of year 2, a $625 cash disbursement occurring at the end of year 3, and a $650 cash disbursement occurring at the end of year 4? The periodic interest rate is compounded annually.

32. At what periodic interest rate is a $5,000 cash receipt occurring at the beginning of year 1 equivalent to five annual cash disbursements? The first four annual cash disbursements are $1,000 each and occur at the end of each of the first four years. The last cash disbursement is $2,000 and occurs at the end of the fifth year. The periodic interest rate is compounded annually.

FINANCING A COMPANY'S FINANCIAL NEEDS

In this chapter you learn about financial instruments that can be used to provide the necessary cash for a construction company's operation. You also learn to compare debt instruments with different conditions and how loan provisions and closing costs can increase the effective interest rate on a loan or line of credit. An understanding of these principles helps you reduce borrowing costs and determine the best way to provide the cash needed to operate a construction company. Success in obtaining financing for a company can allow the company to take on additional projects, whereas failure to obtain financing can spell the doom of a company.

In chapter 14 we found that the construction company in Examples 14-1 through 14-5 needed an additional $60,000 to $100,000 in cash to finance the construction work that it had scheduled for the upcoming year. Raising the required cash could be done through equity financing, the sale of assets, or debt financing. If it were to raise the needed cash through equity financing, the existing owners would need to provide the additional cash or they would need to allow additional owners to invest in the company. Alternately, it could sell surplus assets to generate the cash. Another option is to obtain more cash through debt financing. The company could increase its use of trade financing—the use of subcontractors and its cash—to finance its operations or it could take out a short-term loan, a long-term loan, or a line of credit from a bank or other financial institution.

In this chapter you learn about five common ways of using debt financing to meet a company's cash needs, including loans, lines of credits, leases, trade financing, and credit cards. You also learn to compare debt instruments with different interest rates and provisions. If you were to go from lending institution to lending institution looking for a loan to finance a piece of heavy equipment for your construction company, you would find that the interest rates and provisions of the loans vary from institution to institution. These provisions include the costs associated with setting up the loan and requirements to maintain other accounts with the institution. The comparison of debt instruments will be made by determining the effective annual interest rate (i_a), which incorporates the costs of the instrument's provisions into the interest rate. The effective annual interest rates may then be easily compared. Before we can compare debt instruments we must first understand the basic principles of interest.

INTEREST

Interest may be broken down into two types, simple interest and compound interest. Simple interest does not pay interest on the previous period's interest, whereas compound interest pays interest on the previous period's interest.

Simple Interest

Simple interest is calculated using the following formula:

$$I = P(i)n \qquad (16\text{-}1)$$

where

I = Interest
P = Principal
i = Interest Rate per Year
n = Number of Years

Because simple interest ignores the effects of compounding interest, simple interest is seldom used for loans with terms longer than one year. Because simple interest is most commonly used for loans with a term of shorter than one year, Eq. (16-1) may be written using days in lieu of years as follows:

$$I = P(i)D/365 \qquad (16\text{-}2)$$

where

I = Interest
P = Principal
i = Interest Rate per Year
D = Length of the Loan in Days

Example 16-1: Determine the interest due on a $100,000 short-term loan, with a term of 245 days and a simple interest rate of 10%.

Solution: Using Eq. (16-2) we get the following:

$$I = \$100,000.00(0.10)245/365 = \$6,712.33$$

The interest on the loan for the 245 days would be $6,712.33.

Compound Interest

Compound interest may pay or collect interest at different intervals or compounding periods. The most common compounding periods include annually, semiannually, quarterly, monthly, and daily. A financial instrument that pays interest on a quarterly basis is said to be compounded quarterly.

Compound interest rates are most commonly quoted as nominal interest rate (r), which is also referred to as the annual percentage rate or APR. The nominal interest rate ignores the effects of compounding and is determined by summing the periodic interest rates (i) for all of the compounding periods in one year. To use the nominal interest rate to calculate the interest, the nominal interest rate must be converted to the periodic interest rate. There are two primary methods to perform this conversion. The first method divides the nominal rate by number of compounding periods in a year (c) and pays this interest rate for each of the periods. This conversion method uses the following formula for the periodic interest rate:

$$i = r/c \qquad\qquad (16\text{-}3)$$

where

i = Periodic Interest Rate
r = Nominal Interest Rate per Year or Annual Percentage Rate (APR)
c = Number of Compounding Periods in a Year where $c \geq 1$

Example 16-2: Determine the quarterly interest rate for a loan that charges an annual percentage rate of 12%. The loan charges interest quarterly.

Solution: In this example, the number of compounding periods per year is 4. Using Eq. (16-3) we get the following:

$$i = 0.12/4 = 0.03$$

or 3% interest is paid each quarter.

Example 16-3: Determine the monthly interest rate for a loan that charges an annual percentage rate of 12%. The loan charges interest monthly.

Solution: In this example, the number of compounding periods per year is 12. Using Eq. (16-3) we get the following:

$$i = 0.12/12 = 0.01$$

or 1% interest is charged each month.

The second method divides the nominal interest rate by 365 days per year and multiplies the resultant by the number of days in the billing period. This conversion method uses the following formula for the periodic interest rate:

$$i = (r/365)D \tag{16-4}$$

where

i = Periodic Interest Rate

r = Nominal Interest Rate per Year or Annual Percentage Rate (APR)

$r/365$ = Daily Finance Charge

D = Number of Days in the Billing Period

Using Eq. (16-4) results in periodic interest rates that are different for periods of different lengths. For example, a period with 30 days will have a higher periodic interest rate than a period with 28 days. The number of days in a month and if the billing date falls on a weekend or holiday can affect the number of days in the billing period. For example, a credit card may be billed on the seventh of each month except when the seventh falls on a weekend or holiday, in which case it is billed the next business day. In this case the billing periods would range from 28 days to 33 days.

Example 16-4: Determine the interest rate for a billing period with 28 days for a loan that charges an annual percentage rate of 12%.

Solution: Using Eq. (16-4) we get the following:

$$i = (0.12/365)28 = 0.0092$$

or 0.92% interest will be charged during the billing period.

Yield or Annual Percentage Yield

To compare interest rates with different compounding periods, the interest rates must be converted to a common compounding period. The common compounding period used is one year and the equivalent interest rate is known as the yield (i_a), which is also referred to as the annual percentage yield or APY. In the absence of deposits and withdrawals from an account, paying interest annually at the yield produces the same result as paying the interest each period at the periodic interest rate. In this case, the yield is equivalent to the periodic interest rate.

In the absence of instrument provisions that increase or decrease the interest rate, the yield or annual percentage yield is equal to the effective annual interest rate (i_a). The key difference between the yield and the effective annual interest rate is that the yield ignores loan provisions and closing costs that increase the effective interest rate. In this book, the terms *yield* or *annual percentage yield* are used when the cost of the provisions of the debt instruments are being ignored and the term *effective annual interest rate* is used when the cost of the provisions are included.

The yield for financial instruments is calculated by the following formula:

$$i_a = (1 + r/c)^c - 1 \qquad (16\text{-}5)$$

where

i_a = Yield or Annual Percentage Yield (APY)

r = Nominal Interest Rate per Year or Annual Percentage Rate (APR)

c = Number of Compounding Periods in a Year where $c \geq 1$

Equation (16-5) is valid only when the periodic interest rates are the same for each of the periods. This equation may be used to provide a close approximation of the effective interest rate for monthly payments where the periodic interest rates are not the same, which is the case when Eq. (16-4) is used to calculate the periodic interest rates.

It is important to note that as long as the number of compounding periods in a year is greater than 1, the yield (APY) will be greater than the nominal interest rate (APR). Placing emphasis on the nominal interest rate gives the appearance of a lower interest rate, whereas placing emphasis on the yield gives the appearance of a higher interest rate. This is why loan advertisements often place the emphasis on the nominal interest rate, whereas saving and certificate of deposit advertisements often place the emphasis on the yield.

Example 16-5: Determine the annual percentage yield for a loan that charges an annual percentage rate of 12% compounded quarterly.

Solution: In this problem, the number of compounding periods per year is 4. Using Eq. (16-5) we get the following:

$$i_a = (1 + 0.12/4)^4 - 1 = 0.1255$$

The certificate of deposit has an annual percentage yield of 12.55%.

SIDEBAR 16-1

CONVERTING ANNUAL PERCENTAGE RATE TO ANNUAL PERCENTAGE YIELD USING A TI BA II PLUS CALCULATOR

The annual percentage rate is converted to the annual percentage yield as shown below. For this sidebar we use Example 16-5.

TASK	KEYSTROKES	DISPLAY	
1. Select Interest Worksheet	[2nd] [ICONV]	NOM=	0.00
2. Clear Worksheet	[2nd] [CLR WORK]	NOM=	0.00
3. Enter APR	12 [ENTER]	NOM=	12.00
4. Enter Number of Compounding Periods	[↓][↓] 4 [ENTER]	C/Y=	4.00
5. Calculate Effective Annual Yield	[↑] [CPT]	EFF=	12.55

Example 16-6: Determine the annual percentage yield for a loan that charges an annual percentage rate of 12% and charges interest monthly.

Solution: In this problem, the number of compounding periods per year is 12. Using Eq. (16-5) we get the following:

$$i_a = (1 + 0.12/12)^{12} - 1 = 0.1268$$

The loan has an annual percentage yield of 12.68%.

From Examples 16-5 and 16-6 we can see that the shorter the compounding period, the higher the annual percentage yield for a given annual percentage rate.

Example 16-7: Determine the annual percentage yield for a loan with an annual percentage rate of 18%. The loan charges interest at the end of each billing period. The billing periods end on the twentieth of each month, except for when the twentieth falls on a weekend or holiday, in which case the billing period ends on the next business day.

Solution: In this problem, the compounding periods will be of unequal lengths and will be all about one month long. The number of compounding periods per year is 12. Using Eq. (16-5) to approximate the annual percentage yield, we get the following:

$$i_a = (1 + 0.18/12)^{12} - 1 = 0.1956$$

The loan has an annual percentage yield of 19.56%. In the above example, the error introduced by the unequal compounding period is less than the errors introduced by rounding the yield.

Substituting Eq. (16-3) into Eq. (16-5) we get the following equation, which is used to calculate the annual percentage yield from the periodic interest rate:

$$i_a = (1 + i)^c - 1 \qquad\qquad (16\text{-}6)$$

where

i_a = Yield or Annual Percentage Yield (APY)

i = Periodic Interest Rate

c = Number of Compounding Periods in a Year where $c \geq 1$

Example 16-8: Determine the annual percentage yield for a loan that charges a monthly interest rate of 1% and compounds the interest monthly.

Solution: In this problem the number of compounding periods per year is 12. Using Eq. (16-6) we get the following:

$$i_a = (1 + 0.01)^{12} - 1 = 0.1268$$

The loan has an annual percentage yield of 12.68%.

Fixed versus Variable Interest Rates

Financial instruments may be divided into two classes based on whether their interest rate is fixed or variable. Instruments with a fixed interest rate guarantee the same interest rate for the term of the financial instrument. For example, a thirty-six-month loan that charges an annual percentage rate of 6% compounded quarterly will pay 1.5% at the end of each quarter for thirty-six months (12 quarters). At the end of the financial instrument's term, the financial instrument must be renegotiated.

For instruments with a variable interest rate, the interest rate varies at specified times during the life of the instrument and is tied to some financial index or measure, with the most common index being the prime rate. The prime rate is the base rate for corporate loans based on the lending practices of the nation's largest banks. The prime rate should be tied to a publication—such as the *Wall Street Journal*—for a specified publication date. For example, a loan's interest rate may be 2% above the prime rate and change every six months with the prime rate being tied to the published rate in the *Wall Street Journal* on January 2 and July 1 or the next business day. At the end of six months, if the prime rate were higher than is currently being paid on the loan, the interest rate on the loan would increase. Conversely, if the prime rate had decreased, the interest rate on the loan would decrease. On variable-rate financial instruments, the rates may vary annually, semiannually, quarterly, monthly, or daily. Some variable-rate financial instruments may defer the first rate change for a longer period than the normal time between rate changes. For example, a loan's interest rate may change at the end of the fifth year and semiannually thereafter. Loans with variable interest rates are often attractive despite the risk of the interest rate increasing because they often have a lower interest rate than fixed-rate instruments and, as a result, have a smaller monthly payment.

LOANS AND LINES OF CREDITS

Loans and lines of credit are ways of borrowing money from a bank or financial institution. Each loan or line of credit comes with a set of provisions that must be met by the borrower. Borrowers should carefully read, understand, and be willing to abide by the commitments that they are making when using debt instruments. Any concerns regarding any of the provisions in the documents should be reviewed by a professional familiar with financial documents.

A common provision in a loan or line of credit is that the borrower pledges specific assets as security for the loan or line of credit. In the event the borrower defaults on the debt, the lender has the right to sell the asset to recover the borrowed money. A loan or line of credit with this type of provision is known as a secured instrument or secured debt. With secured debt the borrowers are prohibited from selling or disposing of the asset without using the proceeds to pay off the debt. They are often prohibited from using the same assets as security on additional debt. Real estate is often used as security for mortgages. Where real estate is used as the security for a loan, a copy of the loan documents is filed with the county recorder's office or other public office, where they become available for public inspection. By doing so, the public is put on notice that the real estate has been used as security for a loan. When equipment and vehicles are used as security for a loan, the lending institution often holds the title to the equipment or vehicle until the loan has been paid off, thus preventing the borrower from selling the asset. When assets are used as security for a loan, the lending institution requires that borrowers maintain minimum amounts of insurance on the asset and that the lending institution is often named as an additional insured on the policy. Naming the lending institution as an additional insured under the policy requires the insurance company to notify the lending institution should the insurance be canceled for any reason.

Loans or line of credits that are not secured with assets are known as unsecured instruments or unsecured debt. Should the borrower fail to pay off the debt, the lender is left to recover the debt from the assets remaining after all of the secured debts have been paid. Most loans and lines of credit require some form of security.

Another common provision in a loan or line of credit is that this debt must be paid off before any other debts are paid. This is known as subordinating debt, in that all other debts become subordinate to the debt identified in the instrument. A subordinate debt clause in a loan or line of credit may make it difficult to finalize the debt because all existing lenders must agree for their debts to be subordinated to the new debt. Additionally, having a subordination clause in an existing debt instrument may make it difficult to obtain financing on new assets because the lender will want to use the new assets as security without its debt subordinate to that of any other debt instruments. For example, a construction company has an existing line of credit that has a subordination clause. The company wants to purchase a new piece of equipment using a new loan. The lender wants to use the new piece of equipment as security for the loan, but the new debt may become subordinate to the line of credit. Should the construction company become bankrupt, the new piece of equipment may only be used as security for the loan after the line of credit is paid off. Should the new piece of equipment be sold to satisfy the line of credit, the new lender would be left without security on the loan. It is unlikely that the new lender will make the loan if there is a chance that the debt will become subordinate to any other debt instrument. For these reasons, subordinating debt should be avoided if at all possible.

Another common provision is a third-party guarantee or personal endorsement. Under a third-party guarantee, a company or person other than the borrower becomes a third party to the loan and uses assets to guarantee the loan. This provision is very common when the borrower is seen as a poor credit risk or does not have a credit history. The third party may also be referred to as a cosigner. Under a personal endorsement, the owner or owners of a company pledge personal assets to pay the debts of the company should the company fail to pay the debts. A personal guarantee is almost always required when credit is extended to a small company. A third-party guarantee or personal endorsement is desirable to the lender because it increases the assets available from which to recover the debt should the lender fail to pay the debt. Conversely, these provisions are undesirable from a borrower's perspective because assets other than the company's assets are at risk. Where possible, a third-party guarantee or personal endorsement should be avoided. If it cannot be avoided the third party or personal endorser should try to place a monetary limit on his or her personal liability. Where there are multiple third parties or personal endorsers, they should try to limit their individual liabilities to a percentage of the total liability. For example, if there were two personal endorsers on a loan they should try to limit their individual liability to 50% of the total liability. This is to prevent one of the parties from having to cover the entire liability him- or herself. When signing documentation for a loan or line of credit as an officer of the company, make sure that you are signing as an officer and not as a personal endorser.

Short-term financing should be used to finance short-term financial needs. Long-term financing should be used to finance long-term financial needs. Matching the term of the financing to the length of the financial need is known as maturity matching. For example, if a new piece of equipment with a useful life of five years were purchased with a four- or five-year loan we would say that their maturities match. The key point in maturity matching is that the financing must give the asset time to generate enough cash to pay off the principal and interest from the financial instrument and the financial instrument must be paid off before the end of the useful life of the equipment.

Short-term financing should not be used to finance long-term assets. By using short-term financing, such as a line of credit, to purchase a large piece of equipment, the borrower takes the risk that he or she will be able to renew the short-term financing or find a new source of financing when the short-term financing expires. One exception to this rule is on a real estate development where lending institutions provide a short-term construction loan during construction and then provide a long-term mortgage at the completion of the construction. When developing real estate it is wise to obtain both the construction loan and the long-term financing before beginning the project. Because the long-term financing will not be finalized until construction is complete, it is important to have a written commitment for the financing.

LOANS

Loans typically consist of a fixed amount of money, known as the principal, which is borrowed at the beginning of the loan and is paid back with interest at some point in the future or over a period of time by making periodic payments. Short-term loans are loans with a term of one year or less. Long-term loans are loans with a term of more than a year. Short-term loans may allow that both the principal and interest may be paid off at the maturity of the loan or the loan may require that the interest be paid at regular intervals with the principal being paid at the end of the loan. Long-term loans usually require periodic payments covering both interest and principal, thus reducing the principal over time.

Long-Term Loans

Long-term loans range in length from a few years for equipment and vehicle loans to thirty years for real estate loans. Long-term loans require monthly payments. The proceeds from the monthly payments are first used to pay off the interest on the loan due during the period and then the remaining proceeds are used to reduce the principal or the amount borrowed.

The following equation is used to calculate the monthly payments for loans with a uniform monthly payment and a fixed interest rate:

$$A = P[i(1 + i)^n]/[(1 + i)^n - 1] \qquad (16\text{-}7)$$

where

P = Principal
i = Periodic Interest Rate for One Month
n = Duration of Loan in Months

You should recognize this formula as the uniform-series capital-recovery factor from chapter 15. This is because payments on a loan are equivalent to the principal at the periodic interest rate.

This formula excludes funds included in the payment that are placed in escrow for payment of hazard insurance and property taxes. When using this formula be sure to use the periodic interest rate rather than the annual percentage rate (APR) or annual percentage yield (APY) and be sure to use the number of months rather than the number of years. Ignoring the closing costs, the amount of interest paid over the life of the loan is determined by the following formula:

$$I = An - P \qquad (16\text{-}8)$$

where

I = Total Interest Paid
A = Monthly Payment Determined by Eq. (16-7)
n = Duration of Loan in Months
P = Principal

This formula ignores the rounding of the payment and the interest to whole cents and as a result there will be small differences between the results of this formula and the actual amount of interest paid.

> **Example 16-9:** A $150,000 office building is to be purchased with a thirty-year loan with an annual percentage rate of 9% compounded monthly. Determine the monthly payments and how much interest is paid over the life of the loan.

SIDEBAR 16-2

DETERMINING MONTHLY PAYMENTS FOR A LOAN USING A TI BA II PLUS CALCULATOR

The monthly payment for a loan is calculated as shown below. To perform this calculation, the interest should not be converted to a periodic interest rate but should be entered as an annual percentage rate. In Step 4 the months may be entered in months or years. Steps 2, 3, and 4 may be done in any order. The payment will carry a negative sign, indicating that it is a cash outflow. For this sidebar we use Example 16-9.

TASK	KEYSTROKES		DISPLAY
1. Set Variables to Defaults	[2nd] [RESET] [ENTER]	RST	0.00
2. Enter Principal	150000 [PV]	PV=	150,000.00
3. Enter Annual Percentage Rate	9 [I/Y]	I/Y=	9.00
4. Enter Length of Loan		N=	360.00
in Months	360 [N]		
—OR—			
in Years	30 [2nd] [xP/Y] [N]		
5. Calculate Payment	[CPT] [PMT]	PMT=	−1,206.93

Solution: In this example, the compounding period is one month, with 12 compounding periods per year and 360 compounding periods during the life of the loan. Using Eq. (16-3) to find the monthly interest rate we get the following:

$$i = 0.090/12 = 0.0075 \text{ or } 0.75\%$$

Using Eq. (16-7) to find the monthly payments we get the following:

$$A = \$150,000[0.0075(1 + 0.0075)^{360}]/[(1 + 0.0075)^{360} - 1]$$
$$A = \$1,206.93$$

Using Eq. (16-8) to find the total interest paid during the life of the loan we get the following:

$$I = \$1,206.93(360) - \$150,000 = \$284,494.80$$

Example 16-10: The office building in Example 16-9 is to be purchased with a twenty-year loan with an annual percentage rate of 9% compounded monthly. Determine the monthly payments and how much interest is paid over the life of the loan. What is the difference in the monthly payments for the twenty-year and thirty-year loan in Example 16-9? How much would the company save in interest charges by using the twenty-year loan over the thirty-year loan?

Solution: In this example the compounding period is one month, with 12 compounding periods per year and 240 compounding periods during the life of the loan. The monthly interest is the same as the monthly interest in Example 16-9 or 0.75%.

Using Eq. (16-7) to find the monthly payments we get the following:

$$A = \$150,000[0.0075(1 + 0.0075)^{240}]/[(1 + 0.0075)^{240} - 1]$$
$$A = \$1,349.59$$

Using Eq. (16-8) to find the total interest paid during the life of the loan we get the following:

$$I = \$1,349.59(240) - \$150,000 = \$173,901.60$$

By taking out the twenty-year loan the company would pay an additional $142.66 ($1,349.59 − $1,206.93) per month and would save $110,593.20 ($284,494.80 − $173,901.60) in interest over the life of the loan.

From Examples 16-9 and 16-10 we see that a 12% ($142.66/1,206.93) increase in the monthly payments results in a 33% decrease (1 − 20/30) in the length of the loan and 39% decrease (1 − $173,901.60/$284,494.80) in the total interest paid over the life of the loan. Table 16-1 shows the monthly payment and total interest paid over the life of the loan for a $100,000 loan at 8% interest compounded annually for different lengths of loans.

From Table 16-1 we see that for a twenty-year loan the interest paid over the life of the loan exceeds the amount borrowed and for a thirty-five-year loan the interest paid is almost twice the amount borrowed.

For a loan, the proceeds from the monthly payments are first used to pay off the interest accrued during the previous month and then the remaining proceeds are used to reduce the principal. This is the case even when the monthly payments are not equal. In the case where the monthly payment does not cover the previous month's interest, the unpaid interest is added to the principal. The monthly interest for month t is calculated by using the following formula:

$$I_t = U_{t-1}(i) \tag{16-9}$$

TABLE 16-1 Payment and Interest Comparison for a $100,000 Loan at 8% Compounded Annually

YEARS	MONTHLY PAYMENT ($)	TOTAL INTEREST ($)
5	2,027.64	21,658.40
10	1,213.28	45,593.60
15	955.65	72,017.00
20	836.44	100,745.60
25	771.82	131,546.00
30	733.76	164,153.60
35	710.26	198,309.20

where

It = Interest Due for Month t

U_{t-1} = Outstanding Principal at the End of the Previous Month $(t - 1)$

i = Periodic Interest Rate

The outstanding principal at the end of month t is calculated by the following equation:

$$U_t = U_{t-1} + I_t - A \tag{16-10}$$

where

U_t = Outstanding Principal at the End of Month t

U_{t-1} = Outstanding Principal at the End of the Previous Month $(t - 1)$

I_t = Interest Due for Month t

A = Monthly Payment

By substituting Eq. (16-9) into Eq. (16-10) and combining terms we get the following:

$$U_t = U_{t-1}(1 + i) - A \tag{16-11}$$

The reduction in the outstanding principal equals the outstanding principal balance at the beginning of the month less the outstanding principal balance at the end of the month and may be found by solving Eq. (16-10) for $U_{t-1} - U_t$ as follows:

$$B_t = U_{t-1} - U_t = A - I_t \tag{16-12}$$

where

B_t = Reduction in Outstanding Principal for Payment t

U_t = Outstanding Principal at the End of Month t

U_{t-1} = Outstanding Principal at the End of the Previous Month $(t - 1)$

A = Monthly Payment

I_t = Interest Due for Month t

Example 16-11: For the loan in Example 16-9, determine the monthly interest for the first and second months and the outstanding principal at the end of the first and second month.

Solution: From Example 16-9 the monthly payment is $1,206.93 and the periodic interest rate for the month is 0.75%. Using Eq. (16-9) to find the interest paid on the loan for the first month we get the following:

$$I_1 = \$150,000(0.0075) = \$1,125.00$$

Before calculating the interest for the second month we need to calculate outstanding principal balance at the end of the first month. Using Eq. (16-10) we get the following:

$$U_1 = \$150,000.00 + \$1,125.00 - \$1,206.93 = \$149,918.07$$

Of the first month's payment, $1,125.00 was used to pay the interest and $81.93 ($1,206.93 − $1,125.00) was used to reduce the outstanding principal balance on the loan.

Using Eq. (16-9) to find the interest paid on the loan for the second month we get the following:

$$I_2 = \$149,918.07(0.0075) = \$1,124.39$$

SIDEBAR 16-3

CALCULATING THE MONTHLY INTEREST, PRINCIPAL REDUCTION, AND BALANCE USING A TI BA II PLUS CALCULATOR

The monthly interest, principal reduction, and balance—at the end of the month—are calculated as follows. First you must calculate the monthly payment using the same five steps you used in Sidebar 16-2. For this sidebar we use Example 16-11.

TASK	KEYSTROKES	DISPLAY	
1. Set Variables to Defaults	[2nd] [RESET] [ENTER]	RST	0.00
2. Enter Principal	150000 [PV]	PV=	150,000.00
3. Enter Annual Percentage Rate	9 [I/Y]	I/Y=	9.00
4. Enter Length of Loan		N=	360.00
in Months	360 [N]		
—OR—			
in Years	30 [2nd] [xP/Y] [N]		
5. Calculate Payment	[CPT] [PMT]	PMT=	−1,206.93
6. Select Amortization Worksheet	[2nd] [AMORT]	P1=	1.00
7. View Balance	[↓][↓]	BAL=	149,918.07
8. View Principal Reduction	[↓]	PRN=	−81.93
9. View Interest	[↓]	INT=	−1,125.00
10. Move to Second Year	[↓] [CPT]	P1=	2.00
11. View Balance	[↓][↓]	PRN=	149,835.53
12. View Principal Reduction	[↓]	INT=	−82.54
13. View Interest	[↓]	P1=	−1,124.39
14. Repeat Steps 10 through 13 for the Remaining Years			

Using Eq. (16-10) we get an outstanding principal balance at the end of the second month of the following:

$$U_2 = \$149{,}918.07 + \$1{,}124.39 - \$1{,}206.93 = \$149{,}835.53$$

Of the second month's payment, \$1,124.39 was used to pay the interest and \$82.54 (\$1,206.93 − \$1,124.39) was used to reduce the outstanding principal balance on the loan.

For a loan with a fixed interest rate and equal periods, the interest for each period decreases because the outstanding principal balance decreases and the amount of the payment that is used to reduce the outstanding principal balance on the loan increases. This is not always the case with variable rate loans and for loans with unequal periods because the periodic interest rate can vary from period to period. Figure 16-1 shows the allocation of the payment between principal reduction and interest paid.

The outstanding principal balance for a loan with a fixed payment and interest rate is calculated for any point in time using the following formula:

$$U_t = A[(1 + i)^{(n-t)} - 1]/[i(1 + i)^{(n-t)}] \tag{16-13}$$

where

U_t = Outstanding Principal Balance of the End of Month t

A = Monthly Payment

i = Monthly Interest Rate

n = Duration of Loan in Months

t = Number of Monthly Payments That Have Been Made

FIGURE 16-1 Allocation of Loan Payments

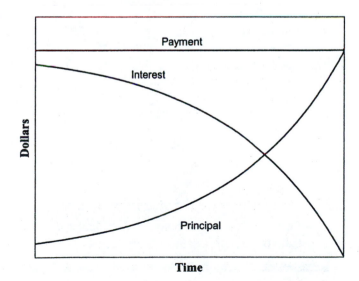

The outstanding principal balance equals the present value of the remaining payments measured at the end of month t.

Example 16-12: The borrowers in Example 16-9 have just made their 180th payment. What is the outstanding principal balance on the loan?

Solution: In this example, the borrowers have made 180 of the required 360 payments, leaving 180 remaining payments. Using Eq. (16-13) to find the outstanding principal balance we get the following:

$$U_{180} = \$1,206.93[(1 + 0.0075)^{(360-180)} - 1]/$$
$$[0.0075(1 + 0.0075)^{(360-180)}]$$
$$U_{180} = \$118,995.34$$

From Example 16-12 we can see that after making payments on the loan for half of the life of the loan, the borrowers have reduced the principal by less than 21% ($1 - \$118,995.34/\$150,000.00$). This is because during the early months of the loan most of the payment is being used to pay the interest. As we approach the

---

SIDEBAR 16-4

CALCULATING THE UNPAID BALANCE AFTER t PAYMENTS USING A TI BA II PLUS CALCULATOR

The unpaid balance after t payments is calculated as follows. First you must calculate the monthly payment using the same five steps you used in Sidebar 16-2. For this sidebar we use Example 16-12.

TASK	KEYSTROKES	DISPLAY	
1. Set Variables to Defaults	[2nd] [RESET] [ENTER]	RST	0.00
2. Enter Principal	150000 [PV]	PV=	150,000.00
3. Enter Annual Percentage Rate	9 [I/Y]	I/Y=	9.00
4. Enter Length of Loan		N=	360.00
in Months	360 [N]		
—OR—			
in Years	30 [2nd] [xP/Y] [N]		
5. Calculate Payment	[CPT] [PMT]	PMT=	−1,206.93
6. Select Amortization Worksheet	[2nd] [AMORT]	P1=	1.00
7. Enter the Payment	180 [ENTER]	P1=	180.00
	[↓] 180 [ENTER]	P2=	180.00
8. View Balance	[↓]	BAL=	118,997.10

There is a small difference between the calculator's answer and Example 16-12 because the calculator rounds the monthly payments and interest to whole pennies.

end of the loan the majority of the payment is being used to pay down the outstanding principal balance.

The interest paid between any two periods is calculated by subtracting the outstanding principal balance at the end of the last period from the outstanding principal balance at the beginning of the first period to determine the reduction in outstanding principal for the periods. The difference between the reduction in principal and the total of the monthly payments made during the periods equals the interest paid. The interest between any two periods is calculated using the following formula:

$$I = N(A) + U_t - U_{t-N} \qquad (16\text{-}14)$$

where

I = Interest Due for a Period of N Months
N = Number of Monthly Payments Made Between Two Periods
A = Monthly Payment
U_t = Outstanding Principal at the End of the Last Period
U_{t-N} = Outstanding Principal at the Beginning of the First Period $(t - N)$

The outstanding principal balances are calculated using Eq. (16-13). Equations (16-13) and (16-14) ignore the rounding of the payment and the interest to whole cents and as a result there will be small differences between the results of Eq. (16-14) and the actual amount of interest paid. This formula is useful when calculating the annual interest paid.

Example 16-13: How much interest do the borrowers in Example 16-9 pay during the fourth year of the loan?

Solution: During the fourth year they will make payments 37 through 48. The outstanding principal balance at the beginning of the fourth year equals the outstanding principal balance after the 36th payment has been made and is calculated using Eq. (16-13) as follows:

$$U_{36} = \$1,206.93[(1 + 0.0075)^{(360-36)} - 1]/$$
$$[0.0075(1 + 0.0075)^{(360-36)}]$$
$$U_{36} = \$146,627.72$$

The outstanding principal balance at the end of the fourth year equals the outstanding principal balance after the 48th payment has been made and is calculated using Eq. (16-13) as follows:

$$U_{48} = \$1,206.93[(1 + 0.0075)^{(360-48)} - 1]/$$
$$[0.0075(1 + 0.0075)^{(360-48)}]$$
$$U_{48} = \$145,286.63$$

The interest for the year is calculated using Eq. (16-14) as follows:

$$I = 12(\$1,206.93) + \$145,286.63 - \$146,627.72 = \$13,142.07$$

> ### SIDEBAR 16-5
>
> ## CALCULATING INTEREST FOR A SERIES OF PAYMENTS USING A TI BA II PLUS CALCULATOR
>
> The interest paid for a series of payments—for example, over the course of a year—is calculated as follows. First you must calculate the monthly payment using the same five steps you used in Sidebar 16-2. For this sidebar we use Example 16-13.
>
> | TASK | KEYSTROKES | DISPLAY | |
> |------|-----------|---------|---|
> | 1. Set Variables to Defaults | [2nd] [RESET] [ENTER] | RST | 0.00 |
> | 2. Enter Principal | 150000 [PV] | PV= | 150,000.00 |
> | 3. Enter Annual Percentage Rate | 9 [I/Y] | I/Y= | 9.00 |
> | 4. Enter Length of Loan | | N= | 360.00 |
> | in Months | 360 [N] | | |
> | —OR— | | | |
> | in Years | 30 [2nd] [xP/Y] [N] | | |
> | 5. Calculate Payment | [CPT] [PMT] | PMT= | −1,206.93 |
> | 6. Select Amortization Worksheet | [2nd] [AMORT] | P1= | 1.00 |
> | 7. Enter the Beginning Payment | 37 [ENTER] | P1= | 37.00 |
> | 8. Enter the Ending Payment | [↓] 48 [ENTER] | P2= | 48.00 |
> | 9. View Interest | [↓][↓][↓] | INT= | −13,142.13 |
>
> There is a small difference between the calculator's answer and Example 16-13 because the calculator rounds the monthly payments and interest to whole pennies.

Amortization Schedule

The monthly reduction in the outstanding principal balance and the interest accrued for each month may be expressed in tabular form as shown in Figure 16-2. Expressing the loan information in this format is known as an amortization schedule. An abbreviated amortization schedule for the loan in Example 16-9 is shown in Figure 16-2. The full amortization schedule is found in Appendix E.

When preparing an amortization schedule like the one found in Figure 16-2, one must keep in mind that payments will be made to the nearest whole penny. In Example 16-9 the monthly payment on the loan was calculated to be $1,206.933925, which was rounded to $1,206.93. Also, the monthly interest reported in the amortization schedule was rounded to the nearest penny. In the amortization schedule shown in Figure 16-2, the last payment has been increased by $6.81 to cover the rounding of the monthly payments and monthly interest. In Figure 16-2 the outstanding (ending) principal after the 180th payment has been made is $118,997.10. The value calculated in Example 16-12 was $118,995.34.

APR: 9.00% Page 1
Term: 360 Months
Monthly Payment: $1,206.93

Month	Beginning Principal	Monthly Payment	Monthly Interest	Principal Reduction	Ending Principal
0					150,000.00
1	150,000.00	1,206.93	1,125.00	81.93	149,918.07
2	149,918.07	1,206.93	1,124.39	82.54	149,835.53
3	149,835.53	1,206.93	1,123.77	83.16	149,752.37
4	149,752.37	1,206.93	1,123.14	83.79	149,668.58
5	149,668.58	1,206.93	1,122.51	84.42	149,584.16
6	149,584.16	1,206.93	1,121.88	85.05	149,499.11
7	149,499.11	1,206.93	1,121.24	85.69	149,413.42
8	149,413.42	1,206.93	1,120.60	86.33	149,327.09
9	149,327.09	1,206.93	1,119.95	86.98	149,240.11
10	149,240.11	1,206.93	1,119.30	87.63	149,152.48
...	...	...	...	...	...
175	120,835.26	1,206.93	906.26	300.67	120,534.59
176	120,534.59	1,206.93	904.01	302.92	120,231.67
177	120,231.67	1,206.93	901.74	305.19	119,926.48
178	119,926.48	1,206.93	899.45	307.48	119,619.00
179	119,619.00	1,206.93	897.14	309.79	119,309.21
180	119,309.21	1,206.93	894.82	312.11	118,997.10
181	118,997.10	1,206.93	892.48	314.45	118,682.65
182	118,682.65	1,206.93	890.12	316.81	118,365.84
183	118,365.84	1,206.93	887.74	319.19	118,046.65
184	118,046.65	1,206.93	885.35	321.58	117,725.07
185	117,725.07	1,206.93	882.94	323.99	117,401.08
...	...	...	...	...	...
350	12,704.00	1,206.93	95.28	1,111.65	11,592.35
351	11,592.35	1,206.93	86.94	1,119.99	10,472.36
352	10,472.36	1,206.93	78.54	1,128.39	9,343.97
353	9,343.97	1,206.93	70.08	1,136.85	8,207.12
354	8,207.12	1,206.93	61.55	1,145.38	7,061.74
355	7,061.74	1,206.93	52.96	1,153.97	5,907.77
356	5,907.77	1,206.93	44.31	1,162.62	4,745.15
357	4,745.15	1,206.93	35.59	1,171.34	3,573.81
358	3,573.81	1,206.93	26.80	1,180.13	2,393.68
359	2,393.68	1,206.93	17.95	1,188.98	1,204.70
360	1,204.70	1,213.74	9.04	1,204.70	0.00
Total		434,501.61	284,501.61	150,000.00	

FIGURE 16-2 Amortization Schedule for Example 16-9

The difference of $1.76 is due to round the payments and interest to the nearest penny in the amortization schedule.

When using a spreadsheet program to prepare an amortization schedule the payment and interest should be rounded to the nearest penny by using a

APR: 9.00%
Term: 36 months
Monthly Payment: $636.07

Payment Date	Monthly Interest Rate	Beginning Principal	Monthly Payment	Monthly Interest	Principal Reduction	Ending Principal
1/19/04						20,000.00
2/19/04	0.0076438	20,000.00	636.07	152.88	483.19	19,516.81
3/19/04	0.0071507	19,516.81	636.07	139.56	496.51	19,020.30
4/19/04	0.0076438	19,020.30	636.07	145.39	490.68	18,529.62
5/19/04	0.0073973	18,529.62	636.07	137.07	499.00	18,030.62
6/21/04	0.0081370	18,030.62	636.07	146.71	489.36	17,541.26
7/19/04	0.0069041	17,541.26	636.07	121.11	514.96	17,026.30
8/19/04	0.0076438	17,026.30	636.07	130.15	505.92	16,520.38
9/20/04	0.0078904	16,520.38	636.07	130.35	505.72	16,014.66
10/18/04	0.0069041	16,014.66	636.07	110.57	525.50	15,489.16
11/19/04	0.0078904	15,489.16	636.07	122.22	513.85	14,975.31
12/20/04	0.0076438	14,975.31	636.07	114.47	521.60	14,453.71
1/19/05	0.0073973	14,453.71	636.07	106.92	529.15	13,924.56
2/21/05	0.0081370	13,924.56	636.07	113.30	522.77	13,401.79
3/21/05	0.0069041	13,401.79	636.07	92.53	543.54	12,858.25
4/18/05	0.0069041	12,858.25	636.07	88.77	547.30	12,310.95
5/19/05	0.0076438	12,310.95	636.07	94.10	541.97	11,768.98
6/20/05	0.0078904	11,768.98	636.07	92.86	543.21	11,225.77
7/18/05	0.0069041	11,225.77	636.07	77.50	558.57	10,667.20
8/19/05	0.0078904	10,667.20	636.07	84.17	551.90	10,115.30
9/19/05	0.0076438	10,115.30	636.07	77.32	558.75	9,556.55
10/19/05	0.0073973	9,556.55	636.07	70.69	565.38	8,991.17
11/21/05	0.0081370	8,991.17	636.07	73.16	562.91	8,428.26
12/19/05	0.0069041	8,428.26	636.07	58.19	577.88	7,850.38
1/19/06	0.0076438	7,850.38	636.07	60.01	576.06	7,274.32
2/20/06	0.0078904	7,274.32	636.07	57.40	578.67	6,695.65
3/20/06	0.0069041	6,695.65	636.07	46.23	589.84	6,105.81
4/19/06	0.0073973	6,105.81	636.07	45.17	590.90	5,514.91
5/19/06	0.0073973	5,514.91	636.07	40.80	595.27	4,919.64
6/19/06	0.0076438	4,919.64	636.07	37.60	598.47	4,321.17
7/19/06	0.0073973	4,321.17	636.07	31.96	604.11	3,717.06
8/21/06	0.0081370	3,717.06	636.07	30.25	605.82	3,111.24
9/18/06	0.0069041	3,111.24	636.07	21.48	614.59	2,496.65
10/19/06	0.0076438	2,496.65	636.07	19.08	616.99	1,879.66
11/20/06	0.0078904	1,879.66	636.07	14.83	621.24	1,258.42
12/18/06	0.0069041	1,258.42	636.07	8.69	627.38	631.04
1/19/07	0.0078904	631.04	636.02	4.98	631.04	0.00
		Totals:	22,898.47	2,898.47	20,000.00	

FIGURE 16-3   Amortization Schedule for Loan with Different Period Lengths

rounding function. A common mistake is to format the cells so the payment and interest are shown to the nearest penny instead of rounding the values to the nearest penny. When formatting the cell to the nearest penny, although the values are only shown to the nearest penny, the values used in the calculations include fractions of a cent.

Amortization schedules for loans, which calculate the interest based on the number of days in the period, are prepared in the same manner as the amortization schedule shown in Figure 16-2, except the monthly interest rate must be calculated using Eq. (16-4). Figure 16-3 shows an amortization schedule for a thirty-six-month loan where the interest rate is based on the number of days in the month.

For the amortization schedule shown in Figure 16-3, both the monthly interest and payment have been rounded to whole pennies. As a result, the last payment has been reduced by $0.05 due to this rounding. The bill due date used in these calculations was the nineteenth of the month. If the nineteenth fell on a weekend or holiday, the bill date was the next business day.

Closing Costs

There are often many fees added to a loan to cover the cost of setting up the loan and to provide a profit for the lending institution. These fees are known as closing costs and include such items as the origination fee, the cost of the appraisal of the property used as security, the cost of the credit report on the applicants, underwriting fees, processing fees, documentation preparation fees, courier fees, title insurance, and other title charges.

When looking for loans, lending institutions should prepare a good faith estimate identifying all of the closing costs and any additional costs to close the loan. These additional costs include the payment of any existing loans that are to be paid off, payment of accrued interest on the existing loans, and funds to be placed in an escrow account for the payment of hazardous insurance and tax assessments. The good faith estimate also shows the estimated monthly payment, including amounts to be placed in escrow. As the name implies, the good faith estimate is an estimate prepared in good faith and the numbers in the estimate are not guaranteed. A sample of a good faith estimate is shown in Figure 16-4.

The closing costs provide the lending institution revenue to cover its costs and make a profit on setting up the loan. The closing costs also act as a deterrent against the borrower changing loans every time the interest rates change a fraction of a percentage. The closing costs also increase the effective interest rate on the loan by decreasing the amount of the principal available to the borrower. For example, if a company borrows $100,000 and pays 2% of the amount borrowed in the form of closing costs, after paying the closing costs, the company has increased its available cash by $98,000 ($100,000 − $100,000 × 0.02). Because the company is paying interest on the full $100,000, the interest rate it is paying on the increase in available cash of

GOOD FAITH ESTIMATE

Lender:			
Base Loan Amount:		$	75,000.00
Total Loan Amount:		$	75,000.00
Term			180 mo
Applicant(s):			
Interest Rate:			7.125%
Type of Loan:			Fixed
Preparation Date:			3/29/02

This Good Faith Estimate of closing costs is a sample form based upon HUD form HUD-1 Settlement Statement which the borrower receives at settlement. The charges are only estimates and may be more or less.

800	Items Payable in Connection with Loan:			1100	Title Charges:		
801	Loan Origination Fee 1.00 %	$	750.00	1101	Settlement or Closing Fee	$	100.00
802	Loan Discount Fee %	$		1102	Abstract or Title Search	$	
803	Appraisal Fee	$	250.00	1103	Title Examination	$	
804	Credit Report	$	20.00	1104	Title Insurance Binder	$	
805	Lender's Inspection Fee	$		1105	Document Preparation Fee	$	
806	Mortgage Insurance			1106	Notary Fee	$	
	Application Fee	$		1107	Attorney's Fee	$	
807	Assumption Fee	$		1108	Title Insurance	$	492.50
808	Mortgage Broker			1109	Lender's Coverage	$	
	Commission/Fee	$		1110	Owner's Coverage	$	
809	Tax Service Fee	$	104.00	1111	Endorsements	$	55.00
810	Processing Fee	$	200.00	1112	Reconveyance Fee	$	65.00
811	Underwriting Fee	$	85.00	1113	Other	$	
812	Wire Transfer Fee	$		1200	Transfer Charges:		
813	Courier Fee	$	35.00	1201	Recording Fee	$	35.00
814	Document Preparation Fee	$	100.00	1202	City/County Tax/Stamps	$	
815	Other	$		1203	State Tax/Stamps	$	
900	Items Required by Lender to Be Paid in Advance:			1204	Intangible Tax	$	
				1205	Other		
901	Interest for 15 days @	$		1300	Additional Settlement Charges:		
	$14.64 /day	$	219.60	1301	Survey	$	
902	Mortgage Insurance Premium	$		1302	Pest Inspection		
903	Hazard Insurance Premium	$		1303	Other	$	
904	County Property Taxes	$		Total Estimated Funds Needed to Close:			
905	Flood Insurance	$		Pay Off Existing Loans/Liens		$	72,612.80
906	Other	$		Estimated Closing Costs (Section 800,			
1000	Reserves Deposited with Lender:			900, 1100 to 1300)		$	2,511.10
1001	Hazard Insurance			Estimated Prepaid Items (Section			
	6 Months @ $ 29.17 /mo	$	175.02	1000)		$	835.97
1002	Mortgage Insurance			Other		$	
	5 Months @ $ 132.19 /mo	$	660.95	Estimated Funds Needed to Close		$	959.87
1003	City Property Taxes			Total Estimated Monthly Payment:			
	Months @ $ /mo	$		Principal and Interest		$	679.37
1004	County Property Taxes			Real Estate Taxes		$	132.19
	Months @ $ /mo	$		Hazard Insurance		$	29.17
1007	Flood Insurance			Flood Insurance		$	
	Months @ $ /mo	$		Mortgage Insurance		$	
1008	Other	$		Other		$	
				Total Estimate Monthly Payment		$	840.73

FIGURE 16-4 Good Faith Estimate

FIGURE 16-5   Cash Flow for
Loan

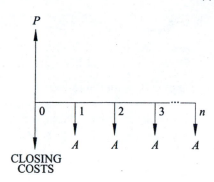

CLOSING
COSTS

$98,000 is greater than the yield on the loan. The cash flow for a loan with closing costs is shown in Figure 16-5.

The effective annual interest rate is calculated solving the following equation for i:

$$A = (P - \text{Closing Costs})[i(1 + i)^n]/[(1 + i)^n - 1] \qquad (16\text{-}15)$$

where

A = Monthly Payment
P = Principal
i = Periodic Interest Rate
n = Duration of Loan in Months

The effective annual interest rate may then be calculated from the periodic interest rate using Eq. (16-6).

Example 16-14:   The bank charges $2,500 for closing costs on a $100,000 loan with an annual percentage rate of 9% compounded monthly and a term of thirty years. The bank will not allow the closing costs to be added to the $100,000 borrowed. What effect do the closing costs have on the effective annual interest rate?

Solution: Using Eq. (16-3) to find the monthly interest rate we get the following:

$$i = 0.090/12 = 0.0075$$

Using Eq. (16-7) to find the monthly payments we get the following:

$$A = \$100,000[0.0075(1 + 0.0075)^{360}]/[(1 + 0.0075)^{360} - 1]$$
$$A = \$804.62$$

Substituting the monthly payments, closing costs, and loan principal into Eq. (16-15) we get the following:

$$\$804.62 = (\$100,000 - \$2,500)[i(1 + i)^{360}]/[(1 + i)^{360} - 1]$$

SIDEBAR 16-6

CALCULATING THE EFFECTIVE ANNUAL INTEREST RATE WITH CLOSING COSTS USING A TI BA II PLUS CALCULATOR

The effective annual interest rate for a loan with closing costs is calculated as follows. First you must calculate the monthly payment using the same five steps you used in Sidebar 16-2. Next you calculate the nominal interest rate that must be converted as was done in Sidebar 16-1. For this sidebar we use Example 16-14.

TASK	KEYSTROKES	DISPLAY	
1. Set Variables to Defaults	[2nd] [RESET] [ENTER]	RST	0.00
2. Enter Principal	100000 [PV]	PV=	100,000.00
3. Enter Annual Percentage Rate	9 [I/Y]	I/Y=	9.00
4. Enter Length of Loan		N=	360.00
in Months	360 [N]		
—OR—			
in Years	30 [2nd] [xP/Y] [N]		
5. Calculate Payment	[CPT] [PMT]	PMT=	−804.62
6. Enter Principal Less Closing Costs	(100000 [−] 2500) [PV]	PV=	97,500.00
7. Calculate APR	[CPT] [I/Y]	I/Y=	9.29
8. Store APR in Memory 1	[STO] 1		9.29
9. Select Interest Worksheet	[2nd] [ICONV]	NOM=	0.00
10. Clear Worksheet	[2nd] [CLR WORK]	NOM=	0.00
11. Enter APR	[RCL] 1 [ENTER]	NOM=	9.29
12. Calculate Effective Annual Yield	[↓] [CPT]	EFF=	9.69

This method may only be used when all of the payments are equal.

Solving for the periodic interest rate by trial and error we get the following:

$$i = 0.0077379 \text{ or } 0.77379\%$$

Using Eq. (16-6) to determine the effective annual interest rate we get the following:

$$i_a = (1 + 0.0077379)^{12} - 1 = 0.0969 \text{ or } 9.69\%$$

The increase in interest rate is due to both the effect of compound interest and the loan closing costs. Without the closing costs the effective annual interest rate could be calculated as follows, using Eq. (16-6):

$$i_a = (1 + 0.0075)^{12} - 1 = 0.0938 \text{ or } 9.38\%$$

The loan closing costs raised the effective annual interest rate from 9.38% to 9.69%.

FIGURE 16-6   Cash Flow for Loan with Shortened Life

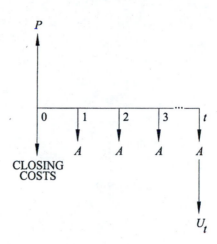

If the bank in Example 16-14 allowed the closing costs to be added to the loan, the principal of the loan would be increased by $2,500 to $102,500.

The effective annual interest rate in Example 16-14 is based on the assumption that the loan is paid off over its thirty-year term. The closing costs have an even greater effect if the loan is paid off early. The cash flow for a loan with closing costs, which is paid off early, is shown in Figure 16-6. The outstanding principal balance at the end of t months will be paid at the time payment t is made.

The effective annual interest rate is calculated for a loan that is paid off after month t by solving the following equation for periodic interest rate:

$$P = \text{Closing Costs} + A[(1 + i)^t - 1]/[i(1 + i)^t] + U_t/(1 + i)^t \qquad (16\text{-}16)$$

where

P = Principal
A = Monthly Payment
i = Periodic Interest Rate
t = Actual Duration of Loan in Months
U_t = Outstanding Principal Balance of the End of Month t

The derivation of Eq. (16-16) is found in Appendix C. The effective annual interest rate is then calculated from the periodic interest rate using Eq. (16-6). If there are penalties for paying off the loan early this formula may be used to find the periodic interest rate by adding the penalties to outstanding principal balance and then substituting the sum into Eq. (16-16) in place of U_t.

Example 16-15:   If the loan in Example 16-14 is paid off at the end of the fifth year (at the time of the 60th payment), what effect does this have on the effective annual interest rate?

Solution: At the time of the 60th payment we will also need to pay off the outstanding balance on the loan. To solve Eq. (16-16) we need P, A, U_t, i, and the closing costs. From Example 16-14 we find the following:

$$P = \$100,000.00$$
$$A = \$804.62$$
$$i = 0.0075 \text{ or } 0.75\%$$

and the closing costs are $2,500.00. Using Eq. (16-13) to find the outstanding principal balance we get the following:

$$U_t = \$804.62[(1 + 0.0075)^{(360-60)} - 1]/$$
$$[0.0075(1 + 0.0075)^{(360-60)}]$$
$$U_t = \$95,879.82$$

The outstanding principal balance is calculated at the monthly interest rate for the loan. Using Eq. (16-16) we get the following:

$$\$100,000 = \$2,500 + \$804.62[(1 + i)^{60} - 1]/[i(1 + i)^{60}]$$
$$+ \$95,879.82/(1 + i)^{60}$$

Solving for the periodic interest rate by trial-and-error we get the following:

$$i = 0.0080359 \text{ or } 0.80359\%$$

Using Eq. (16-6) to solve for the effective annual interest rate we get the following:

$$i_a = (1 + 0.0080359)^{12} = 0.1008 \text{ or } 10.08\%$$

If the loan were paid off after five years, the loan closing costs would have increased the effective interest rate from 9.38% to 10.08%.

Loan closing costs make it difficult to determine if it is worthwhile to change loans when loans with lower interest rates are available. One way of approaching the problem is to identify the interest rate at which the monthly payments for the new loan would be equal to the monthly payments for the existing loan. The monthly interest rate should be expressed as an annual percentage rate (APR) to be consistent with how banks specify interest rates on loans. If the interest rate of the new loan is less than the interest rate at which the monthly payments for the new loan are equal to the payments of the existing loan, then the new loan is financially attractive. If the interest rate of the new loan is equal to or greater than the interest rate at which the monthly payments for the new loan are equal to the payments of the existing loan, then the new loan will cost your company as much or more than the existing loan. For this comparison to work the new loan must have the same number and size of monthly payments as the current loan. The beginning principal for the new loan must include the unpaid balance on the existing loan plus the closing costs for the new loan. This is necessary because if we were to close out our existing loan and replace it with a new loan, the principal

CALCULATING THE EFFECTIVE ANNUAL INTEREST RATE WITH CLOSING COSTS WITH EARLY PAYOFF USING A TI BA II PLUS CALCULATOR

The effective annual interest rate for a loan with closing costs, which is paid off early, is calculated as follows. You cannot use the method in Sidebar 16-6 because the last payment includes paying off the loan. To do this you need to calculate the monthly payment as in Sidebar 16-2 and calculate the unpaid principal as in Sidebar 16-4. The payments and unpaid balance should be negative. For this sidebar we use Example 16-15.

	TASK	KEYSTROKES		DISPLAY
1.	Set Variables to Defaults	[2nd] [RESET] [ENTER]	RST	0.00
2.	Enter Principal	100000 [PV]	PV=	100,000.00
3.	Enter Annual Percentage Rate	9 [I/Y]	I/Y=	9.00
4.	Enter Length of Loan		N=	360.00
	in Months	360 [N]		
	—OR—			
	in Years	30 [2nd] [xP/Y] [N]		
5.	Calculate Payment	[CPT] [PMT]	PMT=	−804.62
6.	Store Payment in Memory 1	[STO] 1		−804.62
7.	Select Amortization Worksheet	[2nd] [AMORT]	P1=	1.00
8.	Enter the Payment	60 [ENTER]	P1=	60.00
		[↓] 60 [ENTER]	P2=	60.00
9.	View Balance	[↓]	BAL=	95,880.34
10.	Store Unpaid Balance in Memory 2	[STO] 2	BAL	95,880.34
11.	Select Cash Flow Worksheet	[CF]	CFo=	0.00
12.	Enter Principal Less Closing Costs	(100000 [−] 2500) [ENTER]	CFo=	97,500.00
13.	Enter All but Last Monthly Payment	[↓] [RCL] 1 [ENTER]	CF1=	−804.62
		[↓] 59 [ENTER]	F01=	59.00
14.	Enter Last Payment	[↓] ([RCL] 1[−] [RCL] 2) [ENTER]	CF2=	−96,684.96
15.	Calculate Monthly Interest Rate	[IRR] [CPT]	IRR=	0.80
16.	Store Interest Rate in Memory 3	[STO] 3	IRR	0.80
17.	Clear Worksheet	[CE/C] [CE/C]		0.80
18.	Convert to Effective Annual Interest Rate	[RCL] 3 [/] 100 [+] 1 [=]		1.01
		[y^x] 12 [=]		1.10
		[−] 1 [=]		0.10
		[×] 100 [=]		10.08

of the new loan would need to pay off the existing loan and cover the closing costs on the new loan to maintain the company's available cash at its current level. If the principal on the new loan only paid off the existing loan, paying the closing costs on the new loan would reduce the company's available cash. These calculation are shown in the following example.

Example 16-16: Your company has an existing loan with monthly payments—principal and interest—of $1,100.00. There are 60 payments left on the loan and the loan has an unpaid balance of $55,000.00. Your company is looking at the possibility of replacing this loan with a loan with closing costs of $1,590.00. At what interest rate would this become attractive?

Solution: To replace this loan with another loan while maintaining your company's available cash at the same level, a loan for $56,590.00 ($55,000.00 + $1,590.00) would need to be secured. Using Eq. (16-7) and setting the new loan's payment equal to the payment of the existing loan we get the following:

$$\$1,100.00 = \$56,590.00[i(1 + i)^{60}]/[(1 + i)^{60} - 1]$$

Solving for the periodic interest rate by trial-and-error we get the following:

$$i = 0.0051884 \text{ or } 0.51884\%$$

CALCULATING INTEREST RATE WHERE REPLACING A LOAN BECOMES ATTRACTIVE USING A TI BA II PLUS CALCULATOR

The annual percentage rate at which it becomes attractive to replace a loan that includes closing costs is calculated as follows. For this sidebar we use Example 16-16.

TASK	KEYSTROKES	DISPLAY	
1. Set Variables to Defaults	[2nd] [RESET] [ENTER]	RST	0.00
2. Enter Unpaid Balance Plus Closing Costs	(55000 [+] 1590) [PV]	PV=	56,590.00
3. Enter Payment	1100 [+/−] [PMT]	PMT=	−1,100.00
4. Enter Length of Loan		N=	60.00
in Months	60 [N]		
—OR—			
in Years	5 [2nd] [xP/Y] [N]		
5. Calculate Interest Rate	[CPT] [[I/Y]	I/Y=	6.23

The annual percentage rate is found by solving Eq. (16-3) for r as follows:

$$r = 0.0051884(12) = 0.0623 \text{ or } 6.23\%$$

In the above calculations, the monthly payments include only the principal and interest. The payments exclude money placed in escrow to pay for insurance and property tax. These are not costs associated with the loan but with owning property.

Short-Term Loans

Short-term loans are loans with a term of one year or less. Simple interest is often used in lieu of compound interest when calculating the interest on a short-term loan. It is common for the interest on short-term loans to be paid at the time the loan is acquired. This is known as discounting the interest. For example, if you were to take out a $100,000 loan with a term of one year and an interest rate of 10%, the lending institution would take $10,000 out of the loan when it was opened as the interest payment and you would receive the remaining $90,000. Because the interest has already been paid, only the principal needs to be paid off at the end of the loan. In the previous example, you would have to pay the lending institution $100,000 at the end of the year. The cash flow for this loan is shown in Figure 16-7.

Discounting interest increases the effective annual interest rate paid on the loan by decreasing the amount of the principal available to the borrower and requiring the interest to be paid at the beginning of the loan. We can determine the effective annual interest rate for a loan where the interest is discounted using the following equation:

$$i = [P/(P - I)] - 1 \tag{16-17}$$

where

i = Period Interest Rate
P = Principal
I = Total Interest Paid

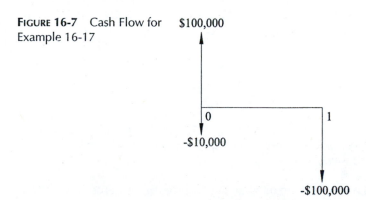

FIGURE 16-7 Cash Flow for Example 16-17

The derivation of Eq. (16-17) is found in Appendix C. The total interest paid on the loan is determined by Eq. (16-1) or (16-2). From this periodic interest rate we may calculate the effective annual interest rate.

Example 16-17: Determine the effective annual interest rate on a $100,000 short-term loan, with a term of one year and a nominal interest rate of 10%. The bank discounts the interest.

Solution: Using Eq. (16-1) to find the total interest paid on the loan we get the following:

$$I = \$100,000(0.10)1 = \$10,000$$

The interest on the loan is $10,000 and will be deducted from the loan proceeds at the time the loan is acquired, leaving the borrower with $90,000 as the net proceeds from the loan. Using Eq. (16-17) to find the periodic interest rate we get the following:

$$i = [\$100,000/(\$100,000 - \$10,000)] - 1$$
$$i = 0.1111 \text{ or } 11.11\%$$

In the absence of any other fees, we can use Eq. (16-6) to get the effective annual interest rate.

$$i_a = (1 + 0.1111)^1 - 1 = 0.1111 \text{ or } 11.11\%$$

We see that when the term of the short-term loan is one year the interest rate calculated from Eq. (16-17) is the same as the effective annual interest rate and we need not perform the last step. This is only the case when the length of the loan is one year, in other words c equals 1.

If there are closing costs associated with the short-term loan they may be added to the total interest paid and used in Eq. (16-16).

Example 16-18: The loan in Example 16-17 has an origination fee of $2,000. Determine the effective annual interest rate on the loan.

Solution: From Example 16-17 the total interest paid on the loan is $10,000. The total of the interest paid and the closing costs—the loan origination fee—on the loan is $12,000 ($10,000 + $2,000) and is substituted into Eq. (16-16) to find the periodic interest rate as follows:

$$i = [\$100,000/(\$100,000 - \$12,000)] - 1$$
$$i = 0.1364 \text{ or } 13.64\%$$

Because the loan length is one year, the effective annual interest rate equals the periodic interest rate; therefore, the effective annual interest rate is 13.64%.

Short-term loans that pay compound interest are evaluated in the same manner as long-term loans.

SIDEBAR 16-9

CALCULATING THE EFFECTIVE ANNUAL INTEREST ON A SIMPLE-INTEREST LOAN WITH DISCOUNTED INTEREST USING A TI BA II PLUS CALCULATOR

The effective annual interest on a simple-interest loan for which the interest is discounted is calculated as follows. First you must calculate the interest due at the beginning of the loan. For this sidebar we use Example 16-17.

TASK	KEYSTROKES		DISPLAY
1. Set Variables to Defaults	[2nd] [RESET] [ENTER]	RST	0.00
2. Store Principal in Memory 1	100000 [STO] 1		100,000.00
3. Calculate Interest Due	[x] 10 [%] [=]		10,000.00
4. Store Interest in Memory 2	[STO] 2		10,000.00
5. Select Cash Flow Worksheet	[CF]	CFo=	0.00
6. Enter Principal Less Interest	([RCL] 1 [−] [RCL] 2) [ENTER]	CFo=	90,000.00
7. Enter Payment	[↓] [RCL] 1 [+/−] [ENTER]	CF1=	−100,000.00
8. Calculate Monthly Interest Rate	[IRR] [CPT]	IRR=	11.11

LINES OF CREDITS

A line of credit consists of a lender committing to loan a borrower up to a specified amount of money on an as needed basis. The borrower may borrow up to the limit of the line of credit one week and pay it off the next week. Lines of credit are used to finance short-term fluctuations in cash flows. The borrower pays interest on the amount of funds borrowed at any given time. The interest rate on a line of credit is usually a variable rate that changes frequently. Interest is usually accrued monthly for lines of credits. Lines of credit may use a monthly interest rate as calculated by Eq. (16-3) using twelve equal periods per year or a monthly interest rate as calculated by Eq. (16-4), taking into account the number of days in each period. To calculate the monthly interest, the average daily balance is multiplied by the monthly interest rate by using the following formula:

$$I_t = ADB_t(i) \qquad\qquad (16\text{-}18)$$

where

$$I_t = \text{Interest Due for Period } t$$
$$i = \text{Periodic Interest Rate}$$
$$ADB_t = \text{Average Daily Balance for Period } t$$

The average daily balance is calculated by summing the daily balances for a period and dividing the sum by the number of days in the period. The monthly interest may be calculated using the average daily balance.

Example 16-19:   How much interest would be charged on a line of credit that charges a monthly interest rate of 1.1% if the average daily balance for the month was $55,100?

Solution: Using Eq. (16-18) to calculate the interest for the month we get the following:

$$I = \$55,100.00\,(0.011) = \$606.10$$

Granting a line of credit requires a lender to commit funds to the line of credit without knowing how much money will be borrowed over the life of the line of credit. Committing these funds to a line of credit prevents the lender from committing the funds to other loans and requires the funds to be invested in less profitable, short-term investments. Two provisions—compensating balance and commitment fee—are often used in lines of credit to compensate the lender for committing these funds.

Compensating Balance

The first provision is to require that percentage of the maximum amount that may be borrowed from the line of credit be placed in a low- or non-interest-bearing account. This is known as a compensating balance. A typical compensating balance is 10%. For example, if you were to set up a $10,000 line of credit with a requirement that a 10% compensating balance be placed in a non-interest-bearing savings account, $1,000 would need to be placed in the savings account leaving $9,000 from the line of credit available for use by your company. From the time the line of credit was set up your company would be paying interest on the $1,000 compensating balance even though you could not use the money. The compensating balance reduces the funds available from the line of credit and increases the effective annual interest rate. The effect the compensating balance has on the actual interest rate is dependent on the amount of money borrowed against the line of credit. In the above example, if the average daily balance were $1,000, we would be using $1,000 and paying interest on $2,000, effectively doubling the interest rate. If the average daily balance increased to $2,000, you would be using $2,000 and paying interest on $3,000. This increases the effective interest rate by 50%. Hence, the more you use the line of credit the smaller the impact of the compensating balance. The requirement for a compensating balance also acts as a deterrent against a company obtaining an excessively large or unneeded line of credit.

When determining the effective annual interest rate for a line of credit, the rate needs to be based on the proceeds from the line of credit used to fund operations and exclude the uses of cash that are associated with the line of credit. The costs associated with the line of credit include interest on the line of credit and the compensating balance. Just as was done with long-term loans, we are interested in finding out what the effective annual interest rate is that a company is paying for the additional capital that is available for daily operations. Each month when interest is paid on the line of credit, this interest payment reduces the cash available for operations and increases the amount of money that is needed to borrow from the line of credit. For example, if a company's operations needed a constant $4,000 from a $10,000 line of credit for three consecutive months and the line of credit required a 10% compensating balance and had a monthly interest rate of 1% collected monthly, the first month the average daily balance would be $5,000, the $4,000 plus a compensating balance of $1,000. The second month the average daily balance would be the $4,000 and the $1,000 compensating balance plus the first month's interest. The first month's interest would be an additional $50 ($5,000.00 × 0.01) for an average daily balance for the second month of $5,050. The first month's interest may be paid out of operating costs, thus increasing the need to borrow against the line of credit to cover our operating costs, or the interest may be paid out of the line of credit. The third month, the average daily balance would be the previous month's balance of $5,050.00 plus the second month's interest. The second month's interest would be an additional $50.50 ($5,050.00 × 0.01) for an average daily balance for the third month of $5,100.50. The third month's interest would be $51.00 ($5,100.50 × 0.01). The total interest paid during the three months would be $150.50. Although the average daily balance for the three months for the line of credit was $5,050.17, the average daily balance of the increase in available cash was only the $4,000. To borrow this $4,000 the company paid $150.50 of interest.

The interest on the line of credit may be calculated as it was in the previous example. The interest paid during the year on the line of credit may be approximated by substituting the yield for the line of credit into Eq. (16-18) in place of i. Unless the average daily balance for each of the months is equal, this is only an approximation. The use of the yield takes into account the increase in the line of credit average daily balance due to the monthly payment of interest.

Example 16-20: Determine the effective annual interest rate on a $50,000 line of credit with an annual percentage rate of 12% compounded monthly. The bank requires a 10% compensating balance be placed in a non-interest-bearing account. The average daily balance is anticipated to be $25,000, excluding the compensating balance and interest due on the line of credit.

Solution: Using Eq. (16-5), we get a yield for the line of credit of the following:

$$i_a = (1 + 0.12/12)^{12} - 1 = 0.12683 \text{ or } 12.683\%$$

The lender requires that 10% of the $50,000 line of credit or $5,000 be placed in a non-interest-bearing account. The average daily balance, including the compensating balance, is $30,000 ($25,000 + $5,000). The interest for the year can be estimated using Eq. (16-18) as follows:

$$I = \$30,000.00(0.12683) = \$3,804.90$$

The interest rate paid on the funds used from the line of credit ($25,000) is calculated by solving Eq. (16-18) for i_a and using the average daily balance of the funds available for operations as follows:

$$i_a = \$3,804.90/\$25,000.00 = 0.15220 \text{ or } 15.220\%$$

In essence, the effective annual interest rate has been increased by over 2.5% (15.220 − 12.683) by the compensating balance.

Example 16-21:   How would the effective annual interest rate change for Example 16-20 if the average daily balance were increased to $35,000?

Solution: From Example 16-20, the yield for the line of credit is 12.683% and the compensating balance is $5,000. The average daily balance, including the compensating balance, is $40,000 ($35,000 + $5,000). The interest for the year can be estimated using Eq. (16-18) as follows:

$$I = \$40,000.00(0.12683) = \$5,073.20$$

The interest rate paid on the funds used from the line of credit ($35,000) is calculated by solving Eq. (16-18) for i_a and using the average daily balance of the funds available for operations as follows:

$$i_a = \$5,073.20/\$35,000.00 = 0.14495 \text{ or } 14.495\%$$

From Examples 16-20 and 16-21 we can see the effect that the compensating balance has on the effective annual interest rate is less dramatic when we use a greater portion of the line of credit. This is due to the fact that the interest being paid on the compensating balance is spread over a larger average daily balance.

Once the line of credit has been set up and interest is being paid on the compensating balance, the cost to borrow additional funds from the line of credit is equal to the yield on the line of credit. In Example 16-21 an additional $10,000 was borrowed that cost an additional $1,268.30 ($5,073.20 − $3,804.90) in interest. The interest rate on these additional funds was 12.683% ($1,268.30/$10,000.00), which is equal to the yield on the line of credit.

Sometimes the compensating balance is placed in an interest-bearing account.

Example 16-22:   Determine the actual annual interest rate on a $50,000 line of credit with an annual percentage rate of 12% compounded monthly. The bank requires that a 10% compensating balance be placed in an interest-bearing account that pays an annual percentage rate of 2% compounded monthly. The average daily balance is anticipated to be $35,000, excluding the compensating balance and interest due on the line of credit.

Solution: Using Eq. (16-5), we get a yield for the line of credit of the following:

$$i_a = (1 + 0.12/12)^{12} - 1 = 0.12683 \text{ or } 12.683\%$$

Using Eq. (16-5), we get a yield for the interest bearing account of the following:

$$i_a = (1 + 0.02/12)^{12} - 1 = 0.02018 \text{ or } 2.018\%$$

The lender requires that 10% of the $50,000 line of credit or $5,000 be placed in an interest-bearing account. The average daily balance for the line of credit, including the compensating balance, is $40,000 ($35,000 + $5000). The interest paid on the line of credit for the year can be estimated using Eq. (16-18) as follows:

$$I = \$40,000.00(0.12683) = \$5,073.20$$

The interest received from the compensating balance is calculated using Eq. (16-18) as follows:

$$I = \$5,000.00(0.02018) = \$100.90$$

The net interest paid on both accounts is as follows:

$$I = \$5,073.20 - \$100.90 = \$4,972.30$$

The interest rate paid on the funds available for use from the line of credit ($35,000) is calculated by solving Eq. (16-18) for i_a and using the average daily balance of the funds available for operations as follows:

$$i_a = \$4,972.30/\$35,000.00 = 0.14207 \text{ or } 14.207\%$$

From Examples 16-21 and 16-22 we can see that the higher the interest rate paid on the compensating balance, the lower the effective annual interest rate was on the line of credit.

Commitment Fee

The second provision is to require that the borrower pay a percentage on the unused balance. This percentage is often 1/2 to 1%. This is known as a commitment fee.

For example, if a company were to set up a $10,000 line of credit with a 1% commitment fee and an annual percentage rate of 8% and the average daily balance were $4,000, the company would pay 8% on the $4,000 and 1% on the unused $6,000. Like the compensating balance, the commitment fee acts as a deterrent against obtaining an excessively large line of credit. The commitment fee also increases the effective annual interest rate. The effect of the commitment fee on the effective annual interest rate is dependent on the amount of money borrowed against the line of credit. The commitment fee uses the same compounding periods as the annual percentage rate on the line of credit.

Example 16-23: Determine the effective annual interest rate on a $50,000 line of credit with an annual percentage rate of 12% compounded monthly. The bank requires a 1% commitment fee be paid on the unused balance of the line of credit. The average daily balance is anticipated to be $25,000.

Solution: Using Eq. (16-5), we get a yield for the line of credit of the following:

$$i = (1 + 0.12/12)^{12} - 1 = 0.12683 \text{ or } 12.683\%$$

Using Eq. (16-5), for the unused portion of the line of credit we get a yield of the following:

$$i = (1 + 0.01/12)^{12} - 1 = 0.01005 \text{ or } 1.005\%$$

The interest paid on the borrowed funds over one year are estimated using Eq. (16-18) as follows:

$$I = \$25,000(0.12683) = \$3,170.75$$

The average daily balance of unused funds equals $50,000 less the average daily balance of the used funds or $25,000. The interest paid on the unused portion of the line of credit over one year is estimated using Eq. (16-18) as follows:

$$I = \$25,000(0.01005) = \$251.25$$

The total interest paid equals the following:

$$I = \$3,170.75 + \$251.25 = \$3,422.00$$

The effective annual interest rate paid on the funds available for use from the line of credit ($25,000) is calculated by solving Eq. (16-18) for i_a and using the average daily balance of the funds available for operations as follows:

$$i_a = \$3,422.00/\$25,000 = 0.13688 \text{ or } 13.688\%$$

In essence, the effective annual interest rate has been increased by 1.005% (13.688 − 12.683) by the commitment fee.

Example 16-24:   How would the effective annual interest rate change for Example 16-23 if the average daily balance were increased to $35,000?

Solution: From Example 16-23 the yield for the line of credit is 12.683% and the yield for the unused portion of the line of credit is 1.005%. The interest paid on the borrowed funds over one year is estimated using Eq. (16-18) as follows:

$$I = \$35,000(0.12683) = \$4,439.05$$

The average daily balance of unused funds equals $50,000 less the average daily balance of the used funds or $15,000. The interest paid on the unused portion of the line of credit over one year is estimated using Eq. (16-18) as follows:

$$I = \$15,000(0.01005) = \$150.75$$

The total interest paid equals the following:

$$I = \$4,439.05 + \$150.75 = \$4,589.80$$

The interest rate paid on the funds available for use from the line of credit ($35,000) is calculated by solving Eq. (16-18) for i_a and using the average daily balance of the funds available for operations as follows:

$$i_a = \$4,589.80/\$35,000 = 0.13114 \text{ or } 13.114\%$$

In essence, the effective annual interest rate has been increased by about 0.43% (13.114% − 12.683%) by the commitment fee.

From Examples 16-23 and 16-24 we can see that the effect of the commitment fee on the effective annual interest rate is less dramatic when we use a greater portion of the line of credit. This is due to the fact that the interest being paid as a commitment fee is smaller and is spread over a larger amount of funds used in the company's operations.

Once the line of credit has been set up and interest is being paid on the compensating balance, the cost to borrow additional funds from the line of credit is equal to the yield on the line of credit less the yield of the commitment fee. In Example 16-24 we borrowed an additional $10,000 that cost an additional $1,167.80 ($4,589.80 − $3,422.00) for an effective annual interest rate of 11.678% ($1,167.80/$10,000). This interest rate is the same as the yield on the line of credit (12.683%) less the yield of the commitment fee (1.005%).

Fixed fees on lines of credit can be handled in the same manner as closing costs on loans. When selecting between lines of credit, all fees, closing costs, compensating balances, and commitment fees as well as the interest rate may be incorporated into the effective annual interest rate. The lines of credits may be compared based on this effective annual interest rate. For example, if we could choose between the line of credit in Example 16-21, Example 16-22, and Example 16-24, we would choose the line of credit in Example 16-24 because it has the lowest effective annual interest rate.

Another common provision in a line of credit is that the line of credit must be paid off for one or two months during the year. This prevents the borrower from using the line of credit to finance capital equipment and requires careful financial planning on the part of the borrower to meet this obligation.

LEASING

Leasing is an alternate to financing equipment and real property through loans. Under a lease, the lessor or landlord retains ownership of the equipment or property during the life of the lease along with any tax benefits from the depreciation of the equipment or property. At the end of the lease, the ownership of the equipment or property may transfer to the company leasing the equipment or property.

Leases are divided into two types, capital leases and operating leases. A lease must be classified as a capital lease if it is noncancelable and meets at least one of the following conditions: (1) the lease extends for 75% or more of the equipment or property's useful life, (2) ownership transfers at the end of the lease, (3) ownership is likely to transfer at the end of the lease through a purchase option with a heavily discounted price, or (4) the present value of the lease payments at market interest rates exceeds 90% of the fair market value of the equipment or property. All cancelable leases and noncancelable leases that fail to meet all four of the above conditions may be considered operating leases. The key difference between capital leases and operating leases is that capital leases must be recognized on the financial statements as liability the same as a loan. An operation lease is not recorded on the financial statements and is often referred to as off-balance-sheet financing because it is a form of financing that does not show up on the balance sheet. Off-balance-sheet financing can be used to improve a company's financial ratios.

Because the tax consequences are different for leases than they are for loans, taxes must be taken into account when comparing leases to loans. Comparison between loans and leases is discussed in chapter 18.

TRADE FINANCING

Another source of short-term financing and probably the most common source of financing for a construction company is trade financing. Trade financing occurs whenever there is a delay between the supplying of material, labor, and equipment to a construction project and the payment for these items. When this happens, the supplier or subcontractors are providing financing to the project in the amount of the materials, labor, and equipment supplied for the time between the delivery of these items and the payment of the bill. We saw extensive use of trade financing in chapters 12 and 14.

When a general contractor pays bills from suppliers and subcontractors prior to being paid by the project's owner for the associated work, the general contractor begins providing financing to the project's owner. For these reasons, it is often in the general contractor's best interest to minimize the amount of financing that is provided to the project's owner. This is often done by arranging for suppliers and subcontractors to wait to be paid until the owner pays the general contractor for the work. This may be included in contracts and supplier agreements in the form of a "Paid when Paid" clause. A paid when paid clause ties the payment of supplier and subcontractor bills to a specified number of days after the general contractor has received payment for the bills in the form of unrestricted funds from the owner. It is not uncommon for a general contractor to finance the majority of a construction project through trade financing rather than their own operating capital.

Some suppliers and subcontractors may offer a discount to construction companies who pay their bill early. Suppliers may provide discounts to improve their cash flows, to reduce their need for operating capital, or to reduce their bill collecting costs. The effective annual interest rate on early payments is calculated by the following formula:

$$i_a = [\text{Discount}\%/(100\% - \text{Discount}\%)](365/\#\,\text{of Days Early}) \qquad (16\text{-}19)$$

where

Discount % = Discount Offered by the Supplier or Subcontractor

\# of Days Early = Number of Days Early the Bill Is Paid

i_a = Effective Annual Interest Rate

This effective annual interest rate of the discount can be compared to the cost to obtain the funds to pay the bills to determine if it is financially advantageous to pay the bills early.

Example 16-25:   A supplier has offered your company a 1% discount for all bills that are paid 10 days after they are billed. The bills would normally be due 30 days after they are billed. What is the return on paying the bills early? If your company can borrow funds from a line of credit at a yield of 14%, is it financially attractive to pay the bills early? The line of credit requires a compensating balance.

Solution: The effective annual interest rate is calculated as follows:

$$i_a = [1.00\%/(100\% - 1.00\%)][365/(30 - 10)] = 18.43\%$$

From Examples 16-20 and 16-21 we saw that the cost to borrow additional funds from a line of credit was equal to the yield on the line of credit when the line of credit is required to have a compensating balance. Because the effective annual interest rate of 18.43% is greater than the yield on the line of credit at 14%, it is financially advantageous to pay the bills early. The saving on the bills will more than offset the interest costs.

To take advantage of trade discounts, the company's accounting system must process bills weekly and be able to identify those bills that offer discounts for early payment.

Although it is financially advantageous to put off paying a bill as long as possible, it is important to pay bills on time to maintain a good credit rating. Suppliers and subcontractors often discontinue extending trade credit or increasing prices to contractors who have a history of slow bill paying. The extra interest earned by putting off paying bills can be quickly offset by a loss of trade credit or by having to pay less favorable prices because your company is a poor credit risk.

CREDIT CARDS

Credit cards may be used to provide a source of financing. Most credit cards do not charge interest on purchases, provided the monthly balance is paid in full by the due date. Credit cards can provide a cheap source of very short-term financing provided the bills are paid in full each month. Because the bills are usually due 20 to 25 days from the date the bill is prepared, items purchased may be financed for up to 55 days interest free, depending on when they are purchased. For example, if you purchased a new copier for your offices on the day after your credit card company prepared its monthly bill, it would be a month before you received a bill for the copier. If the bill was due 20 days after the date the bill was prepared and you paid the bill a few days before the due date, you would have financed the copier for about a month and a half interest free. This time would be reduced to a half a month or so if you purchased the copier just in time for the copier to be billed on the monthly bill. This lag between the date a purchase is made and the date interest is charged is known as a grace period and applies only to those card holders who pay their bill in full each month. Credit cards are a good substitute to trade financing with companies that are not set up to extend financing to your company, provided the bill is paid in full each month.

If the bill is not paid in full, interest is charged based on the average daily balance in the same manner interest is charged on lines of credit. When the balance is not paid in full, the grace period is ignored and interest is charged from the date of the purchase. The interest rate on credits cards is usually much higher than the interest rate on lines of credit and other debit instruments. Credit cards are an expensive source of financing if the bill is not paid in full each month.

SELECTING A BANKER

The most important thing to consider in selecting a banker is to find a banker that you can work with. A little extra interest paid by one bank will not mean much if you cannot get a line of credit or loan that is needed for you to expand your operations. When selecting a bank, be sure that the bank will be responsive to your needs. Here are some things to keep in mind when selecting a banker.

First, bankers like to deal with the complete package. They want your checking account, savings account, certificates of deposit, lines of credits, and loans all with their institution. One reason for this is that it is easier for them to monitor your financial status if all your accounts are with their bank. This is particularly important if they have loaned funds to your company.

Second, some banks specialize in the construction industry. Banks that specialize in the construction industry will be more aware of the unique financial structure and needs of the construction industry.

Third, small banks may be more suitable for a small construction company because they are often more flexible and can offer more personalized service. However, small banks' funds are often more limited, as is their line of services. For this reason, large construction companies often have to look to larger banks to meet their financial needs.

Fourth, choose a bank in a convenient location. Running the deposits to a bank in an out-of-the-way location can waste a lot of time and money.

APPLYING FOR A LOAN

When applying for a loan, it is important for a company to ask the lending institution for the funds it wants rather than leaving it guessing as to what funds are needed. The request should include the amount, duration, and purpose for the loan.

Before a lending institution grants a company a loan or extends a line of credit, the bank want to know that the company is a good credit risk and has the capacity to pay off the debt along with its interest. To determine if a company is good credit risk, the lending institution requests that the company submit an application along with supporting documentation for review. The supporting documentation often includes the following:

Tax Returns: Federal tax returns for the past three years.

Financial Statements: Company financial statements for the past three years. Often the lending institution will require that the financial statements be reviewed or audited by a certified public accountant (CPA). Auditing financial statements provides a more stringent review of the documentation that supports the financial statements than does a review. Having a company's financial statements audited is also more expensive than having them reviewed. If the loan is being guaranteed by a third party or has a personal endorsement, financial statements for the third party will also be required for the past three years.

Work on Hand Report: A report detailing all work on hand, including all work-in-progress, all projects completed in the past twelve months, as well as all potential jobs for the next twelve months. Potential jobs are those jobs for which the contractor was the low bidder but has not been notified that the work has been awarded and jobs that are being negotiated that have a significant chance of being awarded. The status of each of the potential jobs should be clearly and accurately stated in the work on hand report.

Overhead Budget: Overhead budget for the next year. The overhead budget should detail the anticipated costs of operating the construction company for the next year. All costs not associated with specific projects should be included in the overhead budget.

Annual Cash Flow Projection: Cash flow projections for the company for the next year. The purpose of the cash flow projection is to determine if the company has the ability to repay the debt along with its associated interest during the next year. The cash flow projections should be consistent with the work on hand report and the overhead budget.

Project Pro Forma: Project pro forma, including the cash flow projections for the next several years. This is only required if the proceeds from the loan are being used to finance a project or capital facility. The purpose of the pro forma is to determine if the project or capital facility has ability to repay the debt along with its associated interest. The pro forma should cover the entire life of the debt to be serviced.

Business Plan: A business plan detailing how the company will be operated. The business plan should demonstrate management's ability to run the company in a professional manner.

References: Business and trade references that can vouch for the company's payment history.

When applying for a loan, remember the bank is in the business of lending money and it needs to lend money to people and companies who will pay the money back along with interest. Careful preparation of the application package and the associated document will improve your chances of successfully obtaining a loan.

FINANCIAL DOCUMENTS

All financial documents should be carefully read and understood before they are signed. The financial documents are legally binding contracts between the borrower and the lending institution. Concerns about any of the provision in the documents should be reviewed by a professional familiar with financial documents, such as an attorney or certified public accountant.

CONCLUSION

Debt financing is a major source of funding for construction companies. Debt financing includes loans, lines of credit, leases, trade financing, and credit cards. Interest on financing is divided into two types, compound interest and simple interest. Compound interest pays interest on the previous period's interest, whereas simple interest ignores the effects of compound interest. Simple interest is used only on short-term loans. Compound interest is used for long-term loans, lines of credit, credit cards, and trade financing. Compound interest rates are quoted in terms of annual percentage rate (APR) or annual percentage yield (APY). The annual percentage rate ignores the effects of compound interest, whereas the annual percentage yield includes the effects of compound interest. Loan provisions and closing costs may be incorporated into the loan's effective annual interest rate, which may be used to compare the attractiveness of different types of debt financing. During the early years of a loan most of the loan payment is used to pay the interest, whereas during the last years of the loan most of the loan payment is used to reduce the principal. An amortization schedule details how loan payments are divided between interest and principal and how the principal is reduced over time. When obtaining debt financing, the duration of the financial instrument should be matched to the length of the financial need. This is known as maturity matching.

PROBLEMS

1. Determine the interest due on an $85,000 short-term loan, with a term of 300 days and a simple interest rate of 8%.

2. Determine the interest due on a $15,000 short-term loan, with a term of 90 days and a simple interest rate of 11.5%.

3. Determine the quarterly, monthly, and daily interest rates for an annual percentage rate of 10%.

4. Determine the quarterly, monthly, and daily interest rates for an annual percentage rate of 7%.

5. Determine the interest rate for a billing period with 31 days for a loan that charges an annual percentage rate of 9%.

6. Determine the interest rate for a billing period with 30 days for a loan that charges an annual percentage rate of 11.5%.

7. Determine the annual percentage yield for an annual percentage rate of 10% for quarterly and monthly compounding periods.

8. Determine the annual percentage yield for an annual percentage rate of 7% for quarterly and monthly compounding periods.

9. Determine the annual percentage yield for a loan that charges a monthly interest rate of 1.5% and compounds the interest monthly.

10. Determine the annual percentage yield for a loan that charges a monthly interest rate of 3.2% and compounds the interest quarterly.

11. Determine the monthly payment for a thirty-year real estate loan with an annual percentage rate of 8.5% and an initial principal of $200,000. How much interest is paid over the life of the loan?

12. Determine the monthly payment for a sixty-month truck loan with an annual percentage rate of 11% and an initial principal of $17,000. How much interest is paid over the life of the loan?

13. The real estate in Problem 11 is to be purchased with a fifteen-year loan with an annual percentage rate of 8.5%. What is the difference in the monthly payments for the fifteen-year and thirty-year loans? How much does using the fifteen-year loan save in interest?

14. The truck in Problem 12 is to be purchased with a forty-eight-month loan with an annual percentage rate of 11%. What is the difference in the monthly payments for the forty-eight-month and sixty-month loans? How much does using a forty-eight-month loan save in interest?

15. For the loan in Problem 11, determine the monthly interest for the first and second months and the outstanding principal at the end of the first and second months.

16. For the loan in Problem 12, determine the monthly interest for the first and second months and the outstanding principal at the end of the first and second months.

17. Determine the outstanding principal balance on the loan in Problem 11 after 120 payments have been made.

18. Determine the outstanding principal balance on the loan in Problem 12 after 20 payments have been made.

19. How much interest do the borrowers in Problem 11 pay during the tenth year of the loan?

20. How much interest do the borrowers in Problem 12 pay during the second year of the loan?

21. The bank charges $4,000 for closing costs on a $200,000 loan with an annual percentage rate of 8.5% compounded monthly with a term of thirty years. The bank will not allow the closing costs to be added to the $200,000 borrowed. What effect do the closing costs have on the effective annual interest rate?

22. The bank charges $500 for closing costs on a $17,000 loan with an annual percentage rate of 11% compounded monthly with a term of five years. The bank will not allow the closing costs to be added to the $17,000 borrowed. What effect do the closing costs have on the effective annual interest rate?

23. If the loan in Problem 21 is paid off at the end of the tenth year (at the time of the 120th payment) what effect does this have on the effective annual interest rate?

24. If the loan in Problem 22 is paid off at the end of the thirtieth month (at the time of the 30th payment) what effect does this have on the effective annual interest rate?

25. Your company has an existing loan with monthly payments, principal and interest, of $1,888.59. There are 120 payments left on the loan and the loan has an unpaid balance of $155,660.00. Your company is looking at the possibility of replacing this loan with a loan that has estimated closing costs of $3,300.00. At what interest rate would this become attractive?

26. Your company has an existing loan with monthly payments, principal and interest of $1,883.65. There are 48 payments left on the loan and the loan has an unpaid balance of $74,269.00. Your company is looking at the possibility of replacing this loan with a loan that has estimated closing costs of $1,900.00. At what interest rate would this become attractive?

27. Determine the effective annual interest rate on a $75,000 short-term loan, with a term of one year and a nominal interest rate of 12%. The bank discounts the interest.

28. Determine the effective annual interest rate on a $100,000 short-term loan, with a term of 245 days and a nominal interest rate of 8%. The bank discounts the interest.

29. How would the effective annual interest rate for Problem 27 change if the bank charged a 1% loan origination fee?

30. How would the effective annual interest rate for Problem 28 change if the bank charged $1,000 in closing costs?

31. How much interest would be charged on a line of credit that charges a monthly interest rate of 0.75% if the average daily balance for the month were $26,200?

32. How much interest would be charged on a line of credit that charges a monthly interest rate of 0.96% if the average daily balance for the month were $75,000?

33. Determine the actual annual interest rate on a $100,000 line of credit with an annual percentage rate of 10% compounded monthly. The bank requires that a 5% compensating balance be placed in an interest-bearing account that pays an annual percentage rate of 1.5% compounded monthly. The average daily balance is anticipated to be $75,000, excluding the compensating balance and interest due on the line of credit.

34. Determine the actual annual interest rate on a $40,000 line of credit with an annual percentage rate of 12% compounded monthly. The bank requires that a 10% compensating balance be placed in an interest-bearing account that pays an annual percentage rate of 1.25% compounded monthly. The average daily balance is anticipated to be $25,000, excluding the compensating balance and interest due on the line of credit.

35. Determine the effective annual interest rate on an $85,000 line of credit with an annual percentage rate of 9.25% compounded monthly. The bank requires that a 2% commitment fee be paid on the unused balance of the line of credit. The average daily balance is anticipated to be $70,000.

36. Determine the effective annual interest rate on a $25,000 line of credit with an annual percentage rate of 8.75% compounded monthly. The bank requires that a 1.5% commitment fee be paid on the unused balance of the line of credit. The average daily balance is anticipated to be $10,000.

37. A supplier has offered your company a 0.5% discount for all bills that are paid 10 days after they are billed. The bills would normally be due 30 days after they are billed. What is the return on paying the bills early? If your company can borrow funds from a line of credit at a yield of 8%, is it financially attractive to pay the bills early? The line of credit requires a compensating balance.

38. A supplier has offered your company a 1% discount for all bills that are paid 15 days after they are billed. The bills would normally be due 45 days after they are billed. What is the return on paying the bills early? If your company can borrow funds from a line of credit at a yield of 13%, is it financially attractive to pay the bills early? The line of credit requires a compensating balance.

39. Set up a spreadsheet that will calculate the monthly periodic rate and the monthly payment from the annual percentage rate, principal, and the term of the loan in months.

40. Prepare an amortization schedule for Problem 11. Use the same format as was used in Figure 16-2.

41. Prepare an amortization schedule for Problem 12. Use the same format as was used in Figure 16-2.

42. Prepare an amortization schedule for Problem 13. Use the same format as was used in Figure 16-2.

43. Prepare an amortization schedule for Problem 14. Use the same format as was used in Figure 16-2.

44. Prepare an amortization schedule for a sixty-month car loan with an annual percentage rate of 11% and an initial principal of $17,000. The monthly interest rate is based on the number of days in the month multiplied by the daily interest rate. The loan is originated on 10 January 2005 and the payments are due on the tenth of each month. If the payment date falls on a Saturday or Sunday, then the payment is due the following Monday. Use the same format as was used in Figure 16-3.

MAKING FINANCIAL DECISIONS

In this section we look at ways to quantitatively analyze financial decisions. This section includes the following chapters:

TOOLS FOR MAKING FINANCIAL DECISIONS

In this chapter you learn ten quantitative methods that may be used to analyze financial alternatives and to choose the alternative that is best for the company. Without some quantitative method it is often hard for managers to determine which option is best. An understanding of these skills is a necessity for any manager who has to decide where to invest limited capital.

Financial decisions can be viewed as the selection of one or more alternatives from a pool of alternatives. The pool of alternatives may include independent alternatives, mutually exclusive alternatives, contingent alternatives, and the "do nothing" alternative.

Independent alternatives are alternatives where the acceptance of one alternative does not, in and of itself, preclude the selection of the other alternatives. For example, investing part of your surplus capital in heavy equipment does not preclude investing the remaining portion of your surplus capital in a real estate development. Provided there is sufficient capital, you can invest in both of these alternatives.

Mutually exclusive alternatives are alternatives where the acceptance of one of the alternatives precludes investing in the other alternatives. For example, if your company needs to purchase a single backhoe and has narrowed the selection down to three backhoes, when your company purchases one of the backhoes, the need for a backhoe has been fulfilled and the purchase of a second backhoe is no longer an option. Once you have selected one of the three alternatives, the other two alternatives are no longer viable.

Contingent alternatives are alternatives that may be selected only after another alternative has been selected. For example, if your company is looking at purchasing a dump truck and as a second alternative purchasing a dumping trailer to be pulled behind the dump truck, the purchase of the dumping trailer is a contingent alternative because for the dumping trailer to be useful, you must first purchase the dump truck.

The "do nothing" alternative is simply another way of saying that all of the alternatives have been rejected.

Decisions are limited not only by the types of alternatives in the pool but also by external constraints. A common external constraint is the limited supply of capital. With a limited supply of capital, there may be a dozen independent alternatives, but a company may invest in only a fraction of the alternatives because there is not enough capital to invest in all of the alternatives. Another common external constraint is contractual obligations. If a company has a contract to perform excavation work that requires the use of a special backhoe attachment—which the company does not own—management must make a decision that makes the attachment available for use on the contract. When making decisions, both the external constraints and available alternatives must be taken into account.

To use the quantitative methods described in this chapter, one must reduce all decisions to a set of mutually exclusive alternatives. When deciding whether to invest in a single alternative, the decision has two mutually exclusive alternatives: investment in the alternative and the "do nothing" alternative; in other words, reject the alternative. In this situation, the manager must decide if the alternative meets the minimum requirement for profitability. When deciding between mutually exclusive alternatives, the manager must decide which of the alternatives is most financially advantageous while meeting the external constraints. If investment in none of the alternatives is an option, the "do nothing" alternative should be included in the pool of alternatives.

When faced with a decision, which includes contingent or independent alternatives, the decision must be reduced to a set of mutually exclusive alternatives before the alternative may be analyzed quantitatively. This is done by listing all of the possible combinations of alternatives and eliminating infeasible alternatives. A combination of alternatives is infeasible when they (1) contain two or more mutually exclusive alternatives, (2) contain a contingent alternative without containing the alternative that the contingent alternative is contingent on, or (3) do not meet the requirements of the external factors. Converting the decision to a set of mutually exclusive alternatives containing all feasible combinations of alternatives reduces the decision-making process to the selection of a single, best combination of alternatives from a group of all feasible combinations of alternatives. The conversion of alternatives to mutually exclusive alternatives is shown in Example 17-1.

Example 17-1: A manager has up to $200,000 available to invest in new construction equipment for a construction company. The potential new construction equipment has been reduced to the alternatives shown in Table 17-1. The manager must purchase a backhoe to complete an existing contract. A second backhoe is not needed. Prepare a list of the mutually exclusive alternatives and identify which alternatives are not feasible.

TABLE 17-1 Alternatives

No.	Description	Cost ($)
1	Backhoe 1	100,000
2	Backhoe 2	120,000
3	Dump Truck	65,000
4	Dumping Trailer for the Dump Truck	25,000

Solution: Here the manager is faced with two external constraints: The capital available for investment is $200,000 and only one backhoe needs to be purchased. For the manager to analyze the alternatives quantitative, the alternatives must be converted to a group of mutually exclusive combinations of the alternatives that include only the feasible alternatives. Alternatives 1 and 2 are mutually exclusive in that only one backhoe is needed. Alternatives 1 and 3 are independent as are Alternatives 2 and 3. Alternative 4 is contingent on the purchase of Alternative 3. Combinations of the alternatives that do not include Alternative 1 or 2 are unacceptable because the manager must purchase a backhoe. Combinations of the alternatives that include both Alternatives 1 and 2 are unacceptable because the manager needs to purchase only one backhoe, not two. Combinations of the alternatives that include Alternative 4 but do not include Alternative 3 are unacceptable because Alternative 4 is continent on the selection of Alternative 3. Combinations of alternatives that cost more than $200,000 are unacceptable because they exceed the capital available for investment. Table 17-2

TABLE 17-2 Combination of Alternatives

Alternatives	Acceptable	Reasoning
Do nothing	No	Does not contain 1 or 2
1	Yes	
2	Yes	
3	No	Does not contain 1 or 2
4	No	Does not contain 1 or 2
1 and 2	No	Selects both 1 and 2
1 and 3	Yes	
1 and 4	No	Selects 4 without 3
2 and 3	Yes	
2 and 4	No	Selects 4 without 3
3 and 4	No	Does not contain 1 or 2
1, 2 and 3	No	Selects both 1 and 2
1, 2 and 4	No	Selects both 1 and 2
1, 3 and 4	Yes	
2, 3 and 4	No	Exceeds budget
1, 2, 3 and 4	No	Selects both 1 and 2, exceeds budget

contains a list of all possible combinations of alternatives and identifies those that are acceptable.

Thus, the alternatives are reduced to five mutually exclusive combinations of alternatives. These five combinations now may be quantitatively analyzed.

When making decisions, the decision maker may make each decision separately or group them together into one more complex decision. The manager in Example 17-1 has three decisions to make: which backhoe to purchase from Alternatives 1 and 2; should the company invest in a dump truck; and, if the company invests in a dump truck, should it invest in a dumping trailer? The strength of making each of these decisions separately is the simplicity of each of the decisions. In each case there are only two alternatives to select between: Do we purchase Backhoe 1 or Backhoe 2, do we invest in a dump truck or do we do nothing, and do we invest in a dumping trailer or do we do nothing? The weakness of making each of these decisions separately is that the manager does not try to invest the limited supply of capital in the most profitable alternatives but simply selects from the available alternatives for each of the decisions. This may result in a manager choosing to invest in an alternative because it meets the minimum requirements for profitability, only to have to pass up a second, more profitable alternative because of the lack of capital, capital that would have been available if the manager had not chosen to invest in the first alternative. For example, if the manager in Example 17-1 decides to purchase Backhoe 2 because it is more profitable than Backhoe 1, it precludes the manager from investing in the dumping trailer. The most profitable combination may be to purchase Backhoe 1, the dump truck, and the dumping trailer; however, this option has been eliminated because of the decision to purchase Backhoe 2.

By combining the decisions as to which backhoe to purchase, whether to purchase a dump truck, and whether to purchase a dumping trailer into one decision, the profit on the available cash may be optimized. The strength of combining decisions into one decision is that interaction between the decisions is taken into account to reach the best combination of decisions. The weakness of combining decisions into one decision is that the complexity of the decision increases. The number of combinations of alternatives is usually greater than the number of alternatives. In Example 17-1, it has increased from four to five. It is not always possible to combine all of the decisions into one complex decision, but where possible combining decisions will lead to more profitable decisions.

When faced with a decision, a decision maker must decide which alternatives, if any, are the most financially advantageous for the company. A number of quantitative methods have been developed to assist the decision maker in comparing the alternatives. All of the qualitative methods discussed in this chapter are based on some measure of equivalence. Because equivalence is a function of the sizes of the cash flows, the timing of the cash flows, and the interest rate, to qualitatively compare alternatives, we must eliminate two of the variables. In this chapter, we look at qualitative methods that compare alternatives using each of

TABLE 17-3   Qualitative Methods

Method	Basis of Comparison
Net Present Value	Size of Cash Flows
Incremental Net Present Value	Size of Cash Flows
Future Worth	Size of Cash Flows
Annual Equivalent	Size of Cash Flows
Rate of Return	Interest Rate
Incremental Rate of Return	Interest Rate
Capital Recover with Interest	Time
Payback Period without Interest	Time
Payback Period with Interest	Time
Project Balance	Size of Cash Flows and Time

the three variables while eliminating the other two. The methods covered in this chapter along with their basis of comparison are shown in Table 17-3.

To quantitatively evaluate each of the mutually exclusive combinations of alternatives, cost must be assigned to each alternative. These costs should be identified as accurately as possible. One must keep in mind that the results of the quantitative analysis are only as good as the data used in the analysis. Often the data used in the quantitative analysis are estimates of cash flows occurring years in the future and can easily change based on economic and political environment at the time these cash flows occur.

To use the equations in chapter 15 to perform quantitative analysis, one must assume that all cash flows incurred during a period occur at the end of the period. When using a period length of one year in the analysis, one ignores the interest on the cash flow for part of a year. The accuracy of the analysis can be increased by shortening the period from years to months; however, this increase in accuracy requires that all cash flows must be tied to the shorter periods. This change in period length can increase the data by twelvefold and greatly increase the complexity of the calculations. In most cases, the increase in error as a result of trying to guess at which month the cash flow will occur combined with the error introduced by estimating future costs on a monthly basis has a much greater impact on the accuracy of the results than is gained analyzing the alternative on a monthly basis rather than an annual basis. Unless future cash flows can be accurately projected as to their size and timing—for example, they are set forth by contract—using a period of one year for the analysis produces the best results.

SUNK COSTS

Costs that have already been spent are known as sunk costs. Sunk costs also include all costs that have been committed to be spent for which the commitment cannot be canceled. When analyzing investment alternatives, sunk costs should not be included because they must be paid regardless of which alternative is chosen. For example, if a company has just spent $10,000 on an engine overhaul for a front-end loader and is now looking at replacing the loader versus continuing to use the loader, one would not include the cost of the engine overhaul in the alternative that continues to use the loader. This is because the cost of the engine overhaul has been incurred and will still be a cost regardless of which of the two alternatives are chosen. However, if the front-end loader was in need of an engine overhaul and a company was looking at replacing the loader versus continuing to use the loader, one would include the cost of the engine overhaul in the alternative that continues to use the loader. This is because the cost of the engine overhaul has not been incurred and will only be incurred if the company continues to use the loader.

MARR (MINIMUM ATTRACTIVE RATE OF RETURN)

When comparing alternatives based on the size of the cash flow or time, the variable of interest rate must be eliminated from the equivalence equation. To do this one must determine at what interest rate equivalence will be established. Additionally, when deciding whether to proceed with an investment based on the interest rate paid on the investment (also known as the return on investment), one must have a minimum acceptable interest rate to act as a cutoff point. The interest rate used in determining equivalence during the decision-making process and the interest rate used as the minimum acceptable interest rate is known as the minimum attractive rate of return or MARR. The MARR is the lowest rate of return or interest paid by an investment that is acceptable to the investor. The MARR is different for each company.

The MARR is based on the cost of capital plus a profit. For a company that has to borrow money to make investments, the cost of capital is the effective annual interest rate at which the money will have to be borrowed. For example, if a company were looking at replacing a backhoe by taking out a loan, the cost of capital would be the effective annual interest rate on the loan. For a company that will use existing funds to make investments, the cost of capital is the effective annual interest rate on financial instruments that it would store the funds in if it did not make the investment. For example, if a company were looking at replacing a backhoe by turning in a certificate of deposit, the cost of capital is the effective annual interest rate paid on the certificate of deposit. In this case, if the company were to replace the backhoe, rather than paying interest on a loan, it would lose the interest it would have received on the certificate of deposit. This loss of interest is known as the opportunity cost. By replacing the backhoe, the company has lost the opportunity to invest in and receive the interest from the certificate of deposit. The MARR should always be above the company's cost of capital. If the MARR is below the cost of capital, the company is paying or losing more in interest than is generated by investments meeting the MARR and the company would be better off financially not making the investment.

Determining the cost of capital is relatively easy when dealing with financial instruments with fixed interest rates. When dealing with financial instruments with variable interest rates, the cost of capital must include any anticipated changes in the interest rate.

The second component of the MARR is profit. Suppose you were given two options to invest your savings. The first option is government-backed Treasury bonds that pay a guaranteed interest rate of 4% and have little risk of loss. The second option is to invest in a real estate development that is expected to pay an interest rate of 4% but has a significant risk of loss of the invested funds. Which would you invest in? Most people would invest in the Treasury bonds because why risk losing your money on the real estate investment when you can earn the same interest rate on the Treasury bonds? To make the second investment attractive, the potential for increased profits or returns are needed to offset the risk. Determining the desired return level is quite subjective and is often set by management. The MARR should be set at a rate at which the company has many opportunities to invest. Setting the MARR too high will result in the company passing up many good investments. Setting the MARR too low will result in the company making too many bad or marginal investments.

Given that the MARR is the sum of the cost of capital and the subjective profit markup, the MARR is calculated using the following equation:

$$\text{MARR} = \text{Cost of Capital} + \text{Profit Margin} \qquad (18\text{-}1)$$

Example 17-2: Determine the MARR for a company that can borrow funds at 8.5% and requires 7% profit margin or return.

Solution: The MARR is determined by using Eq. (18-1):

$$\text{MARR} = 8.5\% + 7\% = 15.5\%$$

ADJUSTING LIFE SPANS

When comparing alternatives based on the size of the cash flow or interest rate, the variable of time must be eliminated from the equivalence equation. To do this, not only do all cash flows need to be converted to a common point or set of points in time but also the life spans of the alternatives must be equal. Failure to compare the alternatives over equal life spans ignores what happens to the shorter alternative at the end of its life.

Study Period

The time over which alternatives are compared is known as the study period. Determining the study period is as difficult as determining the MARR. The study period is selected in one of the following ways:

1. The study period may be set by company policy. For example, a company may have a policy that all investments are compared over a five-year period.
2. The study period may be matched to the life of one of the investments. A common practice is to match the study period to alternative with either the

longest or shortest life; however, the study period may be set to the life of one of the other alternatives.

3. The study period may be set to the least common denominator of the alternative lives. Using this method allows one to assume that they continue purchasing each of the alternatives until their lives end at the same point in time. The least common denominator is the smallest number when divided by the useful lives of each of the alternatives results in a whole number. For example, when comparing alternatives that have lives of 3 years, 4 years, and 6 years, the least common dominator is 12 years. A period of less than 6 years does not cover the life of at least one of the alternatives. When divided by a period of 4 years, 6 years does not produce a whole number. Numbers between 7 and 11 years do not produce whole numbers when divided by 6 years. Twelve years produces the whole numbers of 4, 3, and 2 when divided by 3, 4, and 6 years, respectively.

4. The study period may be set based on the length of a need. For example, if the company needs to purchase some earthmoving equipment to fulfill its obligation on a highway project with an expected duration of four years, the study period could be set to the life of the project.

The logical next question is, "How long of study period should I use?" There are no clear-cut answers to this question. Depending on your assumptions, different methods may lead to different results. Where possible one should try to match actual conditions as closely as possible. Using a study period equal to the least common denominator and repurchasing the alternative is a good solution if one is trying to set a policy as to how often a company is going to replace its computers, such as every two years or every three years. However, it would not be a suitable method to determine which computer a company should purchase for a three-year project. For this type of problem, one should match the study period to the life of the project.

There are three methods of adjusting the lives of the alternatives so they are equal.

Shortening an Alternative's Life

The life of an investment may be shortened by assuming a price at which the alternative may be sold at the end of the shortened life. This assumed sale price is known as the salvage value. For example, a company needs to purchase a computer and the company has narrowed the choices down to two alternatives. The first alternative is to purchase a computer costing $1,000 with a useful life of two years. The second alternative is to purchase a computer costing $1,500 with a useful life of three years. If the study period were two years, one would shorten the life of the more expensive computer to two years by assuming a salvage value for the more expensive computer at the end of the second year. The cash flows for both computers using a two-year study period are shown in Figure 17-1.

Figure 17-1 Cash Flow for Computers with a Two-Year Study Period

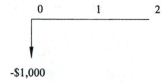

-$1,000

CHEAP COMPUTER

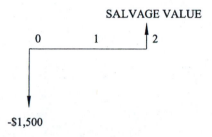

SALVAGE VALUE

-$1,500

EXPENSIVE COMPUTER

Because these cash flows now cover the same period of time, they may be compared based on equivalence. The weakness of this method is that it assumes a salvage value, which may or may not reflect the value of the asset at the end of the study period.

Lengthening an Alternative's Life

The life of an investment may be lengthened by increasing the maintenance costs of the alternative or investing money into the alternative to upgrade it. For example, the computers in Figure 17-1 could be compared with a three-year study period by lengthening the life of the less expensive computer to three years by adding the cost to upgrade the computer at the end of the second year. The cash flows for both computers using a three-year study period are shown in Figure 17-2.

Because these cash flows now cover the same period of time, they may be compared based on equivalence. The weakness of this method is that it assumes a maintenance or upgrade cost, which may or may not reflect the actual costs.

Repurchase an Alternative

The life of an investment may be lengthened by repurchasing the alternative until the study period is equaled or exceeded. If the study period is exceeded, a salvage value may be assumed to allow the life of the alternative to equal the study period. For example, the computers in Figure 17-1 could be compared with a six-year study period by repeatedly purchasing the cheaper computer three times over the six-year period and the more expensive computer two times over the same six-year period. The cash flows for both computers using a six-year study period are shown in Figure 17-3.

FIGURE 17-2   Cash Flow for Computers with a Three-Year Study Period

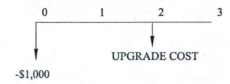

CHEAP COMPUTER

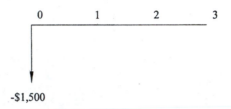

EXPENSIVE COMPUTER

Because these cash flows now cover the same period of time, they may be compared on equivalence. If the same two computers were evaluated over an eight-year period, the cheaper computer would be purchased four times during the study period and the expensive computer would be purchased three times during the study period. At the end of the study period the expensive computer would still have one year left in its useful life; therefore, its life would have to be reduced by including the salvage value at the end of the eighth year. The cash flows for both computers using an eight-year study period are shown in Figure 17-4.

Because these cash flows now cover the same period of time, they may be compared based on equivalence. The weakness of this method is that it assumes that we can repeatedly purchase the same item, with the same cash flows in the future. This is often not the case. Investments and products change over time. Let's look at different qualitative methods for analyzing decisions.

FIGURE 17-3   Cash Flow for Computers with a Six-Year Study Period

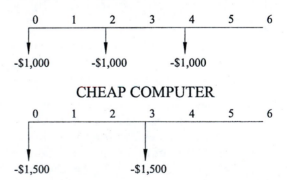

CHEAP COMPUTER

EXPENSIVE COMPUTER

FIGURE 17-4 Cash Flow for
Computers with an Eight-
Year Study Period

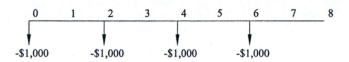

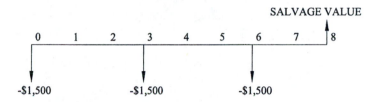

NET PRESENT VALUE OR PRESENT WORTH

The net present value (NPV) or present worth method compares alternatives based
on their present values at the time of the initial investment at the MARR. The net
present value is calculated by determining the equivalent value of the cash receipts
and disbursements at the time of the initial investment using the equations in
chapter 15. If the net present value is positive, the alternative produces a return
greater than the MARR. If the net present value is zero, the alternative produces a return equal to the MARR. If the net present value is negative, the alternative produces
a return less than the MARR and, if possible, the investment should be rejected.

Example 17-3: Your company is looking at purchasing a front-end loader
at a cost of $120,000. The loader would have a useful life of five years with
a salvage value of $12,000 at the end of the fifth year. The loader can be
billed out at $95.00 per hour. It costs $30.00 per hour to operate the front-
end loader and $25.00 per hour for the operator. Using 1,200 billable hours
per year determine the net present value for the purchase of the loader using a MARR of 20%. Should your company purchase the loader?

Solution: The hourly profit on the loader equals the billing rate less the
operation cost and the cost of the operator. The hourly profit is calculated as
follows:

Hourly Profit = $95.00 − $30.00 − $25.00 = $40.00 per hour

The annual profit on the loader equals the hourly profit times the number
of billable hours per year and is calculated as follows:

Annual Profit = $40.00/hour(1,200 hours/year) = $48,000/year

The cash flow for the purchase of the loader in Example 17-3 is shown in
Figure 17-5.

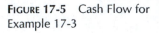

FIGURE 17-5 Cash Flow for
Example 17-3

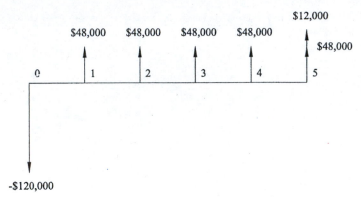

The present value of the annual profits (P_{AP}) is determined by using Eq. (15-9) as follows:

$$P_{AP} = \$48,000[(1 + 0.20)^5 - 1]/[0.20(1 + 0.20)^5] = \$143,549$$

The present value of the annual profit is positive because it is a cash receipt.
The present value of the salvage value (P_{SV}) is determined by using Eq. (15-3) as follows:

$$P_{SV} = \$12,000/(1 + 0.20)^5 = \$4,823$$

The present value of the salvage value is positive because it is a cash receipt.
The present value purchase price (P_{PP}) of the loader is equal to the purchase price because the net present value is measured at the time of the initial investment. The present value of the purchase price is negative because it is a cash disbursement.

The net present value for purchasing the loader equals the sum of the present values of the individual cash flows and is calculated as follows:

$$NPV = \$143,549 + \$4,823 + (-\$120,000) = \$28,372$$

Because the net present value is greater than zero, the purchase of the front-end loader will produce a return greater than the MARR and your company should invest in the front-end loader.

When comparing two alternatives with positive net present values, the alternative with the largest net present value produces the most profit in excess of the MARR.

Example 17-4: Your company is looking at purchasing a front-end loader and has narrowed the choice down to two loaders, the loader in Example 17-3 and a smaller, less powerful loader that costs $110,000. The smaller loader would have a useful life of five years with a salvage value of $10,000 at the end of the fifth year. The smaller loader can be billed out at $90.00 per hour. It costs $28.00 per hour to operate the smaller front-end loader and $25.00 per hour for the operator. Using 1,200 billable hours per year determine the net present

CALCULATING THE NET PRESENT VALUE USING A TI BA II PLUS CALCULATOR

The net present value is calculated as shown below. For this sidebar we use Example 17-3.

TASK	KEYSTROKES	DISPLAY	
1. Set Variables to Defaults	[2nd] [RESET] [ENTER]	RST	0.00
2. Select Cash Flow Worksheet	[CF]	CFo=	0.00
3. Enter Cash Flow at Time Zero	120000 [+/−] [ENTER]	CFo=	−120,000.00
4. Enter Next Four Cash Flows	[↓] 48000 [ENTER]	CF1	48,000.00
	[↓] 4 [ENTER]	F01=	4.00
5. Enter Last Cash Flow	[↓] 60000 [ENTER]	CF2=	60,000.00
	[↓] 1 [ENTER]	F02=	1.00
6. Enter Interest Rate	[NPV]	I=	0.00
	20 [ENTER]	I=	20.00
7. Calculate Present Value	[↓] [CPT]	NPV=	28,371.91

In this example the keystrokes for entering all variables are shown to provide a generic example that can be used for any problem by changing the numbers entered into the calculator. If the display is already shown as indicated you may type [↓] to continue to the next step.

value for the purchase of the smaller loader using a MARR of 20%. Should your company invest in the smaller loader or the loader in Example 17-3?

Solution: The hourly and annual profits on the smaller loader are calculated in the same manner as they were in Example 17-3 and are as follows:

Hourly Profit = $90.00 − $28.00 − $25.00 = $37.00 per hour

Annual Profit = $37.00/hour(1,200 hours/year) = $44,400/year

The present value of the annual profits and the salvage value are determined by using Equations (15-9) and (15-3) as follows:

$$P_{AP} = \$44,400[(1 + 0.20)^5 - 1]/[0.20(1 + 0.20)^5] = \$132,783$$
$$P_{SV} = \$10,000/(1 + 0.20)^5 = \$4,019$$

The net present value for purchasing the loader is calculated as follows:

$$NPV = \$132,783 + \$4,019 + (-\$110,000) = \$26,802$$

The net present value for purchasing the larger loader in Example 17-3 is $28,372. Because the larger loader has a higher net present value, it is a better financial alternative and your company should purchase the larger loader.

TABLE 17-4   Interest Accumulation on $10,000

YEAR	BEGINNING BALANCE ($)	INTEREST ($)	ENDING BALANCE($)
1	10,000	2,000	12,000
2	12,000	2,400	14,400
3	14,400	2,880	17,280
4	17,280	3,456	20,736
5	20,736	4,147	24,883

When comparing two investments that require different initial investments, the underlying assumption is that the difference between the initial investments is invested at the MARR. In Example 17-4, the difference in purchase price between the two pieces of equipment was $10,000. Had this money been invested at the MARR of 20% compounded annually, it would have been worth $24,883 at the end of the fifth year. The interest accumulation on the $10,000 is shown in Table 17-4.

The present value of $24,883 in five years at an interest rate of 20% is calculated using Eq. (15-3) as follows:

$$P = \$24,883/(1 + 0.20)^5 = \$10,000$$

In the analysis of the smaller loader, one could have included an additional $10,000 investment at 20% occurring at the time the loader was purchased, which represents the difference in the purchase price of the two loaders. This investment would generate a cash receipt in the fifth year of $24,883. The present value of this cash receipt is $10,000 and will offset the initial $10,000 investment, leaving the net present value unchanged. Had the difference in purchase prices been invested at a rate other than the MARR, the cash receipt would not have offset the initial investment and the net present value would have changed. Investing the difference in purchase prices in an investment with a return less than the MARR would decrease the net present value, whereas investing the difference in purchase prices in an investment with a return greater than the MARR would increase the net present value.

Some cash flows include only cash disbursements or costs. In this case, the net present value is often referred to as the net present cost. Only cost may be used when the alternatives provide similar services or revenues. For example, when selecting a computer for your office staff, it would be very hard to determine the revenues associated with the purchase of the computer. As long as the computers being compared provide similar benefits they may be compared based on costs. This eliminates the need to estimate revenues and greatly simplifies the calculations. With only costs in the cash flow, the net present cost will always be negative. Here, the objective is to minimize the net present cost or choose the alternative with the least net present cost.

Example 17-5:   Your company needs to purchase a new furnace and has narrowed the choices down to two furnaces. The first furnace cost $3,000 and has an estimated annual operation cost of $1,050. The second furnace cost $3,500 and has an estimated annual operation cost of $950. The estimated life of both furnaces is fifteen years. Using a MARR of 15%, what is the net present cost of each of these furnaces? Which furnace should your company purchase?

Solution: The cash flows for the two furnaces in Example 17-5 are shown in Figure 17-6.

The present value of the annual costs (P_{AC}) for the first furnace is determined by using Eq. (15-9) as follows:

$$P_{AC} = -\$1,050[(1 + 0.15)^{15} - 1]/[0.15(1 + 0.15)^{15}]$$
$$P_{AC} = -\$6,140$$

The present value of the purchase price of the first furnace is equal to the purchase price because the net present value is measured at the time of the initial investment. The net present cost of purchasing the first furnace is calculated as follows:

$$NPV = P_{AC} + P_{PP} = -\$6,140 + (-\$3,000) = -\$9,140$$

The present value of the annual costs for the second furnace is determined by using Eq. (15-9) as follows:

$$P_{AC} = -\$950[(1 + 0.15)^{15}-1]/[0.15(1 + 0.15)^{15}] = -\$5,555$$

The present value purchase price of the second furnace is equal to the purchase price. The net present cost of purchasing the second furnace is calculated as follows:

$$NPV = P_{AC} + P_{PP} = -\$5,555 + (-\$3,500) = -\$9,055$$

Your company should purchase the second furnace because it has the least net present cost.

FIGURE 17-6 Cash Flows for Example 17-5

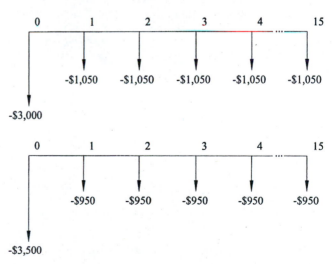

Selection of the study period can have a great effect on the results of a net present value analysis. Because different study periods require different adjustments in the life spans and these adjustments require different assumptions, it is not uncommon to get conflicting results when selecting between two alternatives while analyzing them with different study periods. A longer study period may favor one of the options, whereas a shorter study period may favor another option.

Let's look at a few examples in which the purchase of a new dump truck is compared to the purchase of a used dump truck. The new dump truck has a useful life of seven years. The used dump truck has a useful life of four years. In the first example the study period will be matched to the useful life of the new dump truck and the used dump truck will be overhauled to extend its life to seven years.

Example 17-6: Your company needs to purchase a dump truck and has narrowed the selection down to two alternatives. The first alternative is to purchase a new dump truck for $65,000. At the end of the seventh year the salvage value of the new dump truck is estimated to be $15,000. The second alternative is to purchase a used dump truck for $50,000. At the end of the fourth year the used dump truck will need an overhaul, which is estimated to cost $20,000. At the end of the seventh year the salvage value of the used dump truck is estimated to be $5,000. The annual profits, revenues less operation costs, are $17,000 per year for either truck. Using a MARR of 18% and a seven-year study period, calculate the net present value for each of the dump trucks. Which truck should your company purchase?

Solution: The present value of the annual profits for either truck is determined by using Eq. (15-9) as follows:

$$P_{AP} = \$17,000[(1 + 0.18)^7 - 1]/[0.18(1 + 0.18)^7] = \$64,796$$

The present value of the salvage value for the new dump truck is determined by using Eq. (15-3) as follows:

$$P_{SV} = \$15,000/(1 + 0.18)^7 = \$4,709$$

The net present value for the purchase of the new dump truck is calculated as follows:

$$NPV = \$64,796 + \$4,709 + (-\$65,000) = \$4,505$$

The present value of the overhaul (P_O) and the salvage value for the used dump truck are determined by using Eq. (15-3) as follows:

$$P_O = -\$20,000/(1 + 0.18)^4 = -\$10,316$$
$$P_{SV} = \$5,000/(1 + 0.18)^7 = \$1,570$$

The net present value for the purchase of the used dump truck is calculated as follows:

$$NPV = \$64,796 + (-\$10,316) + \$1,570 + (-\$50,000) = \$6,050$$

The used truck has the highest NPV; therefore, your company should purchase the used truck.

In the second example the study period will be matched to the useful life of the used dump truck.

Example 17-7: Your company needs to purchase a dump truck and has narrowed the selection down to two alternatives. The first alternative is to purchase a new dump truck for $65,000. At the end of the fourth year the salvage value of the new dump truck is estimated to be $40,000. The second alternative is to purchase a used dump truck for $50,000. At the end of the fourth year the salvage value of the used dump truck is estimated to be $5,000. The annual profits, revenues less operation costs, are $17,000 per year for either truck. Using a MARR of 18% and a four-year study period, calculate the net present value for each of the dump trucks. Which truck should your company purchase?

Solution: The present value of the annual profits for either truck is determined by using Eq. (15-9) as follows:

$$P_{AP} = \$17,000[(1 + 0.18)^4 - 1]/[0.18(1 + 0.18)^4] = \$45,731$$

The present value of the salvage value for the new dump truck is determined by using Eq. (15-3) as follows:

$$P_{SV} = \$40,000/(1 + 0.18)^4 = \$20,632$$

The net present value for the purchase of the new dump truck is calculated as follows:

$$NPV = \$45,731 + \$20,632 + (-\$65,000) = \$1,363$$

The present value of the salvage value for the used dump truck is determined by using Eq. (15-3) as follows:

$$P_{SV} = \$5,000/(1 + 0.18)^4 = \$2,579$$

The net present value for the purchase of the used dump truck is calculated as follows:

$$NPV = \$45,731 + \$2,579 + (-\$50,000) = -\$1,690$$

The new truck has the highest NPV; therefore, your company should purchase the new truck.

In Examples 17-6 and 17-7 we see that we selected different alternatives because of the different estimated cash flows used in the net present value analysis.

Let's look at another example. In this example each truck will be repurchased until their useful lives end during the same year, which will occur in the twenty-eighth year.

Example 17-8: Your company needs to purchase a dump truck and has narrowed the selection down to two alternatives. The first alternative is to purchase a new dump truck for $65,000. At the end of the seventh year the salvage value of the new dump truck is estimated to be $15,000. The second alternative is to purchase a used dump truck for $50,000. At the end of the fourth year the salvage value of the used dump truck is estimated to be $5,000. The annual profits, revenues less operation costs, are $17,000 per year for either truck. Using a MARR of 18% and a twenty-eight year study period, calculate the net present value for each of the dump trucks. Which truck should your company purchase?

Solution: The present value of the annual profits for either truck is determined by using Eq. (15-9) as follows:

$$P_{AP} = \$17,000[(1 + 0.18)^{28} - 1]/[0.18(1 + 0.18)^{28}] = \$93,527$$

The present value of the salvage values for the new dump truck is determined by summing the present value of salvage values occurring in years 7, 14, 21, and 28. The present value for each salvage value is calculated using Eq. (15-3) as follows:

$$P_{SV7} = \$15,000/(1 + 0.18)^7 = \$4,709$$
$$P_{SV14} = \$15,000/(1 + 0.18)^{14} = \$1,478$$
$$P_{SV21} = \$15,000/(1 + 0.18)^{21} = \$464$$
$$P_{SV28} = \$15,000/(1 + 0.18)^{28} = \$146$$
$$P_{SV} = \$4,709 + \$1,478 + \$464 + \$146 = \$6,797$$

The present value of the purchase prices for the new dump truck is determined by summing the present value of purchase prices occurring in years 0, 7, 14, and 21. The present value for each purchase price is calculated using Eq. (15-3) as follows:

$$P_{PP0} = -\$65,000/(1 + 0.18)^0 = -\$65,000$$
$$P_{PP7} = -\$65,000/(1 + 0.18)^7 = -\$20,405$$
$$P_{PP14} = -\$65,000/(1 + 0.18)^{14} = -\$6,406$$
$$P_{PP21} = -\$65,000/(1 + 0.18)^{21} = -\$2,011$$
$$P_{PP} = -\$65,000 + (-\$20,405) + (-\$6,406) + (-\$2,011)$$
$$P_{PP} = -\$93,822$$

The net present value for the purchase of the new dump truck is calculated as follows:

$$NPV = \$93,527 + \$6,797 + (-\$93,822) = \$6,502$$

The present value of the salvage values for the used dump truck is determined by summing the present value of salvage values occurring in years 4, 8, 12, 16, 20, 24, and 28. The present value for each salvage value is calculated using Eq. (15-3) as follows:

$$P_{SV4} = \$5,000/(1 + 0.18)^4 = \$2,579$$
$$P_{SV8} = \$5,000/(1 + 0.18)^8 = \$1,330$$

$$P_{SV12} = \$5,000/(1 + 0.18)^{12} = \$686$$
$$P_{SV16} = \$5,000/(1 + 0.18)^{16} = \$354$$
$$P_{SV20} = \$5,000/(1 + 0.18)^{20} = \$183$$
$$P_{SV24} = \$5,000/(1 + 0.18)^{24} = \$94$$
$$P_{SV28} = \$5,000/(1 + 0.18)^{28} = \$49$$
$$P_{SV} = \$2,579 + \$1,330 + \$686 + \$354 + \$183 + \$94 + \$49$$
$$P_{SV} = \$5,275$$

The present value of the purchase prices for the used dump truck is determined by summing the present value of purchase prices occurring in years 0, 4, 8, 12, 16, 20, and 24. The present value for each purchase price is calculated using Eq. (15-3) as follows:

$$P_{PP0} = -\$50,000/(1 + 0.18)^{0} = -\$50,000$$
$$P_{PP4} = -\$50,000/(1 + 0.18)^{4} = -\$25,789$$
$$P_{PP8} = -\$50,000/(1 + 0.18)^{8} = -\$13,302$$
$$P_{PP12} = -\$50,000/(1 + 0.18)^{12} = -\$6,861$$
$$P_{PP16} = -\$50,000/(1 + 0.18)^{16} = -\$3,539$$
$$P_{PP20} = -\$50,000/(1 + 0.18)^{20} = -\$1,825$$
$$P_{PP24} = -\$50,000/(1 + 0.18)^{24} = -\$941$$
$$P_{PP} = -\$50,000 + (-\$25,789) + (-\$13,302) + (-\$6,861)$$
$$+ (-\$3,539) + (-\$1,825) + (-\$941)$$
$$P_{PP} = -\$102,257$$

The net present value for the purchase of the used dump truck is calculated as follows:

$$NPV = \$93,527 + \$5,275 + (-\$102,257) = -\$3,455$$

The new truck has the highest NPV; therefore, your company should purchase the new truck.

INCREMENTAL NET PRESENT VALUE

In Example 17-4 we choose between two mutually exclusive alternatives with different initial capital outlays, $110,000 and $120,000. The incremental net present value is another way to select between mutually exclusive alternatives with different initial costs. The initial cost is the cash disbursement in year 0. The incremental net present value compares two alternatives at a time. The alternative with the higher initial cost is compared to the alternative with the lower initial cost based on the net present value of the difference in the cash receipts and disbursements for the two alternatives. If the incremental net present value is positive, it is financially attractive to invest the extra money and purchase the more expensive alternative. If the incremental net present value is zero, both investments are equally attractive. If incremental net present value is negative, it is financially attractive to purchase the less expensive piece of equipment.

Performing an incremental net present value analysis involves the following steps. First, rank all of the alternatives in order of initial cost from lowest to highest. Second, identify the alternative with the lowest initial cost as the current best alternative. Third, compare the current best alternative with the alternative with the next higher initial cost based on the incremental net present value of the difference in the cash receipts and disbursements for the two alternatives. If the incremental net present value is zero or negative, the current best alternative remains the current best alternative and the competing alternative is eliminated from consideration. If the incremental net present value is positive, the competing alternative becomes the current best alternative and the former current best alternative is eliminated from consideration. This process is repeated until all alternatives have been compared. The current best alternative at the end of the comparison process becomes the selected alternative.

> **Example 17-9:** Your company is looking at purchasing a new front-end loader and has narrowed the choice down to four loaders. The purchase price, annual profit, and salvage value at the end of five years for each of the loaders is found in Table 17-5. Which front-end loader should your company purchase based on the incremental net present values using a MARR of 20% and a useful life of five years?
>
> **Solution:** The first step is to rank the alternative in order of initial cost (purchase price). The loaders are compared in the following order: Loader A, Loader C, Loader B, and Loader D. Because Loader A has the lowest initial cost it is designated the current best alternative.
>
> Next, compare Loader A to Loader C. The difference in the purchase price is $10,000 ($120,000 − $110,000). The difference in annual profit is $3,000 ($40,000 − $37,000). The difference in salvage value is $2,000 ($12,000 − $10,000). The difference in the cash flows for these two alternatives is shown in Figure 17-7.
>
> The present value of the difference in annual profits is determined by using Eq. (15-9) as follows:
>
> $$P_{AP} = \$3,000[(1 + 0.20)^5 - 1]/[0.20(1 + 0.20)^5] = \$8,972$$
>
> The present value of the difference in salvage values is determined by using Eq. (15-3) as follows:
>
> $$P_{SV} = \$2,000/(1 + 0.20)^5 = \$804$$

TABLE 17-5   Cash Flow for Example 17-9

CASH FLOW	LOADER A ($)	LOADER B ($)	LOADER C ($)	LOADER D ($)
Purchase Price	110,000	127,000	120,000	130,000
Annual Profit	37,000	43,000	40,000	44,000
Salvage Value	10,000	13,000	12,000	13,000

Figure 17-7 Incremental Cash Flow for Loaders A and C

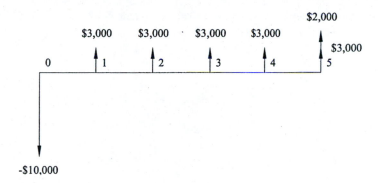

The incremental net present value for the purchase of Loader C in lieu of Loader A is calculated as follows:

$$NPV = \$8,972 + \$804 + (-\$10,000) = -\$224$$

Because the incremental net present value is negative, Loader A continues to be the current best alternative. Next, we compare Loader A to Loader B, the loader with the next lowest initial cost.

The difference in the purchase price is $17,000 ($127,000 − $110,000). The difference in annual profit is $6,000 ($43,000 − $37,000). And the difference in salvage value is $3,000 ($13,000 − $10,000). The difference in the cash flows for these two alternatives is shown in Figure 17-8.

The present value of the difference in annual profits is determined by using Eq. (15-9) as follows:

$$P_{AP} = \$6,000[(1 + 0.20)^5 - 1]/[0.20(1 + 0.20)^5] = \$17,944$$

The present value of the difference in salvage values is determined by using Eq. (15-3) as follows:

$$P_{SV} = \$3,000/(1 + 0.20)^5 = \$1,206$$

The incremental net present value for the purchase of Loader B in lieu of Loader A is calculated as follows:

$$NPV = \$17,944 + \$1,206 + (-\$17,000) = \$2,150$$

Figure 17-8 Incremental Cash Flow for Loaders A and B

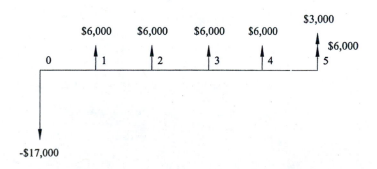

FIGURE 17-9 Incremental Cash Flow for Loaders B and D

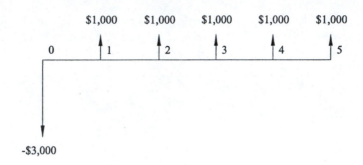

Because the incremental net present value is positive, Loader B becomes the new current best alternative and Loader A is eliminated from comparison. Next, we compare Loader B to Loader D, the only remaining loader not compared.

The difference in the purchase price is $3,000 ($130,000 − $127,000). The difference in annual profit is $1,000 ($44,000 − $43,000). And the difference in salvage value is zero ($13,000 − $13,000). The difference in the cash flows for these two alternatives is shown in Figure 17-9.

The present value of the difference in annual profits is determined by using Eq. (15-9) as follows:

$$P_{AP} = \$1,000[(1 + 0.20)^5 - 1]/[0.20(1 + 0.20)^5] = \$2,991$$

The incremental net present value for the purchase of Loader B in lieu of Loader D is calculated as follows:

$$NPV = \$2,991 + \$0 + (-\$3,000) = -\$8$$

Because the incremental net present value is negative, Loader B continues to be the current best alternative. With no other alternative to compare, Loader B is the selected alternative; therefore, your company should purchase Loader B.

When comparing two alternatives, the incremental net present value equals the difference between the net present values for the alternatives. Let's calculate the net present values for Loader A and Loader C.

The present value of the annual profits for Loader A is determined by using Eq. (15-9) as follows:

$$P_{AP} = \$37,000[(1 + 0.20)^5 - 1]/[0.20(1 + 0.20)^5] = \$110,653$$

The present value of the salvage value for Loader A is determined by using Eq. (15-3) as follows:

$$P_{SV} = \$10,000/(1 + 0.20)^5 = \$4,019$$

The net present value for the purchase of Loader A is calculated as follows:

$$NPV = \$110,653 + \$4,019 + (-\$110,000) = \$4,672$$

The present value of the annual profits for Loader C is determined by using Eq. (15-9) as follows:

$$P_{AP} = \$40,000[(1 + 0.20)^5 - 1]/[0.20(1 + 0.20)^5] = \$119,624$$

The present value of the salvage values for Loader C is determined by using Eq. (15-3) as follows:

$$P_{SV} = \$12,000/(1 + 0.20)^5 = \$4,823$$

The net present value for the purchase of Loader C is calculated as follows:

$$NPV = \$119,624 + \$4,823 + (-\$120,000) = \$4,447$$

The difference in net present value between Loaders A and C is $-\$225$ ($\$4,447 - \$4,672$), which is the incremental net present value for Loaders A and C. The small difference is due to rounding errors. Because we change the current best option only when the incremental net present value is positive, the incremental net present value analysis will select the alternative with the highest net present value.

If the "do nothing" alternative is an acceptable alternative, it must be included in the list of alternatives. Failure to include the "do nothing" alternative may result in the selected alternative having a negative net present value. Because the net present value of any of the alternatives is not included in the calculations, one would have no way of knowing if the net present value of the selected alternative is positive. By including the "do nothing" alternative, we are guaranteed to have an alternative with a nonnegative (zero) net present value.

FUTURE WORTH

The future worth method compares alternatives based on their future values at the end of the study period. Future worth is calculated by determining the equivalent value of the cash receipts and disbursements at the end of the study period using the equations in chapter 15. If the future worth is positive, the alternative produces a return greater than the MARR. If the future worth is zero, the alternative produces a return equal to the MARR. If the future worth is negative, the alternative produces a return less than the MARR and, if possible, the investment should be rejected. Because any present value can be converted to a future value by Equations (15-1) and (15-2) and $(1 + i)^n$ equals a constant for any given i and n, the future worth produces the same result as the net present value for any given i and n.

Example 17-10: Your company is looking at purchasing the front-end loader in Example 17-3 at cost of $120,000. The loader would have a useful life of five years with a salvage value of $12,000 at the end of the fifth year. The loader can be billed out at $95.00 per hour. It costs $30.00 per hour to operate the front-end loader and $25.00 per hour for the operator. Using 1,200 billable hours per year determine the future worth for the purchase of the loader using a MARR of 20%. Should your company purchase the loader?

Solution: The future value of purchase price is determined by using Eq. (15-1) as follows:

$$F_{PP} = -\$120,000(1 + 0.20)^5 = -\$298,598$$

The future value of the purchase price is negative because it is a cash disbursement.

The hourly profit on the loader equals the billing rate less the operation cost and the cost of the operator and is calculated as follows:

$$\text{Hourly Profit} = \$95.00 - \$30.00 - \$25.00 = \$40.00 \text{ per hour}$$

The annual profit on the loader equals the hourly profit times the number of billable hours per year and is calculated as follows:

$$\text{Annual Profit} = \$40.00/\text{hour}(1,200 \text{ hours/year}) = \$48,000/\text{year}$$

The future value of the annual profits is determined by using Eq. (15-5) as follows:

$$F_{AP} = \$48,000[(1 + 0.20)^5 - 1]/0.20 = \$357,197$$

The future value of the annual profits is positive because it is a cash receipt.

The future value of the salvage value is equal to the salvage value because the future value is measured at the end of the study period. The future value of the salvage value is positive because it is a cash receipt.

The future worth for purchasing the loader equals the sum of the future values of the individual cash flows and is calculated as follows:

$$FW = -\$298,598 + \$357,197 + \$12,000 = \$70,599$$

Because the future worth is greater than zero, the purchase of the front-end loader will produce a return greater than the MARR and your company should invest in the front-end loader.

Because all of the costs for Example 17-10 are the same as Example 17-3, the future worth could be calculated from the net present value determined in Example 17-3 using Eq. (15-1) as follows:

$$FW = \$28,372(1 + 0.20)^5 = \$70,599$$

We see that the net present value and the future worth produce the same result and are related by Eq. (15-1).

ANNUAL EQUIVALENT

The annual equivalent method compares alternatives based on their equivalent annual receipts less the equivalent annual disbursements. The annual equivalent is calculated by converting the cash receipts and disbursements into a uniform series of annual cash flows occurring over the study period using the equations in chapter 15. If the annual equivalent is positive, the alternative produces a return greater than the MARR. If the annual equivalent is zero, the alternative produces a return equal to the MARR. If the annual equivalent is negative, the alternative produces a return less than the MARR and, if possible, the investment should be rejected.

Because any present value can be converted to a uniform series by Equations (15-11) and (15-12) and $i(1 + i)^n/[(1 + i)^n - 1]$ equals a constant for any given i and n, the annual equivalent produces the same result as the net present value for any given i and n. Similarly, because any future value can be converted to a uniform series by Equations (15-7) and (15-8) and $i/[(1 + i)^n - 1]$ equals a constant for any given i and n, the annual equivalent produces the same result as the future value for any given i and n.

The annual equivalent method assumes that they are repurchased until the useful lives end in the same period. When dealing with alternatives of different lives, one of the big advantages of using the annual equivalent method over net present value or future value methods is that it produces the same result using a single life for each of the alternatives as assuming each of the alternatives are re-purchases until all of their lives end in the same period. Performing the calculation necessary to complete an annual equivalent analysis using the life of the alternatives is much simpler than performing a net preset value on multiple repurchases of the alternatives. In Example 17-11 we compare the same two alternatives as were compared in Example 17-8. In Example 17-8 they are compared based on net present value using a study period of twenty-eight years. In Example 17-11 they are compared based on annual equivalent. The study period is different for both trucks and is matched to their useful life.

Example 17-11: Your company needs to purchase a dump truck and has narrowed the selection down to two alternatives. The first alternative is to purchase a new dump truck for $65,000. At the end of the seventh year the salvage value of the new dump truck is estimated to be $15,000. The second alternative is to purchase a used dump truck for $50,000. At the end of the fourth year the salvage value of the used dump truck is estimated to be $5,000. The annual profits, revenues less operation costs, are $17,000 per year for either truck. Using a MARR of 18% calculate the annual worth for each of the dump trucks. Which truck should your company purchase?

Solution: The useful life of the new truck is seven years, which is used as the study period for the new truck. The purchase price for the new truck is converted to a uniform series of annual cash flows by Eq. (15-11) as follows:

$$A_{PP} = -\$65,000[0.18(1 + 0.18)^7]/[(1 + 0.18)^7 - 1] = -\$17,054$$

The salvage value for the new truck is converted to a uniform series of annual cash flows by Eq. (15-7) as follows:

$$A_{SV} = \$15,000(0.18)/[(1 + 0.18)^7 - 1] = \$1,235$$

The annual profits for the new truck are already a uniform series. The annual equivalent (AE) for purchasing the loader equals the sum of the uniform series representing each of the individual cash flows and is calculated as follows:

$$AE = -\$17,054 + \$1,235 + \$17,000 = \$1,181$$

The useful life of the used truck is four years, which is used as the study period for the used trucks. The purchase price for the used truck is converted to a uniform series of annual cash flows by Eq. (15-11) as follows:

$$A_{PP} = -\$50,000[0.18(1 + 0.18)^4]/[(1 + 0.18)^4 - 1] = -\$18,587$$

The salvage value for the used truck is converted to a uniform series of annual cash flows by Eq. (15-7) as follows:

$$A_{SV} = \$5,000(0.18)/[(1 + 0.18)^4 - 1] = \$959$$

The annual profits for the used truck are already a uniform series. The annual equivalent for purchasing the truck equals the sum of the uniform series representing each of the individual cash flows and is calculated as follows:

$$AE = -\$18,587 + \$959 + \$17,000 = -\$628$$

The new truck has the highest annual equivalent; therefore, your company should purchase the new truck.

If we convert the net present value for the new truck from Example 17-8 to a uniform series of annual cash flows over the combined life of twenty-eight years by Eq. (15-11) we get the following:

$$A = \$6,502[0.18(1 + 0.18)^{28}]/[(1 + 0.18)^{28} - 1] = \$1,182$$

This value is the same as the annual equivalent calculated for the new truck; however, the calculations are much simpler using the annual equivalent. The same is true for the used truck.

RATE OF RETURN

The rate of return is also known as the internal rate of return or return on investment. The rate of return is the interest rate paid on the unrecovered balance of an investment over the remaining life of the investment. The rate of return is the interest rate that produces a net present value of zero. The rate of return is calculated in the same manner that the unknown interest rate was calculated in Examples 15-13, 15-14, and 15-15. When using the rate of return to choose between investment alternatives, the alternative with the largest rate of return is selected.

If the rate of return on an alternative is greater than the MARR the net present value, future worth, and annual equivalent are greater than zero for the alternative. If the rate of return on an alternative is equal to the MARR the net present value, future worth, and annual equivalent are all equal to zero for the alternative. If the rate of return on an alternative is less than the MARR the net present value, future worth, and annual equivalent are less than zero for the alternative.

Example 17-12: Your company is looking at purchasing a front-end loader at cost of $120,000. The loader would have a useful life of five years with a salvage value of $12,000 at the end of the fifth year. The loader can be billed out at $95.00 per hour. It costs $30.00 per hour to operate the front-end loader and $25.00 per hour for the operator. Using 1,200 billable hours per year determine the rate of return for the purchase of the loader. If your company's MARR was 20%, should your company purchase the loader?

Solution: The hourly profit on the loader equals the billing rate less the operation cost and the cost of the operator and is calculated as follows:

$$\text{Hourly Profit} = \$95.00 - \$30.00 - \$25.00 = \$40.00 \text{ per hour}$$

The annual profit on the loader equals the hourly profit times the number of billable hours per year and is calculated as follows:

$$\text{Annual Profit} = \$40.00/\text{hour}(1,200 \text{ hours/year}) = \$48,000/\text{year}$$

The cash flow for the purchase of the loader in Example 17-12 is shown in Figure 17-10.

The present value of the annual profits is determined by using Eq. (15-9) as follows:

$$P_{AP} = \$48,000[(1 + i)^5 - 1]/[i(1 + i)^5]$$

The present value of the annual profits is positive because it is a cash receipt.

The present value of the salvage value is determined by using Eq. (15-3) as follows:

$$P_{SV} = \$12,000/(1 + i)^5$$

The present value of the salvage value is positive because it is a cash receipt.

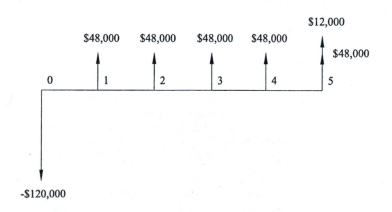

FIGURE 17-10   Cash Flow for Example 17-12

SIDEBAR 17-2

CALCULATING THE RATE OF RETURN USING A TI BA II PLUS CALCULATOR

The net present value is calculated as shown below. For this sidebar we use Example 17-12.

TASK	KEYSTROKES	DISPLAY	
1. Set Variables to Defaults	[2nd] [RESET] [ENTER]	RST	0.00
2. Select Cash Flow Worksheet	[CF]	CFo=	0.00
3. Enter Cash Flow at Time Zero	120000[+/−][ENTER]	CFo=	−120,000.00
4. Enter Next Four Cash Flows	[↓] 48000 [ENTER]	CF1=	48,000.00
	[↓] 4 [ENTER]	F01=	4.00
5. Enter Last Cash Flow	[↓] 60000 [ENTER]	CF2=	60,000.00
	[↓] 1 [ENTER]	F02=	1.00
6. Calculate Rate of Return	[IRR] [CPT]	IRR=	30.06

In this example the keystrokes for entering all variables are shown to provide a generic example that can be used for any problem by changing the numbers entered into the calculator. If the display is already shown as indicated you may type [↓] to continue to the next step.

The present value of the purchase price of the loader is equal to the purchase price because the net present value is measured at the time of the initial investment. The present value of the purchase price is negative because it is a cash disbursement.

To find the rate of return one must write an equation that includes the present values representing all of the cash flows and set the net present value to zero. The net present value for purchasing the loader equals the sum of the present values of the individual cash flows and is calculated as follows:

$$0 = \$48,000[(1 + i)^5 - 1]/[i(1 + i)^5] + \$12,000/(1 + i)^5 + (-\$120,000)$$

Solving for i by trial and error we find that i equals 30.06%. The rate of return for the investment is 30.06%. Because the rate of return is greater than the MARR of 20%, the present value will be positive and your company should invest in the front-end loader.

One weakness of the rate of return method is that a series of cash flows may have multiple rates of returns if one of the following conditions exist: the cash flow in year zero is positive, the sign on the net cash flow changes from period to period more than once, or the disbursements are greater than the receipts.

When using the rate of return method to select between alternatives one must be sure to convert them to mutually exclusive alternatives as shown in the following example.

Example 17-13: Your company has $200,000 to invest and has identified the following three investments. Investment A requires an initial investment of $120,000 and has an annual rate of return of 18%. Investment B requires an initial investment of $80,000 and has an annual rate of return of 22%. Investment C requires an initial investment of $20,000 and has an annual rate of return of 35%. Unused funds will be placed in a bank account with an annual percentage yield of 6%. You may invest in each of the investments only once. All of the investments have a one year life. Which investments should your company invest in?

Solution: In this example one must first combine the investments into mutually exclusive alternatives. A list of the mutually exclusive alternatives is shown in Table 17-6. The option to not invest in any of the investments, the "do nothing" alternative, is included as Alternative 1. For each of these alternatives the unused capital will be placed in a bank account, which earns 6% interest; therefore, whether to invest the excess funds does not need to be included in the alternatives.

Only Alternative 8 is not acceptable because of the limited funds. Alternative 8 would require the investment of $220,000 and the company only has $200,000 available.

The interest earned on Investments A, B, and C is determined by using Eq. (16-1) as follows:

$$I_A = \$120,000(0.18)1 = \$21,600$$
$$I_B = \$80,000(0.22)1 = \$17,600$$
$$I_C = \$20,000(0.35)1 = \$7,000$$

For Alternative 1 the rate of return is 6% because all of the money is invested in a bank account that has an annual percentage yield of 6%.

TABLE 17-6 Mutually Exclusive Alternatives

ALTERNATIVE	INVESTMENTS	ACCEPTABLE
1	None	Yes
2	A	Yes
3	B	Yes
4	C	Yes
5	A & B	Yes
6	B & C	Yes
7	A & C	Yes
8	A, B, & C	No

TABLE 17-7   Rate of Return for Alternatives for
Example 17-13

ALTERNATIVE	INVESTMENTS	ROR (%)
1	None	6.0
2	A	13.2
3	B	12.4
4	C	8.9
5	A & B	19.6
6	B & C	15.3
7	A & C	16.1
8	A, B, & C	NA

For Alternative 2, $120,000 will be invested in Investment A and $80,000 in a bank account that has an annual percentage yield of 6%. The interest earned on the bank account is calculated using Eq. (16-1) as follows:

$$I_{Bank} = \$80,000(0.06)1 = \$4,800$$

The interest earned for Alternative 2 is $26,400 ($21,600 + $4,800), for a total worth of $226,400 at the end of year 1. Using Eq. (15-1) to set the cash investment equivalent to the value of the investment at the end of year 1 we get the following:

$$\$226,400 = \$200,000(1 + i)^1$$

Solving for i we find that i equals 13.2%.

Alternatives 3 through 7 are solved in a similar manner—adding up the interest on the investments and the bank account and then determining the rate of return. Alternative 8 is not a feasible alternative because we lack the funds to invest in all three investments. Table 17-7 shows the rate of return for each of the alternatives. Alternative 5, investment in Investments A and B, has the highest rate of return and is the alternative that should be selected.

In Example 17-13, had we begun by investing in the investment with the highest rate of return and continued doing so until we ran out of money, we would have invested in Investments A and C, which would have a combined return of 16.1%. From Example 17-13 we see the set of investments with the highest return is the combination of Investments A and B, with a combined return of 19.6%. This underscores the importance of setting up mutually exclusive alternatives to be analyzed.

INCREMENTAL RATE OF RETURN

Like the incremental net present value, the incremental rate of return is a way to select between mutually exclusive alternatives with different initial costs. The incremental rate of return compares alternatives by determining the rate of return on the difference in initial costs. The initial cost is the cash disbursement in year 0.

The incremental rate of return is determined by setting the incremental net present value to zero. The incremental rate of return compares two alternatives at a time. The alternative with the higher initial cost is compared with the alternative with the lower cost based on the rate of return for the difference in the cash receipts and disbursements for the two alternatives. If the incremental rate of return is greater than the MARR, it is financially attractive to invest the more expensive alternative. If the incremental rate of return is equal to the MARR, both alternatives are equally attractive. If the incremental rate of return is less than the MARR, it is financially attractive to invest the less expensive alternative.

Performing an incremental rate of return analysis involves the following steps. First, rank all of the alternatives in order of initial cost. Second, identify the alternative with the lowest initial cost as the current best alternative. Third, compare the current best alternative with the alternative with the next higher initial cost based on its incremental rate of return. If the incremental rate of return is equal to or less than the MARR, the current best alternative remains the current best alternative and the competing alternative is eliminated from consideration. If the incremental rate of return is greater than the MARR, the competing alternative becomes the new current best alternative and the former current best alternative is eliminated from consideration. This process is repeated until all alternatives have been compared. The current best alternative at the end of the comparison process becomes the selected alternative. Let's look at Example 17-9 using the incremental rate of return method in lieu of the incremental net present value.

Example 17-14:   Your company is looking at purchasing a new front-end loader and has narrowed the choice down to four loaders. The useful life of the loaders is five years. The purchase price, annual profit, and salvage value at the end of five years for each of the loaders is found in Table 17-8. Which front-end loader should your company purchase based on the incremental rate of return and a MARR of 20%?

Solution: The first step is to rank the alternatives in order of initial capital outlay. The loaders are compared in the following order: Loader A, Loader C, Loader B, and Loader D. Because Loader A has the lowest purchase price it is designated the current best alternative.

Next, compare Loader A to Loader C. The difference in the purchase price is $10,000 ($120,000 − $110,000). The difference in annual profit is $3,000 ($40,000 − $37,000). The difference in salvage value is $2,000 ($12,000 − $10,000).

TABLE 17-8   Cash Flow for Example 17-14

CASH FLOW	LOADER A ($)	LOADER B ($)	LOADER C ($)	LOADER D ($)
Purchase Price	110,000	127,000	120,000	130,000
Annual Profit	37,000	43,000	40,000	44,000
Salvage Value	10,000	13,000	12,000	13,000

The present value of the difference in annual profits is determined by using Eq. (15-9) as follows:

$$P_{AP} = \$3{,}000[(1 + i)^5 - 1]/[i(1 + i)^5]$$

The present value of the difference in salvage values is determined by using Eq. (15-3) as follows:

$$P_{SV} = \$2{,}000/(1 + i)^5$$

The incremental net present value for the purchase of the new loader is calculated as follows:

$$NPV = \$3{,}000[(1 + i)^5 - 1]/[i(1 + i)^5] + \$2{,}000/(1 + i)^5 + (-\$10{,}000)$$

Setting the incremental net present value to zero and solving by trial and error we find the incremental rate of return equals 19.05%. Because the incremental rate of return is less than the MARR, Loader A continues to be the current best alternative.

Next, we compare Loader A to Loader B, the loader with the next lowest cost. The difference in the purchase price is $17,000 ($127,000 − $110,000). The difference in annual profit is $6,000 ($43,000 − $37,000). The difference in salvage value is $3,000 ($13,000 − $10,000).

The present value of the difference in annual profits is determined by using Eq. (15-9) as follows:

$$P_{AP} = \$6{,}000[(1 + i)^5 - 1]/[i(1 + i)^5]$$

The present value of the difference in salvage values is determined by using Eq. (15-3) as follows:

$$P_{SV} = F/(1 + i)^n = \$3{,}000/(1 + i)^5$$

The incremental net present value for the purchase of the new loader is calculated as follows:

$$NPV = \$6{,}000[(1 + i)^5 - 1]/[i(1 + i)^5] + \$3{,}000/(1 + i)^5 + (-\$17{,}000)$$

Setting the incremental net present value to zero and solving by trial and error we find the incremental rate of return equals 25.32%. Because the incremental rate of return is greater than the MARR, Loader B is the new current best alternative and Loader A is eliminated from comparison.

Next, we compare Loader B to Loader D, the only remaining loader not compared. The difference in the purchase price is $3,000 ($130,000 − $127,000). The difference in annual profit is $1,000 ($44,000 − $43,000). The difference in salvage value is zero ($13,000 − $13,000).

The present value of the difference in annual profits is determined by using Eq. (15-9) as follows:

$$P_{AP} = \$1{,}000[(1 + i)^5 - 1]/[i(1 + i)^5]$$

The incremental net present value for the purchase of the new loader is calculated as follows:

$$NPV = \$1,000[(1 + i)^5 - 1]/[i(1 + i)^5] + \$0 + (-\$3,000)$$

Setting the incremental net present value to zero and solving by trial and error we find the incremental rate of return equals 19.86%. Because the incremental rate of return is less than the MARR, Loader B continues to be the current best alternative. With no other alternative to compare, Loader B is the selected alternative; therefore, your company should purchase Loader B.

The incremental rate of return produced the same results as the incremental net present value and the net present value. Because we change the current best option only when the incremental rate of return is greater than the MARR, which corresponds to an incremental positive net present value, the incremental rate of return selects the alternative with the highest net present value.

If the "do nothing" alternative is an acceptable alternative it must be included in the list of alternatives. Failure to include the "do nothing" alternative may result in the selected alternative having a rate of return less than the MARR, which corresponds to a negative net present value. Because the rate of return of any of the alternatives is not included in the calculations, one would have no way of knowing if the net present value of the selected alternative is positive. By including the "do nothing" alternative, we are guaranteed to have an alternative with a nonnegative net present value.

CAPITAL RECOVERY WITH RETURN

The capital recovery with return method is similar to the annual equivalent method, except it looks only at capital costs. The capital costs included in the calculations are the purchase price and salvage value. When using the capital recovery with return method the purchase price and salvage value are converted to their annual equivalents at the MARR. Because the purchase price is almost always larger than the salvage value, the capital recovery with return is usually negative. The capital recovery with return represents the annual equivalent loss in the value of an asset. For an alternative to be financially attractive the loss in value of the asset must be offset by profits (revenue less noncapital expenses) on the alternative. The capital recovery with return is useful when looking at the effects of pricing and volume (e.g., billing hours) on the attractiveness of an alternative.

Example 17-15: Your company is looking at purchasing a new hydraulic excavator. The excavator has a purchase price of $120,000, a useful life of five years, and a salvage value of $12,000 at the end of the fifth year. The excavator can be billed out at $95.00 per hour. It costs $30.00 per hour to operate the excavator and $25.00 per hour for the operator. Using a MARR of 20% and the capital recovery with return method, determine the minimum number of billable hours in a year that will make purchasing the excavator financially attractive. How many hours will need to be billed if the billing rate were reduced to $90.00 per hour?

Solution: For purchase of the excavator to be financially attractive, the annual profit must be equal to the capital recovery with return, which is equal to the annual equivalents of the purchase price and salvage value at the MARR.

The purchase price for the excavator is converted to a uniform series of annual cash flows by Eq. (15-11) as follows:

$$A_{PP} = -\$120,000[0.20(1 + 0.20)^5]/[(1 + 0.20)^5 - 1]$$
$$A_{PP} = -\$40,126$$

The salvage value for the excavator is converted to a uniform series of annual cash flows by Eq. (15-7) as follows:

$$A_{SV} = \$12,000(0.20)/[(1 + 0.20)^5 - 1] = \$1,613$$

The capital recovery with return (CR) for purchasing the excavator equals the sum of the uniform series representing each of the individual cash flows and is calculated as follows:

$$CR = -\$40,126 + \$1,613 = -\$38,513$$

For the purchase of the excavator to be financially attractive, it must generate $38,513 in profit (revenue less noncapital costs) each year. The hourly profit on the excavator equals the billing rate less the operation cost and the cost of the operator and is calculated as follows:

$$\text{Hourly Profit} = \$95.00 - \$30.00 - \$25.00 = \$40.00 \text{ per hour}$$

The annual profit on the loader equals the hourly profit times the number of billable hours per year. Solving for number of billable hours we get the following:

$$\text{Billable Hours} = \text{Annual Profit/Hourly Profit}$$

Calculating the minimum number of billable hours per year required to offset the capital recovery with return we get the following:

$$\text{Billable Hours} = \$38,513 \text{ per year}/\$40.00 \text{ per hour} = 963 \text{ hours/year}$$

At a billing rate of $95.00 per hour, one would need to bill 963 hours per year. If the billing rate were reduced to $90.00 per hour, the hourly profit on the excavator would be:

$$\text{Hourly Profit} = \$90.00 - \$30.00 - \$25.00 = \$35.00 \text{ per hour}$$

Calculating the minimum number of billable hours per year required to offset the capital recovery with return we get the following:

Billable Hours = $38,513 per year/$35.00 per hour
Billable Hours = 1,100 hours/year

At a billing rate of $90.00 per hour, one would need to bill 1,100 hours per year or an additional 137 (1,100 − 963) hours per year.

In Example 17-15, if one believes that the excavator can generate a profit of $38,513 per year, then the investment is financially attractive. We showed that this could be done by billing out 963 hours per year at $95.00 per hour or 1,100 hours per year at $90.00 per hour. If we do not think that the excavator can generate a profit of $38,513 per year, then the investment is not financially attractive.

PAYBACK PERIOD WITHOUT INTEREST

The payback period without interest compares alternatives based on how long it takes to pay back the initial costs. The payback period is determined by finding the first period when the sum of the net cash flows, both receipts and disbursements, to date is nonnegative (zero or positive). The payback period without interest ignores the interest on the initial costs. Unless the payback period equals or exceeds the life of the alternative it also ignores the salvage value. If the payback period is less than or equal to the useful life of the alternative, the alternative will recover the initial costs. Because the time value of money is not included in the calculations, this does not guarantee that the alternative will produce a specific return.

Example 17-16: Your company is looking at purchasing a front-end loader at cost of $120,000. The loader can be billed out at $95.00 per hour. It costs $30.00 per hour to operate the front-end loader and $25.00 per hour for the operator. The useful life of the equipment is five years. Using 1,200 billable hours per year determine the payback period without interest for the front-end loader. Does the front-end loader generate enough revenue to recover the initial cost?

Solution: The hourly profit on the loader equals the billing rate less the operation cost and the cost of the operator and is calculated as follows:

Hourly Profit = $95.00 − $30.00 − $25.00 = $40.00 per hour

The annual profit on the loader equals the hourly profit times the number of billable hours per year and is calculated as follows:

Annual Profit = $40.00/hour(1,200 hours/year) = $48,000/year

The payback period (n') equals the number of years it takes to recover the initial capital outlay and is calculated as follows:

$$n' = \text{Purchase Price/Annual Profit}$$
$$n' = \$120{,}000/\$48{,}000 \text{ per year} = 2.5 \text{ years}$$

The payback period for the investment is three years because the initial cost is paid back during the third year. Because the payback period is less than the five-year useful life of the loader, the purchase of the loader will generate enough revenue to recover the initial costs, the operating costs, and the cost of the operator.

When comparing investments using the payback period without interest method, the alternative with the smallest payback period is selected. The payback period without interest is a good measure of how long the initial investment is at risk and represents how long the initial investment is tied up in an alternative. The weakness of this method is that it ignores interest on the investment, it ignores all cash flows that occur after the payback period, and it ignores the life of the equipment. Because the payback without interest ignores what happens to the investment after the payback period occurs it favors short-term investments. It is a good analytical tool when there is a high degree of uncertainty and one wants to recoup the investment as soon as possible. The payback period without interest is a good supplemental measure to be used in conjunction with other quantitative methods that include analysis of the cash flow over the life of the alternatives, such as the net present value. The payback period without interest can be used to help select between two alternatives with similar net present values by selecting the one that places the initial capital outlay at risk for the shortest period of time.

Example 17-17:   Your company is looking at investing in one of the three investments shown in Table 17-9. Using the payback period without interest method which investment would you choose? How would your decision be different if you used the net present value method and a MARR of 20%? Which investment would you choose if the investments were considered high risks and you used both of the above methods?

TABLE 17-9   Investments for Example 17-17

YEAR	INVESTMENT A ($)	INVESTMENT B ($)	INVESTMENT C ($)
0	−1,000	−2,000	−2,000
1	500	500	900
2	500	600	900
3	0	400	900
4	0	500	900
5	0	3,500	900

Solution: The payback period for Investment A is two years because in year 2 the sum of the cash flows to date ($-\$1,000 + \$500 + \$500 = \$0$) is nonnegative for the first time. The payback period for Investment B is four years because in year 4 the sum of the cash flows to date ($-\$2,000 + \$500 + \$600 + \$400 + \$500 = \$0$) is nonnegative for the first time. The payback period for Investment C is three years because in year 3 the sum of the cash flows to date ($-\$2,000 + \$900 + \$900 + \$900 = \$,700$) is nonnegative for the first time. Based on the payback period without interest Investment A is the most financially attractive investment.

Next, we look at the net present value for each of the investments.

The present value of the uniform series of payments in Investment A is determined by using Eq. (15-9) as follows:

$$P_A = \$500[(1 + 0.20)^2 - 1]/[0.20(1 + 0.20)^2] = \$764$$

The present value of the initial investment is equal to the initial investment. The net present value for Investment A equals the sum of the present values and is calculated as follows:

$$\text{NPV} = \$764 + (-\$1,000) = -\$236$$

The present value of individual cash flows for Investment B is determined by using Eq. (15-3) as follows:

$$P_0 = -\$2,000/(1 + 0.20)^0 = -\$2,000$$
$$P_1 = \$500/(1 + 0.20)^1 = \$417$$
$$P_2 = \$600/(1 + 0.20)^2 = \$417$$
$$P_3 = \$400/(1 + 0.20)^3 = \$231$$
$$P_4 = \$500/(1 + 0.20)^4 = \$241$$
$$P_5 = \$3,500/(1 + 0.20)^5 = \$1,407$$

The net present value for Investment B equals the sum of the present values and is calculated as follows:

$$\text{NPV} = -\$2,000 + \$417 + \$417 + \$231 + \$241 + \$1,407 = \$713$$

The present value of the uniform series of payments in Investment C is determined by using Eq. (15-9) as follows:

$$P_A = \$900[(1 + 0.20)^5 - 1]/[0.20(1 + 0.20)^5] = \$2,692$$

The present value of the initial investment is equal to the initial investment. The net present value for Investment C equals the sum of the present values and is calculated as follows:

$$\text{NPV} = \$2,692 + (-\$2,000) = \$692$$

Based on the net present value at a MARR of 20%, Investment B is the most financially attractive alternative.

For the third part of this example we look at both the net present value and the payback period without interest. Looking at Investment A we see that it has the shortest payback period but has a negative net present value. This is because the cash flows stop in the same year that the payback period occurs. Because the payback period with interest ignores the cash flows that occur after the payback period and ignores interest on the cash flows, it allows one to accept an investment that one would reject based on its net present value.

Looking at Investments B and C we see that Investment B is preferred based on the net present values of the investments by $21 ($713 − $692); however, Investment C is preferred based on the payback period without interest because its payback period is a year less.

Given that the investments are risky and we would like to get our investment back as soon as possible, we will forgo the additional $21 gained on Investment B and invest in Investment C because our investment is exposed to loss for a shorter period of time.

In Example 17-17 we saw that the payback period without interest could be used in conjunction with the net present value to add a measure of how long an investment is at risk to a measure of the return on the investment.

PAYBACK PERIOD WITH INTEREST

The payback period with interest is the same as the payback period without interest, except it takes the time value of money into account when making the calculations. The payback period with interest compares alternatives based on how long it takes to pay back the initial costs including interest on the initial costs at the MARR. The payback period is determined by finding the first period when the sum of the net cash flows—including interest on the outstanding investment—is nonnegative (zero or positive). This is done by determining at what point in time the present value of the net cash flows (both cash receipts and disbursements) are equal to or greater than zero. Unless the payback period is equal to or longer than the useful life of the alternative it ignores the salvage value. If the payback period is less than or equal to the useful life of the alternative, the alternative will recover the initial investment plus interest on the investment at the MARR. Because the time value of money is included in the calculation, a payback period that is less than or equal to the useful life of the alternative guarantees that the investment will have a return equal to or greater than the MARR.

Example 17-18:   Your company is looking at purchasing a front-end loader at cost of $120,000. The loader can be billed out at $95.00 per hour. It costs $30.00 per hour to operate the front-end loader and $25.00 per hour for the operator. The useful life of the equipment is five years. Using 1,200 billable hours per year and a MARR of 20% determine the payback period with interest for the front-end loader. Does the front-end loader generate enough revenue to recover the initial cost while providing a return of at least 20%?

Solution: The hourly profit on the loader equals the billing rate less the operation cost and the cost of the operator and is calculated as follows:

$$\text{Hourly Profit} = \$95.00 - \$30.00 - \$25.00 = \$40.00 \text{ per hour}$$

The annual profit on the loader equals the hourly profit times the number of billable hours per year and is calculated as follows:

$$\text{Annual Profit} = \$40.00/\text{hour}(1{,}200 \text{ hours/year}) = \$48{,}000/\text{year}$$

Convert the annual profits to their present values. The present value of the annual profits is determined by using Eq. (15-3) as follows:

$$P_0 = -\$120{,}000/(1 + 0.20)^0 = -\$120{,}000$$
$$P_1 = \$48{,}000/(1 + 0.20)^1 = \$40{,}000$$
$$P_2 = \$48{,}000/(1 + 0.20)^2 = \$33{,}333$$
$$P_3 = \$48{,}000/(1 + 0.20)^3 = \$27{,}778$$
$$P_4 = \$48{,}000/(1 + 0.20)^4 = \$23{,}148$$
$$P_5 = \$48{,}000/(1 + 0.20)^5 = \$19{,}290$$

The payback period with interest for purchase of the loader is four years because in the fourth year the present value of the net cash flows to date $(-\$120{,}000 + \$40{,}000 + \$33{,}333 + \$27{,}778 + \$23{,}148 = \$4{,}259)$ is positive for the first time. Because the payback period is less than the five-year useful life of the loader, the purchase of the loader will generate enough return to recover the initial costs plus interest on the initial investment at an interest rate greater than 20%. Because interest was included, the payback period of the loader has increased from the three years in Example 17-16 to four years.

When comparing investments using the payback period with interest, the alternative with the smallest payback period is selected. The payback period with interest is a good measure of how long the initial investment plus interest on the investment is at risk and represents how long it takes to recover the initial investment with interest. The weakness of this method is that it ignores the cash flows that occur after the payback period and the life of the equipment. Because the payback period with interest ignores what happens to the investment after the payback period is completed it favors short-term investments. It is a better tool than the payback period without interest because it incorporates interest on the investment. It is a good analytical tool when there is a high degree of uncertainty and one wants to recoup the investment as soon as possible. The payback period with interest is a good supplemental measure to be used in conjunction with other quantitative methods that include analysis of the cash flow over the life of the alternatives, such as the net present value. The payback period with interest can be used to help select between two alternatives with similar net present values by selecting the one that places the initial capital outlay at risk for the shortest period of time.

PROJECT BALANCE

The project balance method is a graphical method that shows the potential profit or exposure to loss for any period during an alternative's life. The project balance incorporates interest at the MARR into its calculations. From the project balance graph, one can read the future worth of the alternative at the end of its life as well as the payback period with interest. The project balance is calculated by determining the net cash flow to date for any alternative including interest on the outstanding investment or project balance (PB) as shown in Example 17-19.

Example 17-19: Your company is looking at purchasing a front-end loader at cost of $120,000. The loader can be billed out at $95.00 per hour. It costs $30.00 per hour to operate the front-end loader and $25.00 per hour for the operator. The useful life of the equipment is five years. The salvage value of the loader at the end of the fifth year is $12,000. Using 1,200 billable hours per year and a MARR of 20% prepare a project balance graph for the front-end loader. What is the future worth of the loader? What is the payback period with interest?

Solution: The hourly profit on the loader equals the billing rate less the operation cost and the cost of the operator and is calculated as follows:

Hourly Profit $= \$95.00 - \$30.00 - \$25.00 = \$40.00$ per hour

The annual profit on the loader equals the hourly profit times the number of billable hours per year and is calculated as follows:

Annual Profit $= \$40.00/\text{hour}(1,200 \text{ hours/year}) = \$48,000/\text{year}$

The project balance at the initial point in time ($t = 0$) is a negative $120,000 or the cost of the front-end loader. If we were to terminate the investment immediately after the purchase of the loader, we would be exposed to a $120,000 loss.

The project balance at the end of the first year is equal to the project balance at the end of the previous period plus interest on the project balance from the previous period plus the annual profit. Because the project balance at the end of year 0 was negative the interest for period one will be negative. The project balance at the end of the first year is calculated as follows:

$$PB_1 = PB_0 + PB_0(i) + \text{Annual Profits}$$
$$PB_1 = -\$120,000 + (-\$120,000)(0.20) + \$48,000 = -\$96,000$$

The project balance at the end of the second year is equal to the project balance at the end of the previous period plus interest on the project balance from the previous period plus the annual profit. The project balance at the end of the second year is calculated as follows:

$$PB_2 = -\$96,000 + (-\$96,000)(0.20) + \$48,000 = -\$67,200$$

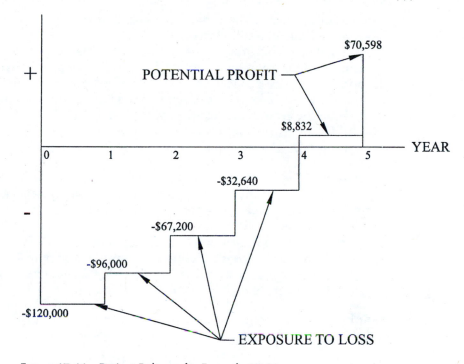

FIGURE 17-11   Project Balance for Example 17-19

Similarly, the project balances at the end of the third and fourth years is calculated as follows:

$$PB_3 = -\$67,200 + (-\$67,200)(0.20) + \$48,000 = -\$32,640$$
$$PB_4 = -\$32,640 + (-\$32,640)(0.20) + \$48,000 = \$8,832$$

In the fifth year the annual profit is increased by salvage value of the equipment or $12,000 for an annual profit of $60,000. The project balance at the end of the fifth year is calculated as follows:

$$PB_5 = \$8,832 + \$8,832(0.20) + \$60,000 = \$70,598$$

The annual project balance for the loader may be graphed as shown in Figure 17-11.

From the project balance graph we see the payback period with interest is four years, which is the same as was calculated for this same loader in Example 17-18. We also see that the loader has a future worth of $70,598, which is the same as was calculated in Example 17-10. The one-dollar difference is due to rounding.

The weakness of the project balance method is that it ignores the salvage value until the end of the study period. In Example 17-19, at the initial point in time our graph shows that we would incur a $120,000 loss if we terminated the investment in the loader. This ignores the possibility that we may sell the loader to offset part of this $120,000 loss.

The strength of the project balance method is that it incorporates both the future worth—which is mathematically related to the net present value—and payback period with interest as well as showing the potential profit or potential loss for each of the years. The project balance method is useful for risky investment because it shows the exposure to loss for the project. The project balance method is also useful for comparing projects with similar future worth (or net present value or annual equivalents) and similar payback periods with interest.

Example 17-20:   Your company is looking at investing in one of two investments, Investment A and Investment B. Both investments are considered risky and your company wants to recoup its investment as soon as possible. The cash flows for both investments are shown in Table 17-10. Using a MARR of 20% the future worth for Investment A is $63,715 and the future worth for Investment B is $63,710. Both investments have a payback period with interest of four years at the MARR. Using the project balance method, which investment should your company invest in?

Solution: The project balance for Investment A is calculated as follows:

$$PB_0 = -\$100,000$$
$$PB_1 = -\$100,000 + (-\$100,000)(0.20) + \$42,000 = -\$78,000$$
$$PB_2 = -\$78,000 + (-\$78,000)(0.20) + \$42,000 = -\$51,600$$
$$PB_3 = -\$51,600 + (-\$51,600)(0.20) + \$42,000 = -\$19,920$$
$$PB_4 = -\$19,920 + (-\$19,920)(0.20) + \$42,000 = \$18,096$$
$$PB_5 = \$18,096 + \$18,096(0.20) + \$42,000 = \$63,715$$

The project balance for Investment B is calculated as follows:

$$PB_0 = -\$100,000$$
$$PB_1 = -\$100,000 + (-\$100,000)(0.20) + \$19,000 = -\$101,000$$
$$PB_2 = -\$101,000 + (-\$101,000)(0.20) + \$48,000 = -\$73,200$$
$$PB_3 = -\$73,200 + (-\$73,200)(0.20) + \$60,000 = -\$27,840$$
$$PB_4 = -\$27,840 + (-\$27,840)(0.20) + \$69,000 = \$35,592$$
$$PB_5 = \$35,592 + \$35,592(0.20) + \$21,000 = \$63,710$$

TABLE 17-10   Cash Flows for Example 17-20

YEAR	INVESTMENT A ($)	INVESTMENT B ($)
0	−100,000	−100,000
1	42,000	19,000
2	42,000	48,000
3	42,000	60,000
4	42,000	69,000
5	42,000	21,000

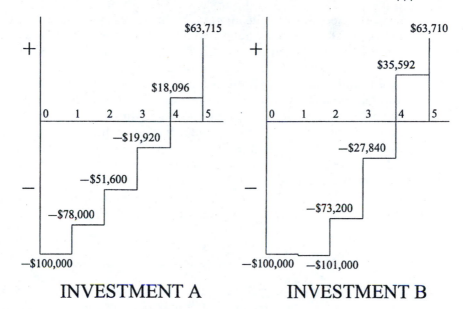

FIGURE 17-12 Project Balance for Example 17-20

The project balance graphs for Investments A and B are shown in Figure 17-12.

Based on the project balance graphs we should invest in Investment A because it has a smaller exposure to loss during the first three years.

NONECONOMIC FACTORS IN DECISION MAKING

Throughout this chapter we looked at the economic factors that make an alternative financially advantageous or financially unviable. When considering alternatives there are other considerations that may sway the decision in one direction or another. These include environmental factors, ergonomic factors, and personal preferences.

CONCLUSION

There are a number of analytical tools that may be used to compare mutually exclusive alternatives. Mutually exclusive alternatives are alternatives where the acceptance of one of the alternatives precludes investing in the other alternatives. To compare alternatives a minimum attractive rate of return (MARR) must be established. Alternatives are worth the effort and risk when they have a return equal to or greater than the MARR. To compare alternatives with different lives, the lives must be made equal. This may be done by shortening the lives of alternatives, lengthening the lives of alternatives, or repurchasing alternatives.

The net present value, incremental net present value, future worth, and annual equivalent methods are related by the equivalence equations and produce the same decisions. When these methods produce a nonnegative numbers the alternative has a return equal to or greater than the MARR. The rate of return for an investment equals the interest rate that produces a net present value equal to zero and may be directly compared to the MARR. The capital recovery method is useful in determining the annual break-even volumes for an alternative. The payback period without interest and payback period with interest select between alternatives based on the speed at which the original investment is recouped and are useful when used in conjunction with the net present value, future worth, annual equivalent, or rate of return. The project balance method incorporates the future value and the payback period with interest while showing the exposure to loss and potential profits graphically for each period.

PROBLEMS

1. A manager has up to $190,000 available to invest in new construction equipment for the company. The manager must purchase a new dump truck and does not have a need for a second dump truck. The dumping trailer can only be purchased along with a dump truck. From the following list of possible equipment, identify all of the mutually exclusive alternatives and identify which of the alternatives are not acceptable.

No.	Description	Cost ($)
1	Loader	125,000
2	Dump Truck 1	70,000
3	Dump Truck 2	65,000
4	Dumping Trailer for the Dump Truck	25,000

2. A manager has up to $200,000 available to invest in new construction equipment for the company. The manager must purchase at least one new dump truck. There are two dumping trailers available. A dump truck must be purchased for each dumping trailer purchased. From the following list of possible equipment, identify all of the mutually exclusive alternatives and identify which of the alternatives are not acceptable.

No.	Description	Cost ($)
1	Dump Truck 1	70,000
2	Dump Truck 2	65,000
3	Dumping Trailer for the Dump Truck	28,000
4	Dumping Trailer for the Dump Truck	25,000

3. Determine the MARR for a company that can borrow funds at 9% and requires 6% profit margin.

4. Determine the MARR for a company that can invest excess funds at 6% and requires 7% profit margin.

5. Your company is looking at purchasing a dump truck at a cost of $65,000. The truck would have a useful life of five years. At the end of the fifth year the salvage value is estimated to be $10,000. The dump truck could be billed out at $55.00 per hour and costs $13.00 per hour to operate. The operator costs $22.00 per hour. Using 1,000 billable hours per year determine the net present value for the purchase of the dump truck using a MARR of 18%. Should your company purchase the dump truck?

6. Your company is looking at purchasing a loader at a cost of $125,000. The loader would have a useful life of seven years. At the end of the seventh year the salvage value is estimated to be $10,000. The loader could be billed out at $85.00 per hour and costs $30.00 per hour to operate. The operator costs $25.00 per hour. Using 1,100 billable hours per year determine the net present value for the purchase of the loader using a MARR of 22%. Should your company purchase the loader?

7. Your company needs to purchase a new track hoe and has narrowed the selection to two pieces of equipment. The first track hoe costs $100,000 and costs $32.00 per hour to operate. The second track hoe costs $110,000 and costs $27.00 per hour to operate. The operator costs $28.00 per hour. The revenue from either track hoe is $95.00 per hour. Using a useful life of four years, a salvage value equal to 20% of the purchase price, 1,200 billable hours per year, and a MARR of 20%, calculate the NPV for both track hoes. Which track hoe should your company choose?

8. Your company needs to purchase a new track hoe and has narrowed the selection to two pieces of equipment. The first track hoe costs $100,000 and has an hourly operation cost of $31.00 and a $35,000 salvage value at the end of three years. The second track hoe costs $65,000 and has an hourly operation cost of $36.00 and no salvage value at the end of three years. The operator cost is $29.00 per hour. The revenue from either track hoe is $95.00 per hour. Using 1,200 billable hours per year and a MARR of 20%, calculate the NPV for both track hoes. Which track hoe should your company choose?

9. Your company needs to purchase a track hoe and has narrowed the selection to two pieces of equipment. The first track hoe costs $100,000 and has an hourly operation cost of $31.00 and a useful life of four years. At the end of four years its salvage value is $20,000. The second track hoe costs $65,000 and has an hourly operation cost of $36.00 and has a useful life of three years. At the end of three years its salvage value is $10,000. The operator cost is $29.00 per hour. The revenue from either track hoe is $95.00 per hour. Using 1,200 billable hours per year and a MARR of 20%, calculate the net present value for both track hoes. Assume that each option is repurchased until their useful lives end in the same year. Which track hoe should your company choose?

10. Your company needs to purchase a truck and has narrowed the selection to two pieces of equipment. The first truck costs $70,000 and has an hourly operation cost of $13.00 and a useful life of six years. At the end of six years its salvage value is $10,000. The second truck costs $40,000 and has an hourly operation cost of $18.00 and has a useful life of four years. At the end of four years its salvage value is $5,000. The operator cost is $22.00 per hour. The revenue from either truck is $55.00 per hour. Using 1,500 billable hours per year and a MARR of 18%, calculate the net present value for both trucks. Assume that each option is repurchased until their useful lives end in the same year. Which truck should your company choose?

11. Determine the incremental net present value for Problem 7. Which track hoe should your company choose?

12. Determine the incremental net present value for Problem 8. Which track hoe should your company choose?

13. Determine the future worth for Problem 5. Should your company purchase the dump truck?

14. Determine the future worth for Problem 6. Should your company purchase the loader?

15. Determine the annual equivalent for Problem 5. Should your company purchase the dump truck?

16. Determine the annual equivalent for Problem 6. Should your company purchase the loader?

17. Determine the rate of return for Problem 5. Should your company purchase the dump truck?

18. Determine the rate of return for Problem 6. Should your company purchase the loader?

19. Your company has $100,000 to invest and has identified the following three investments. Investment A requires an initial investment of $70,000 and has an annual rate of return of 15%. Investment B requires an initial investment of $80,000 and has an annual rate of return of 21%. Investment C requires an initial investment of $30,000 and has an annual rate of return of 29%. Unused funds will be placed in a bank account with an annual percentage rate of 5%. You may invest in each of the investments only once. All of the investments have a life of one year. Which investment should your company invest in?

20. Your company has $200,000 to invest and has identified the following three investments. Investment A requires an initial investment of $130,000 and has an annual rate of return of 12%. Investment B requires an initial investment of $70,000 and has an annual rate of return of 16%. Investment C requires an initial investment of $30,000 and has an annual rate of return of 27%. Unused funds will be placed in a bank account with an annual percentage rate of 4.5%. You may invest in each of the investments only once.

All of the investments have a life of one year. Which investment should your company invest in?

21. Determine the incremental rate of return for Problem 7. Which track hoe should your company choose?

22. Determine the incremental rate of return for Problem 8. Which track hoe should your company choose?

23. Your company has purchased a new track hoe for $100,000. The track hoe can be billed out at $95.00 per hour, has an hourly operation cost of $33.00, and has a useful life of four years. At the end of four years the track hoe has a salvage value of $20,000. The operator cost is $27.00 per hour. Using a MARR of 21%, what is the minimum number of billable hours each year in order for your company to break even?

24. Your company has purchased a new excavator for $210,000. The track hoe can be billed out at $180.00 per hour, has an hourly operation cost of $104.00, and has a useful life of six years. At the end of six years the track hoe has a salvage value of $35,000. The operator cost is $36.00 per hour. Using a MARR of 25%, what is the minimum number of billable hours each year in order for your company to break even?

25. Determine the payback period without interest for Problem 5. If the maximum allowable payback period without interest for your company is three years, should your company purchase the dump truck?

26. Determine the payback period without interest for Problem 6. If the maximum allowable payback period without interest for your company is four years, should your company purchase the loader?

27. Determine the payback period with interest for Problem 5. If the maximum allowable payback period with interest for your company is four years, should your company purchase the dump truck?

28. Determine the payback period with interest for Problem 6. If the maximum allowable payback period with interest for your company is five years, should your company purchase the loader?

29. Draw a project balance chart for Problem 5.

30. Draw a project balance chart for Problem 6.

31. Calculate the net present value for Problem 7 using a computer spreadsheet.

32. Calculate the rate of return for Problem 5 using a computer spreadsheet.

33. Calculate the rate of return for Problem 6 using a computer spreadsheet.

34. Calculate the incremental rate of return for Problem 7 using a computer spreadsheet.

35. Calculate the incremental rate of return for Problem 8 using a computer spreadsheet.

CHAPTER 18

INCOME TAXES AND FINANCIAL DECISIONS

In this chapter you learn how income taxes can affect the attractiveness of financial decisions and how to incorporate income taxes into the decision-making tools from chapter 17. If income taxes affected all alternatives the same, income taxes would not be an issue; however, income taxes prefer some financial alternatives. With income tax rates of up to 38.6% financial managers must take income taxes into account by weighing financial alternatives.

Throughout chapter 17 we ignored the effects of income taxes when making our decisions. In this chapter we look at how income taxes affect the decision process. Because income tax law is constantly changing, the general principles of taxation as they apply to the decision-making process are discussed. Also, there are many exceptions to these rules that are beyond the scope of this chapter. For these two reasons, the reader is advised to consult with a tax accountant or tax attorney for the current regulations regarding any investment.

If all cash flows were treated the same for income tax purposes and taxed at the same rate, income taxes would have little effect on the decision-making process set forth in chapter 17. For the net present value, incremental net present value, future worth, annual equivalent, and capital recovery with return, the after-tax solutions could be calculated by multiplying the before-tax solutions found by the methods in chapter 17 by the result of one minus the tax rate in decimal format. For example, if a company had to pay taxes at a rate of 33%, the after-tax solution from these quantitative methods would be 67% $(1 - 0.33)$ of the before-tax solution found using the methods in chapter 17. Because all alternatives would be multiplied by the same number, the order of their financial attractiveness would not change. Also, all positive values would remain positive and all negative values would remain negative; therefore, these quantitative methods would lead to the same conclusion. The rate of return, incremental rate of return, payback period without interest, and payback period with interest would remain unchanged—because all cash flows would be multiplied by one minus the tax rate—once again leading to the same conclusion. However, this is not the case for the following reasons:

1. Some losses must be carried forward, deferring the tax savings associated with the losses.
2. The tax rates vary based on the size of the taxable income and may vary from year to year.
3. Capital investments—such as investments in equipment and buildings—must be depreciated.
4. Some revenues are taxed at a reduced rate—such as some capital gains.
5. There are tax credits that reduce the actual taxes due rather than reduce the taxable income.

This chapter looks at the effects of each of these on the decision-making process.

LOSSES CARRIED FORWARD

When a company has losses that must be carried forward, the tax benefits of these losses are deferred into future years. Unless there is a change in the marginal tax rate, the deferral of these tax benefits reduces their value due to the time value of money, which in turn reduces the present value for the alternative.

Example 18-1:   A C corporation is looking at investing in one of two investments. Both investments have a before-tax cash flow of −$20,000 for the first year and a before-tax cash flow of $40,000 for the second year. The first investment is a passive investment and the losses from the first year must be carried forward to the second year. For the second investment, the company may write the first year's losses off against other income earned by the company during the first year. Using a marginal tax rate of 34% and a MARR of 15% compare the net present values of the after-tax cash flows for these two investments. How do the after-tax net present values compare to the before-tax net present values?

Solution: No tax savings occur during the first year for the first investment because the loss must be carried forward. The taxable income for the second year is $20,000 ($40,000 − $20,000). The tax liability for the second year is as follows:

$$Tax_2 = \$20,000(0.34) = \$6,800$$

The after-tax cash flows for the first investment are as follows:

$$Cash\ Flow_1 = -\$20,000$$
$$Cash\ Flow_2 = \$40,000 - \$6,800 = \$33,200$$

The net present value for the first investment is calculated using Eq. (15-3) as follows:

$$NPV = -\$20,000/(1 + 0.15)^1 + \$33,200/(1 + 0.15)^2 = \$7,713$$

The second investment may take the tax savings in year 1. The tax liabilities for the second investment are as follows:

$$Tax_1 = -\$20,000(0.34) = -\$6,800$$
$$Tax_2 = \$40,000(0.34) = \$13,600$$

The after-tax cash flows for the second investment are as follows:

$$Cash\ Flow_1 = -\$20,000 - (-\$6,800) = -\$13,200$$
$$Cash\ Flow_2 = \$40,000 - \$13,600 = \$26,400$$

The net present value for the second investment is calculated using Eq. (15-3) as follows:

$$NPV = -\$13,200/(1 + 0.15)^1 + \$26,400/(1 + 0.15)^2 = \$8,484$$

The before-tax net present value for both investments is calculated using Eq. (15-3) as follows:

$$NPV = -\$20,000/(1 + 0.15)^1 + \$40,000/(1 + 0.15)^2 = \$12,854$$

The net present value of the first investment is $771 ($8,484 − $7,713) less than the net present value of the second investment because the company had to carry the first year loss forward. Taxes reduce the net present value of the first investment by $5,141 ($12,854 − $7,713) and the net present value of the second investment by $4,370 ($12,854 − $8,484).

In Example 18-1 we see that both investments have the same pretax net present values and are equally attractive. When taxes are taken into account the second alternative is more attractive because it has a higher net present value. The higher net present value is the result of being able to take the tax loss during the first year.

In chapter 17 we looked at an example where the revenues were ignored because they were similar for all alternatives and the alternatives were compared based on their costs. This may be done when including income taxes in the analysis of alternatives provided that the revenues are similar and the company has sufficient taxable income that may be used to offset the costs. If a company lacks sufficient taxable income to offset the costs, the company will be carrying losses into other tax years and will need to include revenues in the analysis.

DIFFERENT TAX RATES

Fluctuations in a company's tax rate can affect the attractiveness of investments. Investments that produce positive taxable income during years of low tax rates and negative taxable income during years of high tax rates are favored by fluctuations in the tax rate.

> **Example 18-2:**   You are looking at setting up a C corporation to develop real estate. The company is looking at two alternatives. The first alternative produces a taxable income for the company of $10,000, $100,000, and $10,000 for the next three years. The second alternative produces a taxable income for the company of $35,000, $40,000, and $45,000 for the next three years. Compare the net present values before taxes to the net present value after taxes for both of these investments using the corporate federal tax rates for the year 2002 and a MARR of 15%. How do taxes affect the result of the net present value analysis?
>
> **Solution:**   The pretax net present value for the first alternative is calculated using Eq. (15-3) as follows:
>
> $$NPV = (\$10,000)/(1 + 0.15)^1 + (\$100,000)/(1 + 0.15)^2$$
> $$+ (\$10,000)/(1 + 0.15)^3$$
> $$NPV = \$90,885$$
>
> The pretax net present value for the second alternative is calculated using Eq. (15-3) as follows:
>
> $$NPV = (\$35,000)/(1 + 0.15)^1 + (\$40,000)/(1 + 0.15)^2$$
> $$+ (\$45,000)/(1 + 0.15)^3$$
> $$NPV = \$90,269$$
>
> Based on the pretax net present values one would have chosen the first alternative. The annual income taxes for the first alternative are as follows:
>
> $$Tax_1 = \$10,000(0.15) = \$1,500$$
> $$Tax_2 = \$50,000(0.15) + \$25,000(0.25) + \$25,000(0.34) = \$22,250$$
> $$Tax_3 = \$10,000(0.15) = \$1,500$$

The after-tax cash flows for the first alternative are as follows:

$$\text{Cash Flow}_1 = \$10{,}000 - \$1{,}500 = \$8{,}500$$
$$\text{Cash Flow}_2 = \$100{,}000 - \$22{,}250 = \$77{,}750$$
$$\text{Cash Flow}_3 = \$10{,}000 - \$1{,}500 = \$8{,}500$$

The after-tax net present value for the first alternative is calculated using Eq. (15-3) as follows:

$$\text{NPV} = \$8{,}500/(1 + 0.15)^1 + \$77{,}750/(1 + 0.15)^2$$
$$+ \$8{,}500/(1 + 0.15)^3$$
$$\text{NPV} = \$71{,}770$$

The annual income taxes for the second alternative are as follows:

$$\text{Tax}_1 = \$35{,}000(0.15) = \$5{,}250$$
$$\text{Tax}_2 = \$40{,}000(0.15) = \$6{,}000$$
$$\text{Tax}_3 = \$45{,}000(0.15) = \$6{,}750$$

The after-tax cash flows for the second alternative are as follows:

$$\text{Cash Flow}_1 = \$35{,}000 - \$5{,}250 = \$29{,}750$$
$$\text{Cash Flow}_2 = \$40{,}000 - \$6{,}000 = \$34{,}000$$
$$\text{Cash Flow}_3 = \$45{,}000 - \$6{,}750 = \$38{,}250$$

The after-tax net present value for the second alternative is calculated using Eq. (15-3) as follows:

$$\text{NPV} = \$29{,}750/(1 + 0.15)^1 + \$34{,}000/(1 + 0.15)^2$$
$$+ \$38{,}250/(1 + 0.15)^3$$
$$\text{NPV} = \$76{,}728$$

Based on the after-tax net present values one would have chosen the second alternative. We see that the most financially attractive alternative changes from the first alternative to the second alternative after taxes are included in our analysis because the first alternative pays a higher tax rate in the second year due to the effects of the income tax brackets.

DEPRECIATION

Depreciation is not an actual cash flow; therefore, it is not included in the sum of the cash flows used to analyze an alternative. However, because depreciation affects the taxes paid on an alternative, depreciation will affect the taxes due during each period depreciation occurs, which is a cash flow that is included in analysis of an alternative. Depreciation affects the cash flows of the alternatives by deferring the tax savings to future years. For example, when a company purchases a piece of construction equipment, rather than takes the tax savings during the year the equipment was purchased, the company may be required to take the tax savings over a six-year period.

Example 18-3: A company has purchased a small pickup truck for $20,000. Compare writing the truck off in the year it was purchased under Section 179 (see chapter 5) versus depreciating it using 200% declining balance and the half-year convention. The company's marginal tax rate is 34% and its MARR is 15%.

Solution: If the truck were to be written off during the year it was purchased the company's tax savings would be as follows:

$$\text{Tax}_1 = -\$20,000(0.34) = -\$6,800$$

The cash flow for writing the truck off is as follows:

$$\text{Cash Flow}_1 = -\$20,000 - (-\$6,800) = -\$13,200$$

The after-tax net present cost for writing the truck off is calculated using Eq. (15-3) as follows:

$$\text{NPV} = -\$13,200/(1 + 0.15)^1 = -\$11,478$$

Using 5-16, the annual depreciation for the truck is as follows:

$$\text{Depreciation}_1 = \$20,000(0.2000) = \$4,000$$
$$\text{Depreciation}_2 = \$20,000(0.3200) = \$6,400$$
$$\text{Depreciation}_3 = \$20,000(0.1920) = \$3,840$$
$$\text{Depreciation}_4 = \$20,000(0.1152) = \$2,304$$
$$\text{Depreciation}_5 = \$20,000(0.1152) = \$2,304$$
$$\text{Depreciation}_6 = \$20,000(0.0576) = \$1,152$$

The annual tax savings are as follows:

$$\text{Tax}_1 = \$4,000(0.34) = \$1,360$$
$$\text{Tax}_2 = \$6,400(0.34) = \$2,176$$
$$\text{Tax}_3 = \$3,840(0.34) = \$1,306$$
$$\text{Tax}_4 = \$2,304(0.34) = \$783$$
$$\text{Tax}_5 = \$2,304(0.34) = \$783$$
$$\text{Tax}_6 = \$1,152(0.34) = \$392$$

The annual cash flows are as follows:

$$\text{Cash Flow}_1 = -\$20,000 - (-\$1,360) = -\$18,640$$
$$\text{Cash Flow}_2 = \$2,176$$

$$\text{Cash Flow}_3 = \$1,306$$
$$\text{Cash Flow}_4 = \$783$$
$$\text{Cash Flow}_5 = \$783$$
$$\text{Cash Flow}_6 = \$392$$

The after-tax net present cost for depreciating the truck is calculated using Eq. (15-3) as follows:

$$NPV = -\$18,640/(1 + 0.15)^1 + \$2,176/(1 + 0.15)^2 + \$1,306/$$
$$(1 + 0.15)^3 + \$783/(1 + 0.15)^4 + \$783/$$
$$(1 + 0.15)^5 + \$392/(1 + 0.15)^6$$
$$NPV = -\$12,698$$

We see that by depreciating the truck the net present cost has increased by $1,220 ($12,698 − $11,478).

CAPITAL GAINS

Capital gains and losses are gains and losses on the sale or disposition of capital assets, depreciable property, and real property. Throughout history tax breaks have been given to capital gains held for certain lengths of time in order to stimulate long-term investment over short-term investment. Because preferential tax treatment is given to capital investments held for longer periods of time, capital gains often affect the decision-making process when one compares short-term investments to long-term investments.

Example 18-4: On November 30 of last year your company invested $1,000,000 in an office-building complex and has the opportunity to sell its interest in the complex for $1,220,000 in November. If the complex is sold in November, your company will have held the asset for a year or less, and it will be taxed as ordinary income at a rate of 34%. Your company has the option to wait and sell its interest in the complex for $1,200,000 in December. If the complex is sold in December, your company will have held the asset for more than a year and it will be taxed as a long-term capital gain at a rate of 20%. Using an MARR of 15% determine the net present value for each of these sales. Which alternative is more financially attractive?

Solution: For this problem all cash flows that occur during the year will be lumped together. Selling the property in November will result in a capital gain of $220,000 ($1,220,000 − $1,000,000) that will be taxed at a rate of 34%. The income tax due on the sale is $74,800 ($220,000 × 0.34) for an after-tax cash flow of $1,145,200. The net present value for this option is calculated using Eq. (15-3) as follows:

$$NPV = -\$1,000,000 + \$1,145,200/(1 + 0.15)^1 = -\$4,174$$

Selling the property in December will result in a long-term capital gain of $200,000 ($1,200,000 − $1,000,000) that will be taxed at a rate of 20%. The income tax due on the sale is $40,000 ($200,000 × 0.20) for an after-tax cash flow of $1,160,000. The net present value for this option is calculated using Eq. (15-3) as follows:

$$NPV = -\$1,000,000 + \$1,160,000/(1 + 0.15)^1 = \$8,696$$

By waiting a month to sell the asset, although the sale price is reduced by $20,000, the price reduction is more than offset by tax savings. In fact, by waiting a month, the net present value of the sale for the asset goes from an unacceptable (a negative) net present value to an acceptable (a positive) net present value.

TAX CREDITS

Tax credits reduce the tax liability and as a result affect the attractiveness of an investment. For example, when tax credits are given to hire and train members of a targeted group a company may reduce its tax liability by a percentage of the wages paid to the target group, in lieu of writing off that same percentage of wages as an expense, thereby reducing its taxable income and tax liability. This preferential tax treatment favors the alternatives receiving the tax credit.

Example 18-5: Your company is looking at leasing office space for the next three years and has identified two options. The first option is to lease space for $13,200 per year. The second option is to lease space for $10,800 per year; however, the second option will require you to spend $10,000 during the first year to comply with the Americans with Disability Act. Your company can claim a tax credit equal to 50% of the costs of the modifications made to comply with the Americans with Disability Act. Both leases may be treated as an operating lease. Using a MARR of 15% and a marginal tax rate of 35%, determine the before-tax and after-tax net present values (costs) for both options. How do taxes affect your decision?

Solution: Determine the before-tax net present cost for the first option using Eq. (15-3) as follows:

$$NPV = (-\$13,200)/1.15^1 + (-\$13,200)/1.15^2 + (-\$13,200)/1.15^3$$
$$NPV = -\$30,139$$

The cash flow for the first year of the second option is a cash disbursement of $20,800 ($10,800 + $10,000). Determine the before-tax net present cost for the second option using Eq. (15-3) as follows:

$$NPV = (-\$20,800)/1.15^1 + (-\$10,800)/1.15^2 + (-\$10,800)/1.15^3$$
$$NPV = -\$33,354$$

Based on the before-tax net present cost the first option is more attractive. The annual tax savings and the after-tax cash flow for the first option is as follows:

$$Tax_{1-3} = \$13,200(0.35) = \$4,620$$
$$Cash\ Flow_{1-3} = -\$13,200 + \$4,620 = -\$8,580$$

The after-tax net present cost for the first option is calculated using Eq. (15-3) as follows:

$$NPV = (-\$8,580)/1.15^1 + (-\$8,580)/1.15^2 + (-\$8,580)/1.15^3$$
$$NPV = -\$19,590$$

The annual tax savings for the second option are as follows:

$$Tax_1 = \$20,800(0.35) + \$10,000(0.50) = \$12,280$$
$$Tax_{2-3} = \$10,800(0.35) = \$3,780$$

The after-tax cash flows for the second option are as follows:

$$Cash\ Flow_1 = -\$20,800 + \$12,280 = -\$8,520$$
$$Cash\ Flow_{2-3} = -\$10,800 + \$3,780 = -\$7,020$$

The after-tax net present cost for the second option is calculated using Eq. (15-3) as follows:

$$NPV = (-\$8,520)/1.15^1 + (-\$7,020)/1.15^2 + (-\$7,020)/1.15^3$$
$$NPV = -\$17,333$$

Based on the after-tax net present cost the second option is more attractive. The most financially attractive alternative changes from the first alternative to the second alternative after taxes are included in our analysis because the second alternative gets a $5,000 tax credit.

AFTER-TAX CASH FLOWS

Now that we have discussed a number of tax provisions that affect the financial attractiveness of alternatives, we are ready to incorporate them into the comparison of alternatives. A common decision that must be compared on an after-tax basis is the comparison of leasing a vehicle versus purchasing a vehicle. In the next example we compare three alternatives of obtaining a vehicle: the purchase of the vehicle using cash, the purchase of the vehicle through financing, and leasing the vehicle with an operating lease.

Example 18-6: Your S corporation needs a new truck for its operations and is looking at three alternatives. The first alternative is to lease the truck for sixty months. The monthly lease payment is $525 per month with the first payment due in April. At the end of the lease the truck will be returned to the dealer. The lease is considered an operating lease and excludes all maintenance and operational costs. The second alternative is to purchase the truck with a sixty-month loan at an interest rate of 9% (APY 9.38). The loan has $250 in origination fees. The truck's entire sales price of $25,000—including the loan origination fees—can be financed. The first payment is due in April. The third alternative is to purchase the truck with cash for $25,000 in April. If your company purchases the truck, the estimated salvage value of the truck at the end of five years is $5,000. Gains and losses on the sale of the truck will be treated as ordinary income. The truck may be depreciated using the half-year convention. For all three alternatives, the truck is to be placed in service in April. Your company's tax year is the same as the calendar year and its marginal tax rate is 34%. Using the net present value (cost) method, which of the above alternatives is the best for your company if your minimal acceptable rate of return (MARR) is 1% per month? Assume that there is sufficient taxable income to use all tax savings in the year they occur.

Solution: The costs for each month can be easily determined; therefore, we use a period length of one month. Because the company is an S corporation that will pay income taxes at the individual level, periodic tax payments are due in April, June, September, and January of the following year. The useful life of the truck will be from April of the first year to March of the sixth year. The income tax savings or costs for the sixth year will occur in April, June, and September of the sixth year and January of the seventh year; therefore, the study period will be from April of the first year to January of the seventh year. Solving this problem is best done using a spreadsheet because each option will require seventy periods to cover the study period. The spreadsheet solutions are shown in Figures 18-1, 18-4, and 18-5.

First, we calculate the net present value for the first alternative, leasing the truck. The after-tax cost for each month is the lease payment less the tax savings, which occur only in the months of April, June, September, and January. The tax savings for the first year are divided equally among the four months and are calculated as follows:

$$\text{Tax Savings}_1 = \$525.00/\text{month}(9\text{ months})(0.34)/4 = \$401.63$$

The after-tax cost for the first month—April—is calculated as follows:

$$\text{After-Tax Cost}_1 = -\$525.00 + \$401.63 = -\$123.37$$

The present value of the after-tax cost for the first month is calculated using Eq. (15-3) as follows:

$$P_1 = -\$123.37/(1 + 0.01)^1 = -\$122.15$$

Because no tax savings occur in the second month—May—the after-tax cost equals the costs of the lease. The present value of the after-tax cost for the second month is calculated using Eq. (15-3) as follows:

$$P_2 = -\$525.00/(1 + 0.01)^2 = -\$514.66$$

The after-tax costs and present values of the third through seventienth months are calculated in a similar manner. Keep in mind that the lease cost will go to zero in the sixty-first month, the tax savings will change beginning with the thirteenth month—April of the second year and again beginning with the sixty-first month—April of the sixth year. The tax savings for the thirteenth and sixty-first months are calculated as follows:

$$\text{Tax Savings}_{13} = \$525.00/\text{month}(12\,\text{months})(0.34)/4 = \$535.50$$
$$\text{Tax Savings}_{61} = \$525.00/\text{month}(3\,\text{months})(0.34)/4 = \$133.88$$

The spreadsheet solution for the lease option is shown in Figure 18-1. The differences between the spreadsheet solution and this example are because of rounding errors in the example.

Summing the present values, we get a net present cost of $15,686.

Next, we calculate the net present value for the second alternative, purchasing the truck with a sixty-month loan. The after-tax cost for each month is the loan payment less the tax savings. As in the lease option, the tax savings are spread equally among the months of April, June, September, and January. The tax savings result from the interest paid on the loan and the depreciation of the truck. To calculate the tax savings, the interest paid on the loan each year needs to be calculated. This may be done in two ways.

The first way is to use Eq. (16-7) to determine the monthly payment, Eq. (16-13) to determine the outstanding balance at the end of each year, and Eq. (16-14) to determine the annual interest costs. The periodic rate is calculated using Eq. (16-3) as follows:

$$i = 0.09/12 = 0.0075$$

The initial loan value equals $25,250—the cost of the truck plus the loan origination fees. Using Eq. (16-7) to calculate the monthly loan payments we get the following:

$$A = \$25,250[0.0075(1 + 0.0075)^{60}]/[(1 + 0.0075)^{60} - 1] = \$524.15$$

The outstanding balance on the loan for years 1 through 6 is calculated using Eq. (16-13) as follows:

$$U_9 = \$524.15[(1 + 0.0075)^{60-9} - 1]/[0.0075(1 + 0.0075)^{60-9}]$$
$$U_9 = \$22,145.11$$

MARR 1.00%
Marginal Tax Rate 34.00%
Lease Payment 525.00

Leasing

	Jan.	Feb.	March	April	May	June	July	Aug.	Sept.	Oct.	Nov.	Dec.
Period				1	2	3	4	5	6	7	8	9
Lease Payment				(525.00)	(525.00)	(525.00)	(525.00)	(525.00)	(525.00)	(525.00)	(525.00)	(525.00)
Less Tax Savings				401.63	—	401.63	—	—	401.63	—	—	—
After-Tax Cost				(123.38)	(525.00)	(123.38)	(525.00)	(525.00)	(123.38)	(525.00)	(525.00)	(525.00)
Present Value				(122.15)	(514.66)	(119.75)	(504.51)	(499.52)	(116.22)	(489.68)	(484.83)	(480.03)

	Jan.	Feb.	March	April	May	June	July	Aug.	Sept.	Oct.	Nov.	Dec.
Period	10	11	12	13	14	15	16	17	18	19	20	21
Lease Payment	(525.00)	(525.00)	(525.00)	(525.00)	(525.00)	(525.00)	(525.00)	(525.00)	(525.00)	(525.00)	(525.00)	(525.00)
Less Tax Savings	401.63	—	—	535.50	—	535.50	—	—	535.50	—	—	—
After-Tax Cost	(123.38)	(525.00)	(525.00)	10.50	(525.00)	10.50	(525.00)	(525.00)	10.50	(525.00)	(525.00)	(525.00)
Present Value	(111.69)	(470.57)	(465.91)	9.23	(456.73)	9.04	(447.73)	(443.30)	8.78	(434.56)	(430.26)	(426.00)

	Jan.	Feb.	March	April	May	June	July	Aug.	Sept.	Oct.	Nov.	Dec.
Period	22	23	24	25	26	27	28	29	30	31	32	33
Lease Payment	(525.00)	(525.00)	(525.00)	(525.00)	(525.00)	(525.00)	(525.00)	(525.00)	(525.00)	(525.00)	(525.00)	(525.00)
Less Tax Savings	535.50	—	—	535.50	—	535.50	—	—	535.50	—	—	—
After-Tax Cost	10.50	(525.00)	(525.00)	10.50	(525.00)	10.50	(525.00)	(525.00)	10.50	(525.00)	(525.00)	(525.00)
Present Value	8.44	(417.61)	(413.47)	8.19	(405.33)	8.03	(397.34)	(393.40)	7.79	(385.65)	(381.83)	(378.05)

Block 1

Month	Jan.	Feb.	March	April	May	June	July	Aug.	Sept.	Oct.	Nov.	Dec.
Period	34	35	36	37	38	39	40	41	42	43	44	45
Lease Payment	(525.00)	(525.00)	(525.00)	(525.00)	(525.00)	(525.00)	(525.00)	(525.00)	(525.00)	(525.00)	(525.00)	(525.00)
Less Tax Savings	535.50	—	—	535.50	—	535.50	—	—	535.50	—	—	—
After-Tax Cost	10.50	(525.00)	(525.00)	10.50	(525.00)	10.50	(525.00)	(525.00)	10.50	(525.00)	(525.00)	(525.00)
Present Value	7.49	(370.60)	(366.94)	7.27	(359.71)	7.12	(352.62)	(349.13)	6.91	(342.25)	(338.86)	(335.50)

Block 2

Month	Jan.	Feb.	March	April	May	June	July	Aug.	Sept.	Oct.	Nov.	Dec.
Period	46	47	48	49	50	51	52	53	54	55	56	57
Lease Payment	(525.00)	(525.00)	(525.00)	(525.00)	(525.00)	(525.00)	(525.00)	(525.00)	(525.00)	(525.00)	(525.00)	(525.00)
Less Tax Savings	535.50	—	—	535.50	—	535.50	—	—	535.50	—	—	—
After-Tax Cost	10.50	(525.00)	(525.00)	10.50	(525.00)	10.50	(525.00)	(525.00)	10.50	(525.00)	(525.00)	(525.00)
Present Value	6.64	(328.89)	(325.64)	6.45	(319.22)	6.32	(312.93)	(309.83)	6.14	(303.73)	(300.72)	(297.74)

Block 3

Month	Jan.	Feb.	March	April	May	June	July	Aug.	Sept.	Oct.	Nov.	Dec.
Period	58	59	60	61	62	63	64	65	66	67	68	69
Lease Payment	(525.00)	(525.00)	(525.00)	—	—	—	—	—	—	—	—	—
Less Tax Savings	535.50	—	—	133.88	—	133.88	—	—	133.88	—	—	—
After-Tax Cost	10.50	(525.00)	(525.00)	133.88	—	133.88	—	—	133.88	—	—	—
Present Value	5.90	(291.88)	(288.99)	72.96	—	71.52	—	—	69.42	—	—	—

Block 4

Month	Jan.
Period	70
Lease Payment	—
Less Tax Savings	133.88
After-Tax Cost	133.88
Present Value	66.71

Net Present Value	(15,686)

FIGURE 18-1 Spreadsheet Solution for Leasing the Truck

$$U_{21} = \$524.15[(1 + 0.0075)^{60-21} - 1]/[0.0075(1 + 0.0075)^{60-21}]$$
$$U_{21} = \$17,666.63$$
$$U_{33} = \$524.15[(1 + 0.0075)^{60-33} - 1]/[0.0075(1 + 0.0075)^{60-33}]$$
$$U_{33} = \$12,768.03$$
$$U_{45} = \$524.15[(1 + 0.0075)^{60-45} - 1]/[0.0075(1 + 0.0075)^{60-45}]$$
$$U_{45} = \$7,409.91$$
$$U_{57} = \$524.15[(1 + 0.0075)^{60-57} - 1]/[0.0075(1 + 0.0075)^{60-57}]$$
$$U_{57} = \$1,549.15$$
$$U_{60} = \$524.15[(1 + 0.0075)^{60-60} - 1]/[0.0075(1 + 0.0075)^{60-60}]$$
$$= \$0$$

The annual interest paid each year is calculated using Eq. (16-14) as follows:

$$I_{1-9} = 9(\$524.15) + \$22,145.11 - \$25,250.00 = \$1,612.46$$
$$I_{10-21} = 12(\$524.15) + \$17,666.63 - \$22,145.11 = \$1,811.32$$
$$I_{22-33} = 12(\$524.15) + \$12,768.03 - \$17,666.63 = \$1,391.20$$
$$I_{34-45} = 12(\$524.15) + \$7,409.91 - \$12,768.03 = \$931.68$$
$$I_{46-57} = 12(\$524.15) + \$1,549.15 - \$7,409.91 = \$429.04$$
$$I_{58-60} = 3(\$524.15) + \$0 - \$1,549.15 = \$23.30$$

The second way is to prepare a loan amortization schedule. Because the payments are made monthly, the amortization schedule will cover sixty months beginning with April of year 1 and ending in March of year 6. The amortization schedule for the loan is shown in Figures 18-2 and 18-3 and was prepared as shown in chapter 16. Included on the amortization schedule is a column showing the year-to-date totals for both the monthly payments and the interest paid. Note that the last payment is slightly smaller due to rounding of the monthly payment and monthly interest.

For income tax purposes, the loan payment is not deductible; however, the interest on the loan is deductible. The interest itself is not a cash flow because it has already been included in the cash flow for the loan payment.

In addition to interest, depreciation is also tax deductible. Like interest, depreciation is not a cash flow but is necessary to calculate the cash flow due to tax savings. From Table 5-6 the depreciation for the truck is calculated as follows:

$$D_{1-9} = (\$25,000)0.2000 = \$5,000$$
$$D_{10-21} = (\$25,000)0.3200 = \$8,000$$
$$D_{22-33} = (\$25,000)0.1920 = \$4,800$$
$$D_{34-45} = (\$25,000)0.1152 = \$2,880$$
$$D_{46-57} = (\$25,000)0.1152 = \$2,880$$
$$D_{58-60} = (\$25,000)0.0576 = \$1,440$$

APR: 9.00%   Page 1
Term (Months): 60 Months
Loan Amount: $25,250.00
Monthly Payment: $524.15

Year	Month	Beginning Principal	Monthly Interest	Monthly Payment	Ending Principal	Year to Date Interest	Year to Date Payment
	0				25,250.00		
1	1	25,250.00	189.38	524.15	24,915.23	189.38	524.15
1	2	24,915.23	186.86	524.15	24,577.94	376.24	1,048.30
1	3	24,577.94	184.33	524.15	24,238.12	560.57	1,572.45
1	4	24,238.12	181.79	524.15	23,895.76	742.36	2,096.60
1	5	23,895.76	179.22	524.15	23,550.83	921.58	2,620.75
1	6	23,550.83	176.63	524.15	23,203.31	1,098.21	3,144.90
1	7	23,203.31	174.02	524.15	22,853.18	1,272.23	3,669.05
1	8	22,853.18	171.40	524.15	22,500.43	1,443.63	4,193.20
1	9	22,500.43	168.75	524.15	22,145.03	1,612.38	4,717.35
2	10	22,145.03	166.09	524.15	21,786.97	166.09	524.15
2	11	21,786.97	163.40	524.15	21,426.22	329.49	1,048.30
2	12	21,426.22	160.70	524.15	21,062.77	490.19	1,572.45
2	13	21,062.77	157.97	524.15	20,696.59	648.16	2,096.60
2	14	20,696.59	155.22	524.15	20,327.66	803.38	2,620.75
2	15	20,327.66	152.46	524.15	19,955.97	955.84	3,144.90
2	16	19,955.97	149.67	524.15	19,581.49	1,105.51	3,669.05
2	17	19,581.49	146.86	524.15	19,204.20	1,252.37	4,193.20
2	18	19,204.20	144.03	524.15	18,824.08	1,396.40	4,717.35
2	19	18,824.08	141.18	524.15	18,441.11	1,537.58	5,241.50
2	20	18,441.11	138.31	524.15	18,055.27	1,675.89	5,765.65
2	21	18,055.27	135.41	524.15	17,666.53	1,811.30	6,289.80
3	22	17,666.53	132.50	524.15	17,274.88	132.50	524.15
3	23	17,274.88	129.56	524.15	16,880.29	262.06	1,048.30
3	24	16,880.29	126.60	524.15	16,482.74	388.66	1,572.45
3	25	16,482.74	123.62	524.15	16,082.21	512.28	2,096.60
3	26	16,082.21	120.62	524.15	15,678.68	632.90	2,620.75
3	27	15,678.68	117.59	524.15	15,272.12	750.49	3,144.90
3	28	15,272.12	114.54	524.15	14,862.51	865.03	3,669.05
3	29	14,862.51	111.47	524.15	14,449.83	976.50	4,193.20
3	30	14,449.83	108.37	524.15	14,034.05	1,084.87	4,717.35
3	31	14,034.05	105.26	524.15	13,615.16	1,190.13	5,241.50
3	32	13,615.16	102.11	524.15	13,193.12	1,292.24	5,765.65
3	33	13,193.12	98.95	524.15	12,767.92	1,391.19	6,289.80

FIGURE 18-2   Loan Amortization Schedule

The disposal of the truck will result in a gain or loss, which will be treated as ordinary income or ordinary loss. The book value will be equal to the purchase price less the depreciation taken and is calculated as follows:

$$BV_{60} = \$25,000 - \$5,000 - \$8,000 - \$4,800 - \$2,880 - \$2,880 - \$1,440$$

$$BV_{60} = \$0$$

APR: 9.00%
Term (Months): 60 Months
Loan Amount: $25,250.00
Monthly Payment: $524.15

Year	Month	Beginning Principal	Monthly Interest	Monthly Payment	Ending Principal	Year to Date Interest	Year to Date Payment
4	34	12,767.92	95.76	524.15	12,339.53	95.76	524.15
4	35	12,339.53	92.55	524.15	11,907.93	188.31	1,048.30
4	36	11,907.93	89.31	524.15	11,473.09	277.62	1,572.45
4	37	11,473.09	86.05	524.15	11,034.99	363.67	2,096.60
4	38	11,034.99	82.76	524.15	10,593.60	446.43	2,620.75
4	39	10,593.60	79.45	524.15	10,148.90	525.88	3,144.90
4	40	10,148.90	76.12	524.15	9,700.87	602.00	3,669.05
4	41	9,700.87	72.76	524.15	9,249.48	674.76	4,193.20
4	42	9,249.48	69.37	524.15	8,794.70	744.13	4,717.35
4	43	8,794.70	65.96	524.15	8,336.51	810.09	5,241.50
4	44	8,336.51	62.52	524.15	7,874.88	872.61	5,765.65
4	45	7,874.88	59.06	524.15	7,409.79	931.67	6,289.80
5	46	7,409.79	55.57	524.15	6,941.21	55.57	524.15
5	47	6,941.21	52.06	524.15	6,469.12	107.63	1,048.30
5	48	6,469.12	48.52	524.15	5,993.49	156.15	1,572.45
5	49	5,993.49	44.95	524.15	5,514.29	201.10	2,096.60
5	50	5,514.29	41.36	524.15	5,031.50	242.46	2,620.75
5	51	5,031.50	37.74	524.15	4,545.09	280.20	3,144.90
5	52	4,545.09	34.09	524.15	4,055.03	314.29	3,669.05
5	53	4,055.03	30.41	524.15	3,561.29	344.70	4,193.20
5	54	3,561.29	26.71	524.15	3,063.85	371.41	4,717.35
5	55	3,063.85	22.98	524.15	2,562.68	394.39	5,241.50
5	56	2,562.68	19.22	524.15	2,057.75	413.61	5,765.65
5	57	2,057.75	15.43	524.15	1,549.03	429.04	6,289.80
6	58	1,549.03	11.62	524.15	1,036.50	11.62	524.15
6	59	1,036.50	7.77	524.15	520.12	19.39	1,048.30
6	60	520.12	3.90	524.02	—	23.29	1,572.32

FIGURE 18-3 Loan Amoritzation Schedule

Because the truck is sold for more that its book value, a gain will occur in the sixth year. The gain is equal to the difference in the salvage value and the book value and is calculated as follows.

Capital Gain = $5,000 − $0 = $5,000

The tax savings are equal to the sum of the interest paid and the depreciation multiplied by the marginal tax rate. The tax savings are similar to a cash receipt and as such are positive. The tax savings will change at the beginning of the first, thirteenth, twenty-fifth, thirty-seventh, forty-ninth, and sixty-first months and is calculated as follows:

$$\text{Tax Savings}_1 = (\$1,612.46 + \$5,000.00)(0.34)/4 = \$562.05$$
$$\text{Tax Savings}_{13} = (\$1,811.32 + \$8,000.00)(0.34)/4 = \$833.96$$
$$\text{Tax Savings}_{25} = (\$1,391.20 + \$4,800.00)(0.34)/4 = \$526.25$$

$$\text{Tax Savings}_{37} = (\$931.68 + \$2,880.00)(0.34)/4 = \$323.99$$
$$\text{Tax Savings}_{49} = (\$429.04 + \$2,880.00)(0.34)/4 = \$281.27$$

In the sixty-first month there will be an increase in tax liability due to gains on the truck, which will be taxed at the rate of 34%. The tax savings beginning in the sixty-first month is calculated as follows:

$$\text{Tax Savings}_{61} = (\$23.30 + \$1,440.00 - \$5,000.00)(0.34)/4$$
$$\text{Tax Savings}_{61} = -\$300.62$$

The after-tax costs and present value are calculated in the same manner as they were calculated for the lease option. The spreadsheet solution for the purchase of the truck with a loan is shown in Figure 18-4. The differences between the spreadsheet solution and this example are because of rounding errors in the example.

Summing the present values, we get a net present cost of $13,378.

Next, we calculate the net present value for the third alternative, which is to purchase the truck outright for $25,000. The purchase of the truck occurs during April. For this alternative, only depreciation will be tax deductible. The depreciation will be the same for this alternative as for the second alternative. Similar the disposal of the truck in the sixth year will result in a capital gain of $5,000.

The tax savings are equal to the depreciation multiplied by the marginal tax rate and are divided among the four payments that occur during the year. The tax savings are similar to a cash receipt and as such are positive. The tax savings will change at the beginning of the first, thirteenth, twenty-fifth, thirty-seventh, forty-ninth, and sixty-first months and is calculated as follows:

$$\text{Tax Savings}_{1} = \$5,000.00(0.34)/4 = \$425$$
$$\text{Tax Savings}_{13} = \$8,000.00(0.34)/4 = \$680$$
$$\text{Tax Savings}_{25} = \$4,800.00(0.34)/4 = \$408$$
$$\text{Tax Savings}_{37} = \$2,880.00(0.34)/4 = \$244.80$$
$$\text{Tax Savings}_{49} = \$2,880.00(0.34)/4 = \$244.80$$

In the sixty-first month there will be an increase in tax liability due to gains on the truck, which will be taxed at the rate of 34%. The tax savings beginning in the sixty-first month is calculated as follows:

$$\text{Tax Savings}_{61} = (\$1,440.00 - \$5,000.00)(0.34)/4 = -\$302.60$$

The after-tax costs and present value are calculated in the same manner as they were calculated for the lease option. The spreadsheet solution for the purchasing the truck is shown in Figure 18-5. The differences between the spreadsheet solution and this example are because of rounding errors in the example.

Summing the present values, we get a net present cost of $16,265.

The purchase with a loan has the lowest net present cost; therefore, purchasing the truck with the loan is the most financially attractive alternative.

MARR	1.00%	
Marginal Tax Rate	34.00%	
Purchase Price	25,000	
Loan Interest Rate	9.00%	
Loan Fees	250.00	
Salvage Value	5,000	

Loan

Month	April	May	June	July	Aug.	Sept.	Oct.	Nov.	Dec.
Period	1	2	3	4	5	6	7	8	9
Loan Payment	(524.15)	(524.15)	(524.15)	(524.15)	(524.15)	(524.15)	(524.15)	(524.15)	(524.15)
Salvage Value	—	—	—	—	—	—	—	—	—
Less Tax Savings	562.05	—	562.05	—	—	562.05	—	—	—
After-Tax Cost	37.90	(524.15)	37.90	(524.15)	(524.15)	37.90	(524.15)	(524.15)	(524.15)
Present Value	37.53	(513.82)	36.79	(503.70)	(498.71)	35.71	(488.88)	(484.04)	(479.25)

Month	Jan.	Feb.	March	April	May	June	July	Aug.	Sept.	Oct.	Nov.	Dec.
Period	10	11	12	13	14	15	16	17	18	19	20	21
Loan Payment	(524.15)	(524.15)	(524.15)	(524.15)	(524.15)	(524.15)	(524.15)	(524.15)	(524.15)	(524.15)	(524.15)	(524.15)
Salvage Value	—	—	—	—	—	—	—	—	—	—	—	—
Less Tax Savings	562.05	—	—	833.96	—	833.96	—	—	833.96	—	—	—
After-Tax Cost	37.90	(524.15)	(524.15)	309.81	(524.15)	309.81	(524.15)	(524.15)	309.81	(524.15)	(524.15)	(524.15)
Present Value	34.31	(469.81)	(465.16)	272.22	(455.99)	266.86	(447.01)	(442.58)	259.01	(433.86)	(429.56)	(425.31)

Month	Jan.	Feb.	March	April	May	June	July	Aug.	Sept.	Oct.	Nov.	Dec.
Period	22	23	24	25	26	27	28	29	30	31	32	33
Loan Payment	(524.15)	(524.15)	(524.15)	(524.15)	(524.15)	(524.15)	(524.15)	(524.15)	(524.15)	(524.15)	(524.15)	(524.15)
Salvage Value	—	—	—	—	—	—	—	—	—	—	—	—
Less Tax Savings	833.96	—	—	526.25	—	526.25	—	—	526.25	—	—	—
After-Tax Cost	309.81	(524.15)	(524.15)	2.10	(524.15)	2.10	(524.15)	(524.15)	2.10	(524.15)	(524.15)	(524.15)
Present Value	248.90	(416.93)	(412.80)	1.64	(404.67)	1.61	(396.70)	(392.77)	1.56	(385.03)	(381.22)	(377.44)

Month	Jan.	Feb.	March	April	May	June	July	Aug.	Sept.	Oct.	Nov.	Dec.
Period	34	35	36	37	38	39	40	41	42	43	44	45
Loan Payment	(524.15)	(524.15)	(524.15)	(524.15)	(524.15)	(524.15)	(524.15)	(524.15)	(524.15)	(524.15)	(524.15)	(524.15)
Salvage Value	—	—	—	—	—	—	—	—	—	—	—	—
Less Tax Savings	526.25	—	—	323.99	—	323.99	—	—	323.99	—	—	—
After-Tax Cost	2.10	(524.15)	(524.15)	(200.16)	(524.15)	(200.16)	(524.15)	(524.15)	(200.16)	(524.15)	(524.15)	(524.15)
Present Value	1.50	(370.00)	(366.34)	(138.51)	(359.12)	(135.78)	(352.05)	(348.56)	(131.79)	(341.69)	(338.31)	(334.96)

Month	Jan.	Feb.	March	April	May	June	July	Aug.	Sept.	Oct.	Nov.	Dec.
Period	46	47	48	49	50	51	52	53	54	55	56	57
Loan Payment	(524.15)	(524.15)	(524.15)	(524.15)	(524.15)	(524.15)	(524.15)	(524.15)	(524.15)	(524.15)	(524.15)	(524.15)
Salvage Value	—	—	—	—	—	—	—	—	—	—	—	—
Less Tax Savings	323.99	—	—	281.27	—	281.27	—	—	281.27	—	—	—
After-Tax Cost	(200.16)	(524.15)	(524.15)	(242.88)	(524.15)	(242.88)	(524.15)	(524.15)	(242.88)	(524.15)	(524.15)	(524.15)
Present Value	(126.65)	(328.36)	(325.11)	(149.16)	(318.70)	(146.22)	(312.42)	(309.33)	(141.92)	(303.24)	(300.23)	(297.26)

Month	Jan.	Feb.	March	April	May	June	July	Aug.	Sept.	Oct.	Nov.	Dec.
Period	58	59	60	61	62	63	64	65	66	67	68	69
Loan Payment	(524.15)	(524.15)	(524.15)	—	—	—	—	—	—	—	—	—
Salvage Value	—	—	5,000.00	—	—	—	—	—	—	—	—	—
Less Tax Savings	281.27	—	—	(300.62)	—	(300.62)	—	—	(300.62)	—	—	—
After-Tax Cost	(242.88)	(524.15)	4,475.85	(300.62)	—	(300.62)	—	—	(300.62)	—	—	—
Present Value	(136.38)	(291.40)	2,463.73	(163.84)	—	(160.61)	—	—	(155.89)	—	—	—

Month	Jan.
Period	70
Loan Payment	—
Salvage Value	—
Less Tax Savings	(300.62)
After-Tax Cost	(300.62)
Present Value	(149.80)

Net Present Value	(13,378)

FIGURE 18-4 Spreadsheet Solution for Purchasing the Truck with a Loan

MARR	1.00%								
Marginal Tax Rate	34.00%								
Purchase Price	25,000								
Salvage Value	5,000								

Purchase

Month				Apr.	May.	Jun.	Jul.	Aug.	Sep.	Oct.	Nov.	Dec.
Period				1	2	3	4	5	6	7	8	9
Purchase				(25,000.00)	—	—	—	—	—	—	—	—
Salvage Value				—	—	—	—	—	—	—	—	—
Less Tax Savings				425.00	—	425.00	—	—	425.00	—	—	—
After-Tax Cost				(24,575.00)	—	425.00	—	—	425.00	—	—	—
Present Value				(24,331.68)	—	412.50	—	—	400.37	—	—	—

Month	Jan.	Feb.	Mar.	Apr.	May.	Jun.	Jul.	Aug.	Sep.	Oct.	Nov.	Dec.
Period	10	11	12	13	41	15	16	17	18	19	20	21
Purchase	—	—	—	—	—	—	—	—	—	—	—	—
Salvage Value	—	—	—	—	—	—	—	—	—	—	—	—
Less Tax Savings	425.00	—	—	680.00	—	680.00	—	—	680.00	—	—	—
After-Tax Cost	425.00	—	—	680.00	—	680.00	—	—	680.00	—	—	—
Present Value	384.75	—	—	597.49	—	585.72	—	—	568.49	—	—	—

Month	Jan.	Feb.	Mar.	Apr.	May.	Jun.	Jul.	Aug.	Sep.	Oct.	Nov.	Dec.
Period	22	23	24	25	26	27	28	29	30	31	32	33
Purchase	—	—	—	—	—	—	—	—	—	—	—	—
Salvage Value	—	—	—	—	—	—	—	—	—	—	—	—
Less Tax Savings	680.00	—	—	408.00	—	408.00	—	—	408.00	—	—	—
After-Tax Cost	680.00	—	—	408.00	—	408.00	—	—	408.00	—	—	—
Present Value	546.31	—	—	318.15	—	311.88	—	—	302.70	—	—	—

Month	Jan.	Feb.	Mar.	Apr.	May.	Jun.	Jul.	Aug.	Sep.	Oct.	Nov.	Dec.
Period	34	35	36	37	38	39	40	41	42	43	44	45
Purchase	—	—	—	—	—	—	—	—	—	—	—	—
Salvage Value	—	—	—	—	—	—	—	—	—	—	—	—
Less Tax Savings	408.00	—	—	244.80	—	244.80	—	—	244.80	—	—	—
After-Tax Cost	408.00	—	—	244.80	—	244.80	—	—	244.80	—	—	—
Present Value	290.89	—	—	169.40	—	166.06	—	—	161.18	—	—	—

Month	Jan.	Feb.	Mar.	Apr.	May.	Jun.	Jul.	Aug.	Sep.	Oct.	Nov.	Dec.
Period	46	47	48	49	50	51	52	53	54	55	56	57
Purchase	—	—	—	—	—	—	—	—	—	—	—	—
Salvage Value	—	—	—	—	—	—	—	—	—	—	—	—
Less Tax Savings	244.80	—	—	244.80	—	244.80	—	—	244.80	—	—	—
After-Tax Cost	244.80	—	—	244.80	—	244.80	—	—	244.80	—	—	—
Present Value	154.89	—	—	150.34	—	147.37	—	—	143.04	—	—	—

Month	Jan.	Feb.	Mar.	Apr.	May.	Jun.	Jul.	Aug.	Sep.	Oct.	Nov.	Dec.
Period	58	59	60	61	62	63	64	65	66	67	68	69
Purchase	—	—		—	—	—	—	—	—	—	—	—
Salvage Value	—	—	5,000.00	—	—	—	—	—	—	—	—	—
Less Tax Savings	244.80	—	—	(302.60)	—	(302.60)	—	—	(302.60)	—	—	—
After-Tax Cost	244.80	—	5,000.00	(302.60)	—	(302.60)	—	—	(302.60)	—	—	—
Present Value	137.46	—	2,752.25	(164.92)	—	(161.67)	—	—	(156.91)	—	—	—

Month	Jan.
Period	70
Purchase	—
Salvage Value	—
Less Tax Savings	(302.60)
After-Tax Cost	(302.60)
Present Value	(150.79)

Net Present Value	(16,265)

FIGURE 18-5 Spreadsheet Solution for Purchasing the Truck

CONCLUSION

The point in time when cash flows are subject to income tax can greatly change the attractiveness of an investment. This may happen due to a company having to carry losses forward or having to depreciate assets over a specified recovery period. Alternatives that take tax write-offs in the early years of the alternative are usually favored over alternatives that take the tax write-offs in the later years of an alternative's life. Preferential treatment from an income tax standpoint, such as reduced taxes on capital gains and tax credits, favors alternatives which may take advantage of these tax savings. Finally, the tax brackets may favor alternatives with more uniform cash flows over alternatives with highly variable cash flow for all companies that are not in the top tax bracket.

PROBLEMS

1. Solve Example 18-6 using a spreadsheet. You should be able to determine the new net present value by changing the MARR, marginal tax rate, purchase price, salvage value, loan interest rate, loan fees, or lease payment.

2. Solve the following problem using a spreadsheet. Your S corporation needs a new track hoe for its operations and is looking at three alternatives. The first alternative is to lease the track hoe for sixty months. The monthly lease payment is $2,200 per month. At the end of the lease the track hoe will be returned to the dealer. The lease excludes all maintenance and operational costs. The second alternative is to purchase the track hoe with a sixty-month loan at an interest rate of 7.5% (APY 7.76). The loan has $500 in origination fees. The track hoe's entire sales price of $110,000—including the loan origination fees—can be financed. The first payment is due in July. The second alternative is to purchase the track hoe with cash for $110,000. If your company purchases the track hoe, the estimated salvage value of the track hoe at the end of five years is $15,000. Gains and losses on the sale of the track hoe will be treated as ordinary income. The track hoe may be depreciated using the half-year convention. For all three alternatives, the track hoe is to be placed in service on July 1. Your company's tax year is the same as the calendar year and its marginal tax rate is 35%. Using the net present value (cost) method, which of the above alternatives is the best for your company if your minimal acceptable rate of return (MARR) is 1.25% per month? Assume that there is sufficient taxable income to use all tax savings in the year they occur.

3. Solve the following problem using a spreadsheet. Your S corporation needs a specialized piece of excavating equipment to complete a project. The excavator will need to be available for three years beginning in July of this year. Your company is looking at two alternatives. The first alternative is to

lease the excavator for thirty-six months. The monthly lease payment is $7,100 per month. At the end of the lease the excavator will be returned to the dealer. The lease excludes all maintenance and operational costs. The second alternative is to purchase the excavator with cash for $250,000. If your company purchases the excavator, the estimated salvage value of the excavator at the end of three years is $95,000. Gains and losses on the sale of the excavator will be treated as ordinary income. The excavator may be depreciated using the half-year convention. Your company's tax year is the same as the calendar year and its marginal tax rate is 35%. Using the net present value (cost) method, which of the above alternatives is the best for your company if your minimal acceptable rate of return (MARR) is 1.5% per month? Assume that there is sufficient taxable income to use all tax savings in the year they occur.

APPENDIX A

COMPUTERIZED ACCOUNTING SYSTEMS

The following is a list of some of the features that are available in accounting software programs, which may be used when determining what features your accounting system needs.

GENERAL LEDGER

- ❑ Allows for the customization of the general ledger accounts
- ❑ Allows for the customization of financial statements
- ❑ Allows the user to save multiple formats for the financial statements with different levels of detail
- ❑ Allows for the tracking of multiple companies
- ❑ Fully integrated with accounts receivable, accounts payable, payroll, job cost, equipment, inventory, and purchase orders
- ❑ Posts to multiple periods
- ❑ Provides standard balancing and monthly/yearly closeout procedures

ACCOUNTS RECEIVABLE

- ❑ Generates billings using standard AIA forms and company's own custom invoices
- ❑ Generates time and materials billings
- ❑ Time and materials billings are integrated with job cost and inventory to prevent not billing items or the double billing of items

- ❑ Allows for the billing of labor at fixed labor rates or actual labor cost plus markup when preparing time and materials billings
- ❑ Allows for different cost types to be marked up at different rates when preparing time and materials billings
- ❑ Prepares unit prices bills
- ❑ Calculates finance charges for late bills
- ❑ Reports age of accounts receivable
- ❑ Tracks retention
- ❑ Tracks income by project, phase, and/or cost code
- ❑ Tracks sales and use taxes
- ❑ Posts invoices to multiple periods
- ❑ Posts directly to the general ledger, job cost ledger, and equipment ledger

Accounts Payable

- ❑ Allows the user to set up new vendors while entering invoices
- ❑ Warns the user if the invoice exceeds the contract or purchase order amount
- ❑ Allows for holds to be placed on invoices and for invoices to be partially paid
- ❑ Allows user to select invoices to be paid by job, vendor, due date, discount date, suppliers only, subcontractors only, or a combination of these
- ❑ Tracks contract amount, change orders, billings, and payments for subcontracts
- ❑ Tracks license and workers' compensation insurance expiration dates for subcontractors
- ❑ Automatically withholds workers' compensation insurance and retention from subcontractor's invoices
- ❑ Tracks sales and use taxes
- ❑ Posts invoices to multiple periods
- ❑ Posts directly to the general ledger, job cost ledger, and equipment ledger
- ❑ Integrated with purchase order and inventory modules
- ❑ Includes procedures for reconciling outstanding checks
- ❑ Produces 1099s

Payroll

- ❑ Allows different pay rates for private work, union work, and prevailing wage (Davis Bacon) work
- ❑ Allows an employee to be paid different rates for performing work in different work classes

- ❑ Allows an employee to work in different states during a pay period and prepares withholding and state unemployment insurance for each state
- ❑ Allows different workers' compensation and liability insurance rates to be paid for an employee during a pay period based on the state and class of work the employee performed
- ❑ Allows for customized deductions to be deducted from the employee's check and custom fringe benefits to be added to the labor burden
- ❑ Prepares certified payroll and union reports
- ❑ Prepares the payroll checks with detailed check stubs, including hours worked at the different pay rates
- ❑ Prepares federal and state unemployment reports
- ❑ Prepares W2s
- ❑ Tracks vacation accrued for each employee
- ❑ Maintains employee information, such as social security number, driver license number, birthday, and other customized fields
- ❑ Automatically posts payroll and burden to the job cost module, equipment module, and the general ledger
- ❑ Allows for the billing of equipment from the payroll module; for example, the superintendent's truck can be billed at the same time as the superintendent is billed

JOB COST

- ❑ Allows for the customization of the job cost codes
- ❑ Allows the user to duplicate job cost coding structure and/or budgets from existing jobs to new jobs, thus decreasing job setup time
- ❑ Tracks original contract amount, change orders to the contract, current contract amount, and income by project, phase, and/or cost code
- ❑ Tracks and reports original budget, change orders to the budget, and current budget by job, phase, cost code, and cost type
- ❑ Reports over- and undervariances by comparing the current job costs to the current budget
- ❑ Tracks unit pricing for individual cost codes
- ❑ Budgets and tracks labor units (e.g., hours) and production rates (e.g., hours per square foot)
- ❑ Reports over- and undervariance for labor units by comparing the current labor units to the current budget for labor units
- ❑ Reports over- and undervariance for production rates by comparing the current production rates to the current budget production rates
- ❑ Reports burden costs separately
- ❑ Reports overtime costs separately

- ❏ Allows for job cost reports to be customized
- ❏ Tracks unbilled committed costs
- ❏ Automatically receives data from accounts receivable, accounts payable, payroll, equipment, inventory, and purchase order modules
- ❏ Provides standard balancing procedures to balance the job cost ledger against the general ledger

EQUIPMENT

- ❏ Allows for the customization of the equipment cost codes
- ❏ Allows for different billing rates for different types of jobs
- ❏ Tracks profits and losses for each piece of equipment
- ❏ Tracks ownership and operation costs separately
- ❏ Automatically receives data from accounts payable, payroll, inventory, and purchase order modules
- ❏ Equipment can be billed from the payroll module to the job at the same time the operator is billed to the job
- ❏ Tracks license and insurance information for each piece of equipment
- ❏ Tracks and maintains service schedules for each piece of equipment based on mileage or hours of use
- ❏ Allows for equipment reports to be customized
- ❏ Provides standard balancing procedures to balance the job cost ledger against the general ledger

INVENTORY

- ❏ Allows materials to be moved from inventory to the job, from one job to another job, or from the job back to inventory (for unused materials)
- ❏ Allows items bought in bulk to be broken up into smaller units for billing purposes
- ❏ Allows for tracking inventory locations
- ❏ Allows for multiple levels of pricing for different customer classes
- ❏ Tracks inventory on an order that has not been received
- ❏ Integrated with time and materials billings
- ❏ Posts to job cost module, equipment module, and the general ledger
- ❏ Reports profit or loss on inventory
- ❏ Allows for the balancing of actual inventory quantities against reported inventory quantities

PURCHASE ORDERS

- ❏ Includes quantity, description, and unit/total price for each item on the purchase order
- ❏ Allows for lump sum pricing
- ❏ Includes sales tax, delivery charges, and other costs
- ❏ Allows for a purchase order to be divided between multiple projects
- ❏ Integrated with accounts payable, accounts receivable, job cost, and inventory

APPENDIX B

TREND ANALYSIS

When faced with projecting future costs based on a number of years of historical data, it can be difficult to see a trend. For example, Table B-1 shows ten years of historical data along with their annual growth rates, with the first year having a base rate of 1.00. These costs are also graphed in Figure B-1.

It is difficult to identify the trend for these data. This is a result of two factors. First, costs grow exponentially rather than linearly due to inflation. The relationship between costs at time zero and a time in the future may be written as follows:

$$\text{Cost}_n = \text{Cost}_0(1 + f)^n \tag{B-1}$$

TABLE B-1 Annual Costs and Growth Rates

YEAR	COSTS	GROWTH RATE (%)
0	1.00	
1	1.13	13.3
2	1.39	22.4
3	1.90	36.8
4	2.25	18.5
5	2.62	16.4
6	2.73	4.3
7	3.08	13.0
8	4.14	34.3
9	5.16	24.6

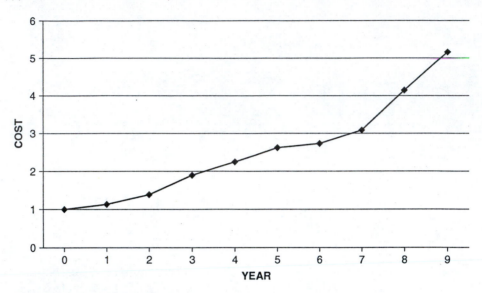

FIGURE B-1   Annual Costs

where

f = Inflation Rate

n = Number of Years

Second, the growth rate is not always constant. To deal with these two issues we may perform an exponential regression, which is a difficult task without computer software. If we take the natural log (ln) of the costs and graph the data, the exponential function forms a straight line. Taking the natural log of the costs in Table B-1 and graphing them as shown in Figure B-2, we see that they more closely follow a straight line.

To simplify the regression analysis we may convert the exponential growth to a linear growth by taking the natural log (ln) of the costs in Eq. (B-1) as follows:

$$\text{Cost}_n = \text{Cost}_0(1 + f)^n$$
$$\ln(\text{Cost}_n) = \ln[\text{Cost}_0(1 + f)^n]$$
$$\ln(\text{Cost}_n) = \ln(\text{Cost}_0) + n\ln(1 + f) \tag{B-2}$$

If we let

$$y = \ln(\text{Cost}_n) \tag{B-3}$$
$$b = \ln(\text{Cost}_0) \tag{B-4}$$
$$m = \ln(1 + f) \tag{B-5}$$
$$x = n \tag{B-6}$$

and substitute Equations (B-3) through (B-6) into Eq. (B-2) we get the following:

$$y = b + mx \tag{B-7}$$

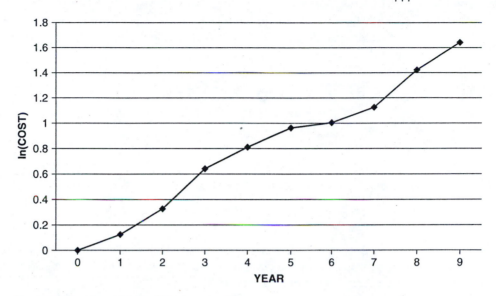

FIGURE B-2   Natural Log of Costs versus Year

This is the standard equation for linear regression, where b and m are constants. The constant m represents the slope of the line and the constant b represents the y intercept. We may then perform linear regression using x and y using the following formulas to find b and m:

$$m = \frac{n\sum xy - \sum x \sum y}{n\sum x^2 - (\sum x)^2}$$

(B-8)[50]

$$b = \frac{\sum y \sum x^2 - \sum x \sum xy}{n\sum x^2 - (\sum x)^2}$$

(B-9)

Solving Eq. (B-4) for the initial estimated cost based on the results of the regression equation we get the following:

$$\text{Cost}_0 = e^b$$

(B-10)

Solving Eq. (B-5) for the inflation rate (f) based on the results of the regression we get the following:

$$f = e^m - 1$$

(B-11)

These values may then be used in Eq. (B-1) to project costs for any year n based on the results of the regression equation.

The accuracy of the regression line may be measured by the coefficient of determination (r^2), which measures the relationship between the actual value of

---

[50]The n in Eq. (B-1) represents the number of years where the n in Eq. (B-8) represents the number of data points. These two should not be confused.

y and the estimated value of y ($\hat{y}$). The coefficient of determination is the square of the correlation coefficient (r). The coefficient of determination is calculated as follows:

$$r^2 = \frac{\left(\sum y\hat{y} - \dfrac{\sum y \sum \hat{y}}{n}\right)^2}{\left[\sum y^2 - \dfrac{(\sum y)^2}{n}\right]\left[\sum \hat{y}^2 - \dfrac{(\sum \hat{y})^2}{n}\right]} \qquad \text{(B-12)}$$

The correlation coefficient is calculated from the coefficient of determination as follows:

$$r = \sqrt{r^2} \qquad \text{(B-13)}$$

Both the coefficient of determination and the correlation coefficient result in a number between 0 and 1, with 1 representing a perfect correlation and 0 representing no correlation at all.

Example B-1:   Determine the inflation factor and initial estimated cost based on the exponential regression for the data in Table B-1. How good is the correlation between the actual cost and the costs based on the regression line? What is the projected cost for the next year?

Solution: First, we take the natural log of the cost so that we may use linear regression. Next, we let x equal the year and y equal the natural log of the cost. To perform linear regression we also need the sum of x, the sum of y, the sum of x^2, and the sum of xy. The results are shown in Table B-2 with the sums being shown at the bottom of each column.

TABLE B-2   Data for Linear Regression

YEAR (x)	COSTS	ln(COSTS) (y)	x^2	yx
0	1.00	0.000	0	0.000
1	1.13	0.122	1	0.122
2	1.39	0.329	4	0.658
3	1.90	0.642	9	1.926
4	2.25	0.811	16	3.244
5	2.62	0.963	25	4.815
6	2.73	1.004	36	6.024
7	3.08	1.125	49	7.875
8	4.14	1.421	64	11.368
9	5.16	1.641	81	14.769
45		8.058	285	50.801

Using Eq. (B-8) we get the following for m:

$$m = \frac{n\sum xy - \sum x \sum y}{n\sum x^2 - (\sum x)^2} = \frac{10(50.801) - 45(8.058)}{10(285) - (45)^2} = 0.1762$$

Using Eq. (B-9) we get the following for b:

$$b = \frac{\sum y \sum x^2 - \sum x \sum xy}{n\sum x^2 - (\sum x)^2} = \frac{8.058(285) - 45(50.801)}{10(285) - (45)^2} = 0.0127$$

Using Eq. (B-10) to find the initial estimated cost based on the results of the regression equation we get the following:

$$Cost_0 = e^b = e^{0.0127} = 1.013$$

This cost is close to our actual cost of 1.000 for year 0.

Using Eq. (B-11) to find the inflation rate based on the results of the regression we get the following:

$$f = e^m - 1 = e^{0.1762} - 1 = 0.193 \text{ or } 19.3\%$$

To calculate the coefficient of determination (r^2) and the correlation coefficient (r) we need to calculate the estimated value of y ($\hat{y}$), the sum of $\hat{y}$, the sum of y, the sum of y^2, and the sum of $y\,\hat{y}$. These values are found in Table B-3, with the sums shown at the bottom of each column.

The values for $\hat{y}$ were calculated as follows:

$$\hat{y}_0 = b + mx = 0.0127 + 0.1762(0) = 0.0129 \quad \text{say } 0.013$$
$$\hat{y}_1 = b + mx = 0.0127 + 0.1762(1) = 0.1889 \quad \text{say } 0.189$$

TABLE B-3   Data for Correlation

Y	y^2	$\hat{y}$	$\hat{y}^2$	$y\hat{y}$
0.000	0.000	0.013	0.000	0.000
0.122	0.015	0.189	0.036	0.023
0.329	0.108	0.365	0.133	0.120
0.642	0.412	0.541	0.293	0.347
0.811	0.658	0.718	0.516	0.582
0.963	0.927	0.894	0.799	0.861
1.004	1.008	1.070	1.145	1.074
1.125	1.266	1.246	1.553	1.402
1.421	2.019	1.422	2.022	2.021
1.641	2.693	1.599	2.557	2.624
8.058	9.106	8.057	9.054	9.054

Using Eq. (B-12) to find the coefficient of determination (r^2) we get the following:

$$r^2 = \frac{\left(\sum y\hat{y} - \dfrac{\sum y \sum \hat{y}}{n}\right)^2}{\left[\sum y^2 - \dfrac{(\sum y)^2}{n}\right]\left[\sum \hat{y}^2 - \dfrac{(\sum \hat{y})^2}{n}\right]}$$

$$r^2 = \frac{\left(9.054 - \dfrac{8.058(8.057)}{10}\right)^2}{\left[9.106 - \dfrac{(8.058)^2}{10}\right]\left[9.054 - \dfrac{(8.057)^2}{10}\right]} = 0.980$$

Using Eq. (B-13) to get the correlation coefficient we get the following:

$$r = \sqrt{r^2} = \sqrt{0.980} = 0.990$$

There is a strong correlation between the regression line and the data in Table B-1.

The relationship between the year and the cost may be described by the following formula:

$$\text{Cost}_n = \text{Cost}_0(1 + f)^n = 1.013(1 + 0.193)^n$$

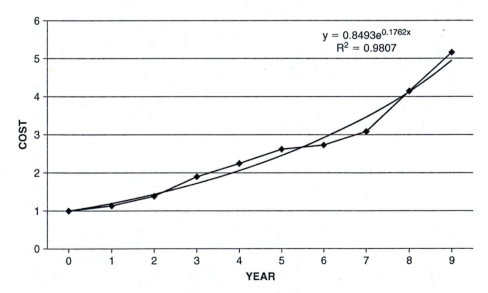

FIGURE B-3   Annual Cost with Regression Line

The cost for the next year (year 10) may be estimated as follows:

$$Cost_{10} = 1.013(1 + 0.193)^{10} = 5.916$$

Alternately, we could have graphed the data in Microsoft Excel and had Excel graph an exponential trend line as shown in Figure B-3.

There are few key differences between the first solution and the solution generated by Excel. First, Excel assumes that the first data point is period 1, the second data point is period 2, and so forth. Excel also assumes that there is a data point for each period. As a result our initial cost for the cost equation generated by Microsoft Excel will occur one year prior to our first set of data (year 0) and in this case x is always one year greater than the actual year. Second, y represents the costs rather than the natural log of the costs. Third, $(1 + f)$ is expressed in the form of e^m; in this case m equals 0.1762 and $(1 + f)$ equals $e^{0.1762}$ or 1.193. By substituting $(1 + f)$ for e^m and $(n + 1)$ for x into the equation generated by Excel we get the following:

$$Cost_n = Cost_0(1 + f)^{(n+1)} = 0.849(1.193)^{(n+1)}$$
$$Cost_n = 0.849(1.193)(1.193)^n$$
$$Cost_n = 1.013(1.193)^n$$

This is the same equation we found by taking the natural log of the costs and using linear regression.

APPENDIX C

DERIVATION OF
SELECTED EQUATIONS

EQUATION (15-1)

The future value at the end of the first year equals the principal plus interest on the principal. Writing the equation for the future value at the end of the first year using the generic variables of P, i, and F we get the following:

$$F_1 = P + Pi$$

Combining terms we get the following:

$$F_1 = P(1 + i)$$

Writing the equation for the future value at the end of the second year using the generic variables of P, i, and F we get the following:

$$F_2 = F_1 + F_1(i)$$

where

$$F_1 = P(1 + i)$$

Substituting $P(1 + i)$ for F_1 and combining terms we get the following:

$$F_2 = F_1 + F_1(i) = P(1 + i) + P(1 + i)i = P(1 + i)(1 + i) = P(1 + i)^2$$

Writing the equation for the future value at the end of the third year using the generic variables of P, i, and F we get the following:

$$F_3 = F_2 + F_2(i)$$

where

$$F_2 = P(1 + i)^2$$

Substituting $P(1 + i)^2$ for F_2 and combining terms we get the following:

$$F_3 = F_2 + F_2(i) = P(1 + i)^2 + P(1 + i)^2 i = P(1 + i)^2(1 + i) = P(1 + i)^3$$

Extrapolating this series out to the nth period we get the following formula:

$$F = P(1 + i)^n \qquad (15\text{-}1)$$

EQUATION (15-5)

Summing the future values of a uniform series we get the following:

$$F = F_1 + F_2 + F_3 + \cdots + F_n \qquad (C\text{-}1)$$

where F and F_n occur at the same point in time. Substituting the present values for F_1 through F_n into Eq. (C-1) we get the following:

$$F = P_1(1 + i)^{n-1} + P_2(1 + i)^{n-2} + P_3(1 + i)^{n-3} + \cdots$$
$$+ P_n(1 + i)^{n-n} \qquad (C\text{-}2)$$

Because $(1 + i)^{n-n}$ equals 1, Eq. (C-2) may be written as follows:

$$F = P_1(1 + i)^{n-1} + P_2(1 + i)^{n-2} + \cdots + P_n$$

Since $P_1 = P_2 = P_3 = \cdots = P_n$ is a uniform series, we may substitute A for each of these values to get the following:

$$F = A(1 + i)^{n-1} + A(1 + i)^{n-2} + \cdots + A$$

Combining terms we get the following:

$$F = A[(1 + i)^{n-1} + (1 + i)^{n-2} + \cdots + 1] \qquad (C\text{-}3)$$

Adding $(1 + i)$ to both sides of Eq. (C-3) we get the following:

$$F(1 + i) = A[(1 + i)^n + (1 + i)^{n-1} + \cdots + (1 + i)] \qquad (C\text{-}4)$$

Subtracting Eq. (C-3) from Eq. (C-4) we get the following:

$$F(1 + i) = A[(1 + i)^n + (1 + i)^{n-1} + \cdots \qquad + (1 + i)]$$
$$- \qquad F = A[\qquad (1 + i)^{n-1} + (1 + i)^{n-2} + \cdots + 1]$$
$$\overline{\qquad\qquad\qquad\qquad\qquad\qquad\qquad\qquad\qquad\qquad\qquad}$$
$$Fi = A[(1 + i)^n \qquad\qquad\qquad\qquad -1]$$
$$Fi = A[(1 + i)^n - 1]$$

And solving for F we get the following:

$$F = A[(1 + i)^n - 1]/i \qquad (15\text{-}5)$$

FIGURE C-1   Cash Flow for
Eq. (16-16)

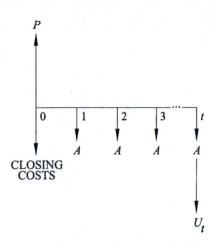

EQUATION (16-16)

Equation (16-16) is derived as follows: The cash flow for the equation is as shown in Figure C-1.

The present value at time zero of the monthly payments is written using Eq. (15-9) as follows:

$$P_{\text{Monthly Payments}} = A[(1 + i)^t - 1]/[i(1 + i)^t]$$

The present value at time zero of the loan payoff at the end of month t is written using Eq. (15-3) as follows:

$$P_{\text{Unpaid Balance}} = F/(1 + i)^t = U_t/(1 + i)^t$$

The present value for the loan should be zero at an interest rate of i; therefore, the present value of the cash receipts must equal the present value of the cash disbursements. Setting the present value of the cash receipts equal to the cash disbursements we get the following:

$$P = \text{Closing Costs} + A[(1 + i)^t - 1]/[i(1 + i)^t] + U_t/(1 + i)^t \qquad (16\text{-}16)$$

EQUATION (16-17)

Equation (16-17) is derived as follows: The cash flow for the equation is as shown in Figure C-2.

The present value at time zero of the principal payment at the end of the period may be written as follows using Eq. (15-3):

$$P_{\text{Principal Payment}} = P/(1 + i)^1 = P/(1 + i)$$

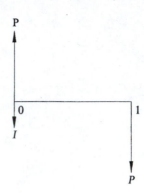

FIGURE C-2   Cash Flow for Eq. (9-17)

The present value for the loan should be zero at an interest rate of i; therefore, the present value of the cash receipts must equal the present value of the cash disbursements. Setting the present value of the cash receipts equal to the cash disbursements we get the following:

$$P = I + P/(1 + i)$$

Subtracting I from both sides of the equation we get the following:

$$P - I = P/(1 + i)$$

Multiplying both sides of the equation by $(1 + i)$ we get the following:

$$(P - I)(1 + i) = P$$

Dividing both sides of the equation by $(P - I)$ we get the following:

$$1 + i = P/(P - I)$$

Subtracting 1 from both sides of the equation we get the following:

$$i = [P/(P - I)] - 1 \tag{16-17}$$

APPENDIX D

INTEREST FACTORS

TABLE D–1   Interest Factors for 0.50%

	SINGLE PAYMENT		UNIFORM SERIES			
	COMPOUND-AMOUNT FACTOR	PRESENT-WORTH FACTOR	COMPOUND-AMOUNT FACTOR	SINKING-FUND FACTOR	PRESENT-WORTH FACTOR	CAPITAL-RECOVERY FACTOR
N	CONVERT P TO F (F/P,I,N)	CONVERT F TO P (P/F,I,N)	CONVERT A TO F (F/A,I,N)	CONVERT F TO A (A/F,I,N)	CONVERT A TO P (P/A,I,N)	CONVERT P TO A (A/P,I,N)
1	1.0050	0.9950	1.0000	1.0000	0.9950	1.0050
2	1.0100	0.9901	2.0050	0.4988	1.9851	0.5038
3	1.0151	0.9851	3.0150	0.3317	2.9702	0.3367
4	1.0202	0.9802	4.0301	0.2481	3.9505	0.2531
5	1.0253	0.9754	5.0503	0.1980	4.9259	0.2030
6	1.0304	0.9705	6.0755	0.1646	5.8964	0.1696
7	1.0355	0.9657	7.1059	0.1407	6.8621	0.1457
8	1.0407	0.9609	8.1414	0.1228	7.8230	0.1278
9	1.0459	0.9561	9.1821	0.1089	8.7791	0.1139
10	1.0511	0.9513	10.2280	0.0978	9.7304	0.1028
11	1.0564	0.9466	11.2792	0.0887	10.6770	0.0937
12	1.0617	0.9419	12.3356	0.0811	11.6189	0.0861
13	1.0670	0.9372	13.3972	0.0746	12.5562	0.0796
14	1.0723	0.9326	14.4642	0.0691	13.4887	0.0741
15	1.0777	0.9279	15.5365	0.0644	14.4166	0.0694
16	1.0831	0.9233	16.6142	0.0602	15.3399	0.0652
17	1.0885	0.9187	17.6973	0.0565	16.2586	0.0615
18	1.0939	0.9141	18.7858	0.0532	17.1728	0.0582
19	1.0994	0.9096	19.8797	0.0503	18.0824	0.0553
20	1.1049	0.9051	20.9791	0.0477	18.9874	0.0527
21	1.1104	0.9006	22.0840	0.0453	19.8880	0.0503
22	1.1160	0.8961	23.1944	0.0431	20.7841	0.0481
23	1.1216	0.8916	24.3104	0.0411	21.6757	0.0461
24	1.1272	0.8872	25.4320	0.0393	22.5629	0.0443
25	1.1328	0.8828	26.5591	0.0377	23.4456	0.0427
26	1.1385	0.8784	27.6919	0.0361	24.3240	0.0411
27	1.1442	0.8740	28.8304	0.0347	25.1980	0.0397
28	1.1499	0.8697	29.9745	0.0334	26.0677	0.0384
29	1.1556	0.8653	31.1244	0.0321	26.9330	0.0371
30	1.1614	0.8610	32.2800	0.0310	27.7941	0.0360
35	1.1907	0.8398	38.1454	0.0262	32.0354	0.0312
40	1.2208	0.8191	44.1588	0.0226	36.1722	0.0276
45	1.2516	0.7990	50.3242	0.0199	40.2072	0.0249
50	1.2832	0.7793	56.6452	0.0177	44.1428	0.0227
55	1.3156	0.7601	63.1258	0.0158	47.9814	0.0208
60	1.3489	0.7414	69.7700	0.0143	51.7256	0.0193
65	1.3829	0.7231	76.5821	0.0131	55.3775	0.0181
70	1.4178	0.7053	83.5661	0.0120	58.9394	0.0170
75	1.4536	0.6879	90.7265	0.0110	62.4136	0.0160
80	1.4903	0.6710	98.0677	0.0102	65.8023	0.0152
85	1.5280	0.6545	105.5943	0.0095	69.1075	0.0145
90	1.5666	0.6383	113.3109	0.0088	72.3313	0.0138
95	1.6061	0.6226	121.2224	0.0082	75.4757	0.0132
100	1.6467	0.6073	129.3337	0.0077	78.5426	0.0127

TABLE D–2 Interest Factors for 0.75%

	SINGLE PAYMENT		UNIFORM SERIES			
	COMPOUND-AMOUNT FACTOR	PRESENT-WORTH FACTOR	COMPOUND-AMOUNT FACTOR	SINKING-FUND FACTOR	PRESENT-WORTH FACTOR	CAPITAL-RECOVERY FACTOR
N	CONVERT P TO F (F/P,I,N)	CONVERT F TO P (P/F,I,N)	CONVERT A TO F (F/A,I,N)	CONVERT F TO A (A/F,I,N)	CONVERT A TO P (P/A,I,N)	CONVERT P TO A (A/P,I,N)
1	1.0075	0.9926	1.0000	1.0000	0.9926	1.0075
2	1.0151	0.9852	2.0075	0.4981	1.9777	0.5056
3	1.0227	0.9778	3.0226	0.3308	2.9556	0.3383
4	1.0303	0.9706	4.0452	0.2472	3.9261	0.2547
5	1.0381	0.9633	5.0756	0.1970	4.8894	0.2045
6	1.0459	0.9562	6.1136	0.1636	5.8456	0.1711
7	1.0537	0.9490	7.1595	0.1397	6.7946	0.1472
8	1.0616	0.9420	8.2132	0.1218	7.7366	0.1293
9	1.0696	0.9350	9.2748	0.1078	8.6716	0.1153
10	1.0776	0.9280	10.3443	0.0967	9.5996	0.1042
11	1.0857	0.9211	11.4219	0.0876	10.5207	0.0951
12	1.0938	0.9142	12.5076	0.0800	11.4349	0.0875
13	1.1020	0.9074	13.6014	0.0735	12.3423	0.0810
14	1.1103	0.9007	14.7034	0.0680	13.2430	0.0755
15	1.1186	0.8940	15.8137	0.0632	14.1370	0.0707
16	1.1270	0.8873	16.9323	0.0591	15.0243	0.0666
17	1.1354	0.8807	18.0593	0.0554	15.9050	0.0629
18	1.1440	0.8742	19.1947	0.0521	16.7792	0.0596
19	1.1525	0.8676	20.3387	0.0492	17.6468	0.0567
20	1.1612	0.8612	21.4912	0.0465	18.5080	0.0540
21	1.1699	0.8548	22.6524	0.0441	19.3628	0.0516
22	1.1787	0.8484	23.8223	0.0420	20.2112	0.0495
23	1.1875	0.8421	25.0010	0.0400	21.0533	0.0475
24	1.1964	0.8358	26.1885	0.0382	21.8891	0.0457
25	1.2054	0.8296	27.3849	0.0365	22.7188	0.0440
26	1.2144	0.8234	28.5903	0.0350	23.5422	0.0425
27	1.2235	0.8173	29.8047	0.0336	24.3595	0.0411
28	1.2327	0.8112	31.0282	0.0322	25.1707	0.0397
29	1.2420	0.8052	32.2609	0.0310	25.9759	0.0385
30	1.2513	0.7992	33.5029	0.0298	26.7751	0.0373
35	1.2989	0.7699	39.8538	0.0251	30.6827	0.0326
40	1.3483	0.7416	46.4465	0.0215	34.4469	0.0290
45	1.3997	0.7145	53.2901	0.0188	38.0732	0.0263
50	1.4530	0.6883	60.3943	0.0166	41.5664	0.0241
55	1.5083	0.6630	67.7688	0.0148	44.9316	0.0223
60	1.5657	0.6387	75.4241	0.0133	48.1734	0.0208
65	1.6253	0.6153	83.3709	0.0120	51.2963	0.0195
70	1.6872	0.5927	91.6201	0.0109	54.3046	0.0184
75	1.7514	0.5710	100.1833	0.0100	57.2027	0.0175
80	1.8180	0.5500	109.0725	0.0092	59.9944	0.0167
85	1.8873	0.5299	118.3001	0.0085	62.6838	0.0160
90	1.9591	0.5104	127.8790	0.0078	65.2746	0.0153
95	2.0337	0.4917	137.8225	0.0073	67.7704	0.0148
100	2.1111	0.4737	148.1445	0.0068	70.1746	0.0143

TABLE D–3   Interest Factors for 1.00%

	SINGLE PAYMENT		UNIFORM SERIES			
	COMPOUND-AMOUNT FACTOR	PRESENT-WORTH FACTOR	COMPOUND-AMOUNT FACTOR	SINKING-FUND FACTOR	PRESENT-WORTH FACTOR	CAPITAL-RECOVERY FACTOR
	CONVERT *P* TO *F*	CONVERT *F* TO *P*	CONVERT *A* TO *F*	CONVERT *F* TO *A*	CONVERT *A* TO *P*	CONVERT *P* TO *A*
N	(F/P,I,N)	(P/F,I,N)	(F/A,I,N)	(A/F,I,N)	(P/A,I,N)	(A/P,I,N)
1	1.0100	0.9901	1.0000	1.0000	0.9901	1.0100
2	1.0201	0.9803	2.0100	0.4975	1.9704	0.5075
3	1.0303	0.9706	3.0301	0.3300	2.9410	0.3400
4	1.0406	0.9610	4.0604	0.2463	3.9020	0.2563
5	1.0510	0.9515	5.1010	0.1960	4.8534	0.2060
6	1.0615	0.9420	6.1520	0.1625	5.7955	0.1725
7	1.0721	0.9327	7.2135	0.1386	6.7282	0.1486
8	1.0829	0.9235	8.2857	0.1207	7.6517	0.1307
9	1.0937	0.9143	9.3685	0.1067	8.5660	0.1167
10	1.1046	0.9053	10.4622	0.0956	9.4713	0.1056
11	1.1157	0.8963	11.5668	0.0865	10.3676	0.0965
12	1.1268	0.8874	12.6825	0.0788	11.2551	0.0888
13	1.1381	0.8787	13.8093	0.0724	12.1337	0.0824
14	1.1495	0.8700	14.9474	0.0669	13.0037	0.0769
15	1.1610	0.8613	16.0969	0.0621	13.8651	0.0721
16	1.1726	0.8528	17.2579	0.0579	14.7179	0.0679
17	1.1843	0.8444	18.4304	0.0543	15.5623	0.0643
18	1.1961	0.8360	19.6147	0.0510	16.3983	0.0610
19	1.2081	0.8277	20.8109	0.0481	17.2260	0.0581
20	1.2202	0.8195	22.0190	0.0454	18.0456	0.0554
21	1.2324	0.8114	23.2392	0.0430	18.8570	0.0530
22	1.2447	0.8034	24.4716	0.0409	19.6604	0.0509
23	1.2572	0.7954	25.7163	0.0389	20.4558	0.0489
24	1.2697	0.7876	26.9735	0.0371	21.2434	0.0471
25	1.2824	0.7798	28.2432	0.0354	22.0232	0.0454
26	1.2953	0.7720	29.5256	0.0339	22.7952	0.0439
27	1.3082	0.7644	30.8209	0.0324	23.5596	0.0424
28	1.3213	0.7568	32.1291	0.0311	24.3164	0.0411
29	1.3345	0.7493	33.4504	0.0299	25.0658	0.0399
30	1.3478	0.7419	34.7849	0.0287	25.8077	0.0387
35	1.4166	0.7059	41.6603	0.0240	29.4086	0.0340
40	1.4889	0.6717	48.8864	0.0205	32.8347	0.0305
45	1.5648	0.6391	56.4811	0.0177	36.0945	0.0277
50	1.6446	0.6080	64.4632	0.0155	39.1961	0.0255
55	1.7285	0.5785	72.8525	0.0137	42.1472	0.0237
60	1.8167	0.5504	81.6697	0.0122	44.9550	0.0222
65	1.9094	0.5237	90.9366	0.0110	47.6266	0.0210
70	2.0068	0.4983	100.6763	0.0099	50.1685	0.0199
75	2.1091	0.4741	110.9128	0.0090	52.5871	0.0190
80	2.2167	0.4511	121.6715	0.0082	54.8882	0.0182
85	2.3298	0.4292	132.9790	0.0075	57.0777	0.0175
90	2.4486	0.4084	144.8633	0.0069	59.1609	0.0169
95	2.5735	0.3886	157.3538	0.0064	61.1430	0.0164
100	2.7048	0.3697	170.4814	0.0059	63.0289	0.0159

TABLE D–4   Interest Factors for 1.25%

	SINGLE PAYMENT		UNIFORM SERIES			
	COMPOUND-AMOUNT FACTOR	PRESENT-WORTH FACTOR	COMPOUND-AMOUNT FACTOR	SINKING-FUND FACTOR	PRESENT-WORTH FACTOR	CAPITAL-RECOVERY FACTOR
	CONVERT P TO F	CONVERT F TO P	CONVERT A TO F	CONVERT F TO A	CONVERT A TO P	CONVERT P TO A
N	(F/P,I,N)	(P/F,I,N)	(F/A,I,N)	(A/F,I,N)	(P/A,I,N)	(A/P,I,N)
1	1.0125	0.9877	1.0000	1.0000	0.9877	1.0125
2	1.0252	0.9755	2.0125	0.4969	1.9631	0.5094
3	1.0380	0.9634	3.0377	0.3292	2.9265	0.3417
4	1.0509	0.9515	4.0756	0.2454	3.8781	0.2579
5	1.0641	0.9398	5.1266	0.1951	4.8178	0.2076
6	1.0774	0.9282	6.1907	0.1615	5.7460	0.1740
7	1.0909	0.9167	7.2680	0.1376	6.6627	0.1501
8	1.1045	0.9054	8.3589	0.1196	7.5681	0.1321
9	1.1183	0.8942	9.4634	0.1057	8.4623	0.1182
10	1.1323	0.8832	10.5817	0.0945	9.3455	0.1070
11	1.1464	0.8723	11.7139	0.0854	10.2178	0.0979
12	1.1608	0.8615	12.8604	0.0778	11.0793	0.0903
13	1.1753	0.8509	14.0211	0.0713	11.9302	0.0838
14	1.1900	0.8404	15.1964	0.0658	12.7706	0.0783
15	1.2048	0.8300	16.3863	0.0610	13.6005	0.0735
16	1.2199	0.8197	17.5912	0.0568	14.4203	0.0693
17	1.2351	0.8096	18.8111	0.0532	15.2299	0.0657
18	1.2506	0.7996	20.0462	0.0499	16.0295	0.0624
19	1.2662	0.7898	21.2968	0.0470	16.8193	0.0595
20	1.2820	0.7800	22.5630	0.0443	17.5993	0.0568
21	1.2981	0.7704	23.8450	0.0419	18.3697	0.0544
22	1.3143	0.7609	25.1431	0.0398	19.1306	0.0523
23	1.3307	0.7515	26.4574	0.0378	19.8820	0.0503
24	1.3474	0.7422	27.7881	0.0360	20.6242	0.0485
25	1.3642	0.7330	29.1354	0.0343	21.3573	0.0468
26	1.3812	0.7240	30.4996	0.0328	22.0813	0.0453
27	1.3985	0.7150	31.8809	0.0314	22.7963	0.0439
28	1.4160	0.7062	33.2794	0.0300	23.5025	0.0425
29	1.4337	0.6975	34.6954	0.0288	24.2000	0.0413
30	1.4516	0.6889	36.1291	0.0277	24.8889	0.0402
35	1.5446	0.6474	43.5709	0.0230	28.2079	0.0355
40	1.6436	0.6084	51.4896	0.0194	31.3269	0.0319
45	1.7489	0.5718	59.9157	0.0167	34.2582	0.0292
50	1.8610	0.5373	68.8818	0.0145	37.0129	0.0270
55	1.9803	0.5050	78.4225	0.0128	39.6017	0.0253
60	2.1072	0.4746	88.5745	0.0113	42.0346	0.0238
65	2.2422	0.4460	99.3771	0.0101	44.3210	0.0226
70	2.3859	0.4191	110.8720	0.0090	46.4697	0.0215
75	2.5388	0.3939	123.1035	0.0081	48.4890	0.0206
80	2.7015	0.3702	136.1188	0.0073	50.3867	0.0198
85	2.8746	0.3479	149.9682	0.0067	52.1701	0.0192
90	3.0588	0.3269	164.7050	0.0061	53.8461	0.0186
95	3.2548	0.3072	180.3862	0.0055	55.4211	0.0180
100	3.4634	0.2887	197.0723	0.0051	56.9013	0.0176

TABLE D–5   Interest Factors for 1.50%

	SINGLE PAYMENT		UNIFORM SERIES			
	COMPOUND-AMOUNT FACTOR	PRESENT-WORTH FACTOR	COMPOUND-AMOUNT FACTOR	SINKING-FUND FACTOR	PRESENT-WORTH FACTOR	CAPITAL-RECOVERY FACTOR
N	CONVERT P TO F $(F/P,I,N)$	CONVERT F TO P $(P/F,I,N)$	CONVERT A TO F $(F/A,I,N)$	CONVERT F TO A $(A/F,I,N)$	CONVERT A TO P $(P/A,I,N)$	CONVERT P TO A $(A/P,I,N)$
1	1.0150	0.9852	1.0000	1.0000	0.9852	1.0150
2	1.0302	0.9707	2.0150	0.4963	1.9559	0.5113
3	1.0457	0.9563	3.0452	0.3284	2.9122	0.3434
4	1.0614	0.9422	4.0909	0.2444	3.8544	0.2594
5	1.0773	0.9283	5.1523	0.1941	4.7826	0.2091
6	1.0934	0.9145	6.2296	0.1605	5.6972	0.1755
7	1.1098	0.9010	7.3230	0.1366	6.5982	0.1516
8	1.1265	0.8877	8.4328	0.1186	7.4859	0.1336
9	1.1434	0.8746	9.5593	0.1046	8.3605	0.1196
10	1.1605	0.8617	10.7027	0.0934	9.2222	0.1084
11	1.1779	0.8489	11.8633	0.0843	10.0711	0.0993
12	1.1956	0.8364	13.0412	0.0767	10.9075	0.0917
13	1.2136	0.8240	14.2368	0.0702	11.7315	0.0852
14	1.2318	0.8118	15.4504	0.0647	12.5434	0.0797
15	1.2502	0.7999	16.6821	0.0599	13.3432	0.0749
16	1.2690	0.7880	17.9324	0.0558	14.1313	0.0708
17	1.2880	0.7764	19.2014	0.0521	14.9076	0.0671
18	1.3073	0.7649	20.4894	0.0488	15.6726	0.0638
19	1.3270	0.7536	21.7967	0.0459	16.4262	0.0609
20	1.3469	0.7425	23.1237	0.0432	17.1686	0.0582
21	1.3671	0.7315	24.4705	0.0409	17.9001	0.0559
22	1.3876	0.7207	25.8376	0.0387	18.6208	0.0537
23	1.4084	0.7100	27.2251	0.0367	19.3309	0.0517
24	1.4295	0.6995	28.6335	0.0349	20.0304	0.0499
25	1.4509	0.6892	30.0630	0.0333	20.7196	0.0483
26	1.4727	0.6790	31.5140	0.0317	21.3986	0.0467
27	1.4948	0.6690	32.9867	0.0303	22.0676	0.0453
28	1.5172	0.6591	34.4815	0.0290	22.7267	0.0440
29	1.5400	0.6494	35.9987	0.0278	23.3761	0.0428
30	1.5631	0.6398	37.5387	0.0266	24.0158	0.0416
35	1.6839	0.5939	45.5921	0.0219	27.0756	0.0369
40	1.8140	0.5513	54.2679	0.0184	29.9158	0.0334
45	1.9542	0.5117	63.6142	0.0157	32.5523	0.0307
50	2.1052	0.4750	73.6828	0.0136	34.9997	0.0286
55	2.2679	0.4409	84.5296	0.0118	37.2715	0.0268
60	2.4432	0.4093	96.2147	0.0104	39.3803	0.0254
65	2.6320	0.3799	108.8028	0.0092	41.3378	0.0242
70	2.8355	0.3527	122.3638	0.0082	43.1549	0.0232
75	3.0546	0.3274	136.9728	0.0073	44.8416	0.0223
80	3.2907	0.3039	152.7109	0.0065	46.4073	0.0215
85	3.5450	0.2821	169.6652	0.0059	47.8607	0.0209
90	3.8189	0.2619	187.9299	0.0053	49.2099	0.0203
95	4.1141	0.2431	207.6061	0.0048	50.4622	0.0198
100	4.4320	0.2256	228.8030	0.0044	51.6247	0.0194

TABLE D–6   Interest Factors for 1.75%

	SINGLE PAYMENT		UNIFORM SERIES			
	COMPOUND-AMOUNT FACTOR	PRESENT-WORTH FACTOR	COMPOUND-AMOUNT FACTOR	SINKING-FUND FACTOR	PRESENT-WORTH FACTOR	CAPITAL-RECOVERY FACTOR
	CONVERT P TO F	CONVERT F TO P	CONVERT A TO F	CONVERT F TO A	CONVERT A TO P	CONVERT P TO A
N	$(F/P,I,N)$	$(P/F,I,N)$	$(F/A,I,N)$	$(A/F,I,N)$	$(P/A,I,N)$	$(A/P,I,N)$
1	1.0175	0.9828	1.0000	1.0000	0.9828	1.0175
2	1.0353	0.9659	2.0175	0.4957	1.9487	0.5132
3	1.0534	0.9493	3.0528	0.3276	2.8980	0.3451
4	1.0719	0.9330	4.1062	0.2435	3.8309	0.2610
5	1.0906	0.9169	5.1781	0.1931	4.7479	0.2106
6	1.1097	0.9011	6.2687	0.1595	5.6490	0.1770
7	1.1291	0.8856	7.3784	0.1355	6.5346	0.1530
8	1.1489	0.8704	8.5075	0.1175	7.4051	0.1350
9	1.1690	0.8554	9.6564	0.1036	8.2605	0.1211
10	1.1894	0.8407	10.8254	0.0924	9.1012	0.1099
11	1.2103	0.8263	12.0148	0.0832	9.9275	0.1007
12	1.2314	0.8121	13.2251	0.0756	10.7395	0.0931
13	1.2530	0.7981	14.4565	0.0692	11.5376	0.0867
14	1.2749	0.7844	15.7095	0.0637	12.3220	0.0812
15	1.2972	0.7709	16.9844	0.0589	13.0929	0.0764
16	1.3199	0.7576	18.2817	0.0547	13.8505	0.0722
17	1.3430	0.7446	19.6016	0.0510	14.5951	0.0685
18	1.3665	0.7318	20.9446	0.0477	15.3269	0.0652
19	1.3904	0.7192	22.3112	0.0448	16.0461	0.0623
20	1.4148	0.7068	23.7016	0.0422	16.7529	0.0597
21	1.4395	0.6947	25.1164	0.0398	17.4475	0.0573
22	1.4647	0.6827	26.5559	0.0377	18.1303	0.0552
23	1.4904	0.6710	28.0207	0.0357	18.8012	0.0532
24	1.5164	0.6594	29.5110	0.0339	19.4607	0.0514
25	1.5430	0.6481	31.0275	0.0322	20.1088	0.0497
26	1.5700	0.6369	32.5704	0.0307	20.7457	0.0482
27	1.5975	0.6260	34.1404	0.0293	21.3717	0.0468
28	1.6254	0.6152	35.7379	0.0280	21.9870	0.0455
29	1.6539	0.6046	37.3633	0.0268	22.5916	0.0443
30	1.6828	0.5942	39.0172	0.0256	23.1858	0.0431
35	1.8353	0.5449	47.7308	0.0210	26.0073	0.0385
40	2.0016	0.4996	57.2341	0.0175	28.5942	0.0350
45	2.1830	0.4581	67.5986	0.0148	30.9663	0.0323
50	2.3808	0.4200	78.9022	0.0127	33.1412	0.0302
55	2.5965	0.3851	91.2302	0.0110	35.1354	0.0285
60	2.8318	0.3531	104.6752	0.0096	36.9640	0.0271
65	3.0884	0.3238	119.3386	0.0084	38.6406	0.0259
70	3.3683	0.2969	135.3308	0.0074	40.1779	0.0249
75	3.6735	0.2722	152.7721	0.0065	41.5875	0.0240
80	4.0064	0.2496	171.7938	0.0058	42.8799	0.0233
85	4.3694	0.2289	192.5393	0.0052	44.0650	0.0227
90	4.7654	0.2098	215.1646	0.0046	45.1516	0.0221
95	5.1972	0.1924	239.8402	0.0042	46.1479	0.0217
100	5.6682	0.1764	266.7518	0.0037	47.0615	0.0212

TABLE D–7   Interest Factors for 2.00%

	SINGLE PAYMENT		UNIFORM SERIES			
	COMPOUND-AMOUNT FACTOR	PRESENT-WORTH FACTOR	COMPOUND-AMOUNT FACTOR	SINKING-FUND FACTOR	PRESENT-WORTH FACTOR	CAPITAL-RECOVERY FACTOR
	CONVERT P TO F	CONVERT F TO P	CONVERT A TO F	CONVERT F TO A	CONVERT A TO P	CONVERT P TO A
N	$(F/P,I,N)$	$(P/F,I,N)$	$(F/A,I,N)$	$(A/F,I,N)$	$(P/A,I,N)$	$(A/P,I,N)$
1	1.0200	0.9804	1.0000	1.0000	0.9804	1.0200
2	1.0404	0.9612	2.0200	0.4950	1.9416	0.5150
3	1.0612	0.9423	3.0604	0.3268	2.8839	0.3468
4	1.0824	0.9238	4.1216	0.2426	3.8077	0.2626
5	1.1041	0.9057	5.2040	0.1922	4.7135	0.2122
6	1.1262	0.8880	6.3081	0.1585	5.6014	0.1785
7	1.1487	0.8706	7.4343	0.1345	6.4720	0.1545
8	1.1717	0.8535	8.5830	0.1165	7.3255	0.1365
9	1.1951	0.8368	9.7546	0.1025	8.1622	0.1225
10	1.2190	0.8203	10.9497	0.0913	8.9826	0.1113
11	1.2434	0.8043	12.1687	0.0822	9.7868	0.1022
12	1.2682	0.7885	13.4121	0.0746	10.5753	0.0946
13	1.2936	0.7730	14.6803	0.0681	11.3484	0.0881
14	1.3195	0.7579	15.9739	0.0626	12.1062	0.0826
15	1.3459	0.7430	17.2934	0.0578	12.8493	0.0778
16	1.3728	0.7284	18.6393	0.0537	13.5777	0.0737
17	1.4002	0.7142	20.0121	0.0500	14.2919	0.0700
18	1.4282	0.7002	21.4123	0.0467	14.9920	0.0667
19	1.4568	0.6864	22.8406	0.0438	15.6785	0.0638
20	1.4859	0.6730	24.2974	0.0412	16.3514	0.0612
21	1.5157	0.6598	25.7833	0.0388	17.0112	0.0588
22	1.5460	0.6468	27.2990	0.0366	17.6580	0.0566
23	1.5769	0.6342	28.8450	0.0347	18.2922	0.0547
24	1.6084	0.6217	30.4219	0.0329	18.9139	0.0529
25	1.6406	0.6095	32.0303	0.0312	19.5235	0.0512
26	1.6734	0.5976	33.6709	0.0297	20.1210	0.0497
27	1.7069	0.5859	35.3443	0.0283	20.7069	0.0483
28	1.7410	0.5744	37.0512	0.0270	21.2813	0.0470
29	1.7758	0.5631	38.7922	0.0258	21.8444	0.0458
30	1.8114	0.5521	40.5681	0.0246	22.3965	0.0446
35	1.9999	0.5000	49.9945	0.0200	24.9986	0.0400
40	2.2080	0.4529	60.4020	0.0166	27.3555	0.0366
45	2.4379	0.4102	71.8927	0.0139	29.4902	0.0339
50	2.6916	0.3715	84.5794	0.0118	31.4236	0.0318
55	2.9717	0.3365	98.5865	0.0101	33.1748	0.0301
60	3.2810	0.3048	114.0515	0.0088	34.7609	0.0288
65	3.6225	0.2761	131.1262	0.0076	36.1975	0.0276
70	3.9996	0.2500	149.9779	0.0067	37.4986	0.0267
75	4.4158	0.2265	170.7918	0.0059	38.6771	0.0259
80	4.8754	0.2051	193.7720	0.0052	39.7445	0.0252
85	5.3829	0.1858	219.1439	0.0046	40.7113	0.0246
90	5.9431	0.1683	247.1567	0.0040	41.5869	0.0240
95	6.5617	0.1524	278.0850	0.0036	42.3800	0.0236
100	7.2446	0.1380	312.2323	0.0032	43.0984	0.0232

TABLE D–8   Interest Factors for 2.50%

	SINGLE PAYMENT		UNIFORM SERIES			
	COMPOUND-AMOUNT FACTOR	PRESENT-WORTH FACTOR	COMPOUND-AMOUNT FACTOR	SINKING-FUND FACTOR	PRESENT-WORTH FACTOR	CAPITAL-RECOVERY FACTOR
	CONVERT P TO F	CONVERT F TO P	CONVERT A TO F	CONVERT F TO A	CONVERT A TO P	CONVERT P TO A
N	$(F/P,I,N)$	$(P/F,I,N)$	$(F/A,I,N)$	$(A/F,I,N)$	$(P/A,I,N)$	$(A/P,I,N)$
1	1.0250	0.9756	1.0000	1.0000	0.9756	1.0250
2	1.0506	0.9518	2.0250	0.4938	1.9274	0.5188
3	1.0769	0.9286	3.0756	0.3251	2.8560	0.3501
4	1.1038	0.9060	4.1525	0.2408	3.7620	0.2658
5	1.1314	0.8839	5.2563	0.1902	4.6458	0.2152
6	1.1597	0.8623	6.3877	0.1565	5.5081	0.1815
7	1.1887	0.8413	7.5474	0.1325	6.3494	0.1575
8	1.2184	0.8207	8.7361	0.1145	7.1701	0.1395
9	1.2489	0.8007	9.9545	0.1005	7.9709	0.1255
10	1.2801	0.7812	11.2034	0.0893	8.7521	0.1143
11	1.3121	0.7621	12.4835	0.0801	9.5142	0.1051
12	1.3449	0.7436	13.7956	0.0725	10.2578	0.0975
13	1.3785	0.7254	15.1404	0.0660	10.9832	0.0910
14	1.4130	0.7077	16.5190	0.0605	11.6909	0.0855
15	1.4483	0.6905	17.9319	0.0558	12.3814	0.0808
16	1.4845	0.6736	19.3802	0.0516	13.0550	0.0766
17	1.5216	0.6572	20.8647	0.0479	13.7122	0.0729
18	1.5597	0.6412	22.3863	0.0447	14.3534	0.0697
19	1.5987	0.6255	23.9460	0.0418	14.9789	0.0668
20	1.6386	0.6103	25.5447	0.0391	15.5892	0.0641
21	1.6796	0.5954	27.1833	0.0368	16.1845	0.0618
22	1.7216	0.5809	28.8629	0.0346	16.7654	0.0596
23	1.7646	0.5667	30.5844	0.0327	17.3321	0.0577
24	1.8087	0.5529	32.3490	0.0309	17.8850	0.0559
25	1.8539	0.5394	34.1578	0.0293	18.4244	0.0543
26	1.9003	0.5262	36.0117	0.0278	18.9506	0.0528
27	1.9478	0.5134	37.9120	0.0264	19.4640	0.0514
28	1.9965	0.5009	39.8598	0.0251	19.9649	0.0501
29	2.0464	0.4887	41.8563	0.0239	20.4535	0.0489
30	2.0976	0.4767	43.9027	0.0228	20.9303	0.0478
35	2.3732	0.4214	54.9282	0.0182	23.1452	0.0432
40	2.6851	0.3724	67.4026	0.0148	25.1028	0.0398
45	3.0379	0.3292	81.5161	0.0123	26.8330	0.0373
50	3.4371	0.2909	97.4843	0.0103	28.3623	0.0353
55	3.8888	0.2572	115.5509	0.0087	29.7140	0.0337
60	4.3998	0.2273	135.9916	0.0074	30.9087	0.0324
65	4.9780	0.2009	159.1183	0.0063	31.9646	0.0313
70	5.6321	0.1776	185.2841	0.0054	32.8979	0.0304
75	6.3722	0.1569	214.8883	0.0047	33.7227	0.0297
80	7.2096	0.1387	248.3827	0.0040	34.4518	0.0290
85	8.1570	0.1226	286.2786	0.0035	35.0962	0.0285
90	9.2289	0.1084	329.1543	0.0030	35.6658	0.0280
95	10.4416	0.0958	377.6642	0.0026	36.1692	0.0276
100	11.8137	0.0846	432.5487	0.0023	36.6141	0.0273

TABLE D–9 Interest Factors for 3.00%

	SINGLE PAYMENT		UNIFORM SERIES			
	COMPOUND-AMOUNT FACTOR	PRESENT-WORTH FACTOR	COMPOUND-AMOUNT FACTOR	SINKING-FUND FACTOR	PRESENT-WORTH FACTOR	CAPITAL-RECOVERY FACTOR
N	CONVERT P TO F $(F/P,I,N)$	CONVERT F TO P $(P/F,I,N)$	CONVERT A TO F $(F/A,I,N)$	CONVERT F TO A $(A/F,I,N)$	CONVERT A TO P $(P/A,I,N)$	CONVERT P TO A $(A/P,I,N)$
1	1.0300	0.9709	1.0000	1.0000	0.9709	1.0300
2	1.0609	0.9426	2.0300	0.4926	1.9135	0.5226
3	1.0927	0.9151	3.0909	0.3235	2.8286	0.3535
4	1.1255	0.8885	4.1836	0.2390	3.7171	0.2690
5	1.1593	0.8626	5.3091	0.1884	4.5797	0.2184
6	1.1941	0.8375	6.4684	0.1546	5.4172	0.1846
7	1.2299	0.8131	7.6625	0.1305	6.2303	0.1605
8	1.2668	0.7894	8.8923	0.1125	7.0197	0.1425
9	1.3048	0.7664	10.1591	0.0984	7.7861	0.1284
10	1.3439	0.7441	11.4639	0.0872	8.5302	0.1172
11	1.3842	0.7224	12.8078	0.0781	9.2526	0.1081
12	1.4258	0.7014	14.1920	0.0705	9.9540	0.1005
13	1.4685	0.6810	15.6178	0.0640	10.6350	0.0940
14	1.5126	0.6611	17.0863	0.0585	11.2961	0.0885
15	1.5580	0.6419	18.5989	0.0538	11.9379	0.0838
16	1.6047	0.6232	20.1569	0.0496	12.5611	0.0796
17	1.6528	0.6050	21.7616	0.0460	13.1661	0.0760
18	1.7024	0.5874	23.4144	0.0427	13.7535	0.0727
19	1.7535	0.5703	25.1169	0.0398	14.3238	0.0698
20	1.8061	0.5537	26.8704	0.0372	14.8775	0.0672
21	1.8603	0.5375	28.6765	0.0349	15.4150	0.0649
22	1.9161	0.5219	30.5368	0.0327	15.9369	0.0627
23	1.9736	0.5067	32.4529	0.0308	16.4436	0.0608
24	2.0328	0.4919	34.4265	0.0290	16.9355	0.0590
25	2.0938	0.4776	36.4593	0.0274	17.4131	0.0574
26	2.1566	0.4637	38.5530	0.0259	17.8768	0.0559
27	2.2213	0.4502	40.7096	0.0246	18.3270	0.0546
28	2.2879	0.4371	42.9309	0.0233	18.7641	0.0533
29	2.3566	0.4243	45.2189	0.0221	19.1885	0.0521
30	2.4273	0.4120	47.5754	0.0210	19.6004	0.0510
35	2.8139	0.3554	60.4621	0.0165	21.4872	0.0465
40	3.2620	0.3066	75.4013	0.0133	23.1148	0.0433
45	3.7816	0.2644	92.7199	0.0108	24.5187	0.0408
50	4.3839	0.2281	112.7969	0.0089	25.7298	0.0389
55	5.0821	0.1968	136.0716	0.0073	26.7744	0.0373
60	5.8916	0.1697	163.0534	0.0061	27.6756	0.0361
65	6.8300	0.1464	194.3328	0.0051	28.4529	0.0351
70	7.9178	0.1263	230.5941	0.0043	29.1234	0.0343
75	9.1789	0.1089	272.6309	0.0037	29.7018	0.0337
80	10.6409	0.0940	321.3630	0.0031	30.2008	0.0331
85	12.3357	0.0811	377.8570	0.0026	30.6312	0.0326
90	14.3005	0.0699	443.3489	0.0023	31.0024	0.0323
95	16.5782	0.0603	519.2720	0.0019	31.3227	0.0319
100	19.2186	0.0520	607.2877	0.0016	31.5989	0.0316

TABLE D–10   Interest Factors for 4.00%

	SINGLE PAYMENT		UNIFORM SERIES			
	COMPOUND-AMOUNT FACTOR	PRESENT-WORTH FACTOR	COMPOUND-AMOUNT FACTOR	SINKING-FUND FACTOR	PRESENT-WORTH FACTOR	CAPITAL-RECOVERY FACTOR
	CONVERT P TO F	CONVERT F TO P	CONVERT A TO F	CONVERT F TO A	CONVERT A TO P	CONVERT P TO A
N	$(F/P,I,N)$	$(P/F,I,N)$	$(F/A,I,N)$	$(A/F,I,N)$	$(P/A,I,N)$	$(A/P,I,N)$
1	1.0400	0.9615	1.0000	1.0000	0.9615	1.0400
2	1.0816	0.9246	2.0400	0.4902	1.8861	0.5302
3	1.1249	0.8890	3.1216	0.3203	2.7751	0.3603
4	1.1699	0.8548	4.2465	0.2355	3.6299	0.2755
5	1.2167	0.8219	5.4163	0.1846	4.4518	0.2246
6	1.2653	0.7903	6.6330	0.1508	5.2421	0.1908
7	1.3159	0.7599	7.8983	0.1266	6.0021	0.1666
8	1.3686	0.7307	9.2142	0.1085	6.7327	0.1485
9	1.4233	0.7026	10.5828	0.0945	7.4353	0.1345
10	1.4802	0.6756	12.0061	0.0833	8.1109	0.1233
11	1.5395	0.6496	13.4864	0.0741	8.7605	0.1141
12	1.6010	0.6246	15.0258	0.0666	9.3851	0.1066
13	1.6651	0.6006	16.6268	0.0601	9.9856	0.1001
14	1.7317	0.5775	18.2919	0.0547	10.5631	0.0947
15	1.8009	0.5553	20.0236	0.0499	11.1184	0.0899
16	1.8730	0.5339	21.8245	0.0458	11.6523	0.0858
17	1.9479	0.5134	23.6975	0.0422	12.1657	0.0822
18	2.0258	0.4936	25.6454	0.0390	12.6593	0.0790
19	2.1068	0.4746	27.6712	0.0361	13.1339	0.0761
20	2.1911	0.4564	29.7781	0.0336	13.5903	0.0736
21	2.2788	0.4388	31.9692	0.0313	14.0292	0.0713
22	2.3699	0.4220	34.2480	0.0292	14.4511	0.0692
23	2.4647	0.4057	36.6179	0.0273	14.8568	0.0673
24	2.5633	0.3901	39.0826	0.0256	15.2470	0.0656
25	2.6658	0.3751	41.6459	0.0240	15.6221	0.0640
26	2.7725	0.3607	44.3117	0.0226	15.9828	0.0626
27	2.8834	0.3468	47.0842	0.0212	16.3296	0.0612
28	2.9987	0.3335	49.9676	0.0200	16.6631	0.0600
29	3.1187	0.3207	52.9663	0.0189	16.9837	0.0589
30	3.2434	0.3083	56.0849	0.0178	17.2920	0.0578
35	3.9461	0.2534	73.6522	0.0136	18.6646	0.0536
40	4.8010	0.2083	95.0255	0.0105	19.7928	0.0505
45	5.8412	0.1712	121.0294	0.0083	20.7200	0.0483
50	7.1067	0.1407	152.6671	0.0066	21.4822	0.0466
55	8.6464	0.1157	191.1592	0.0052	22.1086	0.0452
60	10.5196	0.0951	237.9907	0.0042	22.6235	0.0442
65	12.7987	0.0781	294.9684	0.0034	23.0467	0.0434
70	15.5716	0.0642	364.2905	0.0027	23.3945	0.0427
75	18.9453	0.0528	448.6314	0.0022	23.6804	0.0422
80	23.0498	0.0434	551.2450	0.0018	23.9154	0.0418
85	28.0436	0.0357	676.0901	0.0015	24.1085	0.0415
90	34.1193	0.0293	827.9833	0.0012	24.2673	0.0412

TABLE D–11 Interest Factors for 5.00%

	SINGLE PAYMENT		UNIFORM SERIES			
	COMPOUND-AMOUNT FACTOR	PRESENT-WORTH FACTOR	COMPOUND-AMOUNT FACTOR	SINKING-FUND FACTOR	PRESENT-WORTH FACTOR	CAPITAL-RECOVERY FACTOR
	CONVERT P TO F	CONVERT F TO P	CONVERT A TO F	CONVERT F TO A	CONVERT A TO P	CONVERT P TO A
N	$(F/P,I,N)$	$(P/F,I,N)$	$(F/A,I,N)$	$(A/F,I,N)$	$(P/A,I,N)$	$(A/P,I,N)$
1	1.0500	0.9524	1.0000	1.0000	0.9524	1.0500
2	1.1025	0.9070	2.0500	0.4878	1.8594	0.5378
3	1.1576	0.8638	3.1525	0.3172	2.7232	0.3672
4	1.2155	0.8227	4.3101	0.2320	3.5460	0.2820
5	1.2763	0.7835	5.5256	0.1810	4.3295	0.2310
6	1.3401	0.7462	6.8019	0.1470	5.0757	0.1970
7	1.4071	0.7107	8.1420	0.1228	5.7864	0.1728
8	1.4775	0.6768	9.5491	0.1047	6.4632	0.1547
9	1.5513	0.6446	11.0266	0.0907	7.1078	0.1407
10	1.6289	0.6139	12.5779	0.0795	7.7217	0.1295
11	1.7103	0.5847	14.2068	0.0704	8.3064	0.1204
12	1.7959	0.5568	15.9171	0.0628	8.8633	0.1128
13	1.8856	0.5303	17.7130	0.0565	9.3936	0.1065
14	1.9799	0.5051	19.5986	0.0510	9.8986	0.1010
15	2.0789	0.4810	21.5786	0.0463	10.3797	0.0963
16	2.1829	0.4581	23.6575	0.0423	10.8378	0.0923
17	2.2920	0.4363	25.8404	0.0387	11.2741	0.0887
18	2.4066	0.4155	28.1324	0.0355	11.6896	0.0855
19	2.5270	0.3957	30.5390	0.0327	12.0853	0.0827
20	2.6533	0.3769	33.0660	0.0302	12.4622	0.0802
21	2.7860	0.3589	35.7193	0.0280	12.8212	0.0780
22	2.9253	0.3418	38.5052	0.0260	13.1630	0.0760
23	3.0715	0.3256	41.4305	0.0241	13.4886	0.0741
24	3.2251	0.3101	44.5020	0.0225	13.7986	0.0725
25	3.3864	0.2953	47.7271	0.0210	14.0939	0.0710
26	3.5557	0.2812	51.1135	0.0196	14.3752	0.0696
27	3.7335	0.2678	54.6691	0.0183	14.6430	0.0683
28	3.9201	0.2551	58.4026	0.0171	14.8981	0.0671
29	4.1161	0.2429	62.3227	0.0160	15.1411	0.0660
30	4.3219	0.2314	66.4388	0.0151	15.3725	0.0651
35	5.5160	0.1813	90.3203	0.0111	16.3742	0.0611
40	7.0400	0.1420	120.7998	0.0083	17.1591	0.0583
45	8.9850	0.1113	159.7002	0.0063	17.7741	0.0563
50	11.4674	0.0872	209.3480	0.0048	18.2559	0.0548
55	14.6356	0.0683	272.7126	0.0037	18.6335	0.0537
60	18.6792	0.0535	353.5837	0.0028	18.9293	0.0528
65	23.8399	0.0419	456.7980	0.0022	19.1611	0.0522
70	30.4264	0.0329	588.5285	0.0017	19.3427	0.0517
75	38.8327	0.0258	756.6537	0.0013	19.4850	0.0513
80	49.5614	0.0202	971.2288	0.0010	19.5965	0.0510

TABLE D–12 Interest Factors for 6.00%

	SINGLE PAYMENT		UNIFORM SERIES			
	COMPOUND-AMOUNT FACTOR	PRESENT-WORTH FACTOR	COMPOUND-AMOUNT FACTOR	SINKING-FUND FACTOR	PRESENT-WORTH FACTOR	CAPITAL-RECOVERY FACTOR
	CONVERT P TO F	CONVERT F TO P	CONVERT A TO F	CONVERT F TO A	CONVERT A TO P	CONVERT P TO A
N	$(F/P,I,N)$	$(P/F,I,N)$	$(F/A,I,N)$	$(A/F,I,N)$	$(P/A,I,N)$	$(A/P,I,N)$
1	1.0600	0.9434	1.0000	1.0000	0.9434	1.0600
2	1.1236	0.8900	2.0600	0.4854	1.8334	0.5454
3	1.1910	0.8396	3.1836	0.3141	2.6730	0.3741
4	1.2625	0.7921	4.3746	0.2286	3.4651	0.2886
5	1.3382	0.7473	5.6371	0.1774	4.2124	0.2374
6	1.4185	0.7050	6.9753	0.1434	4.9173	0.2034
7	1.5036	0.6651	8.3938	0.1191	5.5824	0.1791
8	1.5938	0.6274	9.8975	0.1010	6.2098	0.1610
9	1.6895	0.5919	11.4913	0.0870	6.8017	0.1470
10	1.7908	0.5584	13.1808	0.0759	7.3601	0.1359
11	1.8983	0.5268	14.9716	0.0668	7.8869	0.1268
12	2.0122	0.4970	16.8699	0.0593	8.3838	0.1193
13	2.1329	0.4688	18.8821	0.0530	8.8527	0.1130
14	2.2609	0.4423	21.0151	0.0476	9.2950	0.1076
15	2.3966	0.4173	23.2760	0.0430	9.7122	0.1030
16	2.5404	0.3936	25.6725	0.0390	10.1059	0.0990
17	2.6928	0.3714	28.2129	0.0354	10.4773	0.0954
18	2.8543	0.3503	30.9057	0.0324	10.8276	0.0924
19	3.0256	0.3305	33.7600	0.0296	11.1581	0.0896
20	3.2071	0.3118	36.7856	0.0272	11.4699	0.0872
21	3.3996	0.2942	39.9927	0.0250	11.7641	0.0850
22	3.6035	0.2775	43.3923	0.0230	12.0416	0.0830
23	3.8197	0.2618	46.9958	0.0213	12.3034	0.0813
24	4.0489	0.2470	50.8156	0.0197	12.5504	0.0797
25	4.2919	0.2330	54.8645	0.0182	12.7834	0.0782
26	4.5494	0.2198	59.1564	0.0169	13.0032	0.0769
27	4.8223	0.2074	63.7058	0.0157	13.2105	0.0757
28	5.1117	0.1956	68.5281	0.0146	13.4062	0.0746
29	5.4184	0.1846	73.6398	0.0136	13.5907	0.0736
30	5.7435	0.1741	79.0582	0.0126	13.7648	0.0726
35	7.6861	0.1301	111.4348	0.0090	14.4982	0.0690
40	10.2857	0.0972	154.7620	0.0065	15.0463	0.0665
45	13.7646	0.0727	212.7435	0.0047	15.4558	0.0647
50	18.4202	0.0543	290.3359	0.0034	15.7619	0.0634
55	24.6503	0.0406	394.1720	0.0025	15.9905	0.0625
60	32.9877	0.0303	533.1282	0.0019	16.1614	0.0619
65	44.1450	0.0227	719.0829	0.0014	16.2891	0.0614
70	59.0759	0.0169	967.9322	0.0010	16.3845	0.0610

TABLE D–13   Interest Factors for 7.00%

	SINGLE PAYMENT		UNIFORM SERIES			
	COMPOUND-AMOUNT FACTOR	PRESENT-WORTH FACTOR	COMPOUND-AMOUNT FACTOR	SINKING-FUND FACTOR	PRESENT-WORTH FACTOR	CAPITAL-RECOVERY FACTOR
	CONVERT P TO F	CONVERT F TO P	CONVERT A TO F	CONVERT F TO A	CONVERT A TO P	CONVERT P TO A
N	(F/P,I,N)	(P/F,I,N)	(F/A,I,N)	(A/F,I,N)	(P/A,I,N)	(A/P,I,N)
1	1.0700	0.9346	1.0000	1.0000	0.9346	1.0700
2	1.1449	0.8734	2.0700	0.4831	1.8080	0.5531
3	1.2250	0.8163	3.2149	0.3111	2.6243	0.3811
4	1.3108	0.7629	4.4399	0.2252	3.3872	0.2952
5	1.4026	0.7130	5.7507	0.1739	4.1002	0.2439
6	1.5007	0.6663	7.1533	0.1398	4.7665	0.2098
7	1.6058	0.6227	8.6540	0.1156	5.3893	0.1856
8	1.7182	0.5820	10.2598	0.0975	5.9713	0.1675
9	1.8385	0.5439	11.9780	0.0835	6.5152	0.1535
10	1.9672	0.5083	13.8164	0.0724	7.0236	0.1424
11	2.1049	0.4751	15.7836	0.0634	7.4987	0.1334
12	2.2522	0.4440	17.8885	0.0559	7.9427	0.1259
13	2.4098	0.4150	20.1406	0.0497	8.3577	0.1197
14	2.5785	0.3878	22.5505	0.0443	8.7455	0.1143
15	2.7590	0.3624	25.1290	0.0398	9.1079	0.1098
16	2.9522	0.3387	27.8881	0.0359	9.4466	0.1059
17	3.1588	0.3166	30.8402	0.0324	9.7632	0.1024
18	3.3799	0.2959	33.9990	0.0294	10.0591	0.0994
19	3.6165	0.2765	37.3790	0.0268	10.3356	0.0968
20	3.8697	0.2584	40.9955	0.0244	10.5940	0.0944
21	4.1406	0.2415	44.8652	0.0223	10.8355	0.0923
22	4.4304	0.2257	49.0057	0.0204	11.0612	0.0904
23	4.7405	0.2109	53.4361	0.0187	11.2722	0.0887
24	5.0724	0.1971	58.1767	0.0172	11.4693	0.0872
25	5.4274	0.1842	63.2490	0.0158	11.6536	0.0858
26	5.8074	0.1722	68.6765	0.0146	11.8258	0.0846
27	6.2139	0.1609	74.4838	0.0134	11.9867	0.0834
28	6.6488	0.1504	80.6977	0.0124	12.1371	0.0824
29	7.1143	0.1406	87.3465	0.0114	12.2777	0.0814
30	7.6123	0.1314	94.4608	0.0106	12.4090	0.0806
35	10.6766	0.0937	138.2369	0.0072	12.9477	0.0772
40	14.9745	0.0668	199.6351	0.0050	13.3317	0.0750
45	21.0025	0.0476	285.7493	0.0035	13.6055	0.0735
50	29.4570	0.0339	406.5289	0.0025	13.8007	0.0725
55	41.3150	0.0242	575.9286	0.0017	13.9399	0.0717
60	57.9464	0.0173	813.5204	0.0012	14.0392	0.0712

TABLE D–14   Interest Factors for 8.00%

	SINGLE PAYMENT		UNIFORM SERIES			
	COMPOUND-AMOUNT FACTOR	PRESENT-WORTH FACTOR	COMPOUND-AMOUNT FACTOR	SINKING-FUND FACTOR	PRESENT-WORTH FACTOR	CAPITAL-RECOVERY FACTOR
	CONVERT P TO F	CONVERT F TO P	CONVERT A TO F	CONVERT F TO A	CONVERT A TO P	CONVERT P TO A
N	$(F/P,I,N)$	$(P/F,I,N)$	$(F/A,I,N)$	$(A/F,I,N)$	$(P/A,I,N)$	$(A/P,I,N)$
1	1.0800	0.9259	1.0000	1.0000	0.9259	1.0800
2	1.1664	0.8573	2.0800	0.4808	1.7833	0.5608
3	1.2597	0.7938	3.2464	0.3080	2.5771	0.3880
4	1.3605	0.7350	4.5061	0.2219	3.3121	0.3019
5	1.4693	0.6806	5.8666	0.1705	3.9927	0.2505
6	1.5869	0.6302	7.3359	0.1363	4.6229	0.2163
7	1.7138	0.5835	8.9228	0.1121	5.2064	0.1921
8	1.8509	0.5403	10.6366	0.0940	5.7466	0.1740
9	1.9990	0.5002	12.4876	0.0801	6.2469	0.1601
10	2.1589	0.4632	14.4866	0.0690	6.7101	0.1490
11	2.3316	0.4289	16.6455	0.0601	7.1390	0.1401
12	2.5182	0.3971	18.9771	0.0527	7.5361	0.1327
13	2.7196	0.3677	21.4953	0.0465	7.9038	0.1265
14	2.9372	0.3405	24.2149	0.0413	8.2442	0.1213
15	3.1722	0.3152	27.1521	0.0368	8.5595	0.1168
16	3.4259	0.2919	30.3243	0.0330	8.8514	0.1130
17	3.7000	0.2703	33.7502	0.0296	9.1216	0.1096
18	3.9960	0.2502	37.4502	0.0267	9.3719	0.1067
19	4.3157	0.2317	41.4463	0.0241	9.6036	0.1041
20	4.6610	0.2145	45.7620	0.0219	9.8181	0.1019
21	5.0338	0.1987	50.4229	0.0198	10.0168	0.0998
22	5.4365	0.1839	55.4568	0.0180	10.2007	0.0980
23	5.8715	0.1703	60.8933	0.0164	10.3711	0.0964
24	6.3412	0.1577	66.7648	0.0150	10.5288	0.0950
25	6.8485	0.1460	73.1059	0.0137	10.6748	0.0937
26	7.3964	0.1352	79.9544	0.0125	10.8100	0.0925
27	7.9881	0.1252	87.3508	0.0114	10.9352	0.0914
28	8.6271	0.1159	95.3388	0.0105	11.0511	0.0905
29	9.3173	0.1073	103.9659	0.0096	11.1584	0.0896
30	10.0627	0.0994	113.2832	0.0088	11.2578	0.0888
35	14.7853	0.0676	172.3168	0.0058	11.6546	0.0858
40	21.7245	0.0460	259.0565	0.0039	11.9246	0.0839
45	31.9204	0.0313	386.5056	0.0026	12.1084	0.0826
50	46.9016	0.0213	573.7702	0.0017	12.2335	0.0817
55	68.9139	0.0145	848.9232	0.0012	12.3186	0.0812

TABLE D–15 Interest Factors for 9.00%

	SINGLE PAYMENT		UNIFORM SERIES			
	COMPOUND-AMOUNT FACTOR	PRESENT-WORTH FACTOR	COMPOUND-AMOUNT FACTOR	SINKING-FUND FACTOR	PRESENT-WORTH FACTOR	CAPITAL-RECOVERY FACTOR
	CONVERT P TO F	CONVERT F TO P	CONVERT A TO F	CONVERT F TO A	CONVERT A TO P	CONVERT P TO A
N	$(F/P,I,N)$	$(P/F,I,N)$	$(F/A,I,N)$	$(A/F,I,N)$	$(P/A,I,N)$	$(A/P,I,N)$
1	1.0900	0.9174	1.0000	1.0000	0.9174	1.0900
2	1.1881	0.8417	2.0900	0.4785	1.7591	0.5685
3	1.2950	0.7722	3.2781	0.3051	2.5313	0.3951
4	1.4116	0.7084	4.5731	0.2187	3.2397	0.3087
5	1.5386	0.6499	5.9847	0.1671	3.8897	0.2571
6	1.6771	0.5963	7.5233	0.1329	4.4859	0.2229
7	1.8280	0.5470	9.2004	0.1087	5.0330	0.1987
8	1.9926	0.5019	11.0285	0.0907	5.5348	0.1807
9	2.1719	0.4604	13.0210	0.0768	5.9952	0.1668
10	2.3674	0.4224	15.1929	0.0658	6.4177	0.1558
11	2.5804	0.3875	17.5603	0.0569	6.8052	0.1469
12	2.8127	0.3555	20.1407	0.0497	7.1607	0.1397
13	3.0658	0.3262	22.9534	0.0436	7.4869	0.1336
14	3.3417	0.2992	26.0192	0.0384	7.7862	0.1284
15	3.6425	0.2745	29.3609	0.0341	8.0607	0.1241
16	3.9703	0.2519	33.0034	0.0303	8.3126	0.1203
17	4.3276	0.2311	36.9737	0.0270	8.5436	0.1170
18	4.7171	0.2120	41.3013	0.0242	8.7556	0.1142
19	5.1417	0.1945	46.0185	0.0217	8.9501	0.1117
20	5.6044	0.1784	51.1601	0.0195	9.1285	0.1095
21	6.1088	0.1637	56.7645	0.0176	9.2922	0.1076
22	6.6586	0.1502	62.8733	0.0159	9.4424	0.1059
23	7.2579	0.1378	69.5319	0.0144	9.5802	0.1044
24	7.9111	0.1264	76.7898	0.0130	9.7066	0.1030
25	8.6231	0.1160	84.7009	0.0118	9.8226	0.1018
26	9.3992	0.1064	93.3240	0.0107	9.9290	0.1007
27	10.2451	0.0976	102.7231	0.0097	10.0266	0.0997
28	11.1671	0.0895	112.9682	0.0089	10.1161	0.0989
29	12.1722	0.0822	124.1354	0.0081	10.1983	0.0981
30	13.2677	0.0754	136.3075	0.0073	10.2737	0.0973
35	20.4140	0.0490	215.7108	0.0046	10.5668	0.0946
40	31.4094	0.0318	337.8824	0.0030	10.7574	0.0930
45	48.3273	0.0207	525.8587	0.0019	10.8812	0.0919
50	74.3575	0.0134	815.0836	0.0012	10.9617	0.0912

TABLE D–16   Interest Factors for 10.00%

	SINGLE PAYMENT		UNIFORM SERIES			
	COMPOUND-AMOUNT FACTOR	PRESENT-WORTH FACTOR	COMPOUND-AMOUNT FACTOR	SINKING-FUND FACTOR	PRESENT-WORTH FACTOR	CAPITAL-RECOVERY FACTOR
	CONVERT P TO F	CONVERT F TO P	CONVERT A TO F	CONVERT F TO A	CONVERT A TO P	CONVERT P TO A
N	$(F/P,I,N)$	$(P/F,I,N)$	$(F/A,I,N)$	$(A/F,I,N)$	$(P/A,I,N)$	$(A/P,I,N)$
1	1.1000	0.9091	1.0000	1.0000	0.9091	1.1000
2	1.2100	0.8264	2.1000	0.4762	1.7355	0.5762
3	1.3310	0.7513	3.3100	0.3021	2.4869	0.4021
4	1.4641	0.6830	4.6410	0.2155	3.1699	0.3155
5	1.6105	0.6209	6.1051	0.1638	3.7908	0.2638
6	1.7716	0.5645	7.7156	0.1296	4.3553	0.2296
7	1.9487	0.5132	9.4872	0.1054	4.8684	0.2054
8	2.1436	0.4665	11.4359	0.0874	5.3349	0.1874
9	2.3579	0.4241	13.5795	0.0736	5.7590	0.1736
10	2.5937	0.3855	15.9374	0.0627	6.1446	0.1627
11	2.8531	0.3505	18.5312	0.0540	6.4951	0.1540
12	3.1384	0.3186	21.3843	0.0468	6.8137	0.1468
13	3.4523	0.2897	24.5227	0.0408	7.1034	0.1408
14	3.7975	0.2633	27.9750	0.0357	7.3667	0.1357
15	4.1772	0.2394	31.7725	0.0315	7.6061	0.1315
16	4.5950	0.2176	35.9497	0.0278	7.8237	0.1278
17	5.0545	0.1978	40.5447	0.0247	8.0216	0.1247
18	5.5599	0.1799	45.5992	0.0219	8.2014	0.1219
19	6.1159	0.1635	51.1591	0.0195	8.3649	0.1195
20	6.7275	0.1486	57.2750	0.0175	8.5136	0.1175
21	7.4002	0.1351	64.0025	0.0156	8.6487	0.1156
22	8.1403	0.1228	71.4027	0.0140	8.7715	0.1140
23	8.9543	0.1117	79.5430	0.0126	8.8832	0.1126
24	9.8497	0.1015	88.4973	0.0113	8.9847	0.1113
25	10.8347	0.0923	98.3471	0.0102	9.0770	0.1102
26	11.9182	0.0839	109.1818	0.0092	9.1609	0.1092
27	13.1100	0.0763	121.0999	0.0083	9.2372	0.1083
28	14.4210	0.0693	134.2099	0.0075	9.3066	0.1075
29	15.8631	0.0630	148.6309	0.0067	9.3696	0.1067
30	17.4494	0.0573	164.4940	0.0061	9.4269	0.1061
35	28.1024	0.0356	271.0244	0.0037	9.6442	0.1037
40	45.2593	0.0221	442.5926	0.0023	9.7791	0.1023
45	72.8905	0.0137	718.9048	0.0014	9.8628	0.1014

TABLE D–17 Interest Factors for 11.00%

	SINGLE PAYMENT		UNIFORM SERIES			
	COMPOUND-AMOUNT FACTOR	PRESENT-WORTH FACTOR	COMPOUND-AMOUNT FACTOR	SINKING-FUND FACTOR	PRESENT-WORTH FACTOR	CAPITAL-RECOVERY FACTOR
	CONVERT P TO F	CONVERT F TO P	CONVERT A TO F	CONVERT F TO A	CONVERT A TO P	CONVERT P TO A
N	$(F/P,I,N)$	$(P/F,I,N)$	$(F/A,I,N)$	$(A/F,I,N)$	$(P/A,I,N)$	$(A/P,I,N)$
1	1.1100	0.9009	1.0000	1.0000	0.9009	1.1100
2	1.2321	0.8116	2.1100	0.4739	1.7125	0.5839
3	1.3676	0.7312	3.3421	0.2992	2.4437	0.4092
4	1.5181	0.6587	4.7097	0.2123	3.1024	0.3223
5	1.6851	0.5935	6.2278	0.1606	3.6959	0.2706
6	1.8704	0.5346	7.9129	0.1264	4.2305	0.2364
7	2.0762	0.4817	9.7833	0.1022	4.7122	0.2122
8	2.3045	0.4339	11.8594	0.0843	5.1461	0.1943
9	2.5580	0.3909	14.1640	0.0706	5.5370	0.1806
10	2.8394	0.3522	16.7220	0.0598	5.8892	0.1698
11	3.1518	0.3173	19.5614	0.0511	6.2065	0.1611
12	3.4985	0.2858	22.7132	0.0440	6.4924	0.1540
13	3.8833	0.2575	26.2116	0.0382	6.7499	0.1482
14	4.3104	0.2320	30.0949	0.0332	6.9819	0.1432
15	4.7846	0.2090	34.4054	0.0291	7.1909	0.1391
16	5.3109	0.1883	39.1899	0.0255	7.3792	0.1355
17	5.8951	0.1696	44.5008	0.0225	7.5488	0.1325
18	6.5436	0.1528	50.3959	0.0198	7.7016	0.1298
19	7.2633	0.1377	56.9395	0.0176	7.8393	0.1276
20	8.0623	0.1240	64.2028	0.0156	7.9633	0.1256
21	8.9492	0.1117	72.2651	0.0138	8.0751	0.1238
22	9.9336	0.1007	81.2143	0.0123	8.1757	0.1223
23	11.0263	0.0907	91.1479	0.0110	8.2664	0.1210
24	12.2392	0.0817	102.1742	0.0098	8.3481	0.1198
25	13.5855	0.0736	114.4133	0.0087	8.4217	0.1187
26	15.0799	0.0663	127.9988	0.0078	8.4881	0.1178
27	16.7386	0.0597	143.0786	0.0070	8.5478	0.1170
28	18.5799	0.0538	159.8173	0.0063	8.6016	0.1163
29	20.6237	0.0485	178.3972	0.0056	8.6501	0.1156
30	22.8923	0.0437	199.0209	0.0050	8.6938	0.1150
35	38.5749	0.0259	341.5896	0.0029	8.8552	0.1129
40	65.0009	0.0154	581.8261	0.0017	8.9511	0.1117
45	109.5302	0.0091	986.6386	0.0010	9.0079	0.1110

TABLE D–18 Interest Factors for 12.00%

	SINGLE PAYMENT		UNIFORM SERIES			
	COMPOUND-AMOUNT FACTOR	PRESENT-WORTH FACTOR	COMPOUND-AMOUNT FACTOR	SINKING-FUND FACTOR	PRESENT-WORTH FACTOR	CAPITAL-RECOVERY FACTOR
N	CONVERT P TO F (F/P,I,N)	CONVERT F TO P (P/F,I,N)	CONVERT A TO F (F/A,I,N)	CONVERT F TO A (A/F,I,N)	CONVERT A TO P (P/A,I,N)	CONVERT P TO A (A/P,I,N)
1	1.1200	0.8929	1.0000	1.0000	0.8929	1.1200
2	1.2544	0.7972	2.1200	0.4717	1.6901	0.5917
3	1.4049	0.7118	3.3744	0.2963	2.4018	0.4163
4	1.5735	0.6355	4.7793	0.2092	3.0373	0.3292
5	1.7623	0.5674	6.3528	0.1574	3.6048	0.2774
6	1.9738	0.5066	8.1152	0.1232	4.1114	0.2432
7	2.2107	0.4523	10.0890	0.0991	4.5638	0.2191
8	2.4760	0.4039	12.2997	0.0813	4.9676	0.2013
9	2.7731	0.3606	14.7757	0.0677	5.3282	0.1877
10	3.1058	0.3220	17.5487	0.0570	5.6502	0.1770
11	3.4785	0.2875	20.6546	0.0484	5.9377	0.1684
12	3.8960	0.2567	24.1331	0.0414	6.1944	0.1614
13	4.3635	0.2292	28.0291	0.0357	6.4235	0.1557
14	4.8871	0.2046	32.3926	0.0309	6.6282	0.1509
15	5.4736	0.1827	37.2797	0.0268	6.8109	0.1468
16	6.1304	0.1631	42.7533	0.0234	6.9740	0.1434
17	6.8660	0.1456	48.8837	0.0205	7.1196	0.1405
18	7.6900	0.1300	55.7497	0.0179	7.2497	0.1379
19	8.6128	0.1161	63.4397	0.0158	7.3658	0.1358
20	9.6463	0.1037	72.0524	0.0139	7.4694	0.1339
21	10.8038	0.0926	81.6987	0.0122	7.5620	0.1322
22	12.1003	0.0826	92.5026	0.0108	7.6446	0.1308
23	13.5523	0.0738	104.6029	0.0096	7.7184	0.1296
24	15.1786	0.0659	118.1552	0.0085	7.7843	0.1285
25	17.0001	0.0588	133.3339	0.0075	7.8431	0.1275
26	19.0401	0.0525	150.3339	0.0067	7.8957	0.1267
27	21.3249	0.0469	169.3740	0.0059	7.9426	0.1259
28	23.8839	0.0419	190.6989	0.0052	7.9844	0.1252
29	26.7499	0.0374	214.5828	0.0047	8.0218	0.1247
30	29.9599	0.0334	241.3327	0.0041	8.0552	0.1241
35	52.7996	0.0189	431.6635	0.0023	8.1755	0.1223
40	93.0510	0.0107	767.0914	0.0013	8.2438	0.1213

TABLE D–19   Interest Factors for 13.00%

	SINGLE PAYMENT		UNIFORM SERIES			
	COMPOUND-AMOUNT FACTOR	PRESENT-WORTH FACTOR	COMPOUND-AMOUNT FACTOR	SINKING-FUND FACTOR	PRESENT-WORTH FACTOR	CAPITAL-RECOVERY FACTOR
N	CONVERT P TO F (F/P,I,N)	CONVERT F TO P (P/F,I,N)	CONVERT A TO F (F/A,I,N)	CONVERT F TO A (A/F,I,N)	CONVERT A TO P (P/A,I,N)	CONVERT P TO A (A/P,I,N)
1	1.1300	0.8850	1.0000	1.0000	0.8850	1.1300
2	1.2769	0.7831	2.1300	0.4695	1.6681	0.5995
3	1.4429	0.6931	3.4069	0.2935	2.3612	0.4235
4	1.6305	0.6133	4.8498	0.2062	2.9745	0.3362
5	1.8424	0.5428	6.4803	0.1543	3.5172	0.2843
6	2.0820	0.4803	8.3227	0.1202	3.9975	0.2502
7	2.3526	0.4251	10.4047	0.0961	4.4226	0.2261
8	2.6584	0.3762	12.7573	0.0784	4.7988	0.2084
9	3.0040	0.3329	15.4157	0.0649	5.1317	0.1949
10	3.3946	0.2946	18.4197	0.0543	5.4262	0.1843
11	3.8359	0.2607	21.8143	0.0458	5.6869	0.1758
12	4.3345	0.2307	25.6502	0.0390	5.9176	0.1690
13	4.8980	0.2042	29.9847	0.0334	6.1218	0.1634
14	5.5348	0.1807	34.8827	0.0287	6.3025	0.1587
15	6.2543	0.1599	40.4175	0.0247	6.4624	0.1547
16	7.0673	0.1415	46.6717	0.0214	6.6039	0.1514
17	7.9861	0.1252	53.7391	0.0186	6.7291	0.1486
18	9.0243	0.1108	61.7251	0.0162	6.8399	0.1462
19	10.1974	0.0981	70.7494	0.0141	6.9380	0.1441
20	11.5231	0.0868	80.9468	0.0124	7.0248	0.1424
21	13.0211	0.0768	92.4699	0.0108	7.1016	0.1408
22	14.7138	0.0680	105.4910	0.0095	7.1695	0.1395
23	16.6266	0.0601	120.2048	0.0083	7.2297	0.1383
24	18.7881	0.0532	136.8315	0.0073	7.2829	0.1373
25	21.2305	0.0471	155.6196	0.0064	7.3300	0.1364
26	23.9905	0.0417	176.8501	0.0057	7.3717	0.1357
27	27.1093	0.0369	200.8406	0.0050	7.4086	0.1350
28	30.6335	0.0326	227.9499	0.0044	7.4412	0.1344
29	34.6158	0.0289	258.5834	0.0039	7.4701	0.1339
30	39.1159	0.0256	293.1992	0.0034	7.4957	0.1334
35	72.0685	0.0139	546.6808	0.0018	7.5856	0.1318

TABLE D–20   Interest Factors for 14.00%

	SINGLE PAYMENT		UNIFORM SERIES			
	COMPOUND-AMOUNT FACTOR	PRESENT-WORTH FACTOR	COMPOUND-AMOUNT FACTOR	SINKING-FUND FACTOR	PRESENT-WORTH FACTOR	CAPITAL-RECOVERY FACTOR
N	CONVERT P TO F (F/P,I,N)	CONVERT F TO P (P/F,I,N)	CONVERT A TO F (F/A,I,N)	CONVERT F TO A (A/F,I,N)	CONVERT A TO P (P/A,I,N)	CONVERT P TO A (A/P,I,N)
1	1.1400	0.8772	1.0000	1.0000	0.8772	1.1400
2	1.2996	0.7695	2.1400	0.4673	1.6467	0.6073
3	1.4815	0.6750	3.4396	0.2907	2.3216	0.4307
4	1.6890	0.5921	4.9211	0.2032	2.9137	0.3432
5	1.9254	0.5194	6.6101	0.1513	3.4331	0.2913
6	2.1950	0.4556	8.5355	0.1172	3.8887	0.2572
7	2.5023	0.3996	10.7305	0.0932	4.2883	0.2332
8	2.8526	0.3506	13.2328	0.0756	4.6389	0.2156
9	3.2519	0.3075	16.0853	0.0622	4.9464	0.2022
10	3.7072	0.2697	19.3373	0.0517	5.2161	0.1917
11	4.2262	0.2366	23.0445	0.0434	5.4527	0.1834
12	4.8179	0.2076	27.2707	0.0367	5.6603	0.1767
13	5.4924	0.1821	32.0887	0.0312	5.8424	0.1712
14	6.2613	0.1597	37.5811	0.0266	6.0021	0.1666
15	7.1379	0.1401	43.8424	0.0228	6.1422	0.1628
16	8.1372	0.1229	50.9804	0.0196	6.2651	0.1596
17	9.2765	0.1078	59.1176	0.0169	6.3729	0.1569
18	10.5752	0.0946	68.3941	0.0146	6.4674	0.1546
19	12.0557	0.0829	78.9692	0.0127	6.5504	0.1527
20	13.7435	0.0728	91.0249	0.0110	6.6231	0.1510
21	15.6676	0.0638	104.7684	0.0095	6.6870	0.1495
22	17.8610	0.0560	120.4360	0.0083	6.7429	0.1483
23	20.3616	0.0491	138.2970	0.0072	6.7921	0.1472
24	23.2122	0.0431	158.6586	0.0063	6.8351	0.1463
25	26.4619	0.0378	181.8708	0.0055	6.8729	0.1455
26	30.1666	0.0331	208.3327	0.0048	6.9061	0.1448
27	34.3899	0.0291	238.4993	0.0042	6.9352	0.1442
28	39.2045	0.0255	272.8892	0.0037	6.9607	0.1437
29	44.6931	0.0224	312.0937	0.0032	6.9830	0.1432
30	50.9502	0.0196	356.7868	0.0028	7.0027	0.1428
35	98.1002	0.0102	693.5727	0.0014	7.0700	0.1414

TABLE D–21   Interest Factors for 15.00%

	SINGLE PAYMENT		UNIFORM SERIES			
	COMPOUND-AMOUNT FACTOR	PRESENT-WORTH FACTOR	COMPOUND-AMOUNT FACTOR	SINKING-FUND FACTOR	PRESENT-WORTH FACTOR	CAPITAL-RECOVERY FACTOR
N	CONVERT P TO F (F/P,I,N)	CONVERT F TO P (P/F,I,N)	CONVERT A TO F (F/A,I,N)	CONVERT F TO A (A/F,I,N)	CONVERT A TO P (P/A,I,N)	CONVERT P TO A (A/P,I,N)
1	1.1500	0.8696	1.0000	1.0000	0.8696	1.1500
2	1.3225	0.7561	2.1500	0.4651	1.6257	0.6151
3	1.5209	0.6575	3.4725	0.2880	2.2832	0.4380
4	1.7490	0.5718	4.9934	0.2003	2.8550	0.3503
5	2.0114	0.4972	6.7424	0.1483	3.3522	0.2983
6	2.3131	0.4323	8.7537	0.1142	3.7845	0.2642
7	2.6600	0.3759	11.0668	0.0904	4.1604	0.2404
8	3.0590	0.3269	13.7268	0.0729	4.4873	0.2229
9	3.5179	0.2843	16.7858	0.0596	4.7716	0.2096
10	4.0456	0.2472	20.3037	0.0493	5.0188	0.1993
11	4.6524	0.2149	24.3493	0.0411	5.2337	0.1911
12	5.3503	0.1869	29.0017	0.0345	5.4206	0.1845
13	6.1528	0.1625	34.3519	0.0291	5.5831	0.1791
14	7.0757	0.1413	40.5047	0.0247	5.7245	0.1747
15	8.1371	0.1229	47.5804	0.0210	5.8474	0.1710
16	9.3576	0.1069	55.7175	0.0179	5.9542	0.1679
17	10.7613	0.0929	65.0751	0.0154	6.0472	0.1654
18	12.3755	0.0808	75.8364	0.0132	6.1280	0.1632
19	14.2318	0.0703	88.2118	0.0113	6.1982	0.1613
20	16.3665	0.0611	102.4436	0.0098	6.2593	0.1598
21	18.8215	0.0531	118.8101	0.0084	6.3125	0.1584
22	21.6447	0.0462	137.6316	0.0073	6.3587	0.1573
23	24.8915	0.0402	159.2764	0.0063	6.3988	0.1563
24	28.6252	0.0349	184.1678	0.0054	6.4338	0.1554
25	32.9190	0.0304	212.7930	0.0047	6.4641	0.1547
26	37.8568	0.0264	245.7120	0.0041	6.4906	0.1541
27	43.5353	0.0230	283.5688	0.0035	6.5135	0.1535
28	50.0656	0.0200	327.1041	0.0031	6.5335	0.1531
29	57.5755	0.0174	377.1697	0.0027	6.5509	0.1527
30	66.2118	0.0151	434.7451	0.0023	6.5660	0.1523
35	133.1755	0.0075	881.1702	0.0011	6.6166	0.1511

TABLE D–22   Interest Factors for 16.00%

	SINGLE PAYMENT		UNIFORM SERIES			
	COMPOUND-AMOUNT FACTOR	PRESENT-WORTH FACTOR	COMPOUND-AMOUNT FACTOR	SINKING-FUND FACTOR	PRESENT-WORTH FACTOR	CAPITAL-RECOVERY FACTOR
N	CONVERT P TO F (F/P,I,N)	CONVERT F TO P (P/F,I,N)	CONVERT A TO F (F/A,I,N)	CONVERT F TO A (A/F,I,N)	CONVERT A TO P (P/A,I,N)	CONVERT P TO A (A/P,I,N)
1	1.1600	0.8621	1.0000	1.0000	0.8621	1.1600
2	1.3456	0.7432	2.1600	0.4630	1.6052	0.6230
3	1.5609	0.6407	3.5056	0.2853	2.2459	0.4453
4	1.8106	0.5523	5.0665	0.1974	2.7982	0.3574
5	2.1003	0.4761	6.8771	0.1454	3.2743	0.3054
6	2.4364	0.4104	8.9775	0.1114	3.6847	0.2714
7	2.8262	0.3538	11.4139	0.0876	4.0386	0.2476
8	3.2784	0.3050	14.2401	0.0702	4.3436	0.2302
9	3.8030	0.2630	17.5185	0.0571	4.6065	0.2171
10	4.4114	0.2267	21.3215	0.0469	4.8332	0.2069
11	5.1173	0.1954	25.7329	0.0389	5.0286	0.1989
12	5.9360	0.1685	30.8502	0.0324	5.1971	0.1924
13	6.8858	0.1452	36.7862	0.0272	5.3423	0.1872
14	7.9875	0.1252	43.6720	0.0229	5.4675	0.1829
15	9.2655	0.1079	51.6595	0.0194	5.5755	0.1794
16	10.7480	0.0930	60.9250	0.0164	5.6685	0.1764
17	12.4677	0.0802	71.6730	0.0140	5.7487	0.1740
18	14.4625	0.0691	84.1407	0.0119	5.8178	0.1719
19	16.7765	0.0596	98.6032	0.0101	5.8775	0.1701
20	19.4608	0.0514	115.3797	0.0087	5.9288	0.1687
21	22.5745	0.0443	134.8405	0.0074	5.9731	0.1674
22	26.1864	0.0382	157.4150	0.0064	6.0113	0.1664
23	30.3762	0.0329	183.6014	0.0054	6.0442	0.1654
24	35.2364	0.0284	213.9776	0.0047	6.0726	0.1647
25	40.8742	0.0245	249.2140	0.0040	6.0971	0.1640
26	47.4141	0.0211	290.0883	0.0034	6.1182	0.1634
27	55.0004	0.0182	337.5024	0.0030	6.1364	0.1630
28	63.8004	0.0157	392.5028	0.0025	6.1520	0.1625
29	74.0085	0.0135	456.3032	0.0022	6.1656	0.1622
30	85.8499	0.0116	530.3117	0.0019	6.1772	0.1619

TABLE D–23   Interest Factors for 17.00%

	SINGLE PAYMENT		UNIFORM SERIES			
	COMPOUND-AMOUNT FACTOR	PRESENT-WORTH FACTOR	COMPOUND-AMOUNT FACTOR	SINKING-FUND FACTOR	PRESENT-WORTH FACTOR	CAPITAL-RECOVERY FACTOR
N	CONVERT P TO F (F/P,I,N)	CONVERT F TO P (P/F,I,N)	CONVERT A TO F (F/A,I,N)	CONVERT F TO A (A/F,I,N)	CONVERT A TO P (P/A,I,N)	CONVERT P TO A (A/P,I,N)
1	1.1700	0.8547	1.0000	1.0000	0.8547	1.1700
2	1.3689	0.7305	2.1700	0.4608	1.5852	0.6308
3	1.6016	0.6244	3.5389	0.2826	2.2096	0.4526
4	1.8739	0.5337	5.1405	0.1945	2.7432	0.3645
5	2.1924	0.4561	7.0144	0.1426	3.1993	0.3126
6	2.5652	0.3898	9.2068	0.1086	3.5892	0.2786
7	3.0012	0.3332	11.7720	0.0849	3.9224	0.2549
8	3.5115	0.2848	14.7733	0.0677	4.2072	0.2377
9	4.1084	0.2434	18.2847	0.0547	4.4506	0.2247
10	4.8068	0.2080	22.3931	0.0447	4.6586	0.2147
11	5.6240	0.1778	27.1999	0.0368	4.8364	0.2068
12	6.5801	0.1520	32.8239	0.0305	4.9884	0.2005
13	7.6987	0.1299	39.4040	0.0254	5.1183	0.1954
14	9.0075	0.1110	47.1027	0.0212	5.2293	0.1912
15	10.5387	0.0949	56.1101	0.0178	5.3242	0.1878
16	12.3303	0.0811	66.6488	0.0150	5.4053	0.1850
17	14.4265	0.0693	78.9792	0.0127	5.4746	0.1827
18	16.8790	0.0592	93.4056	0.0107	5.5339	0.1807
19	19.7484	0.0506	110.2846	0.0091	5.5845	0.1791
20	23.1056	0.0433	130.0329	0.0077	5.6278	0.1777
21	27.0336	0.0370	153.1385	0.0065	5.6648	0.1765
22	31.6293	0.0316	180.1721	0.0056	5.6964	0.1756
23	37.0062	0.0270	211.8013	0.0047	5.7234	0.1747
24	43.2973	0.0231	248.8076	0.0040	5.7465	0.1740
25	50.6578	0.0197	292.1049	0.0034	5.7662	0.1734
26	59.2697	0.0169	342.7627	0.0029	5.7831	0.1729
27	69.3455	0.0144	402.0323	0.0025	5.7975	0.1725
28	81.1342	0.0123	471.3778	0.0021	5.8099	0.1721
29	94.9271	0.0105	552.5121	0.0018	5.8204	0.1718
30	111.0647	0.0090	647.4391	0.0015	5.8294	0.1715

TABLE **D–24**   Interest Factors for 18.00%

	SINGLE PAYMENT		UNIFORM SERIES			
	COMPOUND-AMOUNT FACTOR	PRESENT-WORTH FACTOR	COMPOUND-AMOUNT FACTOR	SINKING-FUND FACTOR	PRESENT-WORTH FACTOR	CAPITAL-RECOVERY FACTOR
N	CONVERT P TO F $(F/P,I,N)$	CONVERT F TO P $(P/F,I,N)$	CONVERT A TO F $(F/A,I,N)$	CONVERT F TO A $(A/F,I,N)$	CONVERT A TO P $(P/A,I,N)$	CONVERT P TO A $(A/P,I,N)$
1	1.1800	0.8475	1.0000	1.0000	0.8475	1.1800
2	1.3924	0.7182	2.1800	0.4587	1.5656	0.6387
3	1.6430	0.6086	3.5724	0.2799	2.1743	0.4599
4	1.9388	0.5158	5.2154	0.1917	2.6901	0.3717
5	2.2878	0.4371	7.1542	0.1398	3.1272	0.3198
6	2.6996	0.3704	9.4420	0.1059	3.4976	0.2859
7	3.1855	0.3139	12.1415	0.0824	3.8115	0.2624
8	3.7589	0.2660	15.3270	0.0652	4.0776	0.2452
9	4.4355	0.2255	19.0859	0.0524	4.3030	0.2324
10	5.2338	0.1911	23.5213	0.0425	4.4941	0.2225
11	6.1759	0.1619	28.7551	0.0348	4.6560	0.2148
12	7.2876	0.1372	34.9311	0.0286	4.7932	0.2086
13	8.5994	0.1163	42.2187	0.0237	4.9095	0.2037
14	10.1472	0.0985	50.8180	0.0197	5.0081	0.1997
15	11.9737	0.0835	60.9653	0.0164	5.0916	0.1964
16	14.1290	0.0708	72.9390	0.0137	5.1624	0.1937
17	16.6722	0.0600	87.0680	0.0115	5.2223	0.1915
18	19.6733	0.0508	103.7403	0.0096	5.2732	0.1896
19	23.2144	0.0431	123.4135	0.0081	5.3162	0.1881
20	27.3930	0.0365	146.6280	0.0068	5.3527	0.1868
21	32.3238	0.0309	174.0210	0.0057	5.3837	0.1857
22	38.1421	0.0262	206.3448	0.0048	5.4099	0.1848
23	45.0076	0.0222	244.4868	0.0041	5.4321	0.1841
24	53.1090	0.0188	289.4945	0.0035	5.4509	0.1835
25	62.6686	0.0160	342.6035	0.0029	5.4669	0.1829
26	73.9490	0.0135	405.2721	0.0025	5.4804	0.1825
27	87.2598	0.0115	479.2211	0.0021	5.4919	0.1821
28	102.9666	0.0097	566.4809	0.0018	5.5016	0.1818
29	121.5005	0.0082	669.4475	0.0015	5.5098	0.1815
30	143.3706	0.0070	790.9480	0.0013	5.5168	0.1813

TABLE D–25   Interest Factors for 19.00%

	SINGLE PAYMENT		UNIFORM SERIES			
	COMPOUND-AMOUNT FACTOR	PRESENT-WORTH FACTOR	COMPOUND-AMOUNT FACTOR	SINKING-FUND FACTOR	PRESENT-WORTH FACTOR	CAPITAL-RECOVERY FACTOR
	CONVERT P TO F	CONVERT F TO P	CONVERT A TO F	CONVERT F TO A	CONVERT A TO P	CONVERT P TO A
N	$(F/P,I,N)$	$(P/F,I,N)$	$(F/A,I,N)$	$(A/F,I,N)$	$(P/A,I,N)$	$(A/P,I,N)$
1	1.1900	0.8403	1.0000	1.0000	0.8403	1.1900
2	1.4161	0.7062	2.1900	0.4566	1.5465	0.6466
3	1.6852	0.5934	3.6061	0.2773	2.1399	0.4673
4	2.0053	0.4987	5.2913	0.1890	2.6386	0.3790
5	2.3864	0.4190	7.2966	0.1371	3.0576	0.3271
6	2.8398	0.3521	9.6830	0.1033	3.4098	0.2933
7	3.3793	0.2959	12.5227	0.0799	3.7057	0.2699
8	4.0214	0.2487	15.9020	0.0629	3.9544	0.2529
9	4.7854	0.2090	19.9234	0.0502	4.1633	0.2402
10	5.6947	0.1756	24.7089	0.0405	4.3389	0.2305
11	6.7767	0.1476	30.4035	0.0329	4.4865	0.2229
12	8.0642	0.1240	37.1802	0.0269	4.6105	0.2169
13	9.5964	0.1042	45.2445	0.0221	4.7147	0.2121
14	11.4198	0.0876	54.8409	0.0182	4.8023	0.2082
15	13.5895	0.0736	66.2607	0.0151	4.8759	0.2051
16	16.1715	0.0618	79.8502	0.0125	4.9377	0.2025
17	19.2441	0.0520	96.0218	0.0104	4.9897	0.2004
18	22.9005	0.0437	115.2659	0.0087	5.0333	0.1987
19	27.2516	0.0367	138.1664	0.0072	5.0700	0.1972
20	32.4294	0.0308	165.4180	0.0060	5.1009	0.1960
21	38.5910	0.0259	197.8474	0.0051	5.1268	0.1951
22	45.9233	0.0218	236.4385	0.0042	5.1486	0.1942
23	54.6487	0.0183	282.3618	0.0035	5.1668	0.1935
24	65.0320	0.0154	337.0105	0.0030	5.1822	0.1930
25	77.3881	0.0129	402.0425	0.0025	5.1951	0.1925
26	92.0918	0.0109	479.4306	0.0021	5.2060	0.1921
27	109.5893	0.0091	571.5224	0.0017	5.2151	0.1917
28	130.4112	0.0077	681.1116	0.0015	5.2228	0.1915
29	155.1893	0.0064	811.5228	0.0012	5.2292	0.1912
30	184.6753	0.0054	966.7122	0.0010	5.2347	0.1910

TABLE D–26 Interest Factors for 20.00%

	SINGLE PAYMENT		UNIFORM SERIES			
	COMPOUND-AMOUNT FACTOR	PRESENT-WORTH FACTOR	COMPOUND-AMOUNT FACTOR	SINKING-FUND FACTOR	PRESENT-WORTH FACTOR	CAPITAL-RECOVERY FACTOR
	CONVERT P TO F	CONVERT F TO P	CONVERT A TO F	CONVERT F TO A	CONVERT A TO P	CONVERT P TO A
N	(F/P,I,N)	(P/F,I,N)	(F/A,I,N)	(A/F,I,N)	(P/A,I,N)	(A/P,I,N)
1	1.2000	0.8333	1.0000	1.0000	0.8333	1.2000
2	1.4400	0.6944	2.2000	0.4545	1.5278	0.6545
3	1.7280	0.5787	3.6400	0.2747	2.1065	0.4747
4	2.0736	0.4823	5.3680	0.1863	2.5887	0.3863
5	2.4883	0.4019	7.4416	0.1344	2.9906	0.3344
6	2.9860	0.3349	9.9299	0.1007	3.3255	0.3007
7	3.5832	0.2791	12.9159	0.0774	3.6046	0.2774
8	4.2998	0.2326	16.4991	0.0606	3.8372	0.2606
9	5.1598	0.1938	20.7989	0.0481	4.0310	0.2481
10	6.1917	0.1615	25.9587	0.0385	4.1925	0.2385
11	7.4301	0.1346	32.1504	0.0311	4.3271	0.2311
12	8.9161	0.1122	39.5805	0.0253	4.4392	0.2253
13	10.6993	0.0935	48.4966	0.0206	4.5327	0.2206
14	12.8392	0.0779	59.1959	0.0169	4.6106	0.2169
15	15.4070	0.0649	72.0351	0.0139	4.6755	0.2139
16	18.4884	0.0541	87.4421	0.0114	4.7296	0.2114
17	22.1861	0.0451	105.9306	0.0094	4.7746	0.2094
18	26.6233	0.0376	128.1167	0.0078	4.8122	0.2078
19	31.9480	0.0313	154.7400	0.0065	4.8435	0.2065
20	38.3376	0.0261	186.6880	0.0054	4.8696	0.2054
21	46.0051	0.0217	225.0256	0.0044	4.8913	0.2044
22	55.2061	0.0181	271.0307	0.0037	4.9094	0.2037
23	66.2474	0.0151	326.2369	0.0031	4.9245	0.2031
24	79.4968	0.0126	392.4842	0.0025	4.9371	0.2025
25	95.3962	0.0105	471.9811	0.0021	4.9476	0.2021
26	114.4755	0.0087	567.3773	0.0018	4.9563	0.2018
27	137.3706	0.0073	681.8528	0.0015	4.9636	0.2015
28	164.8447	0.0061	819.2233	0.0012	4.9697	0.2012
29	197.8136	0.0051	984.0680	0.0010	4.9747	0.2010
30	237.3763	0.0042	1,181.8816	0.0008	4.9789	0.2008

TABLE D–27   Interest Factors for 25.00%

	SINGLE PAYMENT		UNIFORM SERIES			
	COMPOUND-AMOUNT FACTOR	PRESENT-WORTH FACTOR	COMPOUND-AMOUNT FACTOR	SINKING-FUND FACTOR	PRESENT-WORTH FACTOR	CAPITAL-RECOVERY FACTOR
	CONVERT P TO F	CONVERT F TO P	CONVERT A TO F	CONVERT F TO A	CONVERT A TO P	CONVERT P TO A
N	$(F/P,I,N)$	$(P/F,I,N)$	$(F/A,I,N)$	$(A/F,I,N)$	$(P/A,I,N)$	$(A/P,I,N)$
1	1.2500	0.8000	1.0000	1.0000	0.8000	1.2500
2	1.5625	0.6400	2.2500	0.4444	1.4400	0.6944
3	1.9531	0.5120	3.8125	0.2623	1.9520	0.5123
4	2.4414	0.4096	5.7656	0.1734	2.3616	0.4234
5	3.0518	0.3277	8.2070	0.1218	2.6893	0.3718
6	3.8147	0.2621	11.2588	0.0888	2.9514	0.3388
7	4.7684	0.2097	15.0735	0.0663	3.1611	0.3163
8	5.9605	0.1678	19.8419	0.0504	3.3289	0.3004
9	7.4506	0.1342	25.8023	0.0388	3.4631	0.2888
10	9.3132	0.1074	33.2529	0.0301	3.5705	0.2801
11	11.6415	0.0859	42.5661	0.0235	3.6564	0.2735
12	14.5519	0.0687	54.2077	0.0184	3.7251	0.2684
13	18.1899	0.0550	68.7596	0.0145	3.7801	0.2645
14	22.7374	0.0440	86.9495	0.0115	3.8241	0.2615
15	28.4217	0.0352	109.6868	0.0091	3.8593	0.2591
16	35.5271	0.0281	138.1085	0.0072	3.8874	0.2572
17	44.4089	0.0225	173.6357	0.0058	3.9099	0.2558
18	55.5112	0.0180	218.0446	0.0046	3.9279	0.2546
19	69.3889	0.0144	273.5558	0.0037	3.9424	0.2537
20	86.7362	0.0115	342.9447	0.0029	3.9539	0.2529
21	108.4202	0.0092	429.6809	0.0023	3.9631	0.2523
22	135.5253	0.0074	538.1011	0.0019	3.9705	0.2519
23	169.4066	0.0059	673.6264	0.0015	3.9764	0.2515
24	211.7582	0.0047	843.0329	0.0012	3.9811	0.2512
25	264.6978	0.0038	1,054.7912	0.0009	3.9849	0.2509

TABLE D–28 Interest Factors for 30.00%

	SINGLE PAYMENT		UNIFORM SERIES			
	COMPOUND-AMOUNT FACTOR	PRESENT-WORTH FACTOR	COMPOUND-AMOUNT FACTOR	SINKING-FUND FACTOR	PRESENT-WORTH FACTOR	CAPITAL-RECOVERY FACTOR
	CONVERT P TO F	CONVERT F TO P	CONVERT A TO F	CONVERT F TO A	CONVERT A TO P	CONVERT P TO A
N	$(F/P,I,N)$	$(P/F,I,N)$	$(F/A,I,N)$	$(A/F,I,N)$	$(P/A,I,N)$	$(A/P,I,N)$
1	1.3000	0.7692	1.0000	1.0000	0.7692	1.3000
2	1.6900	0.5917	2.3000	0.4348	1.3609	0.7348
3	2.1970	0.4552	3.9900	0.2506	1.8161	0.5506
4	2.8561	0.3501	6.1870	0.1616	2.1662	0.4616
5	3.7129	0.2693	9.0431	0.1106	2.4356	0.4106
6	4.8268	0.2072	12.7560	0.0784	2.6427	0.3784
7	6.2749	0.1594	17.5828	0.0569	2.8021	0.3569
8	8.1573	0.1226	23.8577	0.0419	2.9247	0.3419
9	10.6045	0.0943	32.0150	0.0312	3.0190	0.3312
10	13.7858	0.0725	42.6195	0.0235	3.0915	0.3235
11	17.9216	0.0558	56.4053	0.0177	3.1473	0.3177
12	23.2981	0.0429	74.3270	0.0135	3.1903	0.3135
13	30.2875	0.0330	97.6250	0.0102	3.2233	0.3102
14	39.3738	0.0254	127.9125	0.0078	3.2487	0.3078
15	51.1859	0.0195	167.2863	0.0060	3.2682	0.3060
16	66.5417	0.0150	218.4722	0.0046	3.2832	0.3046
17	86.5042	0.0116	285.0139	0.0035	3.2948	0.3035
18	112.4554	0.0089	371.5180	0.0027	3.3037	0.3027
19	146.1920	0.0068	483.9734	0.0021	3.3105	0.3021
20	190.0496	0.0053	630.1655	0.0016	3.3158	0.3016

TABLE D–29 Interest Factors for 35.00%

	SINGLE PAYMENT		UNIFORM SERIES			
	COMPOUND-AMOUNT FACTOR	PRESENT-WORTH FACTOR	COMPOUND-AMOUNT FACTOR	SINKING-FUND FACTOR	PRESENT-WORTH FACTOR	CAPITAL-RECOVERY FACTOR
	CONVERT P TO F	CONVERT F TO P	CONVERT A TO F	CONVERT F TO A	CONVERT A TO P	CONVERT P TO A
N	(F/P,I,N)	(P/F,I,N)	(F/A,I,N)	(A/F,I,N)	(P/A,I,N)	(A/P,I,N)
1	1.3500	0.7407	1.0000	1.0000	0.7407	1.3500
2	1.8225	0.5487	2.3500	0.4255	1.2894	0.7755
3	2.4604	0.4064	4.1725	0.2397	1.6959	0.5897
4	3.3215	0.3011	6.6329	0.1508	1.9969	0.5008
5	4.4840	0.2230	9.9544	0.1005	2.2200	0.4505
6	6.0534	0.1652	14.4384	0.0693	2.3852	0.4193
7	8.1722	0.1224	20.4919	0.0488	2.5075	0.3988
8	11.0324	0.0906	28.6640	0.0349	2.5982	0.3849
9	14.8937	0.0671	39.6964	0.0252	2.6653	0.3752
10	20.1066	0.0497	54.5902	0.0183	2.7150	0.3683
11	27.1439	0.0368	74.6967	0.0134	2.7519	0.3634
12	36.6442	0.0273	101.8406	0.0098	2.7792	0.3598
13	49.4697	0.0202	138.4848	0.0072	2.7994	0.3572
14	66.7841	0.0150	187.9544	0.0053	2.8144	0.3553
15	90.1585	0.0111	254.7385	0.0039	2.8255	0.3539
16	121.7139	0.0082	344.8970	0.0029	2.8337	0.3529
17	164.3138	0.0061	466.6109	0.0021	2.8398	0.3521
18	221.8236	0.0045	630.9247	0.0016	2.8443	0.3516
19	299.4619	0.0033	852.7483	0.0012	2.8476	0.3512
20	404.2736	0.0025	1,152.2103	0.0009	2.8501	0.3509

Table D–30 Interest Factors for 40.00%

	SINGLE PAYMENT		UNIFORM SERIES			
	COMPOUND-AMOUNT FACTOR	PRESENT-WORTH FACTOR	COMPOUND-AMOUNT FACTOR	SINKING-FUND FACTOR	PRESENT-WORTH FACTOR	CAPITAL-RECOVERY FACTOR
N	CONVERT P TO F $(F/P,I,N)$	CONVERT F TO P $(P/F,I,N)$	CONVERT A TO F $(F/A,I,N)$	CONVERT F TO A $(A/F,I,N)$	CONVERT A TO P $(P/A,I,N)$	CONVERT P TO A $(A/P,I,N)$
1	1.4000	0.7143	1.0000	1.0000	0.7143	1.4000
2	1.9600	0.5102	2.4000	0.4167	1.2245	0.8167
3	2.7440	0.3644	4.3600	0.2294	1.5889	0.6294
4	3.8416	0.2603	7.1040	0.1408	1.8492	0.5408
5	5.3782	0.1859	10.9456	0.0914	2.0352	0.4914
6	7.5295	0.1328	16.3238	0.0613	2.1680	0.4613
7	10.5414	0.0949	23.8534	0.0419	2.2628	0.4419
8	14.7579	0.0678	34.3947	0.0291	2.3306	0.4291
9	20.6610	0.0484	49.1526	0.0203	2.3790	0.4203
10	28.9255	0.0346	69.8137	0.0143	2.4136	0.4143
11	40.4957	0.0247	98.7391	0.0101	2.4383	0.4101
12	56.6939	0.0176	139.2348	0.0072	2.4559	0.4072
13	79.3715	0.0126	195.9287	0.0051	2.4685	0.4051
14	111.1201	0.0090	275.3002	0.0036	2.4775	0.4036
15	155.5681	0.0064	386.4202	0.0026	2.4839	0.4026

TABLE D–31   Interest Factors for 45.00%

	SINGLE PAYMENT		UNIFORM SERIES			
	COMPOUND-AMOUNT FACTOR	PRESENT-WORTH FACTOR	COMPOUND-AMOUNT FACTOR	SINKING-FUND FACTOR	PRESENT-WORTH FACTOR	CAPITAL-RECOVERY FACTOR
	CONVERT P TO F	CONVERT F TO P	CONVERT A TO F	CONVERT F TO A	CONVERT A TO P	CONVERT P TO A
N	(F/P,I,N)	(P/F,I,N)	(F/A,I,N)	(A/F,I,N)	(P/A,I,N)	(A/P,I,N)
1	1.4500	0.6897	1.0000	1.0000	0.6897	1.4500
2	2.1025	0.4756	2.4500	0.4082	1.1653	0.8582
3	3.0486	0.3280	4.5525	0.2197	1.4933	0.6697
4	4.4205	0.2262	7.6011	0.1316	1.7195	0.5816
5	6.4097	0.1560	12.0216	0.0832	1.8755	0.5332
6	9.2941	0.1076	18.4314	0.0543	1.9831	0.5043
7	13.4765	0.0742	27.7255	0.0361	2.0573	0.4861
8	19.5409	0.0512	41.2019	0.0243	2.1085	0.4743
9	28.3343	0.0353	60.7428	0.0165	2.1438	0.4665
10	41.0847	0.0243	89.0771	0.0112	2.1681	0.4612
11	59.5728	0.0168	130.1618	0.0077	2.1849	0.4577
12	86.3806	0.0116	189.7346	0.0053	2.1965	0.4553
13	125.2518	0.0080	276.1151	0.0036	2.2045	0.4536
14	181.6151	0.0055	401.3670	0.0025	2.2100	0.4525
15	263.3419	0.0038	582.9821	0.0017	2.2138	0.4517

TABLE D–32   Interest Factors for 50.00%

	SINGLE PAYMENT		UNIFORM SERIES			
	COMPOUND-AMOUNT FACTOR	PRESENT-WORTH FACTOR	COMPOUND-AMOUNT FACTOR	SINKING-FUND FACTOR	PRESENT-WORTH FACTOR	CAPITAL-RECOVERY FACTOR
	CONVERT P TO F	CONVERT F TO P	CONVERT A TO F	CONVERT F TO A	CONVERT A TO P	CONVERT P TO A
N	(F/P,I,N)	(P/F,I,N)	(F/A,I,N)	(A/F,I,N)	(P/A,I,N)	(A/P,I,N)
1	1.5000	0.6667	1.0000	1.0000	0.6667	1.5000
2	2.2500	0.4444	2.5000	0.4000	1.1111	0.9000
3	3.3750	0.2963	4.7500	0.2105	1.4074	0.7105
4	5.0625	0.1975	8.1250	0.1231	1.6049	0.6231
5	7.5938	0.1317	13.1875	0.0758	1.7366	0.5758
6	11.3906	0.0878	20.7813	0.0481	1.8244	0.5481
7	17.0859	0.0585	32.1719	0.0311	1.8829	0.5311
8	25.6289	0.0390	49.2578	0.0203	1.9220	0.5203
9	38.4434	0.0260	74.8867	0.0134	1.9480	0.5134
10	57.6650	0.0173	113.3301	0.0088	1.9653	0.5088
11	86.4976	0.0116	170.9951	0.0058	1.9769	0.5058
12	129.7463	0.0077	257.4927	0.0039	1.9846	0.5039
13	194.6195	0.0051	387.2390	0.0026	1.9897	0.5026
14	291.9293	0.0034	581.8585	0.0017	1.9931	0.5017
15	437.8939	0.0023	873.7878	0.0011	1.9954	0.5011

APPENDIX E

AMORTIZATION SCHEDULE

APR: 9.00%
Term: 360 Months
Monthly Payment: $1,206.93

MONTH	BEGINNING PRINCIPAL	MONTHLY PAYMENT	MONTHLY INTEREST	PRINCIPAL REDUCTION	ENDING PRINCIPAL
0					150,000.00
1	150,000.00	1,206.93	1,125.00	81.93	149,918.07
2	149,918.07	1,206.93	1,124.39	82.54	149,835.53
3	149,835.53	1,206.93	1,123.77	83.16	149,752.37
4	149,752.37	1,206.93	1,123.14	83.79	149,668.58
5	149,668.58	1,206.93	1,122.51	84.42	149,584.16
6	149,584.16	1,206.93	1,121.88	85.05	149,499.11
7	149,499.11	1,206.93	1,121.24	85.69	149,413.42
8	149,413.42	1,206.93	1,120.60	86.33	149,327.09
9	149,327.09	1,206.93	1,119.95	86.98	149,240.11
10	149,240.11	1,206.93	1,119.30	87.63	149,152.48
11	149,152.48	1,206.93	1,118.64	88.29	149,064.19
12	149,064.19	1,206.93	1,117.98	88.95	148,975.24
13	148,975.24	1,206.93	1,117.31	89.62	148,885.62
14	148,885.62	1,206.93	1,116.64	90.29	148,795.33
15	148,795.33	1,206.93	1,115.96	90.97	148,704.36
16	148,704.36	1,206.93	1,115.28	91.65	148,612.71
17	148,612.71	1,206.93	1,114.60	92.33	148,520.38
18	148,520.38	1,206.93	1,113.90	93.03	148,427.35
19	148,427.35	1,206.93	1,113.21	93.72	148,333.63
20	148,333.63	1,206.93	1,112.50	94.43	148,239.20
21	148,239.20	1,206.93	1,111.79	95.14	148,144.06

Month	Beginning Principal	Monthly Payment	Monthly Interest	Principal Reduction	Ending Principal
22	148,144.06	1,206.93	1,111.08	95.85	148,048.21
23	148,048.21	1,206.93	1,110.36	96.57	147,951.64
24	147,951.64	1,206.93	1,109.64	97.29	147,854.35
25	147,854.35	1,206.93	1,108.91	98.02	147,756.33
26	147,756.33	1,206.93	1,108.17	98.76	147,657.57
27	147,657.57	1,206.93	1,107.43	99.50	147,558.07
28	147,558.07	1,206.93	1,106.69	100.24	147,457.83
29	147,457.83	1,206.93	1,105.93	101.00	147,356.83
30	147,356.83	1,206.93	1,105.18	101.75	147,255.08
31	147,255.08	1,206.93	1,104.41	102.52	147,152.56
32	147,152.56	1,206.93	1,103.64	103.29	147,049.27
33	147,049.27	1,206.93	1,102.87	104.06	146,945.21
34	146,945.21	1,206.93	1,102.09	104.84	146,840.37
35	146,840.37	1,206.93	1,101.30	105.63	146,734.74
36	146,734.74	1,206.93	1,100.51	106.42	146,628.32
37	146,628.32	1,206.93	1,099.71	107.22	146,521.10
38	146,521.10	1,206.93	1,098.91	108.02	146,413.08
39	146,413.08	1,206.93	1,098.10	108.83	146,304.25
40	146,304.25	1,206.93	1,097.28	109.65	146,194.60
41	146,194.60	1,206.93	1,096.46	110.47	146,084.13
42	146,084.13	1,206.93	1,095.63	111.30	145,972.83
43	145,972.83	1,206.93	1,094.80	112.13	145,860.70
44	145,860.70	1,206.93	1,093.96	112.97	145,747.73
45	145,747.73	1,206.93	1,093.11	113.82	145,633.91
46	145,633.91	1,206.93	1,092.25	114.68	145,519.23
47	145,519.23	1,206.93	1,091.39	115.54	145,403.69
48	145,403.69	1,206.93	1,090.53	116.40	145,287.29
49	145,287.29	1,206.93	1,089.65	117.28	145,170.01
50	145,170.01	1,206.93	1,088.78	118.15	145,051.86
51	145,051.86	1,206.93	1,087.89	119.04	144,932.82
52	144,932.82	1,206.93	1,087.00	119.93	144,812.89
53	144,812.89	1,206.93	1,086.10	120.83	144,692.06
54	144,692.06	1,206.93	1,085.19	121.74	144,570.32
55	144,570.32	1,206.93	1,084.28	122.65	144,447.67
56	144,477.67	1,206.93	1,083.36	123.57	144,324.10
57	144,324.10	1,206.93	1,082.43	124.50	144,199.60
58	144,199.60	1,206.93	1,081.50	125.43	144,074.17
59	144,074.17	1,206.93	1,080.56	126.37	143,947.80
60	143,947.80	1,206.93	1,079.61	127.32	143,820.48

Month	Beginning Principal	Monthly Payment	Monthly Interest	Principal Reduction	Ending Principal
61	143,820.48	1,206.93	1,078.65	128.28	143,692.20
62	143,692.20	1,206.93	1,077.69	129.24	143,562.96
63	143,562.96	1,206.93	1,076.72	130.21	143,432.75
64	143,432.75	1,206.93	1,075.75	131.18	143,301.57
65	143,301.57	1,206.93	1,074.76	132.17	143,169.40
66	143,169.40	1,206.93	1,073.77	133.16	143,036.24
67	143,036.24	1,206.93	1,072.77	134.16	142,902.08
68	142,902.08	1,206.93	1,071.77	135.16	142,766.92
69	142,766.92	1,206.93	1,070.75	136.18	142,630.74
70	142,630.74	1,206.93	1,069.73	137.20	142,493.54
71	142,493.54	1,206.93	1,068.70	138.23	142,355.31
72	142,355.31	1,206.93	1,067.66	139.27	142,216.04
73	142,216.04	1,206.93	1,066.62	140.31	142,075.73
74	142,075.73	1,206.93	1,065.57	141.36	141,934.73
75	141,934.37	1,206.93	1,064.51	142.42	141,791.95
76	141,791.95	1,206.93	1,063.44	143.49	141,648.46
77	141,648.46	1,206.93	1,062.36	144.57	141,503.89
78	141,503.89	1,206.93	1,061.28	145.65	141,358.24
79	141,358.24	1,206.93	1,060.19	146.74	141,211.50
80	141,211.50	1,206.93	1,059.09	147.84	141,063.66
81	141,063.66	1,206.93	1,057.98	148.95	140,914.71
82	140,914.71	1,206.93	1,056.86	150.07	140,764.64
83	140,764.64	1,206.93	1,055.73	151.20	140,613.44
84	140,613.44	1,206.93	1,054.60	152.33	140,461.11
85	140,461.11	1,206.93	1,053.46	153.47	140,307.64
86	140,307.64	1,206.93	1,052.31	154.62	140,153.02
87	140,153.02	1,206.93	1,051.15	155.78	139,997.24
88	139,997.24	1,206.93	1,049.98	156.95	139,840.29
89	139,840.29	1,206.93	1,048.80	158.13	139,682.16
90	139,682.16	1,206.93	1,047.62	159.31	139,522.85
91	139,522.85	1,206.93	1,046.42	160.51	139,362.34
92	139,362.34	1,206.93	1,045.22	161.71	139,200.63
93	139,200.63	1,206.93	1,044.00	162.93	139,037.70
94	139,037.70	1,206.93	1,042.78	164.15	138,873.55
95	138,873.55	1,206.93	1,041.55	165.38	138,708.17
96	138,708.17	1,206.93	1,040.31	166.62	138,541.55
97	138,541.55	1,206.93	1,039.06	167.87	138,373.68
98	138,373.68	1,206.93	1,037.80	169.13	138,204.55
99	138,204.55	1,206.93	1,036.53	170.40	138,034.15

Month	Beginning Principal	Monthly Payment	Monthly Interest	Principal Reduction	Ending Principal
100	138,034.15	1,206.93	1,035.26	171.67	137,862.48
101	137,862.48	1,206.93	1,033.97	172.96	137,689.52
102	137,689.52	1,206.93	1,032.67	174.26	137,515.26
103	137,515.26	1,206.93	1,031.36	175.57	137,339.69
104	137,339.69	1,206.93	1,030.05	176.88	137,162.81
105	137,162.81	1,206.93	1,028.72	178.21	136,984.60
106	136,984.60	1,206.93	1,027.38	179.55	136,805.05
107	136,805.05	1,206.93	1,026.04	180.89	136,624.16
108	136,624.16	1,206.93	1,024.68	182.25	136,441.91
109	136,441.91	1,206.93	1,023.31	183.62	136,258.29
110	136,258.29	1,206.93	1,021.94	184.99	136,073.30
111	136,073.30	1,206.93	1,020.55	186.38	135,886.92
112	135,886.92	1,206.93	1,019.15	187.78	135,699.14
113	135,699.14	1,206.93	1,017.74	189.19	135,509.95
114	135,509.95	1,206.93	1,016.32	190.61	135,319.34
115	135,319.34	1,206.93	1,014.90	192.03	135,127.31
116	135,127.31	1,206.93	1,013.45	193.48	134,933.83
117	134,933.83	1,206.93	1,012.00	194.93	134,738.90
118	134,738.90	1,206.93	1,010.54	196.39	134,542.51
119	134,542.51	1,206.93	1,009.07	197.86	134,344.65
120	134,344.65	1,206.93	1,007.58	199.35	134,145.30
121	134,145.30	1,206.93	1,006.09	200.84	133,944.46
122	133,944.46	1,206.93	1,004.58	202.35	133,742.11
123	133,742.11	1,206.93	1,003.07	203.86	133,538.25
124	133,538.25	1,206.93	1,001.54	205.39	133,332.86
125	133,332.86	1,206.93	1,000.00	206.93	133,125.93
126	133,125.93	1,206.93	998.44	208.49	132,917.44
127	132,917.44	1,206.93	996.88	210.05	132,707.39
128	132,707.39	1,206.93	995.31	211.62	132,495.77
129	132,495.77	1,206.93	993.72	213.21	132,282.56
130	132,282.56	1,206.93	992.12	214.81	132,067.75
131	132,067.75	1,206.93	990.51	216.42	131,851.33
132	131,851.33	1,206.93	988.88	218.05	131,633.28
133	131,633.28	1,206.93	987.25	219.68	131,413.60
134	131,413.60	1,206.93	985.60	221.33	131,192.27
135	131,192.27	1,206.93	983.94	222.99	130,969.28
136	130,969.28	1,206.93	982.27	224.66	130,744.62
137	130,744.62	1,206.93	980.58	226.35	130,518.27
138	130,518.27	1,206.93	978.89	228.04	130,290.23

Month	Beginning Principal	Monthly Payment	Monthly Interest	Principal Reduction	Ending Principal
139	130,290.23	1,206.93	977.18	229.75	130,060.48
140	130,060.48	1,206.93	975.45	231.48	129,829.00
141	129,829.00	1,206.93	973.72	233.21	129,595.79
142	129,595.79	1,206.93	971.97	234.96	129,360.83
143	129,360.83	1,206.93	970.21	236.72	129,124.11
144	129,124.11	1,206.93	968.43	238.50	128,885.61
145	128,885.61	1,206.93	966.64	240.29	128,645.32
146	128,645.32	1,206.93	964.84	242.09	128,403.23
147	128,403.23	1,206.93	963.02	243.91	128,159.32
148	128,159.32	1,206.93	961.19	245.74	127,913.58
149	127,913.58	1,206.93	959.35	247.58	127,666.00
150	127,666.00	1,206.93	957.50	249.43	127,416.57
151	127,416.57	1,206.93	955.62	251.31	127,165.26
152	127,165.26	1,206.93	953.74	253.19	126,912.07
153	126,912.07	1,206.93	951.84	255.09	126,656.98
154	126,656.98	1,206.93	949.93	257.00	126,399.98
155	126,399.98	1,206.93	948.00	258.93	126,141.05
156	126,141.05	1,206.93	946.06	260.87	125,880.18
157	125,880.18	1,206.93	944.10	262.83	125,617.35
158	125,617.35	1,206.93	942.13	264.80	125,352.55
159	125,352.55	1,206.93	940.14	266.79	125,085.76
160	125,085.76	1,206.93	938.14	268.79	124,816.97
161	124,816.97	1,206.93	936.13	270.80	124,546.17
162	124,546.17	1,206.93	934.10	272.83	124,273.34
163	124,273.34	1,206.93	932.05	274.88	123,998.46
164	123,998.46	1,206.93	929.99	276.94	123,721.52
165	123,721.52	1,206.93	927.91	279.02	123,442.50
166	123,442.50	1,206.93	925.82	281.11	123,161.39
167	123,161.39	1,206.93	923.71	283.22	122,878.17
168	122,878.17	1,206.93	921.59	285.34	122,592.83
169	122,592.83	1,206.93	919.45	287.48	122,305.35
170	122,305.35	1,206.93	917.29	289.64	122,015.71
171	122,015.71	1,206.93	915.12	291.81	121,723.90
172	121,723.90	1,206.93	912.93	294.00	121,429.90
173	121,429.90	1,206.93	910.72	296.21	121,133.69
174	121,133.69	1,206.93	908.50	298.43	120,835.26
175	120,835.26	1,206.93	906.26	300.67	120,534.59
176	120,534.59	1,206.93	904.01	302.92	120,231.67
177	120,231.67	1,206.93	901.74	305.19	119,926.48

Month	Beginning Principal	Monthly Payment	Monthly Interest	Principal Reduction	Ending Principal
178	119,926.48	1,206.93	899.45	307.48	119,619.00
179	119,619.00	1,206.93	897.14	309.79	119,309.21
180	119,309.21	1,206.93	894.82	312.11	118,997.10
181	118,997.10	1,206.93	892.48	314.45	118,682.65
182	118,682.65	1,206.93	890.12	316.81	118,365.84
183	118,365.84	1,206.93	887.74	319.19	118,046.65
184	118,046.65	1,206.93	885.35	321.58	117,725.07
185	117,725.07	1,206.93	882.94	323.99	117,401.08
186	117,401.08	1,206.93	880.51	326.42	117,074.66
187	117,074.66	1,206.93	878.06	328.87	116,745.79
188	116,745.79	1,206.93	875.59	331.34	116,414.45
189	116,414.45	1,206.93	873.11	333.82	116,080.63
190	116,080.63	1,206.93	870.60	336.33	115,744.30
191	115,744.30	1,206.93	868.08	338.85	115,405.45
192	115,405.45	1,206.93	865.54	341.39	115,064.06
193	115,064.06	1,206.93	862.98	343.95	114,720.11
194	114,720.11	1,206.93	860.40	346.53	114,373.58
195	114,373.58	1,206.93	857.80	349.13	114,024.45
196	114,024.45	1,206.93	855.18	351.75	113,672.70
197	113,672.70	1,206.93	852.55	354.38	113,318.32
198	113,318.32	1,206.93	849.89	357.04	112,961.28
199	112,961.28	1,206.93	847.21	359.72	112,601.56
200	112,601.56	1,206.93	844.51	362.42	112,239.14
201	112,239.14	1,206.93	841.79	365.14	111,874.00
202	111,874.00	1,206.93	839.06	367.87	111,506.13
203	111,506.13	1,206.93	836.30	370.63	111,135.50
204	111,135.50	1,206.93	833.52	373.41	110,762.09
205	110,762.09	1,206.93	830.72	376.21	110,385.88
206	110,385.88	1,206.93	827.89	379.04	110,006.84
207	110,006.84	1,206.93	825.05	381.88	109,624.96
208	109,624.96	1,206.93	822.19	384.74	109,240.22
209	109,240.22	1,206.93	819.30	387.63	108,852.59
210	108,852.59	1,206.93	816.39	390.54	108,462.05
211	108,462.05	1,206.93	813.47	393.46	108,068.59
212	108,068.59	1,206.93	810.51	396.42	107,672.17
213	107,672.17	1,206.93	807.54	399.39	107,272.78
214	107,272.78	1,206.93	804.55	402.38	106,870.40
215	106,870.40	1,206.93	801.53	405.40	106,465.00
216	106,465.00	1,206.93	798.49	408.44	106,056.56

Month	Beginning Principal	Monthly Payment	Monthly Interest	Principal Reduction	Ending Principal
217	106,056.56	1,206.93	795.42	411.51	105,645.05
218	105,645.05	1,206.93	792.34	414.59	105,230.46
219	105,230.46	1,206.93	789.23	417.70	104,812.76
220	104,812.76	1,206.93	786.10	420.83	104,391.93
221	104,391.93	1,206.93	782.94	423.99	103,967.94
222	103,967.94	1,206.93	779.76	427.17	103,540.77
223	103,540.77	1,206.93	776.56	430.37	103,110.40
224	103,110.40	1,206.93	773.33	433.60	102,676.80
225	102,676.80	1,206.93	770.08	436.85	102,239.95
226	102,239.95	1,206.93	766.80	440.13	101,799.82
227	101,799.82	1,206.93	763.50	443.43	101,356.39
228	101,356.39	1,206.93	760.17	446.76	100,909.63
229	100,909.63	1,206.93	756.82	450.11	100,459.52
230	100,459.52	1,206.93	753.45	453.48	100,006.04
231	100,006.04	1,206.93	750.05	456.88	99,549.16
232	99,549.16	1,206.93	746.62	460.31	99,088.85
233	99,088.85	1,206.93	743.17	463.76	98,625.09
234	98,625.09	1,206.93	739.69	467.24	98,157.85
235	98,157.85	1,206.93	736.18	470.75	97,687.10
236	97,687.10	1,206.93	732.65	474.28	97,212.82
237	97,212.82	1,206.93	729.10	477.83	96,734.99
238	96,734.99	1,206.93	725.51	481.42	96,253.57
239	96,253.57	1,206.93	721.90	485.03	95,768.54
240	95,768.54	1,206.93	718.26	488.67	95,279.87
241	95,279.87	1,206.93	714.60	492.33	94,787.54
242	94,787.54	1,206.93	710.91	496.02	94,291.52
243	94,291.52	1,206.93	707.19	499.74	93,791.78
244	93,791.78	1,206.93	703.44	503.49	93,288.29
245	93,288.29	1,206.93	699.66	507.27	92,781.02
246	92,781.02	1,206.93	695.86	511.07	92,269.95
247	92,269.95	1,206.93	692.02	514.91	91,755.04
248	91,755.04	1,206.93	688.16	518.77	91,236.27
249	91,236.27	1,206.93	684.27	522.66	90,713.61
250	90,713.61	1,206.93	680.35	526.58	90,187.03
251	90,187.03	1,206.93	676.40	530.53	89,656.50
252	89,656.50	1,206.93	672.42	534.51	89,121.99
253	89,121.99	1,206.93	668.41	538.52	88,583.47
254	88,853.47	1,206.93	664.38	542.55	88,040.92
255	88,040.92	1,206.93	660.31	546.62	87,494.30

Month	Beginning Principal	Monthly Payment	Monthly Interest	Principal Reduction	Ending Principal
256	87,494.30	1,206.93	656.21	550.72	86,943.58
257	86,943.58	1,206.93	652.08	554.85	86,388.73
258	86,388.73	1,206.93	647.92	559.01	85,829.72
259	85,829.72	1,206.93	643.72	563.21	85,266.51
260	85,266.51	1,206.93	639.50	567.43	84,699.08
261	84,699.08	1,206.93	635.24	571.69	84,127.39
262	84,127.39	1,206.93	630.96	575.97	83,551.42
263	83,551.42	1,206.93	626.64	580.29	82,971.13
264	82,971.13	1,206.93	622.28	584.65	82,386.48
265	82,386.48	1,206.93	617.90	589.03	81,797.45
266	81,797.45	1,206.93	613.48	593.45	81,204.00
267	81,204.00	1,206.93	609.03	597.90	80,606.10
268	80,606.10	1,206.93	604.55	602.38	80,003.72
269	80,003.72	1,206.93	600.03	606.90	79,396.82
270	79,396.82	1,206.93	596.48	611.45	78,785.37
271	78,785.37	1,206.93	590.89	616.04	78,169.33
272	78,169.33	1,206.93	586.27	620.66	77,548.67
273	77,548.67	1,206.93	581.62	625.31	76,923.36
274	76,923.36	1,206.93	576.93	630.00	76,293.36
275	76,293.36	1,206.93	572.20	634.73	75,658.63
276	75,658.63	1,206.93	567.44	639.49	75,019.14
277	75,019.14	1,206.93	562.64	644.29	74,374.85
278	74,374.85	1,206.93	557.81	649.12	73,725.73
279	73,725.73	1,206.93	552.94	653.99	73,071.74
280	73,071.74	1,206.93	548.04	658.89	72,412.85
281	72,412.85	1,206.93	543.10	663.83	71,749.02
282	71,749.02	1,206.93	538.12	668.81	71,080.21
283	71,080.21	1,206.93	533.10	673.83	70,406.38
284	70,406.38	1,206.93	528.05	678.88	69,727.50
285	69,727.50	1,206.93	522.96	683.97	69,043.53
286	69,043.53	1,206.93	517.83	689.10	68,354.43
287	68,354.43	1,206.93	512.66	694.27	67,660.16
288	67,660.16	1,206.93	507.45	699.48	66,960.68
289	66,960.68	1,206.93	502.21	704.72	66,255.96
290	66,255.96	1,206.93	496.92	710.01	65,545.95
291	65,545.95	1,206.93	491.59	715.34	64,830.61
292	64,830.61	1,206.93	486.23	720.70	64,109.91
293	64,109.91	1,206.93	480.82	726.11	63,383.80
294	63,383.80	1,206.93	475.38	731.55	62,652.25

Month	Beginning Principal	Monthly Payment	Monthly Interest	Principal Reduction	Ending Principal
295	62,652.25	1,206.93	469.89	737.04	61,915.21
296	61,915.21	1,206.93	464.36	742.57	61,172.64
297	61,172.64	1,206.93	458.79	748.14	60,424.50
298	60,424.50	1,206.93	453.18	753.75	59,670.75
299	59,670.75	1,206.93	447.53	759.40	58,911.35
300	58,911.35	1,206.93	441.84	765.09	58,146.26
301	58,146.26	1,206.93	436.10	770.83	57,375.43
302	57,375.43	1,206.93	430.32	776.61	56,598.82
303	56,598.82	1,206.93	424.49	782.44	55,816.38
304	55,816.38	1,206.93	418.62	788.31	55,028.07
305	55,028.07	1,206.93	412.71	794.22	54,233.67
306	54,233.85	1,206.93	406.75	800.18	53,433.67
307	53,433.67	1,206.93	400.75	806.18	52,627.49
308	52,627.49	1,206.93	394.71	812.22	51,815.27
309	51,815.27	1,206.93	388.61	818.32	50,996.95
310	50,996.95	1,206.93	382.48	824.45	50,172.50
311	50,172.50	1,206.93	376.29	830.64	49,341.86
312	49,341.86	1,206.93	370.06	836.87	48,504.99
313	48,504.99	1,206.93	363.79	843.14	47,661.85
314	47,661.85	1,206.93	357.46	849.47	46,812.38
315	46,812.38	1,206.93	351.09	855.84	45,956.54
316	45,956.54	1,206.93	344.67	862.26	45,094.28
317	45,094.28	1,206.93	338.21	868.72	44,225.56
318	44,225.56	1,206.93	331.69	875.24	43,350.32
319	43,350.32	1,206.93	325.13	881.80	42,468.52
320	42,468.52	1,206.93	318.51	888.42	41,580.10
321	41,580.10	1,206.93	311.85	895.08	40,685.02
322	40,685.02	1,206.93	305.14	901.79	39,783.23
323	39,783.23	1,206.93	298.37	908.56	38,874.67
324	38,874.67	1,206.93	291.56	915.37	37,959.30
325	37,959.30	1,206.93	284.69	922.24	37,037.06
326	37,037.06	1,206.93	277.78	929.15	36,107.91
327	36,107.91	1,206.93	270.81	936.12	35,171.79
328	35,171.79	1,206.93	263.79	943.14	34,228.65
329	34,228.65	1,206.93	256.71	950.22	33,278.43
330	33,278.43	1,206.93	249.59	957.34	32,321.09
331	32,321.09	1,206.93	242.41	964.52	31,356.57
332	31,356.57	1,206.93	235.17	971.76	30,384.81
333	30,384.81	1,206.93	227.89	979.04	29,405.77

Month	Beginning Principal	Monthly Payment	Monthly Interest	Principal Reduction	Ending Principal
334	29,405.77	1,206.93	220.54	986.39	28,419.38
335	28,419.38	1,206.93	213.15	993.78	27,425.60
336	27,425.60	1,206.93	205.69	1,001.24	26,424.36
337	26,424.36	1,206.93	198.18	1,008.75	25,415.61
338	25,415.61	1,206.93	190.62	1,016.31	24,399.30
339	24,399.30	1,206.93	182.99	1,023.94	23,375.36
340	23,375.36	1,206.93	175.32	1,031.61	22,343.75
341	22,343.75	1,206.93	167.58	1,039.35	21,304.40
342	21,304.40	1,206.93	159.78	1,047.15	20,257.25
343	20,257.25	1,206.93	151.93	1,055.00	19,202.25
344	19,202.25	1,206.93	144.02	1,062.91	18,139.34
345	18,139.34	1,206.93	136.05	1,070.88	17,068.46
346	17,068.46	1,206.93	128.01	1,078.92	15,989.54
347	15,989.54	1,206.93	119.92	1,087.01	14,902.53
348	14,902.53	1,206.93	111.77	1,095.16	13,807.37
349	13,807.37	1,206.93	103.56	1,103.37	12,704.00
350	12,704.00	1,206.93	95.28	1,111.65	11,592.35
351	11,592.35	1,206.93	86.94	1,119.99	10,472.36
352	10,472.36	1,206.93	78.54	1,128.39	9,343.97
353	9,343.97	1,206.93	70.08	1,136.85	8,207.12
354	8,207.12	1,206.93	61.55	1,145.38	7,061.74
355	7,061.74	1,206.93	52.96	1,153.97	5,907.77
356	5,907.77	1,206.93	44.31	1,162.62	4,745.15
357	4,745.15	1,206.93	35.59	1,171.34	3,573.81
358	3,573.81	1,206.93	26.80	1,180.13	2,393.68
359	2,393.68	1,206.93	17.95	1,188.98	1,204.70
360	1,204.70	1,213.74	9.04	1,204.70	0.00
Total		434,501.61	284,501.61	150,000.00	

APPENDIX F

GLOSSARY

A

Accounts Payable Debts the company owes and expects to pay within one year that are not evidenced by a written promise to pay.

Accounts Payable to Revenue Ratio Accounts payable divided by revenue. Often expressed as a percentage.

Accounts Payable to Sales Ratio See **Accounts Payable to Revenue Ratio**.

Accounts Receivable Invoices owed to the company that will likely be paid within one year and have not been formalized by a written promise to pay. Most commonly these are bills to the project owners.

Accrual Method of Accounting An accounting method where revenue is recognized when the company has the right to receive the revenues and expenses are recognized when the company is obligated to pay the expenses.

Accrued Payables Monies owed for supplies and services that have not been billed, including accrued taxes, rents, wages, and vacation time.

Acid Test Ratio See **Quick Ratio**.

Alternate Minimum Tax An alternate method of calculating income tax liability used to ensure those with large amounts of deductions pay a minimum amount of income tax.

Amortization Schedule The table showing how a loan is paid off, which shows the monthly payment, interest, and outstanding principal balance for each month of a loan's existence.

Annual Equivalent An analytical method where investment alternatives are compared based on their equivalent annual receipts less their equivalent annual disbursements over the study period of the alternatives.

Annual Percentage Rate The nominal or stated interest rate on a financial instrument. The annual percentage rate ignores the effects of compound interest.

Annual Percentage Yield The annually compounded interest rate that produces the same amount of interest as the interest rate that is compounded on a more frequent basis.

Annual Value The value of a single cash flow in a uniform series of cash flows that occurs at the end of each period and continues for a number of periods. These cash flows must be uniform or equal in amount (not equivalent), the cash flows must occur at the end of the each period in the series, and the length of the periods must be the same as the length of the periods for the periodic interest rate.

APR See **Annual Percentage Rate**.

APY See **Annual Percentage Yield**.

Assets Resources held by a company or person that will probably lead to some future cash inflows.

Assets to Revenues Ratio Total assets divided by revenues. Often expressed as a percentage.

Assets to Sales Ratio See **Assets to Revenues Ratio**.

Average Age of Accounts Payable A ratio calculated by multiplying accounts payable by 365 days and dividing the resultant by the total of invoices processed through the accounts payable.

Average Age of Accounts Receivable See **Collection Period**.

Average Daily Balance The average of the daily balances in an account. The average daily balance is determined by summing the daily balances in an account and dividing the result by the number of days in the period.

B

Book Value The value of equipment on the accounting books, which equals the purchase price less depreciation.

Burden See **Labor Burden**.

Buyout The process of hiring subcontractors and procuring materials for a construction project.

C

Capital Gain Gain on the sale or disposition of a capital asset, depreciable property, and real property (real estate).

Capital Lease Leases that are noncancelable and meet at least one of the following conditions: (1) The lease extends for 75% or more of the equipment or property's useful life, (2) ownership transfers at the end of the lease, (3) ownership is likely to transfer at the end of the lease through a purchase option with a heavily discounted price, or (4) the present value of the lease payments at market interest rates exceeds 90% of the fair market value of the equipment or property.

Capital Loss Loss on the sale or disposition of a capital asset, depreciable property, and real property (real estate).

Capital Recovery with Return An analytical method where investment alternatives are compared based on the annual return necessary to cover the annual equivalent of the initial investment less the annual equivalent of the salvage value.

Capital Stock Initial investment in a corporation by the shareholders.

Cash Demand deposits, time deposits with a maturity of one year or less, and petty cash.

Cash Disbursement Cash flow from a company; for example, the payment of a bill.

Cash Equivalents The payment of cash to an employee in lieu of providing certain benefits.

Cash Flow Diagram A diagram showing receipts and disbursements of cash. In a cash flow diagram, the periods are represented along the horizontal axis and the cash flows are drawn as vertical arrows next to the period in which they occur. Arrows drawn in the up direction represent cash receipts and arrows drawn in the down direction represent cash disbursements.

Cash Method of Accounting An accounting method where revenue is recognized when the payments are received and expenses are recognized when bills are paid.

Cash Receipt Cash flow into a company.

Collection Period A ratio calculated by multiplying accounts receivable by 365 days and dividing the resultant by revenues.

Completed Contract Method of Accounting An accounting method where revenues, expenses, and profits are recognized at the completion of the project.

Compound Interest Interest that is paid on interest from the previous periods.

Construction Loan A short-term loan used to cover the costs of construction and must be paid off at or shortly after the completion of construction.

Contingent Alternatives Alternatives that may be selected only after another alternative has been selected.

Contra Account An account that is subtracted from another account.

Contribution Margin The amount of money that a project or projects contributes to the company to be used to pay for the fixed overhead and provide a profit for the stakeholders.

Contribution Margin Ratio The contribution margin expressed as a percentage of the company's revenues from construction operations.

Corporate Income Tax Federal income tax levied to corporations, specifically traditional C corporations and some partnerships.

Cost Performance Index A measure of the success of a project's management team to complete a project under budget, which is based on the ratio of budgeted cost of the work performed to the actual cost of the work performed.

Current Assets Assets that are expected to be converted to cash, exchanged, or consumed within one year.

Current Assets to Total Assets Ratio Current assets divided by total assets.

Current Liabilities Liabilities that are expected to be paid within the next year.

Current Liabilities to Net Worth Ratio Current liabilities divided by net worth. Often expressed as a percentage.

Current Period Net Income Profits or losses incurred during the current accounting period.

Current Ratio A measure of a company's ability to use current assets to pay for current liabilities.

D

Debt to Equity Ratio Total liabilities divided by equity (net worth).

Debt to Worth Ratio See **Debt to Equity Ratio**.

Degree of Fixed Asset Newness A ratio calculated by dividing net fixed assets by total fixed assets.

Depreciation The loss in value of an asset, such as equipment and buildings, due to wear and tear, the age of the asset, and obsolescence.

Depreciation Rate The percentage of an asset's depreciation taken in a specified year.

Depreciation Schedule A table showing each year's book value and depreciation for an asset.

Direct Costs Cost of materials, labor, and equipment that are incorporated into the construction of a project.

Direct Overhead Costs See **Indirect Costs**.

"Do Nothing" Alternative The alternative where all other alternatives have been rejected.

E

Effective Tax Rate The average tax rate paid on the taxable income.

Equal Cash flows that are the same amount. The time value of money is ignored with equal cash flows.

Equity See **Owner's Equity**.

Equivalence Cash flows that produce the same results. Equivalence is a function of the size of the cash flows, the timing of the cash flows, and the interest rate.

Equivalent See **Equivalence**.

External Constraints Constraints outside a pool of alternatives that may limit the number or restrict the alternatives than may be selected from the pool of alternatives, such as a limited supply of money or contractual obligations.

F

FICA Federal Insurance Contribution Act. FICA requires employers and employees to pay social security and Medicare taxes.

FIFO See **First-In/First-Out**.

Financial Management The use of a company's financial resources, encompassing all decisions that affect a company's financial health.

First-In/First-Out A method of pricing inventory where it is assumed that the materials purchased first are the materials that are used first.

Fiscal Year A consecutive twelve-month period used by businesses as their financial year, which may be different from the calendar year.

Fixed Assets Building, land, construction equipment, trucks, autos, and office equipment.

Fixed Asset to Net Worth Ratio Fixed asset divided by net worth (equity). Often expressed as a percentage.

Fixed Overhead Overhead costs that do not change with a change in volume of work over a specified range of volume of work.

FUTA Federal Unemployment Tax Act. FUTA requires employers to pay federal unemployment tax.

Future Value The value of a cash flow(s) at some specific point in the future. The future value occurs at the end of the year. The future value may be at any point in time after a cash flow. The future value may also occur concurrently with the last payment in a uniform series of cash flows.

Future Worth An analytical method where investment alternatives are compared based on their worth at some time in the future.

G

General and Administrative Cost Ratio See **General Overhead Ratio**.

General and Administrative Expense See **General Overhead**.

General Overhead Costs that cannot be charged to a specific construction project or be included in the equipment costs section of the income statement.

General Overhead Ratio General overhead divided by revenues. Usually expressed as a percentage.

Good Faith Estimate An estimate of the closing costs for a loan prepared by the lending institution in good faith.

Grace Period The time between a credit card purchase and the date interest is charged on that purchase. The grace period usually only applies to those cardholders who pay their bill in full each month.

Gross Profit Margin Gross profit divided by revenues. Usually expressed as a percentage.

Gross Profit Ratio See **Gross Profit Margin**.

I

Incremental Net Present Value An analytical method where investment alternatives are compared based on the present worth of the difference in the cash flows of the alternatives at the time of the initial investment.

Incremental Rate of Return An analytical method where investment alternatives are compared based on the rate of return of the difference in the cash flows of the alternatives.

Incremental Tax Rate See **Marginal Tax Rate**.

Independent Alternatives Alternatives where the acceptance of one alternative does not, in and of itself, preclude the selection of the other alternatives.

Indirect Costs Costs that can be specifically identified to the completion of a specific construction project, but cannot be identified with the completion of a specific construction component on that project. Indirect costs may also be referred to as indirect project costs, project overhead, or direct overhead costs.

Indirect Project Costs See **Indirect Costs**.

Indirect Overhead See **General Overhead**.

Interest Money paid by banks or borrowers for the use of money. Interest is generally expressed as an annual percentage rate and annual percentage yield.

Inventory Materials available for sale or are available and expected to be incorporated into a construction project within the next year.

L

Labor Burden Cost to the employer to pay for employee taxes, insurances, and other benefits.

Labor Burden Markup Labor burden expressed as a percentage of the employee's wages excluding wages paid for vacation and sick leave.

Last-In/First-Out A method of pricing inventory where it is assumed that the materials purchased last are the materials that are used first.

Liabilities An obligation to transfer assets or render services at some time in the future for which the commitment has already been made.

LIFO See **Last-In/First-Out**.

Loan Provisions Conditions attached to a loan that require the borrower to perform specific actions, such as maintain a compensating balance.

Long-Term Assets Assets with an expected useful life of more than one year at the time of their purchase.

Long-Term Capital Gain or Loss Gains and losses on capital assets held for more than one year.

Long-Term Contract Any construction contract that is likely to span more than one tax year.

Long-Term Liabilities Debts that are not expected to be paid within one year.

M

Marginal Tax Rate The income tax rate paid on the last dollar of taxable income.

MARR See **Minimum Attractive Rate of Return**.

Maturity Matching Matching the term of the financing to the length of the financial need.

Minimum Attractive Rate of Return The lowest rate of return that is acceptable for an investment alternative or the rate of return at which an investments become attractive.

Mixed Overhead Overhead that has both a variable and fixed component.

Mutually Exclusive Alternatives Alternatives where the acceptance of one of the alternatives precludes investment in the other alternatives.

N

Net Income A positive taxable income.

Net Loss A negative taxable income.

Net Present Value An analytical method where investment alternatives are compared based on their present worth at the time of the initial investment.

Net Worth See **Owner's Equity**

Net Worth Ratio See **Debt to Equity Ratio**.

Nominal Interest Rate See **Annual Percentage Rate**.

Notes Payable Debts that will likely be paid within one year and have been formalized by a written promise to pay.

Notes Receivable Invoices, short-term loans, or employee advances owed to the company that will likely be paid within one year and have been formalized by a written promise to pay.

NPV See **Net Present Value**.

O

Off-Balance-Sheet Financing Financing which does not appear on the balance sheet. An operating lease is one form of off-balance-sheet financing.

Operation Cost The costs associated with operating an asset. For a piece of construction equipment this includes tires and other wear items, fuel, lubricants and filters, and repairs.

Operational Lease Any lease that is not a capital lease.

Opportunity Cost The cost of having to pass on one alternative to select another alternative.

Ordinary Income Income that is not considered capital gains for income tax purposes.

Other Assets Assets not elsewhere classified. This includes inventory that will not be sold within a year, investment in other companies, and the cash value of life insurance policies.

Overhead See **General Overhead**.

Owner's Equity The claim of the company's owner or shareholders on the assets that remain after the liabilities are paid.

Ownership Costs The cost of owing an asset that includes purchase price, salvage value, interest, property taxes, and insurance.

P

Paid When Paid Clause A clause that ties the payment of supplier and subcontractor bills to a specified number of days after the contractor has received payment for the bills in the form of unrestricted funds from the owner. It is used to arrange with suppliers and subcontractors to provide the capital needed to construct a construction project.

Passive Activity Generally passive activities include all business activities in which the taxpayer did not materially participate in during the tax year and most rental activities. Passive activities must meet very specific requirements that are defined by the Internal Revenue Code.

Payable Turns A ratio calculated by dividing 365 by the average age of accounts payable.

Payback Period with Interest The time required to recoup the initial investment plus interest on the investment at the MARR.

Payback Period without Interest The time required to recoup the initial investment while ignoring interest on the investment.

Percentage-of-Completion Method of Accounting An accounting method where revenues, expenses, and estimated profits are recognized as the project is completed, based on the percentage of the project that is completed.

Periodic Interest Rate The interest rate for one period. The period may be any specified amount of time with years, quarters, and months being the most common. The period must be the same as the compounding period for the interest rate.

Prepaid Expenses Payments that have been made for future supplies and services, including prepaid taxes, insurance premiums, rent, and deposits.

Personal Endorsement The owners of a company pledge their personal assets to ensure payment of a debt incurred by the company.

Personal Income Tax Federal income tax levied at the personal level. Limited liability companies (LLCs), S corporations, most partnerships, and sole proprietorships pass their tax on to their shareholders to be paid at the personal level.

Present Value The value of a cash flow at the present time. When used in the equivalence formulas, the present value occurs at the beginning of the year. The present value may be used to refer to any point in time prior to a cash flow.

Present Worth See **Net Present Value**.

Principal The original amount of money deposited in a saving instrument, such as a certificate of deposit, or borrowed from a debt instrument, such as a loan.

Profit and Overhead Markup A markup added to construction costs to cover general overhead and provide for a profit, which is expressed as a percentage of construction costs.

Profit Margin A ratio that is calculated by dividing profit by revenues and may be measured before income taxes or after income taxes. Usually expressed as a percentage of revenues.

Project Balance A graphical method used to analyze investment alternatives, which include the future worth of the investment at the end of the study period and the payback period with interest.

Project Overhead See **Indirect Costs**.

Q

Quick Ratio Sum of cash and accounts receivable divided by the current liabilities. Retention and allowances for bad debts are excluded from the accounts receivable.

R

Rate of Return (1) An analytical method where investment alternatives are compared based on their rates of returns. (2) The interest rate that produces a net present value of zero for an investment alternative.

Ratios The resulting number obtained by dividing one category or a group of categories on the company's financial statement into another category or group of categories on the company's financial statement. Ratios provide insights into a company's ability to pay bills, how efficiently it uses its financial resources, its profitability, and the capital structure of the company.

Real Property Land and the buildings permanently affixed to the land.

Receivable Turns A ratio calculated by dividing 365 by the collection period.

Recovery Period The number of years over which an asset is to be depreciated. For tax purposes the Internal Revenue Code identifies the recovery period for different classes of assets. For other purposes the recovery period is often equal to the useful life of the asset.

Retained Earnings Prior accounting period's profits or earnings retained by the corporation to invest in a company's operations rather than be distributed to the shareholders.

Retention Funds withheld from a payment to ensure that a contractor completes a construction project.

Return on Assets A ratio calculated by dividing net profit after taxes by total assets. Often expressed as a percentage.

Return on Equity A ratio calculated by dividing net profit after taxes by equity and may be measured before or after income tax. Often expressed as a percentage.

Return on Investment See **Return on Equity**.

Return on Revenues See **Profit Margin**.

Return on Sales See **Profit Margin**.

Revenue Income from the completion of part or all of a construction project.

Revenues to Net Working Capital Ratio See **Working Capital Turns**.

S

Sales to Net Working Capital Ratio See **Working Capital Turns**.

Salvage Value The estimated resale value of an asset when the asset is sold at some future time.

Schedule Performance Index A measure of the success of a project's management team to complete a project on time, which is based on the ratio of budgeted cost of the work performed to the budgeted cost of the work scheduled.

Secured Debt A debt where the borrower has pledged specific assets as security for the debt.

Short-Term Capital Gain or Loss Gains and losses on capital assets held for one year or less.

Single-Payment Compound-Amount Factor A function or factor used to convert a present value to a future value at a specified rate of interest.

Single-Payment Present-Worth Factor A function or factor used to convert a future value to a present value at a specified rate of interest.

Study Period The period of time over which investment alternatives are studied.

Subordinate Debt A debt that may be paid off only after another debt—the debt it is subordinate to—has been paid off.

Sunk Costs Cost that have been spent or irrevocably committed.

SUTA State Unemployment Tax Act. SUTA requires employers to pay state unemployment tax.

T

Tax Credits Credits that directly reduce income tax liability.

Taxable Income The amount of income that is subject to income tax and equals the company's income minus tax deductions.

Third-Party Guarantee Where a company or person other than the borrower becomes a party to a loan and guarantees payment of the loan.

Trade Financing Financing provided by suppliers and subcontractors by providing materials, labor, and equipment to a construction project before receiving payment for the materials, labor, or equipment.

U

Unallowed Losses Unused losses from passive income.

Uniform See **Equal**.

Uniform Series A series of cash flows that are uniform or equal in amount and occur at the end of each period in the series, where the periods are the same length as each other and are the same length as the compounding period for the period interest rate.

Uniform-Series Capital-Recovery Factor A function or factor used to convert a present value into a series of uniform cash flows.

Uniform-Series Compounding-Amount Factor A function or factor used to convert a series of uniform cash flows into a future value.

Uniform-Series Present-Worth Factor A function or factor used to convert a series of uniform cash flows into a present value.

Uniform-Series Sinking-Fund Factor A function or factor used to convert a future value into a series of uniform cash flows.

Unsecured Debt A debt where the borrower has not pledged specific assets as security for the debt.

Useful Life The number of years for which an asset is useful. The useful life is most often based on economics rather than the number of years an asset can be used.

V

Variable Overhead Overhead costs that change or vary with a change in volume of work.

W

Warranty Reserves Funds set aside to cover the foreseeable cost of warranty work.

Working Capital Turns A ratio calculated by dividing revenues by net working capital. The revenues are reduced by the subcontractor costs when a company passes payments from the owners to subcontractors.

Y

Yield See **Annual Percentage Yield**.

APPENDIX G

LIST OF VARIABLES

A	Annual Value in a Uniform Series (Time Value of Money)
A	Monthly Payment (Financial Instruments)
AAI	Average Annual Investment
$(A/F,i,n)$	Uniform-Series Sinking-Fund Factor
$(A/P,i,n)$	Uniform-Series Capital-Recovery Factor
ACWP	Actual Cost of Work Performed
ADB_t	Average Daily Balance for Period t
AE	Annual Equivalent
b	Intercept Point of a Linear Line Along the y Axis
BCWP	Budgeted Cost of Work Performed
BCWS	Budgeted Cost of Work Scheduled
B_t	Reduction in Unpaid Principal for Payment t
BV_m	Book Value at the End of Year m
c	Compounding Periods in a Year
CPI	Cost Performance Index
CR	Capital Recovery with Return
D	Number of Days
D_m	Depreciation for Year m
f	Inflation Rate
F	Future Value of a Cash Flow (Time Value of Money)
F	Salvage Value (Depreciation)
$(F/A,i,n)$	Uniform-Series Compound-Amount Factor
$(F/P,i,n)$	Single-Payment Compound-Amount Factor
F'	Constant Dollar Future Value
FW	Future Worth

549

I	Interest
I_t	Interest for Period t
i	Periodic Interest Rate
i'	Constant Dollar Periodic Interest Rate
i_a	Yield, Annual Percentage Yield, or APY (Financial Instruments)
i_a	Effective Annual Interest Rate (Financial Instruments)
m	Slope of a Linear Line (Linear Regression)
m	Year (Depreciation)
MARR	Minimum Attractive Rate of Return
N	Recovery Period (Depreciation)
N	Number of Payments (Financial Instruments)
n	Number of Interest Compounding Periods of Time
n'	Payback Period
NPV	Net Present Value
P	Present Value (Time Value of Money)
P	Purchase Price (Depreciation)
P	Principal (Financial Instruments)
$(P/A,i,n)$	Uniform-Series Present-Worth Factor
$(P/F,i,n)$	Single-Payment Present-Worth Factor
P'	Constant Dollar Present Value
R_m	Depreciation Rate or Percentage of Depreciation Taken in Year m
r	Nominal Interest Rate, Annual Percentage Rate, or APR (Financial Instruments)
r	Correlation Coefficient (Statistics)
r^2	Coefficient of Determination
SPI	Schedule Performance Index
SOY	Sum of the Years
t	Number of Monthly Payments That Have Been Made
U_t	Unpaid Principal at End of Period t
$\hat{y}$	Estimated Value of y

INDEX

551